AF174158

ANTHOLOGY OF
BRITISH LITERATURE

Anthology of
BRITISH LITERATURE

From the Restoration to Modernism

Edited with Introductions by
ANGELA VANBUSKIRK

WHITLOCK PUBLISHING
Alfred, NY

First Whitlock Publishing edition 2019

Whitlock Publishing
Alfred, New York

Editorial matter @ Angela VanBuskirk

ISBN: 978-1-943115-35-8

Cover art from Wikimedia Commons
Lies Thru a Lens/ Old London/ Wikimedia Commons

This books was set in Adobe Garamond Pro on 50# acid-free paper that meets ANSI standards for archival quality.

CONTENTS

RESTORATION AND THE EIGHTEENTH CENTURY
(1660–1785)

ROMANTIC PERIOD
(1785–1832)

VICTORIAN AGE
(1832–1901)

THE TWENTIETH CENTURY AND THE MODERNISTS
(1902–1945)

ACKNOWLEDGEMENTS

I would like to extend my sincerest gratitude to Dr. Allen Grove, who not only proposed this anthology project but also helped me discover work I am truly passionate about.

I am also thankful to the professors at the English Division at Alfred University, especially Dr. Melissa Ryan, Dr. Juliana Gray, and Dr. Robert Reginio. Their literary passion, wisdom, and expertise have cultivated my love of literature. I am additionally grateful to Professor Bob Myers for teaching me the value of a holistic perspective.

A special thank you goes to my family for their infinite interest and encouragement throughout this process. Finally, I'd like to express my appreciation to Tim Corkey, who tirelessly supported me and took me on adventures.

NOTE ON IMAGES

The following images are listed in the order of their appearance:

"Black swirl designs" is a derivative of "Vintage swirl design elements" by KaterynaToporkova, on Flickr, used under CC BY-SA 2.0. "Black swirl designs" is licensed under CC BY-SA 2.0 by Angela VanBuskirk.

Engraving of Aphra Behn after a lost portrait by John Riley by John Riley, on Wikimedia Commons, used under CC BY-1.0/ Reduced dimensions from original

Alexander Pope portrait by Frédéric, on Wikimedia Commons, used under CC BY-SA 3.0/ Reduced dimensions from original

Jonathan Swift portrait by Frédéric, on Wikimedia Commons, used under CC BY-SA 3.0/ Reduced dimensions from original

Portrait of Lady Mary Wortley Montagu; from an enamel miniature by Zink in the possession of Charles Colville. Lithography by A. Deveria, by Wellcome Library, London, on Wikimedia Commons, used under CC BY-4.0/ Reduced dimensions from original

John Keats. Wood engraving after J. Severn, 1819, by Wellcome Library, London, on Wikimedia Commons, used under CC BY-4.0/ Black and white, reduced dimensions from original

Alfred, Lord Tennyson by Julia Margaret Cameron, 1869, printed 1905, on Wikimedia Commons, used under CC BY-1.0/ Black and white, reduced dimensions from original

Robert Brown. Lithograph by T. H. Maguire, 1850, by Wellcome Library, London, on Wikimedia Commons, used under CC BY-4.0/ Black and white, reduced dimensions from original

Illustration of Charles Dickens by Wellcome Library, London, on Wikimedia Commons, used under CC BY-4.0/ Black and white, text cropped, reduced dimensions from original

INTRODUCTION

"Do I dare disturb the universe?"
— T.S. Eliot, "The Love Song of J. Alfred Prufrock"

I F ANY GENERALIZATION CAN BE MADE about the twenty-nine British writers in-
cluded in this anthology, it is that they all did more than disturb their universe.
Over the course of nearly 300 years, they responded to it, provoked it, and
fundamentally changed it.

Irrespective of when they wrote or what they wrote about, the following poets,
playwrights, essayists, and novelists chronicle extraordinary experiences and every-
day ones; share strange dreams and create intricate realities; attest to the literary
norms of their age and explore beyond them; and, perhaps most importantly,
compel us to reexamine ourselves and our societies through the stories they tell.
But just because these texts were written in the past does not mean they bear
any less significance today. As the forces of modernity continuously redesign and
revolutionize our cultures, turning to the past is a strategy for better understanding
the present.

Spanning from the Restoration of King Charles in 1660 to the end of World
War II in 1945, *Anthology of British Literature: From the Restoration to Modernism*
is comprised of writers who witnessed some of the most tumultuous events in
English history. Decades of civil war and political upset came to rest when the
monarchy was reinstated. For a brief time, golden threads of indulgence and
mischievous frivolity shrouded the king's court. The country encountered an even
greater metamorphosis, however, when it became the nation of Great Britain in
1707. Still, prosperity and relative stability could not last forever. Time gave way to
revolution, warfare, and discontent. The French Revolution polarized and inflamed
Britons; many lamented the British government's disfavor for democracy while

others demanded increased human liberties. Yet the French Revolution generated Robespierre's Reign of Terror, bringing waves of unjust arrests, imprisonments, and mass executions in the name of righteousness. As these events and other iniquities unfolded, some British advocates felt painfully disillusioned by humanity and the world at large. A much more personal catastrophe struck Britons in the mid nineteenth century when the theory of evolution seemingly usurped religious beliefs, upending long-held attitudes about the very nature of human existence. Though Britain had become the most powerful nation on earth and its colonial reach extended to all corners of the globe, many grieved for the certainty and familiarity of the past. But time, space, and reality itself had split at the seams by World War II, and certainty was only a construct.

The four major historical literary periods encompassed in this anthology–the Restoration and Eighteenth Century, the Romantic period, the Victorian Age, and the Twentieth Century and the Modernists–chart the interconnectivity between English history, literature, and society. Each section includes an overview of significant political and cultural developments, providing readers with a contextual framework in which to consider the subsequent texts. Concise timelines accompany each overview; the two-column structure aligns key societal events with noteworthy literary works. Brief author biographies and timelines precede the selections. Minor grammatical and spelling corrections have been made, but non-uniform capitalization has not been altered. Footnotes clarifying obsolete language, allusions, and other details have been included when necessary. Aside from these edits and additions, works retain their original integrity.

The *Anthology of British Literature* covers a range of writers and pieces, but a great many more writers and pieces exist beyond these pages. English literature is abundant in quantity, variety, and form, and the works anthologized here familiarize students with some of the most essential and influential texts in the canon. Novels have not been included in this collection, as their length would be impractical. This is an unfortunate misrepresentation since novels were a–if not *the*–dominant form from the late eighteenth century onward. The following texts have been selected for their thematic complexity, creativity, stylistic prowess, and impact on the development of literature. Some works embody themes unique to their specific period while other pieces relate themes that carry across the ages. Texts are multidimensional in meaning and syntax alike. From satire to short stories, novellas to poetry, and essays to plays, the variance of genres presented is a sampling of what has entertained and enlightened English readers for years.

The canon has been historically male-dominated, downplaying the significant contributions of female writers. Most women writers were excluded from the literary canon on the basis of sex alone. For generations, the majority of scholars failed to consider their works seriously, if at all. Consequently, literary women were marginalized or ignored despite their contributions. There were, for example, more female writers during the Romantic period than there were male writers, yet the "Big Six"–William Blake, William Wordsworth, Samuel Taylor Coleridge, Percy Bysshe Shelley, John Keats, and Lord Byron–received the brunt of scholars' attention. Several female writers are incorporated into this anthology, among whom is the formative modernist writer Virginia Woolf. Forced to overcome prejudice, systematic oppression, and a host of further challenges, women writers fought to make their mark and earn a place in literary history.

These writers emerge from an array of class statuses, social backgrounds, and occupations. Some struggled to get published in their own lifetime, and the works of others did not see print until years after the author's death. William Blake, a visionary Romantic poet, spent all the money he had to his name to reproduce his pieces. He lived in relative obscurity, as did the Jesuit priest Gerard Manley Hopkins, who all but refused to expose his writing to public eyes. Some, nevertheless, managed to garner enough public attention to support themselves off their publications alone–a rare and exceptional feat accomplished here by Alexander Pope and Alfred Lord Tennyson. For those born into circles of privilege and power, like Lady Mary Wortley Montagu, writing offered a vein of artistic expression and social commentary. The reality for most writers, however, was that writing was a necessity as well as a passion; whether dependent on patrons or periodical buyers, writers commonly had few options but to place their trust in the hands of their readers. Their works have survived, in part, because readers, reviewers, and scholars continue to recognize their importance.

The ensuing authors and texts carry merit as testaments to history and contemporary trends. Though this anthology preserves a narrative of Britain's ideological and literary evolution, it also fosters conversations between writers and readers. It is a means of continuing and contributing to the discussions that have occurred in the margins of pages for centuries. Literature, at its most powerful, does more than relate stories and ideas. It supersedes geographical and spatial boundaries, imploring readers to experience, introspect, and enact change.

ANGELA VANBUSKIRK, OCTOBER 2019
ALFRED, NY

R ESTORATION
AND THE EIGHTEENTH CENTURY
1660–1785

ABSTRACT

The Restoration of 1660 marked the return of the monarchy, Parliament, and the established Anglican Church. Parliament and the people were faithful to King Charles II until his bias toward Roman Catholics ignited fear. James II ascended to the throne in 1685, but he was soon usurped by William and Mary. They placated the country's religious tensions by ushering in a line of Protestant rulers. As the eighteenth century drew nearer, Britain increased its wealth by seizing commercial and global trade opportunities. A range of literary forms and topics emerged, and satire governed the Restoration period while eighteenth-century pieces accentuated sentimentality. By the mid-1700s, the novel had become a formidable literary form, and writers began exploring the "reality" of specific human characters.

POLITICS

After Parliament beheaded Charles I, it acquired sovereign power in England. Its power was short-lived; the army, with Oliver Cromwell at its helm, seized control. Acting as the supreme Protector, Cromwell dissolved Parliament and governed England until his death in 1658. Cromwell's son, however, was an inadequate ruler, and after he was deposed, Parliament returned. The army then intimidated Parliament until it relinquished its power. In January of 1660, an English general dispatched to Scotland gathered his forces, marched on London, and restored Parliament through negotiations. The old Parliament then dissolved, and the new Parliament granted Charles II the throne. The Restoration of 1660 signified an end to over a decade of civil war and vicious political schemes. Under Charles II, England essentially returned to its system of government and its belief in a divine

1

monarchy. Charles's reinstatement remedied many lingering issues, but England lacked stability due to enduring religious tensions.

As the Church of England regained its former power, people belonging to different religious sects increasingly faced persecution. Puritans especially experienced hostility since they had been in power during Cromwell's regime. Charles pardoned many of those who had revolted against the monarchy, but members of Parliament and clergymen were less forgiving. The 1662 Act of Uniformity required all clergymen and schoolteachers to accept the Anglican Book of Common Prayer. Those who declined were labeled "Dissenters"—a term that included Presbyterians, Independents, Baptists, Quakers, and other new sects—and purged from their offices. Two years later, the Conventicle Act punished anyone who attended a religious gathering that did not conform to the established church. The Test Act of 1673 unleashed more discrimination: Anyone holding civil or military office who refused to receive sacrament in the Anglican Church and deny transubstantiation (the belief that bread and wine served during communion, when consecrated in the Eucharist, change into the body and blood of Christ) was barred from attending university or holding public office. Roman Catholics and Protestant Dissenters could not comply with these demands without violating their beliefs.

Despite Parliament's strong, anti-Catholic agenda, Charles II had secret Catholic sympathies. As Charles had no legitimate heir of his own, his brother James, a Roman Catholic, would eventually succeed to the throne. Threatened by the possibility of a Catholic monarch, Parliament—and the country—plunged into hysteria. Titus Oates, an Anglican priest, and his anti-Catholic aquaintance, Israel Tonge, fostered more panic by spreading rumors that Jesuits intended to assassinate the king in order to ensure James's rule. Though entirely fictitious, this so-called Popish Plot generated genuine fear. Parliament tried to force Charles into denying his brother the Crown. Charles solved the matter by dissolving Parliament. His decision initiated the formation of two opposing political parties, the Whigs and the Tories. Whigs believed Parliament should be more powerful than the monarchy. Nobles, members of the House of Lords, members of the House of Commons, property-owners, and merchants composed the majority of the Whig party. Alternately, the Tory party, which consisted of country gentry and clergymen, supported the king.

Parliament's attempts did not stop James II from ascending to the throne. Unlike Charles, James had no qualms about disagreeing with Parliament. He suspended the Test Act and sought to increase the power of the Catholic Church. But his reign fell short. Secret negotiations to depose James began after the birth of his son. Desperate to prevent a Catholic dynasty, the country searched for a suitable Protestant ruler. James's eldest daughter, Mary, had been reared Protestant at the insistence of Charles II; and in 1688, Mary and her Dutch husband, William of

Orange, invaded England with a small army. James II fled to France in permanent exile, and William and Mary seized the throne. The Glorious, or Bloodless, Revolution concluded with the passage of the Bill of Rights, an instrumental document in the British constitution. The Bill of Rights preserves individual liberties by maintaining the political independence of the House of Commons and limiting the excessive use of executive power by the king.

Queen Anne, Mary's younger sister, ascended to the throne in 1702. Her twelve-year reign marked the beginning of a period brimming with global trade and commercial expansion. The War of Spanish Succession, which spanned almost the entire duration of her rule, led to trading prospects. Most notably, England secured new colonies and was granted an exclusive contract to supply slaves to the Spanish colonies in America. It was also during Anne's administration that the 1707 Act of Union joined England, Scotland, and Wales into the nation of Great Britain. Though determined to rule independently, Anne's chronic ill health and limited experience forced her to rely heavily on Whig ministers and the duke of Marlborough. They initially controlled her regime, but since their interests went against those of the established church, Anne dismissed them and placed Tories in power instead.

Anne had no heirs of her own, leaving the transfer of sovereignty in question. In order to preserve a Protestant line of rulers, she conceded to the 1701 Act of Settlement. Since she was the last of the Stuarts to control Britain, the Crown transferred to the royal house of Hanover when she died. The King Georges (I-IV) ruled for over a hundred years, giving the eighteenth century the title of the Georgian period. Not surprisingly, James's son ("the Old Pretender") and grandson ("the Young Pretender") still tried to claim the throne, and Jacobites (from the Latin word *Jacobus*, "James") supported their cause. The Jacobite rebellions, which mostly occurred in Scotland, persisted well into the reign of George II. A final defeat in 1746 silenced the rebels permanently.

Some secret Jacobite sympathizers existed in the government, but many stayed loyal to the king. During the reign of George II, Robert Walpole, a persuasive and politically-conscious Whig, rose to power within Parliament. Walpole, though active during the administration of George I, found favor under George II. He exerted his influence to fill government offices with like-minded politicians. He became Britain's first prime minister and enjoyed a long, profitable career. Walpole's undoing came in 1742 when he voiced his disapproval of a war against the French and Spanish. Despite his warnings, Britain continued to wage wars in the pursuit of wealth and new territory. The loss of the American colonies did little to damage the nation's prosperity. By the late eighteenth century, Great Britain controlled territories in the Caribbean, Canada, and India, and traded extensively with nations around the world.

LITERATURE

RESTORATION

Since many writers were royalists, Restoration literature often reflected court culture. During the reign of King Charles II, the court promoted a lifestyle of libertinism and indulgence. Literary tastes also changed with the king's return. As Charles had spent his exile in France, he developed a proclivity for French literature, art, fashion, and cuisine. Consequently, writers engaged in French literary and artistic trends. Readers and writers valued restraint and clarity over the elaborate, rhetorical, and complicated forms common in late Renaissance literature. Witty, conversational tones renewed old heroic themes of war and love. Further, heroic couplets experienced a resurrection thanks to John Dryden, whose death in 1700 marked the beginning of a more cosmopolitan, modern English language. The style, form, and content of modern literature differed from what had preceded it. A distinct English literary identity emerged.

The shift attracted new audiences, and literature was enjoyed more widely across class boundaries than ever before. To publish a work in the previous age, one needed to obtain government approval; authorities suppressed many unfavorable, unsavory, and criticizing texts. But manuscript versions still circulated, evidencing the ineffectiveness of publishing laws. Parliament lifted the final restrictions on the press (excluding libel and sedition laws) in 1695. Although Parliament tried to police content into the eighteenth century (for example, the 1737 Stage Licensing Act required plays to be approved before production), it mostly directed its efforts towards controlling defamation, obscenity, and treason. The Statute of Anne, passed in 1710, became the first copyright law in Britain to give book publishers and authors legal protection regardless of whether a text met government approval. Publications diverse in form and topic alike flooded the market, including biographies, histories, travel journals, epics, poetry, and, later in the century, novels.

Not everyone could enjoy freer press, nor was every topic appreciated. Theological works, which had been popular during Cromwell's regime, especially struggled because hedonism replaced rigid moral principles. The dominant culture rejected Puritan ideals, and persecution awaited many writers who voiced Puritan views. Readers ruthlessly scrutinized religious figures and dogmas. Still, texts focusing on religion and faith never left the cannon. Despite animosity towards religious writers and writing, some pieces, such as John Bunyan's allegory *Pilgrim's Progress*, resonated with readers. The role of religion remained a pertinent question even though Charles's court downplayed its significance.

The Restoration period is remembered for its dramas more than any other form. Theaters, which had been shut down since 1642, reopened shortly after Charles reclaimed the throne, and the stage welcomed female actors. Playwrights began penning hilarious and bawdy works. "Comedies of manners" gained popularity; this genre ridicules and questions contemporary societal values by satirizing the behavior of entire social classes. With particular emphasis on the wit and politeness brandished by the upper echelons, comedies of manners focus on the use of trickery and sexual deceit to gain power. Plots typically center on affairs or other illicit situations. Characters are gullible and foolish; alternately, they are selfish and exploitative. The interest in mannerisms foreshadowed social ideas about proper conduct that would emerge in the eighteenth century.

Aside from making social inquiries, writers also discussed arithmetical and political issues through scientific and philosophical prose. Sir Isaac Newton catalyzed efforts to better understand matter, force, and other mathematical laws with the publications of *Principia Mathematica* in 1687 and *Opticks* in 1704. Noting his influence, philosophers propagated empiricism, Francis Bacon's theory that knowledge is a product of direct experience. They applied empirical, scientific observations to their own ideas. One such philosopher was John Locke, who published *Two Treatises of Government* and *An Essay Concerning Human Understanding* in 1689 and 1690, respectively. His writings on the rights of the people and the justification of rebellion against unfair governments became weaponized in the following century as countries staged uprisings around the world.

EIGHTEENTH CENTURY

The eighteenth century was simultaneously a time of forward-thinking and retrospection. Due to the advancement of political, scientific, and philosophical ideas, the period is often called the Age of Enlightenment. However, the period is also called the Augustan age since many writers deliberately imitated Virgil and Horace. Augustan writers injected new energy into Greek and Roman styles to craft neoclassicism, a blend of new and classic elements. Meditating on ruins, neoclassicists paid homage to the feats of ancient civilizations by using traditional literary forms like the pastoral and the epic. Though writers understood they could never accomplish the same polish as famed Greeks and Romans, they still valued the harmony, simplicity, and emotional restraint imbued in early works.

Many middle-class readers protested the aristocratic ideals present in Restoration pieces and demanded more literature that narrated experiences closer to their lives. Writing poetry was no longer exclusively for the upper classes; middle-class people began penning verses. Visual imagery and descriptive metaphors flourished. Sentiment was equally important not only in poetry but in drama as well. Capable of moving an audience to laughter and tears, sentimental comedies accentuated high morals.

Satire, nevertheless, dominated the early eighteenth century. Prose adopted new forms and, at times, barbed edges. Many writers partook in the political environment using overt and covert tactics alike. Periodical journals offered a platform to display polemical skills. Often published on a weekly or monthly basis, periodicals made information more available to readers. *The Spectator, The Gentleman's Magazine, The Examiner,* and other periodicals and literary magazines educated readers on contemporary events and promoted intellectual conversations. Paper wars between rival writers prospered. Hoping to further appeal to readers, some influential essayists such as Swift and Johnson invented personae so realistic that they were mistaken for genuine people. A body of public knowledge formed. Coffeehouses (the first of which had opened in London in 1652) became customary meeting places to discuss political, cultural, and social issues.

By the 1740s, the novel outshined the essay. This new literary form emerged from the prose fiction of writers such as Aphra Behn and Daniel Defoe, whose works in the late seventeenth and early eighteenth centuries contributed to the future structure of the novel. Long prose fiction works were part of cultural conversations regarding political selfhood and roles of government, and features—such as gender, religion, and partisan sympathies—often represented the writer's ideals. Writers also connected with their audiences by using generalized characters who lacked unique, specific details. For example, Behn, a proto-feminist who supported the aristocracy, engineered pro-Stuart characters in her pieces to address contemporary political incidents. Similarly, Defoe responded to economic changes with *Robinson Crusoe,* an adventure story symbolizing the values of capitalism. Cultural reactions to various events brought sentimentalism, domestic themes, and realism to fiction, as well as a continued emphasis on human nature. The rise of individualism also added to the popularity of the embryonic novel. Readers believed that the private life of an individual supplied them with a genuine account of a specific human experience. With the publication of Samuel Richardson's *Pamela* in 1740, audiences witnessed the more psychologically complex characters that define the novel. Henry Fielding developed characters differently by creating character types with redeemable qualities. Since Fielding drew inspiration from comedies of manners, his characters are reminiscent of the Restoration period. Fielding, his predecessors, and future novelists reworked the genre to suit their literary and political ambitions.

Writers explored more sinister ideas later in the eighteenth century. Reacting against neoclassicism, some writers explored the strange, exotic, mysterious, and surreal in a genre that became known as the Gothic novel. The emergence of Gothic novels can be regarded as a counternarrative to Britain's sense of progress and security. With an emphasis on antiquated settings and medieval themes, Gothic novels combine romance with elements of horror, despair, and death. Threads of incest, murder, and necrophilia stitch these nightmarish stories together. Many hallmarks of the Gothic novel can be attributed to Horace Walpole, whose 1765 story *The Castle of Otranto* became the first Gothic novel. Controllable reality is shattered in the opening pages, and characters are trapped in a haunted castle destined to fall to ruin through supernatural agency. The genre would gain more traction in the Romantic period. Over many years, writers moved from a crude depiction of evil to a more psychologized version of it. Characters began suffering from twisted inner conditions and warped power ideals, further displaying the darkness of the human heart. Elements of the Gothic novel inspired Mary Wollstonecraft, Bram Stoker, Edgar Allen Poe, the Brontë sisters, and Charles Dickens.

Novelists eventually surpassed poets in popularity, and the novel would be reexamined and reshaped for centuries to come. Plots shifted from externally-focused events to major characters' psychological conditions, and writers progressively realized the importance of character development. Some writers, such as Dickens, relied on caricatures, while others, like Jane Austen, sought to create more believable, psychologically complex characters. Since the characters' environments can also impact their behavior, setting became central to fiction. Austen, the Brontë sisters, Thomas Hardy, and other nineteenth-century writers reevaluated how elements like plot, character, and setting affect the way a story is told. Through their attention and experimentation, the novel acquired new dimension, depth, and levels of realism.

CONTEXTS		TEXTS
1660	Charles II restored to the throne	
1662	Passage of the Act of Uniformity, requiring clergymen and schoolteachers to accept the Book of Common Prayer	
1664–66	The Great Plague of London kills a recorded 68,596 people, but fatalities likely exceed 100,000 of a population estimated at 460,000	
1664	Passage of the Conventicle Act, punishing those who did not conform to the Church of England	
1666	The Great Fire of London destroys St. Paul's Cathedral and most other buildings dating from the middle ages, Queen Elizabeth's reign, and the early Stuart period	
1667		John Dryden, *Annus Mirabilis* John Milton, *Paradise Lost*
1668	Dryden becomes first official Poet Laureate	
1673	Passage of the Test Act, requiring public officials to deny transubstantiation and receive the sacrament of communion	
1675		William Wycherley, *The Country-Wife*
1678	The "Popish Plot" evokes anti-Catholic hysteria	John Bunyan, *Pilgrim's Progress*, part I
1679	Passage of the Habeas Corpus Act, requiring captors to bring detainees before the court	John Wilmot, Second Earl of Rochester, "A Satyr against Reason and Mankind"

1681	Charles II dissolves Parliament	
1685	Death of Charles II; Accession of James II	
1687	Passage of the Declaration of Indulgence, allowing people the right to worship publicly and freely	Sir Isaac Newton, *Principia Mathematica*
1688	The Glorious Revolution establishes William of Orange and Mary II as joint-ruling monarchs	Aphra Behn, *Oroonoko*
1689	Bill of Rights outlines basic civil rights and resolves inheritance of the Crown	John Locke, *Two Treatises of Government*
1690		Locke, *An Essay Concerning Human Understanding*
1694	Death of Queen Mary Bank of England founded	
1700		William Congreve, *The Way of the World*
1701	Act of Settlement transfers the Crown to the Hanoverian descendants of James I	
1702	Death of William III; succession of Queen Anne. War of the Spanish Succession	
1704		Jonathan Swift, *A Tale of a Tub* Newton, *Opticks*
1707	Act of Union unites England, Scotland, and Wales as Great Britain	
1711		Alexander Pope, *An Essay on Criticism*
1713	Treaty of Utrecht resolves the War of the Spanish Succession	

1714	Death of Queen Anne George of Hanover becomes George I	
1715	Jacobite rising in Scotland	
1716		Lady Mary Wortley Montagu, *Court Poems*
1717		Pope, *The Rape of the Lock* (final version)
1718		Susanna Centlivre, *A Bold Stroke for a Wife*
1719		Daniel Defoe, *Robinson Crusoe*
1726		Swift, *Gulliver's Travels*
1727	Death of George I; Succession of George II	
1728		John Gay, *The Beggar's Opera*
1729		Swift, *A Modest Proposal*
1733		Pope, *An Essay on Man*
1737	Passage of the Licensing Act, censoring plays	
1740		Samuel Richardson, *Pamela*
1742	Prime minister Robert Walpole resigns	
1746	Battle of Culloden, ending the last Jacobite rebellion	
1747		Richardson, *Clarissa*
1749		Henry Fielding, *The History of Tom Jones, a Foundling*
1751		Thomas Gray, "Elegy Written in a Country Church Yard"

1755		Samuel Johnson, *A Dictionary of the English Language*
1756–63	Seven Years' War between Britain and France for control of North America	
1757	British East India Company gains control of India	
1760	George III succeeds to the throne	
1761		Laurence Sterne, *Tristram Shandy* (1760–67)
1763	Peace of Paris ends the Seven Years' War	
1764	Invention of the spinning jenny, a machine for spinning wool or cotton that allows users to spin eight threads at once	
1768	Captain James Cook explores Australia and New Zealand	Encyclopedia Britannica (1768–71)
1775–83	Britain's North American colonies rebel, instigating the American Revolutionary War	
1776	British authority is no longer recognized in the North American colonies after the American Declaration of Independence	Adam Smith, *The Wealth of Nations*
1778		Frances Burney, *Evelina*
1783	William Pitt becomes prime minister	
1785		William Cowper, *The Task*

Aphra Behn
1640?–1689

As a result of either inadequate record-keeping or deliberate measures to obscure her past, Aphra Behn's early years are a mystery. Some scholars believe that Behn was baptized on July 10, 1640, in Kent, England, under the name Aphara Amis. According to one account, she was known as Ayfara or Aphra; during the 1650s, she traveled with the Amis couple to the English colony of Suriname in South America. Other scholars believe she was the daughter of Bartholomew Johnson, a barber, who might have sailed with her to Suriname in 1663. We do know that she acquired a sizeable foundation of literary knowledge and learned several languages in her youth, but the details of her education remain uncertain.

She returned to England in 1664 and married a merchant named Behn, who either separated from her or died by the following year. Scholars suggest that he may have perished during the Great Plague of 1665. In 1666, King Charles II employed Aphra Behn to do secret service work in the Netherlands during the Anglo-Dutch War. Dispatched to Antwerp, Belgium, under the codenames Astrea and Agent 160, she relayed information about Dutch plans back to England. Unfortunately, officials ignored her report that the Dutch intended to attack the English navy. On June 13, 1667, Dutch warships sailed up the River Thames, destroyed part of the English fleet, and towed away the English flagship *Royal Charles*. The naval defeat was utterly humiliating.

Since spies were largely left to fend for themselves, Behn repeatedly requested financial assistance from Charles II. Her appeals went unanswered, and when she returned to London in 1667, she was imprisoned for debt. Lord Arlington, the cabinet member tasked with intelligence, or Thomas Killigrew, Lord Arlington's agent and a dramatist, likely provided support.

Once released, Behn began writing to sustain herself. Since Charles II re-opened the theatres when he was restored to the throne, dramas gained undeniable popularity as the favored literary form of the Restoration period. Behn composed seventeen dramas, but she may have written up to twenty-one. As a writer for the Duke's Company, she had a host of extremely talented actors and actresses to perform in her productions. Behn penned tragicomedies, comedies of wit and intrigue, and political satires. Drawing inspiration from the Jacobean dramatists,

Spanish and French novellas, and contemporary events, she developed complex, action-laced plots. The interplay between sex and power also animates her works, and Behn often emphasizes the need for women to make their own choices in marriage. For example, two women in *The Rover* secure marriages on their own terms, achieving financial independence as well as emotional compatibility in the process. Although the play's title honors the rover Willmore, Behn accentuates female power by having various women indirectly control the play's action. *The Rover*'s humor, wit, and dynamism established it as Behn's most popular drama.

Behn later tried her hand at prose narrative, poetry, and translations. She wrote a total of fourteen prose fiction pieces, most of which were completed after 1684. Since the novel did not develop a more structured form until after her death, her longer works can be recognized as precursors to the novel. Striving for realistic effects, Behn incorporated a plethora of visual details, but her works lack psychological realism and rely heavily on chance. As in her plays, Behn's prose fiction often embraces themes of love. Her longest work, the 200,000 word *Love*

Letters Between a Nobleman and His Sister, uses the epistolary narrative technique to explore a scandalous romance between a nobleman and his sister-in-law. Samuel Richardson and other writers popularized the epistolary form throughout the 18th century. Behn's best-known prose work is *Oroonoko: Or, The History of the Royal Slave*. Set in Suriname, *Oroonoko* is a suspenseful and tragic romance. In addition to asserting the need for women to select their own husbands, Behn expounds an opposition to slavery and the slave trade. The story is fueled by first-person observations and sensory details. Behn depicts local wildlife and incorporates cultural elements, such as words from the Carib language and village healing practices. Her details, however, are at times inaccurate. For example, prince Orookoko's lover Imoinda is likely from the Gold Coast, but her markings do not resemble African tribal scars. Nonetheless, both Daniel Defoe and Jonathan Swift embraced Behn's use of concrete details to promote realism.

Though Behn established her literary presence through drama and prose, playwrights risked charges of libel and sedition, and Behn sought a safer and more respectable way to earn a living. Her poetry and translations receive less acclaim from contemporary scholars than her other works. Her poems lack sharp satire, instead leaning toward pastoral love. In lyrical as well as occasional poems, she utilizes heroic couplets. Financial troubles drove her to take on translation projects in addition to her poetry. The exact nature of Behn's financial situation is unknown, but she accepted both French and Latin texts even though she was not proficient in the latter. By modern standards, Behn took great liberties with her translations; however, John Dryden, the dominant literary figure of her time, believed that translators must paraphrase and alter material to suit readers' demands. Whether working on translations or in other genres, Behn catered her characters to what her audience desired. She attempted panegyrics, songs, prologues, epilogues, and satires, sometimes incorporating her political views into her writing. Unlike many other literary figures, Behn supported a divine-right monarchy and scorned democracy.

After writing a satire against the Duke of Monmouth, King Charles II's illegitimate son, in 1682, Behn was once again imprisoned. Despite this blunder, she maintained her popularity. Restoration writers like Behn led precarious existences unless patrons supplemented their incomes, and Behn likely suffered financial strains when the Stuart monarchy began to lose its power. In spite of her declining health, she continued writing in order to afford basic necessities. She completed *The Widow Ranter: Or, The History of Bacon of Virginia*, a drama based on the accounts of the Virginia colony in North America, before her death in 1689.

Behn's literary career spanned only about twenty years, but over half of her career is considered her golden age. While her primary reason for writing may have been pecuniary, she laid the groundwork for a public space for women writers—a feat female playwrights in the next generation recognized. Behn's peers appreciated her, but writers in the eighteenth and nineteenth centuries typically loathed her. Considered an immoral, mediocre woman writer, Behn's reputation did not recover until the twentieth century. In addition to her literary accomplishments in both drama and prose fiction, contemporary scholars note her contributions to the emerging form of the novel. Behn also holds a major place in the history of women writers: She is believed to be the first Englishwoman writer to earn a living by writing.

1640?	Born in Harbledown?, a town in Kent, England
1664	Marries Behn
1666–67	Employed in secret service to the Netherlands
1670	*The Forc'd Marriage: Or, the Jealous Bridegroom*
1671	*The Amorous Prince*
1676	*Abdelazer*
1677	*The Rover: Or, The Banish'd Cavaliers*
1683–87	*Love Letters Between a Nobleman and His Sister*
1687	Translation of *Aesop's Fables* with Francis Barlow
1688	*Oroonoko: Or, The History of the Royal Slave*; *The Fair Jilt: Or, The History of Prince Tarquin and Miranda*; "To the Fair Clarinda, Who Made to Love Me, Imagined More Than Woman"
1689	*The Widow Ranter: Or, The History of Bacon of Virginia*; dies 16 April and is buried in Westminster Abbey

THE ROVER
OR, THE BANISH'D CAVALIERS

PART I.

PROLOGUE
Written by a Person of Quality

Wits like Physicians never can agree,
When of a different Society.
And Rabels Drops were never more cry'd down
By all the Learned Doctors of the Town,
Than a new Play whose Author is unknown.   5
Nor can those Doctors with more Malice sue
(And powerful Purses) the dissenting Few,
Than those with an insulting Pride, do rail
At all who are not of their own Cabal.
If a Young Poet hit your humour right,   10
You judge him then out of Revenge and Spite.
So amongst men there are Ridiculous Elves,
Who Monkeys hate for being too like themselves.
So that the reason of the grand debate,
Why Wit so oft is damn'd, when good Plays take,   15
Is, that you Censure as you love or hate.
Thus like a Learned Conclave, Poets sit
Catholick Judges both of Sense and Wit,
And Damn or Save, as they themselves think fit.
Yet those who to others faults are so severe,   20
Are not so perfect but themselves may Err.
Some write Correct indeed, but then the whole
(Bating their own dull stuff i'th' Play) is stole:
As Bees do suck from Flowers their Honey-dew,
So they rob others, striving to please you.   25
Some write their Characters genteel and fine,
But then they do so Toil for every line,
That what to you does Easy seem, and Plain,
Is the hard issue of their labouring Brain.

And some th' Effects of all their Pains we see,   30
Is but to Mimick good Extempore.
Others, by long Converse about the Town,
Have Wit enough to write a Lew'd Lampoon,
But their chief skill lies in a Bawdy Song.
In short, the only Wit that's now in Fashion   35
Is but the Gleanings of good Conversation.
As for the Author of this coming Play,
I ask'd him what he thought fit I should say
In thanks for your good Company to day:
He call'd me Fool, and said it was well known,   40
You came not here for our sakes, but your own.
New Plays are stuff'd with Wits, and with Debauches,
That Crowd and sweat like Citts in May Day[1] Coaches.

DRAMATIS PERSONÆ

MEN

DON ANTONIO, *the Vice-Roy's Son*

DON PEDRO, *a Noble* Spaniard, *his Friend*

BELVILE, *an* English *Colonel, in Love with* FLORINDA

WILLMORE, *the* ROVER

FREDERICK, *an* English *Gentleman, and Friend*
    to BELVILE *and* BLUNT

BLUNT, *an* English *Country Gentleman*

STEPHANO, *Servant to* DON PEDRO

PHILIPPO, LUCETTA's *Gallant*

SANCHO, *Pimp to* LUCETTA

BISKEY *and* SEBASTIAN, *two Bravoes to* ANGELLICA

OFFICERS *and* SOLDIERS

PAGE, *to* DON ANTONIO

---

1 A holiday celebrating the arrival of spring. Festivities included making floral garlands, gathering greenery, dancing around a Maypole, and choosing a May queen. Hyde Park became a common gathering place for people of all classes to converge.

WOMEN

FLORINDA, *Sister to* DON PEDRO

HELLENA, *a gay young Woman design'd for a Nun,
and Sister to* FLORINDA

VALERIA, *a Kinswoman to* FLORINDA

ANGELLICA BIANCA, *a famous Curtezan*

MORETTA, *her Woman*

CALLIS, *Governess to* FLORINDA *and* HELLENA

LUCETTA, A JILTING WENCH

SERVANTS, *Other* MASQUERADERS, MEN *and* WOMEN

The SCENE—Naples, in Carnival time.

ACT I.

SCENE I. *A chamber.*

Enter FLORINDA *and* HELLENA.

FLORINDA. What an Impertinent thing is a young Girl bred in a Nunnery! How
full of Questions? Prithee no more, Hellena; I have told thee more than thou
understand'st already.

HELLENA. The more's my grief, I wou'd fain know as much as you, which makes
me so inquisitive; nor is't enough to know you're a Lover, unless you tell me
too, who 'tis you sigh for.

FLORINDA. When you're a Lover, I'll think you fit for a Secret of that Nature.

HELLENA. 'Tis true, I was never a Lover yet—but I begin to have a shrew'd guess,
what 'tis to be so, and fancy it very pretty to sigh, and sing, and blush and
wish, and dream and wish, and long and wish to see the Man; and when I do
look pale and tremble; just as you did when my Brother brought home the
fine English Colonel to see you—what do you call him? Don Belvile.

FLORINDA. Fie Hellena.

HELLENA. That blush betrays you—I am sure 'tis so—or is it Don Antonio the
Vice-Roy's Son?—or perhaps the Rich old Don Vincentio whom my father
designs for your Husband?—Why do you blush again?

FLORINDA. With Indignation, and how near soever my Father thinks I am to Marrying that hated Object, I shall let him see, I understand better, what's due to my Beauty, Birth and Fortune, and more to my Soul, than to obey those unjust Commands.

HELLENA. Now hang me, if I don't love thee for that dear disobedience. I love mischief strangely, as most of our Sex do, who are come to love nothing else—But tell me, dear Florinda, don't you love that fine *Anglese?*—for I vow next to loving him my self, 'twill please me most that you do so, for he is so gay and so handsome.

FLORINDA. Hellena, a Maid design'd for a Nun, ought not to be so Curious in a Discourse of Love.

HELLENA. And dost thou think that ever I'll be a Nun? or at least till I'm so old, I'm fit for nothing else. Faith no, Sister; and that which makes me long to know whether you love Belvile, is because I hope he has some mad Companion or other, that will spoil my devotion, nay, I'm resolv'd to provide my self this Carnival, if there be e'er a handsome proper fellow of my humour above ground, tho I ask first.

FLORINDA. Prithee be not so wild.

HELLENA. Now you have provided your self with a Man, you take no Care for poor me—prithee tell me, what dost thou see about me that is unfit for Love— have not I a World of Youth? a Humour gay? a Beauty passable? a Vigour desirable? well shap'd? clean limb'd? sweet breath'd? and sense enough to know how all these ought to be employ'd to the best Advantage; yes, I do and will, therefore lay aside your hopes of my Fortune, by my being a Devotee, and tell me how you came acquainted with this Belvile; for I perceive you knew him before he came to *Naples*.

FLORINDA. Yes, I knew him at the Seige of *Pampelona*,[1] he was then a Colonel of *French* Horse, who when the Town was Ransack'd, nobly treated my Brother and my self, preserving us from all Insolencies; and I must own, (besides great obligations) I have I know not what, that pleads kindly for him about my Heart, and will suffer no other to enter—But see my Brother.

Enter DON PEDRO, STEPHANO, *with a Masquing Habit, and* CALLIS.

PEDRO. Good morrow Sister. Pray when saw you your Lover Don Vincentio?

FLORINDA. I know not, Sir—Callis, when was he here? for I consider it so little, I know not when it was.

---

1 (Battle of Pamplona) The Spanish had gained control of part of Navarre in 1512. In 1521, with the assistance of French forces, the Navarrese defeated the Spanish garrison and captured Pamplona, the capital. Ignatius of Loyola, a Spanish soldier who was wounded during the battle, later founded the Jesuits.

PEDRO. I have a Command from my Father here to tell you, you ought not to despise him, a Man of so vast a Fortune, and such a Passion for you—Stephano, my things—[*Puts on his Masquing habit.*]

FLORINDA. A Passion for me, 'tis more than e'er I saw, or had a desire should be known—I hate Vincentio, and I wou'd not have a Man so dear to me as my Brother, follow the ill Customs of our Country, and make a slave of his Sister—and Sir, my Father's will, I'm sure, you may divert.

PEDRO. I know not how dear I am to you, but I wish only to be rank'd in your esteem, equal with the *English* Colonel Belvile—why do you frown and blush? Is there any guilt belongs to the Name of that Cavalier?

FLORINDA. I'll not deny I value Belvile, when I was expos'd to such dangers as the licens'd Lust of common Soldiers threatened, when Rage and Conquest flew through the City—then Belvile, this Criminal for my sake, threw him self into all dangers to save my honour, and will you not allow him my esteem?

PEDRO. Yes, pay him what you will in Honour—but you must consider Don Vincentio's Fortune, and the Jointure he'll make you.

FLORINDA. Let him consider my Youth, Beauty and Fortune; which ought not to be thrown away on his Age and Jointure.

PEDRO. 'Tis true, he's not so young and fine a Gentleman as that Belvile—but what Jewels will that Cavalier present you with? those of his Eyes and Heart?

HELLENA. And are not those better than any *Don Vincentio* has brought from the *Indies*?

PEDRO. Why how now! has your Nunnery-breeding taught you to understand the value of Hearts and Eyes?

HELLENA. Better than to believe Vincentio deserves Value from any Woman—he may perhaps encrease her Bags, but not her Family.

PEDRO. This is fine—go up to your Devotion, you are not design'd for the conversation of Lovers.

HELLENA. Nor Saints, yet a while I hope. [*Aside.*] Is't not enough you make a Nun of me, but you must cast my Sister away too? exposing her to a worse confinement than a Religious Life?

PEDRO. The Girl's mad—is it a Confinement to be carry'd into the Country, to an Ancient Villa belonging to the Family of the Vincentio's these five hundred Years, and have no other Prospect than that pleasing one of seeing all her own that meets her Eyes—a fine Air, large Fields and Gardens, where she may walk and gather Flowers?

HELLENA. When? By Moon-Light? For I'm sure she dares not encounter with the heat of the Sun; that were a Task only for Don Vincentio and his *Indian* Breeding, who loves it in the Dog-days—And if these be her daily Divertisements, what are those of the Night, to lie in a wide Moth-eaten Bed-Chamber with Furniture in Fashion in the Reign of King *Sancho*[1] the First; the Bed that which his Forefathers liv'd and dy'd in.

PEDRO. Very well.

HELLENA. This Apartment (new furbisht and fitted out for the young Wife) he (out of Freedom) makes his Dressing-room; and being a frugal and a jealous Coxcomb, instead of a Valet to uncase his feeble Carcass, he desires you to do that Office—Signs of Favour, I'll assure you, and such as you must not hope for, unless your Woman be out of the way.

PEDRO. Have you done yet?

HELLENA. That Honour being past, the Giant stretches it self, yawns and sighs a Belch or two as loud as a Musket, throws himself into Bed, and expects you in his foul Sheets, and e'er you can get your self undrest, calls you with a Snore or two—And are not these fine Blessings to a young Lady?

PEDRO. Have you done yet?

HELLENA. And this Man you must kiss, nay, you must kiss none but him too—and nuzle thro his Beard to find his Lips—and this you must submit to for three-score Years, and all for a Jointure.

PEDRO. For all your Character of Don Vincentio, she is as like to marry him as she was before.

HELLENA. Marry Don Vincentio! hang me, such a Wedlock would be worse than Adultery with another Man: I had rather see her in the *Hostel de Dieu*, to waste her Youth there in Vows, and be a Handmaid to Lazers and Cripples, than to lose it in such a Marriage.

PEDRO. You have consider'd, Sister, that Belvile has no Fortune to bring you to, is banisht his Country, despis'd at home, and pity'd abroad.

HELLENA. What then? the Vice-Roy's Son is better than that Old Sir Fisty. Don Vincentio! Don Indian! he thinks he's trading to *Gambo*[2] still, and wou'd barter himself (that Bell and Bawble) for your Youth and Fortune.

PEDRO. Callis, take her hence, and lock her up all this Carnival, and at Lent she shall begin her everlasting Penance in a Monastery.

HELLENA. I care not, I had rather be a Nun, than be oblig'd to marry as you wou'd have me, if I were design'd for't.

PEDRO. Do not fear the Blessing of that Choice—you shall be a Nun.

HELLENA. Shall I so? you may chance to be mistaken in my way of Devotion—A Nun! yes I am like to make a fine Nun! I have an excellent Humour for a

---

1 King Sancho I, nicknamed Sancho the Fat, ruled the Spanish state of Leon from 956-967.

2 Located in West Africa, Gambo (Gambia) was a British colony.

Grate: No, I'll have a Saint of my own to pray to shortly, if I like any that dares venture on me. [*Aside.*]

PEDRO. Callis, make it your Business to watch this wild Cat. As for you, Florinda, I've only try'd you all this while, and urg'd my Father's Will; but mine is, that you would love Antonio, he is brave and young, and all that can compleat the Happiness of a gallant Maid—This Absence of my Father will give us opportunity to free you from Vincentio, by marrying here, which you must do to morrow.

FLORINDA. To morrow!

PEDRO. To morrow, or 'twill be too late—'tis not my Friendship to Antonio, which makes me urge this, but Love to thee, and Hatred to Vincentio—therefore resolve upon't to morrow.

FLORINDA. Sir, I shall strive to do, as shall become your Sister.

PEDRO. I'll both believe and trust you—Adieu. [*Exit* PEDRO *and* STEPHANO.]

HELLENA. As become his Sister!—That is, to be as resolved your way, as he is his—
     [HELLENA *goes to* CALLIS.]

FLORINDA. I ne'er till now perceiv'd my Ruin near,

     I've no Defence against Antonio's Love,

     For he has all the Advantages of Nature,

     The moving Arguments of Youth and Fortune.

HELLENA. But hark you, Callis, you will not be so cruel to lock me up indeed: will you?

CALLIS. I must obey the Commands I hate—besides, do you consider what a Life you are going to lead?

HELLENA. Yes, Callis, that of a Nun: and till then I'll be indebted a World of Prayers to you, if you let me now see, what I never did, the Divertisements of a Carnival.

CALLIS. What, go in Masquerade? 'twill be a fine farewell to the World I take it— pray what wou'd you do there?

HELLENA. That which all the World does, as I am told, be as mad as the rest, and take all innocent Freedom—Sister, you'll go too, will you not? come prithee be not sad—We'll out-wit twenty Brothers, if you'll be ruled by me—Come put off this dull Humour with your Clothes, and assume one as gay, and as fantastick as the Dress my Cousin Valeria and I have provided, and let's ramble.

FLORINDA. Callis, will you give us leave to go?

CALLIS. I have a youthful Itch of going my self. [*Aside.*]—Madam, if I thought your Brother might not know it, and I might wait on you, for by my troth I'll not trust young Girls alone.

FLORINDA. Thou see'st my Brother's gone already, and thou shalt attend and watch us.

Enter STEPHANO.

STEPHANO. Madam, the Habits are come, and your Cousin Valeria is drest, and stays for you.

FLORINDA. 'Tis well—I'll write a Note, and if I chance to see Belvile, and want an opportunity to speak to him, that shall let him know what I've resolv'd in favour of him.

HELLENA. Come, let's in and dress us. [*Exeunt.*]

SCENE II. *A long Street.*

Enter BELVILE, *melancholy,* BLUNT *and* FREDERICK.

FREDERICK. Why, what the Devil ails the Colonel, in a time when all the World is gay, to look like mere Lent thus? Hadst thou been long enough in *Naples* to have been in love, I should have sworn some such Judgment had befall'n thee.

BELVILE. No, I have made no new Amours since I came to *Naples.*

FREDERICK. You have left none behind you in *Paris.*

BELVILE. Neither.

FREDERICK. I can't divine the Cause then; unless the old Cause, the want of Money.

BLUNT. And another old Cause, the want of a Wench— Wou'd not that revive you?

BELVILE. You're mistaken, Ned.

BLUNT. Nay, 'Sheartlikins, then thou art past Cure.

FREDERICK. I have found it out; thou hast renew'd thy Acquaintance with the Lady that cost thee so many Sighs at the Siege of *Pampelona*—pox on't, what d'ye call her—her Brother's a noble *Spaniard*—Nephew to the dead General— Florinda—ay, Florinda—And will nothing serve thy turn but that damn'd virtuous Woman, whom on my Conscience thou lov'st in spite too, because thou seest little or no possibility of gaining her?

BELVILE. Thou art mistaken, I have Interest enough in that lovely Virgin's Heart, to make me proud and vain, were it not abated by the Severity of a Brother, who perceiving my Happiness—

FREDERICK. Has civilly forbid thee the House?

BELVILE. 'Tis so, to make way for a powerful Rival, the Vice-Roy's Son, who has the advantage of me, in being a Man of Fortune, a *Spaniard*, and her Brother's Friend; which gives him liberty to make his Court, whilst I have recourse only to Letters, and distant Looks from her Window, which are as soft and kind as those which Heav'n sends down on Penitents.

BLUNT. Hey day! 'Sheartlikins, Simile! by this Light the Man is quite spoil'd— Frederick, what the Devil are we made of, that we cannot be thus concern'd for a Wench?—'Sheartlikins, our *Cupids* are like the Cooks of the Camp, they can roast or boil a Woman, but they have none of the fine Tricks to set 'em off, no Hogoes[1] to make the Sauce pleasant, and the Stomach sharp.

FREDERICK. I dare swear I have had a hundred as young, kind and handsome as this Florinda; and Dogs eat me, if they were not as troublesome to me i'th' Morning as they were welcome o'er night.

BLUNT. And yet, I warrant, he wou'd not touch another Woman, if he might have her for nothing.

BELVILE. That's thy Joy, a cheap Whore.

BLUNT. Why, 'dsheartlikins, I love a frank Soul—When did you ever hear of an honest Woman that took a Man's Money? I warrant 'em good ones—But, Gentlemen, you may be free, you have been kept so poor with Parliaments and Protectors, that the little Stock you have is not worth preserving—but I thank my Stars, I have more Grace than to forfeit my Estate by Cavaliering.

BELVILE. Methinks only following the Court should be sufficient to entitle 'em to that.

BLUNT. 'Sheartlikins, they know I follow it to do it no good, unless they pick a hole in my Coat for lending you Money now and then; which is a greater Crime to my Conscience, Gentlemen, than to the Common-wealth.

Enter WILLMORE.

WILLMORE. Ha! Dear Belvile! noble Colonel!

BELVILE. Willmore! welcome ashore, my dear Rover!—what happy Wind blew us this good Fortune?

WILLMORE. Let me salute you my dear Frederick, and then command me—How is't honest Lad?

FREDERICK. Faith, Sir, the old Complement, infinitely the better to see my dear mad Willmore again—Prithee why camest thou ashore? and where's the Prince?

WILLMORE. He's well, and reigns still Lord of the watery Element—I must aboard again within a Day or two, and my Business ashore was only to enjoy my self a little this Carnival.

BELVILE. Pray know our new Friend, Sir, he's but bashful, a raw Traveller, but honest, stout, and one of us. [*Embraces* BLUNT.]

WILLMORE. That you esteem him, gives him an Interest here.

BLUNT. Your Servant, Sir.

WILLMORE. But well— Faith I'm glad to meet you again in a warm Climate, where the kind Sun has its god-like Power still over the Wine and Women.—Love

---

1 An Anglican spelling of the French word haut-goût, meaning a slight taint of decay (found especially in wild game meat) that was once considered desirable.

and Mirth are my Business in *Naples*; and if I mistake not the Place, here's an excellent Market for Chapmen of my Humour.

BELVILE. See here be those kind Merchants of Love you look for.

> *Enter several Men in masquing Habits, some playing on Musick, others dancing after; Women drest like Curtezans, with Papers pinn'd to their Breasts, and Baskets of Flowers in their Hands.*

BLUNT. 'Sheartlikins, what have we here!

FREDERICK. Now the Game begins.

WILLMORE. Fine pretty Creatures! may a stranger have leave to look and love?— What's here—*Roses for every Month!* [*Reads the Paper.*]

BLUNT. Roses for every Month! what means that?

BELVILE. They are, or wou'd have you think they're Curtezans, who here in *Naples* are to be hir'd by the Month.

WILLMORE. Kind and obliging to inform us—Pray where do these Roses grow? I would fain plant some of 'em in a Bed of mine.

WOMAN. Beware such Roses, Sir.

WILLMORE. A Pox of Fear: I'll be bak'd with thee between a pair of Sheets, and that's thy proper Still, so I might but strow such Roses over me and under me—Fair one, wou'd you wou'd give me leave to gather at your Bush this idle Month, I wou'd go near to make some Body smell of it all the Year after.

BELVILE. And thou hast need of such a Remedy, for thou stinkest of Tar and Rope-ends, like a Dock or Pesthouse.

> [*The Woman puts herself into the Hands of a Man, and* Exit.]

WILLMORE. Nay, nay, you shall not leave me so.

BELVILE. By all Means use no Violence here.

WILLMORE. Death! just as I was going to be damnably in love, to have her led off! I could pluck that Rose out of his Hand, and even kiss the Bed, the Bush it grew in.

FREDERICK. No Friend to Love like a long Voyage at Sea.

BLUNT. Except a Nunnery, Frederick.

WILLMORE. Death! but will they not be kind, quickly be kind? Thou know'st I'm no tame Sigher, but a rampant Lion of the Forest.

> *Two Men drest all over with Horns of several sorts, making Grimaces at one another, with Papers pinn'd on their Backs, advance from the farther end of the Scene.*

BELVILE. Oh the fantastical Rogues, how they are dress'd! 'tis a Satire against the whole Sex.

WILLMORE. Is this a Fruit that grows in this warm Country?

BELVILE. Yes: 'Tis pretty to see these *Italian* start, swell, and stab at the Word *Cuckold*, and yet stumble at Horns on every Threshold.

WILLMORE. See what's on their Back—*Flowers for every Night.* [*Reads.*]—Ah Rogue! And more sweet than Roses of ev'ry Month! This is a Gardiner of *Adam's* own breeding. [*They dance.*]

BELVILE. What think you of those grave People?—is a Wake in *Essex* half so mad or extravagant?

WILLMORE. I like their sober grave way, 'tis a kind of legal authoriz'd Fornication, where the Men are not chid for't, nor the Women despis'd, as amongst our dull *English*; even the Monsieurs want that part of good Manners.

BELVILE. But here in *Italy* a Monsieur is the humblest best-bred Gentleman— Duels are so baffled by Bravo's, that an Age shews not one, but between a *Frenchman* and a Hang-man, who is as much too hard for him on the Piazza, as they are for a *Dutchman* on the new Bridge—But see another Crew.

Enter FLORINDA, HELLENA, *and* VALERIA, *drest like Gipsies;* CALLIS *and* STEPHANO, LUCETTA, PHILLIPPO *and* SANCHO *in Masquerade.*

HELLENA. Sister, there's your *Englishman*, and with him a handsome proper Fellow—I'll to him, and instead of telling him his Fortune, try my own.

WILLMORE. Gipsies, on my Life—Sure these will prattle if a Man cross their Hands. [*Goes to* HELLENA]—Dear pretty (and I hope) young Devil, will you tell an amorous Stranger what Luck he's like to have?

HELLENA. Have a care how you venture with me, Sir, lest I pick your Pocket, which will more vex your *English* Humour, than an *Italian* Fortune will please you.

WILLMORE. How the Devil cam'st thou to know my Country and Humour?

HELLENA. The first I guess by a certain forward Impudence, which does not displease me at this time; and the Loss of your Money will vex you, because I hope you have but very little to lose.

WILLMORE. Egad, Child, thou'rt i'th' right; it is so little, I dare not offer it thee for a Kindness—But cannot you divine what other things of more value I have about me, that I would more willingly part with?

HELLENA. Indeed no, that's the Business of a Witch, and I am but a Gipsy yet—Yet, without looking in your Hand, I have a parlous Guess, 'tis some foolish Heart you mean, an inconstant *English* Heart, as little worth stealing as your Purse.

WILLMORE. Nay, then thou dost deal with the Devil, that's certain—Thou hast guess'd as right as if thou hadst been one of that Number it has languisht for—I find you'll be better acquainted with it; nor can you take it in a better time, for I come from Sea, Child; and *Venus* not being propitious to me in her own Element, I have a world of Love in store—Wou'd you would be good-natur'd, and take some on't off my Hands.

HELLENA. Why—I could be inclin'd that way—but for a foolish Vow I am going to make—to die a Maid.

WILLMORE. Then thou art damn'd without Redemption; and as I am a good Christian, I ought in charity to divert so wicked a Design—therefore prithee dear Creature, let me know quickly when and where I shall begin to set a helping hand to so good a Work.

HELLENA. If you should prevail with my tender Heart (as I begin to fear you will, for you have horrible loving Eyes) there will be difficulty in't that you'll hardly undergo for my sake.

WILLMORE. Faith, Child, I have been bred in Dangers, and wear a Sword that has been employ'd in a worse Cause, than for a handsome kind Woman—Name the Danger—let it be any thing but a long Siege, and I'll undertake it.

HELLENA. Can you storm?

WILLMORE. Oh, most furiously.

HELLENA. What think you of a Nunnery-wall? for he that wins me, must gain that first.

WILLMORE. A Nun! Oh how I love thee for't! there's no Sinner like a young Saint—Nay, now there's no denying me: the old Law had no Curse (to a Woman) like dying a Maid; witness *Jephtha's* Daughter.[1]

HELLENA. A very good Text this, if well handled; and I perceive, Father Captain, you would impose no severe Penance on her who was inclin'd to console her self before she took Orders.

WILLMORE. If she be young and handsome.

HELLENA. Ay, there's it—but if she be not—

WILLMORE. By this Hand, Child, I have an implicit Faith, and dare venture on thee with all Faults—besides, 'tis more meritorious to leave the World when thou hast tasted and prov'd the Pleasure on't; then 'twill be a Virtue in thee, which now will be pure Ignorance.

HELLENA. I perceive, good Father Captain, you design only to make me fit for Heaven—but if on the contrary you should quite divert me from it, and bring me back to the World again, I should have a new Man to seek I find; and what a Grief that will be—for when I begin, I fancy I shall love like any thing: I never try'd yet.

WILLMORE. Egad, and that's kind—Prithee, dear Creature, give me Credit for a Heart, for faith I'm a very honest Fellow—Oh, I long to come first to the Banquet of Love; and such a swinging Appetite I bring—Oh, I'm impatient. Thy Lodging, Sweet-heart, thy Lodging, or I'm a dead man.

---

1 Judges 11: 37-40: Jephtha vowed to sacrifice his daughter to God. Before he made the sacrifice, he allowed her to roam the mountains and "bewail [her] virginity" for two months.

HELLENA. Why must we be either guilty of Fornication or Murder, if we converse with you Men?—And is there no difference between leave to love me, and leave to lie with me?

WILLMORE. Faith, Child, they were made to go together.

LUCETTA. Are you sure this is the man? [*Pointing to* BLUNT.]

SANCHO. When did I mistake your Game?

LUCETTA. This is a stranger, I know by his gazing; if he be brisk he'll venture to follow me; and then, if I understand my Trade, he's mine: he's *English* too, and they say that's a sort of good-natur'd loving People, and have generally so kind an Opinion of themselves, that a Woman with any Wit may flatter 'em into any sort of Fool she pleases.

BLUNT. 'Tis so—she is taken—I have Beauties which my false Glass at home did not discover.

[*She often passes by* BLUNT, *and gazes on him; he struts, and cocks, and walks, and gazes on her.*]

FLORINDA. This Woman watches me so, I shall get no Opportunity to discover my self to him, and so miss the intent of my coming—But as I was saying, Sir—by this Line you should be a Lover. [*Looking in his Hand.*]

BELVILE. I thought how right you guess'd, all Men are in love, or pretend to be so—Come, let me go, I'm weary of this fooling. [*Walks away.*]

FLORINDA. I will not, till you have confess'd whether the Passion that you have vow'd Florinda be true or false. [*She holds him, he strives to get from her.*]

BELVILE. Florinda! [*Turns quick towards her.*]

FLORINDA. Softly.

BELVILE. Thou hast nam'd one will fix me here for ever.

FLORINDA. She'll be disappointed then, who expects you this Night at the Garden-gate, and if you'll fail not—as let me see the other Hand—you will go near to do—she vows to die or make you happy. [*Looks on* CALLIS, *who observes 'em.*]

BELVILE. What canst thou mean?

FLORINDA. That which I say—Farewell. [*Offers to go.*]

BELVILE. Oh charming Sybil stay, complete that Joy, which, as it is, will turn into Distraction!—Where must I be? at the Garden-gate? I know it—at night, you say—I'll sooner forfeit Heaven than disobey.

Enter DON PEDRO *and other Masquers, and pass over the Stage.*

CALLIS. Madam, your Brother's here.

FLORINDA. Take this to instruct you farther. [*Gives him a Letter, and goes off.*]

FREDERICK. Have a care, Sir, what you promise; this may be a Trap laid by her Brother to ruin you.

BELVILE. Do not disturb my Happiness with Doubts. [*Opens the Letter.*]

WILLMORE. My dear pretty Creature, a Thousand Blessings on thee; still in this Habit, you say, and after Dinner at this Place.

HELLENA. Yes, if you will swear to keep your Heart, and not bestow it between this time and that.

WILLMORE. By all the little Gods of Love I swear, I'll leave it with you; and if you run away with it, those Deities of Justice will revenge me. [*Exit all the Women except* LUCETTA.]

FREDERICK. Do you know the Hand?

BELVILE. 'Tis Florinda's. All Blessings fall upon the virtuous Maid.

FREDERICK. Nay, no Idolatry, a sober Sacrifice I'll allow you.

BELVILE. Oh Friends! the welcom'st News, the softest Letter!—nay, you shall see it; and could you now be serious, I might be made the happiest Man the Sun shines on.

WILLMORE. The Reason of this mighty Joy?

BELVILE. See how kindly she invites me to deliver her from the threatened Violence of her Brother—will you not assist me?

WILLMORE. I know not what thou mean'st, but I'll make one at any Mischief where a Woman's concern'd—but she'll be grateful to us for the Favour, will she not?

BELVILE. How mean you?

WILLMORE. How should I mean? Thou know'st there's but one way for a Woman to oblige me.

BELVILE. Don't prophane—the Maid is nicely virtuous.

WILLMORE. Who pox, then she's fit for nothing but a Husband; let her e'en go, Colonel.

FREDERICK. Peace, she's the Colonel's Mistress, Sir.

WILLMORE. Let her be the Devil; if she be thy Mistress, I'll serve her—name the way.

BELVILE. Read here this Postscript. [*Gives him a Letter.*]

WILLMORE. [*Reads.*] *At Ten at night—at the Garden-Gate—of which, if I cannot get the Key, I will contrive a way over the Wall—come attended with a Friend or two.*—Kind heart, if we three cannot weave a String to let her down a Garden-Wall, 'twere pity but the Hangman wove one for us all.

FREDERICK. Let her alone for that: your Woman's Wit, your fair kind Woman, will out-trick a Brother or a Jew, and contrive like a Jesuit in Chains—but see, Ned Blunt is stoln out after the Lure of a Damsel. [*Exit* BLUNT *and* LUCETTA.]

BELVILE. So he'll scarce find his way home again, unless we get him cry'd by the Bell-man in the Market-place, and 'twou'd sound prettily—a lost *English* Boy of Thirty.

FREDERICK. I hope 'tis some common crafty Sinner, one that will fit him; it may be she'll sell him for *Peru*, the Rogue's sturdy and would work well in a Mine; at least I hope she'll dress him for our Mirth; cheat him of all, then have him well-favour'dly bang'd, and turn'd out naked at Midnight.

WILLMORE. Prithee what Humour is he of, that you wish him so well?

BELVILE. Why, of an *English* Elder Brother's Humour, educated in a Nursery, with a Maid to tend him till Fifteen, and lies with his Grand-mother till he's of Age; one that knows no pleasure beyond riding to the next Fair, or going up to *London* with his right Worshipful Father in Parliament-time; wearing gay Clothes, or making honourable Love to his Lady Mother's Landry-Maid; gets drunk at a Hunting-Match, and ten to one then gives some Proofs of his Prowess—A pox upon him, he's our Banker, and has all our Cash about him, and if he fail we are all broke.

FREDERICK. Oh let him alone for that matter, he's of a damn'd stingy Quality, that will secure our Stock; I know not in what Danger it were indeed, if the Jilt should pretend she's in love with him, for 'tis a kind believing Coxcomb; otherwise if he part with more than a Piece of Eight—geld him: for which offer he may chance to be beaten, if she be a Whore of the first Rank.

BELVILE. Nay, the Rogue will not be easily beaten, he's stout enough; perhaps if they talk beyond his Capacity, he may chance to exercise his Courage upon some of them; else I'm sure they'll find it as difficult to beat as to please him.

WILLMORE. 'Tis a lucky Devil to light upon so kind a Wench!

FREDERICK. Thou hadst a great deal of talk with thy little Gipsy, coud'st thou do no good upon her? for mine was hard-hearted.

WILLMORE. Hang her, she was some damn'd honest Person of Quality, I'm sure, she was so very free and witty. If her Face be but answerable to her Wit and Humour, I wou'd be bound to Constancy this Month to gain her. In the mean time, have you made no kind Acquaintance since you came to Town?—You do not use to be honest so long, Gentlemen.

FREDERICK. Faith, Love has kept us honest, we have been all fir'd with a Beauty newly come to Town, the famous *Paduana* Angellica Bianca.

WILLMORE. What, the Mistress of the dead *Spanish* General?

BELVILE. Yes, she's now the only ador'd Beauty of all the Youth in *Naples*, who put on all their Charms to appear lovely in her sight, their Coaches, Liveries, and themselves, all gay, as on a Monarch's Birth-Day, to attract the Eyes of this fair Charmer, while she has the Pleasure to behold all languish for her that see her.

FREDERICK. 'Tis pretty to see with how much Love the Men regard her, and how much Envy the Women.

WILLMORE. What Gallant has she?

BELVILE. None, she's exposed to Sale, and four Days in the Week she's yours—for so much a Month.

WILLMORE. The very Thought of it quenches all manner of Fire in me—yet prithee let's see her.

BELVILE. Let's first to Dinner, and after that we'll pass the Day as you please—but at Night ye must all be at my Devotion.

WILLMORE. I will not fail you. [*Exeunt.*]

ACT II.

SCENE I. *The Long Street.*

Enter BELVILE *and* FREDERICK *in Masquing-Habits, and* WILLMORE *in his own Clothes, with a Vizard in his Hand.*

WILLMORE. But why thus disguis'd and muzzl'd?

BELVILE. Because whatever Extravagances we commit in these Faces, our own may not be oblig'd to answer 'em.

WILLMORE. I should have chang'd my Eternal Buff too; but no matter, my little Gipsy wou'd not have found me out then: for if she should change hers, it is impossible I should know her, unless I should hear her prattle—A pox on't, I cannot get her out of my Head: Pray Heaven, if ever I do see her again, she prove damnable ugly, that I may fortify my self against her Tongue.

BELVILE. Have a care of Love, for o' my conscience she was not of a Quality to give thee any hopes.

WILLMORE. Pox on 'em, why do they draw a Man in then? She has play'd with my Heart so, that 'twill never lie still, till I have met with some kind Wench, that will play the Game out with me—Oh for my Arms full of soft, white, kind—Woman! such as I fancy Angellica.

BELVILE. This is her House, if you were but in stock to get admittance; they have not din'd yet; I perceive the Picture is not out.

Enter BLUNT.

WILLMORE. I long to see the Shadow of the fair Substance, a Man may gaze on that for nothing.

BLUNT. Colonel, thy Hand—and thine, Frederick. I have been an Ass, a deluded Fool, a very Coxcomb from my Birth till this Hour, and heartily repent my little Faith.

BELVILE. What the Devil's the matter with thee, Ned?

BLUNT. Oh such a Mistress, Frederick, such a Girl!

WILLMORE. Ha! where?

FREDERICK. Ay where!

BLUNT. So fond, so amorous, so toying and fine! and all for sheer Love, ye Rogue! Oh how she lookt and kiss'd! and sooth'd my Heart from my Bosom. I cannot think I was awake, and yet methinks I see and feel her Charms still—Frederick—Try if she have not left the Taste of her balmy Kisses upon my Lips—[*Kisses him.*]

BELVILE. Ha, ha, ha!

WILLMORE. Death Man, where is she?

BLUNT. What a Dog was I to stay in dull *England* so long—How have I laught at the Colonel when he sigh'd for Love! but now the little Archer has reveng'd him, and by his own Dart, I can guess at all his Joys, which then I took for Fancies, mere Dreams and Fables—Well, I'm resolved to sell all in *Essex*, and plant here for ever.

BELVILE. What a Blessing 'tis, thou hast a Mistress thou dar'st boast of; for I know thy Humour is rather to have a proclaim'd Clap, than a secret Amour.

WILLMORE. Dost know her Name?

BLUNT. Her Name? No, 'sheartlikins: what care I for Names?—She's fair, young, brisk and kind, even to ravishment: and what a pox care I for knowing her by another Title?

WILLMORE. Didst give her anything?

BLUNT. Give her!—Ha, ha, ha! why, she's a Person of Quality—That's a good one, give her! 'sheartlikins dost think such Creatures are to be bought? Or are we provided for such a Purchase? Give her, quoth ye? Why she presented me with this Bracelet, for the Toy of a Diamond I us'd to wear: No, Gentlemen, Ned Blunt is not every Body—She expects me again to night.

WILLMORE. Egad that's well; we'll all go.

BLUNT. Not a Soul: No, Gentlemen, you are Wits; I am a dull Country Rogue, I.

FREDERICK. Well, Sir, for all your Person of Quality, I shall be very glad to understand your Purse be secure; 'tis our whole Estate at present, which we are loth to hazard in one Bottom: come, Sir, unload.

BLUNT. Take the necessary Trifle, useless now to me, that am belov'd by such a Gentlewoman—'sheartlikins Money! Here, take mine too.

FREDERICK. No, keep that to be cozen'd, that we may laugh.

WILLMORE. Cozen'd!—Death! wou'd I cou'd meet with one, that wou'd cozen me of all the Love I cou'd spare to night.

FREDERICK. Pox 'tis some common Whore upon my Life.

BLUNT. A Whore! yes with such Clothes! such Jewels! such a House! such Furniture, and so attended! a Whore!

BELVILE. Why yes, Sir, they are Whores, tho they'll neither entertain you with Drinking, Swearing, or Baudy; are Whores in all those gay Clothes, and right Jewels; are Whores with great Houses richly furnisht with Velvet Beds, Store of Plate, handsome Attendance, and fine Coaches, are Whores and errant ones.

WILLMORE. Pox on't, where do these fine Whores live?

BELVILE. Where no Rogue in Office yclep'd Constables dare give 'em Laws, nor the Wine-inspir'd Bullies of the Town break their Windows; yet they are Whores, tho this *Essex* Calf believe them Persons of Quality.

BLUNT. 'Sheartlikins, y'are all Fools, there are things about this *Essex* Calf, that shall take with the Ladies, beyond all your Wits and Parts—This Shape and Size, Gentlemen, are not to be despis'd; my Waste tolerably long, with other inviting Signs that shall be nameless.

WILLMORE. Egad I believe he may have met with some Person of Quality that may be kind to him.

BELVILE. Dost thou perceive any such tempting things about him, should make a fine Woman, and of Quality, pick him out from all Mankind, to throw away her Youth and Beauty upon, nay, and her dear Heart too?—no, no, Angellica has rais'd the Price too high.

WILLMORE. May she languish for Mankind till she die, and be damn'd for that one Sin alone.

Enter two Bravoes, and hang up a great Picture of ANGELLICA's, *against the Balcony, and two little ones at each side of the Door.*

BELVILE. See there the fair Sign to the Inn, where a Man may lodge that's Fool enough to give her Price. [WILLMORE *gazes on the Picture.*]

BLUNT. 'Sheartlikins, Gentlemen, what's this?

BELVILE. A famous Curtezan that's to be sold.

BLUNT. How! to be sold! nay then I have nothing to say to her—sold! what Impudence is practis'd in this Country?—with Order and Decency Whoring's establish'd here by virtue of the Inquisition—Come let's be gone, I'm sure we're no Chapmen for this Commodity.

FREDERICK. Thou art none, I'm sure, unless thou could'st have her in thy Bed at the Price of a Coach in the Street.

WILLMORE. How wondrous fair she is—a Thousand Crowns a Month—by Heaven as many Kingdoms were too little. A plague of this Poverty—of which I ne'er complain, but when it hinders my Approach to Beauty, which Virtue ne'er could purchase. [*Turns from the Picture.*]

BLUNT. What's this?— [*Reads*] *A Thousand Crowns a Month!*—'Sheartlikins, here's a Sum! sure 'tis a mistake. —Hark you Friend, does she take or give so much by the Month?

FREDERICK. A Thousand Crowns! Why, 'tis a Portion for the *Infanta*.

BLUNT. Hark ye, Friends, won't she trust?

BRAVO. This is a Trade, Sir, that cannot live by Credit.

    Enter DON PEDRO *in Masquerade, follow'd by* STEPHANO.

BELVILE. See, here's more Company, let's walk off a while.

     [PEDRO *Reads.*] [*Exeunt* English.]

 Enter ANGELLICA *and* MORETTA *in the Balcony, and draw a Silk Curtain.*

PEDRO. Fetch me a Thousand Crowns, I never wish to buy this Beauty at an easier Rate. [*Passes off.*]

ANGELLICA. Prithee what said those Fellows to thee?

BRAVO. Madam, the first were Admirers of Beauty only, but no purchasers; they were merry with your Price and Picture, laught at the Sum, and so past off.

ANGELLICA. No matter, I'm not displeas'd with their rallying; their Wonder feeds my Vanity, and he that wishes to buy, gives me more Pride, than he that gives my Price can make me Pleasure.

BRAVO. Madam, the last I knew thro all his Disguises to be Don Pedro, Nephew to the General, and who was with him in *Pampelona*.

ANGELLICA. Don Pedro! my old Gallant's Nephew! When his Uncle dy'd, he left him a vast Sum of Money; it is he who was so in love with me at *Padua*, and who us'd to make the General so jealous.

MORETTA. Is this he that us'd to prance before our Window, and take such care to shew himself an amorous Ass? if I am not mistaken, he is the likeliest Man to give your Price.

ANGELLICA. The Man is brave and generous, but of an Humour so uneasy and inconstant, that the victory over his Heart is as soon lost as won; a Slave that can add little to the Triumph of the Conqueror: but Inconstancy's the Sin of all Mankind, therefore I'm resolv'd that nothing but Gold shall charm my Heart.

MORETTA. I'm glad on't; 'tis only Interest that Women of our Profession ought to consider: tho I wonder what has kept you from that general Disease of our Sex so long, I mean that of being in love.

ANGELLICA. A kind, but sullen Star, under which I had the Happiness to be born; yet I have had no time for Love; the bravest and noblest of Mankind have purchas'd my Favours at so dear a Rate, as if no Coin but Gold were current with our Trade—But here's Don Pedro again, fetch me my Lute—for 'tis for him or Don Antonio the Vice-Roy's Son, that I have spread my Nets.

Enter at one Door DON PEDRO, *and* STEPHANO; DON ANTONIO *and*
DIEGO [*his page*] *at the other Door, with People following him in Mas-
querade, antickly attir'd, some with Musick: they both go up to the Picture.*

ANTONIO. A thousand Crowns! had not the Painter flatter'd her, I shou'd not think
it dear.

PEDRO. Flatter'd her! by Heaven he cannot. I have seen the Original, nor is there
one Charm here more than adorns her Face and Eyes; all this soft and sweet,
with a certain languishing Air, that no Artist can represent.

ANTONIO. What I heard of her Beauty before had fir'd my Soul, but this confirma-
tion of it has blown it into a flame.

PAGE. Sir, I have known you throw away a thousand Crowns on a worse Face, and
tho y' are near your Marriage, you may venture a little Love here; Florinda—
will not miss it.

PEDRO. Ha! Florinda! Sure 'tis Antonio.

ANTONIO. Florinda! name not those distant Joys, there's not one thought of her
will check my Passion here.

PEDRO. Florinda scorn'd! and all my hopes defeated of the possession of Angellica!
[*A Noise of a Lute above.* ANTONIO *gazes up.*] Her Injuries by Heaven he shall
not boast of. [*Song to a Lute above.*]

SONG

When Damon *first began to love,*
He languisht in a soft Desire,
And knew not how the Gods to move,
To lessen or increase his Fire.
For Cælia *in her charming Eyes*
Wore all Love's Sweet, and all his Cruelties.

II.

But as beneath a Shade he lay,
Weaving of Flow'rs for Cælia's *Hair,*
She chanc'd to lead her Flock that way,
And saw the am'rous Shepherd there.
She gaz'd around upon the Place,
And saw the Grove (resembling Night)
To all the Joys of Love invite,
Whilst guilty Smiles and Blushes drest her Face.
At this the bashful Youth all Transport grew,
And with kind Force he taught the Virgin how
To yield what all his Sighs cou'd never do.

ANTONIO. By Heav'n she's charming fair!

> [ANGELLICA *throws open the Curtains, and bows to* ANTONIO, *who pulls off his Vizard, and bows and blows up Kisses.* PEDRO *unseen looks in his Face.*]

PEDRO. 'Tis he, the false Antonio!

ANTONIO. Friend, where must I pay my offering of Love? [*To the* BRAVO.] My Thousand Crowns I mean.

PEDRO. That Offering I have design'd to make,

And yours will come too late.

ANTONIO. Prithee be gone, I shall grow angry else,

And then thou art not safe.

PEDRO. My Anger may be fatal, Sir, as yours;

And he that enters here may prove this Truth.

ANTONIO. I know not who thou art, but I am sure thou'rt worth my killing, and aiming at Angellica. [*They draw and fight.*]

> Enter WILLMORE *and* BLUNT, *who draw and part 'em.*

BLUNT. 'Sheartlikins, here's fine doings.

WILLMORE. Tilting for the Wench I'm sure—nay gad, if that wou'd win her, I have as good a Sword as the best of ye—Put up—put up, and take another time and place, for this is design'd for Lovers only. [*They all put up.*]

PEDRO. We are prevented; dare you meet me to morrow on the *Molo?*

For I've a Title to a better quarrel,

That of Florinda, in whose credulous Heart

Thou'st made an Int'rest, and destroy'd my Hopes.

ANTONIO. Dare?

I'll meet thee there as early as the Day.

PEDRO. We will come thus disguis'd, that whosoever chance to get the better, he may escape unknown.

ANTONIO. It shall be so. [*Exit* PEDRO *and* STEPHANO.] Who shou'd this Rival be? unless the *English* Colonel, of whom I've often heard Don Pedro speak; it must be he, and time he were removed, who lays a Claim to all my Happiness.

> [WILLMORE *having gaz'd all this while on the Picture, pulls down a little one.*]

WILLMORE. This Posture's loose and negligent,

The sight on't wou'd beget a warm desire

In Souls, whom Impotence and Age had chill'd.

—This must along with me.

BRAVO. What means this rudeness, Sir?—restore the Picture.

ANTONIO. Ha! Rudeness committed to the fair Angellica!—Restore the Picture, Sir.

WILLMORE. Indeed I will not, Sir.

ANTONIO. By Heav'n but you shall.

WILLMORE. Nay, do not shew your Sword; if you do, by this dear Beauty—I will shew mine too.

ANTONIO. What right can you pretend to't?

WILLMORE. That of Possession which I will maintain—you perhaps have 1,000 Crowns to give for the Original.

ANTONIO. No matter, Sir, you shall restore the Picture.

ANGELLICA. Oh, Moretta! what's the matter? [ANGELLICA *and* MORETTA *above.*]

ANTONIO. Or leave your Life behind.

WILLMORE. Death! you lye—I will do neither.

ANGELLICA. Hold I command you, if for me you fight.

> [*They fight, the Spaniards join with* ANTONIO, BLUNT *laying on like mad. They leave off and bow.*]

WILLMORE. How heavenly fair she is!—ah Plague of her Price.

ANGELLICA. You Sir in Buff, you that appear a Soldier, that first began this Insolence.

WILLMORE. 'Tis true, I did so, if you call it Insolence for a Man to preserve himself; I saw your charming Picture, and was wounded: quite thro my Soul each pointed Beauty ran; and wanting a Thousand Crowns to procure my Remedy, I laid this little Picture to my Bosom—which if you cannot allow me, I'll resign.

ANGELLICA. No, you may keep the Trifle.

ANTONIO. You shall first ask my leave, and this. [*Fight again as before.*]

> *Enter* BELVILE *and* FREDERICK *who join with the English.*

ANGELLICA. Hold; will you ruin me?—Biskey, Sebastian, part them. [*The* Spaniards *are beaten off.*]

MORETTA. Oh Madam, we're undone, a pox upon that rude Fellow, he's set on to ruin us: we shall never see good days, till all these fighting poor Rogues are sent to the Gallies.

> *Enter* BELVILE, BLUNT *and* WILLMORE, *with his Shirt bloody.*

BLUNT. 'Sheartlikins, beat me at this Sport, and I'll ne'er wear Sword more.

BELVILE. The Devil's in thee for a mad Fellow, thou art always one at an unlucky Adventure.—Come, let's be gone whilst we're safe, and remember these are *Spaniards*, a sort of People that know how to revenge an Affront.

FREDERICK. You bleed; I hope you are not wounded. [*To* WILLMORE.]

WILLMORE. Not much:—a plague upon your Dons, if they fight no better they'll ne'er recover *Flanders*.[1]—What the Devil was't to them that I took down the Picture?

---

1 Flanders, the northern region of Belgium, fought for independence from Spain.

BLUNT. Took it! 'Sheartlikins, we'll have the great one too; 'tis ours by Conquest.—
Prithee help me up, and I'll pull it down.—

ANGELLICA. Stay Sir, and e'er you affront me further, let me know how you durst
commit this Outrage—To you I speak, Sir, for you appear like a Gentleman.

WILLMORE. To me, Madam?—Gentlemen, your Servant. [BELVILE *stays him.*]

BELVILE. Is the Devil in thee? Do'st know the danger of entering the House of an
incens'd Curtezan?

WILLMORE. I thank you for your care—but there are other matters in hand, there
are, tho we have no great Temptation.—Death! let me go.

FREDERICK. Yes, to your Lodging, if you will, but not in here.—Damn these
gay Harlots—by this Hand I'll have as sound and handsome a Whore for a
Patacoone.[1]—Death, Man, she'll murder thee.

WILLMORE. Oh! fear me not, shall I not venture where a Beauty calls? a lovely
charming Beauty? for fear of danger! when by Heaven there's none so great as
to long for her, whilst I want Money to purchase her.

FREDERICK. Therefore 'tis loss of time, unless you had the thousand Crowns to pay.

WILLMORE. It may be she may give a Favour, at least I shall have the pleasure of
saluting her when I enter, and when I depart.

BELVILE. Pox, she'll as soon lie with thee, as kiss thee, and sooner stab than do
either—you shall not go.

ANGELLICA. Fear not, Sir, all I have to wound with, is my Eyes.

BLUNT. Let him go, 'Sheartlikins, I believe the Gentlewoman means well.

BELVILE. Well, take thy Fortune, we'll expect you in the next Street.—Farewell
Fool,—farewell—

WILLMORE. B'ye Colonel—[*Goes in.*]

FREDERICK. The Rogue's stark mad for a Wench. [*Exeunt.*]

SCENE II. *A fine Chamber.*

Enter WILLMORE, ANGELLICA, *and* MORETTA.

ANGELLICA. Insolent Sir, how durst you pull down my Picture?

WILLMORE. Rather, how durst you set it up, to tempt poor amorous Mortals
with so much Excellence? which I find you have but too well consulted by
the unmerciful price you set upon't.—Is all this Heaven of Beauty shewn to
move Despair in those that cannot buy? and can you think the effects of that
Despair shou'd be less extravagant than I have shewn?

1 A Spanish coin.

ANGELLICA. I sent for you to ask my Pardon, Sir, not to aggravate your Crime.—I thought I should have seen you at my Feet imploring it.

WILLMORE. You are deceived, I came to rail at you, and talk such Truths too, as shall let you see the Vanity of that Pride, which taught you how to set such a Price on Sin. For such it is, whilst that which is Love's due is meanly barter'd for.

ANGELLICA. Ha, ha, ha, alas good Captain, what pity 'tis your edifying Doctrine will do no good upon me—Moretta, fetch the Gentleman a Glass, and let him survey himself, to see what Charms he has,—and guess my Business. [*Aside in a soft tone.*]

MORETTA. He knows himself of old, I believe those Breeches and he have been acquainted ever since he was beaten at *Worcester*.

ANGELLICA. Nay, do not abuse the poor Creature.—

MORETTA. Good Weather-beaten Corporal, will you march off? we have no need of your Doctrine, tho you have of our Charity; but at present we have no Scraps, we can afford no kindness for God's sake; in fine, Sirrah, the Price is too high i'th' Mouth for you, therefore troop, I say.

WILLMORE. Here, good Fore-Woman of the Shop, serve me, and I'll be gone.

MORETTA. Keep it to pay your Landress, your Linen stinks of the Gun-Room; for here's no selling by Retail.

WILLMORE. Thou hast sold plenty of thy stale Ware at a cheap Rate.

MORETTA. Ay, the more silly kind Heart I, but this is an Age wherein Beauty is at higher Rates.—In fine, you know the price of this.

WILLMORE. I grant you 'tis here set down a thousand Crowns a Month—Baud, take your black Lead and sum it up, that I may have a Pistole-worth of these vain gay things, and I'll trouble you no more.

MORETTA. Pox on him, he'll fret me to Death:—abominable Fellow, I tell thee, we only sell by the whole Piece.

WILLMORE. 'Tis very hard, the whole Cargo or nothing—Faith, Madam, my Stock will not reach it, I cannot be your Chapman.—Yet I have Countrymen in Town, Merchants of Love, like me; I'll see if they'l put for a share, we cannot lose much by it, and what we have no use for, we'll sell upon the *Friday's* Mart, at—*Who gives more?* I am studying, Madam, how to purchase you, tho at present I am unprovided of Money.

ANGELLICA. Sure this from any other Man would anger me—nor shall he know the Conquest he has made—Poor angry Man, how I despise this railing.

WILLMORE. Yes, I am poor—but I'm a Gentleman,
And one that scorns this Baseness which you practise.
Poor as I am, I would not sell my self,
No, not to gain your charming high-priz'd Person.

Tho I admire you strangely for your Beauty,
Yet I contemn your Mind.
—And yet I wou'd at any rate enjoy you;
At your own rate—but cannot—See here
The only Sum I can command on Earth;
I know not where to eat when this is gone:
Yet such a Slave I am to Love and Beauty,
This last reserve I'll sacrifice to enjoy you.
—Nay, do not frown, I know you are to be bought,
And wou'd be bought by me,
For a mean trifling Sum, if I could pay it down.
Which happy knowledge I will still repeat,
And lay it to my Heart, it has a Virtue in't,
And soon will cure those Wounds your Eyes have made.
—And yet—there's something so divinely powerful there—
Nay, I will gaze—to let you see my Strength. [*Holds her, looks on her, and pauses and sighs.*]
By Heaven, bright Creature—I would not for the World thy Fame were half so fair as is thy Face. [*Turns her away from him.*]

ANGELLICA. His words go thro me to the very Soul. [*Aside.*]—If you have nothing else to say to me.

WILLMORE. Yes, you shall hear how infamous you are—
For which I do not hate thee:
But that secures my Heart, and all the Flames it feels
Are but so many Lusts,
I know it by their sudden bold intrusion.
The Fire's impatient and betrays, 'tis false—
For had it been the purer Flame of Love,
I should have pin'd and languished at your Feet,
E'er found the Impudence to have discover'd it.
I now dare stand your Scorn, and your Denial.

MORETTA. Sure she's bewitcht, that she can stand thus tamely, and hear his saucy railing.—Sirrah, will you be gone?

ANGELLICA. How dare you take this liberty?—Withdraw. [*To* MORETTA.]—Pray, tell me, Sir, are not you guilty of the same mercenary Crime? When a Lady is proposed to you for a Wife, you never ask, how fair, discreet, or virtuous she is; but what's her Fortune—which if but small, you cry—She will not do my business—and basely leave her, tho she languish for you.—Say, is not this as poor?

WILLMORE. It is a barbarous Custom, which I will scorn to defend in our Sex, and
do despise in yours.

ANGELLICA. Thou art a brave Fellow! put up thy Gold, and know,
That were thy Fortune large, as is thy Soul,
Thou shouldst not buy my Love,
Couldst thou forget those mean effects of Vanity,
Which set me out to sale; and as a Lover, prize
My yielding Joys.
Canst thou believe they'l be entirely thine,
Without considering they were mercenary?

WILLMORE. I cannot tell, I must bethink me first—ha, Death, I'm going to believe
her. [*Aside*].

ANGELLICA. Prithee confirm that Faith—or if thou canst not—flatter me a little,
'twill please me from thy Mouth.

WILLMORE. Curse on thy charming Tongue! dost thou return
My feign'd Contempt with so much subtilty? [*Aside.*]
Thou'st found the easiest way into my Heart,
Tho I yet know that all thou say'st is false. [*Turning from her in a Rage.*]

ANGELLICA. By all that's good 'tis real,
I never lov'd before, tho oft a Mistress.
—Shall my first Vows be slighted?

WILLMORE. What can she mean? [*Aside.*]

ANGELLICA. I find you cannot credit me. [*In an angry tone.*]

WILLMORE. I know you take me for an errant Ass,
An Ass that may be sooth'd into Belief,
And then be us'd at pleasure.
—But, Madam I have been so often cheated
By perjur'd, soft, deluding Hypocrites,
That I've no Faith left for the cozening Sex,
Especially for Women of your Trade.

ANGELLICA. The low esteem you have of me, perhaps
May bring my Heart again:
For I have Pride that yet surmounts my Love. [*She turns with Pride, he
holds her.*]

WILLMORE. Throw off this Pride, this Enemy to Bliss,
And shew the Power of Love: 'tis with those Arms
I can be only vanquisht, made a Slave.

ANGELLICA. Is all my mighty Expectation vanisht?
—No, I will not hear thee talk,—thou hast a Charm

In every word, that draws my Heart away.
And all the thousand Trophies I design'd,
Thou hast undone—Why art thou soft?
Thy Looks are bravely rough, and meant for War.
Could thou not storm on still?
I then perhaps had been as free as thou.

WILLMORE. Death! how she throws her Fire about my Soul! [*Aside.*]
—Take heed, fair Creature, how you raise my Hopes,
Which once assum'd pretend to all Dominion.
There's not a Joy thou hast in store
I shall not then command:
For which I'll pay thee back my Soul, my Life.
Come, let's begin th' account this happy minute.

ANGELLICA. And will you pay me then the Price I ask?

WILLMORE. Oh, why dost thou draw me from an awful Worship,
By shewing thou art no Divinity?
Conceal the Fiend, and shew me all the Angel;
Keep me but ignorant, and I'll be devout,
And pay my Vows for ever at this Shrine. [*Kneels, and kisses her Hand.*]

ANGELLICA. The Pay I mean is but thy Love for mine.
—Can you give that?

WILLMORE. Entirely—come, let's withdraw: where I'll renew my Vows,—and
breathe 'em with such Ardour, thou shall not doubt my Zeal.

ANGELLICA. Thou hast a Power too strong to be resisted. [*Exit* WILLMORE *and*
ANGELLICA.]

MORETTA. Now my Curse go with you—Is all our Project fallen to this? to love
the only Enemy to our Trade? Nay, to love such a Shameroon,[1] a very Beggar;
nay, a Pirate-Beggar, whose Business is to rifle and be gone, a No-Purchase,
No-Pay Tatterdemalion, an *English* Piccaroon; a Rogue that fights for daily
Drink, and takes a Pride in being loyally lousy—Oh, I could curse now, if I
durst—This is the Fate of most Whores.

> *Trophies, which from believing Fops we win,*
> *Are Spoils to those who cozen us again.*

---

1 A trickster.

ACT III.

SCENE I. *A Street.*

Enter FLORINDA, VALERIA, HELLENA, *in Antick different Dresses from what they were in before,* CALLIS *attending.*

FLORINDA. I Wonder what should make my Brother in so ill a Humour: I hope he has not found out our Ramble this Morning.

HELLENA. No, if he had, we should have heard on't at both Ears, and have been mew'd up this Afternoon; which I would not for the World should have happen'd—Hey ho! I'm sad as a Lover's Lute.

VALERIA. Well, methinks we have learnt this Trade of Gipsies as readily as if we had been bred upon the Road to *Loretto*; and yet I did so fumble, when I told the Stranger his Fortune, that I was afraid I should have told my own and yours by mistake—But methinks Hellena has been very serious ever since.

FLORINDA. I would give my Garters she were in love, to be reveng'd upon her, for abusing me—How is't, Hellena?

HELLENA. Ah!—would I had never seen my mad Monsieur—and yet for all your laughing I am not in love—and yet this small Acquaintance, o'my Conscience, will never out of my Head.

VALERIA. Ha, ha, ha—I laugh to think how thou art fitted with a Lover, a Fellow that, I warrant, loves every new Face he sees.

HELLENA. Hum—he has not kept his Word with me here—and may be taken up—that Thought is not very pleasant to me—what the Duce should this be now that I feel?

VALERIA. What is't like?

HELLENA. Nay, the Lord knows—but if I should be hanged, I cannot chuse but be angry and afraid, when I think that mad Fellow should be in love with any Body but me—What to think of my self I know not—Would I could meet with some true damn'd Gipsy, that I might know my Fortune.

VALERIA. Know it! why there's nothing so easy: thou wilt love this wandering Inconstant till thou find'st thy self hanged about his Neck, and then be as mad to get free again.

FLORINDA. Yes, Valeria; we shall see her bestride his Baggage-horse, and follow him to the Campaign.

HELLENA. So, so; now you are provided for, there's no care taken of poor me—But since you have set my Heart a wishing, I am resolv'd to know for what. I will not die of the Pip, so I will not.

FLORINDA. Art thou mad to talk so? Who will like thee well enough to have thee, that hears what a mad Wench thou art?

HELLENA. Like me! I don't intend every he that likes me shall have me, but he that I like: I shou'd have staid in the Nunnery still, if I had lik'd my Lady Abbess as well as she lik'd me. No, I came thence, not (as my wise Brother imagines) to take an eternal Farewell of the World, but to love and to be belov'd; and I will be belov'd or I'll get one of your Men, so I will.

VALERIA. Am I put into the Number of Lovers?

HELLENA. You! my Couz, I know thou art too good natur'd to leave us in any Design: Thou wou't venture a Cast, tho thou comest off a Loser, especially with such a Gamester—I observ'd your Man, and your willing Ears incline that way; and if you are not a Lover, 'tis an Art soon learnt—that I find. [Sighs.]

FLORINDA. I wonder how you learnt to love so easily, I had a thousand Charms to meet my Eyes and Ears, e'er I cou'd yield; and 'twas the knowledge of Belvile's Merit, not the surprising Person, took my Soul—Thou art too rash to give a Heart at first sight.

HELLENA. Hang your considering Lover; I ne'er thought beyond the Fancy, that 'twas a very pretty, idle, silly kind of Pleasure to pass one's time with, to write little, soft, nonsensical Billets, and with great difficulty and danger receive Answers; in which I shall have my Beauty prais'd, my Wit admir'd (tho little or none) and have the Vanity and Power to know I am desirable; then I have the more Inclination that way, because I am to be a Nun, and so shall not be suspected to have any such earthly Thoughts about me—But when I walk thus—and sigh thus—they'll think my Mind's upon my Monastery, and cry, how happy 'tis she's so resolv'd!—But not a Word of Man.

FLORINDA. What a mad Creature's this!

HELLENA. I'll warrant, if my Brother hears either of you sigh, he cries (gravely)—I fear you have the Indiscretion to be in love, but take heed of the Honour of our House, and your own unspotted Fame; and so he conjures on till he has laid the soft-wing'd God in your Hearts, or broke the Birds-nest—But see here comes your Lover: but where's my inconstant? let's step aside, and we may learn something. [Go aside.]

Enter BELVILE, FREDERICK, *and* BLUNT.

BELVILE. What means this? the Picture's taken in.

BLUNT. It may be the Wench is good natur'd, and will be kind *gratis.* Your Friend's a proper handsome Fellow.

BELVILE. I rather think she has cut his Throat and is fled: I am mad he should throw himself into Dangers—Pox on't, I shall want him to night—let's knock and ask for him.

HELLENA. My heart goes a-pit a-pat, for fear 'tis my Man they talk of. [*Knock, * MORETTA *above.*]

MORETTA. What would you have?

BELVILE. Tell the Stranger that enter'd here about two Hours ago, that his Friends stay here for him.

MORETTA. A Curse upon him for Moretta, would he were at the Devil—but he's coming to you. [*Enter* WILMORE.]

HELLENA. I, I, 'tis he. Oh how this vexes me.

BELVILE. And how, and how, dear Lad, has Fortune smil'd? Are we to break her Windows, or raise up Altars to her? hah!

WILLMORE. Does not my Fortune sit triumphant on my Brow? dost not see the little wanton God there all gay and smiling? have I not an Air about my Face and Eyes, that distinguish me from the Croud of common Lovers? By Heav'n, *Cupid's* Quiver has not half so many Darts as her Eyes—Oh such a *Bona Roba*, to sleep in her Arms is lying in Fresco, all perfum'd Air about me.

HELLENA. Here's fine encouragement for me to fool on. [*Aside.*]

WILLMORE. Hark ye, where didst thou purchase that rich Canary we drank to-day? Tell me, that I may adore the Spigot, and sacrifice to the Butt: the Juice was divine, into which I must dip my Rosary, and then bless all things that I would have bold or fortunate.

BELVILE. Well, Sir, let's go take a Bottle, and hear the Story of your Success.

FREDERICK. Would not *French* Wine do better?

WILLMORE. Damn the hungry Balderdash; cheerful Sack has a generous Virtue in't, inspiring a successful Confidence, gives Eloquence to the Tongue, and Vigour to the Soul; and has in a few Hours compleated all my Hopes and Wishes. There's nothing left to raise a new Desire in me—Come let's be gay and wanton—and Gentlemen, study, study what you want, for here are Friends,— that will supply, Gentlemen,—hark! what a charming sound they make—'tis he and she Gold whilst here, shall beget new Pleasures every moment.

BLUNT. But hark ye Sir, you are not married, are you?

WILLMORE. All the Honey of Matrimony, but none of the Sting, Friend.

BLUNT. 'Sheartlikins, thou'rt a fortunate Rogue.

WILLMORE. I am so, Sir, let these inform you.—Ha, how sweetly they chime! Pox of Poverty, it makes a Man a Slave, makes Wit and Honour sneak, my Soul grew lean and rusty for want of Credit.

BLUNT. 'Sheartlikins, this I like well, it looks like my lucky Bargain! Oh how I long for the Approach of my Squire, that is to conduct me to her House again. Why! here's two provided for.

FREDERICK. By this Light y're happy Men.

BLUNT. Fortune is pleased to smile on us, Gentlemen,—to smile on us.

Enter SANCHO, *and pulls* BLUNT *by the Sleeve. They go aside.*

SANCHO. Sir, my Lady expects you—she has remov'd all that might oppose your Will and Pleasure—and is impatient till you come.

BLUNT. Sir, I'll attend you—Oh the happiest Rogue! I'll take no leave, lest they either dog me, or stay me. [*Exit with* SANCHO.]

BELVILE. But then the little Gipsy is forgot?

WILLMORE. A Mischief on thee for putting her into my thoughts; I had quite forgot her else, and this Night's Debauch had drunk her quite down.

HELLENA. Had it so, good Captain? [*Claps him on the Back.*]

WILLMORE. Ha! I hope she did not hear.

HELLENA. What, afraid of such a Champion!

WILLMORE. Oh! you're a fine Lady of your word, are you not? to make a Man languish a whole day—

HELLENA. In tedious search of me.

WILLMORE. Egad, Child, thou'rt in the right, hadst thou seen what a melancholy Dog I have been ever since I was a Lover, how I have walkt the Streets like a *Capuchin*, with my Hands in my Sleeves—Faith Sweetheart, thou wouldst pity me.

HELLENA. Now, if I should be hang'd, I can't be angry with him, he dissembles so heartily—Alas good Captain, what pains you have taken—Now were I ungrateful not to reward so true a Servant.

WILLMORE. Poor Soul! that's kindly said, I see thou bearest a Conscience—come then for a beginning shew me thy dear Face.

HELLENA. I'm afraid, my small Acquaintance, you have been staying that swinging stomach you boasted of this morning; I remember then my little Collation would have gone down with you, without the Sauce of a handsome Face—Is your Stomach so queasy now?

WILLMORE. Faith long fasting, Child, spoils a Man's Appetite—yet if you durst treat, I could so lay about me still.

HELLENA. And would you fall to, before a Priest says Grace?

WILLMORE. Oh fie, fie, what an old out-of-fashion'd thing hast thou nam'd? Thou could'st not dash me more out of Countenance, shouldst thou shew me an ugly Face.

Whilst he is seemingly courting HELLENA, *enter* ANGELLICA, MORETTA, BISKEY, *and* SEBASTIAN, *all in Masquerade:* ANGELLICA *sees* WILLMORE *and starts.*

ANGELLICA. Heavens, is't he? and passionately fond to see another Woman?

MORETTA. What cou'd you expect less from such a Swaggerer?

ANGELLICA. Expect! as much as I paid him, a Heart entire,
  Which I had pride enough to think when e'er I gave
  It would have rais'd the Man above the Vulgar,
  Made him all Soul, and that all soft and constant.

HELLENA. You see, Captain, how willing I am to be Friends with you, till Time and Ill-luck make us Lovers; and ask you the Question first, rather than put your Modesty to the blush, by asking me: for alas, I know you Captains are such strict Men, severe Observers of your Vows to Chastity, that 'twill be hard to prevail with your tender Conscience to marry a young willing Maid.

WILLMORE. Do not abuse me, for fear I should take thee at thy Word, and marry thee indeed, which I'm sure will be Revenge sufficient.

HELLENA. O' my Conscience, that will be our Destiny, because we are both of one humour; I am as inconstant as you, for I have considered, Captain, that a handsome Woman has a great deal to do whilst her Face is good, for then is our Harvest-time to gather Friends; and should I in these days of my Youth, catch a fit of foolish Constancy, I were undone; 'tis loitering by day-light in our great Journey: therefore declare, I'll allow but one year for Love, one year for Indifference, and one year for Hate—and then—go hang your self—for I profess myself the gay, the kind, and the inconstant—the Devil's in't if this won't please you.

WILLMORE. Oh most damnably!—I have a Heart with a hole quite thro it too, no Prison like mine to keep a Mistress in.

ANGELLICA. Perjur'd Man! how I believe thee now! [*Aside.*]

HELLENA. Well, I see our Business as well as Humours are alike, yours to cozen as many Maids as will trust you, and I as many Men as have Faith—See if I have not as desperate a lying look, as you can have for the heart of you. [*Pulls off her Vizard; he starts.*]

—How do you like it, Captain?

WILLMORE. Like it! by Heav'n, I never saw so much Beauty. Oh the Charms of those sprightly black Eyes, that strangely fair Face, full of Smiles and Dimples! those soft round melting cherry Lips! and small even white Teeth! not to be exprest, but silently adored!—Oh one Look more, and strike me dumb, or I shall repeat nothing else till I am mad. [*He seems to court her to pull off her Vizard: she refuses.*]

ANGELLICA. I can endure no more—nor is it fit to interrupt him; for if I do, my Jealousy has so destroy'd my Reason,—I shall undo him—Therefore I'll retire. And you Sebastian [*To one of her Bravoes*] follow that Woman, and learn who 'tis; while you tell the Fugitive, I would speak to him instantly. [*To the other Bravo.*] [*Exit.*]

[*This while* FLORINDA *is talking to* BELVILE, *who stands sullenly.* FREDERICK *courting* VALERIA.]

VALERIA. Prithee dear Stranger, be not so sullen; for tho you have lost your Love, you see my Friend frankly offers you hers, to play with in the mean time.

BELVILE. Faith Madam, I am sorry I can't play at her Game.

FREDERICK. Pray leave your Intercession, and mind your own Affair, they'll better agree apart; he's a model Sigher in Company, but alone no Woman escapes him.

FLORINDA. Sure he does but rally—yet if it should be true—I'll tempt him farther— Believe me, noble Stranger, I'm no common Mistress—and for a little proof on't—wear this Jewel—nay, take it, Sir, 'tis right, and Bills of Exchange may sometimes miscarry.

BELVILE. Madam, why am I chose out of all Mankind to be the Object of your Bounty?

VALERIA. There's another civil Question askt.

FREDERICK. Pox of's Modesty, it spoils his own Markets, and hinders mine.

FLORINDA. Sir, from my Window I have often seen you; and Women of Quality have so few opportunities for Love, that we ought to lose none.

FREDERICK. Ay, this is something! here's a Woman!—When shall I be blest with so much kindness from your fair Mouth?—Take the Jewel, Fool. [*Aside to* BELVILE.]

BELVILE. You tempt me strangely, Madam, every way.

FLORINDA. So, if I find him false, my whole Repose is gone. [*Aside.*]

BELVILE. And but for a Vow I've made to a very fine Lady, this Goodness had subdu'd me.

FREDERICK. Pox on't be kind, in pity to me be kind, for I am to thrive here but as you treat her Friend.

HELLENA. Tell me what did you in yonder House, and I'll unmasque.

WILLMORE. Yonder House—oh—I went to—a—to—why, there's a Friend of mine lives there.

HELLENA. What a she, or a he Friend?

WILLMORE. A Man upon my Honour! a Man—A She Friend! no, no, Madam, you have done my Business, I thank you.

HELLENA. And was't your Man Friend, that had more Darts in's Eyes than *Cupid* carries in a whole Budget of Arrows?

WILLMORE. So—

HELLENA. Ah such a *Bona Roba*: to be in her Arms is lying in *Fresco*, all perfumed Air about me—Was this your Man Friend too?

WILLMORE. So—

HELLENA. That gave you the He, and the She—Gold, that begets young Pleasures.

WILLMORE. Well, well, Madam, then you see there are Ladies in the World, that will not be cruel—there are, Madam, there are—

HELLENA. And there be Men too as fine, wild, inconstant Fellows as your self, there be Captain, there be, if you go to that now—therefore I'm resolv'd—

WILLMORE. Oh!

HELLENA. To see your Face no more—

WILLMORE. Oh!

HELLENA. Till to morrow.

WILLMORE. Egad, you frighted me.

HELLENA. Nor then neither, unless you'l swear never to see that Lady more.

WILLMORE. See her!—why! never to think of Womankind again?

HELLENA. Kneel, and swear. [*Kneels, she gives him her hand.*]

WILLMORE. I do, never to think—to see—to love—nor lie with any but thy self.

HELLENA. Kiss the Book.

WILLMORE. Oh, most religiously. [*Kisses her Hand.*]

HELLENA. Now what a wicked Creature am I, to damn a proper Fellow.

CALLIS. Madam, I'll stay no longer, 'tis e'en dark. [*To* FLORINDA.]

FLORINDA. However, Sir, I'll leave this with you—that when I'm gone, you may repent the opportunity you have lost by your Modesty. [*Gives him the Jewel, which is her Picture, and Exits. He gazes after her.*]

WILLMORE. 'Twill be an Age till to morrow,—and till then I will most impatiently expect you—Adieu, my dear pretty Angel. [*Exit all the Women.*]

BELVILE. Ha! Florinda's Picture! 'twas she her self—what a dull Dog was I? I would have given the World for one minute's discourse with her.—

FREDERICK. This comes of your Modesty,—ah pox on your Vow, 'twas ten to one but we had lost the Jewel by't.

BELVILE. Willmore! the blessed'st Opportunity lost!—Florinda, Friends, Florinda!

WILLMORE. Ah Rogue! such black Eyes, such a Face, such a Mouth, such Teeth,— and so much Wit!

BELVILE. All, all, and a thousand Charms besides.

WILLMORE. Why, dost thou know her?

BELVILE. Know her! ay, ay, and a Pox take me with all my Heart for being modest.

WILLMORE. But hark ye, Friend of mine, are you my Rival? and have I been only beating the Bush all this while?

BELVILE. I understand thee not—I'm mad—see here— [*Shews the Picture.*]

WILLMORE. Ha! whose Picture is this?—'tis a fine Wench.

FREDERICK. The Colonel's Mistress, Sir.

WILLMORE. Oh, oh, here—I thought it had been another Prize—come, come, a Bottle will set thee right again. [*Gives the Picture back.*]

BELVILE. I am content to try, and by that time 'twill be late enough for our Design.

WILLMORE. Agreed.

> *Love does all day the Soul's great Empire keep,*
> *But Wine at night lulls the soft God asleep.* [*Exeunt.*]

SCENE II. LUCETTA's *House.*

Enter BLUNT *and* LUCETTA *with a Light.*

LUCETTA. Now we are safe and free, no fears of the coming home of my old jealous Husband, which made me a little thoughtful when you came in first—but now Love is all the business of my Soul.

BLUNT. I am transported—Pox on't, that I had but some fine things to say to her, such as Lovers use—I was a Fool not to learn of Frederick, a little by Heart before I came—something I must say.— [*Aside.*] 'Sheartlikins, sweet Soul, I am not us'd to complement, but I'm an honest Gentleman, and thy humble Servant.

LUCETTA. I have nothing to pay for so great a Favour, but such a Love as cannot but be great, since at first sight of that sweet Face and Shape it made me your absolute Captive.

BLUNT. Kind heart, how prettily she talks! Egad, I'll show her Husband a *Spanish* Trick; send him out of the World, and marry her: she's damnably in love with me, and will ne'er mind Settlements, and so there's that saved. [*Aside.*]

LUCETTA. Well, Sir, I'll go and undress me, and be with you instantly.

BLUNT. Make haste then, for 'dsheartlikins, dear Soul, thou canst not guess at the pain of a longing Lover, when his Joys are drawn within the compass of a few minutes.

LUCETTA. You speak my Sense, and I'll make haste to provide it. [*Exit.*]

BLUNT. 'Tis a rare Girl, and this one night's enjoyment with her will be worth all the days I ever past in *Essex*—Would she'd go with me into *England*, tho to say truth, there's plenty of Whores there already.—But a pox on 'em they are such mercenary prodigal Whores, that they want such a one as this, that's free and generous, to give 'em good Examples:—Why, what a House she has! how rich and fine!

Enter SANCHO.

SANCHO. Sir, my Lady has sent me to conduct you to her Chamber.

BLUNT. Sir, I shall be proud to follow—Here's one of her Servants too: 'dsheart-likins, by his Garb and Gravity he might be a Justice of Peace in *Essex*, and is but a Pimp here. [*Exeunt.*]

The Scene changes to a Chamber with an Alcove-Bed in it, a Table, &c. LUCETTA *in Bed. Enter* SANCHO *and* BLUNT, *who takes the Candle of* SANCHO *at the Door.*

SANCHO. Sir, my Commission reaches no farther.

BLUNT. Sir, I'll excuse your Complement:—what, in Bed, my sweet Mistress?

LUCETTA. You see, I still out-do you in kindness.

BLUNT. And thou shall see what haste I'll make to quit scores—oh the luckiest Rogue! [*Undresses himself.*]

LUCETTA. Shou'd you be false or cruel now!

BLUNT. False, 'Sheartlikins, what dost thou take me for a *Jew?* an insensible Heathen,—A Pox of thy old jealous Husband: and he were dead, egad, sweet Soul, it shou'd be none of my fault, if I did not marry thee.

LUCETTA. It never shou'd be mine.

BLUNT. Good Soul, I'm the fortunatest Dog!

LUCETTA. Are you not undrest yet?

BLUNT. As much as my Impatience will permit. [*Goes towards the Bed in his Shirt and Drawers.*]

LUCETTA. Hold, Sir, put out the Light, it may betray us else.

BLUNT. Any thing, I need no other Light but that of thine Eyes!—'sheartlikins, there I think I had it. [*Aside.*] [*Puts out the Candle, the Bed descends, he gropes about to find it.*]—Why—why—where am I got? what, not yet?—where are you sweetest?—ah, the Rogue's silent now—a pretty Love-trick this—how she'll laugh at me anon!—you need not, my dear Rogue! you need not! I'm all on a fire already—come, come, now call me in for pity—Sure I'm enchanted! I have been round the Chamber, and can find neither Woman, nor Bed—I lockt the Door, I'm sure she cannot go that way; or if she cou'd, the Bed cou'd not—Enough, enough, my pretty Wanton, do not carry the Jest too far—Ha, betray'd! Dogs! Rogues! Pimps! help! help! [*Lights on a Trap, and is let down.*]

Enter LUCETTA, PHILIPPO, *and* SANCHO *with a light.*

PHILIPPO. Ha, ha, ha, he's dispatcht finely.

LUCETTA. Now, Sir, had I been coy, we had mist of this Booty.

PHILIPPO. Nay when I saw 'twas a substantial Fool, I was mollified; but when you doat upon a Serenading Coxcomb, upon a Face, fine Clothes, and a Lute, it makes me rage.

LUCETTA. You know I never was guilty of that Folly, my dear Philippo, but with your self—But come let's see what we have got by this.

PHILIPPO. A rich Coat!—Sword and Hat!—these Breeches too—are well lin'd!—see here a Gold Watch!—a Purse—ha! Gold!—at least two hundred Pistoles![1] a bunch of Diamond Rings; and one with the Family Arms!—a Gold Box!—with a Medal of his King! and his Lady Mother's Picture!—these were sacred Reliques, believe me!—see, the Wasteband of his Breeches have a Mine of Gold!—Old Queen *Bess's*.[2] We have a Quarrel to her ever since *Eighty Eight*,[3] and may therefore justify the Theft, the Inquisition might have committed it.

LUCETTA. See, a Bracelet of bow'd Gold, these his Sister ty'd about his Arm at parting—but well—for all this, I fear his being a Stranger may make a noise, and hinder our Trade with them hereafter.

PHILIPPO. That's our security; he is not only a Stranger to us, but to the Country too—the Common-Shore[4] into which he is descended, thou know'st, conducts him into another Street, which this Light will hinder him from ever finding again—he knows neither your Name, nor the Street where your House is, nay, nor the way to his own Lodgings.

LUCETTA. And art not thou an unmerciful Rogue, not to afford him one Night for all this?—I should not have been such a *Jew*.

PHILIPPO. Blame me not, Lucetta, to keep as much of thee as I can to my self—come, that thought makes me wanton,—let's to Bed,—Sancho, lock up these.

> *This is the Fleece which Fools do bear,*
>
> *Design'd for witty Men to sheer.* [*Exeunt.*]

> *The Scene changes, and discovers* BLUNT, *creeping out of a Common Shore, his Face, &c., all dirty.*

BLUNT. Oh Lord! [*Climbing up.*] I am got out at last, and (which is a Miracle) without a Clue—and now to Damning and Cursing,—but if that would ease me, where shall I begin? with my Fortune, my self, or the Quean that cozen'd me—What a Dog was I to believe in Women! Oh Coxcomb—ignorant conceited Coxcomb! to fancy she cou'd be enamour'd with my Person, at the first sight enamour'd—Oh, I'm a cursed Puppy, 'tis plain, Fool was writ upon my Forehead, she perceiv'd it,—saw the *Essex* Calf there—for what Allurements could there be in this Countenance? which I can indure, because I'm acquainted with it—Oh, dull silly Dog! to be thus sooth'd into a Cozening! Had I been drunk, I might fondly have credited the young Quean! but as I was in my right Wits, to be thus cheated, confirms I am a dull believing *English* Country Fop.—But my Comrades! Death and the Devil, there's the worst of all—then a Ballad will be

---

1 A Spanish gold coin.

2 Elizabeth I, who ruled from 1533-1603.

3 England defeated the Spanish Armada in 1588.

4 Sewer.

sung to Morrow on the *Prado*, to a lousy Tune of the enchanted Squire, and the annihilated Damsel—But Frederick, that Rogue, and the Colonel, will abuse me beyond all Christian patience—had she left me my Clothes, I have a Bill of Exchange at home wou'd have sav'd my Credit—but now all hope is taken from me—Well, I'll home (if I can find the way) with this Consolation, that I am not the first kind believing Coxcomb; but there are, Gallants, many such good Natures amongst ye.

> *And tho you've better Arts to hide your Follies,*
> *Adsheartlikins y'are all as errant Cullies.*

SCENE III. *The Garden, in the Night.*

Enter FLORINDA *undres'd, with a Key, and a little Box.*

FLORINDA. Well, thus far I'm in my way to Happiness; I have got my self free from Callis; my Brother too, I find by yonder light, is gone into his Cabinet, and thinks not of me: I have by good Fortune got the Key of the Garden Back-door,—I'll open it, to prevent Belvile's knocking,—a little noise will now alarm my Brother. Now am I as fearful as a young Thief. [*Unlocks the Door.*]—Hark,—what noise is that?—Oh, 'twas the Wind that plaid amongst the Boughs.—Belvile stays long, methinks—it's time—stay—for fear of a surprize, I'll hide these Jewels in yonder Jessamin. [*She goes to lay down the Box.*]

Enter WILLMORE *drunk.*

WILLMORE. What the Devil is become of these Fellows, Belvile and Frederick? They promis'd to stay at the next corner for me, but who the Devil knows the corner of a full Moon?—Now—whereabouts am I?—hah—what have we here? a Garden!—a very convenient place to sleep in—hah—what has God sent us here?—a Female—by this light, a Woman; I'm a Dog if it be not a very Wench.—

FLORINDA. He's come!—hah—who's there?

WILLMORE. Sweet Soul, let me salute thy Shoe-string.

FLORINDA. 'Tis not my Belvile—good Heavens, I know him not.—Who are you, and from whence come you?

WILLMORE. Prithee—prithee Child—not so many hard Questions—let it suffice I am here, Child—Come, come kiss me.

FLORINDA. Good Gods! what luck is mine?

WILLMORE. Only good luck, Child, parlous good luck—Come hither,—'tis a delicate shining Wench,—by this Hand she's perfum'd, and smells like any

Nosegay.—Prithee dear Soul, let's not play the Fool, and lose time,—precious time—for as Gad shall save me, I'm as honest a Fellow as breathes, tho I am a little disguis'd[1] at present.—Come, I say,—why, thou may'st be free with me, I'll be very secret. I'll not boast who 'twas oblig'd me, not I—for hang me if I know thy Name.

FLORINDA. Heavens! what a filthy beast is this!

WILLMORE. I am so, and thou oughtst the sooner to lie with me for that reason,— for look you Child, there will be no Sin in't, because 'twas neither design'd nor premeditated; 'tis pure Accident on both sides—that's a certain thing now—Indeed should I make love to you, and you vow Fidelity—and swear and lye till you believ'd and yielded—Thou art therefore (as thou art a good Christian) oblig'd in Conscience to deny me nothing. Now—come, be kind, without any more idle prating.

FLORINDA. Oh, I am ruin'd—wicked Man, unhand me.

WILLMORE. Wicked! Egad, Child, a Judge, were he young and vigorous, and saw those Eyes of thine, would know 'twas they gave the first blow—the first provocation.—Come, prithee let's lose no time, I say—this is a fine convenient place.

FLORINDA. Sir, let me go, I conjure you, or I'll call out.

WILLMORE. Ay, ay, you were best to call Witness to see how finely you treat me—do.—

FLORINDA. I'll cry Murder, Rape, or any thing, if you do not instantly let me go.

WILLMORE. A Rape! Come, come, you lye, you Baggage, you lye: What, I'll warrant you would fain have the World believe now that you are not so forward as I. No, not you,—why at this time of Night was your Cobweb-door set open, dear Spider—but to catch Flies?—Hah come—or I shall be damnably angry.—Why what a Coil is here.—

FLORINDA. Sir, can you think—

WILLMORE. That you'd do it for nothing? oh, oh, I find what you'd be at—look here, here's a Pistole for you—here's a work indeed—here—take it, I say.—

FLORINDA. For Heaven's sake, Sir, as you're a Gentleman.

WILLMORE. So—now—she would be wheedling me for more—what, you will not take it then—you're resolv'd you will not.—Come, come, take it, or I'll put it up again; for, look ye, I never give more.—Why, how now, Mistress, are you so high i'th' Mouth, a Pistole won't down with you?—hah—why, what a work's here—in good time—come, no struggling, be gone—But an y'are good at a dumb Wrestle, I'm for ye,—look ye,—I'm for ye.— [*She struggles with him.*]

---

1 A phrase meaning drunk.

Enter BELVILE *and* FREDERICK.

BELVILE. The Door is open, a Pox of this mad Fellow, I'm angry that we've lost him, I durst have sworn he had follow'd us.

FREDERICK. But you were so hasty, Colonel, to be gone.

FLORINDA. Help, help,—Murder!—help—oh, I'm ruin'd.

BELVILE. Ha, sure that's Florinda's Voice. [*Comes up to them.*]—A Man! Villain, let go that Lady. [*A noise.*]

[WILLMORE *turns and draws,* FREDERICK *interposes.*]

FLORINDA. Belvile! Heavens! my Brother too is coming, and 'twill be impossible to escape.—Belvile, I conjure you to walk under my Chamber-window, from whence I'll give you some instructions what to do—This rude Man has undone us. [*Exit.*]

WILLMORE. Belvile!

Enter PEDRO, STEPHANO, *and other Servants with Lights.*

PEDRO. I'm betray'd; run, Stephano, and see if Florinda be safe. [*Exit* STEPHANO.] So whoe'er they be, all is not well, I'll to Florinda's Chamber. [*They fight, and* PEDRO's *Party beats 'em out; going out, meets* STEPHANO.]

STEPHANO. You need not, Sir, the poor Lady's fast asleep, and thinks no harm: I wou'd not wake her, Sir, for fear of frightning her with your danger.

PEDRO. I'm glad she's there—Rascals, how came the Garden-Door open?

STEPHANO. That Question comes too late, Sir, some of my Fellow-Servants Masquerading I'll warrant.

PEDRO. Masquerading! a leud Custom to debauch our Youth—there's something more in this than I imagine. [*Exeunt.*]

SCENE IV. *Changes to the Street.*

Enter BELVILE *in Rage,* FREDERICK *holding him, and* WILLMORE, *melancholy.*

WILLMORE. Why, how the Devil shou'd I know Florinda?

BELVILE. Ah plague of your ignorance! if it had not been Florinda, must you be a Beast?—a Brute, a senseless Swine?

WILLMORE. Well, Sir, you see I am endu'd with Patience—I can bear—tho egad y're very free with me methinks.—I was in good hopes the Quarrel wou'd have been on my side, for so uncivilly interrupting me.

BELVILE. Peace, Brute, whilst thou'rt safe—oh, I'm distracted.

WILLMORE. Nay, nay, I'm an unlucky Dog, that's certain.

BELVILE. Ah curse upon the Star that rul'd my Birth! or whatsoever other Influence that makes me still so wretched.

WILLMORE. Thou break'st my Heart with these Complaints; there is no Star in fault, no Influence but Sack, the cursed Sack I drank.

FREDERICK. Why, how the Devil came you so drunk?

WILLMORE. Why, how the Devil came you so sober?

BELVILE. A curse upon his thin Skull, he was always before-hand that way.

FREDERICK. Prithee, dear Colonel, forgive him, he's sorry for his fault.

BELVILE. He's always so after he has done a mischief—a plague on all such Brutes.

WILLMORE. By this Light I took her for an errant Harlot.

BELVILE. Damn your debaucht Opinion: tell me, Sot, hadst thou so much sense and light about thee to distinguish her to be a Woman, and could'st not see something about her Face and Person, to strike an awful Reverence into thy Soul?

WILLMORE. Faith no, I consider'd her as mere a Woman as I could wish.

BELVILE. 'Sdeath I have no patience—draw, or I'll kill you.

WILLMORE. Let that alone till to morrow, and if I set not all right again, use your Pleasure.

BELVILE. To morrow, damn it.

The spiteful Light will lead me to no happiness.

To morrow is Antonio's, and perhaps

Guides him to my undoing;—oh that I could meet

This Rival, this powerful Fortunate.

WILLMORE. What then?

BELVILE. Let thy own Reason, or my Rage instruct thee.

WILLMORE. I shall be finely inform'd then, no doubt; hear me, Colonel—hear me—shew me the Man and I'll do his Business.

BELVILE. I know him no more than thou, or if I did, I should not need thy aid.

WILLMORE. This you say is Angellica's House, I promis'd the kind Baggage to lie with her to Night. [*Offers to go in.*]

Enter ANTONIO *and his Page.* ANTONIO *knocks on the Hilt of his Sword.*

ANTONIO. You paid the thousand Crowns I directed?

PAGE. To the Lady's old Woman, Sir, I did.

WILLMORE. Who the Devil have we here?

BELVILE. I'll now plant my self under Florinda's Window, and if I find no comfort there, I'll die. [*Exit* BELVILE *and* FREDERICK.]

Enter MORETTA.

MORETTA. Page!

PAGE. Here's my Lord.

WILLMORE. How is this, a Piccaroon going to board my Frigate! here's one Chase-Gun for you. [*Drawing his Sword, justles* ANTONIO *who turns and draws. They fight,* ANTONIO *falls.*]

MORETTA. Oh, bless us, we are all undone! [*Runs in, and shuts the Door.*]

PAGE. Help, Murder! [BELVILE *returns at the noise of fighting.*]

BELVILE. Ha, the mad Rogue's engag'd in some unlucky Adventure again.

Enter two or three Masqueraders.

MASQUERADER. Ha, a Man kill'd!

WILLMORE. How! a Man kill'd! then I'll go home to sleep. [*Puts up, and reels out. Exit Masquers another way.*]

BELVILE. Who shou'd it be! pray Heaven the Rogue is safe, for all my Quarrel to him. [*As* BELVILE *is groping about, enter an Officer and six Soldiers.*]

SOLDIER. Who's there?

OFFICER. So, here's one dispatcht—secure the Murderer.

BELVILE. Do not mistake my Charity for Murder:
I came to his Assistance. [*Soldiers seize on* BELVILE.]

OFFICER. That shall be tried, Sir.—St. *Jago*, Swords drawn in the Carnival time! [*Goes to* ANTONIO.]

ANTONIO. Thy Hand prithee.

OFFICER. Ha, Don Antonio! look well to the Villain there.—How is't, Sir?

ANTONIO. I'm hurt.

BELVILE. Has my Humanity made me a Criminal?

OFFICER. Away with him.

BELVILE. What a curst Chance is this! [*Exit Soldiers with* BELVILE.]

ANTONIO. This is the Man that has set upon me twice—carry him to my Apartment till you have further Orders from me. [*To the Officer. Exit.* ANTONIO *led.*]

ACT IV.

SCENE I. *A fine Room.*

Discovers BELVILE, *as by Dark alone.*

BELVILE. When shall I be weary of railing on Fortune, who is resolv'd never to turn with Smiles upon me?—Two such Defeats in one Night—none but the Devil and that mad Rogue could have contriv'd to have plagued me with—I am here a Prisoner—but where?—Heaven knows—and if there be Murder done, I can soon decide the Fate of a Stranger in a Nation without Mercy—Yet this is nothing to the Torture my Soul bows with, when I think of losing my fair, my dear Florinda.—Hark—my Door opens—a Light—a Man—and seems of Quality—arm'd too.—Now shall I die like a Dog without defence.

Enter ANTONIO *in a Night-Gown, with a Light; his Arm in a Scarf, and a Sword under his Arm: He sets the Candle on the Table.*

ANTONIO. Sir, I come to know what Injuries I have done you, that could provoke you to so mean an Action, as to attack me basely, without allowing time for my Defence.

BELVILE. Sir, for a Man in my Circumstances to plead Innocence, would look like Fear—but view me well, and you will find no marks of a Coward on me, nor any thing that betrays that Brutality you accuse me of.

ANTONIO. In vain, Sir, you impose upon my Sense,

   You are not only he who drew on me last Night,

   But yesterday before the same House, that of Angellica.

   Yet there is something in your Face and Mein—

BELVILE. I own I fought to day in the defence of a Friend of mine, with whom you (if you're the same) and your Party were first engag'd.

   Perhaps you think this Crime enough to kill me,

   But if you do, I cannot fear you'll do it basely.

ANTONIO. No, Sir, I'll make you fit for a Defence with this. [*Gives him the Sword.*]

BELVILE. This Gallantry surprizes me—nor know I how to use this Present, Sir, against a Man so brave.

ANTONIO. You shall not need;

   For know, I come to snatch you from a Danger

   That is decreed against you;

   Perhaps your Life, or long Imprisonment:

   And 'twas with so much Courage you offended,

   I cannot see you punisht.

BELVILE. How shall I pay this Generosity?

ANTONIO. It had been safer to have killed another,

   Than have attempted me:

   To shew your danger, Sir, I'll let you know my Quality;

   And 'tis the Vice-Roy's Son whom you have wounded.

BELVILE. The Vice-Roy's Son!

   Death and Confusion! was this Plague reserved

   To compleat all the rest?—oblig'd by him!

   The Man of all the World I wou'd destroy. [*Aside.*]

ANTONIO. You seem disorder'd, Sir.

BELVILE. Yes, trust me, Sir, I am, and 'tis with pain

   That Man receives such Bounties,

   Who wants the pow'r to pay 'em back again.

ANTONIO. To gallant Spirits 'tis indeed uneasy;

    —But you may quickly over-pay me, Sir.

BELVILE. Then I am well—kind Heaven! but set us even,

    That I may fight with him, and keep my Honour safe. [*Aside.*]

    —Oh, I'm impatient, Sir, to be discounting

    The mighty Debt I owe you; command me quickly—

ANTONIO. I have a Quarrel with a Rival, Sir,

    About the Maid we love.

BELVILE. Death, 'tis Florinda he means—

    That Thought destroys my Reason, and I shall kill him—[*Aside.*]

ANTONIO. My Rival, Sir,

    Is one has all the Virtues Man can boast of.

BELVILE. Death! who shou'd this be? [*Aside.*]

ANTONIO. He challeng'd me to meet him on the *Molo*,

    As soon as Day appear'd; but last Night's quarrel

    Has made my Arm unfit to guide a Sword.

BELVILE. I apprehend you, Sir, you'd have me kill the Man

    That lays a claim to the Maid you speak of.

    —I'll do't—I'll fly to do it.

ANTONIO. Sir, do you know her?

BELVILE. —No, Sir, but 'tis enough she is admired by you.

ANTONIO. Sir, I shall rob you of the Glory on't,

    For you must fight under my Name and Dress.

BELVILE. That Opinion must be strangely obliging that makes you think I can personate the brave Antonio, whom I can but strive to imitate.

ANTONIO. You say too much to my Advantage.

    Come, Sir, the Day appears that calls you forth.

    Within, Sir, is the Habit. [*Exit* ANTONIO.]

BELVILE. Fantastick Fortune, thou deceitful Light,

    That cheats the wearied Traveller by Night,

    Tho on a Precipice each step you tread,

    I am resolv'd to follow where you lead. [*Exit.*]

SCENE II. *The Molo.*

Enter FLORINDA *and* CALLIS *in Masques, with* STEPHANO.

FLORINDA. I'm dying with my fears; Belvile's not coming,

As I expected, underneath my Window,

Makes me believe that all those Fears are true. [*Aside.*]

—Canst thou not tell with whom my Brother fights?

STEPHANO. No Madam, they were both in Masquerade, I was by when they
challeng'd one another, and they had decided the Quarrel then, but were
prevented by some Cavaliers; which made 'em put it off till now—but I am
sure 'tis about you they fight.

FLORINDA. Nay then 'tis with Belvile, for what other Lover have I that dares fight
for me, except Antonio? and he is too much in favour with my Brother—If it
be he, for whom shall I direct my Prayers to Heaven?

STEPHANO. Madam, I must leave you; for if my Master see me, I shall be hang'd
for being your Conductor.—I escap'd narrowly for the Excuse I made for you
last night i'th' Garden.

FLORINDA. And I'll reward thee for't—prithee no more. [*Exit* STEPHANO.]

Enter DON PEDRO *in his Masquing Habit.*

PEDRO. Antonio's late to day, the place will fill, and we may be prevented.
[*Walks about.*]

FLORINDA. Antonio! sure I heard amiss. [*Aside.*]

PEDRO. But who would not excuse a happy Lover,

When soft fair Arms confine the yielding Neck;

And the kind Whisper languishingly breathes,

Must you be gone so soon?

Sure I had dwelt for ever on her Bosom.

—But stay, he's here.

Enter BELVILE *drest in* Antonio's *Clothes.*

FLORINDA. 'Tis not Belvile, half my Fears are vanisht.

PEDRO. Antonio!—

BELVILE. This must be he. [*Aside.*] You're early, Sir,—I do not use to be out-done
this way.

PEDRO. The wretched, Sir, are watchful, and 'tis enough

You have the advantage of me in Angellica.

BELVILE. Angellica! or I've mistook my Man! Or else Antonio,

    Can he forget his Interest in Florinda,

    And fight for common Prize? [*Aside.*]

PEDRO. Come, Sir, you know our terms—

BELVILE. By Heaven, not I. [*Aside.*]

    —No talking, I am ready, Sir.

                  [*Offers to fight,* FLORINDA *runs in.*]

FLORINDA. Oh, hold! whoe'er you be, I do conjure you hold. [*To* BELVILE.]

PEDRO. Florinda!

BELVILE. Florinda imploring for my Rival!

PEDRO. Away, this Kindness is unseasonable. [*Puts her by, they fight; she runs in just
as* BELVILE *disarms* PEDRO.]

FLORINDA. Who are you, Sir, that dare deny my Prayers?

BELVILE. Thy Prayers destroy him; if thou wouldst preserve him,

    Do that thou'rt unacquainted with, and curse him. [*She holds him.*]

FLORINDA. By all you hold most dear, by her you love,

      I do conjure you, touch him not.

BELVILE. By her I love!

    See—I obey—and at your Feet resign

    The useless Trophy of my Victory. [*Lays his sword at her Feet.*]

PEDRO. Antonio, you've done enough to prove you love Florinda.

BELVILE. Love Florinda!

    Does Heaven love Adoration, Pray'r, or Penitence?

    Love her! here Sir,—your Sword again. [*Snatches up the Sword, and gives it him.*]

    Upon this Truth I'll fight my Life away.

PEDRO. No, you've redeem'd my Sister, and my Friendship.

BELVILE. Don Pedro! [*He gives him* FLORINDA *and pulls off his Vizard to shew his
Face, and puts it on again.*]

PEDRO. Can you resign your Claims to other Women,

    And give your Heart entirely to Florinda?

BELVILE. Entire, as dying Saints Confessions are.

    I can delay my happiness no longer.

    This minute let me make Florinda mine:

PEDRO. This minute let it be—no time so proper,

    This Night my Father will arrive from *Rome*,

    And possibly may hinder what we propose.

FLORINDA. Oh Heavens! this Minute! [*Enter Masqueraders, and pass over.*]

BELVILE. Oh, do not ruin me!

PEDRO. The place begins to fill; and that we may not be observ'd, do you walk off to St. *Peter's* Church, where I will meet you, and conclude your Happiness.

BELVILE. I'll meet you there—if there be no more Saints Churches in *Naples*. [*Aside.*]

FLORINDA. Oh stay, Sir, and recall your hasty Doom:

Alas I have not yet prepar'd my Heart

To entertain so strange a Guest.

PEDRO. Away, this silly Modesty is assum'd too late.

BELVILE. Heaven, Madam! what do you do?

FLORINDA. Do! despise the Man that lays a Tyrant's Claim

To what he ought to conquer by Submission.

BELVILE. You do not know me—move a little this way. [*Draws her aside.*]

FLORINDA. Yes, you may even force me to the Altar,

But not the holy Man that offers there

Shall force me to be thine. [PEDRO *talks to* CALLIS *this while.*]

BELVILE. Oh do not lose so blest an opportunity!

See—'tis your Belvile—not Antonio,

Whom your mistaken Scorn and Anger ruins. [*Pulls off his Vizard.*]

FLORINDA. Belvile!

Where was my Soul it cou'd not meet thy Voice,

And take this knowledge in? [*As they are talking, enter* WILLMORE *finely drest, and* FREDERICK.]

WILLMORE. No Intelligence! no News of Belvile yet—well I am the most unlucky Rascal in Nature—ha!—am I deceiv'd—or is it he—look.

FREDERICK. —'Tis he—my dear Belvile. [*Vizard falls out on's hand, runs and embraces him.*]

BELVILE. Hell and Confusion seize thee!

PEDRO. Ha! Belvile! I beg your Pardon, Sir. [*Takes* FLORINDA *from him.*]

BELVILE. Nay, touch her not, she's mine by Conquest, Sir. I won her by my Sword.

WILLMORE. Did'st thou so—and egad, Child, we'll keep her by the Sword. [*Draws on* PEDRO, BELVILE *goes between.*]

BELVILE. Stand off.

Thou'rt so profanely leud, so curst by Heaven,

All Quarrels thou espousest must be fatal.

WILLMORE. Nay, an you be so hot, my Valour's coy, and shall be courted when you want it next. [*Puts up his Sword.*]

BELVILE. You know I ought to claim a Victor's Right, [*To* PEDRO.]

But you're the Brother to divine Florinda,

To whom I'm such a Slave—to purchase her,

I durst not hurt the Man she holds so dear.

PEDRO. 'Twas by Antonio's, not by Belvile's Sword,

This Question should have been decided, Sir:

I must confess much to your Bravery's due,

Both now, and when I met you last in Arms.

But I am nicely punctual in my word,

As Men of Honour ought, and beg your Pardon.

—For this Mistake another Time shall clear.

—This was some Plot between you and Belvile:

But I'll prevent you. [*Aside to* FLORINDA *as they are going out.*] [BELVILE *looks after her, and begins to walk up and down in a Rage.*]

WILLMORE. Do not be modest now, and lose the Woman: but if we shall fetch her back, so—

BELVILE. Do not speak to me.

WILLMORE. Not speak to you!—Egad, I'll speak to you, and will be answered too.

BELVILE. Will you, Sir?

WILLMORE. I know I've done some mischief, but I'm so dull a Puppy, that I am the Son of a Whore, if I know how, or where—prithee inform my Understanding.—

BELVILE. Leave me I say, and leave me instantly.

WILLMORE. I will not leave you in this humour, nor till I know my Crime.

BELVILE. Death, I'll tell you, Sir—[*Draws and runs at* WILLMORE, *he runs out; *BELVILE *after him,* FREDERICK *interposes.*]

Enter ANGELLICA, MORETTA, *and* SEBASTIAN.

ANGELLICA. Ha—Sebastian—Is not that Willmore? haste, haste, and bring him back.

FREDERICK. The Colonel's mad—I never saw him thus before; I'll after 'em, lest he do some mischief, for I am sure Willmore will not draw on him. [*Exit.*]

ANGELLICA. I am all Rage! my first desires defeated for one, for ought he knows, that has no other Merit than her Quality,—her being Don Pedro's Sister—He loves her:

I know 'tis so—dull, dull, insensible—

He will not see me now tho oft invited;

And broke his Word last night—false perjur'd Man!

—He that but yesterday fought for my Favours,

And would have made his Life a Sacrifice

To've gain'd one Night with me,

Must now be hired and courted to my Arms.

MORETTA. I told you what wou'd come on't, but Moretta's an old doating Fool—
Why did you give him five hundred Crowns, but to set himself out for other
Lovers? You shou'd have kept him poor, if you had meant to have had any
good from him.

ANGELLICA. Oh, name not such mean Trifles.—Had I given him all my Youth has
earn'd from Sin,

I had not lost a Thought nor Sigh upon't.

But I have given him my eternal Rest,

My whole Repose, my future Joys, my Heart;

My Virgin Heart. Moretta! oh 'tis gone!

MORETTA. Curse on him, here he comes;

How fine she has made him too!

Enter WILLMORE *and* SEBASTAIN. ANGELLICA *turns and walks away.*

WILLMORE. How now, turn'd Shadow?

Fly when I pursue, and follow when I fly!

> *Stay gentle Shadow of my Dove,* [*Sings.*]
> *And tell me e'er I go,*
> *Whether the Substance may not prove*
> *A fleeting Thing like you.*

There's a soft kind Look remaining yet. [*As she turns she looks on him.*]

ANGELLICA. Well, Sir, you may be gay; all Happiness, all Joys pursue you still,
Fortune's your Slave, and gives you every hour choice of new Hearts and
Beauties, till you are cloy'd with the repeated Bliss, which others vainly languish
for—But know, false Man, that I shall be reveng'd. [*Turns away in a Rage.*]

WILLMORE. So, 'gad, there are of those faint-hearted Lovers, whom such a sharp
Lesson next their Hearts would make as impotent as Fourscore—pox o' this
whining—my Bus'ness is to laugh and love—a pox on't; I hate your sullen
Lover, a Man shall lose as much time to put you in Humour now, as would
serve to gain a new Woman.

ANGELLICA. I scorn to cool that Fire I cannot raise,

Or do the Drudgery of your virtuous Mistress.

WILLMORE. A virtuous Mistress! Death, what a thing thou hast found out for
me! why what the Devil should I do with a virtuous Woman?—a sort of
ill-natur'd Creatures, that take a Pride to torment a Lover. Virtue is but an
infirmity in Women, a Disease that renders even the handsome ungrateful;
whilst the ill-favour'd, for want of Solicitations and Address, only fancy them-
selves so.—I have lain with a Woman of Quality, who has all the while been
railing at Whores.

ANGELLICA. I will not answer for your Mistress's Virtue,

> Tho she be young enough to know no Guilt:
>
> And I could wish you would persuade my Heart,
>
> 'Twas the two hundred thousand Crowns you courted.

WILLMORE. Two hundred thousand Crowns! what Story's this?—what Trick?—what Woman?—ha.

ANGELLICA. How strange you make it! have you forgot the Creature you entertain'd on the Piazza last night?

WILLMORE. Ha, my Gipsy worth two hundred thousand Crowns!—oh how I long to be with her—pox, I knew she was of Quality. [*Aside.*]

ANGELLICA. False Man, I see my Ruin in thy Face.

> How many vows you breath'd upon my Bosom,
>
> Never to be unjust—have you forgot so soon?

WILLMORE. Faith no, I was just coming to repeat 'em—but here's a Humour indeed—would make a Man a Saint—Wou'd she'd be angry enough to leave me, and command me not to wait on her. [*Aside.*]

Enter HELLENA, *drest in Man's Clothes.*

HELLENA. This must be Angellica, I know it by her mumping Matron here—Ay, ay, 'tis she: my mad Captain's with her too, for all his swearing—how this unconstant Humour makes me love him:—pray, good grave Gentlewoman, is not this Angellica?

MORETTA. My too young Sir, it is—I hope 'tis one from Don Antonio. [*Goes to* ANGELLICA.]

HELLENA. Well, something I'll do to vex him for this. [*Aside.*]

ANGELLICA. I will not speak with him; am I in humour to receive a Lover?

WILLMORE. Not speak with him! why I'll be gone—and wait your idler minutes— Can I shew less Obedience to the thing I love so fondly? [*Offers to go.*]

ANGELLICA. A fine Excuse this—stay—

WILLMORE. And hinder your Advantage: should I repay your Bounties so ungratefully?

ANGELLICA. Come hither, Boy,—that I may let you see

> How much above the Advantages you name
>
> I prize one Minute's Joy with you.

WILLMORE. Oh, you destroy me with this Endearment. [*Impatient to be gone.*]— Death, how shall I get away?—Madam, 'twill not be fit I should be seen with you—besides, it will not be convenient—and I've a Friend—that's dangerously sick.

ANGELLICA. I see you're impatient—yet you shall stay.

WILLMORE. And miss my Assignation with my Gipsy. [*Aside, and walks about impatiently.*]

HELLENA. Madam, [MORETTA *brings* HELLENA, *who addresses her self to* ANGELLICA.]

You'll hardly pardon my Intrusion,

When you shall know my Business;

And I'm too young to tell my Tale with Art:

But there must be a wondrous store of Goodness

Where so much Beauty dwells.

ANGELLICA. A pretty Advocate, whoever sent thee,

—Prithee proceed—Nay, Sir, you shall not go. [*To* WILLMORE *who is stealing off.*]

WILLMORE. Then shall I lose my dear Gipsy for ever.

—Pox on't, she stays me out of spite. [*Aside.*]

HELLENA. I am related to a Lady, Madam,

Young, rich, and nobly born, but has the fate

To be in love with a young *English* Gentleman.

Strangely she loves him, at first sight she lov'd him,

But did adore him when she heard him speak;

For he, she said, had Charms in every word,

That fail'd not to surprize, to wound, and conquer—

WILLMORE. Ha, Egad I hope this concerns me. [*Aside.*]

ANGELLICA. 'Tis my false Man, he means—wou'd he were gone. This Praise will raise his Pride and ruin me—Well, since you are so impatient to be gone, I will release you, Sir. [*To* WILLMORE.]

WILLMORE. Nay, then I'm sure 'twas me he spoke of, this cannot be the Effects of Kindness in her. [*Aside.*]

—No, Madam, I've consider'd better on't,

And will not give you cause of Jealousy.

ANGELLICA. But, Sir, I've—business, that—

WILLMORE. This shall not do, I know 'tis but to try me.

ANGELLICA. Well, to your Story, Boy,—tho 'twill undo me. [*Aside.*]

HELLENA. With this Addition to his other Beauties,

He won her unresisting tender Heart,

He vow'd and sigh'd, and swore he lov'd her dearly;

And she believ'd the cunning Flatterer,

And thought her self the happiest Maid alive:

To day was the appointed time by both,

To consummate their bliss;

The Virgin, Altar, and the Priest were drest,

And whilst she languisht for the expected Bridegroom,

She heard, he paid his broken Vows to you.

WILLMORE. So, this is some dear Rogue that's in love with me, and this way lets me know it; or if it be not me, she means some one whose place I may supply. [*Aside.*]

ANGELLICA. Now I perceive the cause of thy Impatience to be gone, and all the business of this glorious Dress.

WILLMORE. Damn the young Prater, I know not what he means.

HELLENA. Madam,

In your fair Eyes I read too much concern

To tell my farther Business.

ANGELLICA. Prithee sweet. Youth, talk on, thou may'st perhaps

Raise here a Storm that may undo my Passion,

And then I'll grant thee any thing.

HELLENA. Madam,'tis to entreat you, (oh unreasonable!)

You wou'd not see this Stranger;

For if you do, she vows you are undone,

Tho Nature never made a Man so excellent;

And sure he'ad been a God, but for Inconstancy.

WILLMORE. Ah, Rogue, how finely he's instructed! [*Aside.*]—'Tis plain some Woman that has seen me *en passant*.

ANGELLICA. Oh, I shall burst with Jealousy! do you know the Man you speak of?—

HELLENA. Yes, Madam, he us'd to be in Buff and Scarlet.

ANGELLICA. Thou, false as Hell, what canst thou say to this? [*To* WILLMORE.]

WILLMORE. By Heaven—

ANGELLICA. Hold, do not damn thy self—

HELLENA. Nor hope to be believ'd. [*He walks about, they follow.*]

ANGELLICA. Oh, perjur'd Man!

Is't thus you pay my generous Passion back?

HELLENA. Why wou'd you, Sir, abuse my Lady's Faith?

ANGELLICA. And use me so inhumanly?

HELLENA. A Maid so young, so innocent—

WILLMORE. Ah, young Devil!

ANGELLICA. Dost thou not know thy Life is in my Power?

HELLENA. Or think my Lady cannot be reveng'd?

WILLMORE. So, so, the Storm comes finely on. [*Aside.*]

ANGELLICA. Now thou art silent, Guilt has struck thee dumb. Oh, hadst thou still been so, I'd liv'd in safety. [*She turns away and weeps.*]

WILLMORE. Sweetheart, the Lady's Name and House—quickly: I'm impatient to be with her.—[*Aside to* HELLENA, *looks towards* ANGELLICA *to watch her turning; and as she comes towards them, he meets her.*]

HELLENA. So now is he for another Woman. [*Aside.*]

WILLMORE. The impudent'st young thing in Nature!

     I cannot persuade him out of his Error, Madam.

ANGELLICA. I know he's in the right,—yet thou'st a Tongue

     That wou'd persuade him to deny his Faith. [*In Rage walks away.*]

WILLMORE. Her Name, her Name, dear Boy—[*Said softly to* HELLENA.]

HELLENA. Have you forgot it, Sir?

WILLMORE. Oh, I perceive he's not to know I am a Stranger to his Lady. [*Aside.*]

     —Yes, yes, I do know—but—I have forgot the— [ANGELLICA *turns.*]

     —By Heaven, such early Confidence I never saw.

ANGELLICA. Did I not charge you with this Mistress, Sir?

     Which you denied, tho I beheld your Perjury.

     This little Generosity of thine has render'd back my Heart. [*Walks away.*]

WILLMORE. So, you have made sweet work here, my little Mischief; look your Lady be kind and good-natur'd now, or I shall have but a cursed Bargain on't. [ANGELLICA *turns towards them.*]

     —The Rogue's bred up to Mischief,

     Art thou so great a Fool to credit him?

ANGELLICA. Yes, I do; and you in vain impose upon me.—Come hither, Boy—Is not this he you speak of?

HELLENA. I think—it is; I cannot swear, but I vow he has just such another lying Lover's look. [HELLENA *looks in his Face, he gazes on her.*]

WILLMORE. Hah! do not I know that Face?—

     By Heaven, my little Gipsy! what a dull Dog was I?

     Had I but lookt that way, I'd known her.

     Are all my hopes of a new Woman banisht? [*Aside.*]

     —Egad, if I don't fit thee for this, hang me.

     —Madam, I have found out the Plot.

HELLENA. Oh Lord, what does he say? am I discover'd now?

WILLMORE. Do you see this young Spark here?

HELLENA. He'll tell her who I am.

WILLMORE. Who do you think this is?

HELLENA. Ay, ay, he does know me.—Nay, dear Captain, I'm undone if you discover me.

WILLMORE. Nay, nay, no cogging;[1] she shall know what a precious Mistress I have.

HELLENA. Will you be such a Devil?

WILLMORE. Nay, nay, I'll teach you to spoil sport you will not make.—This small Ambassador comes not from a Person of Quality, as you imagine, and he says; but from a very errant Gipsy, the talkingst, pratingst, cantingst little Animal thou ever saw'st.

ANGELLICA. What news you tell me! that's the thing I mean.

HELLENA. Wou'd I were well off the place.—If ever I go a Captain-hunting again.—[*Aside.*]

WILLMORE. Mean that thing? that Gipsy thing? thou may'st as well be jealous of thy Monkey, or Parrot, as her: a *German* Motion were worth a dozen of her, and a Dream were a better Enjoyment, a Creature of Constitution fitter for Heaven than Man.

HELLENA. Tho I'm sure he lyes, yet this vexes me. [*Aside.*]

ANGELLICA. You are mistaken, she's a *Spanish* Woman made up of no such dull Materials.

WILLMORE. Materials! Egad, and she be made of any that will either dispense, or admit of Love, I'll be bound to continence.

HELLENA. Unreasonable Man, do you think so? [*Aside to him.*]

WILLMORE. You may return, my little Brazen Head, and tell your Lady, that till she be handsome enough to be belov'd, or I dull enough to be religious, there will be small hopes of me.

ANGELLICA. Did you not promise then to marry her?

WILLMORE. Not I by Heaven.

ANGELLICA. You cannot undeceive my fears and torments, till you have vow'd you will not marry her.

HELLENA. If he swears that, he'll be reveng'd on me indeed for all my Rogueries.

ANGELLICA. I know what Arguments you'll bring against me, Fortune and Honour.

WILLMORE. Honour! I tell you, I hate it in your Sex; and those that fancy themselves possest of that Foppery, are the most impertinently troublesome of all Woman-kind, and will transgress nine Commandments to keep one: and to satisfy your Jealousy I swear—

HELLENA. Oh, no swearing, dear Captain—[*Aside to him.*]

---

1 To deceive or trick.

WILLMORE. If it were possible I should ever be inclin'd to marry, it should be some kind young Sinner, one that has Generosity enough to give a favour handsomely to one that can ask it discreetly, one that has Wit enough to manage an Intrigue of Love—oh, how civil such a Wench is, to a Man than does her the Honour to marry her.

ANGELLICA. By Heaven, there's no Faith in any thing he says.

Enter SEBASTIAN.

SEBASTIAN. Madam, Don Antonio—

ANGELLICA. Come hither.

HELLENA. Ha, Antonio! he may be coming hither, and he'll certainly discover me, I'll therefore retire without a Ceremony. [*Exit* HELLENA.]

ANGELLICA. I'll see him, get my Coach ready.

SEBASTIAN. It waits you, Madam.

WILLMORE. This is lucky: what, Madam, now I may be gone and leave you to the enjoyment of my Rival?

ANGELLICA. Dull Man, that canst not see how ill, how poor

That false dissimulation looks—Be gone,

And never let me see thy cozening Face again,

Lest I relapse and kill thee.

WILLMORE. Yes, you can spare me now,—farewell till you are in a better Humour—I'm glad of this release—

Now for my Gipsy:

For tho to worse we change, yet still we find

New Joys, New Charms, in a new Miss that's kind. [*Exit* WILLMORE.]

ANGELLICA. He's gone, and in this Ague of My Soul

The shivering Fit returns;

Oh with what willing haste he took his leave,

As if the long'd for Minute were arriv'd,

Of some blest Assignation.

In vain I have consulted all my Charms,

In vain this Beauty priz'd, in vain believ'd

My Eyes cou'd kindle any lasting Fires.

I had forgot my Name, my Infamy,

And the Reproach that Honour lays on those

That dare pretend a sober passion here.

Nice Reputation, tho it leave behind

More Virtues than inhabit where that dwells,

Yet that once gone, those Virtues shine no more.

—Then since I am not fit to be belov'd,

I am resolv'd to think on a Revenge

On him that sooth'd me thus to my undoing. [*Exeunt.*]

SCENE III. *A Street.*

Enter FLORINDA *and* VALERIA *in Habits different from what they have been seen in.*

FLORINDA. We're happily escap'd, yet I tremble still.

VALERIA. A Lover and fear! why, I am but half a one, and yet I have Courage for any Attempt. Would Hellena were here. I wou'd fain have had her as deep in this Mischief as we, she'll fare but ill else I doubt.

FLORINDA. She pretended a Visit to the *Augustine* Nuns, but I believe some other design carried her out, pray Heavens we light on her.

—Prithee what didst do with Callis?

VALERIA. When I saw no Reason wou'd do good on her, I follow'd her into the Wardrobe, and as she was looking for something in a great Chest, I tumbled her in by the Heels, snatcht the Key of the Apartment where you were confin'd, lockt her in, and left her bauling for help.

FLORINDA. 'Tis well you resolve to follow my Fortunes, for thou darest never appear at home again after such an Action.

VALERIA. That's according as the young Stranger and I shall agree—But to our Business—I deliver'd your Letter, your Note to Belvile, when I got out under pretence of going to Mass, I found him at his Lodging, and believe me it came seasonably; for never was Man in so desperate a Condition. I told him of your Resolution of making your escape to day, if your Brother would be absent long enough to permit you; if not, die rather than be Antonio's.

FLORINDA. Thou shou'dst have told him I was confin'd to my Chamber upon my Brother's suspicion, that the Business on the *Molo* was a Plot laid between him and I.

VALERIA. I said all this, and told him your Brother was now gone to his Devotion, and he resolves to visit every Church till he find him; and not only undeceive him in that, but caress him so as shall delay his return home.

FLORINDA. Oh Heavens! he's here, and Belvile with him too. [*They put on their Vizards.*]

Enter DON PEDRO, BELVILE, WILLMORE; BELVILE *and* DON PEDRO *seeming in serious Discourse.*

VALERIA. Walk boldly by them, I'll come at a distance, lest he suspect us. [*She walks by them, and looks back on them.*]

WILLMORE. Ha! Woman! and of an excellent Mien!

PEDRO. She throws a kind look back on you.

WILLMORE. Death, 'tis a likely Wench, and that kind look shall not be cast away— I'll follow her.

BELVILE. Prithee do not.

WILLMORE. Do not! By Heavens to the Antipodes, with such an Invitation. [*She goes out, and* WILLMORE *follows her.*]

BELVILE. 'Tis a mad Fellow for a Wench.

Enter FREDERICK.

FREDERICK. Oh Colonel, such News!

BELVILE. Prithee what?

FREDERICK. News that will make you laugh in spite of Fortune.

BELVILE. What, Blunt has had some damn'd Trick put upon him, cheated, bang'd, or clapt?

FREDERICK. Cheated, Sir, rarely cheated of all but his Shirt and Drawers; the unconscionable Whore too turn'd him out before, so that traversing the Streets at Midnight, the Watch found him in this *Fresco*, and conducted him home: By Heaven 'tis such a slight, and yet I durst as well have been hang'd as laugh at him, or pity him; he beats all that do but ask him a Question, and is in such an Humour—

PEDRO. Who is't has met with this ill usage, Sir?

BELVILE. A Friend of ours, whom you must see for Mirth's sake. I'll imploy him to give Florinda time for an escape. [*Aside.*]

PEDRO. What is he?

BELVILE. A young Countryman of ours, one that has been educated at so plentiful a rate, he yet ne'er knew the want of Money, and 'twill be a great Jest to see how simply he'll look without it. For my part I'll lend him none, and the Rogue knows not how to put on a borrowing Face, and ask first. I'll let him see how good 'tis to play our parts whilst I play his—Prithee, Frederick do go home and keep him in that posture till we come. [*Exeunt.*]

Enter FLORINDA *from the farther end of the Scene, looking behind her.*

FLORINDA. I am follow'd still—hah—my Brother too advancing this way, good Heavens defend me from being seen by him. [*She goes off.*]

Enter WILLMORE, *and after him* VALERIA, *at a little distance.*

WILLMORE. Ah! There she sails, she looks back as she were willing to be boarded, I'll warrant her Prize. [*He goes out,* VALERIA *following.*]

Enter HELLENA, *just as he goes out, with a Page.*

HELLENA. Hah, is not that my Captain that has a Woman in chase?—'tis not Angellica. Boy, follow those People at a distance, and bring me an Account where they go in.—I'll find his Haunts, and plague him every where.—ha—my Brother! [*Exit* PAGE.]

[BELVILE, WILLMORE, PEDRO *cross the Stage:* HELLENA *runs off.*]

Scene changes to another Street. Enter FLORINDA.

FLORINDA. What shall I do, my Brother now pursues me.

Will no kind Power protect me from his Tyranny?

—Hah, here's a Door open, I'll venture in, since nothing can be worse than to fall into his Hands, my Life and Honour are at stake, and my Necessity has no choice. [*She goes in.*]

Enter VALERIA, *and* HELLENA's *Page peeping after* FLORINDA.

PAGE. Here she went in, I shall remember this House. [*Exit* BOY.]

VALERIA. This is Belvile's Lodgings; she's gone in as readily as if she knew it—hah—here's that mad Fellow again, I dare not venture in—I'll watch my Opportunity. [*Goes aside.*]

Enter WILLMORE, *gazing about him.*

WILLMORE. I have lost her hereabouts—Pox on't she must not scape me so. [*Goes out.*]

Scene changes to BLUNT's *Chamber, discovers him sitting on a Couch in his Shirt and Drawers, reading.*

BLUNT. So, now my Mind's a little at Peace, since I have resolv'd Revenge—A Pox on this Tailor tho, for not bringing home the Clothes I bespoke; and a Pox of all poor Cavaliers, a Man can never keep a spare Suit for 'em; and I shall have these Rogues come in and find me naked; and then I'm undone; but I'm resolv'd to arm my self—the Rascals shall not insult over me too much. [*Puts on an old rusty Sword and Buff-Belt.*]—Now, how like a Morrice-Dancer I am equipt—a fine Lady-like Whore to cheat me thus, without affording me a Kindness for my Money, a Pox light on her, I shall never be reconciled to the Sex more, she has made me as faithless as a Physician, as uncharitable as a Churchman, and as ill-natur'd as a Poet. O how I'll use all Women-kind hereafter! what wou'd I give to have one of 'em within my reach now! any Mortal thing in Petticoats, kind Fortune, send me; and I'll forgive thy last Night's Malice—Here's a cursed Book too, (a Warning to all young Travellers) that can instruct me how to prevent such Mischiefs now 'tis too late. Well, 'tis a rare convenient thing to read a little now and then, as well as hawk and hunt. [*Sits down again and reads.*]

Enter to him FLORINDA.

FLORINDA. This House is haunted sure, 'tis well furnisht and no living thing inhabits it—hah—a Man! Heavens how he's attir'd! sure 'tis some Rope-dancer, or Fencing-Master; I tremble now for fear, and yet I must venture now to speak to him—Sir, if I may not interrupt your Meditations—[*He starts up and gazes.*]

BLUNT. Hah—what's here? Are my wishes granted? and is not that a she Creature? Adsheartlikins 'tis! what wretched thing art thou—hah!

FLORINDA. Charitable Sir, you've told your self already what I am; a very wretched Maid, forc'd by a strange unlucky Accident, to seek a safety here, and must be ruin'd, if you do not grant it.

BLUNT. Ruin'd! Is there any Ruin so inevitable as that which now threatens thee? Dost thou know, miserable Woman, into what Den of Mischiefs thou art fall'n? what a Bliss of Confusion?—hah—dost not see something in my looks that frights thy guilty Soul, and makes thee wish to change that Shape of Woman for any humble Animal, or Devil? for those were safer for thee, and less mischievous.

FLORINDA. Alas, what mean you, Sir? I must confess your Looks have something in 'em makes me fear; but I beseech you, as you seem a Gentleman, pity a harmless Virgin, that takes your House for Sanctuary.

BLUNT. Talk on, talk on, and weep too, till my faith return. Do, flatter me out of my Senses again—a harmless Virgin with a Pox, as much one as t'other, adsheartlikins. Why, what the Devil can I not be safe in my House for you? not in my Chamber? nay, even being naked too cannot secure me. This is an Impudence greater than has invaded me yet.—Come, no Resistance. [*Pulls her rudely.*]

FLORINDA. Dare you be so cruel?

BLUNT. Cruel, adsheartlikins as a Gally-slave, or a *Spanish* Whore: Cruel, yes, I will kiss and beat thee all over; kiss, and see thee all over; thou shalt lie with me too, not that I care for the Enjoyment, but to let you see I have ta'en deliberated Malice to thee, and will be revenged on one Whore for the Sins of another; I will smile and deceive thee, flatter thee, and beat thee, kiss and swear, and lye to thee, embrace thee and rob thee, as she did me, fawn on thee, and strip thee stark naked, then hang thee out at my Window by the Heels, with a Paper of scurvey Verses fasten'd to thy Breast, in praise of damnable Women—Come, come along.

FLORINDA. Alas, Sir, must I be sacrific'd for the Crimes of the most infamous of my Sex? I never understood the Sins you name.

BLUNT. Do, persuade the Fool you love him, or that one of you can be just or honest; tell me I was not an easy Coxcomb, or any strange impossible Tale: it will be believ'd sooner than thy false Showers or Protestations. A Generation of damn'd Hypocrites, to flatter my very Clothes from my back! dissembling Witches! are these the Returns you make an honest Gentleman that trusts, believes, and loves you?—But if I be not even with you—Come along, or I shall—[*Pulls her again.*]

Enter FREDERICK.

FREDERICK. Hah, what's here to do?

BLUNT. Adsheartlikins, Frederick. I am glad thou art come, to be a Witness of my dire Revenge.

FREDERICK. What's this, a Person of Quality too, who is upon the Ramble to supply the Defects of some grave impotent Husband?

BLUNT. No, this has another Pretence, some very unfortunate Accident brought her hither, to save a Life pursued by I know not who, or why, and forc'd to take Sanctuary here at Fools Haven. Adsheartlikins to me of all Mankind for Protection? Is the Ass to be cajol'd again, think ye? No, young one, no Prayers or Tears shall mitigate my Rage; therefore prepare for both my Pleasure of Enjoyment and Revenge, for I am resolved to make up my Loss here on thy Body, I'll take it out in kindness and in beating.

FREDERICK. Now Mistress of mine, what do you think of this?

FLORINDA. I think he will not—dares not be so barbarous.

FREDERICK. Have a care, Blunt, she fetch'd a deep Sigh, she is inamour'd with thy Shirt and Drawers, she'll strip thee even of that. There are of her Calling such unconscionable Baggages, and such dexterous Thieves, they'll flea a Man, and he shall ne'er miss his Skin, till he feels the Cold. There was a Country-man of ours robb'd of a Row of Teeth whilst he was sleeping, which the Jilt made him buy again when he wak'd—You see, Lady, how little Reason we have to trust you.

BLUNT. 'Dsheartlikins, why, this is most abominable.

FLORINDA. Some such Devils there may be, but by all that's holy I am none such, I entered here to save a Life in danger.

BLUNT. For no goodness I'll warrant her.

FREDERICK. Faith, Damsel, you had e'en confess the plain Truth, for we are Fellows not to be caught twice in the same Trap: Look on that Wreck, a tight Vessel when he set out of Haven, well trim'd and laden, and see how a Female Piccaroon of this Island of Rogues has shatter'd him, and canst thou hope for any Mercy?

BLUNT. No, no, Gentlewoman, come along, adsheartlikins we must be better acquainted—we'll both lie with her, and then let me alone to bang her.

FREDERICK. I am ready to serve you in matters of Revenge, that has a double Pleasure in't.

BLUNT. Well said. You hear, little one, how you are condemn'd by publick Vote to the Bed within, there's no resisting your Destiny, Sweetheart. [*Pulls her.*]

FLORINDA. Stay, Sir, I have seen you with Belvile, an *English* Cavalier, for his sake use me kindly; you know how, Sir.

BLUNT. Belvile! why, yes, Sweeting, we do know Belvile, and wish he were with us now, he's a Cormorant at Whore and Bacon, he'd have a Limb or two of thee, my Virgin Pullet: but 'tis no matter, we'll leave him the Bones to pick.

FLORINDA. Sir, if you have any Esteem for that Belvile, I conjure you to treat me with more Gentleness; he'll thank you for the Justice.

FREDERICK. Hark ye, Blunt, I doubt we are mistaken in this matter.

FLORINDA. Sir, If you find me not worth Belvile's Care, use me as you please; and that you may think I merit better treatment than you threaten—pray take this Present—[*Gives him a Ring: He looks on it.*]

BLUNT. Hum—A Diamond! why, 'tis a wonderful Virtue now that lies in this Ring, a mollifying Virtue; adsheartlikins there's more persuasive Rhetorick in't, than all her Sex can utter.

FREDERICK. I begin to suspect something; and 'twou'd anger us vilely to be truss'd up for a Rape upon a Maid of Quality, when we only believe we ruffle a Harlot.

BLUNT. Thou art a credulous Fellow, but adsheartlikins I have no Faith yet; why, my Saint prattled as parlously as this does, she gave me a Bracelet too, a Devil on her: but I sent my Man to sell it to day for Necessaries, and it prov'd as counterfeit as her Vows of Love.

FREDERICK. However, let it reprieve her till we see Belvile.

BLUNT. That's hard, yet I will grant it.

Enter a Servant.

SERVANT. Oh, Sir, the Colonel is just come with his new Friend and a *Spaniard* of Quality, and talks of having you to Dinner with 'em.

BLUNT. 'Dsheartlikins, I'm undone!—I would not see 'em for the World: Harkye, Frederick, lock up the Wench in your Chamber.

FREDERICK. Fear nothing, Madam, whate'er he threatens, you're safe whilst in my Hands. [*Exit* FREDERICK *and* FLORINDA.]

BLUNT. And Sirrah—upon your Life, say—I am not at home—or that I am asleep—or—or any thing—away—I'll, prevent them coming this way. [*Locks the Door and Exeunt.*]

ACT V.

SCENE I. BLUNT's *Room.*

After a great knocking at his Chamber-door, enter BLUNT *softly, crossing the Stage in his Shirt and Drawers, as before.*

Ned, Ned Blunt, Ned Blunt. [*Call within.*]

BLUNT. The Rogues are up in Arms, 'dsheartlikins, this villainous Frederick has betray'd me, they have heard of my blessed Fortune.

Ned Blunt, Ned, Ned—[*and knocking within.*]

BELVILE. Why, he's dead, Sir, without dispute dead, he has not been seen to day; let's break open the Door—here—Boy—

BLUNT. Ha, break open the Door! 'dsheartlikins that mad Fellow will be as good as his word.

BELVILE. Boy, bring something to force the Door. [*A great noise within at the Door again.*]

BLUNT. So, now must I speak in my own Defence, I'll try what Rhetorick will do—hold—hold, what do you mean, Gentlemen, what do you mean?

BELVILE. Oh Rogue, art alive? prithee open the Door, and convince us.

BLUNT. Yes, I am alive, Gentlemen—but at present a little busy.

BELVILE. How! Blunt grown a man of Business! come, come, open, and let's see this Miracle. [*Within.*]

BLUNT. No, no, no, no Gentlemen, 'tis no great Business—but—I am—at—my Devotion,—'dsheartlikins, will you not allow a man time to pray?

BELVILE. Turn'd religious! a greater Wonder than the first, therefore open quickly, or we shall unhinge, we shall. [*Within.*]

BLUNT. This won't do—Why, hark ye, Colonel; to tell you the plain Truth, I am about a necessary Affair of Life.—I have a Wench with me—you apprehend me? the Devil's in't if they be so uncivil as to disturb me now.

WILLMORE. How, a Wench! Nay, then we must enter and partake; no Resistance,— unless it be your Lady of Quality, and then we'll keep our distance.

BLUNT. So, the Business is out.

WILLMORE. Come, come, lend more hands to the Door,—now heave altogether— so, well done, my Boys—[*Breaks open the Door.*]

Enter BELVILE, WILLMORE, FREDERICK, PEDRO, *and* BELVILE's *Page:* BLUNT *looks simply, they all laugh at him, he lays his hand on his Sword, and comes up to* WILLMORE.

BLUNT. Hark ye, Sir, laugh out your laugh quickly, d'ye hear, and be gone, I shall spoil your sport else; 'dsheartlikins, Sir, I shall—the Jest has been carried on too long,—a Plague upon my Tailor—[*Aside.*]

WILLMORE. 'Sdeath, how the Whore has drest him! Faith, Sir, I'm sorry.

BLUNT. Are you so, Sir? keep't to your self then Sir, I advise you, d'ye hear? for I can as little endure your Pity as his Mirth. [*Lays his Hand on's Sword.*]

BELVILE. Indeed, Willmore, thou wert a little too rough with Ned Blunt's Mistress; call a Person of Quality Whore, and one so young, so handsome, and so eloquent!—ha, ha, ha.

BLUNT. Hark ye, Sir, you know me, and know I can be angry; have a care—for 'dsheartlikins I can fight too—I can, Sir,—do you mark me—no more.

BELVILE. Why so peevish, good Ned? some Disappointments, I'll warrant—What! did the jealous Count her Husband return just in the nick?

BLUNT. Or the Devil, Sir,—d'ye laugh? [*They laugh.*] Look ye, settle me a good sober Countenance, and that quickly too, or you shall know Ned Blunt is not—

BELVILE. Not every Body, we know that.

BLUNT. Not an Ass, to be laught at, Sir.

WILLMORE. Unconscionable Sinner, to bring a Lover so near his Happiness, a vigorous passionate Lover, and then not only cheat him of his Moveables, but his Desires too.

BELVILE. Ah, Sir, a Mistress is a Trifle with Blunt, he'll have a dozen the next time he looks abroad; his Eyes have Charms not to be resisted: There needs no more than to expose that taking Person to the view of the Fair, and he leads 'em all in Triumph.

PEDRO. Sir, tho I'm a stranger to you, I'm asham'd at the rudeness of my Nation, and could you learn who did it, would assist you to make an Example of 'em.

BLUNT. Why, ay, there's one speaks sense now, and handsomely; and let me tell you Gentlemen, I should not have shew'd my self like a Jack-Pudding, thus to have made you Mirth, but that I have revenge within my power; for know, I have got into my possession a Female, who had better have fallen under any Curse, than the Ruin I design her: 'dsheartlikins, she assaulted me here in my own Lodgings, and had doubtless committed a Rape upon me, had not this Sword defended me.

FREDERICK. I knew not that, but o' my Conscience thou hadst ravisht her, had she not redeem'd her self with a Ring—let's see't, Blunt. [BLUNT *shews the Ring.*]

BELVILE. Hah!—the Ring I gave Florinda when we exchang'd our Vows!—hark ye, Blunt—[*Goes to whisper to him.*]

WILLMORE. No whispering, good Colonel, there's a Woman in the case, no whispering.

BELVILE. Hark ye, Fool, be advis'd, and conceal both the Ring and the Story, for your Reputation's sake; don't let People know what despis'd Cullies we *English* are: to be cheated and abus'd by one Whore, and another rather bribe thee than be kind to thee, is an Infamy to our Nation.

WILLMORE. Come, come, where's the Wench? we'll see her, let her be what she will, we'll see her.

PEDRO. Ay, ay, let us see her, I can soon discover whether she be of Quality, or for your Diversion.

BLUNT. She's in Frederick's Custody.

WILLMORE. Come, come, the Key. [*To* FREDERICK, *who gives him the Key, they are going.*]

BELVILE. Death! what shall I do?—stay Gentlemen—yet if I hinder 'em, I shall discover all—hold, let's go one at once—give me the Key.

WILLMORE. Nay, hold there, Colonel, I'll go first.

FREDERICK. Nay, no Dispute, Ned and I have the property of her.

WILLMORE. Damn Property—then we'll draw Cuts. [BELVILE *goes to whisper* WILLMORE.] Nay, no Corruption, good Colonel: come, the longest Sword carries her.—[*They all draw, forgetting* DON PEDRO, *being a* Spaniard, *had the longest.*]

BLUNT. I yield up my Interest to you Gentlemen, and that will be Revenge sufficient.

WILLMORE. The Wench is yours—(*To* PEDRO.) Pox of his *Toledo*, I had forgot that.

FREDERICK. Come, Sir, I'll conduct you to the Lady. [*Exit* FREDERICK *and* PEDRO.]

BELVILE. To hinder him will certainly discover—[*Aside.*] Dost know, dull Beast, what Mischief thou hast done? [WILLMORE *walking up and down out of Humour.*]

WILLMORE. Ay, ay, to trust our Fortune to Lots, a Devil on't, 'twas madness, that's the Truth on't.

BELVILE. Oh intolerable Sot!

Enter FLORINDA, *running masqu'd,* PEDRO *after her,* WILLMORE *gazing round her.*

FLORINDA. Good Heaven, defend me from discovery. [*Aside.*]

PEDRO. 'Tis but in vain to fly me, you are fallen to my Lot.

BELVILE. Sure she is undiscover'd yet, but now I fear there is no way to bring her off.

WILLMORE. Why, what a Pox is not this my Woman, the same I follow'd but now? [PEDRO *talking to* FLORINDA, *who walks up and down.*]

PEDRO. As if I did not know ye, and your Business here.

FLORINDA. Good Heaven! I fear he does indeed—[*Aside.*]

PEDRO. Come, pray be kind, I know you meant to be so when you enter'd here, for these are proper Gentlemen.

WILLMORE. But, Sir—perhaps the Lady will not be impos'd upon, she'll chuse her Man.

PEDRO. I am better bred, than not to leave her Choice free.

Enter VALERIA, *and is surprized at the sight of* DON PEDRO.

VALERIA. Don Pedro here! there's no avoiding him. [*Aside.*]

FLORINDA. Valeria! then I'm undone—[*Aside.*]

VALERIA. Oh! have I found you, Sir—[*To* PEDRO, *running to him.*]—The strangest Accident—if I had breath—to tell it.

PEDRO. Speak—is Florinda safe? Hellena well?

VALERIA. Ay, ay, Sir—Florinda—is safe—from any fears of you.

PEDRO. Why, where's Florinda?—speak.

VALERIA. Ay, where indeed, Sir? I wish I could inform you,—But to hold you no longer in doubt—

FLORINDA. Oh, what will she say! [*Aside.*]

VALERIA. She's fled away in the Habit of one of her Pages, Sir—but Callis thinks you may retrieve her yet, if you make haste away; she'll tell you, Sir, the rest—if you can find her out. [*Aside.*]

PEDRO. Dishonourable Girl, she has undone my Aim—Sir—you see my necessity of leaving you, and I hope you'll pardon it: my Sister, I know, will make her flight to you; and if she do, I shall expect she should be render'd back.

BELVILE. I shall consult my Love and Honour, Sir. [*Exit* PEDRO.]

FLORINDA. My dear Preserver, let me embrace thee. [*To* VALERIA.]

WILLMORE. What the Devil's all this?

BLUNT. Mystery by this Light.

VALERIA. Come, come, make haste and get your selves married quickly, for your Brother will return again.

BELVILE. I am so surpriz'd with Fears and Joys, so amaz'd to find you here in safety, I can scarce persuade my Heart into a Faith of what I see—

WILLMORE. Harkye, Colonel, is this that Mistress who has cost you so many Sighs, and me so many Quarrels with you?

BELVILE. It is—Pray give him the Honour of your Hand. [*To* FLORINDA.]

WILLMORE. Thus it must be receiv'd then. [*Kneels and kisses her Hand.*] And with it give your Pardon too.

FLORINDA. The Friend to Belvile may command me any thing.

WILLMORE. Death, wou'd I might, 'tis a surprizing Beauty. [*Aside.*]

BELVILE. Boy, run and fetch a Father instantly. [*Exit* BOY.]

FREDERICK. So, now do I stand like a Dog, and have not a Syllable to plead my own Cause with: by this Hand, Madam, I was never thorowly confounded before, nor shall I ever more dare look up with Confidence, till you are pleased to pardon me.

FLORINDA. Sir, I'll be reconcil'd to you on one Condition, that you'll follow the Example of your Friend, in marrying a Maid that does not hate you, and whose Fortune (I believe) will not be unwelcome to you.

FREDERICK. Madam, had I no inclinations that way, I shou'd obey your kind Commands.

BELVILE. Who, Frederick marry; he has so few Inclinations for Womankind, that had he been possest of Paradise, he might have continu'd there to this Day, if no Crime but Love cou'd have disinherited him.

FREDERICK. Oh, I do not use to boast of my Intrigues.

BELVILE. Boast! why thou do'st nothing but boast; and I dare swear, wer't thou as Innocent from the Sin of the Grape, as thou art from the Apple, thou might'st yet claim that right in *Eden* which our first Parents lost by too much loving.

FREDERICK. I wish this Lady would think me so modest a Man.

VALERIA. She shou'd be sorry then, and not like you half so well, and I shou'd be loth to break my Word with you; which was, That if your Friend and mine are agreed, it shou'd be a Match between you and I. [*She gives him her Hand.*]

FREDERICK. Bear witness, Colonel, 'tis a Bargain. [*Kisses her Hand.*]

BLUNT. I have a Pardon to beg too; but adsheartlikins I am so out of Countenance, that I am a Dog if I can say any thing to purpose. [*To* FLORINDA.]

FLORINDA. Sir, I heartily forgive you all.

BLUNT. That's nobly said, sweet Lady—Belvile, prithee present her her Ring again, for I find I have not Courage to approach her my self. [*Gives him the Ring, he gives it to* FLORINDA.]

Enter BOY.

BOY. Sir, I have brought the Father that you sent for.

BELVILE. 'Tis well, and now my dear Florinda, let's fly to compleat that mighty Joy we have so long wish'd and sigh'd for.—Come, Frederick, you'll follow?

FREDERICK. Your Example, Sir, 'twas ever my Ambition in War, and must be so in Love.

WILLMORE. And must not I see this juggling Knot tied?

BELVILE. No, thou shalt do us better Service, and be our Guard, lest Don Pedro's sudden Return interrupt the Ceremony.

WILLMORE. Content; I'll secure this Pass. [*Exit* BELVILE, FLORINDA, FREDERICK, *and* VALERIA.]

Enter BOY.

BOY. Sir, there's a Lady without wou'd speak to you. [*To* WILLMORE.]

WILLMORE. Conduct her in, I dare not quit my Post.

BOY. And, Sir, your Tailor waits you in your Chamber.

BLUNT. Some comfort yet, I shall not dance naked at the Wedding. [*Exit* BLUNT *and* BOY.]

> *Enter again the* BOY, *conducting in* ANGELLICA *in a masquing Habit and a Vizard,* WILLMORE *runs to her.*

WILLMORE. This can be none but my pretty Gipsy—Oh, I see you can follow as well as fly—Come, confess thy self the most malicious Devil in Nature, you think you have done my Bus'ness with Angellica—

ANGELLICA. Stand off, base Villain—[*She draws a Pistol and holds to his Breast.*]

WILLMORE. Hah, 'tis not she: who art thou? and what's thy Business?

ANGELLICA. One thou hast injur'd, and who comes to kill thee for't.

WILLMORE. What the Devil canst thou mean?

ANGELLICA. By all my Hopes to kill thee—[*Holds still the Pistol to his Breast, he going back, she following still.*]

WILLMORE. Prithee on what Acquaintance? for I know thee not.

ANGELLICA. Behold this Face!—so lost to thy Remembrance!

And then call all thy Sins about thy Soul,

And let them die with thee. [*Pulls off her Vizard.*]

WILLMORE. Angellica!

ANGELLICA. Yes, Traitor.

Does not thy guilty Blood run shivering thro thy Veins?

Hast thou no Horrour at this Sight, that tells thee,

Thou hast not long to boast thy shameful Conquest?

WILLMORE. Faith, no Child, my Blood keeps its old Ebbs and Flows still, and that usual Heat too, that cou'd oblige thee with a Kindness, had I but opportunity.

ANGELLICA. Devil! dost wanton with my Pain—have at thy Heart.

WILLMORE. Hold, dear Virago! hold thy Hand a little,

I am not now at leisure to be kill'd—hold and hear me—

Death, I think she's in earnest. [*Aside.*]

ANGELLICA. Oh if I take not heed,

My coward Heart will leave me to his Mercy. [*Aside, turning from him.*]

—What have you, Sir, to say?—but should I hear thee,

Thoud'st talk away all that is brave about me: [*Follows him with the Pistol to his Breast.*]

And I have vow'd thy Death, by all that's sacred.

WILLMORE. Why, then there's an end of a proper handsome Fellow, that might have liv'd to have done good Service yet:—That's all I can say to't.

ANGELLICA. Yet—I wou'd give thee—time for Penitence. [*Pausingly.*]

WILLMORE. Faith, Child, I thank God, I have ever took care to lead a good, sober, hopeful Life, and am of a Religion that teaches me to believe, I shall depart in Peace.

ANGELLICA. So will the Devil: tell me

How many poor believing Fools thou hast undone;

How many Hearts thou hast betray'd to ruin!

— Yet these are little Mischiefs to the Ills

Thou'st taught mine to commit: thou'st taught it Love.

WILLMORE. Egad, 'twas shrewdly hurt the while.

ANGELLICA. —Love, that has robb'd it of its Unconcern,

Of all that Pride that taught me how to value it,

And in its room a mean submissive Passion was convey'd,

That made me humbly bow, which I ne'er did

To any thing but Heaven.

—Thou, perjur'd Man, didst this, and with thy Oaths,

Which on thy Knees thou didst devoutly make,

Soften'd my yielding Heart—And then, I was a Slave—

Yet still had been content to've worn my Chains,

Worn 'em with Vanity and Joy for ever,

Hadst thou not broke those Vows that put them on.

—'Twas then I was undone. [*All this while follows him with a Pistol to his Breast.*]

WILLMORE. Broke my Vows! why, where hast thou lived?

Amongst the Gods! For I never heard of mortal Man,

That has not broke a thousand Vows.

ANGELLICA. Oh, Impudence!

WILLMORE. Angellica! that Beauty has been too long tempting,

Not to have made a thousand Lovers languish,

Who in the amorous Favour, no doubt have sworn

Like me; did they all die in that Faith? still adoring?

I do not think they did.

ANGELLICA. No, faithless Man: had I repaid their Vows, as I did thine, I wou'd have kill'd the ungrateful that had abandon'd me.

WILLMORE. This old General has quite spoil'd thee, nothing makes a Woman so vain, as being flatter'd; your old Lover ever supplies the Defects of Age, with intolerable Dotage, vast Charge, and that which you call Constancy; and attributing all this to your own Merits, you domineer, and throw your Favours in's Teeth, upbraiding him still with the Defects of Age, and cuckold him as often as he deceives your Expectations. But the gay, young, brisk Lover, that brings his equal Fires, and can give you Dart for Dart, he'll be as nice as you sometimes.

ANGELLICA. All this thou'st made me know, for which I hate thee.

Had I remain'd in innocent Security,

I shou'd have thought all Men were born my Slaves;

And worn my Pow'r like Lightning in my Eyes,

To have destroy'd at Pleasure when offended.

—But when Love held the Mirror, the undeceiving Glass

Reflected all the Weakness of my Soul, and made me know,

My richest Treasure being lost, my Honour,

All the remaining Spoil cou'd not be worth

The Conqueror's Care or Value.

—Oh how I fell like a long worship'd Idol,

Discovering all the Cheat!

Wou'd not the Incense and rich Sacrifice,

Which blind Devotion offer'd at my Altars,

Have fall'n to thee?

Why woud'st thou then destroy my fancy'd Power?

WILLMORE. By Heaven thou art brave, and I admire thee strangely.

I wish I were that dull, that constant thing,

Which thou woud'st have, and Nature never meant me:

I must, like chearful Birds, sing in all Groves,

And perch on every Bough,

Billing the next kind She that flies to meet me;

Yet after all cou'd build my Nest with thee,

Thither repairing when I'd lov'd my round,

And still reserve a tributary Flame.

—To gain your Credit, I'll pay you back your Charity,

And be oblig'd for nothing but for Love. [*Offers her a Purse of Gold.*]

ANGELLICA. Oh that thou wert in earnest!

So mean a Thought of me,

Wou'd turn my Rage to Scorn, and I shou'd pity thee,

And give thee leave to live;

Which for the publick Safety of our Sex,

And my own private Injuries, I dare not do.

Prepare—[*Follows, still, as before.*]

—I will no more be tempted with Replies.

WILLMORE. Sure—

ANGELLICA. Another Word will damn thee! I've heard thee talk too long. [*She follows him with a Pistol ready to shoot: he retires still amaz'd.*]

    Enter DON ANTONIO, *his Arm in a Scarf, and lays hold on the Pistol.*

ANTONIO. Hah! Angellica!

ANGELLICA. Antonio! What Devil brought thee hither?

ANTONIO. Love and Curiosity, seeing your Coach at Door. Let me disarm you of this unbecoming Instrument of Death.—[*Takes away the Pistol.*] Amongst the Number of your Slaves, was there not one worthy the Honour to have fought your Quarrel?

—Who are you, Sir, that are so very wretched

To merit Death from her?

WILLMORE. One, Sir, that cou'd have made a better End of an amorous Quarrel without you, than with you.

ANTONIO. Sure 'tis some Rival—hah—the very Man took down her Picture yesterday—the very same that set on me last night—Blest opportunity—[*Offers to shoot him.*]

ANGELLICA. Hold, you're mistaken, Sir.

ANTONIO. By Heaven the very same!

—Sir, what pretensions have you to this Lady?

WILLMORE. Sir, I don't use to be examin'd, and am ill at all Disputes but this— [*Draws,* ANTONIO *offers to shoot.*]

ANGELLICA. Oh, hold! you see he's arm'd with certain Death: [*To* WILLMORE.]

—And you, Antonio, I command you hold,

By all the Passion you've so lately vow'd me.

    Enter DON PEDRO, *sees* ANTONIO *and stays.*

PEDRO. Hah, Antonio! and Angellica! [*Aside.*]

ANTONIO. When I refuse Obedience to your Will,

May you destroy me with your mortal Hate.

By all that's Holy I adore you so,

That even my Rival, who has Charms enough

To make him fall a Victim to my Jealousy,

Shall live, nay, and have leave to love on still.

PEDRO. What's this I hear? [*Aside.*]

ANGELLICA. Ah thus, 'twas thus he talk'd, and I believ'd. [*Pointing to* WILLMORE.]

—Antonio, yesterday,

I'd not have sold my Interest in his Heart,

For all the Sword has won and lost in Battle.
—But now to show my utmost of Contempt,
I give thee Life—which if thou would'st preserve,
Live where my Eyes may never see thee more,
Live to undo some one, whose Soul may prove
So bravely constant to revenge my Love. [*Goes out,* ANTONIO *follows, but* PEDRO *pulls him back.*]

PEDRO. Antonio—stay.

ANTONIO. Don Pedro—

PEDRO. What Coward Fear was that prevented thee
From meeting me this Morning on the *Molo?*

ANTONIO. Meet thee?

PEDRO. Yes me; I was the Man that dar'd thee to't.

ANTONIO. Hast thou so often seen me fight in War,
To find no better Cause to excuse my Absence?
—I sent my Sword and one to do thee Right,
Finding my self uncapable to use a Sword.

PEDRO. But 'twas Florinda's Quarrel that we fought,
And you, to shew how little you esteem'd her,
Sent me your Rival, giving him your Interest.
—But I have found the Cause of this Affront,
But when I meet you fit for the Dispute,
—I'll tell you my Resentment.

ANTONIO. I shall be ready, Sir, e'er long to do you Reason. [*Exit* ANTONIO.]

PEDRO. If I cou'd find Florinda, now whilst my Anger's high, I think I shou'd be kind, and give her to Belvile in Revenge.

WILLMORE. Faith, Sir, I know not what you wou'd do, but I believe the Priest within has been so kind.

PEDRO. How! my Sister married?

WILLMORE. I hope by this time she is, and bedded too, or he has not my longings about him.

PEDRO. Dares he do thus? Does he not fear my Pow'r?

WILLMORE. Faith not at all. If you will go in, and thank him for the Favour he has done your Sister, so; if not, Sir, my Power's greater in this House than yours; I have a damn'd surly Crew here, that will keep you till the next Tide, and then clap you an board my Prize; my Ship lies but a League off the *Molo,* and we shall show your Donship a damn'd *Tramontana*[1] Rover's Trick.

---

1 A cold, dry north wind.

Enter BELVILE.

BELVILE. This Rogue's in some new Mischief—hah, Pedro return'd!

PEDRO. Colonel Belvile, I hear you have married my Sister.

BELVILE. You have heard truth then, Sir.

PEDRO. Have I so? then, Sir, I wish you Joy.

BELVILE. How!

PEDRO. By this Embrace I do, and I glad on't.

BELVILE. Are you in earnest?

PEDRO. By our long Friendship and my Obligations to thee, I am. The sudden Change I'll give you Reasons for anon. Come lead me into my Sister, that she may know I now approve her Choice. [*Exit* BELVILE *with* PEDRO.]

[WILLMORE *goes to follow them. Enter* HELLENA *as before in Boy's Clothes, and pulls him back.*

WILLMORE. Ha! my Gipsy—Now a thousand Blessings on thee for this Kindness. Egad, Child, I was e'en in despair of ever seeing thee again; my Friends are all provided for within, each Man his kind Woman.

HELLENA. Hah! I thought they had serv'd me some such Trick.

WILLMORE. And I was e'en resolv'd to go aboard, condemn my self to my lone Cabin, and the Thoughts of thee.

HELLENA. And cou'd you have left me behind? wou'd you have been so ill-natur'd?

WILLMORE. Why, 'twou'd have broke my Heart, Child—but since we are met again, I defy foul Weather to part us.

HELLENA. And wou'd you be a faithful Friend now, if a Maid shou'd trust you?

WILLMORE. For a Friend I cannot promise, thou art of a Form so excellent, a Face and Humour too good for cold dull Friendship; I am parlously afraid of being in love Child, and you have not forgot how severely you have us'd me.

HELLENA. That's all one, such Usage you must still look for, to find out all your Haunts, to rail at you to all that love you, till I have made you love only me in your own Defence, because no body else will love.

WILLMORE. But hast thou no better Quality to recommend thy self by?

HELLENA. Faith none, Captain—Why, 'twill be the greater Charity to take me for thy Mistress, I am a lone Child, a kind of Orphan Lover; and why I shou'd die a Maid, and in a Captain's Hands too, I do not understand.

WILLMORE. Egad, I was never claw'd away with Broad Sides from any Female before, thou hast one Virtue I adore, good-Nature; I hate a coy demure Mistress, she's as troublesome as a Colt, I'll break none; no, give me a mad Mistress when mew'd, and in flying on I dare trust upon the Wing, that whilst she's kind will come to the Lure.

HELLENA. Nay, as kind as you will, good Captain, whilst it lasts, but let's lose no time.

WILLMORE. My time's as precious to me, as thine can be; therefore dear Creature, since we are so well agreed, let's retire to my Chamber, and if ever thou wert treated with such savory Love—Come—My Bed's prepar'd for such a Guest, all clean and sweet as thy fair self; I love to steal a Dish and a Bottle with a Friend, and hate long Graces—Come, let's retire and fall to.

HELLENA. 'Tis but getting my Consent, and the Business is soon done; let but old Gaffer *Hymen* and his Priest say Amen to't, and I dare lay my Mother's Daughter by as proper a Fellow as your Father's Son, without fear or blushing.

WILLMORE. Hold, hold, no Bugg Words, Child, Priest and *Hymen*: prithee add Hangman to 'em to make up the Consort—No, no, we'll have no Vows but Love, Child, nor Witness but the Lover; the kind Diety enjoins naught but love and enjoy. *Hymen* and Priest wait still upon Portion, and Joynture; Love and Beauty have their own Ceremonies. Marriage is as certain a Bane to Love, as lending Money is to Friendship: I'll neither ask nor give a Vow, tho I could be content to turn Gipsy, and become a Left-hand Bridegroom, to have the Pleasure of working that great Miracle of making a Maid a Mother, if you durst venture; 'tis upse Gipsy that, and if I miss, I'll lose my Labour.

HELLENA. And if you do not lose, what shall I get? A Cradle full of Noise and Mischief, with a Pack of Repentance at my Back? Can you teach me to weave Incle[1] to pass my time with? 'Tis upse Gipsy that too.

WILLMORE. I can teach thee to weave a true Love's Knot better.

HELLENA. So can my Dog.

WILLMORE. Well, I see we are both upon our Guard, and I see there's no way to conquer good Nature, but by yielding—here—give me thy Hand—one Kiss and I am thine—

HELLENA. One Kiss! How like my Page he speaks; I am resolv'd you shall have none, for asking such a sneaking Sum—He that will be satisfied with one Kiss will never die of that Longing; good Friend single-Kiss, is all your talking come to this? A Kiss, a Caudle! farewell, Captain single-Kiss. [*Going out he stays her.*]

WILLMORE. Nay, if we part so, let me die like a Bird upon a Bough, at the Sheriff's Charge. By Heaven, both the *Indies* shall not buy thee from me. I adore thy Humour and will marry thee, and we are so of one Humour, it must be a Bargain—give me thy Hand— [*Kisses her Hand.*] And now let the blind ones (Love and Fortune) do their worst.

HELLENA. Why, God-a-mercy, Captain!

---

1 A woven linen tape or braid once used for trimming.

WILLMORE. But harkye—The Bargain is now made; but is it not fit we shou'd know each other's Names? That when we have Reason to curse one another hereafter, and People ask me who 'tis I give to the Devil, I may at least be able to tell what Family you came of.

HELLENA. Good reason, Captain; and where I have cause, (as I doubt not but I shall have plentiful) that I may know at whom to throw my—Blessings—I beseech ye your Name.

WILLMORE. I am call'd *Robert the Constant.*

HELLENA. A very fine Name! pray was it your Faulkner or Butler that christen'd you? Do they not use to whistle when then call you?

WILLMORE. I hope you have a better, that a Man may name without crossing himself, you are so merry with mine.

HELLENA. I am call'd *Hellena the Inconstant.*

Enter PEDRO, BELVILE, FLORINDA, FREDERICK, VALERIA.

PEDRO. Ha! Hellena!

FLORINDA. Hellena!

HELLENA. The very same—hah my Brother! now Captain, shew your Love and Courage; stand to your Arms, and defend me bravely, or I am lost for ever.

PEDRO. What's this I hear? false Girl, how came you hither, and what's your Business? Speak. [*Goes roughly to her.*]

WILLMORE. Hold off, Sir, you have leave to parly only. [*Puts himself between.*]

HELLENA. I had e'en as good tell it, as you guess it. Faith, Brother, my Business is the same with all living Creatures of my Age, to love, and be loved, and here's the Man.

PEDRO. Perfidious Maid, hast thou deceiv'd me too, deceiv'd thy self and Heaven?

HELLENA. 'Tis time enough to make my Peace with that: Be you but kind, let me alone with Heaven.

PEDRO. Belvile, I did not expect this false Play from you; was't not enough you'd gain Florinda (which I pardon'd) but your leud Friends too must be inrich'd with the Spoils of a noble Family?

BELVILE. Faith, Sir, I am as much surpriz'd at this as you can be: Yet, Sir, my Friends are Gentlemen, and ought to be esteem'd for their Misfortunes, since they have the Glory to suffer with the best of Men and Kings; 'tis true, he's a Rover of Fortune, yet a Prince aboard his little wooden World.

PEDRO. What's this to the maintenance of a Woman or her Birth and Quality?

WILLMORE. Faith, Sir, I can boast of nothing but a Sword which does me Right where-e'er I come, and has defended a worse Cause than a Woman's: and since I lov'd her before I either knew her Birth or Name, I must pursue my Resolution, and marry her.

PEDRO. And is all your holy Intent of becoming a Nun debauch'd into a Desire of Man?

HELLENA. Why—I have consider'd the matter, Brother, and find the Three hundred thousand Crowns my Uncle left me (and you cannot keep from me) will be better laid out in Love than in Religion, and turn to as good an Account—let most Voices carry it, for Heaven or the Captain?

ALL CRY. A Captain, a Captain.

HELLENA. Look ye, Sir, 'tis a clear Case.

PEDRO. Oh I am mad—if I refuse, my Life's in Danger—[*Aside.*]—Come—There's one motive induces me—take her—I shall now be free from the fear of her Honour; guard it you now, if you can, I have been a Slave to't long enough. [*Gives her to him.*]

WILLMORE. Faith, Sir, I am of a Nation that are of opinion a Woman's Honour is not worth guarding, when she has a mind to part with it.

HELLENA. Well said, Captain.

PEDRO. This was your Plot, Mistress, but I hope you have married one that will revenge my Quarrel to you—[*To* VALERIA.]

VALERIA. There's no altering Destiny, Sir.

PEDRO. Sooner than a Woman's Will, therefore I forgive you all—and wish you may get my Father's Pardon as easily; which I fear.

　　Enter BLUNT *drest in a* Spanish *Habit, looking very ridiculously; his Man adjusting his Band.*

MAN. 'Tis very well, Sir.

BLUNT. Well Sir, 'dsheartlikins I tell you 'tis damnable ill, Sir—a Spanish Habit, good Lord! Cou'd the Devil and my Tailor devise no other Punishment for me, but the Mode of a Nation I abominate?

BELVILE. What's the matter, Ned?

BLUNT. Pray view me round, and judge—[*Turns round.*]

BELVILE. I must confess thou art a kind of an odd Figure.

BLUNT. In a *Spanish* Habit with a Vengeance! I had rather be in the Inquisition for Judaism, than in this Doublet and Breeches; a Pillory were an easy Collar to this, three Handfuls high; and these Shoes too are worse than the Stocks, with the Sole an Inch shorter than my Foot: In fine, Gentlemen, methinks I look altogether like a Bag of Bays stuff'd full of Fools Flesh.

BELVILE. Methinks 'tis well, and makes thee look *en Cavalier:* Come, Sir, settle your Face, and salute our Friends, Lady—

BLUNT. Hah! Say'st thou so, my little Rover? [*To* HELLENA.] Lady—(if you be one) give me leave to kiss your Hand, and tell you, adsheartlikins, for all I look so, I am your humble Servant—A Pox of my *Spanish* Habit.

WILLMORE. Hark—what's this? [*Musick is heard to Play.*]

Enter BOY.

BOY. Sir, as the Custom is, the gay People in Masquerade, who make every Man's House their own, are coming up.

> *Enter several Men and Women in masquing Habits, with Musick, they put themselves in order and dance.*

BLUNT. Adsheartlikins, wou'd 'twere lawful to pull off their false Faces, that I might see if my Doxy were not amongst 'em.

BELVILE. Ladies and Gentlemen, since you are come so *a propos*, you must take a small Collation with us. [*To the Masquers.*]

WILLMORE. Whilst we'll to the Good Man within, who stays to give us a Cast of his Office. [*To* HELLENA.]

—Have you no trembling at the near approach?

HELLENA. No more than you have in an Engagement or a Tempest.

WILLMORE. Egad, thou'rt a brave Girl, and I admire thy Love and Courage.

Lead on, no other Dangers they can dread,

Who venture in the Storms o'th' Marriage-Bed. [*Exeunt.*]

EPILOGUE

The banisht Cavaliers! a Roving Blade!
A popish Carnival! a Masquerade!
The Devil's in't if this will please the Nation,
In these our blessed Times of Reformation,
When Conventicling is so much in Fashion.   5
And yet—
That mutinous Tribe less Factions do beget,
Than your continual differing in Wit;
Your Judgment's (as your Passions) a Disease:
Nor Muse nor Miss your Appetite can please;   10
You're grown as nice as queasy Consciences,
Whose each Convulsion, when the Spirit moves,
Damns every thing that Maggot disapproves.
    With canting Rule you wou'd the Stage refine,
And to dull Method all our Sense confine.   15

With th' Insolence of Common-wealths you rule,
Where each gay Fop, and politick brave Fool
On Monarch Wit impose without controul.
As for the last who seldom sees a Play,
Unless it be the old Black-Fryers way,   20
Shaking his empty Noddle o'er Bamboo,
He crys—Good Faith, these Plays will never do.
—Ah, Sir, in my young days, what lofty Wit,
What high-strain'd Scenes of Fighting there were writ:
These are slight airy Toys. But tell me, pray,   25
What has the House of Commons[1] done to day?
Then shews his Politicks, to let you see
Of State Affairs he'll judge as notably,
As he can do of Wit and Poetry.
The younger Sparks, who hither do resort,   30
Cry—
Pox o' your gentle things, give us more Sport;
—Damn me, I'm sure 'twill never please the Court.
    Such Fops are never pleas'd, unless the Play
Be stuff'd with Fools, as brisk and dull as they: 35
Such might the Half-Crown spare, and in a Glass
At home behold a more accomplisht Ass,
Where they may set their Cravats, Wigs and Faces,
And practice all their Buffoonry Grimaces;
See how this—Huff becomes—this Dammy—flare—   40
Which they at home may act, because they dare,
But—must with prudent Caution do elsewhere.
Oh that our Nokes, or Tony Lee[2] could show
A Fop but half so much to th' Life as you.

1677

---

1 The elected legislative body of the British Parliament.
2 James Nokes and Tony Lee were famous comedic actors.

WILLIAM WYCHERLEY
1641?–1716

William Wycherley's father, steward to the Marquess of Winchester, did not want his son to receive a Puritan education and sent the boy to France when he was fifteen. While there, the young Wycherley converted to Roman Catholicism. He returned to England in 1660 to attend the University of Oxford, but he left without a degree. In his brief time at college, however, he reverted to Protestantism. Wycherley entered the Inner Temple although he had no genuine interest in law. Finding his surroundings far more stimulating than his studies, he frequented the theatre, coffee houses, taverns, and St. James's Park where he observed people and events that he would later integrate into his plays.

Little is certain about Wycherley's life during the 1660s. His biographers believe that he fought in the navy during the Second Anglo-Dutch War, a conflict over trade and maritime rights. He also may have ventured to Spain in 1665. In 1671, however, his first play called *Love in a Wood; or, St. James's Park* was performed in London. With a complicated plot centered around idealized lovers and a bawdy subplot typical of Restoration comedy, *Love in a Wood* had its structural flaws. Even with its shortcomings, Wycherley's play clearly evidenced that the young, inexperienced playwright knew what his audience wanted to see. The play's success brought him into the company of court wits. His next play, a farce called *The Gentleman Dancing-Master*, overcorrected his previous failings. Focusing on only one plot and containing too few characters, the production was condemned as uninventive. Still, the first strands of Wycherley's satirical qualities emerged, becoming especially evident in his portraits of fops, rakes, would-be wits, and overly serious characters.

Three years after the unsuccessful production of *The Gentleman Dancing-Master*, Wycherley completed another play, this time amending his novice missteps. *The Country Wife* exposes the marriage system's impact on honor, virtue, and innocence in a comic satire about jealousy and self-satisfaction. Critics label Horner, the play's protagonist, as one of the most immoral characters in Restoration theatre. Most scholars agree that *The Country Wife* is Wycherley's strongest play, but many of Wycherley's contemporaries insisted that his finest piece was his final play. In *The Plain Dealer*, the misanthrope Captain Manly values plain dealing, but others in his life do not; his mistress marries his best friend, and Manly's shipmate, a young woman who is secretly in love with him, pretends to be a boy. Despite Manly's morals, he, like most of his fellow characters, acts in dishonest and deceitful ways. In spite of the inconsistencies of characterization, the play brutally and effectively satirizes greed. Wycherley's style is callous, powerful, and dark.

Wycherley fell ill two years after *The Plain Dealer*'s initial performance. King Charles II sent him to Montpellier to recover and offered him a pension upon his return, but Wycherley squandered the opportunity. He instead secretly married the Countess of Drogheda, a jealous woman whose rigid and controlling behavior caused him to lose favor in the court. The Countess died a year after their union, leaving Wycherley to inherit her fortune as well as her debts. But her will was contested, and Wycherley was thrown in a debtor's prison. Seven years passed before King James II, believing that Manly from *The Plain Dealer* was a representation of himself, freed Wycherley from prison and paid off most of the playwright's debts. James II granted him a small pension, but Wycherley lost his money after the king was deposed in 1688.

Wycherley's life was financially precarious. His father bestowed the family estate to a relative and provided Wycherley with such a small income that the playwright could scarcely sustain himself. In 1715, Wycherley married Elizabeth Jackson for the sole purpose of disinheriting his nephew, who would receive the family estate, but Wycherley died eleven days after his wedding. He had reverted to Roman Catholicism at his time of death. He left a limited canon behind; his literary reputation rests on four plays and a single volume of poetry that had been edited by the fledgling Alexander Pope. Wycherley's plays document his evolution from technical weaknesses to a precise mastery of drama. Fond of experimenting with theatrical elements, Wycherley unearthed a method that allowed him to reveal foolishness and failure in his productions.

1641?	William Wycherley likely born 28 May
1655–1660	Sent to France for his education
1660	Enters Queen's College, University of Oxford
1671	*Love in a Wood; or, St. James's Park*
1672	*The Gentleman Dancing-Master*
1675	*The Country-Wife*
1676	*The Plain Dealer*
1678	Falls ill and is sent to Montpellier at the expense of King Charles II
1680	Secretly marries Laetitia Isabella, the Countess of Drogheda
1681	Laetitia Isabella, The Countess of Drogheda dies
1685	Imprisoned in Fleet Prison, a debtor's prison
1704	*Miscellany Poems*
1715	Marries Elizabeth Jackson
1716	Dies 1 January and is buried in St. Paul's, Covent Garden

THE COUNTRY WIFE

A COMEDY

Indignor quidquam reprehendi, non quia crasse
Compositum illepideve putetur, sed quia nuper:
nec veniuam antiquis, sed honorem & proemia posci.[1]

HORACE

PROLOGUE

SPOKEN BY MR. HART[2]

Poets, like Cudgell'd Bullies, never do
At first or Second Blow submit to you;
But will provoke you still, and ne'er have done,
Till you are weary first with laying on:
The late so baffled Scribbler of this Day,   5
Tho he stands trembling, bids me boldly say,
What we before most Plays are us'd to do,
For Poets out of fear first draw on you;
In a fierce Prologue the still Pit defy,
And e're you speak, like Castril[3] *give the Lye;*   10
But tho our Bayes's *Battles oft I've fought,*
And with bruis'd Knuckels their dear Conquests bought;
Nay, never yet fear'd Odds upon the Stage,
In Prologue dare not hector with the Age;
But wou'd take Quarter from your saving Hands,   15
Tho Bays *within all yielding countermands,*
Says, you confed'rate Wits, no Quarter give,

---

1 It raises my indignation to see a work undervalued, not because gross and ungenteel, but because of modern date; and that we demand for the ancients, not barely indulgence, but honors and rewards [Horace].

2 Charles Hart (ca. 1628-83) was an esteemed Restoration actor. He is best known for his performances at Drury Lane Theatre, where he played in both tragedies and comedies. He played Horner in the Theatre-Royal performance of *The Country Wife*.

3 The "angry boy" in Ben Johnson's comedy *The Alchemist*.

Therefore his Play shan't ask your Leave to live.
Well, let the vain rash Fop by huffing so,
Think to obtain the better terms of you;   20
But we, the Actors, humbly will submit,
Now, and at any time, to a full Pit;
Nay, often we anticipate your Rage,
And murder Poets for you on our Stage:
We set no Guards upon our Tyring-Room,   25
But when with flying Colours there you come,
We patiently, you see, give up to you
Our Poets, Virgins, nay our Matrons too.

DRAMATIS PERSONÆ

MR. HORNER	MRS. MARGERY PINCHWIFE
MR. HARCOURT	MRS. ALITHEA
MR. DORILANT	MY LADY FIDGET
MR. PINCHWIFE	MRS. DAINTY FIDGET
MR. SPARKISH	MRS. SQUEAMISH
SIR JASPER FIDGET	OLD LADY SQUEAMISH

WAITERS, SERVANTS, *and* ATTENDANTS

A BOY

A QUACK

LUCY, ALITHEA's *Maid*

The SCENE—*London.*

ACT I.

SCENE I—HORNER's *Lodging.*

Enter HORNER, *and* QUACK *following him at a distance.*

HORNER. [*Aside.*] A quack is as fit for a pimp, as a midwife for a bawd; they are still but in their way, both helpers of nature.—[*Aloud.*] Well, my dear doctor, hast thou done what I desired?

QUACK. I have undone you for ever with the women, and reported you throughout the whole town as bad as an eunuch, with as much trouble as if I had made you one in earnest.

HORNER. But have you told all the midwives you know, the orange wenches at the playhouses, the city husbands, and old fumbling keepers of this end of the town? for they'll be the readiest to report it.

QUACK. I have told all the chambermaids, waiting-women, tire-women, and old women of my acquaintance; nay, and whispered it as a secret to 'em, and to the whisperers of Whitehall;[1] so that you need not doubt 'twill spread, and you will be as odious to the handsome young women, as—

HORNER. As the small-pox. Well—

QUACK. And to the married women of this end of the town, as—

HORNER. As the great ones; nay, as their own husbands.

QUACK. And to the city dames, as aniseed Robin,[2] of filthy and contemptible memory; and they will frighten their children with your name, especially their females.

HORNER. And cry, Horner's coming to carry you away. I am only afraid 'twill not be believed. You told 'em it was by an English-French disaster, and an English-French chirurgeon,[3] who has given me at once not only a cure, but an antidote for the future against that damned malady, and that worse distemper, love, and all other women's evils?

QUACK. Your late journey into France has made it the more credible, and your being here a fortnight before you appeared in public, looks as if you apprehended the shame, which I wonder you do not. Well, I have been hired by young gallants to belie 'em t'other way; but you are the first would be thought a man unfit for women.

---

1 A section of Westminster filled governmental offices.

2 According to the writings of Samuel Pepys, Robin (d. 1651) was an aniseed-water seller who was well-known as a hermaphrodite.

3 Surgeon or doctor.

HORNER. Dear Mr. doctor, let vain rogues be contented only to be thought abler men than they are, generally 'tis all the pleasure they have; but mine lies another way.

QUACK. You take, methinks, a very preposterous way to it, and as ridiculous as if we operators in physic should put forth bills to disparage our medicaments, with hopes to gain customers.

HORNER. Doctor, there are quacks in love as well as physic, who get but the fewer and worse patients for their boasting; a good name is seldom got by giving it one's self; and women, no more than honour, are compassed by bragging. Come, come, doctor, the wisest lawyer never discovers the merits of his cause till the trial; the wealthiest man conceals his riches, and the cunning gamester his play. Shy husbands and keepers, like old rooks, are not to be cheated but by a new unpractised trick: false friendship will pass now no more than false dice upon 'em; no, not in the city.

Enter BOY.

BOY. There are two ladies and a gentleman coming up. [*Exit.*]

HORNER. A pox! some unbelieving sisters of my former acquaintance, who, I am afraid, expect their sense should be satisfied of the falsity of the report. No—this formal fool and women!

Enter SIR JASPER FIDGET, LADY FIDGET, *and* MRS. DAINTY FIDGET.

QUACK. His wife and sister.

SIR JASPER. My coach breaking just now before your door, sir, I look upon as an occasional reprimand to me, sir, for not kissing your hands, sir, since your coming out of France, sir; and so my disaster, sir, has been my good fortune, sir; and this is my wife and sister, sir.

HORNER. What then, sir?

SIR JASPER. My lady, and sister, sir.—Wife, this is Master Horner.

LADY FIDGET. Master Horner, husband!

SIR JASPER. My lady, my lady Fidget, sir.

HORNER. So, sir.

SIR JASPER. Won't you be acquainted with her, sir?—[*Aside.*] So, the report is true, I find, by his coldness or aversion to the sex; but I'll play the wag with him.— [*Aloud.*] Pray salute my wife, my lady, sir.

HORNER. I will kiss no man's wife, sir, for him, sir; I have taken my eternal leave, sir, of the sex already, sir.

SIR JASPER. [*Aside.*] Ha! ha! ha! I'll plague him yet.—[*Aloud.*] Not know my wife, sir?

HORNER. I do know your wife, sir; she's a woman, sir, and consequently a monster, sir, a greater monster than a husband, sir.

SIR JASPER. A husband! how, sir?

HORNER. So, sir; but I make no more cuckolds, sir. [*Makes horns.*[1]]

SIR JASPER. Ha! ha! ha! Mercury! Mercury!

LADY FIDGET. Pray, sir Jasper, let us be gone from this rude fellow.

MRS. DAINTY. Who, by his breeding, would think he had ever been in France?

LADY FIDGET. Foh! he's but too much a French fellow, such as hate women of quality and virtue for their love to their husbands. Sir Jasper, a woman is hated by 'em as much for loving her husband as for loving their money. But pray let's be gone.

HORNER. You do well, madam; for I have nothing that you came for. I have brought over not so much as a bawdy picture, no new postures, nor the second part of the *Ecole des Filles*; nor—

QUACK. Hold, for shame, sir! what d'ye mean? you'll ruin yourself for ever with the sex—[*Apart to* HORNER.]

SIR JASPER. Ha! ha! ha! he hates women perfectly, I find.

MRS. DAINTY. What pity 'tis he should!

LADY FIDGET. Ay, he's a base fellow for't. But affectation makes not a woman more odious to them than virtue.

HORNER. Because your virtue is your greatest affectation, madam.

LADY FIDGET. How, you saucy fellow! would you wrong my honour?

HORNER. If I could.

LADY FIDGET. How d'ye mean, sir?

SIR JASPER. Ha! ha! ha! no, he can't wrong your ladyship's honour, upon my honour. He, poor man—hark you in your ear—a mere eunuch. [*Whispers.*]

LADY FIDGET. O filthy French beast! foh! foh! why do we stay? let's be gone: I can't endure the sight of him.

SIR JASPER. Stay but till the chairs come; they'll be here presently.

LADY FIDGET. No, no.

SIR JASPER. Nor can I stay longer. 'Tis, let me see, a quarter and half quarter of a minute past eleven. The council will be set; I must away. Business must be preferred always before love and ceremony with the wise, Mr. Horner.

HORNER. And the impotent, sir Jasper.

SIR JASPER. Ay, ay, the impotent, Master Horner; hah! hah! hah!

LADY FIDGET. What, leave us with a filthy man alone in his lodgings?

SIR JASPER. He's an innocent man now, you know. Pray stay, I'll hasten the chairs to you.—Mr. Horner, your servant; I should be glad to see you at my house.

---

1 Horns are the sign of a cuckold.

Pray come and dine with me, and play at cards with my wife after dinner; you are fit for women at that game yet, ha! ha!—[*Aside.*] 'Tis as much a husband's prudence to provide innocent diversion for a wife as to hinder her unlawful pleasures; and he had better employ her than let her employ herself.—[*Aloud.*] Farewell.

HORNER. Your servant, sir Jasper. [*Exit* SIR JASPER.]

LADY FIDGET. I will not stay with him, foh!—

HORNER. Nay, madam, I beseech you stay, if it be but to see I can be as civil to ladies yet as they would desire.

LADY FIDGET. No, no, foh! you cannot be civil to ladies.

MRS. DAINTY. You as civil as ladies would desire?

LADY FIDGET. No, no, no, foh! foh! foh! [*Exeunt* LADY FIDGET *and* MRS. DAINTY FIDGET.]

QUACK. Now, I think, I, or you yourself, rather, have done your business with the women.

HORNER. Thou art an ass. Don't you see already, upon the report and my carriage, this grave man of business leaves his wife in my lodgings, invites me to his house and wife, who before would not be acquainted with me out of jealousy?

QUACK. Nay, by this means you may be the more acquainted with the husbands, but the less with the wives.

HORNER. Let me alone; if I can but abuse the husbands, I'll soon disabuse the wives. Stay—I'll reckon you up the advantages I am like to have by my stratagem. First, I shall be rid of all my old acquaintances, the most insatiable sort of duns, that invade our lodgings in a morning; and next to the pleasure of making a new mistress is that of being rid of an old one, and of all old debts. Love, when it comes to be so, is paid the most unwillingly.

QUACK. Well, you may be so rid of your old acquaintances; but how will you get any new ones?

HORNER. Doctor, thou wilt never make a good chemist, thou art so incredulous and impatient. Ask but all the young fellows of the town if they do not lose more time, like huntsmen, in starting the game, than in running it down. One knows not where to find 'em; who will or will not. Women of quality are so civil, you can hardly distinguish love from good breeding, and a man is often mistaken: but now I can be sure she that shows an aversion to me loves the sport, as those women that are gone, whom I warrant to be right. And then the next thing is, your women of honour, as you call 'em, are only chary of their reputations, not their persons; and 'tis scandal they would avoid, not men. Now may I have, by the reputation of a eunuch, the privileges of one, and be seen in a lady's chamber in a morning as early as her husband; kiss virgins before their parents or lovers; and may be, in short, the *pars-par-tout* of the town. Now, doctor.

QUACK. Nay, now you shall be the doctor; and your process is so new that we do not know but it may succeed.

HORNER. Not so new neither; *probatum est*,[1] doctor.

QUACK. Well, I wish you luck, and many patients, whilst I go to mine. [*Exit.*]

Enter HARCOURT *and* DORILANT.

HARCOURT. Come, your appearance at the play yesterday, has, I hope, hardened you for the future against the women's contempt and the men's raillery; and now you'll abroad as you were wont.

HORNER. Did I not bear it bravely?

DORILANT. With a most theatrical impudence, nay, more than the orange-wenches show there, or a drunken vizard-mask, or a great-bellied actress; nay, or the most impudent of creatures, an ill poet; or what is yet more impudent, a second-hand critic.

HORNER. But what say the ladies? have they no pity?

HARCOURT. What ladies? The vizard-masks, you know, never pity a man when all's gone, though in their service.

DORILANT. And for the women in the boxes, you'd never pity them when 'twas in your power.

HARCOURT. They say 'tis pity but all that deal with common women should be served so.

DORILANT. Nay, I dare swear they won't admit you to play at cards with them, go to plays with 'em, or do the little duties which other shadows of men are wont to do for 'em.

HORNER. What do you call shadows of men?

DORILANT. Half-men.

HORNER. What, boys?

DORILANT. Ay, your old boys, old *beaux garçons*, who, like superannuated stallions, are suffered to run, feed, and whinny with the mares as long as they live, though they can do nothing else.

HORNER. Well, a pox on love and wenching! Women serve but to keep a man from better company. Though I can't enjoy them, I shall you the more. Good fellowship and friendship are lasting, rational, and manly pleasures.

HARCOURT. For all that, give me some of those pleasures you call effeminate too; they help to relish one another.

HORNER. They disturb one another.

---

1 It is proved.

HARCOURT. No, mistresses are like books. If you pore upon them too much, they doze you, and make you unfit for company; but if used discreetly, you are the fitter for conversation by 'em.

DORILANT. A mistress should be like a little country retreat near the town; not to dwell in constantly, but only for a night and away, to taste the town the better when a man returns.

HORNER. I tell you, 'tis as hard to be a good fellow, a good friend, and a lover of women, as 'tis to be a good fellow, a good friend, and a lover of money. You cannot follow both, then choose your side. Wine gives you liberty, love takes it away.

DORILANT. Gad, he's in the right on't.

HORNER. Wine gives you joy; love, grief and tortures, besides surgeons. Wine makes us witty; love, only sots. Wine makes us sleep; love breaks it.

DORILANT. By the world he has reason, Harcourt.

HORNER. Wine makes—

DORILANT. Ay, wine makes us—makes us princes; love makes us beggars, poor rogues, egad—and wine—

HORNER. So, there's one converted.—No, no, love and wine, oil and vinegar.

HARCOURT. I grant it; love will still be uppermost.

HORNER. Come, for my part, I will have only those glorious manly pleasures of being very drunk and very slovenly.

Enter BOY.

BOY. Mr. Sparkish is below, sir. [*Exit.*]

HARCOURT. What, my dear friend! a rogue that is fond of me only, I think, for abusing him.

DORILANT. No, he can no more think the men laugh at him than that women jilt him; his opinion of himself is so good.

HORNER. Well, there's another pleasure by drinking I thought not of,—I shall lose his acquaintance, because he cannot drink: and you know 'tis a very hard thing to be rid of him; for he's one of those nauseous offerers at wit, who, like the worst fiddlers, run themselves into all companies.

HARCOURT. One that, by being in the company of men of sense, would pass for one.

HORNER. And may so to the short-sighted world; as a false jewel amongst true ones is not discerned at a distance. His company is as troublesome to us as a cuckold's when you have a mind to his wife's.

HARCOURT. No, the rogue will not let us enjoy one another, but ravishes our conversation; though he signifies no more to't than Sir Martin Mar-all's[2] gaping, and awkward thrumming upon the lute, does to his man's voice and music.

---

2 A Restoration comedy by John Dryden.

DORILANT. And to pass for a wit in town shows himself a fool every night to us, that are guilty of the plot.

HORNER. Such wits as he are, to a company of reasonable men, like rooks to the gamesters; who only fill a room at the table, but are so far from contributing to the play, that they only serve to spoil the fancy of those that do.

DORILANT. Nay, they are used like rooks too, snubbed, checked, and abused; yet the rogues will hang on.

HORNER. A pox on 'em, and all that force nature, and would be still what she forbids 'em! Affectation is her greatest monster.

HARCOURT. Most men are the contraries to that they would seem. Your bully, you see, is a coward with a long sword; the little humbly-fawning physician, with his ebony cane, is he that destroys men.

DORILANT. The usurer, a poor rogue, possessed of mouldy bonds and mortgages; and we they call spendthrifts, are only wealthy, who lay out his money upon daily new purchases of pleasure.

HORNER. Ay, your arrantest cheat is your trustee or executor; your jealous man, the greatest cuckold; your churchman the greatest atheist; and your noisy pert rogue of a wit, the greatest fop, dullest ass, and worst company, as you shall see; for here he comes.

Enter SPARKISH.

SPARKISH. How is't, sparks? how is't? Well, faith, Harry, I must rally thee a little, ha! ha! ha! upon the report in town of thee, ha! ha! ha! I can't hold i'faith; shall I speak?

HORNER. Yes; but you'll be so bitter then.

SPARKISH. Honest Dick and Frank here shall answer for me; I will not be extreme bitter, by the universe.

HARCOURT. We will be bound in a ten thousand pound bond, he shall not be bitter at all.

DORILANT. Nor sharp, nor sweet.

HORNER. What, not downright insipid?

SPARKISH. Nay then, since you are so brisk, and provoke me, take what follows. You must know, I was discoursing and rallying with some ladies yesterday, and they happened to talk of the fine new signs in town—

HORNER. Very fine ladies, I believe.

SPARKISH. Said I, I know where the best new sign is.—Where? says one of the ladies.—In Covent-Garden, I replied.—Said another, In what street?—In Russel-street, answered I.—Lord, says another, I'm sure there was never a fine new sign there yesterday.—Yes, but there was, said I again; and it came out of France, and has been there a fortnight.

DORILANT. A pox! I can hear no more, prithee.

HORNER. No, hear him out; let him tune his crowd a while.

HARCOURT. The worst music, the greatest preparation.

SPARKISH. Nay, faith, I'll make you laugh.—It cannot be, says a third lady.—Yes, yes, quoth I again.—Says a fourth lady—

HORNER. Look to't, we'll have no more ladies.

SPARKISH. No—then mark, mark, now. Said I to the fourth, Did you never see Mr. Horner? he lodges in Russel-street, and he's a sign of a man, you know, since he came out of France; ha! ha! ha!

HORNER. But the devil take me if thine be the sign of a jest.

SPARKISH. With that they all fell a-laughing, till they bepissed themselves. What, but it does not move you, methinks? Well, I see one had as good go to law without a witness, as break a jest without a laugher on one's side.—Come, come, sparks, but where do we dine? I have left at Whitehall an earl, to dine with you.

DORILANT. Why, I thought thou hadst loved a man with a title, better than a suit with a French trimming to't.

HARCOURT. Go to him again.

SPARKISH. No, sir, a wit to me is the greatest title in the world.

HORNER. But go dine with your earl, sir; he may be exceptious. We are your friends, and will not take it ill to be left, I do assure you.

HARCOURT. Nay, faith, he shall go to him.

SPARKISH. Nay, pray, gentlemen.

DORILANT. We'll thrust you out, if you won't; what, disappoint anybody for us?

SPARKISH. Nay, dear gentlemen, hear me.

HORNER. No, no, sir, by no means; pray go, sir.

SPARKISH. Why, dear rogues—

DORILANT. No, no. [*They all thrust him out of the room.*]

ALL. Ha! ha! ha!

Re-enter SPARKISH.

SPARKISH. But, sparks, pray hear me. What, d'ye think I'll eat then with gay shallow fops and silent coxcombs? I think wit as necessary at dinner, as a glass of good wine; and that's the reason I never have any stomach when I eat alone.—Come, but where do we dine?

HORNER. Even where you will.

SPARKISH. At Chateline's?

DORILANT. Yes, if you will.

SPARKISH. Or at the Cock?[1]

DORILANT. Yes, if you please.

SPARKISH. Or at the Dog and Partridge?

HORNER. Ay, if you have a mind to't; for we shall dine at neither.

SPARKISH. Pshaw! with your fooling we shall lose the new play; and I would no more miss seeing a new play the first day, than I would miss sitting in the wits' row. Therefore I'll go fetch my mistress, and away. [*Exit.*]

Enter MR. PINCHWIFE.

HORNER. Who have we here? Pinchwife?

PINCHWIFE. Gentlemen, your humble servant.

HORNER. Well, Jack, by thy long absence from the town, the grumness of thy countenance, and the slovenliness of thy habit, I should give thee joy, should I not, of marriage?

PINCHWIFE. [*Aside.*] Death! does he know I'm married too? I thought to have concealed it from him at least.—[*Aloud.*] My long stay in the country will excuse my dress; and I have a suit of law that brings me up to town, that puts me out of humour. Besides, I must give Sparkish to-morrow five thousand pounds to lie with my sister.

HORNER. Nay, you country gentlemen, rather than not purchase, will buy anything; and he is a cracked title, if we may quibble. Well, but am I to give thee joy? I heard thou wert married.

PINCHWIFE. What then?

HORNER. Why, the next thing that is to be heard, is, thou'rt a cuckold.

PINCHWIFE. Insupportable name! [*Aside.*]

HORNER. But I did not expect marriage from such a whoremaster as you; one that knew the town so much, and women so well.

PINCHWIFE. Why, I have married no London wife.

HORNER. Pshaw! that's all one. That grave circumspection in marrying a country wife, is like refusing a deceitful pampered Smithfield jade, to go and be cheated by a friend in the country.

PINCHWIFE. [*Aside.*] A pox on him and his simile!—[*Aloud.*] At least we are a little surer of the breed there, know what her keeping has been, whether foiled or unsound.

HORNER. Come, come, I have known a clap gotten in Wales; and there are cousins, justices' clerks, and chaplains in the country, I won't say coachmen. But she's handsome and young?

---

1 Wycherley and his first wife, the Countess of Drogheda, lived near the infamous Cock Tavern. When Wycherley ventured there with his friends, he left the windows of his residence open to assure his jealous wife that there was no woman with him.

PINCHWIFE. [*Aside.*] I'll answer as I should do.—[*Aloud.*] No, no; she has no beauty but her youth, no attraction but her modesty: wholesome, homely, and huswifely; that's all.

DORILANT. He talks as like a grazier as he looks.

PINCHWIFE. She's too awkward, ill-favoured, and silly to bring to town.

HARCOURT. Then methinks you should bring her to be taught breeding.

PINCHWIFE. To be taught! no, sir, I thank you. Good wives and private soldiers should be ignorant—I'll keep her from your instructions, I warrant you.

HARCOURT. The rogue is as jealous as if his wife were not ignorant. [*Aside.*]

HORNER. Why, if she be ill-favoured, there will be less danger here for you than by leaving her in the country. We have such variety of dainties that we are seldom hungry.

DORILANT. But they have always coarse, constant, swinging stomachs in the country.

HARCOURT. Foul feeders indeed!

DORILANT. And your hospitality is great there.

HARCOURT. Open house; every man's welcome.

PINCHWIFE. So, so, gentlemen.

HORNER. But prithee, why shouldst thou marry her? If she be ugly, ill-bred, and silly, she must be rich then.

PINCHWIFE. As rich as if she brought me twenty thousand pound out of this town; for she'll be as sure not to spend her moderate portion, as a London baggage would be to spend hers, let it be what it would: so 'tis all one. Then, because she's ugly, she's the likelier to be my own; and being ill-bred, she'll hate conversation; and since silly and innocent, will not know the difference betwixt a man of one-and-twenty and one of forty.

HORNER. Nine—to my knowledge. But if she be silly, she'll expect as much from a man of forty-nine, as from him of one-and-twenty. But methinks wit is more necessary than beauty; and I think no young woman ugly that has it, and no handsome woman agreeable without it.

PINCHWIFE. 'Tis my maxim, he's a fool that marries; but he's a greater that does not marry a fool. What is wit in a wife good for, but to make a man a cuckold?

HORNER. Yes, to keep it from his knowledge.

PINCHWIFE. A fool cannot contrive to make her husband a cuckold.

HORNER. No; but she'll club with a man that can: and what is worse, if she cannot make her husband a cuckold, she'll make him jealous, and pass for one: and then 'tis all one.

PINCHWIFE. Well, well, I'll take care for one. My wife shall make me no cuckold, though she had your help, Mr. Horner. I understand the town, sir.

DORILANT. His help! [*Aside.*]

HARCOURT. He's come newly to town, it seems, and has not heard how things are with him. [*Aside.*]

HORNER. But tell me, has marriage cured thee of whoring, which it seldom does?

HARCOURT. 'Tis more than age can do.

HORNER. No, the word is, I'll marry and live honest: but a marriage vow is like a penitent gamester's oath, and entering into bonds and penalties to stint himself to such a particular small sum at play for the future, which makes him but the more eager; and not being able to hold out, loses his money again, and his forfeit to boot.

DORILANT. Ay, ay, a gamester will be a gamester whilst his money lasts, and a whoremaster whilst his vigour.

HARCOURT. Nay, I have known 'em, when they are broke, and can lose no more, keep a fumbling with the box in their hands to fool with only, and hinder other gamesters.

DORILANT. That had wherewithal to make lusty stakes.

PINCHWIFE. Well, gentlemen, you may laugh at me; but you shall never lie with my wife: I know the town.

HORNER. But prithee, was not the way you were in better? is not keeping better than marriage?

PINCHWIFE. A pox on't! the jades would jilt me, I could never keep a whore to myself.

HORNER. So, then you only married to keep a whore to yourself. Well, but let me tell you, women, as you say, are like soldiers, made constant and loyal by good pay, rather than by oaths and covenants. Therefore I'd advise my friends to keep rather than marry, since too I find, by your example, it does not serve one's turn; for I saw you yesterday in the eighteenpenny place with a pretty country-wench.

PINCHWIFE. How the devil! did he see my wife then? I sat there that she might not be seen. But she shall never go to a play again. [*Aside.*]

HORNER. What! dost thou blush, at nine-and-forty, for having been seen with a wench?

DORILANT. No, faith, I warrant 'twas his wife, which he seated there out of sight; for he's a cunning rogue, and understands the town.

HARCOURT. He blushes. Then 'twas his wife; for men are now more ashamed to be seen with them in public than with a wench.

PINCHWIFE. Hell and damnation! I'm undone, since Horner has seen her, and they know 'twas she. [*Aside.*]

HORNER. But prithee, was it thy wife? She was exceeding pretty: I was in love with her at that distance.

PINCHWIFE. You are like never to be nearer to her. Your servant, gentlemen. [*Offers to go.*]

HORNER. Nay, prithee stay.

PINCHWIFE. I cannot; I will not.

HORNER. Come, you shall dine with us.

PINCHWIFE. I have dined already.

HORNER. Come, I know thou hast not: I'll treat thee, dear rogue; thou sha't spend none of thy Hampshire money to-day.

PINCHWIFE. Treat me! So, he uses me already like his cuckold. [*Aside.*]

HORNER. Nay, you shall not go.

PINCHWIFE. I must; I have business at home. [*Exit.*]

HARCOURT. To beat his wife. He's as jealous of her, as a Cheapside husband of a Covent-garden wife.

HORNER. Why, 'tis as hard to find an old whoremaster without jealousy and the gout, as a young one without fear, or the pox:—

> As gout in age from pox in youth proceeds,
>
> So wenching past, then jealousy succeeds;
>
> The worst disease that love and wenching breeds. [*Exeunt.*]

[Handwritten note:] Three rhyming lines to end act; differs from couplets bc it's first act?

ACT II.

SCENE I.—*A Room in* PINCHWIFE'S *House.*

MRS. MARGERY PINCHWIFE *and* ALITHEA. MR. PINCHWIFE *peeping behind at the door.*

MRS. PINCHWIFE. Pray, sister, where are the best fields and woods to walk in, in London?

ALITHEA. [*Aside.*] A pretty question!—[*Aloud.*] Why, sister, Mulberry-garden and St. James's park; and, for close walks, the New Exchange.[1]

MRS. PINCHWIFE. Pray, sister, tell me why my husband looks so grum here in town, and keeps me up so close, and will not let me go a-walking, nor let me wear my best gown yesterday.

---

1 Located on The Strand, the New Exchange offered a popular venue to socialize and shop. It was torn down in 1737.

ALITHEA. O, he's jealous, sister.

MRS. PINCHWIFE. Jealous! what's that?

ALITHEA. He's afraid you should love another man.

MRS. PINCHWIFE. How should he be afraid of my loving another man, when he will not let me see any but himself?

ALITHEA. Did he not carry you yesterday to a play?

MRS. PINCHWIFE. Ay; but we sat amongst ugly people. He would not let me come near the gentry, who sat under us, so that I could not see 'em. He told me, none but naughty women sat there, whom they toused and moused. But I would have ventured, for all that.

ALITHEA. But how did you like the play?

MRS. PINCHWIFE. Indeed I was weary of the play; but I liked hugeously the actors. They are the goodliest, properest men, sister!

ALITHEA. O, but you must not like the actors, sister.

MRS. PINCHWIFE. Ay, how should I help it, sister? Pray, sister, when my husband comes in, will you ask leave for me to go a-walking?

ALITHEA. A-walking! ha! ha! Lord, a country-gentlewoman's pleasure is the drudgery of a footpost; and she requires as much airing as her husband's horses.—[*Aside.*] But here comes your husband: I'll ask, though I'm sure he'll not grant it.

MRS. PINCHWIFE. He says he won't let me go abroad for fear of catching the pox.

ALITHEA. Fy! the small-pox you should say.

Enter PINCHWIFE.

MRS. PINCHWIFE. O my dear, dear bud, welcome home! Why dost thou look so fropish? who has hangered thee?

PINCHWIFE. You're a fool. [MRS. PINCHWIFE *goes aside, and cries.*]

ALITHEA. Faith, so she is, for crying for no fault, poor tender creature!

PINCHWIFE. What, you would have her as impudent as yourself, as arrant a jilflirt, a gadder, a magpie; and to say all, a mere notorious town-woman?

ALITHEA. Brother, you are my only censurer; and the honour of your family will sooner suffer in your wife there than in me, though I take the innocent liberty of the town.

PINCHWIFE. Hark you, mistress, do not talk so before my wife.—The innocent liberty of the town!

ALITHEA. Why, pray, who boasts of any intrigue with me? what lampoon has made my name notorious? what ill women frequent my lodgings? I keep no company with any women of scandalous reputations.

PINCHWIFE. No, you keep the men of scandalous reputations company.

ALITHEA. Where? would you not have me civil? answer 'em in a box at the plays, in the drawing-room at Whitehall, in St James'-park, Mulberry-garden, or—

PINCHWIFE. Hold, hold! do not teach my wife where the men are to be found: I believe she's the worse for your town-documents already. I bid you keep her in ignorance, as I do.

MRS. PINCHWIFE. Indeed, be not angry with her, bud, she will tell me nothing of the town, though I ask her a thousand times a day.

PINCHWIFE. Then you are very inquisitive to know, I find?

MRS. PINCHWIFE. Not I indeed, dear; I hate London. Our place-house in the country is worth a thousand of't: would I were there again!

PINCHWIFE. So you shall, I warrant. But were you not talking of plays and players when I came in?—[*To* ALITHEA.] You are her encourager in such discourses.

MRS. PINCHWIFE. No, indeed, dear; she chid me just now for liking the playermen.

PINCHWIFE. [*Aside.*] Nay, if she be so innocent as to own to me her liking them, there is no hurt in't.—[*Aloud.*] Come, my poor rogue, but thou likest none better than me?

MRS. PINCHWIFE. Yes, indeed, but I do. The playermen are finer folks.

PINCHWIFE. But you love none better than me?

MRS. PINCHWIFE. You are my own dear bud, and I know you. I hate a stranger.

PINCHWIFE. Ay, my dear, you must love me only; and not be like the naughty town-women, who only hate their husbands, and love every man else; love plays, visits, fine coaches, fine clothes, fiddles, balls, treats, and so lead a wicked town-life.

MRS. PINCHWIFE. Nay, if to enjoy all these things be a town-life, London is not so bad a place, dear.

PINCHWIFE. How! if you love me, you must hate London.

ALITHEA. The fool has forbid me discovering to her the pleasures of the town, and he is now setting her agog upon them himself. [*Aside.*]

MRS. PINCHWIFE. But, husband, do the town-women love the playermen too?

PINCHWIFE. Yes, I warrant you.

MRS. PINCHWIFE. Ay, I warrant you.

PINCHWIFE. Why, you do not, I hope?

MRS. PINCHWIFE. No, no, bud. But why have we no playermen in the country?

PINCHWIFE. Ha!—Mrs. Minx, ask me no more to go to a play.

MRS. PINCHWIFE. Nay, why, love? I did not care for going: but when you forbid me, you make me, as 'twere, desire it.

ALITHEA. So 'twill be in other things, I warrant. [*Aside.*]

MRS. PINCHWIFE. Pray let me go to a play, dear.

PINCHWIFE. Hold your peace, I wo' not.

MRS. PINCHWIFE. Why, love?

PINCHWIFE. Why, I'll tell you.

ALITHEA. Nay, if he tell her, she'll give him more cause to forbid her that place. [*Aside.*]

MRS. PINCHWIFE. Pray why, dear?

PINCHWIFE. First, you like the actors; and the gallants may like you.

MRS. PINCHWIFE. What, a homely country girl! No, bud, nobody will like me.

PINCHWIFE. I tell you yes, they may.

MRS. PINCHWIFE. No, no, you jest—I won't believe you: I will go.

PINCHWIFE. I tell you then, that one of the lewdest fellows in town, who saw you there, told me he was in love with you.

MRS. PINCHWIFE. Indeed! who, who, pray who was't?

PINCHWIFE. I've gone too far, and slipped before I was aware; how overjoyed she is! [*Aside.*]

MRS. PINCHWIFE. Was it any Hampshire gallant, any of our neighbours? I promise you, I am beholden to him.

PINCHWIFE. I promise you, you lie; for he would but ruin you, as he has done hundreds. He has no other love for women but that; such as he look upon women, like basilisks, only to destroy 'em.

MRS. PINCHWIFE. Ay, but if he loves me, why should he ruin me? answer me to that. Methinks he should not, I would do him no harm.

ALITHEA. Ha! ha! ha!

PINCHWIFE. 'Tis very well; but I'll keep him from doing you any harm, or me either. But here comes company; get you in, get you in.

MRS. PINCHWIFE. But, pray, husband, is he a pretty gentleman that loves me?

PINCHWIFE. In, baggage, in. [*Thrusts her in, and shuts the door.*]

Enter SPARKISH *and* HARCOURT.

What, all the lewd libertines of the town brought to my lodging by this easy coxcomb! 'sdeath, I'll not suffer it.

SPARKISH. Here, Harcourt, do you approve my choice?—[*To* ALITHEA.] Dear little rogue, I told you I'd bring you acquainted with all my friends, the wits and— [HARCOURT *salutes her.*]

PINCHWIFE. Ay, they shall know her, as well as you yourself will, I warrant you.

SPARKISH. This is one of those, my pretty rogue, that are to dance at your wedding to-morrow; and him you must bid welcome ever, to what you and I have.

PINCHWIFE. Monstrous! [*Aside.*]

SPARKISH. Harcourt, how dost thou like her, faith? Nay, dear, do not look down; I should hate to have a wife of mine out of countenance at anything.

PINCHWIFE. Wonderful! [*Aside.*]

SPARKISH. Tell me, I say, Harcourt, how dost thou like her? Thou hast stared upon her enough, to resolve me.

HARCOURT. So infinitely well, that I could wish I had a mistress too, that might differ from her in nothing but her love and engagement to you.

ALITHEA. Sir, Master Sparkish has often told me that his acquaintance were all wits and raillieurs, and now I find it.

SPARKISH. No, by the universe, madam, he does not rally now; you may believe him. I do assure you, he is the honestest, worthiest, true-hearted gentlemen—a man of such perfect honour, he would say nothing to a lady he does not mean.

PINCHWIFE. Praising another man to his mistress! [*Aside.*]

HARCOURT. Sir, you are so beyond expectation obliging, that—

SPARKISH. Nay, egad, I am sure you do admire her extremely; I see't in your eyes.— He does admire you, madam.—By the world, don't you?

HARCOURT. Yes, above the world, or the most glorious part of it, her whole sex: and till now I never thought I should have envied you, or any man about to marry, but you have the best excuse for marriage I ever knew.

ALITHEA. Nay, now, sir, I'm satisfied you are of the society of the wits and raillieurs, since you cannot spare your friend, even when he is but too civil to you; but the surest sign is, since you are an enemy to marriage,—for that I hear you hate as much as business or bad wine.

HARCOURT. Truly, madam, I was never an enemy to marriage till now, because marriage was never an enemy to me before.

ALITHEA. But why, sir, is marriage an enemy to you now? because it robs you of your friend here? for you look upon a friend married, as one gone into a monastery, that is, dead to the world.

HARCOURT. 'Tis indeed, because you marry him; I see, madam, you can guess my meaning. I do confess heartily and openly, I wish it were in my power to break the match; by heavens I would.

SPARKISH. Poor Frank!

ALITHEA. Would you be so unkind to me?

HARCOURT. No, no, 'tis not because I would be unkind to you.

SPARKISH. Poor Frank! no gad, 'tis only his kindness to me.

PINCHWIFE. Great kindness to you indeed! Insensible fop, let a man make love to his wife to his face! [*Aside.*]

SPARKISH. Come, dear Frank, for all my wife there, that shall be, thou shalt enjoy me sometimes, dear rogue. By my honour, we men of wit condole for our deceased brother in marriage, as much as for one dead in earnest: I think that was prettily said of me, ha, Harcourt?—But come, Frank, be not melancholy for me.

HARCOURT. No, I assure you, I am not melancholy for you.

SPARKISH. Prithee, Frank, dost think my wife that shall be there, a fine person?

HARCOURT. I could gaze upon her till I became as blind as you are.

SPARKISH. How as I am? how?

HARCOURT. Because you are a lover, and true lovers are blind, stock blind.

SPARKISH. True, true; but by the world she has wit too, as well as beauty: go, go with her into a corner, and try if she has wit; talk to her anything, she's bashful before me.

HARCOURT. Indeed if a woman wants wit in a corner, she has it nowhere.

ALITHEA. Sir, you dispose of me a little before your time—[*Aside to* SPARKISH.]

SPARKISH. Nay, nay, madam, let me have an earnest of your obedience, or—go, go, madam—[HARCOURT *courts* ALITHEA *aside.*]

PINCHWIFE. How, sir! if you are not concerned for the honour of a wife, I am for that of a sister; he shall not debauch her. Be a pander to your own wife! bring men to her! let 'em make love before your face! thrust 'em into a corner together, then leave 'em in private! Is this your town wit and conduct?

SPARKISH. Ha! ha! ha! a silly wise rogue would make one laugh more than a stark fool, ha! ha! I shall burst. Nay, you shall not disturb 'em; I'll vex thee, by the world. [*Struggles with* PINCHWIFE *to keep him from* HARCOURT *and* ALITHEA.]

ALITHEA. The writings are drawn, sir, settlements made; 'tis too late, sir, and past all revocation.

HARCOURT. Then so is my death.

ALITHEA. I would not be unjust to him.

HARCOURT. Then why to me so?

ALITHEA. I have no obligation to you.

HARCOURT. My love.

ALITHEA. I had his before.

HARCOURT. You never had it; he wants, you see, jealousy, the only infallible sign of it.

ALITHEA. Love proceeds from esteem; he cannot distrust my virtue: besides, he loves me, or he would not marry me.

HARCOURT. Marrying you is no more sign of his love than bribing your woman, that he may marry you, is a sign of his generosity. Marriage is rather a sign of interest than love; and he that marries a fortune covets a mistress, not loves her. But if you take marriage for a sign of love, take it from me immediately.

ALITHEA. No, now you have put a scruple in my head; but in short, sir, to end our dispute, I must marry him, my reputation would suffer in the world else.

HARCOURT. No; if you do marry him, with your pardon, madam, your reputation suffers in the world, and you would be thought in necessity for a cloak.

ALITHEA. Nay, now you are rude, sir.—Mr. Sparkish, pray come hither, your friend here is very troublesome, and very loving.

HARCOURT. Hold! hold!—[*Aside to* ALITHEA.]

PINCHWIFE. D'ye hear that?

SPARKISH. Why, d'ye think I'll seem to be jealous, like a country bumpkin?

PINCHWIFE. No, rather be a cuckold, like a credulous cit.

HARCOURT. Madam, you would not have been so little generous as to have told him.

ALITHEA. Yes, since you could be so little generous as to wrong him.

HARCOURT. Wrong him! no man can do't, he's beneath an injury: a bubble, a coward, a senseless idiot, a wretch so contemptible to all the world but you, that—

ALITHEA. Hold, do not rail at him, for since he is like to be my husband, I am resolved to like him: nay, I think I am obliged to tell him you are not his friend.—Master Sparkish, Master Sparkish!

SPARKISH. What, what?—[*To* HARCOURT.] Now, dear rogue, has not she wit?

HARCOURT. Not so much as I thought, and hoped she had. [*Speaks surlily.*]

ALITHEA. Mr. Sparkish, do you bring people to rail at you?

HARCOURT. Madam—

SPARKISH. How! no; but if he does rail at me, 'tis but in jest, I warrant: what we wits do for one another, and never take any notice of it.

ALITHEA. He spoke so scurrilously of you, I had no patience to hear him; besides, he has been making love to me.

HARCOURT. True, damned tell-tale woman! [*Aside.*]

SPARKISH. Pshaw! to show his parts—we wits rail and make love often, but to show our parts: as we have no affections, so we have no malice, we—

ALITHEA. He said you were a wretch below an injury—

SPARKISH. Pshaw!

HARCOURT. Damned, senseless, impudent, virtuous jade! Well, since she won't let me have her, she'll do as good, she'll make me hate her. [*Aside.*]

ALITHEA. A common bubble—

SPARKISH. Pshaw!

ALITHEA. A coward—

SPARKISH. Pshaw, pshaw!

ALITHEA. A senseless, drivelling idiot—

SPARKISH. How! did he disparage my parts? Nay, then, my honour's concerned, I can't put up that, sir, by the world—brother, help me to kill him—[*Aside*] I may draw now, since we have the odds of him:—'tis a good occasion, too, before my mistress—[*Offers to draw.*]

ALITHEA. Hold, hold!

SPARKISH. What, what?

ALITHEA. [*Aside.*] I must not let 'em kill the gentleman neither, for his kindness to me: I am so far from hating him, that I wish my gallant had his person and understanding. Nay, if my honour—

SPARKISH. I'll be thy death.

ALITHEA. Hold, hold! Indeed, to tell the truth, the gentleman said after all, that what he spoke was but out of friendship to you.

SPARKISH. How! say, I am, I am a fool, that is, no wit, out of friendship to me?

ALITHEA. Yes, to try whether I was concerned enough for you; and made love to me only to be satisfied of my virtue, for your sake.

HARCOURT. Kind, however. [*Aside.*]

SPARKISH. Nay, if it were so, my dear rogue, I ask thee pardon; but why would not you tell me so, faith?

HARCOURT. Because I did not think on't, faith.

SPARKISH. Come, Horner does not come; Harcourt, let's be gone to the new play.—Come, madam.

ALITHEA. I will not go, if you intend to leave me alone in the box, and run into the pit, as you use to do.

SPARKISH. Pshaw! I'll leave Harcourt with you in the box to entertain you, and that's as good; if I sat in the box, I should be thought no judge but of trimmings.—Come away, Harcourt, lead her down. [*Exeunt* SPARKISH, HARCOURT, *and* ALITHEA.]

PINCHWIFE. Well, go thy ways, for the flower of the true town fops, such as spend their estates before they come to 'em, and are cuckolds before they're married. But let me go look to my own freehold.—How!

Enter LADY FIDGET, MRS. DAINTY FIDGET, *and* MRS. SQUEAMISH.

LADY FIDGET. Your servant, sir: where is your lady? We are come to wait upon her to the new play.

PINCHWIFE. New play!

LADY FIDGET. And my husband will wait upon you presently.

PINCHWIFE. [*Aside.*] Damn your civility.—[*Aloud.*] Madam, by no means; I will not see sir Jasper here, till I have waited upon him at home; nor shall my wife see you till she has waited upon your ladyship at your lodgings.

LADY FIDGET. Now we are here, sir?

PINCHWIFE. No, madam.

MRS. DAINTY. Pray, let us see her.

MRS. SQUEAMISH. We will not stir till we see her.

PINCHWIFE. [*Aside.*] A pox on you all!—[*Goes to the door, and returns.*] She has locked the door, and is gone abroad.

LADY FIDGET. No, you have locked the door, and she's within.

MRS. DAINTY. They told us below she was here.

PINCHWIFE. [*Aside.*] Will nothing do?—[*Aloud.*] Well, it must out then. To tell you the truth, ladies, which I was afraid to let you know before, lest it might endanger your lives, my wife has just now the small-pox come out upon her; do not be frightened; but pray be gone, ladies; you shall not stay here in danger of your lives; pray get you gone, ladies.

LADY FIDGET. No, no, we have all had 'em.

MRS. SQUEAMISH. Alack, alack!

MRS. DAINTY. Come, come, we must see how it goes with her; I understand the disease.

LADY FIDGET. Come!

PINCHWIFE. [*Aside.*] Well, there is no being too hard for women at their own weapon, lying, therefore I'll quit the field. [*Exit.*]

MRS. SQUEAMISH. Here's an example of jealousy!

LADY FIDGET. Indeed, as the world goes, I wonder there are no more jealous, since wives are so neglected.

MRS. DAINTY. Pshaw! as the world goes, to what end should they be jealous?

LADY FIDGET. Foh! 'tis a nasty world.

MRS. SQUEAMISH. That men of parts, great acquaintance, and quality, should take up with and spend themselves and fortunes in keeping little playhouse creatures, foh!

LADY FIDGET. Nay, that women of understanding, great acquaintance, and good quality, should fall a-keeping too of little creatures, foh!

MRS. SQUEAMISH. Why, 'tis the men of quality's fault; they never visit women of honour and reputation as they used to do; and have not so much as common civility for ladies of our rank, but use us with the same indifferency and ill-breeding as if we were all married to 'em.

LADY FIDGET. She says true; 'tis an arrant shame women of quality should be so slighted; methinks birth—birth should go for something; I have known men admired, courted, and followed for their titles only.

MRS. SQUEAMISH. Ay, one would think men of honour should not love, no more than marry, out of their own rank.

MRS. DAINTY. Fy, fy, upon 'em! they are come to think cross breeding for themselves best, as well as for their dogs and horses.

LADY FIDGET. They are dogs and horses for't.

MRS. SQUEAMISH. One would think, if not for love, for vanity a little.

MRS. DAINTY. Nay, they do satisfy their vanity upon us sometimes; and are kind to us in their report, tell all the world they lie with us.

LADY FIDGET. Damned rascals, that we should be only wronged by 'em! To report a man has had a person, when he has not had a person, is the greatest wrong in the whole world that can be done to a person.

MRS. SQUEAMISH. Well, 'tis an arrant shame noble persons should be so wronged and neglected.

LADY FIDGET. But still 'tis an arranter shame for a noble person to neglect her own honour, and defame her own noble person with little inconsiderable fellows, foh!

MRS. DAINTY. I suppose the crime against our honour is the same with a man of quality as with another.

LADY FIDGET. How! no sure, the man of quality is likest one's husband, and therefore the fault should be the less.

MRS. DAINTY. But then the pleasure should be the less.

LADY FIDGET. Fy, fy, fy, for shame, sister! whither shall we ramble? Be continent in your discourse, or I shall hate you.

MRS. DAINTY. Besides, an intrigue is so much the more notorious for the man's quality.

MRS. SQUEAMISH. 'Tis true nobody takes notice of a private man, and therefore with him 'tis more secret; and the crime's the less when 'tis not known.

LADY FIDGET. You say true; i'faith, I think you are in the right on't: 'tis not an injury to a husband, till it be an injury to our honours; so that a woman of honour loses no honour with a private person; and to say truth—

MRS. DAINTY. So, the little fellow is grown a private person—with her—[Apart to MRS. SQUEAMISH.]

LADY FIDGET. But still my dear, dear honour—

Enter SIR JASPER FIDGET, HORNER, and DORILANT.

SIR JASPER. Ay, my dear, dear of honour, thou hast still so much honour in thy mouth—

HORNER. That she has none elsewhere, [Aside.]

LADY FIDGET. Oh, what d'ye mean to bring in these upon us?

MRS. DAINTY. Foh! these are as bad as wits.

MRS. SQUEAMISH. Foh!

LADY FIDGET. Let us leave the room.

SIR JASPER. Stay, stay; faith, to tell you the naked truth—

LADY FIDGET. Fy, Sir Jasper! do not use that word naked.

SIR JASPER. Well, well, in short I have business at Whitehall, and cannot go to the play with you, therefore would have you go—

LADY FIDGET. With those two to a play?

SIR JASPER. No, not with t'other, but with Mr. Horner; there can be no more scandal to go with him than with Mr. Tattle, or Master Limberham.[1]

LADY FIDGET. With that nasty fellow! no—no.

SIR JASPER. Nay, prithee, dear, hear me. [*Whispers to* LADY FIDGET.]

HORNER. Ladies—[HORNER *and* DORILANT *draw near* MRS. SQUEAMISH *and* MRS. DAINTY FIDGET.]

MRS. DAINTY. Stand off.

MRS. SQUEAMISH. Do not approach us.

MRS. DAINTY. You herd with the wits, you are obscenity all over.

MRS. SQUEAMISH. And I would as soon look upon a picture of Adam and Eve, without fig-leaves, as any of you, if I could help it; therefore keep off, and do not make us sick.

DORILANT. What a devil are these?

HORNER. Why, these are pretenders to honour, as critics to wit, only by censuring others; and as every raw, peevish, out-of-humoured, affected, dull, tea-drinking, arithmetical fop, sets up for a wit by railing at men of sense, so these for honour, by railing at the court, and ladies of as great honour as quality.

SIR JASPER. Come, Mr. Horner, I must desire you to go with these ladies to the play, sir.

HORNER. I, sir?

SIR JASPER. Ay, ay, come, sir.

HORNER. I must beg your pardon, sir, and theirs; I will not be seen in women's company in public again for the world.

SIR JASPER. Ha, ha, strange aversion!

MRS. SQUEAMISH. No, he's for women's company in private.

SIR JASPER. He—poor man—he—ha! ha! ha!

MRS. DAINTY. 'Tis a greater shame amongst lewd fellows to be seen in virtuous women's company, than for the women to be seen with them.

HORNER. Indeed, madam, the time was I only hated virtuous women, but now I hate the other too; I beg your pardon, ladies.

LADY FIDGET. You are very obliging, sir, because we would not be troubled with you.

SIR JASPER. In sober sadness, he shall go.

DORILANT. Nay, if he wo' not, I am ready to wait upon the ladies, and I think I am the fitter man.

SIR JASPER. You sir! no, I thank you for that. Master Horner is a privileged man amongst the virtuous ladies, 'twill be a great while before you are so; he! he!

---

1 Generalized names for men who would be unthreatening companions to city wives. Mr. Limberham is also a character in Dryden's *The Kind Keeper, or Mr. Limberham* (1678).

he! he's my wife's gallant; he! he! he! No, pray withdraw, sir, for as I take it, the virtuous ladies have no business with you.

DORILANT. And I am sure he can have none with them. 'Tis strange a man can't come amongst virtuous women now, but upon the same terms as men are admitted into the Great Turk's seraglio. But heavens keep me from being an ombre player with 'em!—But where is Pinchwife? [*Exit.*]

SIR JASPER. Come, come, man; what, avoid the sweet society of womankind? that sweet, soft, gentle, tame, noble creature, woman, made for man's companion—

HORNER. So is that soft, gentle, tame, and more noble creature a spaniel, and has all their tricks; can fawn, lie down, suffer beating, and fawn the more; barks at your friends when they come to see you, makes your bed hard, gives you fleas, and the mange sometimes. And all the difference is, the spaniel's the more faithful animal, and fawns but upon one master.

SIR JASPER. He! he! he!

MRS. SQUEAMISH. O the rude beast!

MRS. DAINTY. Insolent brute!

LADY FIDGET. Brute! stinking, mortified, rotten French wether, to dare—

SIR JASPER. Hold, an't please your ladyship.—For shame, master Horner! your mother was a woman—[*Aside.*] Now shall I never reconcile 'em.—[*Aside to* LADY FIDGET.] Hark you, madam, take my advice in your anger. You know you often want one to make up your drolling pack of ombre players, and you may cheat him easily; for he's an ill gamester, and consequently loves play. Besides, you know you have but two old civil gentlemen (with stinking breaths too) to wait upon you abroad; take in the third into your service. The other are but crazy; and a lady should have a supernumerary gentleman-usher as a supernumerary coach-horse, lest sometimes you should be forced to stay at home.

LADY FIDGET. But are you sure he loves play, and has money?

SIR JASPER. He loves play as much as you, and has money as much as I.

LADY FIDGET. Then I am contented to make him pay for his scurrility. Money makes up in a measure all other wants in men.—Those whom we cannot make hold for gallants, we make fine. [*Aside.*]

SIR JASPER. [*Aside.*] So, so; now to mollify, wheedle him.—[*Aside to* HORNER.] Master Horner, will you never keep civil company? methinks 'tis time now, since you are only fit for them. Come, come, man, you must e'en fall to visiting our wives, eating at our tables, drinking tea with our virtuous relations after dinner, dealing cards to 'em, reading plays and gazettes to 'em, picking fleas out of their smocks for 'em, collecting receipts, new songs, women, pages, and footmen for 'em.

HORNER. I hope they'll afford me better employment, sir.

SIR JASPER. He! he! he! 'tis fit you know your work before you come into your place. And since you are unprovided of a lady to flatter, and a good house to eat at, pray frequent mine, and call my wife mistress, and she shall call you gallant, according to the custom.

HORNER. Who, I?

SIR JASPER. Faith, thou sha't for my sake; come, for my sake only.

HORNER. For your sake—

SIR JASPER. Come, come, here's a gamester for you; let him be a little familiar sometimes; nay, what if a little rude? Gamesters may be rude with ladies, you know.

LADY FIDGET. Yes; losing gamesters have a privilege with women.

HORNER. I always thought the contrary, that the winning gamester had most privilege with women; for when you have lost your money to a man, you'll lose anything you have, all you have, they say, and he may use you as he pleases.

SIR JASPER. He! he! he! well, win or lose, you shall have your liberty with her.

LADY FIDGET. As he behaves himself; and for your sake I'll give him admittance and freedom.

HORNER. All sorts of freedom, madam?

SIR JASPER. Ay, ay, ay, all sorts of freedom thou canst take. And so go to her, begin thy new employment; wheedle her, jest with her, and be better acquainted one with another.

HORNER. [Aside.] I think I know her already; therefore may venture with her my secret for hers. [HORNER and LADY FIDGET whisper.]

SIR JASPER. Sister cuz, I have provided an innocent playfellow for you there.

MRS. DAINTY. Who, he?

MRS. SQUEAMISH. There's a playfellow, indeed!

SIR JASPER. Yes sure.—What, he is good enough to play at cards, blindman's-buff, or the fool with, sometimes!

MRS. SQUEAMISH. Foh! we'll have no such playfellows.

MRS. DAINTY. No, sir; you shan't choose playfellows for us, we thank you.

SIR JASPER. Nay, pray hear me. [Whispering to them.]

LADY FIDGET. But, poor gentleman, could you be so generous, so truly a man of honour, as for the sakes of us women of honour, to cause yourself to be reported no man? No man! and to suffer yourself the greatest shame that could fall upon a man, that none might fall upon us women by your conversation? but, indeed, sir, as perfectly, perfectly the same man as before your going into France, sir? as perfectly, perfectly, sir?

HORNER. As perfectly, perfectly, madam. Nay, I scorn you should take my word; I desire to be tried only, madam.

LADY FIDGET. Well, that's spoken again like a man of honour: all men of honour desire to come to the test. But, indeed, generally you men report such things of yourselves, one does not know how or whom to believe; and it is come to that pass, we dare not take your words no more than your tailor's, without some staid servant of yours be bound with you. But I have so strong a faith in your honour, dear, dear, noble sir, that I'd forfeit mine for yours, at any time, dear sir.

HORNER. No, madam, you should not need to forfeit it for me; I have given you security already to save you harmless, my late reputation being so well known in the world, madam.

LADY FIDGET. But if upon any future falling-out, or upon a suspicion of my taking the trust out of your hands, to employ some other, you yourself should betray your trust, dear sir? I mean, if you'll give me leave to speak obscenely, you might tell, dear sir.

HORNER. If I did, nobody would believe me. The reputation of impotency is as hardly recovered again in the world as that of cowardice, dear madam.

LADY FIDGET. Nay, then, as one may say, you may do your worst, dear, dear sir.

SIR JASPER. Come, is your ladyship reconciled to him yet? have you agreed on matters? for I must be gone to Whitehall.

LADY FIDGET. Why, indeed, sir Jasper, master Horner is a thousand, thousand times a better man than I thought him. Cousin Squeamish, sister Dainty, I can name him now. Truly, not long ago, you know, I thought his very name obscenity; and I would as soon have lain with him as have named him.

SIR JASPER. Very likely, poor madam.

MRS. DAINTY. I believe it.

MRS. SQUEAMISH. No doubt on't.

SIR JASPER. Well, well—that your ladyship is as virtuous as any she, I know, and him all the town knows—he! he! he! therefore now you like him, get you gone to your business together, go, go to your business, I say, pleasure, whilst I go to my pleasure, business.

LADY FIDGET. Come, then, dear gallant.

HORNER. Come away, my dearest mistress.

SIR JASPER. So, so; why, 'tis as I'd have it. [*Exit.*]

HORNER. And as I'd have it.

LADY FIDGET. Who for his business from his wife will run,

    Takes the best care to have her business done. [*Exeunt.*]

ACT III.

SCENE I.—*A Room in* PINCHWIFE'S *House.*

Enter ALITHEA *and* MRS. PINCHWIFE.

ALITHEA. Sister, what ails you? you are grown melancholy.

MRS. PINCHWIFE. Would it not make any one melancholy to see you go every day fluttering about abroad, whilst I must stay at home like a poor, lonely, sullen bird in a cage?

ALITHEA. Ay, sister; but you came young, and just from the nest to your cage: so that I thought you liked it, and could be as cheerful in't as others that took their flight themselves early, and are hopping abroad in the open air.

MRS. PINCHWIFE. Nay, I confess I was quiet enough till my husband told me what pure lives the London ladies live abroad, with their dancing, meetings, and junketings, and dressed every day in their best gowns; and I warrant you, play at nine-pins every day of the week, so they do.

Enter PINCHWIFE.

PINCHWIFE. Come, what's here to do? you are putting the town-pleasures in her head, and setting her a-longing.

ALITHEA. Yes, after nine-pins. You suffer none to give her those longings you mean but yourself.

PINCHWIFE. I tell her of the vanities of the town like a confessor.

ALITHEA. A confessor! just such a confessor as he that, by forbidding a silly hostler to grease the horse's teeth, taught him to do't.

PINCHWIFE. Come, Mrs. Flippant, good precepts are lost when bad examples are still before us: the liberty you take abroad makes her hanker after it, and out of humour at home. Poor wretch! she desired not to come to London; I would bring her.

ALITHEA. Very well.

PINCHWIFE. She has been this week in town, and never desired till this afternoon to go abroad.

ALITHEA. Was she not at a play yesterday?

PINCHWIFE. Yes; but she ne'er asked me; I was myself the cause of her going.

ALITHEA. Then if she ask you again, you are the cause of her asking, and not my example.

PINCHWIFE. Well, to-morrow night I shall be rid of you; and the next day, before 'tis light, she and I'll be rid of the town, and my dreadful apprehensions.—Come, be not melancholy; for thou sha't go into the country after to-morrow, dearest.

ALITHEA. Great comfort!

MRS. PINCHWIFE. Pish! what d'ye tell me of the country for?

PINCHWIFE. How's this! what, pish at the country?

MRS. PINCHWIFE. Let me alone; I am not well.

PINCHWIFE. O, if that be all—what ails my dearest?

MRS. PINCHWIFE. Truly, I don't know: but I have not been well since you told me there was a gallant at the play in love with me.

PINCHWIFE. Ha!—

ALITHEA. That's by my example too!

PINCHWIFE. Nay, if you are not well, but are so concerned, because a lewd fellow chanced to lie, and say he liked you, you'll make me sick too.

MRS. PINCHWIFE. Of what sickness?

PINCHWIFE. O, of that which is worse than the plague, jealousy.

MRS. PINCHWIFE. Pish, you jeer! I'm sure there's no such disease in our receipt-book at home.

PINCHWIFE. No, thou never met'st with it, poor innocent.—Well, if thou cuckold me, 'twill be my own fault—for cuckolds and bastards are generally makers of their own fortune. [*Aside.*]

MRS. PINCHWIFE. Well, but pray, bud, let's go to a play to-night.

PINCHWIFE. 'Tis just done, she comes from it. But why are you so eager to see a play?

MRS. PINCHWIFE. Faith, dear, not that I care one pin for their talk there; but I like to look upon the player-men, and would see, if I could, the gallant you say loves me: that's all, dear bud.

PINCHWIFE. Is that all, dear bud?

ALITHEA. This proceeds from my example!

MRS. PINCHWIFE. But if the play be done, let's go abroad, however, dear bud.

PINCHWIFE. Come, have a little patience, and thou shalt go into the country on Friday.

MRS. PINCHWIFE. Therefore I would see first some sights to tell my neighbours of. Nay, I will go abroad, that's once.

ALITHEA. I'm the cause of this desire too!

PINCHWIFE. But now I think on't, who, who was the cause of Horner's coming to my lodgings to-day? That was you.

ALITHEA. No, you, because you would not let him see your handsome wife out of your lodging.

MRS. PINCHWIFE. Why, O Lord! did the gentleman come hither to see me indeed?

PINCHWIFE. No, no.—You are not the cause of that damned question too, mistress Alithea?—[*Aside.*] Well, she's in the right of it. He is in love with my wife—

and comes after her—'tis so—but I'll nip his love in the bud; lest he should follow us into the country, and break his chariot-wheel near our house, on purpose for an excuse to come to't. But I think I know the town.

MRS. PINCHWIFE. Come, pray, bud, let's go abroad before 'tis late; for I will go, that's flat and plain.

PINCHWIFE. [*Aside.*] So! the obstinacy already of the town-wife; and I must, whilst she's here, humour her like one.—[*Aloud.*] Sister, how shall we do, that she may not be seen, or known?

ALITHEA. Let her put on her mask.

PINCHWIFE. Pshaw! a mask makes people but the more inquisitive, and is as ridiculous a disguise as a stage-beard: her shape, stature, habit, will be known. And if we should meet with Horner, he would be sure to take acquaintance with us, must wish her joy, kiss her, talk to her, leer upon her, and the devil and all. No, I'll not use her to a mask, 'tis dangerous; for masks have made more cuckolds than the best faces that ever were known.

ALITHEA. How will you do then?

MRS. PINCHWIFE. Nay, shall we go? The Exchange will be shut, and I have a mind to see that.

PINCHWIFE. So—I have it—I'll dress her up in the suit we are to carry down to her brother, little Sir James; nay, I understand the town-tricks. Come, let's go dress her. A mask! no—a woman masked, like a covered dish, gives a man curiosity and appetite; when, it may be, uncovered, 'twould turn his stomach: no, no.

ALITHEA. Indeed your comparison is something a greasy one: but I had a gentle gallant used to say, A beauty masked, like the sun in eclipse, gathers together more gazers than if it shined out. [*Exeunt.*]

SCENE II.—*The New Exchange.*

Enter HORNER, HARCOURT, *and* DORILANT.

DORILANT. Engaged to women, and not sup with us!

HORNER. Ay, a pox on 'em all!

HARCOURT. You were much a more reasonable man in the morning, and had as noble resolutions against 'em, as a widower of a week's liberty.

DORILANT. Did I ever think to see you keep company with women in vain?

HORNER. In vain: no—'tis since I can't love 'em, to be revenged on 'em.

HARCOURT. Now your sting is gone, you looked in the box amongst all those women like a drone in the hive; all upon you, shoved and ill-used by 'em all, and thrust from one side to t'other.

DORILANT. Yet he must be buzzing amongst 'em still, like other beetle-headed liquorish drones. Avoid 'em, and hate 'em, as they hate you.

HORNER. Because I do hate 'em, and would hate 'em yet more, I'll frequent 'em. You may see by marriage, nothing makes a man hate a woman more than her constant conversation. In short, I converse with 'em, as you do with rich fools, to laugh at 'em and use 'em ill.

DORILANT. But I would no more sup with women, unless I could lie with 'em, than sup with a rich coxcomb, unless I could cheat him.

HORNER. Yes, I have known thee sup with a fool for his drinking; if he could set out your hand that way only, you were satisfied, and if he were a wine-swallowing mouth, 'twas enough.

HARCOURT. Yes, a man drinks often with a fool, as he tosses with a marker, only to keep his hand in use. But do the ladies drink?

HORNER. Yes, sir; and I shall have the pleasure at least of laying 'em flat with a bottle, and bring as much scandal that way upon 'em as formerly t'other.

HARCOURT. Perhaps you may prove as weak a brother among 'em that way as t'other.

DORILANT. Foh! drinking with women is as unnatural as scolding with 'em. But 'tis a pleasure of decayed fornicators, and the basest way of quenching love.

HARCOURT. Nay, 'tis drowning love, instead of quenching it. But leave us for civil women too!

DORILANT. Ay, when he can't be the better for 'em. We hardly pardon a man that leaves his friend for a wench, and that's a pretty lawful call.

HORNER. Faith, I would not leave you for 'em, if they would not drink.

DORILANT. Who would disappoint his company at Lewis's for a gossiping?

HARCOURT. Foh! Wine and women, good apart, together are as nauseous as sack and sugar. But hark you, sir, before you go, a little of your advice; an old maimed general, when unfit for action, is fittest for counsel. I have other designs upon women than eating and drinking with them; I am in love with Sparkish's mistress, whom he is to marry to-morrow: now how shall I get her?

Enter SPARKISH, *looking about.*

HORNER. Why here comes one will help you to her.

HARCOURT. He! he, I tell you, is my rival, and will hinder my love.

HORNER. No; a foolish rival and a jealous husband assist their rival's designs; for they are sure to make their women hate them, which is the first step to their love for another man.

HARCOURT. But I cannot come near his mistress but in his company.

HORNER. Still the better for you; for fools are most easily cheated when they themselves are accessories: and he is to be bubbled of his mistress as of his money, the common mistress, by keeping him company.

SPARKISH. Who is that that is to be bubbled? Faith, let me snack; I han't met with a bubble since Christmas. 'Gad, I think bubbles are like their brother woodcocks, go out with the cold weather.

HARCOURT. A pox! he did not hear all, I hope. [*Apart to* HORNER.]

SPARKISH. Come, you bubbling rogues you, where do we sup?—Oh, Harcourt, my mistress tells me you have been making fierce love to her all the play long: ha! ha!—But I—

HARCOURT. I make love to her!

SPARKISH. Nay, I forgive thee, for I think I know thee, and I know her; but I am sure I know myself.

HARCOURT. Did she tell you so? I see all women are like these of the Exchange; who, to enhance the prize of their commodities, report to their fond customers offers which were never made 'em.

HORNER. Ay, women are apt to tell before the intrigue, as men after it, and so show themselves the vainer sex. But hast thou a mistress, Sparkish? 'Tis as hard for me to believe it, as that thou ever hadst a bubble, as you bragged just now.

SPARKISH. O, your servant, sir: are you at your raillery, sir? But we are some of us beforehand with you to-day at the play. The wits were something bold with you, sir; did you not hear us laugh?

HORNER. Yes; but I thought you had gone to plays, to laugh at the poet's wit, not at your own.

SPARKISH. Your servant, sir: no, I thank you. 'Gad I go to a play as to a country treat; I carry my own wine to one, and my own wit to t'other, or else I'm sure I should not be merry at either. And the reason why we are so often louder than the players, is, because we think we speak more wit, and so become the poet's rivals in his audience: for to tell you the truth, we hate the silly rogues; nay, so much, that we find fault even with their bawdy upon the stage, whilst we talk nothing else in the pit as loud.

HORNER. But why shouldst thou hate the silly poets? Thou hast too much wit to be one; and they, like whores, are only hated by each other: and thou dost scorn writing, I'm sure,

SPARKISH. Yes; I'd have you to know I scorn writing; but women, women, that make men do all foolish things, make 'em write songs too. Everybody does it. 'Tis even as common with lovers, as playing with fans; and you can no more help rhyming to your Phillis, than drinking to your Phillis.

HARCOURT. Nay, poetry in love is no more to be avoided than jealousy.

DORILANT. But the poets damned your songs, did they?

SPARKISH. Damn the poets! they have turned 'em into burlesque, as they call it. That burlesque is a hocus-pocus trick they have got, which, by the virtue of *Hictius doctius topsy turvy*, they make a wise and witty man in the world, a fool upon the stage you know not how: and 'tis therefore I hate 'em too, for I know not but it may be my own case; for they'll put a man into a play for looking asquint. Their predecessors were contented to make serving-men only their stage-fools: but these rogues must have gentlemen, with a pox to 'em, nay, knights; and, indeed, you shall hardly see a fool upon the stage but he's a knight. And to tell you the truth, they have kept me these six years from being a knight in earnest, for fear of being knighted in a play, and dubbed a fool.

DORILANT. Blame 'em not, they must follow their copy, the age.

HARCOURT. But why shouldst thou be afraid of being in a play, who expose yourself every day in the play-houses, and at public places?

HORNER. 'Tis but being on the stage, instead of standing on a bench in the pit.

DORILANT. Don't you give money to painters to draw you like? and are you afraid of your pictures at length in a playhouse, where all your mistresses may see you?

SPARKISH. A pox! painters don't draw the small-pox or pimples in one's face. Come, damn all your silly authors whatever, all books and booksellers, by the world; and all readers, courteous or uncourteous!

HARCOURT. But who comes here, Sparkish?

Enter PINCHWIFE *and* MRS. PINCHWIFE *in man's clothes,* ALITHEA *and* LUCY.

SPARKISH. Oh, hide me! There's my mistress too. [SPARKISH *hides himself behind* HARCOURT.]

HARCOURT. She sees you.

SPARKISH. But I will not see her. 'Tis time to go to Whitehall, and I must not fail the drawing-room.

HARCOURT. Pray, first carry me, and reconcile me to her.

SPARKISH. Another time. Faith, the king will have supped.

HARCOURT. Not with the worse stomach for thy absence. Thou art one of those fools that think their attendance at the king's meals as necessary as his physicians, when you are more troublesome to him than his doctors or his dogs.

SPARKISH. Pshaw! I know my interest, sir. Prithee hide me.

HORNER. Your servant, Pinchwife.—What, he knows us not!

PINCHWIFE. Come along. [*To his wife aside.*]

MRS. PINCHWIFE. Pray, have you any ballads? give me sixpenny worth.

BOOKSELLER. We have no ballads.

MRS. PINCHWIFE. Then give me *Covent Garden Drollery*, and a play or two—Oh, here's *Tarugo's Wiles*, and the *Slighted Maiden*; I'll have them.

PINCHWIFE. No; plays are not for your reading. Come along; will you discover yourself? [*Apart to her.*]

HORNER. Who is that pretty youth with him, Sparkish?

SPARKISH. I believe his wife's brother, because he's something like her: but I never saw her but once.

HORNER. Extremely handsome; I have seen a face like it too. Let us follow 'em.

[*Exeunt* PINCHWIFE, MRS. PINCHWIFE, ALITHEA, *and* LUCY; HORNER *and* DORILANT *following them.*]

HARCOURT. Come, Sparkish, your mistress saw you, and will be angry you go not to her. Besides, I would fain be reconciled to her, which none but you can do, dear friend.

SPARKISH. Well, that's a better reason, dear friend. I would not go near her now for her's or my own sake; but I can deny you nothing: for though I have known thee a great while, never go, if I do not love thee as well as a new acquaintance.

HARCOURT. I am obliged to you indeed, dear friend. I would be well with her, only to be well with thee still; for these ties to wives usually dissolve all ties to friends. I would be contented she should enjoy you a-nights, but I would have you to myself a-days as I have had, dear friend.

SPARKISH. And thou shalt enjoy me a-days, dear, dear friend, never stir: and I'll be divorced from her, sooner than from thee. Come along.

HARCOURT. [*Aside.*] So, we are hard put to't, when we make our rival our procurer; but neither she nor her brother would let me come near her now. When all's done, a rival is the best cloak to steal to a mistress under, without suspicion; and when we have once got to her as we desire, we throw him off like other cloaks. [*Exit* SPARKISH, HARCOURT *following him.*]

Re-enter MR. PINCHWIFE *and* MRS. PINCHWIFE.

PINCHWIFE. [*To* ALITHEA.] Sister, if you will not go, we must leave you.—[*Aside.*] The fool her gallant and she will muster up all the young saunterers of this place, and they will leave their dear sempstresses to follow us. What a swarm of cuckolds and cuckold-makers are here!—Come, let's be gone, mistress Margery.

MRS. PINCHWIFE. Don't you believe that; I han't half my bellyfull of sights yet.

PINCHWIFE. Then walk this way.

MRS. PINCHWIFE. Lord, what a power of brave signs are here! stay—the Bull's-Head, the Ram's-Head, and the Stag's-Head, dear—

PINCHWIFE. Nay, if every husband's proper sign here were visible, they would be all alike.

MRS. PINCHWIFE. What d'ye mean by that, bud?

PINCHWIFE. 'Tis no matter—no matter, bud.

MRS. PINCHWIFE. Pray tell me: nay, I will know.

PINCHWIFE. They would be all Bulls, Stags, and Rams-heads. [*Exeunt* PINCHWIFE *and* MRS. PINCHWIFE.]

Re-enter SPARKISH, HARCOURT, ALITHEA, *and* LUCY, *at the other door.*

SPARKISH. Come, dear madam, for my sake you shall be reconciled to him.

ALITHEA. For your sake I hate him.

HARCOURT. That's something too cruel, madam, to hate me for his sake.

SPARKISH. Ay indeed, madam, too, too cruel to me, to hate my friend for my sake.

ALITHEA. I hate him because he is your enemy; and you ought to hate him too, for making love to me, if you love me.

SPARKISH. That's a good one! I hate a man for loving you! If he did love you, 'tis but what he can't help; and 'tis your fault, not his, if he admires you. I hate a man for being of my opinion! I'll n'er do't, by the world.

ALITHEA. Is it for your honour, or mine, to suffer a man to make love to me, who am to marry you to-morrow?

SPARKISH. Is it for your honour, or mine, to have me jealous? That he makes love to you, is a sign you are handsome; and that I am not jealous, is a sign you are virtuous. That I think is for your honour.

ALITHEA. But 'tis your honour too I am concerned for.

HARCOURT. But why, dearest madam, will you be more concerned for his honour than he is himself? Let his honour alone, for my sake and his. He! he has no honour—

SPARKISH. How's that?

HARCOURT. But what my dear friend can guard himself.

SPARKISH. O ho—that's right again.

HARCOURT. Your care of his honour argues his neglect of it, which is no honour to my dear friend here. Therefore once more, let his honour go which way it will, dear madam.

SPARKISH. Ay, ay; were it for my honour to marry a woman whose virtue I suspected, and could not trust her in a friend's hands?

ALITHEA. Are you not afraid to lose me?

HARCOURT. He afraid to lose you, madam! No, no—you may see how the most estimable and most glorious creature in the world is valued by him. Will you not see it?

SPARKISH. Right, honest Frank, I have that noble value for her that I cannot be jealous of her.

ALITHEA. You mistake him. He means, you care not for me, nor who has me.

SPARKISH. Lord, madam, I see you are jealous! Will you wrest a poor man's meaning from his words?

ALITHEA. You astonish me, sir, with your want of jealousy.

SPARKISH. And you make me giddy, madam, with your jealousy and fears, and virtue and honour. 'Gad, I see virtue makes a woman as troublesome as a little reading or learning.

ALITHEA. Monstrous!

LUCY. Well, to see what easy husbands these women of quality can meet with! a poor chambermaid can never have such ladylike luck. Besides, he's thrown away upon her. She'll make no use of her fortune, her blessing, none to a gentleman, for a pure cuckold; for it requires good breeding to be a cuckold. [*Aside.*]

ALITHEA. I tell you then plainly, he pursues me to marry me.

SPARKISH. Pshaw!

HARCOURT. Come, madam, you see you strive in vain to make him jealous of me. My dear friend is the kindest creature in the world to me.

SPARKISH. Poor fellow!

HARCOURT. But his kindness only is not enough for me, without your favour, your good opinion, dear madam: 'tis that must perfect my happiness. Good gentleman, he believes all I say: would you would do so! Jealous of me! I would not wrong him nor you for the world.

SPARKISH. Look you there. Hear him, hear him, and do not walk away so. [ALITHEA *walks carelessly to and fro.*]

HARCOURT. I love you, madam, so—

SPARKISH. How's that? Nay, now you begin to go too far indeed.

HARCOURT. So much, I confess, I say, I love you, that I would not have you miserable, and cast yourself away upon so unworthy and inconsiderable a thing as what you see here. [*Clapping his hand on his breast, points at* SPARKISH.]

SPARKISH. No, faith, I believe thou wouldst not: now his meaning is plain; but I knew before thou wouldst not wrong me, nor her.

HARCOURT. No, no, Heavens forbid the glory of her sex should fall so low, as into the embraces of such a contemptible wretch, the least of mankind—my friend here—I injure him! [*Embracing* SPARKISH.]

ALITHEA. Very well.

SPARKISH. No, no, dear friend, I knew it.—Madam, you see he will rather wrong himself than me, in giving himself such names.

ALITHEA. Do not you understand him yet?

SPARKISH. Yes: how modestly he speaks of himself, poor fellow!

ALITHEA. Methinks he speaks impudently of yourself, since—before yourself too; insomuch that I can no longer suffer his scurrilous abusiveness to you, no more than his love to me. [*Offers to go.*]

SPARKISH. Nay, nay, madam, pray stay—his love to you! Lord, madam, has he not spoke yet plain enough?

ALITHEA. Yes, indeed, I should think so.

SPARKISH. Well then, by the world, a man can't speak civilly to a woman now, but presently she says, he makes love to her. Nay, madam, you shall stay, with your pardon, since you have not yet understood him, till he has made an eclaircissement of his love to you, that is, what kind of love it is. Answer to thy catechism, friend; do you love my mistress here?

HARCOURT. Yes, I wish she would not doubt it.

SPARKISH. But how do you love her?

HARCOURT. With all my soul.

ALITHEA. I thank him, methinks he speaks plain enough now.

SPARKISH. [*To* ALITHEA.] You are out still.—But with what kind of love, Harcourt?

HARCOURT. With the best and the truest love in the world.

SPARKISH. Look you there then, that is with no matrimonial love, I'm sure.

ALITHEA. How's that? do you say matrimonial love is not best?

SPARKISH. 'Gad, I went too far ere I was aware. But speak for thyself, Harcourt, you said you would not wrong me nor her.

HARCOURT. No, so, madam, e'en take him for Heaven's sake.

SPARKISH. Look you there, madam.

HARCOURT. Who should in all justice be yours, he that loves you most. [*Claps his hand on his breast.*]

ALITHEA. Look you there, Mr. Sparkish, who's that?

SPARKISH. Who should it be?—Go on, Harcourt.

HARCOURT. Who loves you more than women titles, or fortune fools. [*Points at* SPARKISH.]

SPARKISH. Look you there, he means me still, for he points at me.

ALITHEA. Ridiculous!

HARCOURT. Who can only match your faith and constancy in love.

SPARKISH. Ay.

HARCOURT. Who knows, if it be possible, how to value so much beauty and virtue.

SPARKISH. Ay.

HARCOURT. Whose love can no more be equalled in the world, than that heavenly form of yours.

SPARKISH. No.

HARCOURT. Who could no more suffer a rival, than your absence, and yet could no more suspect your virtue, than his own constancy in his love to you.

SPARKISH. No.

HARCOURT. Who, in fine, loves you better than his eyes, that first made him love you.

SPARKISH. Ay—Nay, madam, faith, you shan't go till—

ALITHEA. Have a care, lest you make me stay too long.

SPARKISH. But till he has saluted you; that I may be assured you are friends, after
- his honest advice and declaration. Come, pray, madam, be friends with him.

Re-enter PINCHWIFE *and* MRS. PINCHWIFE.

ALITHEA. You must pardon me, sir, that I am not yet so obedient to you.

PINCHWIFE. What, invite your wife to kiss men? Monstrous! are you not ashamed?
I will never forgive you.

SPARKISH. Are you not ashamed, that I should have more confidence in the chastity
of your family than you have? You must not teach me, I am a man of honour,
sir, though I am frank and free; I am frank, sir—

PINCHWIFE. Very frank, sir, to share your wife with your friends.

SPARKISH. He is an humble, menial friend, such as reconciles the differences of the
marriage bed; you know man and wife do not always agree; I design him for
that use, therefore would have him well with my wife.

PINCHWIFE. A menial friend!—you will get a great many menial friends, by
showing your wife as you do.

SPARKISH. What then? It may be I have a pleasure in't, as I have to show fine
clothes at a play-house, the first day, and count money before poor rogues.

PINCHWIFE. He that shows his wife or money, will be in danger of having them
borrowed sometimes.

SPARKISH. I love to be envied, and would not marry a wife that I alone could love;
loving alone is as dull as eating alone. Is it not a frank age? and I am a frank
person; and to tell you the truth, it may be, I love to have rivals in a wife, they
make her seem to a man still but as a kept mistress; and so good night, for I
must to Whitehall.—Madam, I hope you are now reconciled to my friend;
and so I wish you a good night, madam, and sleep if you can; for to-morrow
you know I must visit you early with a canonical gentleman. Good night, dear
Harcourt. [*Exit.*]

HARCOURT. Madam, I hope you will not refuse my visit to-morrow, if it should be
earlier with a canonical gentleman than Mr. Sparkish's.

PINCHWIFE. This gentlewoman is yet under my care, therefore you must yet forbear
your freedom with her, sir. [*Coming between* ALITHEA *and* HARCOURT.]

HARCOURT. Must, sir?

PINCHWIFE. Yes, sir, she is my sister.

HARCOURT. 'Tis well she is, sir—for I must be her servant, sir.—Madam—

PINCHWIFE. Come away, sister, we had been gone, if it had not been for you, and so avoided these lewd rake-hells, who seem to haunt us.

Re-enter HORNER *and* DORILANT.

HORNER. How now, Pinchwife!

PINCHWIFE. Your servant.

HORNER. What! I see a little time in the country makes a man turn wild and unsociable, and only fit to converse with his horses, dogs, and his herds.

PINCHWIFE. I have business, sir, and must mind it; your business is pleasure, therefore you and I must go different ways.

HORNER. Well, you may go on, but this pretty young gentleman—[*Takes hold of* MRS. PINCHWIFE.]

HARCOURT. The lady—

DORILANT. And the maid—

HORNER. Shall stay with us; for I suppose their business is the same with ours, pleasure.

PINCHWIFE. 'Sdeath, he knows her, she carries it so sillily! yet if he does not, I should be more silly to discover it first. [*Aside.*]

ALITHEA. Pray, let us go, sir.

PINCHWIFE. Come, come—

HORNER. [*To* MRS. PINCHWIFE.] Had you not rather stay with us?—Prithee, Pinchwife, who is this pretty young gentleman?

PINCHWIFE. One to whom I'm a guardian.—[*Aside.*] I wish I could keep her out of your hands.

HORNER. Who is he? I never saw anything so pretty in all my life.

PINCHWIFE. Pshaw! do not look upon him so much, he's a poor bashful youth, you'll put him out of countenance.—Come away, brother. [*Offers to take her away.*]

HORNER. O, your brother!

PINCHWIFE. Yes, my wife's brother.—Come, come, she'll stay supper for us.

HORNER. I thought so, for he is very like her I saw you at the play with, whom I told you I was in love with.

MRS. PINCHWIFE. [*Aside.*] O jeminy! is that he that was in love with me? I am glad on't, I vow, for he's a curious fine gentleman, and I love him already, too.—[*To* PINCHWIFE.] Is this he, bud?

PINCHWIFE. Come away, come away. [*To his wife.*]

HORNER. Why, what haste are you in? why won't you let me talk with him?

PINCHWIFE. Because you'll debauch him; he's yet young and innocent, and I would not have him debauched for anything in the world.—[*Aside.*] How she gazes on him! the devil!

HORNER. Harcourt, Dorilant, look you here, this is the likeness of that dowdy he told us of, his wife; did you ever see a lovelier creature? The rogue has reason to be jealous of his wife, since she is like him, for she would make all that see her in love with her.

HARCOURT. And, as I remember now, she is as like him here as can be.

DORILANT. She is indeed very pretty, if she be like him.

HORNER. Very pretty? a very pretty commendation!—she is a glorious creature, beautiful beyond all things I ever beheld.

PINCHWIFE. So, so.

HARCOURT. More beautiful than a poet's first mistress of imagination.

HORNER. Or another man's last mistress of flesh and blood.

MRS. PINCHWIFE. Nay, now you jeer, sir; pray don't jeer me.

PINCHWIFE. Come, come.—[Aside.] By Heavens, she'll discover herself!

HORNER. I speak of your sister, sir.

PINCHWIFE. Ay, but saying she was handsome, if like him, made him blush.—[Aside.] I am upon a rack!

HORNER. Methinks he is so handsome he should not be a man.

PINCHWIFE. [Aside.] O, there 'tis out! he has discovered her! I am not able to suffer any longer.—[To his wife.] Come, come away, I say.

HORNER. Nay, by your leave, sir, he shall not go yet.—[Aside to them.] Harcourt, Dorilant, let us torment this jealous rogue a little.

HARCOURT. ⎫
DORILANT. ⎬ How?

HORNER. I'll show you.

PINCHWIFE. Come, pray let him go, I cannot stay fooling any longer; I tell you his sister stays supper for us.

HORNER. Does she? Come then, we'll all go to sup with he and thee.

PINCHWIFE. No, now I think on't, having stayed so long for us, I warrant she's gone to bed.—[Aside.] I wish she and I were well out of their hands.—[To his wife.] Come, I must rise early to-morrow, come.

HORNER. Well then, if she be gone to bed, I wish her and you a good night. But pray, young gentleman, present my humble service to her.

MRS. PINCHWIFE. Thank you heartily, sir.

PINCHWIFE. [Aside.] 'Sdeath, she will discover herself yet in spite of me—[Aloud.] He is something more civil to you, for your kindness to his sister, than I am, it seems.

HORNER. Tell her, dear sweet little gentleman, for all your brother there, that you have revived the love I had for her at first sight in the playhouse.

MRS. PINCHWIFE. But did you love her indeed, and indeed?

PINCHWIFE. [*Aside.*] So, so.—[*Aloud.*] Away, I say.

HORNER. Nay, stay.—Yes, indeed, and indeed, pray do you tell her so, and give her this kiss from me. [*Kisses her.*]

PINCHWIFE. [*Aside.*] O Heavens! what do I suffer? Now 'tis too plain he knows her, and yet—

HORNER. And this, and this—[*Kisses her again.*]

MRS. PINCHWIFE. What do you kiss me for? I am no woman.

PINCHWIFE. [*Aside.*] So, there, 'tis out.—[*Aloud.*] Come, I cannot, nor will stay any longer.

HORNER. Nay, they shall send your lady a kiss too. Here, Harcourt, Dorilant, will you not? [*They kiss her.*]

PINCHWIFE. [*Aside.*] How! do I suffer this? Was I not accusing another just now for this rascally patience, in permitting his wife to be kissed before his face? Ten thousand ulcers gnaw away their lips.—[*Aloud.*] Come, come.

HORNER. Good night, dear little gentleman; madam, good night: farewell, Pinchwife.—[*Apart to* HARCOURT *and* DORILANT.] Did not I tell you I would raise his jealous gall? [*Exeunt* HORNER, HARCOURT, *and* DORILANT.]

PINCHWIFE. So, they are gone at last; stay, let me see first if the coach be at this door. [*Exit.*]

Re-enter HORNER, HARCOURT, *and* DORILANT.

HORNER. What, not gone yet? Will you be sure to do as I desired you, sweet sir?

MRS. PINCHWIFE. Sweet sir, but what will you give me then?

HORNER. Anything. Come away into the next walk. [*Exit, haling away* MRS. PINCHWIFE.]

ALITHEA. Hold! hold! what d'ye do?

LUCY. Stay, stay, hold—

HARCOURT. Hold, madam, hold, let him present him—he'll come presently; nay, I will never let you go till you answer my question.

LUCY. For God's sake, sir, I must follow 'em. [ALITHEA *and* LUCY, *struggling with* HARCOURT *and* DORILANT.]

DORILANT. No, I have something to present you with too, you shan't follow them.

Re-enter PINCHWIFE.

PINCHWIFE. Where?—how—what's become of?—gone!—whither?

LUCY. He's only gone with the gentleman, who will give him something, an't please your worship.

PINCHWIFE. Something!—give him something, with a pox!—where are they?

ALITHEA. In the next walk only, brother.

PINCHWIFE. Only, only! where, where? [*Exit and returns presently, then goes out again.*]

HARCOURT. What's the matter with him? why so much concerned? But, dearest madam—

ALITHEA. Pray let me go, sir; I have said and suffered enough already.

HARCOURT. Then you will not look upon, nor pity, my sufferings?

ALITHEA. To look upon 'em, when I cannot help 'em, were cruelty, not pity; therefore, I will never see you more.

HARCOURT. Let me then, madam, have my privilege of a banished lover, complaining or railing, and giving you but a farewell reason why, if you cannot condescend to marry me, you should not take that wretch, my rival.

ALITHEA. He only, not you, since my honour is engaged so far to him, can give me a reason why I should not marry him; but if he be true, and what I think him to me, I must be so to him. Your servant, sir.

HARCOURT. Have women only constancy when l'tis a vice, and are, like Fortune, only true to fools?

DORILANT. Thou sha't not stir, thou robust creature; you see I can deal with you, therefore you should stay the rather, and be kind. [*To* LUCY, *who struggles to get from him.*]

Re-enter PINCHWIFE.

PINCHWIFE. Gone, gone, not to be found! quite gone! ten thousand plagues go with 'em! Which way went they?

ALITHEA. But into t'other walk, brother.

LUCY. Their business will be done presently sure, an't please your worship; it can't be long in doing, I'm sure on't.

ALITHEA. Are they not there?

PINCHWIFE. No, you know where they are, you infamous wretch, eternal shame of your family, which you do not dishonour enough yourself you think, but you must help her to do it too, thou legion of bawds!

ALITHEA. Good brother—

PINCHWIFE. Damned, damned sister!

ALITHEA. Look you here, she's coming.

Re-enter MRS. PINCHWIFE, *running with her hat under her arm, full of oranges and dried fruit,* HORNER *following.*

MRS. PINCHWIFE. O dear bud, look you here what I have got, see!

PINCHWIFE. And what I have got here too, which you can't see! [*Aside, rubbing his forehead.*]

MRS. PINCHWIFE. The fine gentleman has given me better things yet.

PINCHWIFE. Has he so?—[*Aside.*] Out of breath and coloured!—I must hold yet.

HORNER. I have only given your little brother an orange, sir.

PINCHWIFE. [*To* HORNER.] Thank you, sir.—[*Aside.*] You have only squeezed my orange, I suppose, and given it me again; yet I must have a city patience.—[*To his wife.*] Come, come away.

MRS. PINCHWIFE. Stay, till I have put up my fine things, bud.

Enter SIR JASPER FIDGET.

SIR JASPER. O, master Horner, come, come, the ladies stay for you; your mistress, my wife, wonders you make not more haste to her.

HORNER. I have stayed this half hour for you here, and 'tis your fault I am not now with your wife.

SIR JASPER. But, pray, don't let her know so much; the truth on't is, I was advancing a certain project to his majesty about—I'll tell you.

HORNER. No, let's go, and hear it at your house. Good night, sweet little gentleman; one kiss more, you'll remember me now, I hope. [*Kisses her.*]

DORILANT. What, sir Jasper, will you separate friends? He promised to sup with us, and if you take him to your house, you'll be in danger of our company too.

SIR JASPER. Alas! gentlemen, my house is not fit for you; there are none but civil women there, which are not for your turn. He, you know, can bear with the society of civil women now, ha! ha! ha! besides, he's one of my family—he's— he! he! he!

DORILANT. What is he?

SIR JASPER. Faith, my eunuch, since you'll have it; he! he! he! [*Exeunt* SIR JASPER FIDGET *and* HORNER.]

DORILANT. I rather wish thou wert his or my cuckold. Harcourt, what a good cuckold is lost there for want of a man to make him one? Thee and I cannot have Horner's privilege, who can make use of it.

HARCOURT. Ay, to poor Horner 'tis like coming to an estate at threescore, when a man can't be the better for't.

PINCHWIFE. Come.

MRS. PINCHWIFE. Presently, bud.

DORILANT. Come, let us go too.—[*To* ALITHEA.] Madam, your servant.—[*To* LUCY.] Good night, strapper.

HARCOURT. Madam, though you will not let me have a good day or night, I wish you one; but dare not name the other half of my wish.

ALITHEA. Good night, sir, for ever.

MRS. PINCHWIFE. I don't know where to put this here, dear bud, you shall eat it; nay, you shall have part of the fine gentleman's good things, or treat, as you call it, when we come home.

PINCHWIFE. Indeed I deserve it, since I furnished the best part of it. [*Strikes away the orange.*]

> The gallant treats presents, and gives the ball;
> But 'tis the absent cuckold pays for all. [*Exeunt.*]

ACT IV.

SCENE I.—PINCHWIFE'S *House in the Morning.*

Enter ALITHEA *dressed in new Clothes, and* LUCY.

LUCY. Well—madam, now have I dressed you, and set you out with so many ornaments, and spent upon you ounces of essence and pulvillio;[1] and all this for no other purpose but as people adorn and perfume a corpse for a stinking second-hand grave: such, or as bad, I think master Sparkish's bed.

ALITHEA. Hold your peace.

LUCY. Nay, madam, I will ask you the reason why you would banish poor master Harcourt for ever from your sight; how could you be so hard-hearted?

ALITHEA. 'Twas because I was not hard-hearted.

LUCY. No, no; 'twas stark love and kindness, I warrant.

ALITHEA. It was so; I would see him no more because I love him.

LUCY. Hey day, a very pretty reason!

ALITHEA. You do not understand me.

LUCY. I wish you may yourself.

ALITHEA. I was engaged to marry, you see, another man, whom my justice will not suffer me to deceive or injure.

LUCY. Can there be a greater cheat or wrong done to a man than to give him your person without your heart? I should make a conscience of it.

ALITHEA. I'll retrieve it for him after I am married a while.

LUCY. The woman that marries to love better, will be as much mistaken as the wencher that marries to live better. No, madam, marrying to increase love is like gaming to become rich; alas! you only lose what little stock you had before.

ALITHEA. I find by your rhetoric you have been bribed to betray me.

LUCY. Only by his merit, that has bribed your heart, you see, against your word and rigid honour. But what a devil is this honour! 'tis sure a disease in the head, like the megrim or falling-sickness, that always hurries people away to do themselves mischief. Men lose their lives by it; women, what's dearer to 'em, their love, the life of life.

ALITHEA. Come, pray talk you no more of honour, nor master Harcourt; I wish the other would come to secure my fidelity to him and his right in me.

LUCY. You will marry him then?

---

1 Perfume in the form of powder.

ALITHEA. Certainly, I have given him already my word, and will my hand too, to make it good, when he comes.

LUCY. Well, I wish I may never stick pin more, if he be not an arrant natural, to t'other fine gentleman.

ALITHEA. I own he wants the wit of Harcourt, which I will dispense withal for another want he has, which is want of jealousy, which men of wit seldom want.

LUCY. Lord, madam, what should you do with a fool to your husband? You intend to be honest, don't you? then that husbandly virtue, credulity, is thrown away upon you.

ALITHEA. He only that could suspect my virtue should have cause to do it; 'tis Sparkish's confidence in my truth that obliges me to be so faithful to him.

LUCY. You are not sure his opinion may last.

ALITHEA. I am satisfied, 'tis impossible for him to be jealous after the proofs I have had of him. Jealousy in a husband—Heaven defend me from it! it begets a thousand plagues to a poor woman, the loss of her honour, her quiet, and her—

LUCY. And her pleasure.

ALITHEA. What d'ye mean, impertinent?

LUCY. Liberty is a great pleasure, madam.

ALITHEA. I say, loss of her honour, her quiet, nay, her life sometimes; and what's as bad almost, the loss of this town; that is, she is sent into the country, which is the last ill-usage of a husband to a wife, I think.

LUCY. [Aside.] O, does the wind lie there?—[Aloud.] Then of necessity, madam, you think a man must carry his wife into the country, if he be wise. The country is as terrible, I find, to our young English ladies, as a monastery to those abroad; and on my virginity, I think they would rather marry a London jailer, than a high sheriff of a county, since neither can stir from his employment. Formerly women of wit married fools for a great estate, a fine seat, or the like; but now 'tis for a pretty seat only in Lincoln's-Inn-Fields, St. James's-Fields, or the Pall-Mall.

Enter SPARKISH, *and* HARCOURT, *dressed like a parson.*

SPARKISH. Madam, your humble servant, a happy day to you, and to us all.

HARCOURT. Amen.

ALITHEA. Who have we here?

SPARKISH. My chaplain, faith—O madam, poor Harcourt remembers his humble service to you; and, in obedience to your last commands, refrains coming into your sight.

ALITHEA. Is not that he?

SPARKISH. No, fy, no; but to show that he ne'er intended to hinder our match, has sent his brother here to join our hands. When I get me a wife, I must get her a chaplain, according to the custom; this is his brother, and my chaplain.

ALITHEA. His brother!

LUCY. And your chaplain, to preach in your pulpit then—[*Aside.*]

ALITHEA. His brother!

SPARKISH. Nay, I knew you would not believe it.—I told you, sir, she would take you for your brother Frank.

ALITHEA. Believe it!

LUCY. His brother! ha! ha! he! he has a trick left still, it seems. [*Aside.*]

SPARKISH. Come, my dearest, pray let us go to church before the canonical hour is past.

ALITHEA. For shame, you are abused still.

SPARKISH. By the world, 'tis strange now you are so incredulous.

ALITHEA. 'Tis strange you are so credulous.

SPARKISH. Dearest of my life, hear me. I tell you this is Ned Harcourt of Cambridge, by the world; you see he has a sneaking college look. 'Tis true he's something like his brother Frank; and they differ from each other no more than in their age, for they were twins.

LUCY. Ha! ha! ha!

ALITHEA. Your servant, sir; I cannot be so deceived, though you are. But come, let's hear, how do you know what you affirm so confidently?

SPARKISH. Why, I'll tell you all. Frank Harcourt coming to me this morning to wish me joy, and present his service to you, I asked him if he could help me to a parson. Whereupon he told me, he had a brother in town who was in orders; and he went straight away, and sent him, you see there, to me.

ALITHEA. Yes, Frank goes and puts on a black coat, then tells you he is Ned; that's all you have for't.

SPARKISH. Pshaw! pshaw! I tell you, by the same token, the midwife put her garter about Frank's neck, to know 'em asunder, they were so like.

ALITHEA. Frank tells you this too?

SPARKISH. Ay, and Ned there too: nay, they are both in a story.

ALITHEA. So, so; very foolish.

SPARKISH. Lord, if you won't believe one, you had best try him by your chambermaid there; for chambermaids must needs know chaplains from other men, they are so used to 'em.

LUCY. Let's see: nay, I'll be sworn he has the canonical smirk, and the filthy clammy palm of a chaplain.

ALITHEA. Well, most reverend doctor, pray let us make an end of this fooling.

HARCOURT. With all my soul, divine heavenly creature, when you please.

ALITHEA. He speaks like a chaplain indeed.

SPARKISH. Why, was there not soul, divine, heavenly, in what he said?

ALITHEA. Once more, most impertinent black coat, cease your persecution, and let us have a conclusion of this ridiculous love.

HARCOURT. I had forgot, I must suit my style to my coat, or I wear it in vain. [*Aside.*]

ALITHEA. I have no more patience left; let us make once an end of this troublesome love, I say.

HARCOURT. So be it, seraphic lady, when your honour shall think it meet and convenient so to do.

SPARKISH. 'Gad I'm sure none but a chaplain could speak so, I think.

ALITHEA. Let me tell you, sir, this dull trick will not serve your turn; though you delay our marriage, you shall not hinder it.

HARCOURT. Far be it from me, munificent patroness, to delay your marriage; I desire nothing more than to marry you presently, which I might do, if you yourself would; for my noble, good-natured, and thrice generous patron here would not hinder it.

SPARKISH. No, poor man, not I, faith.

HARCOURT. And now, madam, let me tell you plainly nobody else shall marry you; by heavens, I'll die first, for I'm sure I should die after it.

LUCY. How his love has made him forget his function, as I have seen it in real parsons!

ALITHEA. That was spoken like a chaplain too? now you understand him, I hope.

SPARKISH. Poor man, he takes it heinously to be refused; I can't blame him, 'tis putting an indignity upon him, not to be suffered; but you'll pardon me, madam, it shan't be; he shall marry us: come away, pray madam.

LUCY. Ha! ha! he! more ado! 'tis late.

ALITHEA. Invincible stupidity! I tell you, he would marry me as your rival, not as your chaplain.

SPARKISH. Come, come, madam. [*Pulling her away.*]

LUCY. I pray, madam, do not refuse this reverend divine the honour and satisfaction of marrying you; for I dare say, he has set his heart upon't, good doctor.

ALITHEA. What can you hope or design by this?

HARCOURT. I could answer her, a reprieve for a day only, often revokes a hasty doom. At worst, if she will not take mercy on me, and let me marry her, I have at least the lover's second pleasure, hindering my rival's enjoyment, though but for a time. [*Aside.*]

SPARKISH. Come, madam, 'tis e'en twelve o'clock, and my mother charged me never to be married out of the canonical hours. Come, come; Lord, here's such a deal of modesty, I warrant, the first day.

LUCY. Yes, an't please your worship, married women show all their modesty the first day, because married men show all their love the first day. [*Exeunt.*]

SCENE II.—*A Bedchamber in* MR. PINCHWIFE's *House.*

MR. PINCHWIFE *and* MRS. PINCHWIFE *discovered.*

PINCHWIFE. Come, tell me, I say.

MRS. PINCHWIFE. Lord! han't I told it a hundred times over?

PINCHWIFE. [*Aside.*] I would try, if in the repetition of the ungrateful tale, I could find her altering it in the least circumstance; for if her story be false, she is so too.—[*Aloud.*] Come, how was't, baggage?

MRS. PINCHWIFE. Lord, what pleasure you take to hear it sure!

PINCHWIFE. No, you take more in telling it I find; but speak, how was't?

MRS. PINCHWIFE. He carried me up into the house next to the Exchange.

PINCHWIFE. So, and you two were only in the room!

MRS. PINCHWIFE. Yes, for he sent away a youth that was there, for some dried fruit, and China oranges.

PINCHWIFE. Did he so? Damn him for it—and for—

MRS. PINCHWIFE. But presently came up the gentlewoman of the house.

PINCHWIFE. O, 'twas well she did; but what did he do whilst the fruit came?

MRS. PINCHWIFE. He kissed me a hundred times, and told me he fancied he kissed my fine sister, meaning me, you know, whom he said he loved with all his soul, and bid me be sure to tell her so, and to desire her to be at her window, by eleven of the clock this morning, and he would walk under it at that time.

PINCHWIFE. And he was as good as his word, very punctual; a pox reward him for't. [*Aside.*]

MRS. PINCHWIFE. Well, and he said if you were not within, he would come up to her, meaning me, you know, bud, still.

PINCHWIFE. [*Aside.*] So—he knew her certainly; but for this confession, I am obliged to her simplicity.—[*Aloud.*] But what, you stood very still when he kissed you?

MRS. PINCHWIFE. Yes, I warrant you; would you have had me discovered myself?

PINCHWIFE. But you told me he did some beastliness to you, as you call it; what was't?

MRS. PINCHWIFE. Why, he put—

PINCHWIFE. What?

MRS. PINCHWIFE. Why, he put the tip of his tongue between my lips, and so mousled me—and I said, I'd bite it.

PINCHWIFE. An eternal canker seize it, for a dog!

MRS. PINCHWIFE. Nay, you need not be so angry with him neither, for to say truth, he has the sweetest breath I ever knew.

PINCHWIFE. The devil! you were satisfied with it then, and would do it again?

MRS. PINCHWIFE. Not unless he should force me.

PINCHWIFE. Force you, changeling! I tell you, no woman can be forced.

MRS. PINCHWIFE. Yes, but she may sure, by such a one as he, for he's a proper, goodly, strong man; 'tis hard, let me tell you, to resist him.

PINCHWIFE. [*Aside.*] So, 'tis plain she loves him, yet she has not love enough to make her conceal it from me; but the sight of him will increase her aversion for me and love for him; and that love instruct her how to deceive me and satisfy him, all idiot as she is. Love! 'twas he gave women first their craft, their art of deluding. Out of Nature's hands they came plain, open, silly, and fit for slaves, as she and heaven intended 'em; but damned Love—well—I must strangle that little monster whilst I can deal with him.—[*Aloud.*] Go fetch pen, ink, and paper out of the next room.

MRS. PINCHWIFE. Yes, bud. [*Exit.*]

PINCHWIFE. Why should women have more invention in love than men? It can only be, because they have more desires, more soliciting passions, more lust, and more of the devil.

Re-enter MRS. PINCHWIFE.

Come, minx, sit down and write.

MRS. PINCHWIFE. Ay, dear bud, but I can't do't very well.

PINCHWIFE. I wish you could not at all.

MRS. PINCHWIFE. But what should I write for?

PINCHWIFE. I'll have you write a letter to your lover.

MRS. PINCHWIFE. O Lord, to the fine gentleman a letter!

PINCHWIFE. Yes, to the fine gentleman.

MRS. PINCHWIFE. Lord, you do but jeer; sure you jest.

PINCHWIFE. I am not so merry: come, write as I bid you.

MRS. PINCHWIFE. What, do you think I am a fool?

PINCHWIFE. [*Aside.*] She's afraid I would not dictate any love to him, therefore she's unwilling.—[*Aloud.*] But you had best begin.

MRS. PINCHWIFE. Indeed, and indeed, but I won't so I won't.

PINCHWIFE. Why?

MRS. PINCHWIFE. Because he's in town; you may send for him if you will.

PINCHWIFE. Very well, you would have him brought to you; is it come to this? I say, take the pen and write, or you'll provoke me.

MRS. PINCHWIFE. Lord, what d'ye make a fool of me for? Don't I know that letters are never writ but from the country to London, and from London into the country? Now he's in town, and I am in town too; therefore I can't write to him, you know.

PINCHWIFE. [*Aside.*] So, I am glad it is no worse; she is innocent enough yet.—[*Aloud.*] Yes, you may, when your husband bids you, write letters to people that are in town.

MRS. PINCHWIFE. O, may I so? then I'm satisfied.

PINCHWIFE. Come, begin:—*Sir*—[*Dictates.*]

MRS. PINCHWIFE. Shan't I say, *Dear Sir?*—You know one says always something more than bare *sir*.

PINCHWIFE. Write as I bid you, or I will write whore with this penknife in your face.

MRS. PINCHWIFE. Nay, good bud—*Sir*—[*Writes.*]

PINCHWIFE. *Though I suffered last night your nauseous, loathed kisses and embraces*—Write!

MRS. PINCHWIFE. Nay, why should I say so? You know I told you he had a sweet breath.

PINCHWIFE. Write!

MRS. PINCHWIFE. Let me but put out *loathed*.

PINCHWIFE. Write, I say!

MRS. PINCHWIFE. Well then. [*Writes.*]

PINCHWIFE. Let's see, what have you writ?—[*Takes the paper and reads.*] *Though I suffered last night your kisses and embraces*—Thou impudent creature! where is *nauseous* and *loathed?*

MRS. PINCHWIFE. I can't abide to write such filthy words.

PINCHWIFE. Once more write as I'd have you, and question it not, or I will spoil thy writing with this. I will stab out those eyes that cause my mischief. [*Holds up the penknife.*]

MRS. PINCHWIFE. O Lord! I will.

PINCHWIFE. So—so—let's see now.—[*Reads.*] *Though I suffered last night your nauseous, loathed kisses and embraces*—go on—*yet I would not have you presume that you shall ever repeat them*—so—[*She writes.*]

MRS. PINCHWIFE. I have writ it.

PINCHWIFE. On, then—*I then concealed myself from your knowledge, to avoid your insolencies.*—[*She writes.*]

MRS. PINCHWIFE. So—

PINCHWIFE. *The same reason, now I am out of your hands*— [*She writes.*]

MRS. PINCHWIFE. So—

PINCHWIFE. *Makes me own to you my unfortunate, though innocent frolic, of being in man's clothes*—[*She writes.*]

MRS. PINCHWIFE. So—

PINCHWIFE. *That you may for evermore cease to pursue her, who hates and detests you*—[*She writes on.*]

MRS. PINCHWIFE. So. Heigh! [*Sighs.*]

PINCHWIFE. What, do you sigh?—*detests you—as much as she loves her husband and her honour*—

MRS. PINCHWIFE. I vow, husband, he'll ne'er believe I should write such a letter.

PINCHWIFE. What, he'd expect a kinder from you? Come, now your name only.

MRS. PINCHWIFE. What, shan't I say *Your most faithful humble servant till death?*

PINCHWIFE. No, tormenting fiend!—[*Aside.*] Her style, I find, would be very soft.—[*Aloud.*] Come, wrap it up now, whilst I go fetch wax and a candle; and write on the backside, *For Mr. Horner.* [*Exit.*]

MRS. PINCHWIFE. *For Mr. Horner*—So, I am glad he has told me his name. Dear Mr. Horner! but why should I send thee such a letter that will vex thee, and make thee angry with me?—Well, I will not send it.—Ay, but then my husband will kill me—for I see plainly he won't let me love Mr. Horner—but what care I for my husband?—I won't, so I won't, send poor Mr. Horner such a letter—But then my husband—but oh, what if I writ at bottom my husband made me write it?—Ay, but then my husband would see't—Can one have no shift? ah, a London woman would have had a hundred presently. Stay—what if I should write a letter, and wrap it up like this, and write upon't too? Ay, but then my husband would see't—I don't know what to do.—But yet evads I'll try, so I will—for I will not send this letter to poor Mr. Horner, come what will on't.

Dear, sweet Mr. Horner—[*Writes, and repeats what she writes.*]—so—*my husband would have me send you a base, rude, unmannerly letter; but I won't— so—and would have me forbid you loving me; but I won't—so—and would have me say to you, I hate you, poor Mr. Horner; but I won't tell a lie for him—there— for I'm sure if you and I were in the country at cards together—so—I could not help treading on your toe under the table—so—or rubbing knees with you, and staring in your face, till you saw me—very well—and then looking down, and blushing for an hour together—so—but I must make haste before my husband comes: and now he has taught me to write letters, you shall have longer ones from me, who am, dear, dear, poor, dear Mr. Horner, your most humble friend, and servant to command till death,—*MARGERY PINCHWIFE.

Stay, I must give him a hint at bottom—so—now wrap it up just like t'other— so—now write *For Mr. Horner*—But oh now, what shall I do with it? for here comes my husband.

Re-enter PINCHWIFE.

PINCHWIFE. [*Aside.*] I have been detained by a sparkish coxcomb, who pretended a visit to me; but I fear 'twas to my wife—[*Aloud.*] What, have you done?

MRS. PINCHWIFE. Ay, ay, bud, just now.

PINCHWIFE. Let's see't: what d'ye tremble for? what, you would not have it go?

MRS. PINCHWIFE. Here—[*Aside.*] No, I must not give him that: so I had been served if I had given him this. [*He opens and reads the first letter.*]

PINCHWIFE. Come, where's the wax and seal?

MRS. PINCHWIFE. [*Aside.*] Lord, what shall I do now? Nay, then I have it—[*Aloud.*] Pray let me see't. Lord, you think me so arrant a fool, I cannot seal a letter; I will do't, so I will. [*Snatches the letter from him, changes it for the other, seals it, and delivers it to him.*]

PINCHWIFE. Nay, I believe you will learn that, and other things too, which I would not have you.

MRS. PINCHWIFE. So, han't I done it curiously?—[*Aside.*] I think I have; there's my letter going to Mr. Horner, since he'll needs have me send letters to folks.

PINCHWIFE. 'Tis very well; but I warrant, you would not have it go now?

MRS. PINCHWIFE. Yes, indeed, but I would, bud, now.

PINCHWIFE. Well, you are a good girl then. Come, let me lock you up in your chamber, till I come back; and be sure you come not within three strides of the window when I am gone, for I have a spy in the street.—[*Exit* MRS. PINCHWIFE, PINCHWIFE *locks the door.*] At least 'tis fit she thinks so. If we do not cheat women, they'll cheat us, and fraud may be justly used with secret enemies, of which a wife is the most dangerous; and he that has a handsome one to keep, and a frontier town, must provide against treachery, rather than open force. Now I have secured all within, I'll deal with the foe without, with false intelligence. [*Holds up the letter. Exit.*]

SCENE III.—HORNER's *Lodging.*

Enter HORNER *and* QUACK.

QUACK. Well, sir, how fadges[1] the new design? have you not the luck of all your brother projectors, to deceive only yourself at last?

HORNER. No, good domine doctor, I deceive you, it seems, and others too; for the grave matrons, and old rigid husbands think me as unfit for love, as they are; but their wives, sisters, and daughters know, some of 'em, better things already.

QUACK. Already!

HORNER. Already, I say. Last night I was drunk with half-a-dozen of your civil persons, as you call 'em, and people of honour, and so was made free of their society and dressing-rooms for ever hereafter; and am already come to the

---

1 Succeeds.

privileges of sleeping upon their pallets, warming smocks, tying shoes and garters, and the like, doctor, already, already, doctor.

QUACK. You have made good use of your time, sir.

HORNER. I tell thee, I am now no more interruption to 'em, when they sing, or talk bawdy, than a little squab French page who speaks no English.

QUACK. But do civil persons and women of honour drink, and sing bawdy songs?

HORNER. O, amongst friends, amongst friend. For your bigots in honour are just like those in religion; they fear the eye of the world more than the eye of Heaven; and think there is no virtue, but railing at vice, and no sin, but giving scandal. They rail at a poor, little, kept player, and keep themselves some young, modest pulpit comedian to be privy to their sins in their closets, not to tell 'em of them in their chapels.

QUACK. Nay, the truth on't is, priests, amongst the women now, have quite got the better of us lay-confessors, physicians.

HORNER. And they are rather their patients; but—

Enter LADY FIDGET, *looking about her.*

Now we talk of women of honour, here comes one. Step behind the screen there, and but observe, if I have not particular privileges with the women of reputation already, doctor, already. [QUACK *retires.*]

LADY FIDGET. Well, Horner, am not I a woman of honour? you see, I'm as good as my word.

HORNER. And you shall see, madam, I'll not be behind-hand with you in honour; and I'll be as good as my word too, if you please but to withdraw into the next room.

LADY FIDGET. But first, my dear sir, you must promise to have a care of my dear honour.

HORNER. If you talk a word more of your honour, you'll make me incapable to wrong it. To talk of honour in the mysteries of love, is like talking of Heaven or the Deity, in an operation of witchcraft, just when you are employing the devil: it makes the charm impotent.

LADY FIDGET. Nay, fy! let us not be smutty. But you talk of mysteries and bewitching to me; I don't understand you.

HORNER. I tell you, madam, the word money in a mistress's mouth, at such a nick of time, is not a more disheartening sound to a younger brother, than that of honour to an eager lover like myself.

LADY FIDGET. But you can't blame a lady of my reputation to be chary.

HORNER. Chary! I have been chary of it already, by the report I have caused of myself.

LADY FIDGET. Ay, but if you should ever let other women know that dear secret, it would come out. Nay, you must have a great care of your conduct; for my acquaintance are so censorious, (oh, 'tis a wicked, censorious world, Mr. Horner!) I say, are so censorious, and detracting, that perhaps they'll talk to the prejudice of my honour, though you should not let them know the dear secret.

HORNER. Nay, madam, rather than they shall prejudice your honour, I'll prejudice theirs; and, to serve you, I'll lie with 'em all, make the secret their own, and then they'll keep it. I am a Machiavel[1] in love, madam.

LADY FIDGET. O, no sir, not that way.

HORNER. Nay, the devil take me, if censorious women are to be silenced any other way.

LADY FIDGET. A secret is better kept, I hope, by a single person than a multitude; therefore pray do not trust any body else with it, dear, dear Mr. Horner.

Enter SIR JASPER FIDGET.

SIR JASPER. How now!

LADY FIDGET. [*Aside.*] O my husband!—prevented—and what's almost as bad, found with my arms about another man—that will appear too much—what shall I say?—[*Aloud.*] Sir Jasper, come hither: I am trying if Mr. Horner were ticklish, and he's as ticklish as can be. I love to torment the confounded toad; let you and I tickle him.

SIR JASPER. No, your ladyship will tickle him better without me, I suppose. But is this your buying china? I thought you had been at the china-house.

HORNER. [*Aside.*] China-house! that's my cue, I must take it.—[*Aloud.*] A pox! can't you keep your impertinent wives at home? Some men are troubled with the husbands, but I with the wives; but I'd have you to know, since I cannot be your journeyman by night, I will not be your drudge by day, to squire your wife about, and be your man of straw, or scarecrow only to pies and jays, that would be nibbling at your forbidden fruit; I shall be shortly the hackney gentleman-usher of the town.

SIR JASPER. [*Aside.*] He! he! he! poor fellow, he's in the right on't, faith. To squire women about for other folks, is as ungrateful an employment, as to tell money for other folks.—[*Aloud.*] He! he! he! be'n't angry, Horner.

LADY FIDGET. No, 'tis I have more reason to be angry, who am left by you, to go abroad indecently alone; or, what is more indecent, to pin myself upon such ill-bred people of your acquaintance as this is.

SIR JASPER. Nay, prithee, what has he done?

LADY FIDGET. Nay, he has done nothing.

SIR JASPER. But what d'ye take ill, if he has done nothing?

---

1 In *The Prince* (1532), the Italian philosopher Niccolò Machiavelli (1469-1527) promoted sly, deceitful, and expedient behavior, rather than moral action, to achieve one's goals.

LADY FIDGET. Ha! ha! ha! faith, I can't but laugh however; why, d'ye think the unmannerly toad would come down to me to the coach? I was fain to come up to fetch him, or go without him, which I was resolved not to do; for he knows china very well, and has himself very good, but will not let me see it, lest I should beg some; but I will find it out, and have what I came for yet.

HORNER. [*Apart to* LADY FIDGET, *as he follows her to the door.*] Lock the door, madam.—[*Exit* LADY FIDGET, *and locks the door.*]—[*Aloud.*] So, she has got into my chamber and locked me out. Oh the impertinency of woman-kind! Well, sir Jasper, plain-dealing is a jewel; if ever you suffer your wife to trouble me again here, she shall carry you home a pair of horns; by my lord mayor she shall; though I cannot furnish you myself, you are sure, yet I'll find a way.

SIR JASPER. Ha! ha! he!—[*Aside.*] At my first coming in, and finding her arms about him, tickling him it seems, I was half jealous, but now I see my folly.— [*Aloud.*] He! he! he! poor Horner.

HORNER. Nay, though you laugh now, 'twill be my turn ere long. Oh women, more impertinent, more cunning, and more mischievous than their monkeys, and to me almost as ugly!—Now is she throwing my things about, and rifling all I have; but I'll get into her the back way, and so rifle her for it.

SIR JASPER. Ha! ha! ha! poor angry Horner.

HORNER. Stay here a little, I'll ferret her out to you presently, I warrant. [*Exit at the other door.*]

    [SIR JASPER *talks through the door to his wife, she answers from within.*]

SIR JASPER. Wife! my lady Fidget! wife! he is coming in to you the back way.

LADY FIDGET. Let him come, and welcome, which way he will.

SIR JASPER. He'll catch you, and use you roughly, and be too strong for you.

LADY FIDGET. Don't you trouble yourself, let him if he can.

QUACK. [*Aside.*] This indeed I could not have believed from him, nor any but my own eyes.

Enter MRS. SQUEAMISH.

MRS. SQUEAMISH. Where's this woman-hater, this toad, this ugly, greasy, dirty sloven?

SIR JASPER. [*Aside.*] So, the women all will have him ugly: methinks he is a comely person, but his wants make his form contemptible to 'em; and 'tis e'en as my wife said yesterday, talking of him, that a proper handsome eunuch was as ridiculous a thing as a gigantic coward.

MRS. SQUEAMISH. Sir Jasper, your servant: where is the odious beast?

SIR JASPER. He's within in his chamber, with my wife; she's playing the wag with him.

MRS. SQUEAMISH. Is she so? and he's a clownish beast, he'll give her no quarter, he'll play the wag with her again, let me tell you: come, let's go help her—What, the door's locked?

SIR JASPER. Ay, my wife locked it.

MRS. SQUEAMISH. Did she so? let's break it open then.

SIR JASPER. No, no, he'll do her no hurt.

MRS. SQUEAMISH. [*Aside.*] But is there no other way to get in to 'em? whither goes this? I will disturb 'em. [*Exit at another door.*]

Enter OLD LADY SQUEAMISH.

LADY SQUEAMISH. Where is this harlotry, this impudent baggage, this rambling Tomrigg?[1] O sir Jasper, I'm glad to see you here; did you not see my vile grandchild come in hither just now?

SIR JASPER. Yes.

LADY SQUEAMISH. Ay, but where is she then? where is she? Lord, sir Jasper, I have e'en rattled myself to pieces in pursuit of her: but can you tell what she makes here? they say below, no woman lodges here.

SIR JASPER. No.

LADY SQUEAMISH. No! what does she here then? say, if it be not a woman's lodging, what makes she here? But are you sure no woman lodges here?

SIR JASPER. No, nor no man neither, this is Mr. Horner's lodging.

LADY SQUEAMISH. Is it so, are you sure?

SIR JASPER. Yes, yes.

LADY SQUEAMISH. So; then there's no hurt in't, I hope. But where is he?

SIR JASPER. He's in the next room with my wife.

LADY SQUEAMISH. Nay, if you trust him with your wife, I may with my Biddy. They say, he's a merry harmless man now, e'en as harmless a man as ever came out of Italy with a good voice, and as pretty, harmless company for a lady, as a snake without his teeth.

SIR JASPER. Ay, ay, poor man.

Re-enter MRS. SQUEAMISH.

MRS. SQUEAMISH. I can't find 'em.—Oh, are you here, grandmother? I followed, you must know, my lady Fidget hither; 'tis the prettiest lodging, and I have been staring on the prettiest pictures—

Re-enter LADY FIDGET *with a piece of china in her hand, and* HORNER *following.*

LADY FIDGET. And I have been toiling and moiling for the prettiest piece of china, my dear.

HORNER. Nay, she has been too hard for me, do what I could.

MRS. SQUEAMISH. Oh, lord, I'll have some china too. Good Mr. Horner, don't think to give other people china, and me none; come in with me too.

---

1 A wanton girl; a tomboy.

HORNER. Upon my honour, I have none left now.

MRS. SQUEAMISH. Nay, nay, I have known you deny your china before now, but you shan't put me off so. Come.

HORNER. This lady had the last there.

LADY FIDGET. Yes indeed, madam, to my certain knowledge, he has no more left.

MRS. SQUEAMISH. O, but it may be he may have some you could not find.

LADY FIDGET. What, d'ye think if he had had any left, I would not have had it too? for we women of quality never think we have china enough.

HORNER. Do not take it ill, I cannot make china for you all, but I will have a roll-waggon for you too, another time.

MRS. SQUEAMISH. Thank you, dear toad.

LADY FIDGET. What do you mean by that promise? [*Aside to* HORNER.]

HORNER. Alas, she has an innocent, literal understanding. [*Aside to* LADY FIDGET.]

LADY SQUEAMISH. Poor Mr. Horner! he has enough to do to please you all, I see.

HORNER. Ay, madam, you see how they use me.

LADY SQUEAMISH. Poor gentleman, I pity you.

HORNER. I thank you, madam: I could never find pity, but from such reverend ladies as you are; the young ones will never spare a man.

MRS. SQUEAMISH. Come, come, beast, and go dine with us; for we shall want a man at ombre after dinner.

HORNER. That's all their use of me, madam, you see.

MRS. SQUEAMISH. Come, sloven, I'll lead you, to be sure of you. [*Pulls him by the cravat.*]

LADY SQUEAMISH. Alas, poor man, how she tugs him! Kiss, kiss her; that's the way to make such nice women quiet.

HORNER. No, madam, that remedy is worse than the torment; they know I dare suffer anything rather than do it.

LADY SQUEAMISH. Prithee kiss her, and I'll give you her picture in little, that you admired so last night; prithee do.

HORNER. Well, nothing but that could bribe me: I love a woman only in effigy, and good painting as much as I hate them.—I'll do't, for I could adore the devil well painted. [*Kisses* MRS. SQUEAMISH.]

MRS. SQUEAMISH. Foh, you filthy toad! nay, now I've done jesting.

LADY SQUEAMISH. Ha! ha I ha! I told you so.

MRS. SQUEAMISH. Foh! a kiss of his—

SIR JASPER. Has no more hurt in't than one of my spaniel's.

MRS. SQUEAMISH. Nor no more good neither.

QUACK. I will now believe anything he tells me. [*Aside.*]

Enter PINCHWIFE.

LADY FIDGET. O lord, here's a man! Sir Jasper, my mask, my mask! I would not be seen here for the world.

SIR JASPER. What, not when I am with you?

LADY FIDGET. No, no, my honour—let's be gone.

MRS. SQUEAMISH. Oh grandmother, let's be gone; make haste, make haste, I know not how he may censure us.

LADY FIDGET. Be found in the lodging of anything like a man!—Away. [*Exeunt* SIR JASPER FIDGET, LADY FIDGET, OLD LADY SQUEAMISH, *and* MRS. SQUEAMISH.]

QUACK. What's here? another cuckold? he looks like one, and none else sure have any business with him. [*Aside.*]

HORNER. Well, what brings my dear friend hither?

PINCHWIFE. Your impertinency.

HORNER. My impertinency!—why, you gentlemen that have got handsome wives, think you have a privilege of saying anything to your friends, and are as brutish as if you were our creditors.

PINCHWIFE. No, sir, I'll ne'er trust you any way.

HORNER. But why not, dear Jack? why diffide in me thou know'st so well?

PINCHWIFE. Because I do know you so well.

HORNER. Han't I been always thy friend, honest Jack, always ready to serve thee, in love or battle, before thou wert married, and am so still?

PINCHWIFE. I believe so, you would be my second now, indeed.

HORNER. Well then, dear Jack, why so unkind, so grum, so strange to me? Come, prithee kiss me, dear rogue: gad I was always, I say, and am still as much thy servant as—

PINCHWIFE. As I am yours, sir. What, you would send a kiss to my wife, is that it?

HORNER. So, there 'tis—a man can't show his friendship to a married man, but presently he talks of his wife to you. Prithee, let thy wife alone, and let thee and I be all one, as we were wont. What, thou art as shy of my kindness, as a Lombard-street alderman of a courtier's civility at Locket's!

PINCHWIFE. But you are over-kind to me, as kind as if I were your cuckold already; yet I must confess you ought to be kind and civil to me, since I am so kind, so civil to you, as to bring you this: look you there, sir. [*Delivers him a letter.*]

HORNER. What is't?

PINCHWIFE. Only a love-letter, sir.

HORNER. From whom?—how! this is from your wife—hum—and hum—[*Reads.*]

PINCHWIFE. Even from my wife, sir: am I not wondrous kind and civil to you now too?—[*Aside.*] But you'll not think her so.

HORNER. Ha! is this a trick of his or hers? [*Aside.*]

PINCHWIFE. The gentleman's surprised I find.—What, you expected a kinder letter?

HORNER. No faith, not I, how could I?

PINCHWIFE. Yes, yes, I'm sure you did. A man so well made as you are, must needs be disappointed, if the women declare not their passion at first sight or opportunity.

HORNER. [*Aside.*] But what should this mean? Stay, the postscript.—[*Reads aside.*] *Be sure you love me, whatsoever my husband says to the contrary, and let him not see this, lest he should come home and pinch me, or kill my squirrel.*—It seems he knows not what the letter contains.

PINCHWIFE. Come, ne'er wonder at it so much.

HORNER. Faith, I can't help it.

PINCHWIFE. Now, I think I have deserved your infinite friendship and kindness, and have showed myself sufficiently an obliging kind friend and husband; am I not so, to bring a letter from my wife to her gallant?

HORNER. Ay, the devil take me, art thou, the most obliging, kind friend and husband in the world, ha! ha!

PINCHWIFE. Well, you may be merry, sir; but in short I must tell you, sir, my honour will suffer no jesting.

HORNER. What dost thou mean?

PINCHWIFE. Does the letter want a comment? Then, know, sir, though I have been so civil a husband, as to bring you a letter from my wife, to let you kiss and court her to my face, I will not be a cuckold, sir, I will not.

HORNER. Thou art mad with jealousy. I never saw thy wife in my life but at the play yesterday, and I know not if it were she or no. I court her, kiss her!

PINCHWIFE. I will not be a cuckold, I say; there will be danger in making me a cuckold.

HORNER. Why, wert thou not well cured of thy last clap?

PINCHWIFE. I wear a sword.

HORNER. It should be taken from thee, lest thou shouldst do thyself a mischief with it; thou art mad, man.

PINCHWIFE. As mad as I am, and as merry as you are, I must have more reason from you ere we part. I say again, though you kissed and courted last night my wife in man's clothes, as she confesses in her letter—

HORNER. Ha! [*Aside.*]

PINCHWIFE. Both she and I say, you must not design it again, for you have mistaken your woman, as you have done your man.

HORNER. [*Aside.*] O—I understand something now—[*Aloud.*] Was that thy wife! Why wouldst thou not tell me 'twas she? Faith, my freedom with her was your fault, not mine.

PINCHWIFE. Faith, so 'twas. [*Aside.*]

HORNER. Fy! I'd never do't to a woman before her husband's face, sure.

PINCHWIFE. But I had rather you should do't to my wife before my face, than behind my back; and that you shall never do.

HORNER. No—you will hinder me.

PINCHWIFE. If I would not hinder you, you see by her letter she would.

HORNER. Well, I must e'en acquiesce then, and be contented with what she writes.

PINCHWIFE. I'll assure you 'twas voluntarily writ; I had no hand in't you may believe me.

HORNER. I do believe thee, faith.

PINCHWIFE. And believe her too, for she's an innocent creature, has no dissembling in her: and so fare you well, sir.

HORNER. Pray, however, present my humble service to her, and tell her, I will obey her letter to a tittle, and fulfil her desires, be what they will, or with what difficulty soever I do't; and you shall be no more jealous of me, I warrant her, and you.

PINCHWIFE. Well then, fare you well; and play with any man's honour but mine, kiss any man's wife but mine, and welcome. [*Exit.*]

HORNER. Ha! ha! ha! doctor.

QUACK. It seems, he has not heard the report of you, or does not believe it.

HORNER. Ha! ha!—now, doctor, what think you?

QUACK. Pray let's see the letter—hum—*for—dear—love you*—[*Reads the letter.*]

HORNER. I wonder how she could contrive it! What say'st thou to't? 'tis an original.

QUACK. So are your cuckolds too originals: for they are like no other common cuckolds, and I will henceforth believe it not impossible for you to cuckold the Grand Signior amidst his guards of eunuchs, that I say.

HORNER. And I say for the letter, 'tis the first love-letter that ever was without flames, darts, fates, destinies, lying and dissembling in't.

Enter SPARKISH *pulling in* MR. PINCHWIFE.

SPARKISH. Come back, you are a pretty brother-in-law, neither go to church nor to dinner with your sister bride!

PINCHWIFE. My sister denies her marriage, and you see is gone away from you dissatisfied.

SPARKISH. Pshaw! upon a foolish scruple, that our parson was not in lawful orders, and did not say all the common-prayer; but 'tis her modesty only, I believe. But let all women be never so modest the first day, they'll be sure to come to themselves by night, and I shall have enough of her then. In the mean time,

Harry Horner, you must dine with me: I keep my wedding at my aunt's in the Piazza.[1]

HORNER. Thy wedding! what stale maid has lived to despair of a husband, or what young one of a gallant?

SPARKISH. O, your servant, sir—this gentleman's sister then,—no stale maid.

HORNER. I'm sorry for't.

PINCHWIFE. How comes he so concerned for her? [*Aside.*]

SPARKISH. You sorry for't? why, do you know any ill by her?

HORNER. No, I know none but by thee; 'tis for her sake, not yours, and another man's sake that might have hoped, I thought.

SPARKISH. Another man! another man! what is his name?

HORNER. Nay, since 'tis past, he shall be nameless.—[*Aside.*] Poor Harcourt! I am sorry thou hast missed her.

PINCHWIFE. He seems to be much troubled at the match. [*Aside.*]

SPARKISH. Prithee, tell me—Nay, you shan't go, brother.

PINCHWIFE. I must of necessity, but I'll come to you to dinner. [*Exit.*]

SPARKISH. But, Harry, what, have I a rival in my wife already? But with all my heart, for he may be of use to me hereafter; for though my hunger is now my sauce, and I can fall on heartily without, the time will come, when a rival will be as good sauce for a married man to a wife, as an orange to veal.

HORNER. O thou damned rogue! thou hast set my teeth on edge with thy orange.

SPARKISH. Then let's to dinner—there I was with you again. Come.

HORNER. But who dines with thee?

SPARKISH. My friends and relations, my brother Pinchwife, you see, of your acquaintance.

HORNER. And his wife?

SPARKISH. No, 'gad, he'll ne'er let her come amongst us good fellows; your stingy country coxcomb keeps his wife from his friends, as he does his little firkin of ale, for his own drinking, and a gentleman can't get a smack on't; but his servants, when his back is turned, broach it at their pleasures, and dust it away, ha! ha! ha!—'Gad, I am witty, I think, considering I was married to-day, by the world; but come—

HORNER. No, I will not dine with you, unless you can fetch her too.

SPARKISH. Pshaw! what pleasure canst thou have with women now, Harry?

HORNER. My eyes are not gone; I love a good prospect yet, and will not dine with you unless she does too; go fetch her, therefore, but do not tell her husband 'tis for my sake.

---

1 The Piazza at Covent Garden housed various businesses, coffee houses, and the only two theatres in London. Aristocrats and other distinguished people resided there.

SPARKISH. Well, I'll go try what I can do; in the meantime, come away to my aunt's lodging, 'tis in the way to Pinchwife's.

HORNER. The poor woman has called for aid, and stretched forth her hand, doctor; I cannot but help her over the pale out of the briars. [*Exeunt.*]

SCENE IV.—*A Room in* PINCHWIFE'S *House.*

MRS. PINCHWIFE *alone, leaning on her elbow.—A Table, Pen, Ink and Paper.*

MRS. PINCHWIFE. Well, 'tis e'en so, I have got the London disease they call love; I am sick of my husband, and for my gallant. I have heard this distemper called a fever, but methinks 'tis like an ague; for when I think of my husband, I tremble, and am in a cold sweat, and have inclinations to vomit; but when I think of my gallant, dear Mr. Horner, my hot fit comes, and I am all in a fever indeed; and, as in other fevers, my own chamber is tedious to me, and I would fain be removed to his, and then methinks I should be well. Ah, poor Mr. Horner! Well, I cannot, will not stay here; therefore I'll make an end of my letter to him, which shall be a finer letter than my last, because I have studied it like anything. Oh sick, sick! [*Takes the pen and writes.*]

Enter PINCHWIFE, *who seeing her writing, steals softly behind her and looking over her shoulder, snatches the paper from her.*

PINCHWIFE. What, writing more letters?

MRS. PINCHWIFE. O Lord, bud, why d'ye fright me so? [*She offers to run out; he stops her, and reads.*]

PINCHWIFE. How's this? nay, you shall not stir, madam:—*Dear, dear, dear Mr. Horner*—very well—I have taught you to write letters to good purpose—but let us see't.

First, I am to beg your pardon for my boldness in writing to you, which I'd have you to know I would not have done, had not you said first you loved me so extremely, which if you do, you will never suffer me to lie in the arms of another man whom I loathe, nauseate, and detest.—Now you can't write these filthy words? But what follows?—*Therefore, I hope you will speedily find some way to free me from this unfortunate match, which was never, I assure you, of my choice, but I'm afraid 'tis already too far gone; however, if you love me, as I do you, you will try what you can do: but you must help me away before to-morrow, or else, alas! I shall be for ever out of your reach, for I can defer no longer our—our—what is to follow* our?—speak, what—our journey into the country I suppose—Oh woman, damned woman! and Love, damned Love, their old tempter! for this is one of his miracles; in a moment he can make those blind that could see, and those see that were blind, those dumb that could speak, and those prattle who were dumb before; nay, what is more than all, make these dough-baked, senseless, indocile animals, women, too hard for us their politic lords and rulers, in a moment. But make an end of your letter, and then I'll make an end of you thus, and all my plagues together. [*Draws his sword.*]

MRS. PINCHWIFE. O Lord, O Lord, you are such a passionate man, bud!

Enter SPARKISH.

SPARKISH. How now, what's here to do?

PINCHWIFE. This fool here now!

SPARKISH. What! drawn upon your wife? You should never do that, but at night in the dark, when you can't hurt her. This is my sister-in-law, is it not? ay, faith, e'en our country Margery; [*Pulls aside her handkerchief*] one may know her. Come, she and you must go dine with me; dinner's ready, come. But where's my wife? is she not come home yet? where is she?

PINCHWIFE. Making you a cuckold; 'tis that they all do, as soon as they can.

SPARKISH. What, the wedding-day? no, a wife that designs to make a cully of her husband will be sure to let him win the first stake of love, by the world. But come, they stay dinner for us: come, I'll lead down our Margery.

PINCHWIFE. No—sir, go, we'll follow you.

SPARKISH. I will not wag without you.

PINCHWIFE. This coxcomb is a sensible torment to me amidst the greatest in the world. [*Aside.*]

SPARKISH. Come, come, madam Margery.

PINCHWIFE. No; I'll lead her my way: what, would you treat your friends with mine, for want of your own wife?—[*Leads her to the other door, and locks her in and returns.*] I am contented my rage should take breath—[*Aside.*]

SPARKISH. I told Horner this.

PINCHWIFE. Come now.

SPARKISH. Lord, how shy you are of your wife! but let me tell you, brother, we men of wit have amongst us a saying, that cuckolding, like the small-pox, comes with a fear; and you may keep your wife as much as you will out of danger of infection, but if her constitution incline her to't, she'll have it sooner or later, by the world, say they.

PINCHWIFE. [*Aside.*] What a thing is a cuckold, that every fool can make him ridiculous!—[*Aloud.*] Well, sir—but let me advise you, now you are come to be concerned, because you suspect the danger, not to neglect the means to prevent it, especially when the greatest share of the malady will light upon your own head, for

> Hows'e'er the kind wife's belly comes to swell,
> The husband breeds for her, and first is ill. [*Exeunt.*]

ACT V.

SCENE I.—MR. PINCHWIFE'S *House.*

Enter MR. PINCHWIFE *and* MRS. PINCHWIFE—*A Table and Candle.*

PINCHWIFE. Come, take the pen and make an end of the letter, just as you intended; if you are false in a tittle, I shall soon perceive it, and punish you as you deserve.—[*Lays his hand on his sword.*] Write what was to follow—let's see—*You must make haste, and help me away before to-morrow, or else I shall be for ever out of your reach, for I can defer no longer our*—What follows *our?*

MRS. PINCHWIFE. Must all out, then, bud?—Look you there, then. [MRS. PINCHWIFE *takes the pen and writes.*]

PINCHWIFE. Let's see—*For I can defer no longer our*—*wedding*—*Your slighted* ALITHEA.—What's the meaning of this? my sister's name to't? speak, unriddle.

MRS. PINCHWIFE. Yes, indeed, bud.

PINCHWIFE. But why her name to't? speak—speak, I say.

MRS. PINCHWIFE. Ay, but you'll tell her then again. If you would not tell her again—

PINCHWIFE. I will not:—I am stunned, my head turns round.—Speak.

MRS. PINCHWIFE. Won't you tell her, indeed, and indeed?

PINCHWIFE. No; speak, I say.

MRS. PINCHWIFE. She'll be angry with me; but I had rather she should be angry with me than you, bud. And, to tell you the truth, 'twas she made me write the letter, and taught me what I should write.

PINCHWIFE. [*Aside.*] Ha!—I thought the style was somewhat better than her own.—[*Aloud.*] Could she come to you to teach you, since I had locked you up alone?

MRS. PINCHWIFE. O, through the key-hole, bud.

PINCHWIFE. But why should she make you write a letter for her to him, since she can write herself?

MRS. PINCHWIFE. Why, she said because—for I was unwilling to do it.

PINCHWIFE. Because what—because?

MRS. PINCHWIFE. Because, lest Mr. Horner should be cruel, and refuse her; or be vain afterwards, and show the letter, she might disown it, the hand not being hers.

PINCHWIFE. [*Aside.*] How's this? Ha!—then I think I shall come to myself again.— This changeling could not invent this lie: but if she could, why should she? she might think I should soon discover it.—Stay—now I think on't too, Horner said he was sorry she had married Sparkish; and her disowning her marriage to me makes me think she has evaded it for Horner's sake: yet why should she take this course? But men in love are fools; women may well be so—[*Aloud.*] But hark you, madam, your sister went out in the morning, and I have not seen her within since.

MRS. PINCHWIFE. Alack-a-day, she has been crying all day above, it seems, in a corner.

PINCHWIFE. Where is she? let me speak with her.

MRS. PINCHWIFE. [*Aside.*] O Lord, then she'll discover all!—[*Aloud.*] Pray hold, bud; what, d'ye mean to discover me? she'll know I have told you then. Pray, bud, let me talk with her first.

PINCHWIFE. I must speak with her, to know whether Horner ever made her any promise, and whether she be married to Sparkish or no.

MRS. PINCHWIFE. Pray, dear bud, don't, till I have spoken with her, and told her that I have told you all; for she'll kill me else.

PINCHWIFE. Go then, and bid her come out to me.

MRS. PINCHWIFE. Yes, yes, bud.

PINCHWIFE. Let me see—[*Pausing.*]

MRS. PINCHWIFE. [*Aside.*] I'll go, but she is not within to come to him: I have just got time to know of Lucy her maid, who first set me on work, what lie I shall tell next; for I am e'en at my wit's end. [*Exit.*]

PINCHWIFE. Well, I resolve it, Horner shall have her: I'd rather give him my sister than lend him my wife; and such an alliance will prevent his pretensions to my wife, sure. I'll make him of kin to her, and then he won't care for her.

Re-enter MRS. PINCHWIFE.

MRS. PINCHWIFE. O Lord, bud! I told you what anger you would make me with my sister.

PINCHWIFE. Won't she come hither?

MRS. PINCHWIFE. No, no. Lack-a-day, she's ashamed to look you in the face; and she says, if you go in to her, she'll run away down stairs, and shamefully go

herself to Mr. Horner, who has promised her marriage, she says; and she will
have no other, so she won't.

PINCHWIFE. Did he so?—promise her marriage!—then she shall have no other. Go
tell her so; and if she will come and discourse with me a little concerning the
means, I will about it immediately. Go.—[*Exit* MRS. PINCHWIFE.] His estate
is equal to Sparkish's, and his extraction as much better than his, as his parts
are; but my chief reason is, I'd rather be akin to him by the name of brother-
in-law than that of cuckold.

Re-enter MRS. PINCHWIFE.

Well, what says she now?

MRS. PINCHWIFE. Why, she says, she would only have you lead her to Horner's
lodging; with whom she first will discourse the matter before she talks with
you, which yet she cannot do; for alack, poor creature, she says she can't so
much as look you in the face, therefore she'll come to you in a mask. And you
must excuse her, if she make you no answer to any question of yours, till you
have brought her to Mr. Horner; and if you will not chide her, nor question
her, she'll come out to you immediately.

PINCHWIFE. Let her come: I will not speak a word to her, nor require a word
from her.

MRS. PINCHWIFE. Oh, I forgot: besides she says, she cannot look you in the face,
though through a mask; therefore would desire you to put out the candle.

PINCHWIFE. I agree to all. Let her make haste.—There, 'tis out—[*Puts out the
candle. Exit* MRS. PINCHWIFE.] My case is something better: I'd rather fight
with Horner for not lying with my sister, than for lying with my wife; and of
the two, I had rather find my sister too forward than my wife. I expected no
other from her free education, as she calls it, and her passion for the town.
Well, wife and sister are names which make us expect love and duty, pleasure
and comfort; but we find 'em plagues and torments, and are equally, though
differently, troublesome to their keeper; for we have as much ado to get people
to lie with our sisters as to keep 'em from lying with our wives.

Re-enter MRS. PINCHWIFE *masked, and in hoods and scarfs, and a night-
gown and petticoat of* ALITHEA's.

What, are you come, sister? let us go then.—But first, let me lock up my wife.
Mrs. Margery, where are you?

MRS. PINCHWIFE. Here, bud.

PINCHWIFE. Come hither, that I may lock you up: get you in.—[*Locks the door.*]
Come, sister, where are you now? [MRS. PINCHWIFE *gives him her hand; but
when he lets her go, she steals softly on to the other side of him, and is led away by
him for his sister,* ALITHEA.]

SCENE II.—HORNER's *Lodging.*

HORNER *and* QUACK.

QUACK. What, all alone? not so much as one of your cuckolds here, nor one of their wives! They use to take their turns with you, as if they were to watch you.

HORNER. Yes, it often happens that a cuckold is but his wife's spy, and is more upon family duty when he is with her gallant abroad, hindering his pleasure, than when he is at home with her playing the gallant. But the hardest duty a married woman imposes upon a lover is keeping her husband company always.

QUACK. And his fondness wearies you almost as soon as hers.

HORNER. A pox! keeping a cuckold company, after you have had his wife, is as tiresome as the company of a country squire to a witty fellow of the town, when he has got all his money.

QUACK. And as at first a man makes a friend of the husband to get the wife, so at last you are fain to fall out with the wife to be rid of the husband.

HORNER. Ay, most cuckold-makers are true courtiers; when once a poor man has cracked his credit for 'em, they can't abide to come near him.

QUACK. But at first, to draw him in, are so sweet, so kind, so dear! just as you are to Pinchwife. But what becomes of that intrigue with his wife?

HORNER. A pox! he's as surly as an alderman that has been bit; and since he's so coy, his wife's kindness is in vain, for she's a silly innocent.

QUACK. Did she not send you a letter by him?

HORNER. Yes; but that's a riddle I have not yet solved. Allow the poor creature to be willing, she is silly too, and he keeps her up so close—

QUACK. Yes, so close, that he makes her but the more willing, and adds but revenge to her love; which two, when met, seldom fail of satisfying each other one way or other.

HORNER. What! here's the man we are talking of, I think.

Enter MR. PINCHWIFE, *leading in his Wife masked, muffled, and in her Sister's gown.*

Pshaw!

QUACK. Bringing his wife to you is the next thing to bringing a love-letter from her.

HORNER. What means this?

PINCHWIFE. The last time, you know, sir, I brought you a love-letter; now, you see, a mistress; I think you'll say I am a civil man to you.

HORNER. Ay, the devil take me, will I say thou art the civilest man I ever met with; and I have known some. I fancy I understand thee now better than I did the letter. But, hark thee, in thy ear—

PINCHWIFE. What?

HORNER. Nothing but the usual question, man: is she sound, on thy word?

PINCHWIFE. What, you take her for a wench, and me for a pimp?

HORNER. Pshaw! wench and pimp, paw words; I know thou art an honest fellow, and hast a great acquaintance among the ladies, and perhaps hast made love for me, rather than let me make love to thy wife.

PINCHWIFE. Come, sir, in short, I am for no fooling.

HORNER. Nor I neither: therefore prithee, let's see her face presently. Make her show, man: art thou sure I don't know her?

PINCHWIFE. I am sure you do know her.

HORNER. A pox! why dost thou bring her to me then?

PINCHWIFE. Because she's a relation of mine—

HORNER. Is she, faith, man? then thou art still more civil and obliging, dear rogue.

PINCHWIFE. Who desired me to bring her to you.

HORNER. Then she is obliging, dear rogue.

PINCHWIFE. You'll make her welcome for my sake, I hope.

HORNER. I hope she is handsome enough to make herself welcome. Prithee let her unmask.

PINCHWIFE. Do you speak to her; she would never be ruled by me.

HORNER. Madam—[MRS. PINCHWIFE *whispers to* HORNER.] She says she must speak with me in private. Withdraw, prithee.

PINCHWIFE. [*Aside.*] She's unwilling, it seems, I should know all her undecent conduct in this business—[*Aloud.*] Well then, I'll leave you together, and hope when I am gone, you'll agree; if not, you and I shan't agree, sir.

HORNER. What means the fool? if she and I agree 'tis no matter what you and I do. [*Whispers to* MRS. PINCHWIFE, *who makes signs with her hand for him to be gone.*]

PINCHWIFE. In the mean time I'll fetch a parson, and find out Sparkish, and disabuse him. You would have me fetch a parson, would you not? Well then—now I think I am rid of her, and shall have no more trouble with her—our sisters and daughters, like usurers' money, are safest when put out; but our wives, like their writings, never safe, but in our closets under lock and key. [*Exit.*]

Enter BOY.

BOY. Sir Jasper Fidget, sir, is coming up. [*Exit.*]

HORNER. Here's the trouble of a cuckold now we are talking of. A pox on him! has he not enough to do to hinder his wife's sport, but he must other women's too?—Step in here, madam. [*Exit* MRS. PINCHWIFE.]

Enter SIR JASPER FIDGET.

SIR JASPER. My best and dearest friend.

HORNER. [*Aside to* QUACK.] The old style, doctor.—[*Aloud.*] Well, be short, for I am busy. What would your impertinent wife have now?

SIR JASPER. Well guessed, i'faith; for I do come from her.

HORNER. To invite me to supper! Tell her, I can't come: go.

SIR JASPER. Nay, now you are out, faith; for my lady, and the whole knot of the virtuous gang, as they call themselves, are resolved upon a frolic of coming to you to-night in masquerade, and are all dressed already.

HORNER. I shan't be at home.

SIR JASPER. [*Aside.*] Lord, how churlish he is to women!—[*Aloud.*] Nay, prithee don't disappoint 'em; they'll think 'tis my fault: prithee don't. I'll send in the banquet and the fiddles. But make no noise on't; for the poor virtuous rogues would not have it known, for the world, that they go a-masquerading; and they would come to no man's ball but yours.

HORNER. Well, well—get you gone; and tell 'em, if they come, 'twill be at the peril of their honour and yours.

SIR JASPER. He! he! he!—we'll trust you for that: farewell. [*Exit.*]

HORNER. Doctor, anon you too shall be my guest,

But now I'm going to a private feast. [*Exeunt.*]

SCENE III.—*The Piazza of Covent Garden.*

Enter SPARKISH *with a letter in his hand,* MR. PINCHWIFE *following.*

SPARKISH. But who would have thought a woman could have been false to me? By the world, I could not have thought it.

PINCHWIFE. You were for giving and taking liberty: she has taken it only, sir, now you find in that letter. You are a frank person, and so is she, you see there.

SPARKISH. Nay, if this be her hand—for I never saw it.

PINCHWIFE. 'Tis no matter whether that be her hand or no; I am sure this hand, at her desire, led her to Mr. Horner, with whom I left her just now, to go fetch a parson to 'em at their desire too, to deprive you of her for ever; for it seems yours was but a mock marriage.

SPARKISH. Indeed, she would needs have it that 'twas Harcourt himself, in a parson's habit, that married us; but I'm sure he told me 'twas his brother Ned.

PINCHWIFE. O, there 'tis out; and you were deceived, not she: for you are such a frank person. But I must be gone.—You'll find her at Mr. Horner's. Go, and believe your eyes. [*Exit.*]

SPARKISH. Nay, I'll to her, and call her as many crocodiles, sirens, harpies, and other heathenish names, as a poet would do a mistress who had refused to hear his suit, nay more, his verses on her.—But stay, is not that she following a torch at t'other end of the Piazza? and from Horner's certainly—'tis so.

Enter ALITHEA *following a torch, and* LUCY *behind.*

You are well met, madam, though you don't think so. What, you have made a short visit to Mr. Horner? but I suppose you'll return to him presently, by that time the parson can be with him.

ALITHEA. Mr. Horner and the parson, sir!

SPARKISH. Come, madam, no more dissembling, no more jilting; for I am no more a frank person.

ALITHEA. How's this?

LUCY. So, 'twill work, I see. [*Aside.*]

SPARKISH. Could you find out no easy country fool to abuse? none but me, a gentleman of wit and pleasure about the town? But it was your pride to be too hard for a man of parts, unworthy false woman! false as a friend that lends a man money to lose; false as dice, who undo those that trust all they have to 'em.

LUCY. He has been a great bubble, by his similes, as they say. [*Aside.*]

ALITHEA. You have been too merry, sir, at your wedding-dinner, sure.

SPARKISH. What, d'ye mock me too?

ALITHEA. Or you have been deluded.

SPARKISH. By you.

ALITHEA. Let me understand you.

SPARKISH. Have you the confidence, (I should call it something else, since you know your guilt,) to stand my just reproaches? you did not write an impudent letter to Mr. Horner? who I find now has clubbed with you in deluding me with his aversion for women, that I might not, forsooth, suspect him for my rival.

LUCY. D'ye think the gentleman can be jealous now, madam? [*Aside.*]

ALITHEA. I write a letter to Mr. Horner!

SPARKISH. Nay, madam, do not deny it. Your brother showed it me just now; and told me likewise, he left you at Horner's lodging to fetch a parson to marry you to him; and I wish you joy, madam, joy, joy; and to him too, much joy; and to myself more joy, for not marrying you.

ALITHEA. [*Aside.*] So, I find my brother would break off the match; and I can consent to't, since I see this gentleman can be made jealous.—[*Aloud.*] O Lucy, by his rude usage and jealousy, he makes me almost afraid I am married to him. Art thou sure 'twas Harcourt himself, and no parson, that married us?

SPARKISH. No, madam, I thank you. I suppose, that was a contrivance too of Mr. Horner's and yours, to make Harcourt play the parson; but I would as little as you have him one now, no, not for the world. For, shall I tell you another truth? I never had any passion for you till now, for now I hate you. 'Tis true, I might have married your portion, as other men of parts of the town do sometimes; and so, your servant. And to show my unconcernedness, I'll come to your wedding, and resign you with as much joy, as I would a stale wench to a new cully; nay, with as much joy as I would after the first night, if I had been married to you. There's for you; and so your servant, servant. [*Exit.*]

ALITHEA. How was I deceived in a man!

LUCY. You'll believe then a fool may be made jealous now? for that easiness in him that suffers him to be led by a wife, will likewise permit him to be persuaded against her by others.

ALITHEA. But marry Mr. Horner! my brother does not intend it, sure: if I thought he did, I would take thy advice, and Mr. Harcourt for my husband. And now I wish, that if there be any over-wise woman of the town, who, like me, would marry a fool for fortune, liberty, or title, first, that her husband may love play, and be a cully to all the town but her, and suffer none but Fortune to be mistress of his purse; then, if for liberty, that he may send her into the country, under the conduct of some huswifely mother-in-law; and if for title, may the world give 'em none but that of cuckold.

LUCY. And for her greater curse, madam, may he not deserve it.

ALITHEA. Away, impertinent! Is not this my old lady Lanterlu's?[1]

LUCY. Yes, madam.—[*Aside.*] And here I hope we shall find Mr. Harcourt. [*Exeunt.*]

SCENE IV.—HORNER's *Lodging. A Table, Banquet, and Bottles.*

Enter HORNER, LADY FIDGET, MRS. DAINTY FIDGET, *and* MRS. SQUEAMISH.

HORNER. A pox! they are come too soon—before I have sent back my new mistress. All that I have now to do is to lock her in, that they may not see her. [*Aside.*]

LADY FIDGET. That we may be sure of our welcome, we have brought our entertainment with us, and are resolved to treat thee, dear toad.

MRS. DAINTY. And that we may be merry to purpose, have left sir Jasper and my old lady Squeamish, quarrelling at home at backgammon.

MRS. SQUEAMISH. Therefore let us make use of our time, lest they should chance to interrupt us.

LADY FIDGET. Let us sit then.

---

1 A card game.

HORNER. First, that you may be private, let me lock this door and that, and I'll wait upon you presently.

LADY FIDGET. No, sir, shut 'em only, and your lips for ever; for we must trust you as much as our women.

HORNER. You know all vanity's killed in me; I have no occasion for talking.

LADY FIDGET. Now, ladies, supposing we had drank each of us our two bottles, let us speak the truth of our hearts.

MRS. DAINTY *and* MRS. SQUEAMISH. Agreed.

LADY FIDGET. By this brimmer, for truth is nowhere else to be found—[*Aside to* HORNER.] not in thy heart, false man!

HORNER. You have found me a true man, I'm sure. [*Aside to* LADY FIDGET.]

LADY FIDGET. [*Aside to* HORNER.] Not every way.—But let us sit and be merry. [*Sings.*]
Why should our damn'd tyrants oblige us to live
On the pittance of pleasure which they only give?
   We must not rejoice
   With wine and with noise:
In vain we must wake in a dull bed alone,
Whilst to our warm rival the bottle they're gone.
   Then lay aside charms,
   And take up these arms.[2]
'Tis wine only gives 'em their courage and wit;
Because we live sober, to men we submit.
   If for beauties you'd pass,
   Take a lick of the glass,
'Twill mend your complexions, and when they are gone,
The best red we have is the red of the grape:
   Then, sisters, lay't on,
   And damn a good shape.

MRS. DAINTY. Dear brimmer! Well, in token of our openness and plain-dealing, let us throw our masks over our heads.

HORNER. So, 'twill come to the glasses anon. [*Aside.*]

MRS. SQUEAMISH. Lovely brimmer! let me enjoy him first.

LADY FIDGET. No, I never part with a gallant till I've tried him. Dear brimmer! that makest our husbands short-sighted.

MRS. DAINTY. And our bashful gallants bold.

MRS. SQUEAMISH. And, for want of a gallant, the butler lovely in our eyes.— Drink, eunuch.

---

2 The glasses.

LADY FIDGET. Drink, thou representative of a husband.—Damn a husband!

MRS. DAINTY. And, as it were a husband, an old keeper.

MRS. SQUEAMISH. And an old grandmother.

HORNER. And an English bawd, and a French surgeon.

LADY FIDGET. Ay, we have all reason to curse 'em.

HORNER. For my sake, ladies?

LADY FIDGET. No, for our own; for the first spoils all young gallants' industry.

MRS. DAINTY. And the other's art makes 'em bold only with common women.

MRS. SQUEAMISH. And rather run the hazard of the vile distemper amongst them, than of a denial amongst us.

MRS. DAINTY. The filthy toads choose mistresses now as they do stuffs, for having been fancied and worn by others.

MRS. SQUEAMISH. For being common and cheap.

LADY FIDGET. Whilst women of quality, like the richest stuffs, lie untumbled, and unasked for.

HORNER. Ay, neat, and cheap, and new, often they think best.

MRS. DAINTY. No, sir, the beasts will be known by a mistress longer than by a suit.

MRS. SQUEAMISH. And 'tis not for cheapness neither.

LADY FIDGET. No; for the vain fops will take up druggets, and embroider 'em. But I wonder at the depraved appetites of witty men; they use to be out of the common road, and hate imitation. Pray tell me, beast, when you were a man, why you rather chose to club with a multitude in a common house for an entertainment, than to be the only guest at a good table.

HORNER. Why, faith, ceremony and expectation are unsufferable to those that are sharp bent. People always eat with the best stomach at an ordinary, where every man is snatching for the best bit.

LADY FIDGET. Though he get a cut over the fingers.—But I have heard, that people eat most heartily of another man's meat, that is, what they do not pay for.

HORNER. When they are sure of their welcome and freedom; for ceremony in love and eating is as ridiculous as in fighting: falling on briskly is all should be done on those occasions.

LADY FIDGET. Well then, let me tell you, sir, there is nowhere more freedom than in our houses; and we take freedom from a young person as a sign of good breeding; and a person may be as free as he pleases with us, as frolic, as gamesome, as wild as he will.

HORNER. Han't I heard you all declaim against wild men?

LADY FIDGET. Yes; but for all that, we think wildness in a man as desirable a quality as in a duck or rabbit: a tame man! foh!

HORNER. I know not, but your reputations frightened me as much as your faces invited me.

LADY FIDGET. Our reputation! Lord, why should you not think that we women make use of our reputation, as you men of yours, only to deceive the world with less suspicion? Our virtue is like the statesman's religion, the quaker's word, the gamester's oath, and the great man's honour; but to cheat those that trust us.

MRS. SQUEAMISH. And that demureness, coyness, and modesty, that you see in our faces in the boxes at plays, is as much a sign of a kind woman, as a vizard-mask in the pit.

MRS. DAINTY. For, I assure you, women are least masked when they have the velvet vizard on.

LADY FIDGET. You would have found us modest women in our denials only.

MRS. SQUEAMISH. Our bashfulness is only the reflection of the men's.

MRS. DAINTY. We blush when they are shamefaced.

HORNER. I beg your pardon, ladies, I was deceived in you devilishly. But why that mighty pretence to honour?

LADY FIDGET. We have told you; but sometimes 'twas for the same reason you men pretend business often, to avoid ill company, to enjoy the better and more privately those you love.

HORNER. But why would you ne'er give a friend a wink then?

LADY FIDGET. Faith, your reputation frightened us, as much as ours did you, you were so notoriously lewd.

HORNER. And you so seemingly honest.

LADY FIDGET. Was that all that deterred you?

HORNER. And so expensive—you allow freedom, you say.

LADY FIDGET. Ay, ay.

HORNER. That I was afraid of losing my little money, as well as my little time, both which my other pleasures required.

LADY FIDGET. Money! foh! you talk like a little fellow now: do such as we expect money?

HORNER. I beg your pardon, madam, I must confess, I have heard that great ladies, like great merchants, set but the higher prices upon what they have, because they are not in necessity of taking the first offer.

MRS. DAINTY. Such as we make sale of our hearts?

MRS. SQUEAMISH. We bribed for our love? foh!

HORNER. With your pardon ladies, I know, like great men in offices, you seem to exact flattery and attendance only from your followers; but you have receivers about you, and such fees to pay, a man is afraid to pass your grants. Besides, we must let you win at cards, or we lose your hearts; and if you make an assignation, 'tis at a goldsmith's, jeweller's, or china-house; where for your honour you deposit to him, he must pawn his to the punctual cit, and so paying for what you take up, pays for what he takes up.

MRS. DAINTY. Would you not have us assured of our gallants' love?

MRS. SQUEAMISH. For love is better known by liberality than by jealousy.

LADY FIDGET. For one may be dissembled, the other not.—[*Aside.*] But my jealousy can be no longer dissembled, and they are telling ripe.—[*Aloud.*]—Come, here's to our gallants in waiting, whom we must name, and I'll begin. This is my false rogue. [*Claps him on the back.*]

MRS. SQUEAMISH. How!

HORNER. So, all will out now. [*Aside.*]

MRS. SQUEAMISH. Did you not tell me, 'twas for my sake only you reported yourself no man? [*Aside to* HORNER.]

MRS. DAINTY. Oh, wretch! did you not swear to me, 'twas for my love and honour you passed for that thing you do? [*Aside to* HORNER.]

HORNER. So, so.

LADY FIDGET. Come, speak, ladies: this is my false villain.

MRS. SQUEAMISH. And mine too.

MRS. DAINTY. And mine.

HORNER. Well then, you are all three my false rogues too, and there's an end on't.

LADY FIDGET. Well then, there's no remedy; sister sharers, let us not fall out, but have a care of our honour. Though we get no presents, no jewels of him, we are savers of our honour, the jewel of most value and use, which shines yet to the world unsuspected, though it be counterfeit.

HORNER. Nay, and is e'en as good as if it were true, provided the world think so; for honour, like beauty now, only depends on the opinion of others.

LADY FIDGET. Well, Harry Common, I hope you can be true to three. Swear; but 'tis to no purpose to require your oath, for you are as often forsworn as you swear to new women.

HORNER. Come, faith, madam, let us e'en pardon one another; for all the difference I find betwixt we men and you women, we forswear ourselves at the beginning of an amour, you as long as it lasts.

Enter SIR JASPER FIDGET, *and* OLD LADY SQUEAMISH.

SIR JASPER. Oh, my lady Fidget, was this your cunning, to come to Mr. Horner without me? but you have been nowhere else, I hope.

LADY FIDGET. No, sir Jasper.

LADY SQUEAMISH. And you came straight hither, Biddy?

MRS. SQUEAMISH. Yes, indeed, lady grandmother.

SIR JASPER. 'Tis well, 'tis well; I knew when once they were thoroughly acquainted with poor Horner, they'd ne'er be from him: you may let her masquerade it with my wife and Horner, and I warrant her reputation safe.

Enter BOY.

BOY. O, sir, here's the gentleman come, whom you bid me not suffer to come up, without giving you notice, with a lady too, and other gentlemen.

HORNER. Do you all go in there, whilst I send 'em away; and, boy, do you desire 'em to stay below till I come, which shall be immediately. [*Exeunt* SIR JASPER FIDGET, LADY FIDGET, LADY SQUEAMISH, MRS. SQUEAMISH, *and* MRS. DAINTY FIDGET.]

BOY. Yes, sir. [*Exit.*]

[*Exit* HORNER *at the other door, and returns with* MRS. PINCHWIFE.]

HORNER. You would not take my advice, to be gone home before your husband came back, he'll now discover all; yet pray, my dearest, be persuaded to go home, and leave the rest to my management; I'll let you down the back way.

MRS. PINCHWIFE. I don't know the way home, so I don't.

HORNER. My man shall wait upon you.

MRS. PINCHWIFE. No, don't you believe that I'll go at all; what, are you weary of me already?

HORNER. No, my life, 'tis that I may love you long, 'tis to secure my love, and your reputation with your husband; he'll never receive you again else.

MRS. PINCHWIFE. What care I? d'ye think to frighten me with that? I don't intend to go to him again; you shall be my husband now.

HORNER. I cannot be your husband, dearest, since you are married to him.

MRS. PINCHWIFE. O, would you make me believe that? Don't I see every day at London here, women leave their first husbands, and go and live with other men as their wives? pish, pshaw! you'd make me angry, but that I love you so mainly.

HORNER. So, they are coming up—In again, in, I hear 'em.—[*Exit* MRS. PINCHWIFE.] Well, a silly mistress is like a weak place, soon got, soon lost, a man has scarce time for plunder; she betrays her husband first to her gallant, and then her gallant to her husband.

Enter PINCHWIFE, ALITHEA, HARCOURT, SPARKISH, LUCY, *and a* PARSON.

PINCHWIFE. Come, madam, 'tis not the sudden change of your dress, the confidence of your asseverations, and your false witness there, shall persuade me I did not bring you hither just now; here's my witness, who cannot deny it, since you must be confronted.—Mr. Horner, did not I bring this lady to you just now?

HORNER. Now must I wrong one woman for another's sake,—but that's no new thing with me, for in these cases I am still on the criminal's side against the innocent. [*Aside.*]

ALITHEA. Pray speak, sir.

HORNER. It must be so. I must be impudent, and try my luck; impudence uses to be too hard for truth. [*Aside.*]

PINCHWIFE. What, you are studying an evasion or excuse for her! Speak, sir.

HORNER. No, faith, I am something backward only to speak in women's affairs or disputes.

PINCHWIFE. She bids you speak.

ALITHEA. Ay, pray, sir, do, pray satisfy him.

HORNER. Then truly, you did bring that lady to me just now.

PINCHWIFE. O ho!

ALITHEA. How, sir?

HARCOURT. How, Horner?

ALITHEA. What mean you, sir? I always took you for a man of honour.

HORNER. Ay, so much a man of honour, that I must save my mistress, I thank you, come what will on't. [*Aside.*]

SPARKISH. So, if I had had her, she'd have made me believe the moon had been made of a Christmas pie.

LUCY. Now could I speak, if I durst, and solve the riddle, who am the author of it. [*Aside.*]

ALITHEA. O unfortunate woman! A combination against my honour! which most concerns me now, because you share in my disgrace, sir, and it is your censure, which I must now suffer, that troubles me, not theirs.

HARCOURT. Madam, then have no trouble, you shall now see 'tis possible for me to love too, without being jealous; I will not only believe your innocence myself, but make all the world believe it.—[*Aside to* HORNER.] Horner, I must now be concerned for his lady's honour.

HORNER. And I must be concerned for a lady's honour too.

HARCOURT. This lady has her honour, and I will protect it.

HORNER. My lady has not her honour, but has given it me to keep, and I will preserve it.

HARCOURT. I understand you not.

HORNER. I would not have you.

MRS. PINCHWIFE. What's the matter with 'em all? [*Peeping in behind.*]

PINCHWIFE. Come, come, Mr. Horner, no more disputing; here's the parson, I brought him not in vain.

HARCOURT. No, sir, I'll employ him, if this lady please.

PINCHWIFE. How! what d'ye mean?

SPARKISH. Ay, what does he mean?

HORNER. Why, I have resigned your sister to him, he has my consent.

PINCHWIFE. But he has not mine, sir: a woman's injured honour, no more than a man's, can be repaired or satisfied by any but him that first wronged it; and you shall marry her presently, or—[*Lays his hand on his sword.*]

Re-enter MRS. PINCHWIFE.

MRS. PINCHWIFE. O Lord, they'll kill poor Mr. Horner! besides, he shan't marry her whilst I stand by, and look on; I'll not lose my second husband so.

PINCHWIFE. What do I see?

ALITHEA. My sister in my clothes!

SPARKISH. Ha!

MRS. PINCHWIFE. Nay, pray now don't quarrel about finding work for the parson, he shall marry me to Mr. Horner; or now, I believe, you have enough of me. [*To* MR. PINCHWIFE.]

HORNER. Damned, damned loving changeling! [*Aside.*]

MRS. PINCHWIFE. Pray, sister, pardon me for telling so many lies of you.

HORNER. I suppose the riddle is plain now.

LUCY. No, that must be my work.—Good sir, hear me. [*Kneels to* MR. PINCHWIFE, *who stands doggedly with his hat over his eyes.*]

PINCHWIFE. I will never hear woman again, but make 'em all silent thus—[*Offers to draw upon his wife.*]

HORNER. No, that must not be.

PINCHWIFE. You then shall go first, 'tis all one to me. [*Offers to draw on* HORNER, *stopped by* HARCOURT.]

HARCOURT. Hold!

Re-enter SIR JASPER FIDGET, LADY FIDGET, LADY SQUEAMISH, MRS. DAINTY FIDGET, *and* MRS. SQUEAMISH.

SIR JASPER. What's the matter? what's the matter? pray, what's the matter, sir? I beseech you communicate, sir.

PINCHWIFE. Why, my wife has communicated, sir, as your wife may have done too, sir, if she knows him, sir.

SIR JASPER. Pshaw, with him! ha! ha! he!

PINCHWIFE. D'ye mock me, sir? a cuckold is a kind of a wild beast; have a care, sir.

SIR JASPER. No, sure, you mock me, sir. He cuckold you! it can't be, ha! ha! he! why, I'll tell you, sir—[*Offers to whisper.*]

PINCHWIFE. I tell you again, he has whored my wife, and yours too, if he knows her, and all the women he comes near; 'tis not his dissembling, his hypocrisy, can wheedle me.

SIR JASPER. How! does he dissemble? is he a hypocrite? Nay, then—how—wife—sister, is he a hypocrite?

LADY SQUEAMISH. A hypocrite! a dissembler! Speak, young harlotry, speak, how?

SIR JASPER. Nay, then—O my head too!—O thou libidinous lady!

LADY SQUEAMISH. O thou harloting harlotry! hast thou done't then?

SIR JASPER. Speak, good Horner, art thou a dissembler, a rogue? hast thou—

HORNER. So!

LUCY. I'll fetch you off, and her too, if she will but hold her tongue. [*Apart to* HORNER.]

HORNER. Canst thou? I'll give thee—[*Apart to* LUCY.]

LUCY. [*To* MR. PINCHWIFE.] Pray have but patience to hear me, sir, who am the unfortunate cause of all this confusion. Your wife is innocent, I only culpable; for I put her upon telling you all these lies concerning my mistress, in order to the breaking off the match between Mr. Sparkish and her, to make way for Mr. Harcourt.

SPARKISH. Did you so, eternal rotten tooth? Then, it seems, my mistress was not false to me, I was only deceived by you. Brother, that should have been, now man of conduct, who is a frank person now, to bring your wife to her lover, ha?

LUCY. I assure you, sir, she came not to Mr. Horner out of love, for she loves him no more—

MRS. PINCHWIFE. Hold, I told lies for you, but you shall tell none for me, for I do love Mr. Horner with all my soul, and nobody shall say me nay; pray, don't you go to make poor Mr. Horner believe to the contrary; 'tis spitefully done of you, I'm sure.

HORNER. Peace, dear idiot. [*Aside to* MRS. PINCHWIFE.]

MRS. PINCHWIFE. Nay, I will not peace.

PINCHWIFE. Not till I make you.

Enter DORILANT *and* QUACK.

DORILANT. Horner, your servant; I am the doctor's guest, he must excuse our intrusion.

QUACK. But what's the matter, gentlemen? for heaven's sake, what's the matter?

HORNER. Oh, 'tis well you are come. 'Tis a censorious world we live in; you may have brought me a reprieve, or else I had died for a crime I never committed, and these innocent ladies had suffered with me; therefore, pray satisfy these worthy, honourable, jealous gentlemen—that—[*Whispers.*]

QUACK. O, I understand you, is that all?—Sir Jasper, by heavens, and upon the word of a physician, sir—[*Whispers to* SIR JASPER.]

SIR JASPER. Nay, I do believe you truly.—Pardon me, my virtuous lady, and dear of honour.

LADY SQUEAMISH. What, then all's right again?

SIR JASPER. Ay, ay, and now let us satisfy him too. [*They whisper with* MR. PINCHWIFE.]

PINCHWIFE. An eunuch! Pray, no fooling with me.

QUACK. I'll bring half the chirurgeons in town to swear it.

PINCHWIFE. They!—they'll swear a man that bled to death through his wounds, died of an apoplexy.

QUACK. Pray, hear me, sir—why, all the town has heard the report of him.

PINCHWIFE. But does all the town believe it?

QUACK. Pray, inquire a little, and first of all these.

PINCHWIFE. I'm sure when I left the town, he was the lewdest fellow in't.

QUACK. I tell you, sir, he has been in France since; pray, ask but these ladies and gentlemen, your friend Mr. Dorilant. Gentlemen and ladies, han't you all heard the late sad report of poor Mr. Horner?

ALL THE LADIES. Ay, ay, ay.

DORILANT. Why, thou jealous fool, dost thou doubt it? he's an arrant French capon.

MRS. PINCHWIFE. 'Tis false, sir, you shall not disparage poor Mr. Horner, for to my certain knowledge—

LUCY. O, hold!

MRS. SQUEAMISH. Stop her mouth! [*Aside to* LUCY.]

LADY FIDGET. Upon my honour, sir, 'tis as true—[*To* MR. PINCHWIFE.]

MRS. DAINTY. D'ye think we would have been seen in his company?

MRS. SQUEAMISH. Trust our unspotted reputations with him?

LADY FIDGET. This you get, and we too, by trusting your secret to a fool. [*Aside to* HORNER.]

HORNER. Peace, madam.—[*Aside to* QUACK.] Well, doctor, is not this a good design, that carries a man on unsuspected, and brings him off safe?

PINCHWIFE. Well, if this were true—but my wife—[*Aside.*]

[DORILANT *whispers with* MRS. PINCHWIFE.]

ALITHEA. Come, brother, your wife is yet innocent, you see; but have a care of too strong an imagination, lest, like an over-concerned timorous gamester, by fancying an unlucky cast, it should come. Women and fortune are truest still to those that trust 'em.

LUCY. And any wild thing grows but the more fierce and hungry for being kept up, and more dangerous to the keeper.

ALITHEA. There's doctrine for all husbands, Mr. Harcourt.

HARCOURT. I edify, madam, so much, that I am impatient till I am one.

DORILANT. And I edify so much by example, I will never be one.

SPARKISH. And because I will not disparage my parts, I'll ne'er be one.

HORNER. And I, alas! can't be one.

PINCHWIFE. But I must be one—against my will to a country wife, with a country murrain to me!

MRS. PINCHWIFE. And I must be a country wife still too, I find; for I can't, like a city one, be rid of my musty husband, and do what I list. [*Aside.*]

HORNER. Now, sir, I must pronounce your wife innocent, though I blush whilst I do it; and I am the only man by her now exposed to shame, which I will straight drown in wine, as you shall your suspicion; and the ladies' troubles we'll divert with a ballad.—Doctor, where are your maskers?

LUCY. Indeed, she's innocent, sir, I am her witness; and her end of coming out was but to see her sister's wedding; and what she has said to your face of her love to Mr. Horner, was but the usual innocent revenge on a husband's jealousy;— was it not, madam, speak?

MRS. PINCHWIFE. [*Aside to* LUCY *and* HORNER.] Since you'll have me tell more lies—[*Aloud.*] Yes, indeed, bud.

PINCHWIFE. For my own sake fain I would all believe;

Cuckolds, like lovers, should themselves deceive.

But—[*Sighs*]

His honour is least safe (too late I find)

Who trusts it with a foolish wife or friend.

A Dance of Cuckolds.

HORNER. Vain fops but court and dress, and keep a pother,

To pass for women's men with one another;

But he who aims by women to be prized,

First by the men, you see, must be despised. [*Exeunt omnes.*]

EPILOGUE

SPOKEN BY MRS. KNEP[1]

Now you the vigorous, who daily here
O'er vizard-mask in public domineer,
And what you'd do to her, if in place where;
Nay, have the confidence to cry, *Come out!*
Yet when she says, *Lead on!* you are not stout;   5
But to your well-dress'd brother straight turn round,
And cry, *Pox on her, Ned, she can't be sound!*
Then slink away, a fresh one to engage,
With so much seeming heat and loving rage,
You'd frighten listening actress on the stage;   10
Till she at last has seen you huffing come,
And talk of keeping in the tiring-room,
Yet cannot be provoked to lead her home.
Next, you Falstaffs of fifty, who beset
Your buckram maidenheads, which your friends get;   15
And whilst to them you of achievements boast,
They share the booty, and laugh at your cost.
In fine, you essenced boys, both old and young,
Who would be thought so eager, brisk, and strong,
Yet do the ladies, not their husbands wrong;   20
Whose purses for your manhood make excuse,
And keep your Flanders mares for show not use;
Encouraged by our woman's man to-day,
A Horner's part may vainly think to play;
And may intrigues so bashfully disown,   25
That they may doubted be by few or none;
May kiss the cards at picquet, ombre, loo,
And so be taught to kiss the lady too;
But, gallants, have a care, faith, what you do.
The world, which to no man his due will give,   30
You by experience know you can deceive,
And men may still believe you vigorous,
But then we women—there's no cozening us.

1675

---

1 Mary Knep played Lady Fidget in the Drury Lane Theatre production of *The Country Wife*.

JOHN WILMOT, SECOND EARL OF ROCHESTER
1647–1680

John Wilmot, Second Earl of Rochester, was born on April 1, 1647. His mother was a severe Puritan, and his father, a heavy-drinking and battle-hardened cavalry officer, was a loyal confidante to Charles II. The boy was transferred earldom upon his father's death in 1658. A country-bred aristocrat, he entered Oxford when he was twelve years old and was given his MA two years later. In 1661, Sir Andrew Balfour, a Scottish physician and scholar, was appointed as Rochester's guide on a Grand Tour of Europe. The seventeen-year-old Rochester presented himself at court shortly after returning.

His career was marked by a pattern of reckless decisions, beginning with an attempt to abduct Elizabeth Malet, an heiress, after she refused his proposal. The two eventually married, but Rochester was briefly imprisoned in the Tower of London for the incident. He joined the British naval fleet after his release and fought during the Second Anglo-Dutch War. His bravery was rewarded with a series of duties to the king and country; he first took a seat in the House of Lords, and he then successively held positions as gamekeeper, ranger, and keeper of various regions in England. Still, Rochester's notorious behavior persisted. He had numerous affairs, drank excessively, vandalized, and constantly disputed with others.

Rochester's irascible conduct and literary finesse secured him a reputation as a famous court wit. Second only to John Dryden, Rochester was esteemed for his intellectual acuity and ability to effortlessly turn a phrase. In many of his pieces, he successfully invents personae that allow him to entertain his reader while maintaining personal distance from his topic. Cynical, ironic, and humorous, Rochester's work is simultaneously playful and powerful. His contemporaries deemed him "our great bawdy poet" because his writing celebrated the glories of what society considered immoral behavior. He particularly emphasized indulging in the pleasures of the flesh. Often daring and scatological, his poetry epitomizes scandalousness. Yet despite its frequent crudeness, Rochester's work is philosophical. Though he provides a reductive view of sexual relations, which regards sex as an animal act, he refuses to omit or simplify the emotional and moral complexities involved. He instead exposes feelings of uncertainty and inadequacy. At times Rochester considered sexual love paramount; at other times he denounced it as utterly unfulfilling and insufficient at cultivating security and stability.

Rochester revealed the arbitrariness and irrationality behind unexamined beliefs about religion, wealth, class, gender, and social and sexual restraint. He reveled in flipping conventional stances, as in his most famous poem, "A Satire against Reason and Mankind," which mocks the pride humans take in being rational creatures. Rochester denounced attempts to control or stifle natural human desires and instead promoted a lifestyle driven by self-interest. It was only on his deathbed that Rochester changed his mindset. Dangerously ill from the combined effects of a bladder ulcer, venereal diseases, and alcoholism, he converted to Christianity and demanded all his profane writings be burned. His decision shocked the court and church. The same dramatic flair which characterized his work exaggerated the significance of his salvation. He died when he was thirty-three, legendary for both his debauchery and his repentance.

1647	John Wilmot born 1 April
1658	Succeeds to earldom
1660–61	Attends Wadham College, Oxford University
1661–64	Grand Tour of Europe guided by Sir Andrew Balfour
1667	Marries Elizabeth Malet; Accepts post of Gentleman of the Bedchamber; Takes seat in the House of Lords
1671	"All things submit themselves"; "Caelia, that faithfull Servant"
1673	"Att five this Morn"; "As some brave Admiral"; "The Gods, by right of Nature"; "Wit has of late"; "In the Isle of Brittain"
1674	Appointed Ranger and Keeper of Woodstock Park; "What, Timon, does old Age, begin"; "Strephon, there sighs not"; *A Satyr Against Mankind*
1675	Appointed Master, Surveyor, and Keeper of Charles II's hawks; "Well Sir 'tis granted"
1677	"Some few from Wit"; Daughter born to actress Elizabeth Barry
1678	"Upon Nothing"
1679	"Deare friend I hear this Towne"
1680	Rochester dies 26 July due to syphilis, gonorrhea, and alcoholism and is buried in Spelburys Church, Spelsbury; *Poems on Several Occasions*

THE DISABLED DEBAUCHEE[1]

I.

As some brave Admiral in former War
   Depriv'd of Force, but pressed with Courage still,
Two rival Fleets appearing from afar,
   Crawls to the Top of an adjacent Hill.

II.

From whence (with Thoughts full of Concern) he views   5
   The wise, and daring Conduct, of the Fight:
Whilst each bold Action to his Mind renews,
   His present Glory, and his past Delight.

III.

From his fierce Eyes flashes of Rage he throws,
   As from black Clouds when Lightning breaks away,   10
Transported thinks himself amidst the Foes,
   And absent yet enjoys the bloody Day.

IV.

So when my Days of Impotence approach,
   And I'm by Love and Wine's unlucky Chance,
Driv'n from the pleasing Billows of Debauch,   15
   On the dull Shore of lazy Temperance.

V.

My Pains at least some Respite shall afford,
   While I behold the Battles you maintain;
When Fleets of Glasses sail about the Board,
   From whose Broad-sides Volleys of Wit shall rain.   20

VI.

Nor shall the Sight of honorable Scars,
   Which my too forward Valor did procure,
Frighten new-listed Soldiers from the Wars:
   Past Joys have more than paid what I endure.

---

1 Sometimes titled "The Maim'd Debauchee."

VII.

Shou'd some brave Youth (worth being drunk) prove nice,   25
   And from his fair Inviter meanly shrink,
'Twould please the Ghost of my departed Vice
   If at my Counsel he repent and drink.

VIII.

Or shou'd some cold complexion'd Sot forbid,
   With his dull Morals, our Nights brisk Alarms,   30
I'll fire his Blood by telling what I did,
   When I was strong, and able to bear Arms.

IX.

I'll tell of Whores attack'd their Lords at home,
   Bawds Quarters beaten up, and Fortress won;
Windows demolish'd, Watches overcome,   35
   And handsome Ills by my Contrivance done.

X.

With Tales like these I will such Heat inspire.
   As to important Mischief shall incline;
I'll make him long some ancient Church to fire,
   And fear no Lewdness they're call'd to by Wine.   40

XI.

Thus Statesman-like I'll saucily impose,
   And safe from Danger valiantly advise;
Shelter'd in Impotence urge you to Blows,
   And being good for nothing else be wise.

1675?

THE IMPERFECT ENJOYMENT

Naked she lay, clasped in my longing arms,
I filled with love, and she all over charms;
Both equally inspired with eager fire,
Melting through kindness, flaming in desire.
With arms, legs, lips close clinging to embrace,   5
She clips me to her breast, and sucks me to her face.
Her nimble tongue, Love's lesser lightning, played
Within my mouth, and to my thoughts conveyed
Swift orders that I should prepare to throw
The all-dissolving thunderbolt below.   10
My fluttering soul, sprung with the pointed kiss,
Hangs hovering o'er her balmy brinks of bliss.
But whilst her busy hand would guide that part
Which should convey my soul up to her heart,
In liquid raptures I dissolve all o'er,   15
Melt into sperm, and spend at every pore.
A touch from any part of her had done 't:
Her hand, her foot, her very look's a cunt.
    Smiling, she chides in a kind murmuring noise,
And from her body wipes the clammy joys,   20
When, with a thousand kisses wandering o'er
My panting bosom, "Is there then no more?"
She cries. "All this to love and rapture's due;
Must we not pay a debt to pleasure too?"
    But I, the most forlorn, lost man alive,   25
To show my wished obedience vainly strive:
I sigh, alas! and kiss, but cannot swive.
Eager desires confound my first intent,
Succeeding shame does more success prevent,
And rage at last confirms me impotent.   30
Ev'n her fair hand, which might bid heat return
To frozen age, and make cold hermits burn,
Applied to my dear cinder, warms no more
Than fire to ashes could past flames restore.
Trembling, confused, despairing, limber, dry,   35

A wishing, weak, unmoving lump I lie.
This dart of love, whose piercing point, oft tried,
With virgin blood ten thousand maids has dyed;
Which nature still directed with such art
That it through every cunt reached every heart—   40
Stiffly resolved, 'twould carelessly invade
Woman or man, nor ought its fury stayed:
Where'er it pierced, a cunt it found or made—
Now languid lies in this unhappy hour,
Shrunk up and sapless like a withered flower.   45

   Thou treacherous, base deserter of my flame,
False to my passion, fatal to my fame,
Through what mistaken magic dost thou prove
So true to lewdness, so untrue to love?
What oyster-cinder-beggar-common whore   50
Didst thou e'er fail in all thy life before?
When vice, disease, and scandal lead the way,
With what officious haste doest thou obey!
Like a rude, roaring hector in the streets
Who scuffles, cuffs, and justles all he meets,   55
But if his King or country claim his aid,
The rakehell villain shrinks and hides his head;
Ev'n so thy brutal valor is displayed,
Breaks every stew, does each small whore invade,
But when great Love the onset does command,   60
Base recreant to thy prince, thou dar'st not stand.
Worst part of me, and henceforth hated most,
Through all the town a common fucking post,
On whom each whore relieves her tingling cunt
As hogs on gates do rub themselves and grunt,   65
Mayst thou to ravenous chancres be a prey,
Or in consuming weepings waste away;
May strangury and stone thy days attend;
May'st thou never piss, who didst refuse to spend
When all my joys did on false thee depend.   70
   And may ten thousand abler pricks agree
   To do the wronged Corinna right for thee.

1680

JONATHAN SWIFT
1667–1745

Jonathan Swift was a man of secrecy and stark contradictions. No definitive date attests to his birth, and the other details of his early years are shrouded in mystery. Born of English parents living in Dublin, Swift grew up virtually an orphan; the man who was allegedly his father died seven months before Swift's birth, and his mother and sister moved to England to live with relatives when he was still a child. An uncle sent Swift to Kilkenny College and then to Trinity College in Dublin, two of Ireland's most exalted academic institutions, where the boy received rigorous schooling. Though an undeniably brilliant student, Swift was somewhat rebellious and scarcely earned his degree. Political unrest soon prevented him from choosing a career or continuing his studies. Following James II's abdication and the invasion of Ireland, Swift, along with other Anglo-Irish, made an exodus to England for safety. With little money, an unremarkable degree, and no patrons, Swift was in a poor position to advance himself. Until he could solidify his future course, he settled in the household of Sir William Temple, a retired diplomat and close friend of William III. Throughout his stay, Swift enjoyed constant contact with people of nobility.

Swift craved an occupation in politics or government service, but his degree qualified him for ministry. He grudgingly accepted orders and later became dean of St. Patrick's Cathedral in Dublin. Religion and politics were closely interwoven, however, and it was through the Anglican Church that Swift first uncovered his power as a satirist. In 1701, he plunged into the political atmosphere with a lengthy pamphlet titled *Contests and Dissensions*. The pamphlet constructed an obvious but unstated parallel between the ancient world of Athens and Rome and modern England. Three years later, he anonymously published *A Tale of a Tub*. It was immediately recognized for its brilliance, but the satire ultimately ruined Swift's career hopes of an English bishopric. Targeting the corruption of churches and schools, *A Tale* was accused of being subversive to the very religion it supposedly defended. Nevertheless, Swift's loyalties to the Anglican Church were overt. He aligned himself with the Tories—supporters of the monarchy and the Church of England—and employed his prose skills to advance their agenda. From 1710 to 1711, he was editor of a Tory periodical, the *Examiner*, and one of its most prominent authors.

The demands of political writing exhausted Swift, and his pamphlets hindered his career. When he began *Gulliver's Travels* in 1721, he welcomed the challenge. *Gulliver's Travels* was his first full-length piece since *A Tale*. Some five years of writing resulted in a delightful story for children and a barbed satire for adults. A critique of humankind's faltering political, social, and economic systems, *Gulliver's Travels* scrutinizes human nature through the eyes of an adaptable, unassuming narrator named Lemuel Gulliver. Across four books, Gulliver chronicles his ill-fated voyages in nations of vivid, whimsical design that are reminiscent of the real world. Swift deliberately distorts size, suggesting that meaning is merely a product of perspective, and he toys with the extremes of reason and passion. By instigating double-binds, incorporating allusions to past and present events, and deploying an acute sense of irony, Swift underscores the similarities between ourselves and the peoples of his book, provoking readers to inspect their own absurdity and reassess their worldview.

Swift's irony is fueled by personal emotional suffering. In "A Modest Proposal," he unites irony with satire to protest England's exploitation of Ireland; he simultaneously chastises Ireland for its complicity in being ruled as a dependent colony. For example, Irish people contributed to their own poverty and ill treatment by

purchasing luxurious English goods rather than buying local products. Though other writers offered solutions to Ireland's economic crisis, Swift's proposal adopted a cutting edge. His "project for eating children," as he deemed "A Modest Proposal," mocks overly-objective political positions. Swift's cynicism is often difficult to separate from his earnestness. Swift is charged with misogyny for scatalogical poems such as "The Lady's Dressing Room," and some critics claim Gulliver from *Gulliver's Travels* is a misanthrope. While it may seem that he was indeed disgusted with humanity, the playful notes underlying his works cannot be overlooked. Illustrious and ordinary people alike esteemed Swift, and those who knew him personally never doubted his integrity. Hailed a national hero for his political writings under the pseudonym M.B. Drapier and conscientious of the struggles of the mentally ill, Swift deeply sympathized with the plight of those around him.

As he aged, Swift developed an especially intimate friendship with Esther Johnson, a woman who had once been his tutee. In the letters and poems he exchanged with "Stella" (as he affectionately called her), Swift asserted that intelligent women were doing themselves a disservice by spelling poorly. He amended Stella's mistakes, offering himself as a mentor as well as a friend and perhaps as a lover. Stella became the woman Swift adored above all others. The exact nature of their relationship, however, is unknown. It may have been purely platonic; it may have been romantic. The two were rumored to have married, but it is unknown if they actually did. Stella moved to Dublin at Swift's urging, and though they saw one another frequently, they were careful never to meet alone. The *Journal to Stella*, which is composed of sixty-five letters and was published posthumously, evidences Swift's side of their correspondence. Swift also had relations with Esther Vanhomrigh, a woman he named "Vanessa." Vanessa was enamored by the writer and yearned for his affections. She sought to publicize their letters, but only "Cadenus and Vanessa," a poem Swift intended to keep private, was printed. Their surviving letters were not published until 1921.

Swift's gender views may seem somewhat progressive for their time, but by today's standards, he harbored many misogynistic opinions. He indeed believed women should be educated, but not for their own individual and intellectual gain; he hoped educated women would fill their roles more capably, and, consequently, provide more stimulating company for men. Like many men of his time, Swift's interests were male-centered: He feared that independent women would threaten patriarchal power. Resultantly, women who challenged gender boundaries through wit and conversation received the brunt of Swift's criticism.

Swift's poor health tormented him particularly during the latter years of his life. In addition to an illness now known as Ménière's disease, which had afflicted Swift with nausea, vertigo, and deafness since his youth, he displayed symptoms of dementia. His behavior fluctuated between geniality and irritability; many of his final writings are rife with bitterness and wrath. In 1742, his condition grew grave after he suffered a stroke. He was relieved of his deanship and placed under guardianship. His failing mental state agonized him so severely that he felt estranged from himself.

In his epitaph, Swift relates that indignation wounded his heart. His satires reflect exasperation without overshadowing his dedication to justice. Masterfully injecting passion into politics and weaving eccentric narratives, Swift used his talents to captivate and unnerve his audience. He devised seemingly implausible situations that mirrored realities his readers recognized and understood.

1667	Jonathan Swift believed to have been born 30 November
1682–86	Attends Trinity College, Dublin, and graduates *speciali gratia* ("by special favor")
1689	Flees Ireland just before James II lands in Ireland and begins the War of the Two Kings
1692	Stops by Oxford University to purchase his M.A., a prerequisite for ordination that required no studying
1694	Ordained deacon in Christ Church Cathedral in Dublin
1695	Appointed rector of Ballynure and vicar of Kilroot and Templecorran
1701	*Contests and Dissensions*
1704	*A Tale of a Tub*, *The Battle of the Books*, and *The Mechanical Operation of the Spirit* in a single volume
1710–11	Editor and author for the *Examiner*
1710	Fifth edition of *A Tale of a Tub*, with added "Apology"
1713	Installed as dean of St. Patrick's Cathedral, Dublin
1726	*Gulliver's Travels*; "Cadenus and Vanessa" published without Swift's permission
1729	"A Modest Proposal"
1732	"The Lady's Dressing Room"
1745	Swift dies 19 October shortly after suffering a stroke and is buried near Stella inside St. Patrick's Cathedral, Dublin, Ireland

GULLIVER'S TRAVELS
INTO SEVERAL REMOTE NATIONS OF THE WORLD

THE PUBLISHER TO THE READER

THE AUTHOR OF THESE TRAVELS, Mr. *Lemuel Gulliver*, is my ancient and intimate Friend; there is likewise some Relation between us by the Mother's Side. About three Years ago, Mr. *Gulliver* growing weary of the Concourse of curious People coming to him at his House in *Redriff*, made a small Purchase of Land, with a convenient House, near *Newark* in *Nottingham-shire*, his Native Country; where he now lives retired, yet in good Esteem among his Neighbours.

Although Mr. *Gulliver* was born in *Nottinghamshire*, where his Father dwelt, yet I have heard him say, his Family came from *Oxfordshire*; to confirm which, I have observed in the Church-Yard at *Banbury*, in that County, several Tombs and Monuments of the *Gullivers*.

Before he quitted *Redriff*, he left the Custody of the following Papers in my Hands, with the liberty to dispose of them as I should think fit. I have carefully perused them three Times: The Style is very plain and simple; and the only Fault I find is, that the Author, after the Manner of Travellers, is a little too Circumstantial. There is an Air of Truth apparent through the Whole; and indeed, the Author was so distinguished for his VeraCity, that it became a sort of Proverb among his Neighbours at *Redriff*, when any one affirm'd a Thing, to say, it was as true as if Mr. *Gulliver* had spoken it.

By the Advice of several worthy Persons, to whom, with the Author's Permission, I communicated these Papers, I now venture to send them into the World, hoping they may be at least, for some time, a better Entertainment to our young Noblemen, than the common Scribbles of Politicks and Party.

This Volume would have been at least twice as large, if I had not made bold to strike out innumerable Passages relating to the Winds and Tides, as well as to the Variations and Bearings in the several Voyages; together with the minute Descriptions of the Management of the Ship in Storms, in the Style of Sailors: Likewise the Account of Longitudes and Latitudes; wherein I have Reason to apprehend, that Mr. *Gulliver* may be a little dissatisfied: But I was resolved to fit the Work as much as possible to the general CapaCity of Readers. However, if my own Ignorance in Sea-Affairs shall have led me to commit some Mistakes, I alone am answerable for them: And if any Traveller hath a Curiosity to see the whole Work at large, as it came from the Hand of the Author, I will be ready to gratify him.

As for any further Particulars relating to the Author, the Reader will receive Satisfaction from the first Pages of the Book.

RICHARD SYMPSON.

A LETTER FROM CAPTAIN GULLIVER TO HIS COUSIN SYMPSON

Written in the year 1727

I Hope you will be ready to own publickly, whenever you shall be called to it, that by your great and frequent urgency you prevailed on me to publish a very loose and uncorrect account of my travels, with directions to hire some young gentleman of either university to put them in order, and correct the style, as my cousin *Dampier* did by my advice in his book called, *A Voyage round the World*. But I do not remember I gave you power to consent, that any thing should be omitted, and much less that any thing should be inserted; therefore, as to the latter, I do here renounce every thing of that kind; particularly a paragraph about her majesty Queen *Anne* of most pious and glorious memory; although I did reverence and esteem her more than any of human species. But you, or your interpolator, ought to have considered, that as it was not my inclination, so was it not decent to praise any animal of our composition before my Master *Houyhnhnm*:[1] And besides, the fact was altogether false; for to my knowledge, being in *England* during some part of her majesty's reign, she did govern by a chief minister; nay even by two successively, the first whereof was the lord of *Godolphin*,[2] and the second the lord of *Oxford*;[3] so that you have made me *say the thing that was not*. Likewise in the account of the academy of projectors, and several passages of my discourse to my Master *Houyhnhnm*, you have either omitted some material circumstances, or minced or changed them in such a manner, that I do hardly know my own work. When I formerly hinted to you something of this in a letter, you were pleased to answer that you were afraid of giving offence; that people in power were very watchful over the press, and apt not only to interpret, but to punish every thing which looked like an *Innuendo* (as I think you call it). But, pray how could that which I spoke so many Years ago, and at about five thousand

---

1 A fictional race of intelligent, rational horses that Gulliver encounters in Part IV of his travels.

2 Sidney Godolphin, 1st Earl of Godolphin, served as lord treasurer for Queen Anne from 1702 to 1710. A trusted member of the queen's ministry, Godolphin convinced Queen Anne to stock government offices with Whigs.

3 Robert Harley, 1st Earl of Oxford, controlled Queen Anne's government along with Godolphin and the 1st Duke of Marlborough. Queen Anne favored Oxford, but conflicts with Godolphin and Marlborough forced him to resign.

leagues distance, in another reign, be applied to any of the *Yahoos*,[1] who now are said to govern the herd; especially at a time when I little thought, or feared, the unhappiness of living under them? Have not I the most reason to complain, when I see these very *Yahoos* carried by *Houyhnhnms* in a vehicle, as if they were brutes and those the rational creatures? And indeed to avoid so monstrous and detestable a sight was one principal motive of my retirement hither.

Thus much I thought proper to tell you in relation to yourself, and to the trust I reposed in you.

I do in the next place complain of my own great want of judgment in being prevailed upon by the entreaties and false reasoning of you and some others, very much against my own opinion, to suffer my travels to be published. Pray bring to your mind how often I desired you to consider, when you insisted on the motive of *Publick Good*, that the *Yahoos* were a species of animals utterly incapable of amendment by precepts or example: And so it hath proved; for, instead of seeing a full stop put to all abuses and corruptions, at least in this little island, as I had reason to expect; behold, after above six Months warning, I cannot learn that my book has produced one single effect according to my intentions. I desired, you would let me know by a letter, when party and faction were extinguished; judges learned and upright; pleaders honest and modest with some tincture of common sense, and *Smithfield*[2] blazing with pyramids of law-books; the young nobility's education entirely changed; the physicians banished; the female *Yahoos* abounding in virtue, honour, truth, and good sense; courts and levees of great ministers thoroughly weeded and swept; wit, merit, and learning rewarded; all disgracers of the press in prose and verse condemned to eat nothing but their own cotton, and quench their thirst with their own ink. These, and a thousand other reformations, I firmly counted upon by your encouragement; as indeed they were plainly deducible from the precepts delivered in my book. And it must be owned, that seven Months were a sufficient time to correct every vice and folly to which *Yahoos* are subject, if their natures had been capable of the least disposition to virtue or wisdom: Yet, so far have you been from answering my expectation in any of your letters; that on the contrary you are loading our carrier every week with libels, and keys, and reflections, and memoirs, and second parts; wherein I see myself accused of reflecting upon great states-folk; of degrading human nature (for so they have still the confidence to style it) and of abusing the female sex. I find likewise, that the writers of those bundles are not agreed among themselves; for some of them will not allow me to be the Author of my own travels; and others make me Author of books, to which I am wholly a stranger.

---

1 A race of filthy, degenerate, human-like brutes tamed by the Houyhnhnms.

2 A marketplace in London.

I find likewise, that your printer has been so careless as to confound the times, and mistake the dates of my several Voyages and returns; neither assigning the true year, nor the true month, nor day of the month: And I hear the original manuscript is all destroyed since the publication of my book; neither have I any copy left; however, I have sent you some corrections, which you may insert, if ever there should be a second edition: And yet I cannot stand to them; but shall leave that matter to my judicious and candid readers to adjust it as they please.

I hear some of our sea-*Yahoos* find fault with my sea-language, as not proper in many parts, nor now in use. I cannot help it. In my first Voyages, while I was young, I was instructed by the oldest mariners, and learned to speak as they did. But I have since found that the sea-*Yahoos* are apt, like the land ones, to become new-fangled in their words, which the latter change every year; insomuch, as I remember upon each return to my own Country, their old dialect was so altered, that I could hardly understand the new. And I observe, when any *Yahoo* comes from *London* out of curiosity to visit me at mine House, we neither of us are able to deliver our conceptions in a manner intelligible to the other.

If the censure of the *Yahoos* could any way affect me, I should have great reason to complain, that some of them are so bold as to think my book of travels a mere fiction out of mine own brain; and have gone so far as to drop hints, that the *Houyhnhnms* and *Yahoos* have no more existence than the inhabitants of Utopia.

Indeed I must confess, that as to the People of *Lilliput, Brobdingrag*[3] (for so the word should have been spelt, and not erroneously *Brobdingnag*) and *Laputa,*[4] I have never yet heard of any *Yahoo* so presumptuous as to dispute their being, or the facts I have related concerning them; because the truth immediately strikes every reader with conviction. And is there less probability in my account of the *Houyhnhnms* or *Yahoos*, when it is manifest as to the latter, there are so many thousands, even in this City, who only differ from their brother brutes in *Houyhnhnm-land*, because they use a sort of *Jabber*, and do not go naked? I wrote for their amendment, and not their approbation. The united praise of the whole race would be of less consequence to me, than the neighing of those two degenerate *Houyhnhnms* I keep in my stable; because from these, degenerate as they are, I still improve in some virtues without any mixture of vice.

Do these miserable animals presume to think, that I am so degenerated as to defend my veracity? *Yahoo* as I am, it is well known through all *Houyhnhnm-land*, that, by the instructions and example of my illustrious Master, I was able in the compass of two Years (although I confess with the utmost difficulty) to remove

---

3 A utopian land inhabited by giants that Gulliver visits in Part II.
4 A flying island that appears in Part III.

that infernal habit of lying, shuffling, deceiving, and equivocating, so deeply rooted in the very souls of all my species; especially the *Europeans*.

I have other complaints to make upon this vexatious occasion; but I forbear troubling myself or you any further. I must freely confess, that since my last return some corruptions of my *Yahoo* nature have revived in me by conversing with a few of your species, and particularly those of my own family, by an un-avoidable necessity; else I should never have attempted so absurd a project as that of reforming the *Yahoo* race in this kingdom: But I have now done with all such visionary schemes for ever.

April 2, 1727

PART I.

A VOYAGE TO LILLIPUT

CHAPTER I.

The Author gives some Account of himself and Family, his first Inducements to travel. He is shipwrecked, and swims for his Life, gets safe on shore in the Country of Lilliput, *is made a Prisoner, and carried up the Country.*

M Y FATHER HAD A SMALL ESTATE in *Nottinghamshire*; I was the Third of Five Sons. He sent me to *Emanuel College* in *Cambridge*, at Fourteen Years old, where I resided three Years, and applied my self close to my Studies; But the Charge of maintaining me (although I had a very scanty Allowance) being too great for a narrow Fortune, I was bound Apprentice to Mr. *James Bates*, an eminent Surgeon in *London*, with whom I continued four Years; and my Father now and then sending me small Sums of Money, I laid them out in learning Navigation, and other Parts of the Mathematics, useful to those who intend to travel, as I always believed it would be some time or other my fortune to do. When I left Mr. *Bates*, I went down to my Father: where by the Assistance of Him and my Uncle *John*, and some other Relations, I got Forty Pounds, and a Promise of Thirty Pounds a Year to maintain me at *Leyden*: There I studied Physick two Years and seven Months, knowing it would be useful in long Voyages.

Soon after my Return from *Leyden*, I was recommended by my good Master Mr. *Bates*, to be Surgeon to the *Swallow*, Captain *Abraham Pannel* Commander; with whom I continued three Years and a half, making a Voyage or two into the

Levant, and some other Parts. When I came back I resolved to settle in *London*, to which Mr. *Bates*, my Master, encouraged me, and by him I was recommended to several Patients. I took Part of a small House in the *Old Jewry*; and being advised to alter my Condition, I married Mrs. *Mary Burton*, second Daughter to Mr. *Edmund Burton* Hosier in *Newgate-Street*, with whom I received four hundred Pounds for a Portion.

But, my good Master *Bates* dying in two Years after, and I having few Friends, my Business began to fail; for my Conscience would not suffer me to imitate the bad Practice of too many among my Brethren. Having therefore consulted with my Wife, and some of my Acquaintance, I determined to go again to Sea. I was Surgeon successively in two Ships, and made several Voyages, for six Years, to the *East* and *West-Indies*, by which I got some Addition to my Fortune. My Hours of Leisure I spent in reading the best Authors ancient and modern, being always provided with a good Number of Books; and when I was ashore, in observing the Manners and Dispositions of the People, as well as learning their Language, wherein I had a great Facility by the Strength of my Memory.

The last of these Voyages not proving very fortunate, I grew weary of the Sea, and intended to stay at home with my Wife and Family. I removed from the *Old Jewry* to *Fetter-Lane*, and from thence to *Wapping*, hoping to get Business among the Sailors; but it would not turn to account. After three Years Expectation that things would mend, I accepted an advantageous Offer from Captain *William Prichard*, Master of the *Antelope*, who was making a Voyage to the *South-Sea*. We set sail from *Bristol May* 4th, 1699, and our Voyage was at first very prosperous.

It would not be proper, for some Reasons, to trouble the Reader with the Particulars of our Adventures in those Seas: Let it suffice to inform him, that in our Passage from thence to the *East-Indies*, we were driven by a violent Storm to the North west of *Van Diemen*'s Land. By an Observation, we found ourselves in the Latitude of 30 Degrees 2 Minutes South. Twelve of our Crew were dead by immoderate Labour, and ill Food, the rest were in a very weak Condition. On the fifth of *November*, which was the Beginning of Summer in those Parts, the Weather being very hazy, the Seamen spied a Rock, within half a Cable's Length of the Ship; but the Wind was so strong, that we were driven directly upon it, and immediately split. Six of the Crew, of whom I was one, having let down the Boat into the Sea, made a shift to get clear of the Ship, and the Rock. We rowed by my Computation about three Leagues, till we were able to work no longer, being already spent with Labour while we were in the Ship. We therefore trusted ourselves to the Mercy of the Waves, and in about half an Hour the Boat was overset by a sudden Flurry from the North. What became of my Companions in the Boat, as well as of those who escaped on the Rock, or were left in the Vessel, I cannot tell; but conclude they were all lost. For my own part, I swam as Fortune directed me, and was pushed forward by Wind and Tide. I often let my Legs drop, and could feel no Bottom: But when I was almost gone, and able to struggle no longer, I found myself within my Depth; and by this time the Storm was much abated. The Declivity was so small, that I walked near a Mile before I got to the Shore, which I conjectur'd was about eight o'clock in the Evening. I then advanced forward near half a Mile, but could not discover any sign of Houses or Inhabitants; at least I was in so weak a Condition, that I did not observe them. I was extremely tired, and with that, and the Heat of the Weather, and about half a Pint of Brandy that I drank as I left the Ship, I found myself much inclined to sleep. I lay down on the Grass, which was very short and soft, where I slept sounder than ever I remembered to have done in my Life, and as I reckoned, about nine Hours; for when I awaked, it was just Day-light. I attempted to rise, but was not able to stir: For as I happen'd to lie on my Back, I found my Arms and Legs were strongly fastened on each side to the Ground; and my Hair, which was long and thick, tied down in the same manner. I likewise felt several slender Ligatures across my Body, from my Arm-pits to my Thighs. I could only look upwards, the Sun began to grow hot, and the Light offended mine Eyes. I heard a confused Noise about me, but in the Posture I lay, could see nothing except the Sky. In a little Time I felt something alive moving on my left Leg, which advancing gently forward over my Breast, came almost up to my Chin; when bending mine Eyes downwards as much as I could, I perceived it to be a human Creature not six Inches high, with a Bow and Arrow in his Hands, and a Quiver at his Back. In the mean time, I felt at least forty more of the same kind (as I conjectured) following the first. I was in the utmost Astonishment, and roared so loud, that they all ran back in a Fright; and some of them, as I was afterwards told, were hurt with the Falls they got by leaping from my Sides upon the Ground. However, they soon returned, and one of them, who ventured so far as to get a full sight of my Face, lifting up his Hands and Eyes by Way of Admiration, cried out in a shrill but distinct Voice, *Hekinah Degul*: The others repeated the same Words several times, but I then knew not what they meant. I lay all this while, as the Reader may believe, in great Uneasiness: at length, struggling to get loose, I had the fortune to break the Strings, and wrench out the Pegs that fastened my left Arm to the Ground; for, by lifting it up to my Face, I discover'd the Methods they had taken to bind me, and, at the same Time with a violent Pull, which gave me excessive Pain, I a little loosened the Strings that tied down my Hair on the left Side, so that I was just able to turn my head about two Inches. But the Creatures ran off a second time, before I could seize them; whereupon there was a great Shout in a very shrill Accent, and after it ceased I heard one of them cry aloud, *Tolgo Phonac*; when in an instant I felt above a hundred Arrows discharged on my left Hand, which pricked me like so many Needles; and besides they shot another Flight into the Air, as we do Bombs in

Europe, whereof many, I suppose, fell on my Body, (though I felt them not) and some on my Face, which I immediately covered with my left Hand. When this Shower of Arrows was over, I fell a groaning with Grief and Pain, and then striving again to get loose, they discharged another Volly larger than the first, and some of them attempted with Spears to stick me in the Sides; but, by good luck, I had on me a Buff Jerkin, which they could not pierce. I thought it the most prudent Method to lie still, and my design was to continue so till Night, when my left Hand being already loose, I could easily free myself: And as for the Inhabitants, I had reason to believe I might be a match for the greatest Armies they could bring against me, if they were all of the same Size with him that I saw. But Fortune disposed otherwise of me. When the People observed I was quiet, they discharged no more Arrows: But by the Noise I heard, I knew their Numbers increased; and about four Yards from me, over-against my right Ear, I heard a knocking for above an Hour, like that of People at work; when turning my Head that Way as well as the Pegs and Strings would permit me, I saw a Stage erected about a foot and a half from the Ground, capable of holding four of the Inhabitants, with two or three Ladders to mount it: From whence one of them, who seemed to be a Person of Quality, made me a long Speech, whereof I understood not one Syllable. But I should have mentioned, that before the principal Person began his Oration, he cryed out three times, *Langro Dehul San*: (these Words and the former were afterwards repeated and explained to me.) Whereupon immediately about fifty of the Inhabitants, came and cut the Strings that fastened the left Side of my Head, which gave me the Liberty of turning it to the right, and of observing the Person and Gesture of him that was to speak. He appeared to be of a middle Age, and taller than any of the other three who attended him, whereof one was a Page that held up his Train, and seemed to be somewhat longer than my middle Finger; the other two stood one on each side to support him. He acted every part of an Orator, and I could observe many Periods of Threatenings, and others of Promises, Pity and Kindness. I answered in a few Words, but in the most submissive Manner, lifting up my Left Hand and both mine Eyes to the Sun, as calling him for a Witness; and being almost famished with Hunger, having not eaten a Morsel for some Hours before I left the Ship, I found the Demands of Nature so strong upon me, that I could not forbear showing my Impatience (perhaps against the strict Rules of Decency) by putting my Finger frequently on my Mouth, to signify that I wanted Food. The *Hurgo* (for so they call a great Lord, as I afterwards learnt) understood me very well. He descended from the Stage, and commanded that several Ladders should be applied to my Sides, on which above a hundred of the Inhabitants mounted and walked towards my Mouth, laden with Baskets full of Meat, which had been provided and sent thither by the King's Orders, upon the first Intelligence he received of me. I observed there was the Flesh of several Animals, but could not distinguish them by the Taste. There were Shoulders, Legs and Loins shaped like those of Mutton, and very well dressed, but smaller than the Wings of a Lark. I ate them by two or three at a mouthful, and took three Loaves at a time, about the Bigness of Musket Bullets. They supplied me as fast as they could, showing a thousand Marks of wonder and astonishment at my Bulk and Appetite. I then made another Sign that I wanted Drink. They found by my eating that a small Quantity would not suffice me, and being a most ingenious People, they slung up with great Dexterity one of their largest Hogsheads, then rolled it towards my Hand, and beat out the Top; I drank it off at a Draught, which I might well do, for it did not hold half a Pint, and tasted like a small Wine of *Burgundy*, but much more delicious. They brought me a second Hogshead, which I drank in the same manner, and made Signs for more, but they had none to give me. When I had performed these Wonders, they shouted for Joy, and danced upon my Breast, repeating several times as they did at first, *Hekinah Degul*. They made me a Sign that I should throw down the two Hogsheads, but first warning the People below to stand out of the way, crying aloud, *Borach Mivola*, and when they saw the Vessels in the Air, there was a universal shout of *Hekinah Degul*. I confess I was often tempted, while they were passing backwards and forwards on my Body, to seize Forty or Fifty of the first that came in my reach, and dash them against the Ground. But the Remembrance of what I had felt, which probably might not be the worst they could do, and the Promise of Honour I made them, for so I interpreted my submissive Behaviour, soon drove out these Imaginations. Besides, I now consider'd my self as bound by the Laws of Hospitality to a People who had treated me with so much Expence and Magnificence. However, in my Thoughts I could not sufficiently wonder at the Intrepidity of these diminutive Mortals, who durst venture to mount and walk upon my Body, while one of my Hands was at liberty, without trembling at the very sight of so prodigious a Creature as I must appear to them. After some time, when they observ'd that I made no more Demands for Meat, there appeared before me a Person of high Rank from his Imperial Majesty. His excellency having mounted on the small of my right Leg, advanced forwards up to my Face, with about a Dozen of his Retinue. And producing his Credentials under the Signet Royal, which he applied close to mine eyes, spoke about ten Minutes, without any Signs of Anger, but with a kind of determinate Resolution; often pointing forwards, which as I afterwards found, was towards the Capital City, about half a Mile distant, whither it was agreed by his Majesty in Council that I must be conveyed. I answered in few words, but to no purpose, and made a Sign with my Hand that was loose, putting it to the other (but over his Excellency's Head, for fear of hurting him or his Train) and then to my own Head and Body, to signify that I desired my Liberty. It appeared that he understood me well enough, for he shook his Head by way of Disapprobation, and held his Hand in a Posture to show that I must be carried as a Prisoner. However, he made other Signs to let me understand that I should have Meat and Drink enough, and very good Treatment. Whereupon I once more thought of attempting to break my Bonds, but again, when I felt the Smart of their Arrows, upon my Face and Hands, which were all in Blisters, and many of the Darts still sticking in them, and observing likewise that the Number of my Enemies increased, I gave Tokens to let them know that they might do with me what they pleased. Upon this the *Hurgo* and his Train withdrew with much Civility and chearful Countenances. Soon after I heard a general Shout, with frequent repetitions of the Words, *Peplom Selan*, and I felt great Numbers of People on my Left Side relaxing the Cords to such a degree, that I was able to turn upon my Right, and to ease myself with making Water; which I very plentifully did, to the great Astonishment of the People, who conjecturing by my Motion what I was going to do, immediately opened to the right and left on that side to avoid the Torrent which fell with such noise and violence from me. But before this, they had daubed my Face and both my Hands with a sort of Ointment very pleasant to the Smell, which in a few Minutes removed all the Smart of their Arrows. These Circumstances added to the Refreshment I had received by their Victuals and Drink, which were very nourishing, disposed me to sleep. I slept about eight Hours, as I was afterwards assured; and it was no wonder, for the Physicians, by the Emperor's Order, had mingled a sleepy Potion in the Hogsheads of Wine.

It seems that upon the first Moment I was discovered sleeping on the Ground, after my Landing, the Emperor had early Notice of it by an Express, and determined in Council that I should be tied in the Manner I have related (which was done in the Night while I slept) that Plenty of Meat and Drink should be sent to me, and a Machine prepared to carry me to the Capital City.

This Resolution perhaps may appear very bold and dangerous, and I am confident would not be imitated by any Prince in *Europe* on the like Occasion; however, in my Opinion it was extremely Prudent as well as generous. For supposing these People had endeavour'd to kill me with their Spears and Arrows while I was asleep, I should certainly have awaked with the first sense of Smart, which might so far have roused my Rage and Strength, as to have enabled me to break the Strings wherewith I was tied; after which, as they were not able to make Resistance, so they could expect no Mercy.

These People are most excellent Mathematicians, and arriv'd to a great Perfection in Mechanicks by the Countenance and Encouragement of the Emperor, who is a renowned Patron of Learning. This Prince hath several Machines fixed on Wheels for the Carriage of Trees and other great Weights. He often builds his largest Men of War, whereof some are nine Foot long, in the Woods where the Timber grows, and has them carried on these Engines three or four hundred

Yards to the Sea. Five Hundred Carpenters and Engineers were immediately set at work to prepare the greatest Engine they had. It was a Frame of Wood raised three Inches from the Ground, about seven Foot long and four wide, moving upon twenty-two Wheels. The Shout I heard was upon the Arrival of this Engine, which it seems set out in four Hours after my Landing. It was brought parallel to me as I lay. But the principal Difficulty was to raise and place me in this Vehicle. Eighty Poles, each of one Foot high, were erected for this purpose, and very strong Cords of the bigness of Packthread were fastened by Hooks to many Bandages, which the Workmen had girt round my Neck, my Hands, my Body, and my Legs. Nine hundred of the strongest Men were employed to draw up these Cords by many Pulleys fastened on the Poles, and thus in less than three Hours, I was raised and slung into the Engine, and there tied fast. All this I was told, for while the Operation was performing, I lay in a profound sleep, by the force of that soporiferous Medicine infused into my Liquor. Fifteen Hundred of the Emperor's largest Horses, each about four Inches and a half high, were employed to draw me towards the Metropolis, which, as I said, was half a Mile distant.

About four Hours after we began our Journey, I awaked by a very ridiculous Accident; for the Carriage being stopt a while to adjust something that was out of order, two or three of the young Natives had the Curiosity to see how I looked when I was asleep; they climbed up into the Engine, and advancing very softly to my Face, one of them, an Officer in the Guards, put the sharp end of his Half-pike a good way up into my left Nostril, which tickled my Nose like a Straw, and made me sneeze violently: whereupon they stole off unperceived, and it was three Weeks before I knew the cause of my waking so suddenly. We made a long March the remaining part of that Day, and rested at Night with five hundred Guards on each side of me, half with Torches, and half with Bows and Arrows, ready to shoot me if I should offer to stir. The next Morning at Sun-rise we continued our March, and arrived within two hundred Yards of the City-Gates about noon. The Emperor, and all his Court came out to meet us, but his great Officers would by no means suffer his Majesty to endanger his Person by mounting on my Body.

At the Place where the Carriage stopt, there stood an ancient Temple, esteemed to be the largest in the whole Kingdom, which having been polluted some Years before by an unnatural Murder, was, according to the Zeal of those People, looked upon as Profane, and therefore had been applied to common Use, and all the Ornaments and Furniture carried away. In this Edifice it was determined I should lodge. The great Gate fronting to the North, was about four Foot high, and almost two Foot wide, through which I could easily creep. On each Side of the Gate was a small Window not above six Inches from the Ground into that on the Left Side, the King's Smiths conveyed fourscore and eleven Chains, like those that hang to a Lady's Watch in *Europe*, and almost as large, which were locked to my left Leg with six-and-thirty Padlocks. Over against this Temple, on the other side of the great Highway, at twenty Foot distance, there was a Turret at least five Foot high. Here the Emperor ascended with many principal Lords of his Court, to have an opportunity of viewing me, as I was told, for I could not see them. It was reckoned that above a hundred thousand Inhabitants came out of the Town upon the same Errand; and in spite of my Guards, I believe there could not be fewer than ten thousand, at several times, who mounted my Body by the help of Ladders. But a Proclamation was soon issued to forbid it upon pain of Death. When the Workmen found it was impossible for me to break loose, they cut all the Strings that bound me; whereupon I rose up with as melancholy a Disposition as ever I had in my Life. But the noise and astonishment of the People at seeing me rise and walk are not to be expressed. The Chains that held my left Leg were about two Yards long, and gave me not only the Liberty of walking backwards and forwards in a Semicircle; but being fixed within four Inches of the Gate, allowed me to creep in, and lie at my full length in the Temple.

CHAPTER II.

The Emperor of Lilliput, *attended by several of the Nobility, comes to see the Author in his confinement. The Emperor's Person and Habit describ'd. Learned Men appointed to teach the Author their Language. He gains Favour by his mild Disposition. His Pockets are searched, and his Sword and Pistols taken from him.*

WHEN I FOUND MYSELF ON MY FEET, I looked about me, and must confess I never beheld a more entertaining Prospect. The Country round appeared like a continued Garden, and the inclosed Fields, which were generally forty Foot square, resembled so many Beds of Flowers. These Fields were intermingled with Woods of half a Stang,[1] and the tallest Trees, as I could judge, appeared to be seven Foot high. I viewed the Town on my left hand, which looked like the painted Scene of a City in a Theatre.

I had been for some Hours extremely pressed by the Necessities of Nature; which was no wonder, it being almost two Days since I had last disburdened myself. I was under great Difficulties between Urgency and Shame. The best Expedient I could think on, was to creep into my House, which I accordingly did; and shutting the Gate after me, I went as far as the length of my Chain would suffer, and discharged my Body of that uneasy Load. But this was the only time I was ever

---

1 A long pole or perch.

guilty of so uncleanly an Action; for which I cannot but hope the candid Reader will give some Allowance, after he has maturely and impartially considered my Case, and the Distress I was in. From this time my constant Practice was, as soon as I rose, to perform that Business in open Air, at the full Extent of my Chain, and due Care was taken every Morning before Company came, that the offensive Matter should be carried off in Wheel-barrows, by two Servants appointed for that Purpose. I would not have dwelt so long upon a Circumstance, that perhaps at first sight may appear not very momentous, if I had not thought it necessary to justify my Character in point of Cleanliness to the World; which I am told some of my Maligners have been pleased, upon this and other Occasions, to call in question.

When this Adventure was at an end, I came back out of my House, having occasion for fresh Air. The Emperor was already descended from the Tower, and advancing on Horse-back towards me, which had like to have cost him dear; for the Beast, though very well trained, yet wholly unused to such a Sight, which appeared as if a Mountain moved before him, reared up on its hinder Feet: But that Prince, who is an excellent Horse-Man, kept his Seat, till his Attendants ran in, and held the Bridle, while his Majesty had time to dismount. When he alighted, he surveyed me round with great Admiration, but kept beyond the length of my Chain. He ordered his Cooks and Butlers, who were already prepared to give me Victuals and Drink, which they pushed forward in a sort of Vehicles upon Wheels till I could reach them. I took these Vehicles, and soon emptied them all; twenty of them were filled with Meat, and ten with Liquor; each of the former afforded me two or three good Mouthfuls, and I emptied the Liquor of ten Vessels, which was contained in earthen Vials, into one Vehicle, drinking it off at a Draught, and so I did with the rest. The Empress, and young Princes of the Blood, of both Sexes, attended by many Ladies, sat at some distance in their Chairs, but upon the Accident that happened to the Emperor's Horse, they alighted, and came near his Person, which I am now going to describe. He is taller by almost the breadth of my Nail, than any of his Court, which alone is enough to strike an Awe into the Beholders. His Features are strong and masculine, with an *Austrian* Lip and arched Nose, his Complexion olive, his Countenance erect, his Body and Limbs well proportioned, all his Motions graceful, and his Deportment majestick. He was then past his Prime, being twenty-eight Years and three Quarters old, of which he had reigned about seven, in great Felicity, and generally victorious. For the better convenience of beholding him, I lay on my Side, so that my Face was parallel to his, and he stood but three Yards off: However, I have had him since many times in my Hand, and therefore cannot be deceived in the Description. His Dress was very plain and simple, and the Fashion of it between the *Asiatic* and the *European*: but he had on his Head a light Helmet of Gold, adorned with Jewels, and a Plume on the Crest. He held his Sword drawn in his Hand to defend himself, if I should happen to break loose; it was almost three Inches long, the Hilt and Scabbard were Gold enriched with Diamonds. His Voice was shrill, but very clear and articulate, and I could distinctly hear it when I stood up. The Ladies and Courtiers were all most magnificently clad, so that the Spot they stood upon seemed to resemble a Petticoat spread upon the Ground, embroidered with Figures of Gold and Silver. His Imperial Majesty spoke often to me, and I returned Answers, but neither of us could understand a Syllable. There were several of his Priests and Lawyers present (as I conjectured by their Habits) who were commanded to address themselves to me, and I spoke to them in as many Languages as I had the least smattering of, which were *High* and *Low Dutch, Latin, French, Spanish, Italian,* and *Lingua Franca*; but all to no purpose. After about two Hours the Court retired, and I was left with a strong Guard, to prevent the Impertinence, and probably the Malice of the Rabble, who were very impatient to crowd about me as near as they durst, and some of them had the Impudence to shoot their Arrows at me as I sat on the Ground by the Door of my House, whereof one very narrowly missed my left Eye. But the Colonel ordered six of the Ring-leaders to be seized, and thought no Punishment so proper as to deliver them bound into my Hands, which some of his Soldiers accordingly did, pushing them forward with the Butt-Ends of their Pikes into my reach; I took them all in my right Hand, put five of them into my Coat-Pocket, and as to the sixth, I made a Countenance as if I would eat him alive. The poor man squalled terribly and the Colonel and his Officers were in much Pain, especially when they saw me take out my Penknife: But I soon put them out of fear; for, looking mildly and immediately cutting the Strings he was bound with, I set him gently on the Ground, and away he ran; I treated the rest in the same manner, taking them one by one out of my Pocket, and I observed both the Soldiers and People were highly obliged at this Mark of my Clemency, which was represented very much to my Advantage at Court.

Towards Night I got with some difficulty into my House, where I lay on the Ground, and continued to do so about a Fortnight; during which time, the Emperor gave Orders to have a Bed prepared for me. Six hundred Beds of the common Measure, were brought in Carriages and worked up in my House, a hundred and fifty of their Beds sown together made up the Breadth and Length, and these were four double, which however kept me but very indifferently from the Hardness of the Floor, that was of smooth Stone. By the same Computation they provided me with Sheets, Blankets, and Coverlets, tolerable enough for one who had been so long inured to Hardships as I.

As the News of my Arrival spread through the Kingdom, it brought prodigious Numbers of rich, idle, and curious People to see me; so that the Villages were almost emptied, and great Neglect of Tillage and Household Affairs must have

ensued, if his Imperial Majesty had not provided by several Proclamations and
Orders of State, against this Inconveniency. He directed that those, who had
already beheld me, should return Home, and not presume to come within fifty
Yards of my House, without License from the Court; whereby the Secretaries of
State got considerable Fees.

In the mean time, the Emperor held frequent Councils to debate what Course
should be taken with me; and I was afterwards assured by a particular Friend, a
Person of great Quality, who was looked upon to be as much in the Secret as any,
that the Court was under many Difficulties concerning me. They apprehended my
breaking loose, that my Diet would be very expensive, and might cause a Famine.
Sometimes they determined to starve me, or at least to shoot me in the Face and
Hands with poisoned Arrows, which would soon despatch me: But again they
consider'd, that the Stench of so large a Carcass might produce a Plague in the
Metropolis, and probably spread through the whole Kingdom. In the midst of
these Consultations, several Officers of the Army went to the Door of the great
Council Chamber; and two of them being admitted, gave an account of my
Behaviour to the six Criminals above-mentioned, which made so favourable an
Impression in the Breast of his Majesty and the whole Board in my behalf, that
an Imperial Commission was issued out, obliging all the Villages nine hundred
Yards round the City, to deliver in every Morning six Beeves, forty Sheep, and
other Victuals for my Sustenance; together with a proportionable Quantity of
Bread, and Wine, and other Liquors: for the due Payment of which, his Majesty
gave Assignments upon his Treasury. For this Prince lives chiefly upon his own
Demesnes, seldom, except upon great Occasions raising any subsidies upon his
Subjects, who are bound to attend him in his Wars at their own Expence. An
Establishment was also made of six hundred Persons to be my Domesticks, who
had Board-Wages allowed for their Maintenance, and Tents built for them very
conveniently on each side of my Door. It was likewise ordered, that three hundred
Tailors should make me a Suit of Clothes after the Fashion of the Country: That
six of his Majesty's greatest Scholars should be employ'd to instruct me in their
Language: And, lastly, that the Emperor's Horses, and those of the Nobility, and
Troops of Guards, should be frequently exercised in my sight, to accustom them-
selves to me. All these Orders were duly put in Execution, and in about three
Weeks I made a great Progress in learning their Language; during which time, the
Emperor frequently honoured me with his Visits, and was pleased to assist my
Masters in teaching me. We began already to converse together in some sort;
and the first Words I learnt were to express my Desire that he would please give
me my Liberty, which I every day repeated on my Knees. His Answer, as I could
comprehend it, was, that this must be a Work of Time, not to be thought on
without the Advice of his Council, and that first I must *Lumos Kelmin pesso desmar*

lon Emposo; that is, swear a Peace with him and his Kingdom. However, that I should be used with all Kindness, and he advised me to acquire by my Patience, and discreet Behaviour, the good Opinion of himself and his Subjects. He desired I would not take it ill if he gave Orders to certain proper Officers to search me; for probably I might carry about me several Weapons, which must needs be dangerous things, if they answered the Bulk of so prodigious a Person. I said, his Majesty should be satisfied, for I was ready to strip myself, and turn up my Pockets before him. This I delivered part in Words, and part in Signs. He replied, that by the Laws of the Kingdom I must be searched by two of his Officers; that he knew this could not be done without my Consent and Assistance; that he had so good an Opinion of my Generosity and Justice, as to trust their Persons in my Hands: That whatever they took from me should be returned when I left the Country, or paid for at the Rate which I would set upon them. I took up the two Officers in my Hands, put them first into my Coat-Pockets, and then into every other Pocket about me, except my two Fobs, and another secret Pocket I had no mind should be searched, wherein I had some little Necessaries that were of no consequence to any but myself. In one of my Fobs there was a silver Watch, and in the other a small Quantity of Gold in a Purse. These gentlemen, having Pen Ink and Paper about them, made an exact Inventory of every thing they saw; and when they had done, desired I would set them down, that they might deliver it to the Emperor. This Inventory I afterwards translated into *English*, and is word for word as follows.

IMPRIMIS, In the right Coat-Pocket of the *Great Man Mountain* (for so I interpret the Words *Quinbus Flestrin*,) after the strictest search, we found only one great Piece of coarse Cloath, large enough to be a Foot-Cloth for your Majesty's chief Room of State. In the left Pocket we saw a huge Silver Chest, with a Cover of the same Metal, which we the Searchers were not able to lift. We desired it should be opened, and one of us stepping into it, found himself up to the mid Leg in a sort of Dust, some part whereof flying up to our Faces, set us both a sneezing for several times together. In his right Waistcoat-Pocket we found a prodigious Bundle of white thin Substances, folded one over another, about the Bigness of three Men, tied with a strong Cable, and marked with black Figures; which we humbly conceive to be Writings, every Letter almost half as large as the Palm of our Hands. In the left there was a sort of Engine, from the Back of which were extended twenty long Poles, resembling the Pallisado's before your Majesty's Court; wherewith we conjecture the *Man Mountain* combs his Head, for we did not always trouble him with Questions, because we found it a great Difficulty to make him understand us. In the large Pocket, on the right side of his middle Cover, (so I translate the Word *Ranfu-Lo*, by which they meant my Breeches) we saw a hollow Pillar of Iron, about the length of a Man, fastened to a strong piece of Timber, larger than the Pillar; and upon one side of the Pillar were huge Pieces of

Iron sticking out, cut into strange Figures, which we know not what to make of. In the left Pocket, another Engine of the same kind. In the smaller Pocket on the right side, were several round flat Pieces of white and red Metal, of different Bulk; some of the white, which seemed to be Silver, were so large and heavy, that my Comrade and I could hardly lift them. In the left Pocket were two black Pillars irregularly shaped: we could not, without Difficulty reach the Top of them as we stood at the Bottom of his Pocket. One of them was covered, and seemed all of a Piece: But at the upper End of the other there appeared a white round Substance, about twice the bigness of our Heads. Within each of these was inclosed a prodigious Plate of Steel; which, by our Orders, we obliged him to show us, because we apprehended they might be dangerous Engines. He took them out of their Cases, and told us, that in his own Country his Practice was to shave his Beard with one of these, and cut his Meat with the other. There were two Pockets which we could not enter: These he called his Fobs; they were two large Slits cut into the top of his middle Cover, but squeez'd close by the pressure of his Belly. Out of the right Fob hung a great silver Chain, with a wonderful kind of Engine at the bottom. We directed him to draw out whatever was at the end of that Chain; which appeared to be a Globe, half Silver, and half of some transparent Metal: For on the transparent side we saw certain strange Figures circularly drawn, and thought we could touch them, till we found our Fingers stopped by the lucid Substance. He put this Engine into our Ears, which made an incessant Noise, like that of a Water-Mill. And we conjecture it is either some unknown Animal, or the God that he worships: But we are more inclined to the latter Opinion, because he assured us, (if we understood him right, for he expressed himself very imperfectly) that he seldom did any thing without consulting it. He called it his Oracle, and said it pointed out the Time for every Action of his Life. From the left Fob he took out a Net almost large enough for a Fisherman, but contrived to open and shut like a Purse, and served him for the same use: We found therein several massy Pieces of yellow Metal, which if they be real Gold, must be of immense Value.

HAVING thus, in obedience to your Majesty's Commands, diligently searched all his Pockets, we observed a Girdle about his Waist made of the Hide of some prodigious Animal; from which, on the left Side, hung a Sword of the length of five Men; and on the right, a Bag or Pouch divided into two Cells, each Cell capable of holding three of your Majesty's Subjects. In one of these Cells were several Globes or Balls of a most ponderous Metal, about the bigness of our Heads, and requiring a strong Hand to lift them; The other Cell contained a Heap of certain black Grains, but of no great Bulk or Weight, for we could hold above fifty of them in the Palms of our Hands.

THIS is an exact Inventory of what we found about the Body of the *Man-Mountain*, who used us with great Civility, and due Respect to your Majesty's

Commission. Signed and Sealed on the fourth Day of the eighty-ninth Moon of your Majesty's auspicious Reign.

Clefren Frelock, Marsi Frelock.

When this Inventory was read over to the Emperor, he directed me, although in very gentle Terms, to deliver up the several Particulars. He first called for my Scimitar, which I took out, Scabbard and all. In the mean time he ordered three thousand of his choicest Troops (who then attended him) to surround me at a distance, with their Bows and Arrows just ready to discharge: but I did not observe it, for mine Eyes were wholly fixed upon his Majesty. He then desired me to draw my Scimitar, which, although it had got some Rust by the Sea Water, was in most parts exceeding bright. I did so, and immediately all the Troops gave a Shout between Terror and Surprise; for the Sun shone clear, and the Reflexion dazzled their Eyes as I waved the Scimitar to and fro in my Hand. His Majesty, who is a most magnanimous Prince, was less daunted than I could expect; he ordered me to return it into the Scabbard, and cast in on the Ground as gently as I could, about six Foot from the end of my Chain. The next thing he demanded, was one of the hollow Iron Pillars, by which he meant my Pocket-Pistols. I drew it out, and at his desire, as well as I could, expressed to him the Use of it; and charging it only with Powder, which by the closeness of my Pouch happened to escape wetting in the Sea, (an Inconvenience against which all prudent Mariners take special care to provide) I first cautioned the Emperor not to be afraid, and then I let it off in the Air. The Astonishment here was much greater than at the sight of my Scimitar. Hundreds fell down as if they had been struck dead; and even the Emperor, although he stood his Ground, could not recover himself for some time. I delivered up both my Pistols in the same Manner, as I had done my Scimitar, and then my Pouch of Powder and Bullets; begging him that the former might be kept from Fire, for it would kindle with the smallest Spark, and blow up his Imperial Palace into the Air. I likewise delivered up my Watch, which the Emperor was very curious to see, and commanded two of his tallest Yeomen of the Guards to bear it on a Pole upon their shoulders, as Dray-Men in *England* do a Barrel of Ale. He was amazed at the continual Noise it made, and the Motion of the Minute-Hand, which he could easily discern; for their Sight is much more acute than ours: and asked the Opinions of his learned Men about it, which were various and remote, as the Reader may well imagine without my repeating; although indeed I could not very perfectly understand them. I then gave up my Silver and Copper Money, my Purse with nine large Pieces of Gold, and some smaller ones; my Knife and Razor, my Comb and Silver Snuff-Box, my Handkerchief and Journal Book. My Scimitar, Pistols, and Pouch, were conveyed in Carriages to his Majesty's Stores; but the rest of my Goods were returned me.

I had, as I before observed, one private Pocket which escaped their Search, wherein there was a pair of Spectacles (which I sometimes use for the Weakness of mine Eyes) a Pocket Perspective, and several other little Conveniences; which being of no consequence to the Emperor, I did not think myself bound in Honour to discover, and I apprehended they might be lost or spoiled if I ventured them out of my Possession.

CHAPTER III.

The Author diverts the Emperor and his Nobility of both Sexes in a very uncommon Manner. The Diversions of the Court of Lilliput described. The Author has his Liberty granted him upon certain Conditions.

MY GENTLENESS AND GOOD BEHAVIOUR had gained so far on the Emperor and his Court, and indeed upon the Army and People in general, that I began to conceive Hopes of getting my Liberty in a short time. I took all possible Methods to cultivate this favourable Disposition. The Natives came by degrees to be less apprehensive of any Danger from me. I would sometimes lie down, and let five or six of them dance on my Hand. And at last the Boys and Girls would venture to come and play at Hide and Seek in my Hair. I had now made a good Progress in understanding and speaking their Language. The Emperor had a mind one day to entertain me with several of the Country Shows, wherein they exceed all Nations I have known, both for Dexterity and Magnificence. I was diverted with none so much as that of the Rope-Dancers, performed upon a slender white Thread, extended about two Foot, and twelve Inches from the Ground. Upon which I shall desire liberty, with the Reader's Patience, to enlarge a little.

This Diversion is only practised by those Persons who are Candidates for great Employments, and high Favour, at Court. They are trained in this Art from their Youth, and are not always of noble Birth, or liberal Education. When a great Office is vacant, either by Death or Disgrace (which often happens) five or six of those Candidates petition the Emperor to entertain his Majesty and the Court with a Dance on the Rope, and whoever jumps the highest without falling, succeeds in the Office. Very often the Chief Ministers themselves are commanded to show their Skill and to convince the Emperor that they have not lost their Faculty. *Flimnap*, the Treasurer, is allowed to cut a Caper on the straight Rope, at least an Inch higher than any other Lord in the whole empire. I have seen him do the Summerset several times together upon a Trencher fixed on the Rope, which is no thicker than a common Packthread in *England*. My Friend *Reldresal*, principal Secretary for private Affairs, is, in my Opinion, if I am not partial, the second after the Treasurer; the rest of the great Officers are much upon a Par.

These Diversions are often attended with fatal Accidents, whereof great Numbers are on Record. I myself have seen two or three Candidates break a Limb. But the Danger is much greater when the Ministers themselves are commanded to show their Dexterity; for by contending to excel themselves and their Fellows, they strain so far, that there is hardly one of them who has not received a Fall, and some of them two or three. I was assured that a Year or two before my Arrival, *Flimnap* would have infallibly broke his Neck, if one of the King's Cushions, that accidentally lay on the Ground, had not weakened the Force of his Fall.

There is likewise another Diversion which is only shown before the Emperor and Empress, and first Minister, upon particular Occasions. The Emperor lays on the Table three fine silken Threads of six Inches long. One is Purple, the other Yellow, and the third White. These Threads are proposed as Prizes for those Persons whom the Emperor has a mind to distinguish by a peculiar Mark of his Favour. The Ceremony is performed in his Majesty's great Chamber of State, where the Candidates are to undergo a Trial of Dexterity very different from the former, and such as I have not observed the least Resemblance of in any other Country of the old or the new World. The Emperor holds a Stick in his Hands, both ends parallel to the Horizon, while the Candidates advancing one by one, sometimes leap over the Stick, sometimes creep under it backwards and forwards several times, according as the Stick is advanced or depressed. Sometimes the Emperor holds one end of the Stick, and his first Minister the other; sometimes the Minister has it entirely to himself. Whoever performs his Part with most Agility, and holds out the longest in leaping and creeping, is rewarded with the Purple coloured Silk; the Yellow is given to the next, and the White to the third, which they all wear girt twice round about the middle; and you see few great Persons about this Court, who are not adorned with one of these Girdles.

The Horses of the Army, and those of the royal Stables, having been daily led before me, were no longer shy, but would come up to my very Feet without starting. The Riders would leap them over my Hand as I held it on the Ground, and one of the Emperor's Huntsmen, upon a large Courser, took my Foot, Shoe and all; which was indeed a prodigious Leap. I had the good fortune to divert the Emperor one Day after a very extraordinary manner. I desired he would order several Sticks of two Foot high, and the thickness of an ordinary Cane, to be brought me; whereupon his Majesty commanded the Master of his Woods to give Directions accordingly, and the next Morning six Wood-men arrived with as many Carriages, drawn by eight Horses to each. I took nine of these Sticks, and fixing them firmly in the Ground in a Quadrangular Figure, two foot and a half Square. I took four other Sticks, and tied them parallel at each Corner, about two foot from the Ground;

then I fastened my Handkerchief to the nine Sticks that stood erect, and extended it on all sides till it was tight as the top of a Drum; and the four parallel Sticks rising about five Inches higher than the Handkerchief, served as Ledges on each side. When I had finished my Work, I desired the Emperor to let a Troop of his best Horse, twenty-four in number, come and exercise upon this Plain. His Majesty approved of the Proposal, and I took them up one by one in my hands, ready mounted and armed, with the proper Officers to exercise them. As soon as they got into order, they divided into two Parties, performed mock Skirmishes, discharged blunt Arrows, drew their Swords, fled and pursued, attacked and retired, and in short discovered the best Military Discipline I ever beheld. The parallel Sticks secured them and their Horses from falling over the Stage; and the Emperor was so much delighted, that he ordered this Entertainment to be repeated several days, and once was pleased to be lifted up, and give the word of Command; and, with great difficulty, persuaded even the Empress her self to let me hold her in her close Chair within two Yards of the Stage, whence she was able to take a full View of the whole Performance. It was my good fortune that no ill Accident happened in these Entertainments, only once a fiery Horse that belonged to one of the Captains pawing with his Hoof struck a Hole in my Handkerchief, and his Foot slipping, he overthrew his Rider and himself; but I immediately relieved them both, and covering the Hole with one Hand, I set down the Troop with the other, in the same manner as I took them up. The Horse that fell was strained in the left Shoulder, but the Rider got no hurt, and I repaired my Handkerchief as well as I could; however, I would not trust to the Strength of it any more in such dangerous Enterprises.

About two or three days before I was set at liberty, as I was entertaining the Court with this kind of Feats, there arrived an Express to inform his Majesty, that some of his Subjects riding near the Place where I was first taken up, had seen a great black Substance lying on the Ground very oddly shaped, extending its Edges round as wide as his Majesty's Bedchamber, and rising up in the middle as high as a Man; that it was no living Creature, as they at first apprehended, for it lay on the Grass without Motion, and some of them had walked round it several times: That by mounting upon each other's Shoulders, they had got to the top, which was flat and even, and stamping upon it they found that it was hollow within; that they humbly conceived it might be something belonging to the *Man-Mountain*, and if his Majesty pleased, they would undertake to bring it with only five Horses. I presently knew what they meant, and was glad at heart to receive this Intelligence. It seems upon my first reaching the Shore after our Shipwreck, I was in such confusion, that before I came to the Place where I went to sleep, my Hat which I had fastened with a String to my Head while I was rowing, and had stuck on all the time I was swimming, fell off after I came to Land; the String, as I conjecture, breaking by some Accident which I never observed, but thought my Hat had been lost at Sea. I entreated his Imperial Majesty to give Orders it might be brought to me as soon as possible, describing to him the Use and the Nature of it: And the next Day the Waggoners arrived with it, but not in a very good condition; they had bored two Holes in the Brim, within an Inch and half of the Edge, and fastened two Hooks in the Holes; these Hooks were tied by a long Cord to the Harness, and thus my Hat was dragged along for above half an *English* Mile: but the Ground in that Country being extremely smooth and level, it receiv'd less Damage than I expected.

Two days after this Adventure, the Emperor having ordered that Part of his Army which quarters in and about his Metropolis to be in readiness, took a fancy of diverting himself in a very singular manner. He desired I would stand like a *Colossus*, with my Legs as far asunder as I conveniently could. He then commanded his General, (who was an old experienced Leader, and a great Patron of mine) to draw up the Troops in close Order, and march them under me, the Foot by Twenty-four in a Breast, and the Horse by Sixteen, with Drums beating, Colours flying, and Pikes advanced. This Body consisted of three thousand Foot, and a thousand Horse. His Majesty gave Orders, upon pain of Death, that every Soldier in his March should observe the strictest Decency, with regard to my Person; which, however could not prevent some of the younger Officers from turning up their Eyes as they passed under me. And, to confess the Truth, my Breeches were at that time in so ill a Condition, that they afforded some Opportunities for Laughter and Admiration.

I had sent so many Memorials and Petitions for my Liberty, that his Majesty at length mentioned the Matter first in the Cabinet, and then in a full Council; where it was opposed by none, except *Skyresh Bolgolam*, who was pleased, without any Provocation, to be my mortal Enemy. But it was carried against him by the whole Board, and confirmed by the Emperor. That minister was *Galbet*, or Admiral of the Realm, very much in his Master's Confidence, and a Person well versed in Affairs, but of a morose and sour Complexion. However, he was at length persuaded to comply; but prevailed that the Articles and Conditions upon which I should be set free, and to which I must swear, should be drawn up by himself. These Articles were brought to me by *Skyresh Bolgolam* in Person attended by two Under-Secretaries, and several Persons of Distinction. After they were read, I was demanded to swear to the Performance of them; first in the manner of my own Country, and after-wards in the method prescribed by their Laws which was to hold my right Foot in my left Hand, and to place the middle Finger of my right Hand on the Crown of my Head, and my Thumb on the Tip of my right Ear. But because the Reader may be curious to have some Idea of the Style and Manner of Expression peculiar to that People, as well as to know the Article upon which I recovered my Liberty,

I have made a Translation of the whole Instrument word for word, as near as I was able, which I here offer to the Publick.

"Golbasto Momarem Evlame Gurdilo Shefin Mully Ully Gue, most Mighty Emperor of *Lilliput*, Delight and Terror of the Universe, whose Dominions extend five thousand *Blustrugs* (about twelve Miles in Circumference) to the Extremitys of the Globe; Monarch of all Monarchs, taller than the Sons of Men; whose Feet press down to the Center, and whose Head strikes against the Sun: At whose Nod the Princes of the Earth shake their Knees; pleasant as the Spring, comfortable as the Summer, fruitful as Autumn, dreadful as Winter. His most sublime Majesty proposeth to the *Man-Mountain*, lately arrived at our Celestial Dominions, the following Articles, which by a solemn Oath, he shall be obliged to perform.

FIRST, The *Man-Mountain* shall not depart from our Dominions, without our License under our Great Seal.

SECOND, He shall not presume to come into our Metropolis, without our express Order; at which time the Inhabitants shall have two hours warning to keep within their doors.

THIRD, The said *Man-Mountain* shall confine his Walks to our principal High Roads, and not offer to walk, or lie down in a Meadow or Field of Corn.

FOURTH, As he walks the said Roads, he shall take the utmost care not to trample upon the Bodies of any of our loving Subjects, their Horses, or Carriages, nor take any of our Subjects into his hands without their own Consent.

FIFTH, If an Express requires extraordinary Dispatch, the *Man-Mountain* shall be obliged to carry in his Pocket, the Messenger and Horse a Six Days Journey once in every Moon, and return the said Messenger back (if so required) safe to our Imperial Presence.

SIXTH, He shall be our Ally against our Enemies in the Island of *Blefuscu*, and do his utmost to destroy their Fleet, which is now preparing to invade Us.

SEVENTH, That the said *Man-Mountain* shall, at his times of leisure, be aiding and assisting to our Workmen, in helping to raise certain great Stones, towards covering the Wall of the principal Park, and other our Royal Buildings.

EIGHTH, That the said *Man-Mountain* shall, in two Moons time, deliver in an exact Survey of the Circumference of our Dominions, by a Computation of his own Paces round the Coast.

LASTLY, That upon his solemn Oath to observe all the above Articles, the said *Man-Mountain* shall have a daily Allowance of Meat and Drink sufficient for the Support of 1724 of our Subjects, with free Access to our Royal Person, and other Marks of our Favour. Given at our Palace at *Belfaborac* the twelfth Day of the Ninety-first Moon of our Reign."

I swore and subscribed to these Articles with great Cheerfulness and Content, although some of them were not so honourable as I could have wished; which proceeded wholly from the Malice of *Skyresh Bolgolam* the High Admiral: whereupon my Chains were immediately unlocked, and I was at full liberty; the Emperor himself in Person did me the Honour to be by at the whole Ceremony. I made my Acknowledgements by prostrating myself at his Majesty's Feet: But he commanded me to rise; and after many gracious Expressions, which, to avoid the Censure of Vanity, I shall not repeat, he added, that he hoped I should prove a useful Servant, and well deserve all the Favours he had already conferred upon me, or might do for the future.

The reader may please to observe, that in the last Article of the Recovery of my Liberty, the Emperor stipulates to allow me a Quantity of Meat and Drink sufficient for the Support of 1724 *Lilliputians*. Some time after, asking a Friend at Court how they came to fix on that determinate Number; he told me, that his Majesty's Mathematicians, having taken the Height of my Body by the help of a *Quadrant*, and finding it to exceed theirs in the Proportion of Twelve to One, they concluded from the Similarity of their Bodies, that mine must contain at least 1724 of theirs, and consequently would require as much Food as was necessary to support that number of *Lilliputians*. By which, the Reader may conceive an Idea of the Ingenuity of that People, as well as the prudent and exact economy of so great a Prince.

CHAPTER IV.

Mildendo, *the Metropolis of* Lilliput, *described, together with the Emperor's Palace. A Conversation between the Author and a Principal Secretary, concerning the Affairs of that Empire. The Author's Offers to serve the Emperor in his Wars.*

THE FIRST REQUEST I MADE, after I had obtained my Liberty, was, that I might have license to see *Mildendo*, the Metropolis; which the Emperor easily granted me, but with a special Charge to do no hurt, either to the Inhabitants, or their Houses. The People had notice by Proclamation of my design to visit the Town. The Wall which encompassed it, is two foot and a half high, and at least eleven Inches broad, so that a Coach and Horses may be driven very safely round it; and it is flanked with strong Towers at ten foot distance. I stepped over the great Western Gate, and passed very gently, and sidling through the two principal Streets, only in my short Waistcoat, for fear of damaging the Roofs and Eaves of the Houses with the Skirts of my Coat. I walked with the utmost Circumspection, to avoid treading on any Stragglers, that might remain in the Streets, although the Orders were very strict, that all People should keep in their Houses, at their own peril. The Garret-windows and Tops of Houses were so crowded with Spectators, that I thought in all my Travels I had not seen a more populous Place. The City is an exact Square, each side of the Wall being five hundred foot long. The two great Streets which run cross and divide it into four Quarters, are five foot wide. The Lanes and Alleys which I could not enter, but only viewed them as I passed, are from twelve to eighteen Inches. The Town is capable of holding five hundred thousand Souls. The Houses are from three to five Stories. The Shops and Markets well provided.

The Emperor's Palace is in the Center of the City, where the two great Streets meet. It is inclosed by a Wall of two foot high, and twenty feet distant from the Buildings. I had his Majesty's Permission to step over this Wall; and the Space being so wide between that and the Palace, I could easily view it on every side. The outward Court is a Square of forty foot, and includes two other Courts: In the inmost are the Royal Apartments, which I was very desirous to see, but found it extremely difficult; for the great Gates, from one Square into another, were but eighteen Inches high, and seven Inches wide. Now the Buildings of the outer Court were at least five foot high, and it was impossible for me to stride over them, without infinite Damage to the Pile, though the Walls were strongly built of hewn Stone, and four Inches thick. At the same time the Emperor had a great desire that I should see the Magnificence of his Palace; but this I was not able to do till three Days after, which I spent in cutting down with my Knife some of the largest Trees in the Royal Park, about a hundred Yards distant from the City. Of these Trees I made two Stools, each about three foot high, and strong enough to bear my Weight. The People having received notice a second time, I went again through the City to the Palace, with my two Stools in my Hands. When I came to the side of the outer Court, I stood upon one Stool, and took the other in my hand: This I lifted over the Roof, and gently set it down on the Space between the first and second Court, which was eight foot wide. I then stept over the Building very conveniently from one Stool to the other, and drew up the first after me with a hooked Stick. By this Contrivance I got into the inmost Court; and lying down upon my Side, I applied my Face to the Windows of the middle Stories, which were left open on purpose, and discovered the most splendid Apartments that can be imagined. There I saw the Empress, and the young Princes in their several Lodgings, with their chief Attendants about them. Her Imperial Majesty was pleased to smile very graciously upon me, and gave me out of the Window her Hand to kiss.

But I shall not anticipate the Reader with further Descriptions of this kind, because I reserve them for a greater Work, which is now almost ready for the Press;

containing a general Description of this Empire, from its first Erection, through along Series of Princes, with a particular Account of their Wars and Politicks, Laws, Learning, and Religion: their Plants and Animals, their peculiar Manners and Customs, with other Matters very curious and useful; my chief design at present being only to relate such Events and Transactions as happened to the Publick, or to myself, during a Residence of about nine Months in that Empire.

One Morning, about a Fortnight after I had obtain'd my Liberty, *Reldresal*, Principal Secretary (as they style him) for private Affairs, came to my House, attended only by one Servant. He ordered his Coach to wait at a distance, and desired I would give him an Hour's Audience; which I readily consented to, on account of his Quality, and Personal Merits, as well as of the many good Offices he had done me during my Sollicitations at Court. I offered to lie down, that he might the more conveniently reach my Ear; but he chose rather to let me hold him in my hand during our Conversation. He began with Compliments on my Liberty, said he might pretend to some Merit in it: but, however, added, that if it had not been for the present Situation of things at Court, perhaps I might not have obtained it so soon. "For," said he, "as flourishing a Condition as we may appear to be in to Foreigners, we labour under two mighty Evils; a violent Faction at home, and the Danger of an Invasion by a most potent Enemy from abroad. As to the first, you are to understand, that for about seventy Moons past, there have been two struggling Parties in this Empire, under the Names of *Tramecksan*, and *Slamecksan*, from the high and low Heels of their Shoes, by which they distinguish themselves. It is alleged indeed, that the high Heels are most agreeable to our ancient Constitution: But however this be, his Majesty has determined to make use only of low Heels in the Administration of the Government, and all Offices in the Gift of the Crown, as you cannot but observe; and particularly, that his Majesty's Imperial Heels are lower at least by a *Drurr* than any of his Court; (*Drurr* is a Measure about the fourteenth Part of an Inch). The Animositys between these two Partys run so high, that they will neither eat nor drink, nor talk with each other. We compute the *Tramecksan*, or High Heels, to exceed us in number; but the Power is wholly on our side. We apprehend his Imperial Highness, the Heir to the Crown, to have some Tendency towards the High-Heels; at least we can plainly discover that one of his Heels higher than the other, which gives him a Hobble in his Gait. Now, in the midst of these intestine Disquiets, we are threatened with an Invasion from the island of *Blefuscu*, which is the other great Empire of the Universe, almost as large and powerful as this of his Majesty. For as to what we have heard you affirm, that there are other Kingdoms and States in the World, inhabited by human Creatures as large as yourself, our Philosophers are in much doubt, and would rather conjecture that you dropt from the Moon, or one of the Stars; because it is certain, that a hundred Mortals of your Bulk would, in a short time, destroy all the Fruits and Cattle of his Majesty's Dominions. Besides, our Historys of six thousand Moons make no mention of any other Regions, than the two great Empires of *Lilliput* and *Blefuscu*. Which two mighty Powers have, as I was going to tell you, been engaged in a most obstinate War for six-and-thirty Moons past. It began upon the following Occasion. It is allowed on all hands, that the primitive way of breaking Eggs before we eat them, was upon the larger End: But his present Majesty's Grandfather, while he was a Boy, going to eat an Egg, and breaking it according to the ancient Practice, happened to cut one of his Fingers. Whereupon the Emperor his Father published an Edict, commanding all his Subjects, upon great Penaltys, to break the smaller End of their Eggs. The People so highly resented this Law, that our Historys tell us there have been six Rebellions raised on that account; wherein one Emperor lost his Life, and another his Crown. These civil Commotions were constantly fomented by the Monarchs of *Blefuscu*; and when they were quelled, the Exiles always fled for Refuge to that Empire. It is computed, that eleven thousand Persons have, at several times suffered Death, rather than submit to break their Eggs at the smaller End. Many hundred large Volumes have been published upon this Controversy: But the Books of the *Big-Endians* have been long forbidden, and the whole Party rendered incapable by Law of holding Employments. During the Course of these Troubles, the Emperors of *Blefuscu* did frequently expostulate by their Embassadors, accusing us of making a Schism in Religion, by offending against a fundamental Doctrine of our great Prophet *Lustrog*, in the fifty-fourth Chapter of the *Blundecral*, (which is their *Alcoran*.) This, however, is thought to be a mere Strain upon the Text: For the Words are these; *That all true Believers break their Eggs at the convenient End*: and which is the convenient End, seems, in my humble Opinion to be left to every Man's Conscience, or at least in the power of the Chief Magistrate to determine. Now, the *Big-Endian* Exiles have found so much Credit in the Emperor of *Blefuscu*'s Court, and so much private Assistance and Encouragement from their Party here at home, that a bloody War has been carried on between the two Empires for six-and-thirty Moons with various Success; during which time we have lost forty Capital Ships, and a much a greater number of smaller Vessels, together with thirty thousand of our best Seamen and Soldiers; and the Damage received by the Enemy is reckon'd to be somewhat greater than Ours. However, they have now equipped a numerous Fleet, and are just preparing to make a Descent upon us; and his Imperial Majesty placing great Confidence in your Valour and Strength, hath commanded Me to lay this Account of his Affairs before You."

I desired the Secretary to present my humble Duty to the Emperor, and to let him know, that I thought it would not become Me, who was a Foreigner, to interfere with Parties; but I was ready, with the hazard of my Life, to defend his Person and State against all Invaders.

CHAPTER V.

The Author by an extraordinary Stratagem prevents an Invasion. A high Title of Honour is conferred upon him. Ambassadors arrive from the Emperor of Blefuscu, *and sue for Peace. The Empress's Apartment on fire by an Accident; the Author instrumental in saving the rest of the Palace.*

THE EMPIRE OF *BLEFUSCU* IS AN ISLAND, situated to the North North-East of *Lilliput*, from whence it is parted only by a Channel of eight hundred Yards wide. I had not yet seen it, and upon this Notice of an intended Invasion, I avoided appearing on that side of the Coast, for fear of being discovered, by some of the Enemy's Ships, who had received no Intelligence of me, all Intercourse between the two Empires having been strictly forbidden during the War, upon pain of Death, and an Embargo laid by our Emperor upon all Vessels whatsoever. I communicated to his Majesty a Project I had formed of seizing the Enemy's whole Fleet: which, as our Scouts assured us, lay at Anchor in the Harbour, ready to sail with the first fair Wind. I consulted the most experienced Seamen upon the Depth of the Channel, which they had often plummed, who told me, that in the middle, at High-water, it was seventy *Glumgluffs* deep, which is about six Foot of *European* Measure; and the rest of it fifty *Glumgluffs* at most. I walked towards the North-East Coast over against *Blefuscu*; and lying down behind a Hillock, took out my small Pocket Perspective-Glass, and viewed the Enemy's Fleet at Anchor, consisting of about fifty Men of War, and a great Number of Transports: I then came back to my House, and gave Order (for which I had a Warrant) for a great Quantity of the strongest Cable and Bars of Iron. The Cable was about as thick as Packthread, and the Bars of the length and size of a Knitting-Needle. I trebled the Cable to make it stronger, and for the same reason I twisted three of the Iron Bars together, bending the Extremities into a Hook. Having thus fixed fifty Hooks to as many Cables, I went back to the North-East Coast, and putting off my Coat, Shoes, and Stockings, walked into the Sea, in my Leathern Jerkin, about half an hour before high Water. I waded with what haste I could, and swam in the middle about thirty Yards, till I felt ground; I arrived at the Fleet in less than half an hour. The Enemy was so frightened when they saw me, that they leaped out of their Ships, and swam to shore, where there could not be fewer than thirty thousand Souls. I then took my Tackling, and fastening a Hook to the hole at the Prow of each, I tied all the Cords together at the End. While I was thus employed, the Enemy discharged several thousand Arrows, many of which stuck in my Hands and Face; and besides the excessive smart, gave me much disturbance in my Work. My greatest Apprehension was for mine Eyes, which I should have infallibly lost, if I had not suddenly thought of an Expedient. I kept, among other little Necessaries, a pair of Spectacles in a private Pocket, which, as I observed before, had escaped the Emperor's Searchers. These I took out and fastened as strongly as I could upon my Nose, and thus armed went on boldly with my Work in spite of the Enemy's Arrows, many of which struck against the Glasses of my Spectacles, but without any other Effect, further than a little to discompose them. I had now fastened all the Hooks, and, taking the Knot in my hand, began to pull; but not a Ship would stir, for they were all too fast held by their Anchors, so that the bold part of my Enterprise remained. I therefore let go the Cord, and leaving the Hooks fixed to the Ships, I resolutely cut with my Knife the Cables that fastened the Anchors, receiving about two hundred Shots in my Face and Hands; then I took up the knotted End of the Cables to which my Hooks were tied, and with great ease drew fifty of the Enemy's largest Men of War after me.

The *Blefuscudians*, who had not the least Imagination of what I intended, were at first confounded with Astonishment. They had seen me cut the Cables, and thought my Design was only to let the Ships run a-drift, or fall foul on each other: but when they perceived the whole Fleet moving in Order, and saw me pulling at the End, they set up such a scream of Grief and Despair as it is almost impossible to describe or conceive. When I had got out of danger, I stopt awhile to pick out the Arrows that stuck in my Hands and Face, and rubbed on some of the same Ointment that was given me at my first arrival, as I have formerly mentioned. I then took off my Spectacles, and waiting about an hour, till the Tide was a little fallen, I waded through the middle with my Cargo, and arrived safe at the Royal Port of *Lilliput*.

The Emperor and his whole Court stood on the Shore expecting the Issue of this great Adventure. They saw the Ships move forward in a large Half-Moon, but could not discern me, who was up to my Breast in Water. When I advanced to the middle of the Channel, they were yet more in pain because I was under Water to my Neck. The Emperor concluded me to be drowned, and that the Enemy's Fleet was approaching in a hostile manner: But he was soon eased of his Fears, for the Channel growing shallower every step I made, I came in a short time within hearing, and holding up the end of the Cable by which the Fleet was fastened, I cryed in a loud Voice, *Long live the most puissant Emperor of Lilliput!* This great Prince received me at my Landing with all possible Encomiums, and created me a *Nardac* upon the spot, which is the highest Title of Honour among them.

His Majesty desired I would take some other Opportunity of bringing all the rest of his Enemy's Ships into his Ports. And so unmeasureable is the Ambition of Princes, that he seemed to think of nothing less than reducing the whole Empire of *Blefuscu* into a Province, and governing it by a Vice-Roy; of destroying the

Big-Endian Exiles, and compelling that People to break the smaller end of their Eggs, by which he would remain the sole Monarch of the whole World. But I endeavour'd to divert him from this Design, by many Arguments drawn from the Topicks of Policy as well as Justice: And I plainly protested, that I would never be an Instrument of bringing a Free and Brave People into Slavery. And, when the Matter was debated in Council, the wisest part of the Ministry were of my Opinion.

This open bold Declaration of mine was so opposite to the Schemes and Politicks of his Imperial Majesty, that he could never forgive it; he mentioned it in a very artful manner at Council, where I was told that some of the wisest appeared, at least by their Silence, to be of my Opinion; but others, who were my secret Enemies, could not forbear some Expressions, which by a side-wind reflected on me. And from this time began an Intrigue between his Majesty and a Junto of ministers maliciously bent against me, which broke out in less than two Months, and had like to have ended in my utter Destruction. Of so little weight are the greatest Services to Princes, when put into the Balance with a Refusal to gratify their Passions.

About three Weeks after this Exploit, there arrived a solemn Embassy from *Blefuscu*, with humble Offers of a Peace; which was soon concluded upon Conditions very advantageous to our Emperor, wherewith I shall not trouble the Reader. There were six Ambassadors, with a Train of about five hundred Persons, and their Entry was very magnificent, suitable to the Grandeur of their Master, and the Importance of their Business. When their Treaty was finished, wherein I did them several good Offices by the Credit I now had, or at least appeared to have at Court, their Excellencies, who were privately told how much I had been their Friend, made me a Visit in Form. They began with many Compliments upon my Valour and Generosity, invited me to that Kingdom in the Emperor their Master's Name, and desired me to show them some Proofs of my prodigious Strength, of which they had heard so many Wonders; wherein I readily obliged them, but shall not trouble the Reader with the Particulars.

When I had for some time entertained their Excellencies, to their infinite Satisfaction and Surprise, I desired they would do me the Honour to present my most humble Respects to the Emperor their Master, the Renown of whose Virtues had so justly filled the whole World with Admiration, and whose Royal Person I resolved to attend before I returned to my own Country: accordingly, the next time I had the honour to see our Emperor, I desired his general License to wait on the *Blefuscudian* Monarch, which he was pleas'd to grant me, as I could plainly perceive, in a very cold manner; but could not guess the Reason, till I had a Whisper from a certain Person, that *Flimnap* and *Bolgolam* had represented my Intercourse with those Ambassadors as a mark of Disaffection, from which I am sure my Heart was wholly free. And this was the first time I began to conceive some imperfect Idea of Courts and Ministers.

It is to be observed, that these Ambassadors spoke to me by an Interpreter, the Languages of both Empires differing as much from each other as any two in *Europe*, and each Nation priding itself upon the Antiquity, Beauty, and Energy of their own Tongues, with an avowed Contempt for that of their Neighbour; yet our Emperor standing upon the advantage he had got by the seizure of their Fleet, obliged them to deliver their Credentials, and make their Speech in the *Lilliputian* Tongue. And it must be confessed, that from the great Intercourse of Trade and Commerce between both Realms, from the continual Reception of Exiles, which is mutual among them, and from the Custom in each Empire to send their young Nobility and richer Gentry to the other, in order to polish themselves by seeing the World, and understanding Men and Manners; there are few Persons of Distinction, or Merchants, or Seamen, who dwell in the Maritime Parts, but what can hold Conversation in both Tongues; as I found some Weeks after, when I went to pay my respects to the Emperor of *Blefuscu*, which in the midst of great Misfortunes, through the Malice of my Enemies, proved a very happy adventure to me, as I shall relate in its proper place.

The Reader may remember that when I signed those Articles upon which I recovered my Liberty, there were some which I disliked upon account of their being too servile, neither could any thing but an extreme Necessity have forced me to submit. But being now a *Nardac* of the highest Rank in that Empire, such Offices were looked upon as below my Dignity, and the Emperor (to do him Justice), never once mentioned them to me. However, it was not long before I had an Opportunity of doing his Majesty, at least as I then thought, a most signal Service. I was alarmed at Midnight with the Cries of many hundred People at my Door; by which being suddenly awaked, I was in some kind of Terror. I heard the word *Burglum* repeated incessantly: several of the Emperor's Court making their Way through the Crowd, intreated me to come immediately to the Palace, where her Imperial Majesty's Apartment was on fire, by the carelessness of a Maid of Honour, who fell asleep while she was reading a Romance. I got up in an instant; and Orders being given to clear the way before me, and it being likewise a Moonshine Night, I made a shift to get to the Palace without trampling on any of the People. I found they had already applied Ladders to the Walls of the Apartment, and were well provided with Buckets, but the Water was at some distance. These Buckets were about the size of a large Thimble, and the poor People supplied me with them as fast as they could; but the Flame was so violent, that they did little good. I might easily have stifled it with my Coat, which I unfortunately left behind me for haste, and came away only in my Leathern Jerkin. The Case seemed wholly desperate and deplorable, and this magnificent Palace would have infallibly been burnt down to the ground, if, by a Presence of Mind, unusual to me, I had not suddenly thought of an Expedient. I had the Evening before drank plentifully of a most delicious Wine, called *Glimigrim*, (the *Blefuscudians* call it *Flunec*, but ours is esteemed the better sort) which is very diuretick. By the luckiest Chance in the World, I had not discharged myself of any part of it. The Heat I had contracted by coming very near the Flames, and by labouring to quench them, made the Wine begin to operate by Urine; which I voided in such a Quantity, and applied so well to the proper Places, that in three Minutes the Fire was wholly extinguished, and the rest of that noble Pile, which had cost so many Ages in erecting, preserved from Destruction.

It was now Day-light, and I returned to my House, without waiting to congratulate with the Emperor; because, although I had done a very eminent piece of Service, yet I could not tell how his Majesty might resent the manner by which I had performed it: For, by the fundamental Laws of the Realm, it is Capital in any Person, of what Quality soever, to make water within the Precincts of the Palace. But I was a little comforted by a Message from his Majesty, that he would give Orders to the Grand Justiciary for passing my Pardon in form; which, however, I could not obtain. And I was privately assured, the Empress conceiving the greatest Abhorrence of what I had done, removed to the most distant side of the Court, firmly resolved that those Buildings should never be repaired for her Use; and, in the presence of her chief Confidents could not forbear vowing Revenge.

CHAPTER VI.

Of the Inhabitants of Lilliput; *their Learning, Laws, and Customs; the Manner of Educating their Children. The Author's way of living in that Country. His Vindication of a great Lady.*

ALTHOUGH I INTEND TO LEAVE the Description of this Empire to a particular Treatise, yet, in the mean time I am content to gratify the curious Reader with some general Ideas. As the common Size of the Natives is somewhat under six Inches high, so there is an exact Proportion in all other Animals, as well as Plants and Trees: For instance, the tallest Horses and Oxen are between four and five Inches in height, the Sheep an Inch and a half, more or less; their Geese about the bigness of a Sparrow, and so the several Gradations downwards, till you come to the smallest, which, to my sight, were almost invisible; but Nature has adapted the Eyes of the *Lilliputians* to all Objects proper for their view: They see with great exactness, but at no great distance. And to show the sharpness of their Sight toward Objects that are near, I have been much pleased with observing a Cook pulling a Lark, which was not so large as a common Fly; and a young Girl threading an invisible Needle with invisible Silk. Their tallest Trees are about seven foot high: I mean some of those in the great Royal Park, the Tops whereof I could but just reach with my Fist clenched. The other Vegetables are in the same Proportion; but this I leave to the Reader's Imagination.

I shall say but little at present of their Learning, which for many Ages hath flourished in all its Branches among them: But their manner of Writing is very peculiar, being neither from the Left to the Right, like the *Europeans*; nor from the Right to the Left, like the *Arabians*; nor from up to down, like the *Chinese*; nor from down to up, like the *Cascagians*: but aslant from one Corner of the Paper to the other, like Ladies in *England*.

They bury their Dead with their Heads directly downwards, because they hold an Opinion, that in eleven thousand Moons they are all to rise again, in which Period the Earth (which they conceive to be flat) will turn upside down, and by this means they shall, at their Resurrection, be found ready standing on their Feet. The Learned among them confess the Absurdity of this Doctrine, but the Practice still continues in compliance to the Vulgar.

There are some Laws and Customs in this Empire very peculiar; and if they were not so directly contrary to those of my own dear Country, I should be tempted to say a little in their justification. It is only to be wished, that they were as well executed. The first I shall mention, relates to Informers. All Crimes against the State are punished here with the utmost severity; but if the Person accused maketh his Innocence plainly to appear upon his Trial, the Accuser is immediately put to an ignominious Death; and out of his Goods or Lands, the innocent Person is quadruply recompensed for the Loss of his Time, for the Danger he underwent, for the Hardship of his Imprisonment, and for all the Charges he hath been at in making his Defence. Or, if that Fund be deficient, it is largely supplied by the Crown. The Emperor does also confer on him some publick Mark of his Favour, and Proclamation is made of his Innocence through the whole City.

They look upon Fraud as a greater Crime than Theft, and therefore seldom fail to punish it with Death; for they allege, that Care and Vigilance, with a very common Understanding, may preserve a Man's Goods from Thieves, but Honesty has no defence against superior Cunning: and since it is necessary that there should be a perpetual Intercourse of Buying and Selling, and dealing upon Credit, where Fraud is permitted or connived at, or hath no Law to punish it, the honest Dealer is always undone, and the Knave gets the advantage. I remember when I was once interceding with the King for a Criminal who had wronged his Master of a great Sum of Money, which he had received by Order, and ran away with; and happening to tell his Majesty, by way of Extenuation, that it was only a Breach of Trust; the Emperor thought it monstrous in me to offer, as a Defence, the greatest Aggravation of the Crime: and truly I had little to say in return, farther than the common Answer, that different Nations had different Customs; for, I confess, I was heartily ashamed.

Although we usually call Reward and Punishment the two Hinges upon which all Government turns, yet I could never observe this Maxim to be put in practice by any Nation except that of *Lilliput*. Whoever can there bring sufficient Proof that he hath strictly observed the Laws of his Country for seventy-three Moons, hath a claim to certain Privileges, according to his Quality and Condition of Life, with a proportionable Sum of Money out of a Fund appropriated for that Use: He likewise acquires the Title of *Snilpall*, or *Legal*, which is added to his Name, but does not descend to his Posterity. And these People thought it a prodigious Defect of Policy among us, when I told them that our Laws were enforced only by Penalties without any mention of Reward. It is upon this account that the Image of Justice, in their Courts of Judicature, is formed with six Eyes, two before, as many behind, and on each side one, to signify Circumspection; with a Bag of Gold open in her Right Hand, and a Sword sheathed in her Left, to show she is more disposed to Reward than to Punish.

In choosing Persons for all Employments, they have more regard to good Morals than to great Abilities; for, since Government is necessary to Mankind, they believe that the common Size of Human Understandings, is fitted to some Station or other, and that Providence never intended to make the Management of publick Affairs a Mystery, to be comprehended only by a few Persons of sublime Genius, of which there seldom are three born in an Age: but they suppose Truth, Justice, Temperance, and the like, to be in every Man's power; the Practice of which Virtues, assisted by Experience and a good Intention, would qualify any Man for the service of his Country, except where a Course of Study is required. But they thought the want of Moral Virtues was so far from being supplied by superior Endowments of the Mind, that Employments could never be put into such dangerous Hands as those of Persons so qualify'd; and at least, that the Mistakes committed by Ignorance in a virtuous Disposition, would never be of such fatal Consequence to the Publick Weal, as the Practices of a Man whose Inclinations led him to be corrupt, and who had great Abilities to manage and multiply, and defend his Corruptions.

In like manner, the Disbelief of a Divine Providence renders a man incapable of holding any Publick Station; for since Kings avow themselves to be the Deputies of Providence, the *Lilliputians* think nothing can be more absurd than for a Prince to employ such Men as disown the Authority under which he acts.

In relating these and the following Laws, I would only be understood to mean the original Institutions, and not the most scandalous Corruptions into which these People are fallen by the degenerate Nature of Man. For as to that infamous Practice of acquiring great Employments by dancing on the Ropes, or Badges of Favour and Distinction by leaping over Sticks, and creeping under them, the Reader is to observe, that they were first introduced by the Grand-father of the Emperor now reigning, and grew to the present height by the gradual increase of Party and Faction.

Ingratitude is among them a capital Crime, as we read it to have been in some other Countries; for they reason thus, that whoever makes ill Returns to his Benefactor, must needs be a common Enemy to the rest of Mankind, from whom he has received no Obligation, and therefore such a Man is not fit to live.

Their Notions relating to the Duties of Parents and Children differ extremely from ours. For, since the Conjunction of Male and Female is founded upon the great Law of Nature, in order to propagate and continue the Species, the *Lilliputians* will needs have it, that Men and Women are joined together like other Animals, by the Motives of Concupiscence; and that their Tenderness towards their Young proceeds from the like natural Principle: for which reason they will never allow, that a Child is under any Obligation to his Father for begetting him, or to his Mother for bringing him into the World; which, considering the Miseries of human Life, was neither a Benefit in itself, or intended so by his Parents, whose Thoughts in their Love-Encounters were otherwise employ'd. Upon these, and the like Reasonings, their Opinion is, that Parents are the last of all others to be trusted with the Education of their own Children: and therefore they have in every Town publick Nurseries, where all Parents, except Cottagers and Labourers, are obliged to send their Infants of both Sexes to be reared and educated when they come to the Age of twenty Moons, at which time they are supposed to have some Rudiments of Docility. These Schools are of several kinds, suited to different Qualities, and both Sexes. They have certain Professors well skilled in preparing Children for such a condition of Life as befits the Rank of their Parents, and their own Capacities as well as Inclinations. I shall first say something of the Male Nurseries, and then of the Female.

The nurseries for Males of Noble or Eminent Birth, are provided with Grave and Learned Professors, and their several Deputies. The Clothes and Food of the Children are plain and simple. They are bred up in the Principles of Honour, Justice, Courage, Modesty, Clemency, Religion, and Love of their Country; they are always employed in some Business, except in the times of Eating and Sleeping, which are very short, and two Hours for Diversions, consisting of bodily Exercises. They are dressed by Men till four Years of Age, and then are obliged to dress themselves, although their Quality be ever so great; and the Women Attendants, who are aged proportionably to ours at fifty, perform only the most menial Offices. They are never suffered to converse with Servants, but go together in small or greater numbers to take their Diversions, and always in the presence of a Professor, or one of his Deputies; whereby they avoid those early bad Impressions of Folly and Vice to which our Children are subject. Their Parents are suffered to see them only twice a Year; the Visit is to last but an hour. They are allowed to kiss the Child at Meeting and Parting; but a Professor, who always stands by on those occasions, will not suffer them to whisper, or use any fondling Expressions, or bring any Presents of Toys, Sweet-meats, and the like.

The Pension from each Family for the Education and Entertainment of a Child, upon failure of due payment, is levyed by the Emperor's Officers.

The Nurseries for Children of ordinary Gentlemen, Merchants, Traders, and Handicrafts, are managed proportionably after the same manner; only those designed for Trades are put out Apprentices at Eleven years old, whereas those of Persons of Quality continue in their Nurseries till Fifteen, which answers to One-and-Twenty with us: but the Confinement is gradually lessened for the last three Years.

In the Female Nurseries, the young Girls of Quality are educated much like the Males, only they are dressed by orderly Servants of their own Sex, but always in the presence of a Professor or Deputy, till they come to dress themselves, which is at five Years old. And if it be found that these Nurses ever presume to entertain the Girls with frightful or foolish Stories, or the common Follies practised by Chamber-Maids among us, they are publickly whipped thrice about the City, imprisoned for a Year, and banished for Life to the most desolate Part of the Country. Thus the young Ladies are as much ashamed of being Cowards and Fools, as the Men, and despise all personal Ornaments beyond Decency and Cleanliness: Neither did I perceive any Difference in their Education, made by their Difference of Sex, only that the Exercises of the Females were not altogether so robust; and that some Rules were given them relating to domestick Life, and a smaller Compass of Learning was enjoined them: For the Maxim is, that among People of Quality, a Wife should be always a reasonable and agreeable Companion, because she cannot always be young. When the Girls are twelve Years old, which among them is the marriageable Age, their Parents or Guardians take them home, with great Expressions of Gratitude to the Professors, and seldom without Tears of the young Lady and her Companions.

In the Nurseries of Females of the meaner sort, the Children are instructed in all kinds of Works proper for their Sex, and their several degrees: Those intended for Apprentices, are dismissed at nine Years old, the rest are kept to thirteen.

The meaner Families, who have Children at these Nurseries, are obliged, besides their annual Pension, which is as low as possible, to return to the Steward of the Nursery a small monthly Share of their Gettings, to be a Portion for the Child; and therefore all Parents are limited in their Expences by the Law. For the *Lilliputians* think nothing can be more unjust, than for People, in subservience to their own Appetites, to bring Children into the World, and leave the Burthen of supporting them on the Publick. As to Persons of Quality, they give Security to appropriate a certain Sum for each Child, suitable to their Condition; and these Funds are always managed with good Husbandry, and the most exact Justice.

The Cottagers and Labourers keep their Children at home, their Business being only to till and cultivate the Earth, and therefore their Education is of little consequence to the Publick: but the Old and Diseased among them are supported by Hospitals: for Begging is a Trade unknown in this Kingdom.

And here it may perhaps divert the curious Reader, to give some account of my Domestick, and my manner of living in this Country, during a Residence of nine Months and thirteen Days. Having a Head mechanically turned, and being likewise forced by necessity, I had made for myself a Table and Chair convenient enough, out of the largest Trees in the Royal Park. Two hundred Sempstresses were employed to make me Shirts, and Linnen for my Bed and Table, all of the strongest and coarsest kind they could get; which, however, they were forced to quilt together in several Folds, for the thickest was some degrees finer than Lawn. Their Linnen is usually three Inches wide, and three Foot make a Piece. The Sempstresses took my Measure as I lay on the ground, one standing at my Neck, and another at my Mid Leg, with a strong Cord extended, that each held by the end, while a third measured the length of the Cord with a Rule of an Inch long. Then they measured my right Thumb, and desired no more; for by a mathematical Computation, that twice round the Thumb is once round the Wrist, and so on to the Neck and the Waist, and by the help of my old Shirt, which I displayed on the Ground before them for a Pattern, they fitted me exactly. Three hundred Tailors were employed in the same manner to make me Clothes; but they had another Contrivance for taking my Measure. I kneeled down, and they raised a Ladder from the Ground to my Neck; upon this Ladder one of them mounted, and let fall a Plumb-Line from my Collar to the Floor, which just answered the length of my Coat; but my Waist and Arms I measured myself. When my Clothes were finished, which was done in my House (for the largest of theirs would not have been able to hold them) they looked like the Patch-Work made by the Ladies in *England*, only that mine were all of a Colour.

I had three hundred Cooks to dress my Victuals, in little convenient Huts built about my House, where they and their Families lived, and prepared me two Dishes a-piece. I took up twenty Waiters in my Hand, and placed them on the Table, a hundred more attended below on the Ground, some with Dishes of Meat, and some with Barrels of Wine and other Liquors, slung on their Shoulders; all which the Waiters above drew up as I wanted, in a very ingenious manner, by certain Cords, as we draw the bucket up a Well in *Europe*. A Dish of their Meat was a good Mouthful, and a Barrel of their Liquor a reasonable Draught. Their Mutton yields to ours, but their Beef is excellent. I have had a Sirloin so large, that I have been forced to make three Bits of it; but this is rare. My Servants were astonished to see me eat it Bones and all, as in our Country we do the Leg of a Lark. Their Geese and Turkeys I usually eat at a Mouthful, and I confess they far exceed ours. Of their smaller Fowl I could take up twenty or thirty at the end of my Knife.

One day his Imperial Majesty being informed of my way of living, desired that himself, and his Royal Consort, with the young Princes of the Blood of both Sexes, might have the Happiness (as he was pleased to call it) of dining with me. They came accordingly, and I placed 'em in Chairs of State on my Table, just over-against me, with their Guards about them. *Flimnap* the Lord High Treasurer attended there likewise, with his white Staff; and I observed he often looked on me with a sour Countenance, which I would not seem to regard, but ate more than usual, in honour to my dear Country, as well as to fill the Court with Admiration. I have some private Reasons to believe, that this Visit from his Majesty gave *Flimnap* an opportunity of doing me ill Offices to his Master. That Minister had always been my secret Enemy, though he outwardly caressed me more than was usual to the Moroseness of his Nature. He represented to the Emperor the low Condition of his Treasury; that he was forced to take up Money at a great Discount; that Exchequer Bills would not circulate under nine *per Cent* below Par; that in short I had cost his Majesty above a Million and a half of *Sprugs*, (their greatest Gold Coin, about the bigness of a Spangle;) and, upon the whole, that it would be advisable in the Emperor to take the first fair Occasion of dismissing me.

I am here obliged to vindicate the Reputation of an excellent Lady, who was an innocent Sufferer upon my account. The Treasurer took a fancy to be jealous of his Wife, from the Malice of some Evil Tongues, who informed him that her Grace had taken a violent Affection for my Person, and the Court-Scandal ran for some time, that she once came privately to my Lodging. This I solemnly declare to be a most infamous Falsehood, without any Grounds, further than that her Grace was pleased to treat me with all innocent Marks of Freedom and Friendship. I own she came often to my House, but always publickly, nor ever without three more in the Coach, who were usually her Sister and young Daughter, and some particular Acquaintance; but this was common to many other Ladies of the Court. And I still appeal to my Servants round, whether they at any time saw a Coach at my Door without knowing what Persons were in it. On those Occasions, when a Servant had given me notice, my Custom was to go immediately to the Door: and, after paying my Respects, to take up the Coach and two Horses very carefully in my Hands, (for if there were six Horses, the Postillion always unharnessed four) and place them on a Table, where I had fixed a movable Rim quite round, of five Inches high, to prevent Accidents. And I have often had four Coaches and Horses at once on my Table full of Company, while I sat in my Chair, leaning my Face towards them; and when I was engaged with one Set, the Coachmen would gently drive the others round my Table. I have passed many an Afternoon very agreeably in these Conversations. But I defy the Treasurer, or his two Informers, (I will name them and let 'em make the best of it) *Clustril* and *Drunlo*, to prove that any Person ever came to me *incognito*, except the Secretary *Reldresal*, who was sent by express Command of his Imperial Majesty, as I have before related. I should not have dwelt so long upon this Particular, if it had not been a Point wherein the Reputation of a great Lady is so nearly concerned, to say nothing of my own; though I then had the Honour to be a *Nardac*, which the Treasurer himself is not; for all the World knows he is only a *Glumglum*, a Title inferior by one Degree, as that of a Marquis is to a Duke in *England*, although though I allow he preceded me in right of his Post. These false Informations, which I afterwards came to the knowledge of, by an Accident not proper to mention, made *Flimnap*, the Treasurer, show his Lady for some time an ill Countenance, and me a worse; and although he was at last undeceived and reconciled to her, yet I lost all Credit with him, and found my Interest decline very fast with the Emperor himself, who was indeed too much governed by that Favourite.

CHAPTER VII.

The Author, being informed of a Design to accuse him of High-Treason, makes his Escape to Blefuscu. *His Reception there.*

BEFORE I PROCEED to give an account of my leaving this Kingdom, it may be proper to inform the Reader of a private Intrigue which had been for two Months forming against me.

I had been hitherto all my Life a Stranger to Courts, for which I was unqualified by the Meanness of my Condition. I had indeed heard and read enough of the Dispositions of great Princes and Ministers; but never expected to have found such terrible Effects of them in so remote a Country, governed, as I thought, by very different Maxims from those in *Europe*.

When I was just preparing to pay my Attendance on the Emperor of *Blefuscu*, a considerable Person at Court (to whom I had been very serviceable at a time when he lay under the highest Displeasure of his Imperial Majesty) came to my House very privately at Night, in a close Chair, and, without sending his Name, desired admittance: The Chairmen were dismissed; I put the Chair, with his Lordship in it, into my Coat-Pocket: and giving Orders to a trusty Servant to say I was indisposed and gone to sleep, I fastened the Door of my House, placed the chair on the Table, according to my usual Custom, and sat down by it. After the common Salutations were over, observing his Lordship's Countenance full of Concern; and enquiring into the reason, he desired I would hear him with patience in a Matter that highly concerned my Honour and my Life. His speech was to the following effect, for I took Notes of it as soon as he left me.

"You are to know," said he, "that several Committees of Council have been lately called in the most private manner on your account: And it is but two days since his Majesty came to a full Resolution.

"You are very sensible that *Skyris Bolgolam* (*Galbet*, or High Admiral) hath been your mortal Enemy almost ever since your Arrival: His original Reasons I know not; but his Hatred is increased since your great Success against *Blefuscu*, by which his Glory, as Admiral, is much obscur'd. This Lord, in conjunction with *Flimnap* the High Treasurer, whose Enmity against you is notorious on account of his Lady, *Limtoc* the General, *Lalcon* the Chamberlain, and *Balmuff* the grand Justiciary, have prepared Articles of impeachment against you, for Treason and other capital Crimes."

This Preface made me so impatient, being conscious of my own Merits and Innocence, that I was going to interrupt him; when he entreated me to be silent, and thus proceeded.

"Out of Gratitude for the Favours you have done me, I procured Information of the whole Proceedings, and a Copy of the Articles, wherein I venture my Head for your Service.

"'*Articles of Impeachment against* Quinbus Flestrin (*the* Man-Mountain.)

ARTICLE I.

WHEREAS, by a Statute made in the Reign of his Imperial Majesty *Calin Deffar Plune*, it is enacted, That whoever shall make water within the Precincts of the Royal Palace, shall be liable to the Pains and Penalties of High Treason: Notwithstanding, the said *Quinbus Flestrin*, in open breach of the said Law, under colour of extinguishing the Fire kindled in the Apartment of his Majesty's most dear Imperial Consort, did maliciously, traitorously, and devilishly, by discharge of his Urine, put out the said Fire kindled in the said Apartment, lying and being within the Precincts of the said Royal Palace, against the Statute in that case pro-vided, *etc.* against the Duty, *etc.*

ARTICLE II.

THAT the said *Quinbus Flestrin* having brought the Imperial Fleet of *Blefuscu* into the Royal Port, and being afterwards commanded by his Imperial Majesty to seize all the other Ships of the said Empire of *Blefuscu*, and reduce that Empire to a Province, to be governed by a Vice-Roy from hence, and to destroy and put to death not only all the *Big-Endian Exiles*, but likewise all the People of that Empire who would not immediately forsake the *Big-Endian* Heresy: He the said *Flestrin*, like a false Traitor against his most Auspicious, Serene, Imperial Majesty, did petition to be excused from the said Service, upon pretence of unwillingness to force the Consciences, or destroy the Liberties and Lives of an innocent People.

ARTICLE III.

THAT, whereas certain Ambassadors arrived from the Court of *Blefuscu*, to sue for Peace in his Majesty's Court: He the said *Flestrin* did, like a false Traitor, aid, abet, comfort, and divert, the said Ambassadors, although he knew them to be Servants to a Prince who was lately an open Enemy to his Imperial Majesty, and in open War against his said Majesty.

ARTICLE IV.

THAT the said *Quinbus Flestrin*, contrary to the Duty of a faithful Subject, is now preparing to make a Voyage to the Court and Empire of *Blefuscu*, for which he hath received only verbal License from his Imperial Majesty; and under colour of the said License doth falsely and traitorously intend to take the said Voyage, and thereby to aid, comfort, and abet the Emperor of *Blefuscu*, so lately an Enemy, and in open War with his Imperial Majesty aforesaid.'

"There are some other Articles, but these are the most important, of which I have read you an Abstract.

"In the several Debates upon this Impeachment, it must be confessed that his Majesty gave many marks of his great Lenity, often urging the Services you had done him, and endeavouring to extenuate your Crimes. The Treasurer and Admiral insisted that you should be put to the most painful and ignominious Death, by setting fire to your House at Night, and the General was to attend with twenty thousand Men, armed with poisoned Arrows, to shoot you on the Face and Hands. Some of your Servants were to have private Orders to strew a poisonous Juice on your Shirts, which would soon make you tear your own Flesh, and die in the utmost Torture. The General came into the same Opinion; so that for a long time there was a Majority against you: But his Majesty resolving, if possible, to spare your Life, at last brought off the Chamberlain.

"Upon this Incident, *Reldresal*, Principal Secretary for private Affairs, who always approved himself your true Friend, was commanded by the Emperor to deliver his Opinion, which he accordingly did: and therein justify'd the good Thoughts you have of him. He allowed your Crimes to be great, but that still there was room for Mercy, the most commendable Virtue in a Prince, and for which his Majesty was so justly celebrated. He said, the Friendship between you and him was so well known to the World, that perhaps the most honourable Board might think him partial: However, in obedience to the Command he had received, he would freely offer his Sentiments. That if his Majesty, in consideration of your Services, and pursuant to his own merciful Disposition, would please to spare your Life, and only give orders to put out both your Eyes, he humbly conceived, that by this Expedient Justice might in some measure be satisfied, and all the

World would applaud the Lenity of the Emperor, as well as the fair and generous Proceedings of those who have the Honour to be his Counsellors. That the loss of your Eyes would be no Impediment to your bodily Strength, by which you might still be useful to his Majesty. That Blindness is an addition to Courage, by concealing Dangers from us; that the Fear you had for your Eyes, was the greatest Difficulty in bringing over the Enemy's Fleet, and it would be sufficient for you to see by the Eyes of the Ministers, since the greatest Princes do no more.

"This Proposal was received with the utmost Disapprobation by the whole Board. *Bolgolam*, the Admiral, could not preserve his Temper; but, rising up in Fury, said, he wondered how the Secretary durst presume to give his Opinion for preserving the Life of a Traitor: That the Services you had performed, were, by all true Reasons of State, the great Aggravation of your Crimes; that you, who were able to extinguish the Fire, by discharge of Urine in her Majesty's Apartment (which he mentioned with horror) might, at another time, raise an Inundation by the same means, to drown the whole Palace; and the same Strength which enabled you to bring over the Enemy's Fleet, might serve, upon the first Discontent to carry it back: That he had good Reasons to think you were a *Big-Endian* in your Heart; and as Treason begins in the Heart before it appears in Overt-Acts, so he accused you as a Traitor on that account, and therefore insisted you should be put to death.

"The Treasurer was of the same Opinion; he showed to what straits his Majesty's Revenue was reduced by the charge of maintaining you, which would soon grow insupportable: That the Secretary's Expedient of putting out your Eyes was so far from being a Remedy against this Evil, that it would probably increase it, as is manifest from the common practice of blinding some kind of Fowl, after which they fed the faster, and grew sooner fat: That his sacred Majesty, and the Council, who are your Judges, were in their own Consciences fully convinced of your Guilt, which was a sufficient Argument to condemn you to Death, without the formal Proofs required by the strict Letter of the Law.

"But his Imperial Majesty fully determined against capital Punishment, was graciously pleased to say, that since the Council thought the loss of your Eyes too easy a Censure, some other may be inflicted hereafter. And your Friend the Secretary humbly desiring to be heard again, in answer to what the Treasurer had objected concerning the great Charge his Majesty was at in maintaining you, said, that his Excellency, who had the sole disposal of the Emperor's Revenue, might easily provide against that Evil, by gradually lessening your Establishment; by which, for want of sufficient Food, you would grow weak and faint, and lose your Appetite, and consequently decay and consume in a few Months; neither would the Stench of your Carcass be then so dangerous, when it should become more than half diminished; and immediately upon your Death, five or six Thousand of his Majesty's Subjects might, in two or three days, cut your Flesh from your Bones, take it away by Cart-loads, and bury it in distant parts to prevent Infection, leaving the Skeleton as a Monument of Admiration to Posterity.

"Thus by the great Friendship of the Secretary, the whole Affair was compromised. It was strictly enjoin'd, that the Project of starving you by degrees should be kept a Secret, but the Sentence of putting out your Eyes was entered on the Books; none dissenting except *Bolgolam* the Admiral, who being a Creature of the Empress, was perpetually instigated by her Majesty to insist upon your Death, she having borne perpetual Malice against you, on account of that infamous and illegal Method you took to extinguish the Fire in her Apartment.

"In three days your Friend the Secretary will be directed to come to your House, and read before you the Articles of Impeachment; and then to signify the great Lenity and Favour of his Majesty and Council, whereby you are only condemned to the loss of your Eyes, which his Majesty does not question you will gratefully and humbly submit to; and twenty of his Majesty's Surgeons will attend, in order to see the Operation well performed, by discharging very sharp-pointed Arrows into the Balls of your Eyes, as you lie on the Ground.

"I leave to your Prudence what Measures you will take; and to avoid Suspicion, I must immediately return in as private a manner as I came."

His Lordship did so, and I remained alone, under many Doubts and Perplexities of Mind.

It was a Custom introduced by this Prince and his Ministry, (very different, as I have been assured, from the Practices of former Times) that after the Court had decreed any cruel Execution, either to gratify the Monarch's Resentment, or the Malice of a Favourite, the Emperor made a Speech to his whole Council, expressing his great Lenity and Tenderness, as Qualities known and confessed by all the World. This Speech was immediately published through the Kingdom; nor did any thing terrify the People so much as those Encomiums on his Majesty's Mercy; because it was observed, that the more these Praises were enlarged and insisted on, the more inhuman was the Punishment, and the Sufferer more innocent. And as to myself, I must confess, having never been designed for a Courtier, either by my Birth or Education, I was so ill a Judge of Things, that I could not discover the Lenity and Favour of this Sentence, but conceived it (perhaps erroneously) rather to be rigorous than gentle. I sometimes thought of standing my Trial, for, although I could not deny the Facts alleged in the several Articles, yet I hoped they would admit of some Extenuation. But having in my Life perused many State-Trials, which I ever observed to terminate as the Judges thought fit to direct, I durst not rely on so dangerous a Decision, in so critical a Juncture, and against such powerful Enemies. Once I was strongly bent upon Resistance, for while I had Liberty the whole Strength of that Empire could hardly subdue me, and I might easily with Stones pelt the Metropolis to pieces; but I soon rejected that Project with Horror, by remembering the Oath I had made to the Emperor, the Favours I received from him, and the high Title of *Nardac* he conferred upon me. Neither had I so soon learned the Gratitude of Courtiers, to persuade myself that his Majesty's present Severities acquitted me of all past Obligations.

At last I fixed upon a Resolution, for which it is probable I may incur some Censure, and not unjustly; for I confess I owe the preserving of mine Eyes, and consequently my Liberty, to my own great Rashness and want of Experience: because if I had then known the Nature of Princes and Ministers, which I have since observed in many other Courts, and their Methods of treating Criminals less obnoxious than myself, I should, with great alacrity and readiness, have submitted to so easy a Punishment. But hurry'd on by the Precipitancy of Youth, and having his Imperial Majesty's License to pay my Attendance upon the Emperor of *Blefuscu*, I took this Opportunity, before the three Days were elapsed, to send a Letter to my Friend the Secretary, signifying my Resolution of setting out that Morning for *Blefuscu* pursuant to the leave I had got; and without waiting for an Answer, I went to that side of the Island where our Fleet lay. I seized a large Man of War, tied a Cable to the Prow, and lifting up the Anchors, I stript myself, put my Clothes (together with my Coverlet, which I brought under my Arm) into the Vessel, and drawing it after me between wading and swimming, arrived at the Royal Port of *Blefuscu*, where the People had long expected me; they lent me two Guides to direct me to the Capital City, which is of the same Name. I held them in my Hands till I came within two hundred Yards of the Gate, and desired them to signify my Arrival to one of the Secretaries, and let him know, I there waited his Majesty's Command. I had an Answer in about an Hour, that his Majesty, attended by the Royal Family, and great Officers of the Court, was coming out to receive me. I advanced a Hundred Yards. The Emperor, and his Train, alighted from their Horses, the Empress and Ladies from their Coaches, and I did not perceive they were in any Fright or Concern. I lay on the Ground to kiss his Majesty's and the Empress's Hand. I told his Majesty that I was come according to my Promise, and with the License of the Emperor my Master, to have the Honour of seeing so Mighty a Monarch, and to offer him any Service in my power, consistent with my Duty to my own Prince; not mentioning a Word of my Disgrace, because I had hitherto no regular Information of it, and might suppose myself wholly ignorant of any such Design; neither could I reasonably conceive that the Emperor would discover the Secret while I was out of his power; wherein, however, it soon appeared I was deceived.

I shall not trouble the Reader with the particular Account of my Reception at this Court, which was suitable to the Generosity of so great a Prince; nor of the Difficulties I was in for want of a House and Bed, being forced to lie on the Ground, wrapt up in my Coverlet.

CHAPTER VIII.

The Author, by a lucky Accident, finds means to leave Blefuscu; *and, after some Difficulties, returns safe to his Native Country.*

THREE DAYS AFTER MY ARRIVAL, walking out of Curiosity to the North-East Coast of the Island, I observed, about half a League off, in the Sea, somewhat that looked like a Boat overturned. I pulled off my Shoes and Stockings, and wading two or three Hundred Yards, I found the Object to approach nearer by force of the Tide; and then plainly saw it to be a real Boat, which I supposed might by some Tempest, have been driven from a Ship: whereupon I returned immediately towards the City, and desired his Imperial Majesty to lend me twenty of the tallest Vessels he had left after the Loss of his Fleet, and three thousand Seamen, under the Command of his Vice-Admiral. This Fleet sailed round, while I went back the shortest way to the Coast where I first discovered the Boat; I found the Tide had driven it still nearer. The Seamen were all provided with Cordage, which I had beforehand twisted to a sufficient strength. When the Ships came up, I stript myself, and waded till I came within a hundred Yards of the Boat, after which I was forced to swim till I got up to it. The Seamen threw me the end of the Cord, which I fastened to a Hole in the fore-part of the Boat, and the other end to a Man of War: But I found all my Labour to little purpose; for being out of my depth, I was not able to work. In this Necessity, I was forced to swim behind, and push the Boat forwards as often as I could, with one of my Hands; and the Tide favouring me, I advanced so far, that I could just hold up my Chin and feel the Ground. I rested two or three Minutes and then gave the Boat another Shove, and so on till the Sea was no higher than my Arm-pits; and now the most laborious part being over, I took out my other Cables which were stowed in one of the Ships, and fastened them first to the Boat, and then to nine of the Vessels which attended me; the Wind being favourable, the Seamen towed, and I shoved till we arrived within forty Yards of the Shore, and waiting till the Tide was out, I got dry to the Boat, and by the assistance of two thousand Men, with Ropes and Engines, I made a shift to turn it on its Bottom, and found it was but little damaged.

I shall not trouble the Reader with the Difficulties I was under by the help of certain Paddles, which cost me ten days making, to get my Boat to the Royal Port of *Blefuscu*, where a mighty concourse of People appeared upon my arrival, full of Wonder at the sight of so prodigious a Vessel. I told the Emperor that my good Fortune had thrown this Boat in my way, to carry me to some place whence I might return into my native Country; and begged his Majesty's Orders for getting Materials to fit it up, together with his License to depart; which, after some kind Expostulations, he was pleased to grant.

I did very much wonder, in all this time, not to have heard of any Express relating to me from our Emperor to the Court of *Blefuscu*. But I was afterward given privately to understand, that his Imperial Majesty, never imagining I had the least notice of his Designs, believed I was only gone to *Blefuscu* in performance of my Promise, according to the License he had given me, which was well known at our Court, and would return in a few days when the Ceremony was ended. But he was at last in pain at my long absence; and, after consulting with the Treasurer and the rest of that Cabal, a Person of Quality was dispatched with the Copy of the Articles against me. This Envoy had Instructions to represent to the Monarch of *Blefuscu*, the great Lenity of his Master, who was content to punish me no further than with the loss of mine Eyes; that I had fled from Justice, and if I did not return in two Hours, I should be deprived of my title of *Nardac*, and declared a Traitor. The Envoy further added, that in order to maintain the Peace and Amity between both Empires, his Master expected, that his Brother of *Blefuscu* would give Orders to have me sent back to *Lilliput*, bound Hand and Foot, to be punished as a Traitor.

The Emperor of *Blefuscu* having taken three Days to consult, returned an Answer consisting of many Civilities and Excuses. He said, that as for sending me bound, his Brother knew it was impossible; that although I had deprived him of his Fleet, yet he owed great Obligations to me for many good Offices I had done him in making the Peace. That however both their Majesties would soon be made easy; for I had found a prodigious Vessel on the Shore, able to carry me on the Sea, which he had given orders to fit up with my own Assistance and Direction; and he hoped in a few Weeks both Empires would be freed from so insupportable an Encumbrance.

With this Answer the Envoy returned to *Lilliput*, and the Monarch of *Blefuscu* related to me all that had passed; offering me at the same time (but under the strictest Confidence) his gracious Protection, if I would continue in his Service; wherein although I believed him sincere, yet I resolved never more to put any Confidence in Princes or Ministers, where I could possibly avoid it; and therefore, with all due Acknowledgments for his favourable Intentions, I humbly begged to be excused. I told him, that since Fortune, whether good or evil, had thrown a Vessel in my way, I was resolved to venture myself on the Ocean, rather than be an occasion of Difference between two such mighty Monarchs. Neither did I find the Emperor at all displeased; and I discover'd by a certain Accident, that he was very glad of my Resolution, and so were most of his Ministers.

These Considerations moved me to hasten my Departure somewhat sooner than I intended; to which the Court, impatient to have me gone, very readily contributed. Five Hundred Workmen were employed to make two Sails to my Boat, according to my Directions, by quilting thirteen fold of their strongest Linnen together. I was at the pains of making Ropes and Cables, by twisting ten, twenty or thirty of the thickest and strongest of theirs. A great Stone that I happen'd to find, after a long Search by the Sea-shore, served me for an Anchor. I had the Tallow of three hundred Cows for greasing my Boat, and other Uses. I was at incredible pains in cutting down some of the largest Timber-Trees for Oars and Masts, wherein I was, however, much assisted by his Majesty's Ship-Carpenters, who helped me in smoothing them, after I had done the rough Work.

In about a Month, when all was prepared, I sent to receive his Majesty's Commands, and to take my leave. The Emperor and Royal Family came out of the Palace; I lay down on my Face to kiss his Hand, which he very graciously gave me; so did the Empress, and young Princes of the Blood. His Majesty presented me with fifty Purses of two hundred *Sprugs* a-piece, together with his Picture at full length, which I put immediately into one of my Gloves, to keep it from being hurt. The Ceremonies at my Departure were too many to trouble the Reader with at this time.

I stored the Boat with the Carcasses of a hundred Oxen, and three hundred Sheep, with Bread and Drink proportionable, and as much Meat ready dressed as four hundred Cooks could provide. I took with me six Cows and two Bulls alive, with as many Ewes and Rams, intending to carry them into my own Country, and propagate the Breed. And to feed them on board, I had a good Bundle of Hay, and a Bag of Corn. I would gladly have taken a Dozen of the Natives, but this was a thing the Emperor would by no means permit; and besides a diligent Search into my Pockets, his Majesty engaged my Honour not to carry away any of his Subjects, although with their own Consent and Desire.

Having thus prepared all things as well as I was able, I set sail on the twenty-fourth day of *September* 1701, at six in the Morning; and when I had gone about four Leagues to the Northward, the Wind being at South-East, at six in the Evening, I descryed a small Island about half a League to the North-West. I advanced forward, and cast Anchor on the Lee-side of the Island, which seemed to be uninhabited. I then took some Refreshment, and went to my rest. I slept well, and as I conjectured at least six Hours, for I found the day broke in two Hours after I awaked. It was a clear Night. I ate my breakfast before the sun was up; and heaving Anchor, the Wind being favourable, I steered the same Course that I had done the Day before, wherein I was directed by my Pocket-Compass. My Intention was to reach, if possible, one of those Islands, which I had reason to believe lay to the North-East of *Van Diemen*'s Land. I discovered nothing all that Day; but upon the next, about three in the Afternoon, when I had by my Computation made twenty-four Leagues from *Blefuscu*, I descryed a Sail steering to the South-East; my Course was due East. I hailed her, but could get no Answer; yet I found I gained upon her, for the Wind slackened. I made all the sail I could, and in half an hour she spied me, then hung out her Ancient, and discharged a Gun. It is not easy to express the Joy I was in upon the unexpected hope of once more seeing my beloved Country, and the dear Pledges I left in it. The Ship slackened her Sails, and I came up with her between five and six in the Evening, *September* 26; but my Heart leapt within me to see her *English* Colours. I put my Cows and Sheep into my Coat-Pockets, and got on board with all my little Cargo of Provisions. The Vessel was an *English* Merchant-Man, returning from *Japan* by the *North* and *South Seas*; the Captain, Mr. *John Biddel* of *Deptford*, a very civil Man, and an excellent Sailor. We were now in the Latitude of 30 Degrees South, there were about fifty Men in the Ship; and here I met an old Comrade of mine, one *Peter Williams*, who gave me a good Character to the Captain. This Gentleman treated me with Kindness, and desired I would let him know what place I came from last, and whither I was bound; which I did in a few Words, but he thought I was raving, and that the Dangers I underwent had disturbed my Head; whereupon I took my black Cattle and Sheep out of my Pocket, which, after great Astonishment, clearly convinced him of my Veracity. I then showed him the Gold given me by the Emperor of *Blefuscu*, together with his Majesty's Picture at full length, and some other Rarities of that Country. I gave him two Purses of two hundreds *Sprugs* each, and promised, when we arrived in *England*, to make him a Present of a Cow and a Sheep big with Young.

I shall not trouble the Reader with a particular Account of this Voyage, which was very prosperous for the most part. We arrived in the *Downs* on the 13th of *April* 1702. I had only one Misfortune, that the Rats on board carried away one of my Sheep; I found her Bones in a Hole, picked clean from the Flesh. The rest of my Cattle I got safe on shore, and set them a-grazing in a Bowling-Green at *Greenwich*, where the Fineness of the Grass made them feed very heartily, though I had always feared the contrary: neither could I possibly have preserved them in so long a Voyage, if the Captain had not allowed me some of his best Biscuit, which rubbed to Powder, and mingled with Water, was their constant Food. The short time I continued in *England*, I made a considerable Profit by showing my Cattle to many Persons of Quality, and others: and before I began my second Voyage, I sold them for six hundred Pounds. Since my last return, I find the Breed is considerably increased, especially the Sheep; which I hope will prove much to the Advantage of the Woollen Manufacture, by the Fineness of the Fleeces.

I stayed but two Months with my Wife and Family; for my insatiable Desire of seeing foreign Countries would suffer me to continue no longer. I left fifteen hundred Pounds with my Wife, and fixed her in a good House at *Redriff.* My remaining Stock I carried with me, part in Money and part in Goods, in hopes to improve my Fortunes. My eldest Uncle *John* had left me an Estate in Land, near *Epping*, of about Thirty Pounds a Year; and I had a long Lease of the *Black-Bull* in *Fetter-Lane*, which yielded me as much more: so that I was not in any danger of leaving my Family upon the Parish. My son *Johnny*, named so after his Uncle, was at the Grammar School, and a towardly Child. My Daughter *Betty* (who is now well married, and has Children) was then at her Needle-Work. I took leave of my Wife, and Boy and Girl, with Tears on both sides, and went on board the *Adventure*, a Merchant Ship of three hundred Tons, bound for *Surat*, Captain *John Nicholas* of *Liverpool* Commander. But my Account of this Voyage must be referred to the Second Part of my Travels.

1727

A MODEST PROPOSAL

For Preventing the CHILDREN OF POOR PEOPLE From being a Burden on their
PARENTS or the COUNTRY, And for making them Beneficial to the PUBLICK

IT IS A MELANCHOLY OBJECT to those who walk thro' this great Town, or travel
in the Country, when they see the *Streets*, the *Roads*, and *Cabbin-Doors* crowded
with Beggars of the Female Sex, followed by three, four, or six Children *all in Rags*,
and importuning every Passenger for an Alms. These *Mothers*, instead of being
able to work for their honest Livelihood, are forced to employ all their Time in
stroling to beg Sustenance for their *helpless Infants*; who, as they grow up, either
turn *Thieves* for want of Work, or leave their *dear native Country to fight for the
Pretender in Spain*,[1] or sell themselves to the *Barbadoes*.

I think it is agreed by all Parties, that this prodigious Number of Children, in
the Arms, or on the Backs, or at the *Heels* of their *Mothers*, and frequently of their
Fathers, is *in the present deplorable State of the Kingdom*, a very great additional
Grievance; and therefore whoever could find out a Fair, Cheap and Easy Method
of making these Children Sound and Useful Members of the Common-wealth,
would deserve so well of the Publick, as to have his Statue set up for a Preserver
of the Nation.

But my Intention is very far from being confined to provide only for the
Children of *professed Beggars*; it is of a much greater Extent, and shall take in the
whole Number of Infants at a certain Age, who are born of Parents in effect as
little able to support them, as those who demand our Charity in the Streets.

As to my own Part, having turned my Thoughts for many Years upon this
important Subject, and maturely weighed the several *Schemes of our Projectors*, I
have always found them grossly mistaken in their *Computation*. 'Tis true, a Child
just dropt from its Dam, may be supported by her Milk, for a Solar Year, with
little other Nourishment, at most not above the Value of two Shillings, which
the Mother may certainly get, or the Value in *Scraps*, by *her lawful Occupation
of Begging*; and it is exactly at one Year old that I propose to provide for them, in
such a manner, as, instead of being a *Charge* upon their *Parents*, or the *Parish*, or
wanting Food and Raiment for the rest of their Lives, they shall, on the contrary,
contribute to the *Feeding*, and partly to the *Cloathing* of many Thousands.

---

1 James Francis Edward Stuart (1688–1766), the Old Pretender, was the son of the deposed king
James II. He wanted to reclaim the English throne.

There is likewise another great Advantage in my Scheme, that it will prevent those *voluntary Abortions*, and that horrid Practice of *Women murdering their Bastard Children*, alas! too frequent among us; Sacrificing the poor innocent Babes, I doubt, more to avoid the Expence than the Shame, which would move Tears and Pity in the most savage and inhuman Breast.

The Number of Souls in this Kingdom being usually reckon'd One million and a half; of these I calculate there may be about Two hundred Thousand Couple whose Wives are Breeders; from which Number I subtract Thirty thousand Couples, who are able to maintain their own Children; although I apprehend there cannot be so many under *the present Distresses of the Kingdom*: but this being granted, there will remain One hundred and seventy thousand Breeders.

I again subtract Fifty thousand, for those Women who miscarry, or whose Children die by Accident or Disease within the Year; there only remain One hundred and twenty thousand Children of poor Parents annually born: the Question therefore is, *How this Number shall be reared and provided for*; which, as I have already said, *under the present Situation of Affairs*, is utterly impossible, by all the Methods hitherto proposed: for we can *neither employ them in Handicraft or Agriculture*; we neither build Houses (*I mean in the Country*) nor cultivate Land? They can very seldom pick up a Livelihood *by Stealing*, till they arrive at six Years old, except where they are of Towardly Parts; although, I confess they learn the Rudiments much earlier, during which time they can however be properly look'd upon only as *Probationers*; as I have been informed by a principal Gentleman in the County of *Cavan*, who protested to me, that he never knew above one or two Instances under the Age of Six, even in a part of the Kingdom *so renowned for the quickest Proficiency in that Art.*

I am assured by our Merchants, that a Boy or a Girl, *before twelve Years old*, is no saleable Commodity; and even when they come to this Age, they will not yield above three Pounds, or three Pounds and half a Crown at most, on the Exchange: which cannot turn to Account either to the *Parents* or the *Kingdom*, the Charge of Nutriments and Rags having been at least four times that Value.

I shall now therefore humbly propose my own Thoughts, which I hope will not be liable to the least Objection.

I have been assured by a very knowing *American* of my Acquaintance in *London*, that a young healthy Child well nurs'd, is, at a Year old, a most *delicious, nourishing*, and *wholesome* Food, whether *stewed, roasted, baked*, or *boyled*; and I make no doubt, that it will equally serve in a *Fricassee*, or a *Ragoust*.

I do therefore humbly offer it to *publick Consideration*, that of the Hundred and twenty thousand Children already computed, Twenty thousand may be reserved for *Breed*, whereof only one Fourth part to be Males, which is more than we allow to *Sheep, black Cattle, or Swine*; and my Reason is, that these Children are seldom the Fruits of Marriage, *a Circumstance not much regarded by our Savages,* therefore *one Male* will be sufficient to serve *four Females.* That the remaining Hundred thousand may, at a Year old, be offered in *Sale* to the *Persons of Quality* and *Fortune* through the Kingdom, always advising the Mother to let them suck plentifully in the last Month, so as to *render them plump and fat for a good Table.* A Child will make two Dishes at an Entertainment for Friends, and when the Family dines alone, the fore or hind *Quarter* will make a reasonable Dish, and seasoned with a little *Pepper* or *Salt,* will be very good boiled on the fourth Day, especially in *Winter.*

I have reckoned upon a Medium, that a Child just born will weigh twelve Pounds, and, in a solar Year, if tolerably nursed, encreaseth to Twenty-eight Pounds.

I grant this Food will be somewhat dear, and therefore *very proper for Landlords,* who, as they have already devoured most of the *Parents,* seem to have the best Title to the *Children.*

Infants Flesh will be in Season throughout the Year, but more plentiful in *March,* and a little *before* and *after,* for we are told by a grave Author, an eminent *French* Physician, that *Fish being a prolifick Diet,* there are more Children born in *Roman Catholick Countries* about nine Months after *Lent,* than at any other Season: therefore, reckoning a Year after *Lent,* the Markets will be more glutted than usual, because the Number of *Popish Infants,* is at least three to one in this Kingdom, and therefore it will have one other collateral Advantage by lessening the Number of Papists among us.

I have already computed the Charge of Nursing a Beggar's Child (in which List I reckon all *Cottagers, Labourers,* and Four Fifths of the *Farmers*) to be about two Shillings *per Annum,* Rags included; and I believe no Gentleman would repine to give Ten Shillings for the *Carcass of a good fat Child,* which, as I have said, will make four Dishes of excellent Nutritive Meat, when he hath only some particular Friend, or his own Family to dine with him. Thus the Esquire will learn to be a good Landlord, and grow popular among his Tenants, the Mother will have Eight Shillings neat Profit, and be fit for Work till she produces another Child.

Those who are more thrifty (*as I must confess the Times require*) may flay the Carcass; the Skin of which, artificially dressed, will make admirable *Gloves for Ladies,* and *Summer Boots for fine Gentlemen.*

As to our City of *Dublin,* Shambles may be appointed for this Purpose, in the most convenient Parts of it, and Butchers we may be assured will not be wanting; although I rather recommend buying the Children alive, and dressing them hot from the Knife, as we do *Roasting-Pigs.*

A very worthy Person, *a true Lover of his Country,* and whose Virtues I highly esteem, was lately pleased, in discoursing on this Matter, to offer a Refinement upon my Scheme. He said, that many Gentlemen of this Kingdom having of late destroyed their Deer, he conceived that the want of Venison might be well supplied by the Bodies of young Lads and Maidens, not exceeding fourteen Years of age, nor under twelve; so great a Number of both Sexes in every Country being now ready to starve for want of Work and Service: And these to be disposed of by their Parents, if alive, or otherwise by their nearest Relations. But with due deference to so excellent a Friend, and so deserving a Patriot, I cannot be altogether in his Sentiments: for as to the Males, my *American* Acquaintance assured me from frequent Experience, that their Flesh was generally Tough and Lean, like that of our School-Boys, by continual Exercise, and their Taste disagreeable; and to Fatten them, would not answer the Charge. Then as to the Females, it would, I think, with humble Submission, *be a Loss to the Publick*, because they soon would become Breeders themselves: And besides, it is not improbable that some scrupulous People might be apt to censure such a Practice, (although indeed very unjustly) as a little bordering upon Cruelty; which, I confess, hath always been with me the strongest Objection against any Project, however well intended.

But in order to justify my Friend, he confessed, that this Expedient was put into his Head by the famous *Salmanaazor,* a Native of the Island *Formosa,*[1] who came from thence to *London* above twenty Years ago; and in Conversation told my Friend, that in his Country when any young Person happened to be put to death, the Executioner sold the Carcass to *Persons of Quality,* as a prime Dainty, and that, in his Time, the Body of a plump Girl of fifteen, who was crucify'd for an Attempt to poison the Emperor, was sold to his Imperial *Majesty's Prime Minister of State,* and other great *Mandarins* of the Court, *in Joints from the Gibbet,* at four hundred Crowns. Neither indeed can I deny, that if the same Use were made of several plump young Girls in this Town, who, without one single Groat to their Fortunes, cannot stir abroad without a Chair, and appear at the *Play-House,* and *Assemblies,* in foreign Fineries which they never will pay for; the Kingdom would not be the worse.

Some Persons of a desponding Spirit are in great concern about that vast Number of poor People, who are aged, diseased, or maimed; and I have been desired to employ my Thoughts what Course may be taken, to ease the Nation of so grievous an Incumbrance. But I am not in the least Pain upon that Matter, because it is very well known, that they are every Day *dying,* and *rotting,* by *Cold,* and *Famine,* and *Filth,* and *Vermine,* as fast as can be reasonably expected. And as to the young Labourers, they are now in almost as hopeful a Condition. They cannot get Work, and consequently pine away from want of Nourishment, to a Degree, that if at any time they are accidentally hired to common Labour, they

---

1 George Psalmanazar, a Caucasian man, pretended to be a native of Formosa (now known as Taiwan). In his book *Description of Formosa,* he claimed that Formosan ate children. His hoax was discovered.

have not Strength to perform it: and thus the Country and themselves are happily delivered from the Evils to come.

I have too long digressed, and therefore shall return to my Subject. I think the Advantages by the Proposal which I have made, are obvious and many, as well as of the highest Importance.

For first, as I have already observed, it would greatly lessen the *Number of Papists*, with whom we are yearly overrun, being the principal Breeders of the Nation, as well as our most dangerous Enemies; and who stay at Home on purpose with a design *to deliver the Kingdom to the Pretender*, hoping to take their Advantage by the Absence *of so many good Protestants*, who have chosen rather to leave their Country, than stay at home and pay Tithes against their Conscience, to an *Episcopal Curate*.

Secondly, The poorer Tenants will have something valuable of their own, which by Law may be made liable to a Distress, and help to pay their Landlords Rent; their Corn and Cattle being already seized, and *Money a thing unknown*.

Thirdly, Whereas the Maintenance of an hundred thousand Children, from two Years old, and upwards, cannot be computed at less than ten Shillings a piece *per Annum*, the Nation's Stock will be thereby encreased fifty thousand Pounds *per Annum*, besides the Profit of a new Dish, introduced to the Tables of all *Gentlemen of Fortune* in the Kingdom, who have any Refinement in Taste; and the Money will circulate among our selves, the Goods being entirely of our own Growth and Manufacture.

Fourthly, The constant Breeders, besides the Gain of eight Shillings sterling *per Annum*, by the Sale of their Children, will be rid of the Charge of maintaining them after the first Year.

Fifthly, This Food would likewise bring great *Custom to Taverns*, where the Vintners will certainly be so prudent as to procure the best Receipts for dressing it to Perfection, and consequently have their Houses frequented by all the *fine Gentlemen*, who justly value themselves upon their Knowledge in good Eating; and a skilful Cook, who will contrive to make it as expensive as they please.

Sixthly, This would be a great Inducement to Marriage, which all wise Nations have either encouraged by Rewards, or enforced by Laws and Penalties. It would encrease the Care and Tenderness of Mothers towards their Children, when they were sure of a Settlement for Life to the poor Babes, provided in some Sort by the Publick, to their annual Profit instead of Expence; we should soon see an honest Emulation among the married Women, *which of them could bring the fattest Child to the Market*; Men would become as fond of their *Wives*, during the Time of their Pregnancy, as they are now of their *Mares* in Foal, their *Cows* in Calf, or *Sows* when they are ready to farrow, nor offer to beat or kick them (as it is too frequent a Practice) for fear of a Miscarriage.

Many other Advantages might be enumerated: for Instance, the Addition of some thousand Carcasses in our Exportation of barrel'd Beef: the Propagation of *Swine's Flesh*, and Improvement in the Art of making good *Bacon*, so much wanted among us by the great Destruction of *Pigs*, too frequent at our Tables, which are no way comparable in Taste, or Magnificence, to a well-grown, fat Yearling Child, which roasted whole will make a considerable Figure at a *Lord Mayor's Feast*, or any other publick Entertainment. But this and many others I omit, being studious of Brevity.

Supposing that One thousand Families in this City, would be constant Customers for Infants Flesh, besides others who might have it at Merry-meetings, particularly *Weddings* and *Christenings*; I compute that *Dublin* would take off annually about Twenty thousand Carcasses, and the rest of the Kingdom (where probably they will be sold somewhat cheaper) the remaining Eighty thousand.

I can think of no one Objection that will possibly be raised against this Proposal, unless it should be urged, that the Number of People will be thereby much lessened in the Kingdom. This I freely own, and was indeed one principal Design in offering it to the World.

I desire the Reader will observe, that I calculate my Remedy *for this one individual Kingdom of* Ireland, *and for no other that ever was, is, or I think ever can be upon Earth. Therefore let no Man talk to me of other Expedients: Of taxing our Absentees at five Shillings a Pound: Of using neither Clothes nor Houshold Furniture, except what is of our own Growth and Manufacture: Of utterly rejecting the Materials and Instruments that promote Foreign Luxury: Of curing the Expensiveness of Pride, Vanity, Idleness, and Gaming in our Women: Of introducing a Vein of Parsimony, Prudence and Temperance: Of learning to love our Country, wherein we differ even from* Laplanders,[1] *and the Inhabitants of* Topinamboo: *Of quitting our Animosities and Factions, nor acting any longer like the Jews, who were murdering one another at the very moment their City was taken: Of being a little cautious not to sell our Country and Consciences for nothing: Of teaching Landlords to have at least one Degree of* Mercy *towards their Tenants: Lastly, Of putting a Spirit of Honesty, Industry and Skill into our Shop-Keepers,* who, if a Resolution could now be taken to buy only our Native Goods, would immediately unite to cheat and exact upon us in the Price, the Measure, and the Goodness, nor could ever yet be brought to make one fair Proposal of just Dealing, though often and earnestly invited to it.

Therefore I repeat, let no Man talk to me of these and the like Expedients, till he hath at least some Glympse of Hope, that there will ever be some hearty and sincere Attempt to put them into practice.

But, as to my self, having been wearied out for many Years, with offering vain, idle, visionary Thoughts, and at length utterly despairing of Success, I fortunately

---

1 A derogatory term for inhabitants of the Finnish province of Lapland, in northern Europe.

fell upon this Proposal; which, as it is wholly new, so it hath something solid and real, of no Expence and little Trouble, full in our own Power, and whereby we can incur no Danger in disobliging *England*. For this kind of Commodity will not bear Exportation, the Flesh being of too tender a Consistence, to admit a long Continuance in Salt; *although perhaps I could name a Country, which would be glad to eat up our whole Nation without it.*

After all, I am not so violently bent upon my own Opinion, as to reject any Offer proposed by wise Men, which shall be found equally innocent, cheap, easy, and effectual.

But before something of that kind shall be advanced in contradiction to my Scheme, and offering a better, I desire the Author or Authors will be pleased maturely to consider two Points.

First, As things now stand, how they will be able to find Food and Raiment for One hundred thousand useless Mouths and Backs.

And *secondly*, There being a round Million of Creatures in human Figure, throughout this Kingdom, whose whole Subsistence put into a common Stock, would leave them in Debt Two million of Pounds *Sterling*, adding those, who are Beggars by Profession, to the Bulk of Farmers, Cottagers and Labourers, with their Wives and Children, who are Beggars in effect.

I desire those *Politicians* who dislike my Overture, and may perhaps be so bold to attempt an Answer, that they will first ask the Parents of these Mortals, whether they would not at this Day think it a great Happiness to have been sold for Food at a Year old, in the manner I prescribe, and thereby have avoided such a perpetual Scene of Misfortunes as they have since gone thro', by *the Oppression of Landlords*, the Impossibility of paying Rent without Money or Trade, the want of common Sustenance, with neither House nor Clothes to cover them from Inclemencies of Weather, and the most inevitable Prospect of intailing the like, or greater Miseries upon their *Breed* for ever.

I profess, in the Sincerity of my Heart, that I have not the least Personal Interest in endeavouring to promote this necessary Work, having no other Motive than the *Publick Good of my Country*, by *advancing our Trade, providing for Infants, relieving the Poor, and giving some Pleasure to the Rich*. I have no Children by which I can propose to get a single Penny, the youngest being nine Years old, and my Wife past Child-bearing.

1729

THE LADY'S DRESSING ROOM

Five Hours, (and who can do it less in?)
By haughty *Celia* spent in Dressing;
The Goddess from her Chamber issues,
Array'd in Lace, Brocade, and Tissues:
Strephon, who found the Room was void,   5
And *Betty* otherwise employ'd,
Stole in, and took a strict Survey
Of all the Litter, as it lay,
Whereof, to make the Matter clear,
An *Inventory* follows here.   10

   And, first, a dirty Smock appear'd,
Beneath the Armpits well besmear'd,
Strephon, the Rogue, display'd it wide,
And turn'd it round on ev'ry Side,
In such a Case, few Words are best,   15
And *Strephon* bids us guess the rest;
But swears how damnably the Men lie,
In calling *Celia* sweet and cleanly.

   Now listen while he next produces,
The various Combs for various Uses,   20
Fill'd up with Dirt so closely fixt,
No Brush cou'd force a Way betwixt.
A Paste of Composition rare,
Sweat, Dandriff, Powder, Lead, and Hair.
A Forehead Cloth with Oil upon't,   25
To smooth the Wrinkles on her Front;
Here Alum Flour to stop the Steams,
Exhal'd from sour unsavoury Streams:
There Night-Gloves made of *Tripsey's* Hide,
Bequeath'd by *Tripsey* when she died,   30
With Puppy-Water,[1] Beauty's Help,
Distill'd from *Tripsey's* darling Whelp.

---

1 A cosmetic and healing product made from boiling whelps (puppies). Tripsey was Celia's dog.

Here Gally-pots and Vials plac't,
Some fill'd with Washes, some with Paste;
Some with Pomatums,[2] Paints, and Slops,   35
And Ointments good for scabby Chops.
Hard by, a filthy Bason stands,
Foul'd with the scouring of her Hands;
The Bason takes whatever comes,
The Scrapings from her Teeth and Gums,   40
A nasty Compound of all Hues,
For here she spits, and here she spues.

But, O! it turn'd poor *Strephon*'s Bowels,
When he beheld and smelt the Towels,
Begumm'd, bematter'd, and beslim'd,   45
With Dirt, and Sweat, and Ear-wax grim'd.
No Object *Strephon*'s Eye escapes;
Here, Petticoats in frowzy Heaps;
Nor be the Handkerchiefs forgot,
All varnish'd o'er with Snuff and Snot.   50
The Stockings why should I expose,
Stain'd with the Moisture of her Toes;
Or greasy Coifs, and Pinners[3] reeking,
Which *Celia* slept at least a Week in.
A Pair of Tweezers next he found,   55
To pluck her Brows in Arches round,
Or Hairs that sink the Forehead low,
Or on her Chin like Bristles grow.

The Virtues we must not let pass
Of *Celia*'s Magnifying-Glass;   60
When frighted *Strephon* cast his Eye on't,
It shew'd the Visage of a Giant:
A Glass that can to Sight disclose
The smallest Worm in *Celia*'s Nose,
And faithfully direct her Nail,   65
To squeeze it out from Head to Tail;
For, catch it nicely by the Head,
It must come out alive or dead.

---

2 Pomade.

3 A woman's cap.

Why *Strephon*, will you tell the rest?
And must you needs describe the Chest?   70
That careless Wench! No Creature warn her,
To move it out from yonder Corner,
But leave it standing full in Sight,
For you to exercise your Spite!
In vain the Workman shew'd his Wit,   75
With Rings and Hinges counterfeit,
To make it seem, in this Disguise,
A Cabinet to vulgar Eyes,
Which *Strephon* ventur'd to look in,
Resolv'd to go thro' *thick and thin*,   80
He lifts the Lid: there needs no more,
He smelt it all the Time before.
As, from within *Pandora*'s Box,[1]
When *Epimetheus* op'd the Locks,
A sudden universal Crew   85
Of human Evils, upwards flew;
He still was comforted to find,
That *Hope* at last remain'd behind:

So, *Strephon* lifting up the Lid,
To view what in the Chest was hid,   90
The Vapours flew from up the Vent,
But *Strephon*, cautious, never meant
The Bottom of the *Pan* to grope,
And foul his Hands in search of *Hope*.

O! ne'er may such a vile Machine   95
Be once in *Celia*'s Chamber seen!
O! may she better learn to keep
Those *Secrets of the hoary Deep!*[2]

---

1 According to Greek mythology, Pandora held a jar (in translation, a box) containing the world's evils. Though instructed not to open it, she did; subsequently, she released evil into the world. Only Hope remained in the box.

2 The secrets of the hoary deep, a dark/ Illimitable Ocean without bound/ Without dimension, where length, breadth, and heighth,/ And time and place are lost; where Endless Night/ And Chaos, ancestors of Nature, hold/ Eternal anarchy, amidst the noise/ Of endless wars, and by confusion stand [Milton's Paradise Lost 2.891-7].

As Mutton-Cutlets, *prime of Meat*,
Which, tho' with Art you salt and beat, 100
As Laws of Cookery require,
And toast them at the clearest Fire;
If from upon the hopeful Chops,
The Fat upon a Cinder drops,
To stinking Smoke it turns the Flame, 105
Pois'ning the Flesh from whence it came,
And up exhales a greasy Stench,
For which you curse the careless Wench:
So things which must not be exprest,
When drop'd into the reeking Chest, 110
Send up an excremental Smell
To taint the Part from whence they fell,
The Petticoats and Gown perfume,
And waft a Stink round ev'ry Room.

   Thus finishing his grand Survey, 115
The Swain disgusted slunk away:
Repeating in his am'rous Fits,
"Oh! *Celia, Celia, Celia* sh—!"

   But *Vengeance*, Goddess, never sleeping,
Soon punish'd *Strephon* for his peeping. 120
His foul Imagination links
Each Dame he sees with all her Stinks;
And, if unsavoury Odours fly,
Conceives a Lady standing by.
All women his Description fits, 125
And both Ideas jump like Wits,
By vicious Fancy coupled fast,
And still appearing in *Contrast*.

   I pity wretched *Strephon*, blind
To all the Charms of Female Kind. 130
Should I the *Queen* of *Love* refuse,
Because she rose from stinking Ooze?
To him that looks behind the Scene
Statira's[3] but some pocky Quean.

---

3 One of the widows of Alexander the Great in Nathaniel Lee's play *Rival Queens*.

When *Celia* in her Glory shows,   135
If *Strephon* would but stop his Nose,
Who now so impiously blasphemes
Her Ointments, Daubs, and Paints, and Creams;
Her Washes, Slops, and every Clout,[1]
With which he makes so foul a Rout,   140
He soon would learn to think like me,
And bless his ravish'd Eyes to see
Such Order from Confusion sprung,
Such gaudy *Tulips* rais'd from *Dung*.

1732

---

1 Cloth used as a rag.

ALEXANDER POPE
1688–1744

To survive in a society where the odds were against him, Alexander Pope needed to be imaginative, cunning, and self-confident. As a Roman Catholic in Protestant England, he was denied the right to vote, hold public office, attend a university, and have patrons, all factors which may have benefitted his career. Pope's health also disadvantaged him. Spinal tuberculosis elicited fevers, stunted his growth, and caused severe lung and heart problems. Pope's literary enemies often jeered at his condition. Though physically frail, he was far from weak in character; he met derision with defiance.

Pope's first teachers were his aunt and local Catholic priests. After learning how to read and write, he began self-educating and continued to do so all of his life. He displayed an early affinity for the works of Virgil and Homer, whose styles greatly influenced his own. Pope's first extant poem, "Ode on Solitude," was composed when he was twelve years old. By the end of his teenage years, several of his pieces had already been printed. Pastorals, published in 1709, and *An Essay on Criticism*, published in 1711, boosted his budding reputation. By his early twenties, he had already achieved remarkable poetic success.

Pope's use of the rhyming heroic couplet became a signature of his major works. He gained the attention of several prominent writers of his time, particularly Jonathan Swift. Swift's friendship increasingly drew the poet away from Whig writers, who wanted to limit royal authority, and placed Pope in the company of Tories, who favored Britain's traditional political structure. In 1714, Pope prompted the formation of a group jokingly called the Scriblerus Club. The group included Swift's Tory friends: Dr. John Arbuthnot, a physician to Queen Anne; Thomas Parnell, a poet; and the poet John Gay, who would write the century's greatest theatrical success, *The Beggar's Opera*. Co-writing accounts of a fictional character named Martinus Scriblerus (Martin the Scribbler), the group investigated and parodied false learning. Satire, characteristic of the Scriblerians, resonates in Pope's *The Dunciad*. Pope's involvement in the club was not without its troubles. The Whigs he formerly associated with were infuriated by his writings. When Pope signed a contract for a translation of the Iliad, the rival political party sought to discredit him. Their attempts were futile; the *Iliad* translation, as well as Pope's translation of the *Odyssey*, established his fortune. He is the first English poet in history who could live off the proceeds of published works alone.

Poetry was his vocation. In his "heroi-comical poem" *The Rape of the Lock*, Pope melds his talents as a poet with his satirical skills to weave meaning into a seemingly trivial event. The poem was inspired by a dispute between two Catholic families, wherein Lord Petre cut a lock of hair from Arabella Fermor's head. Arabella and her relatives were appalled. John Caryll, a friend of both parties, suggested that Pope should write a poem about the incident. Caryll hoped that laughter would ease the tensions between the families and reunite them. Pope's two-canto poem was published anonymously in 1711. An expanded version was published in 1714, this time including five cantos and crediting Pope as the author. It was immensely popular.

The Rape of the Lock is a social satire of epic proportions. An afternoon in a drawing room becomes a high-stakes situation when a game of ombre morphs into a battle between ladies and gentlemen. Sylphs, spirits of the air, stand as agents of the supernatural. The gnome Umbriel descends into the underworld, represented as the Cave of Spleen, and unleashes the heroine's fury. Pope's subject matter mocks the exaggeration and aggrandization of mundane events, indicating that the gravity once reserved for serious matters is now applied to marginal ones. Although this farcical poem wears a guise of inconsequentiality, Pope uses it to contemplate beauty, anger, love, and conquest.

Several years and literary ventures after *The Rape of the Lock*, Pope pursued philosophical works. *An Essay on Man* (a four-epistle poem) and *The Dunciad* (which underwent several expansions before its publication as *The Dunciad in Four Books*) explore religion, societal order, and the limits of human reason, knowledge, and ethics. *An Essay on Man* seeks to "vindicate the ways of God

to man," yet it references no specific religion. Rather, it aims for universality and remains abstract in nature. Pope believed humans were inherently flawed. Despite this, he asserted that people have a duty to strive for goodness and love themselves and others. He also encouraged people to accept their place in the Great Chain of Being (the hierarchical structure that classifies all life and matter). Pope planned to include *An Essay on Man* in a longer work, but he never completed his project. He instead continued extending *The Dun-ciad*, which he claimed authorship of in 1735. In his first three versions of *The Dunciad*—the 1728 *Dunciad*, the 1729 *Dunciad Variorum*, and the 1742 *New Dunciad*—Pope lashed out at bad writers and retaliated against his critics in typical

Scriblerian-satire style. He superseded literary feuds in the final version of *The Dunciad*; published as a single volume in 1743, *The Dunciad in Four Books* cuts at rulers, education, and religion. Public reaction was volatile. Pope faced such hostility that he allegedly did not leave his house without two loaded pistols.

For Pope, satire was a means of exposing and countering cruelty, regardless of how it manifested. His pieces commonly provoked hostile responses, yet even when threatened, Pope continued to write. The influences of writers such as Homer, Dryden, and Milton echo in his finest works. A poet, critic, and religious humanist, Pope esteemed moral virtue above his poetic reputation. He is celebrated for the intricacies of his technique and his distinctive poetic style.

1688	Alexander Pope born 21 May
1711	*An Essay on Criticism*
1712	*Messiah*; *The Rape of the Lock* (expanded 1714)
1713	*Windsor-Forest*
1715–20	*The Iliad of Homer* translation
1717	*Works of Mr. Alexander Pope* (expanded 1727)
1725–26	*The Odyssey of Homer* translation
1725	*The Works of Shakespear, in Six Volumes*
1733	*An Essay on Man*; *Imitations of Horace*
1743	*The Dunciad in Four Books*
1744	Pope dies 30 May and is buried beside his parents at St. Mary's Church, Twickenham

THE RAPE OF THE LOCK
An Heroi-Comical Poem

Nolueram, Belinda, tuos violare capillos,
Sed juvat, hoc precibus me tribuisse tuis.[1]

—MARTIAL

To Mrs. *Arabella Fermor*

MADAM,

It will be in vain to deny that I have some Regard for this Piece, since I dedicate it to You. Yet You may bear me Witness, it was intended only to divert a few young Ladies, who have good Sense and good Humour enough to laugh not only at their Sex's little unguarded Follies, but at their own. But as it was communicated with the Air of a Secret, it soon found its Way into the World. An imperfect Copy having been offer'd to a Bookseller, You had the Good-Nature for my Sake to consent to the Publication of one more correct: This I was forc'd to before I had executed half my Design, for the Machinery was entirely wanting to compleat it.

The Machinery, Madam, is a Term invented by the Criticks, to signify that Part which the Deities, Angels, or Dæmons, are made to act in a Poem: For the ancient Poets are in one respect like many modern Ladies; Let an Action be never so trivial in it self, they always make it appear of the utmost Importance. These Machines I determin'd to raise on a very new and odd Foundation, the *Rosicrucian*[2] Doctrine of Spirits.

I know how disagreeable it is to make use of hard Words before a Lady; but 'tis so much the Concern of a Poet to have his Works understood, and particularly by Your Sex, that You must give me leave to explain two or three difficult Terms.

The *Rosicrucians* are a People I must bring You acquainted with. The best Account I know of them is in a *French* Book call'd *Le Comte de Gabalis*, which both in its Title and Size is so like a Novel, that many of the Fair Sex have read it for one by Mistake. According to these Gentlemen, the four Elements are inhabited by Spirits, which they call *Sylphs, Gnomes, Nymphs,* and *Salamanders.* The *Gnomes,* or Dæmons of Earth, delight in Mischief; but the Sylphs, whose Habitation is

---

1 I was unwilling, [Polytimus], to violate your hairs; but, now, I am glad that I yielded to your entreaties in doing so [Martial, *Epigram*, XII. 85]. Pope substitutes Polytimus with Belinda.

2 Rosicrucian teachings combine occultism with mysticism and other religious beliefs. Rosicrucians believe that those in the order have secret wisdom that has been passed down since ancient times.

Air, are the best-condition'd Creatures imaginable. For they say, any Mortals may enjoy the most intimate Familiarities with these gentle Spirits, upon a Condition very easy to all true *Adepts*, an inviolate Preservation of Chastity.

As to the following Canto's all the Passages of them are as Fabulous, as the Vision at the Beginning, or the Transformation at the End; (except the Loss of Your Hair, which I always mention with Reverence) the Human Persons are as Fictitious as the Airy ones; and the Character of *Belinda*, as it is now manag'd, resembles You in nothing but in Beauty.

If this Poem had as many Graces as there are in Your Person, or in your Mind, yet I could never hope it should pass thro' the World half so Uncensured as You have done. But let its Fortune be what it will, mine is happy enough, to have given me this Occasion of assuring You that I am, with the truest Esteem,

MADAM,

Your Most Obedient,

Humble Servant,

A. POPE

CANTO I.

[handwritten: — Heroic couplets (mimics epic)]

What dire Offence from am'rous Causes springs,
What mighty Contests rise from trivial Things,
I sing—This Verse to *C—*,[3] Muse! is due:
This, ev'n *Belinda* may vouchsafe to view:
Slight is the Subject, but not so the Praise,   5
If She inspire, and He approve my Lays.

Say what strange Motive, Goddess! cou'd compel
A well-bred Lord t'assault a gentle *Belle?*
Oh say what stranger Cause, yet unexplor'd,
Could make a gentle *Belle* reject a Lord?   10
And dwells such Rage in softest Bosoms then?
And lodge such daring Souls in Little Men?

Sol thro' white Curtains shot a tim'rous Ray,
And op'd those Eyes that must eclipse the Day;
Now Lapdogs give themselves the rousing shake,   15

---

3 Pope honors John Caryll, who suggested the creation of this poem.

And sleepless Lovers, just at Twelve, awake:
Thrice rung the Bell, the Slipper knock'd the Ground,
And the press'd Watch[1] return'd a silver Sound.
Belinda still her downy pillow prest,
Her guardian *Sylph* prolong'd the balmy rest.   20
'Twas He had summon'd to her silent Bed
The Morning-Dream that hover o'er her Head.
A Youth more glitt'ring than a Birth-night Beau,[2]
(That ev'n in Slumber caus'd her Cheek to glow)
Seem'd to her Ear his winning Lips to lay,   25
And thus in Whispers said, or seem'd to say.

"Fairest of Mortals, thou distinguish'd Care
Of thousand bright Inhabitants of Air!
If e'er one vision touch'd thy infant Thought,
Of all the Nurse and all the Priest have taught,   30
Of Airy Elves by Moonlight Shadows seen,
The silver Token, and the Circled Green,
Or Virgins visited by Angel-Pow'rs,
With Golden Crowns, and Wreaths of heavenly flow'rs,
Hear and believe! thy own Importance know,   35
Nor bound thy narrow Views to things below.
Some secret Truths, from Learned Pride conceal'd,
To Maids alone and Children are reveal'd:
What tho' no Credit doubting Wits may give?
The Fair and Innocent shall still believe.   40
Know then, unnumber'd Spirits round thee fly,
The light Militia of the lower Sky;
These, tho' unseen, are ever on the Wing,
Hang o'er the Box,[3] and hover round the Ring:[4]
Think what an Equipage thou hast in Air,   45
And view with scorn two Pages and a Chair.[5]
As now your own, our Beings were of old,
And once inclos'd in Woman's beauteous Mold;

---

1 A repeater watch strikes the hour.

2 Men of the nobility donned lavish clothing when attending a birth-night party for a member of the British royal family.

3 A reserved-seating area in a theatre.

4 The fashionable inner drive at Hyde Park.

5 A sedan chair, carried by two or more people.

Thence by a soft Transition, we repair
From Earthly Vehicles to these of Air.   50
Think not, when Woman's transient Breath is fled,
That all her Vanities at once are dead:
Succeeding Vanities she still regards,
And tho' she plays no more, o'erlooks the Cards.
Her Joy in gilded Chariots, when alive,   55
And Love of *Ombre*,[6] after Death survive.
For when the Fair in all their Pride expire,
To their first Elements their Souls retire:
The Sprites of fiery Termagants[7] in Flame
Mount up, and take a *Salamander's*[8] Name.   60
Soft yielding Minds to Water glide away,
And sip, with *Nymphs*, their Elemental Tea.
The graver Prude sinks downward to a *Gnome*,
In search of Mischief still on Earth to roam.
The light Coquettes in *Sylphs* aloft repair,   65
And sport and flutter in the Fields of Air.

"Know further yet; whoever fair and chaste
Rejects Mankind, is by some *Sylph* embrac'd:
For Spirits, freed from mortal Laws, with ease
Assume what Sexes and what Shapes they please.   70
What guards the Purity of melting Maids,
In Courtly Balls, and Midnight Masquerades,
Safe from the treach'rous Friend, the daring Spark,
The Glance by Day, the Whisper in the Dark;
When kind Occasion prompts their warm Desires,   75
When Music softens, and when Dancing fires?
'Tis but their *Sylph*, the wise Celestials know,
Tho' *Honour* is the Word with Men below.

"Some Nymphs[9] there are, too conscious of their Face,
For Life predestin'd to the *Gnomes* Embrace.   80
These swell their Prospects and exalt their Pride,
When Offers are disdain'd, and Love deny'd.

---

6 A card game for three players.

7 A harsh-tempered and domineering woman.

8 Lizard-like creatures once thought to live in or withstand fire.

9 In classical mythology, nymphs are beautiful maidens who dwell in nature. Here Pope uses "nymph" as a term for a young woman.

Then gay Ideas crowd the vacant Brain,
While Peers and Dukes, and all their sweeping Train;
And Garters, Stars, and Coronets[1] appear,   85
And in soft Sounds, '*Your Grace*'[2] salutes their Ear.
'Tis these that Early taint the Female Soul,
Instruct the Eyes of young Coquettes to roll,
Teach Infant Cheeks a bidden Blush to know,
And little Hearts to flutter at a Beau.   90

   "Oft' when the World imagine Women stray,
The *Sylph* thro' mystic Mazes guide their Way,
Thro' all the giddy Circle they pursue,
And old Impertinence expel by new.
What tender Maid but must a Victim fall   95
To one Man's Treat, but for another's Ball?
When *Florio* speaks, what Virgin could withstand,
If gentle *Damon* did not squeeze her Hand?
With varying Vanities, from ev'r Part,
They shift the moving Toyshop of their Heart;   100
Where Wigs with Wigs, with Sword-knots Sword-knots strive,
Beaus banish Beaus, and Coaches Coaches drive.
This erring Mortals Levity may call,
Oh blind to Truth! the *Sylphs* contrive it all.

   "Of these am I, who thy Protection claim,   105
A watchful Sprite, and *Ariel* is my Name.
Late, as I rang'd the Crystal Wilds of Air,
In the clear Mirror of thy ruling Star
I saw, alas! some dread Event impend,
E're to the Main this Morning Sun descend,   110
But Heav'n reveals not what, or how, or where:
Warn'd by thy *Sylph*, Oh pious Maid, beware!
This to disclose is all thy Guardian can:
Beware of all, but most beware of Man!"

   He said; when *Shock*,[3] who thought she slept too long,   115
Leap'd up, and wak'd his Mistress with his Tongue.

---

1 Emblems of nobility.

2 Used to address or describe a duchess, duke, or archbishop.

3 A lapdog.

'Twas then, *Belinda*! if Report say true,
Thy Eyes first open'd on a Billet-doux;
Wounds, Charms, and Ardors were no sooner read,
But all the Vision vanish'd from thy Head.   120

   And now, unveil'd, the Toilet stands display'd,
Each Silver Vase in mystic Order laid.
First, rob'd in White, the Nymph intent adores
With Head uncover'd, the Cosmetic Pow'rs.
A heav'nly Image in the Glass appears,   125
To that she bends, to that her Eyes she rears;
Th' inferior Priestess, at her Altar's Side,
Trembling, begins the sacred Rites of Pride.
Unnumber'd Treasures ope at once, and here
The various Off'rings of the World appear;   130
From each she nicely culls with curious Toil,
And Decks the Goddess with the glitt'ring Spoil.
This Casket *India*'s glowing Gems unlocks,
And all *Arabia* breaths from yonder Box.
The Tortoise here and Elephant unite,   135
Transform'd to Combs, the speckled and the white.
Here Files of Pins extend their shining Rows,
Puffs, Powders, Patches, Bibles, Billet-doux.[4]
Now awful Beauty puts on all its Arms;
The Fair each moment rises in her Charms,   140
Repairs her Smiles, awakens ev'ry Grace,
And calls forth all the Wonders of her Face;
Sees by Degrees a purer Blush arise,
And keener Lightnings quicken in her Eyes.
The busy *Sylphs* surround their darling Care,   145
These set the Head, and those divide the Hair,
Some fold the Sleeve, whilst others plait the Gown;
And *Betty*'s prais'd for Labours not her own.

CANTO II.

   Not with more Glories, in th' Etherial Plain,
The Sun first rises o'er the purpled Main,
Than, issuing forth, the rival of his beams

---

4 A love letter.

Launch'd on the Bosom of the Silver *Thames*.
Fair Nymphs, and well-drest Youths around her shone,   5
But ev'ry Eye was fix'd on her alone.
On her white Breast a sparkling Cross she wore,
Which Jews might kiss, and Infidels adore.
Her lively Looks a sprightly Mind disclose,
Quick as her Eyes, and as unfix'd as those: 10
Favours to none, to all she Smiles extends,
Oft she rejects, but never once offends.
Bright as the Sun, her Eyes the Gazers strike,
And, like the Sun, they shine on all alike.
Yet graceful Ease, and Sweetness void of Pride,   15
Might hide her Faults, if *Belles* had Faults to hide:
If to her share some Female Errors fall,
Look on her Face, and you'll forget 'em all.

This Nymph, to the Destruction of Mankind,
Nourish'd two Locks, which graceful hung behind   20
In equal Curls, and well conspir'd to deck
With shining Ringlets the smooth Iv'ry Neck:
Love in these Labyrinths his Slaves detains,
And mighty Hearts are held in slender Chains.
With Hairy Sprindges[1] we the Birds betray,   25
Slight Lines of Hair surprise the Finny-Prey,
Fair Tresses Man's Imperial Race ensnare,
And Beauty draws us with a single Hair.

Th' Advent'rous *Baron* the bright Locks admir'd,
He saw, he wish'd, and to the Prize aspir'd: 30
Resolv'd to win, he meditates the Way,
By Force to ravish, or by Fraud betray;
For when Success a Lover's Toil attends,
Few ask, if Fraud or Force attain'd his Ends.

For this, e're *Phœbus*[2] rose, he had implor'd   35
Propitious Heav'n, and ev'ry Pow'r ador'd,
But chiefly Love—to Love an Altar built,
Of twelve vast *French* Romances, neatly gilt.

---

1 Snares.

2 The sun.

There lay three Garters, half a Pair of Gloves;
And all the Trophies of his former Loves.   40
With tender Billet-doux he lights the Pyre,
And breaths three am'rous Sighs to raise the Fire.
Then prostrate falls, and begs with ardent Eyes
Soon to obtain, and long possess the Prize:
The Pow'rs gave Ear, and granted half his Pray'r,   45
The rest, the Winds dispers'd in empty Air.

   But now secure the painted Vessel glides,
The Sun-beams trembling on the floating Tydes,
While melting Music steals upon the Sky,
And soften'd Sounds along the Waters die.   50
Smooth flow the Waves, the Zephyrs³ gently play,
Belinda smil'd, and all the World was gay.
All but the *Sylph*—with careful Thoughts opprest,
Th' impending Woe sat heavy on his Breast.
He summons strait his Denizens of Air;   55
The lucid Squadrons round the Sails repair:
Soft o'er the Shrouds Aerial Whispers breath,
That seem'd but Zephyrs to the Train beneath.
Some to the Sun their Insect-Wings unfold,
Waft on the Breeze, or sink in Clouds of Gold.   60
Transparent Forms, too fine for mortal Sight,
Their fluid Bodies half dissolv'd in Light.
Loose to the Wind their airy Garments flew,
Thin glitt'ring Textures of the filmy Dew;
Dipt in the richest Tincture of the Skies,   65
Where Light disports in ever-mingling Dies,
While ev'ry Beam new transient Colours flings,
Colours that change whene'er they wave their Wings.
Amid the Circle, on the gilded mast,
Superior by the Head, was *Ariel* plac'd;   70
His purple Pinions⁴ opening to the Sun,
He rais'd his azure Wand, and thus begun.

   "Ye *Sylphs* and *Sylphids*, to your Chief give Ear,
Fays, Fairies, Genii, Elves, and *Dæmons* hear!

---

3 A soft breeze.
4 Wings.

Ye know the Spheres and various Tasks assign'd,   75
By Laws Eternal, to th' Aerial Kind.
Some in the Fields of purest *Æther* play,
And bask and whiten in the Blaze of Day.
Some guide the Course of wandring Orbs on high,
Or roll the Planets thro' the boundless Sky.   80
Some less refin'd, beneath the Moon's pale Light
Hover, and catch the shooting Stars by Night;
Or suck the Mists in grosser Air below,
Or dip their Pinions in the painted Bow,
Or brew fierce Tempests on the wintry Main,   85
Or o'er the Glebe[1] distil the kindly Rain.
Others on Earth o'er human Race preside,
Watch all their Ways, and all their Actions guide:
Of these the Chief the Care of Nations own,
And guard with Arms Divine the *British* Throne.   90

    "Our humbler province is to tend the Fair,
Not a less pleasing, tho' less glorious Care.
To save the Powder from too rude a Gale,
Nor let th' imprison'd Essences exhale,
To draw fresh Colours from the vernal Flow'rs,   95
To steal from Rainbows e'er they drop in Show'rs
A brighter Wash, to curl their waving Hairs,
Assist their Blushes, and inspire their Airs;
Nay oft', in Dreams, Invention we bestow,
To change a Flounce, or add a Furbelo.[2]   100

    "This Day, black Omens threat the brightest Fair,
That e'er deserv'd a watchful Spirit's Care;
Some dire Disaster, or by Force, or Slight;
But what, or where, the Fates have wrapt in Night.
Whether the Nymph shall break *Diana*'s Law,[3]   105
Or some frail *China* Jar receive a Flaw,
Or stain her honour or her new brocade;
Forget her Pray'rs, or miss a Masquerade,
Or lose her Heart, or Necklace, at a Ball;

1 Fields.
2 An ornamental addition to a garment.
3 Diana is the Roman goddess of chastity.

Or whether Heav'n has doom'd that *Shock* must fall.   110
Haste, then, ye Spirits! to your Charge repair;
The flutt'ring Fan be *Zephyretta's* Care;

"The Drops[4] to thee, *Brillante*, we consign;
And, *Momentilla*, let the Watch be thine;
Do thou, *Crispissa*, tend her fav'rite Lock;   115
Ariel himself shall be the Guard of *Shock*.

"To Fifty chosen *Sylphs*, of special Note,
We trust th'important Charge, the *Petticoat*:
Oft' have we known that sev'nfold Fence to fail,
Tho' stiff with Hoops, and arm'd with Ribs of Whale.   120
Form a strong Line about the silver Bound,
And guard the wide Circumference around.

"Whatever Spirit, careless of his Charge,
His Post neglects, or leaves the Fair at large,
Shall feel sharp Vengeance soon o'ertake his Sins,   125
Be stopt in Vials, or transfix'd with Pins;
Or plung'd in Lakes of bitter Washes lie,
Or wedg'd whole Ages in a Bodkin's Eye:[5]
Gums and Pomatums shall his Flight restrain,
While clogg'd he beats his silken Wings in vain;   130
Or Alum-styptics with contracting Pow'r
Shrink his thin Essence like a rivell'd Flow'r:
Or as *Ixion*[6] fix'd, the Wretch shall feel
The giddy Motion of the whirling Mill,
In Fumes of burning Chocolate shall glow,   135
And tremble at the Sea that froths below!"

He spoke; the Spirits from the Sails descend;
Some, Orb in Orb, around the Nymph extend,
Some thrid the mazy Ringlets of her Hair,
Some hang upon the Pendants of her Ear;   140
With beating Hearts the dire Event they wait,
Anxious, and trembling for the Birth of Fate.

---

4 Earrings that dangle from the earlobe.

5 A blunt needle with a large eye used to pull material through a hem.

6 In Greek legend, Zeus bound Ixion, king of the Lapiths, to an ever-turning fiery wheel as punishment for trying to seduce Hera.

CANTO III.

Close by those Meads, for ever crown'd with Flow'rs,
Where *Thames* with Pride surveys his rising Tow'rs,
There stands a structure of Majestic Frame,
Which from the neighb'ring *Hampton*[1] takes its Name.
Here *Britain*'s Statesmen oft' the Fall foredoom   5
Of Foreign Tyrants, and of Nymphs at home;
Here Thou, Great *Anna!*[2] whom three Realms obey,
Dost sometimes Counsel take—and sometimes Tea.

Hither the Heroes and the Nymphs resort,
To taste awhile the Pleasures of a Court;   10
In various Talk th' instructive Hours they past,
Who gave the Ball, or paid the Visit last:
One speaks the Glory of the *British* Queen,
And one describes a charming *Indian* Screen;
A third interprets Motions, Looks, and Eyes;   15
At ev'ry Word a Reputation dies.
Snuff, or the Fan, supply each Pause of Chat,
With singing, laughing, ogling, and all that.

Mean while, declining from the Noon of Day,
The Sun obliquely shoots his burning Ray;   20
The hungry Judges soon the Sentence sign,
And Wretches hang that Jury-men may dine;
The Merchant from th' *Exchange* returns in Peace,
And the long Labours of the Toilet cease—
Belinda now, whom Thirst of Fame invites,   25
Burns to encounter Two advent'rous Knights,
At *Ombre* singly to decide their Doom;
And swells her Breast with Conquests yet to come.
Straight the three Bands prepare in Arms to join,
Each Band the Number of the Sacred Nine.[3]   30
Soon as she spreads her Hand, th' Aerial Guard

---

1 Hampton Court Palace is beside the River Thames.
2 Queen Anne reigned from 1702-1707.
3 The Muses.

Descend, and sit on each important Card:
First *Ariel* perch'd upon a Matadore,[4]
Then each, according to the Rank they bore;
For *Sylphs*, yet mindful of their ancient Race,   35
Are, as when Women, wond'rous fond of Place.

   Behold, four Kings in Majesty rever'd,[5]
With hoary Whiskers and a forky Beard:
And four fair Queens whose hands sustain a Flow'r,
Th' expressive Emblem of their softer Pow'r;   40
Four Knaves[6] in Garbs succinct, a trusty Band,
Caps on their Heads, and Halberts in their Hand;
And particolour'd Troops, a shining Train,
Draw forth to Combat on the Velvet Plain.

   The skilful Nymph reviews her Force with Care;   45
"Let Spades be Trumps," she said, and Trumps they were.

   Now move to War her Sable Matadores,
In Show like Leaders of the swarthy Moors.
Spadillio first, unconquerable Lord!
Led off two captive Trumps, and swept the Board.   50
As many more *Manillio* forc'd to yield,
And march'd a Victor from the verdant Field.
Him *Basto* follow'd, but his Fate more hard,
Gain'd but one Trump and one *Plebeian* Card.
With his broad Sabre next, a Chief in Years,   55
The hoary Majesty of Spades appears;
Puts forth one manly Leg, to sight reveal'd;
The rest his many-colour'd Robe conceal'd.
The Rebel-Knave, who dares his Prince engage,
Proves the just Victim of his Royal Rage.   60
Ev'n mighty *Pam* that Kings and Queens o'erthrew,
And mow'd down Armies in the Fights of *Lu*,[7]

---

4 The highest trumps in ombre.

5 A detailed account of the game ensues. Matadores, spadillio, manillio, and basto are terms associated with the game. Belinda has a promising and powerful hand, but the Baron's hand is furnished for defense. Since the third player's cards are negligible, Belinda and the Baron fight for victory. Belinda wins.

6 Jacks.

7 A game of cards.

Sad Chance of War! now, destitute of Aid,
Falls undistinguish'd by the Victor Spade!

    Thus far both Armies to *Belinda* yield;   65
Now to the Baron Fate inclines the Field.
His warlike *Amazon* her Host invades,
Th' imperial Consort of the Crown of Spades.
The Club's black Tyrant first her Victim dy'd,
Spite of his haughty Mien, and barb'rous Pride: 70
What boots[1] the Regal Circle on his Head,
His Giant Limbs, in State unwieldy spread;
That long behind he trails his pompous Robe,
And of all Monarchs only grasps the Globe?

    The Baron now his Diamonds pours apace;   75
Th' embroider'd King who shows but half his Face,
And his refulgent Queen, with Pow'rs combin'd
Of broken Troops an easy Conquest find.
Clubs, Diamonds, Hearts, in wild Disorder seen,
With Throngs promiscuous strow the level Green.   80
Thus when dispers'd a routed Army runs,
Of *Asia*'s Troops, and *Afric*'s Sable Sons,
With like Confusion different Nations fly,
Of various Habits and of various Dye,
The pierc'd Battalions dis-united fall,   85
In Heaps on Heaps; one Fate o'erwhelms them all.

    The Knave of Diamonds tries his wily Arts,
And wins (oh shameful Chance!) the Queen of Hearts.
At this, the Blood the Virgin's Cheek forsook,
A livid Paleness spreads o'er all her Look;   90
She sees, and trembles at th' approaching Ill,
Just in the Jaws of Ruin, and *Codille*.[2]
And now, (as oft' in some distemper'd State)
On one nice Trick depends the gen'ral Fate.
An Ace of Hearts steps forth: The King unseen   95
Lurk'd in her Hand, and mourn'd his Captive Queen:
He springs to Vengeance with an eager Pace,

---

1 Avails or profits.

2 Losing.

And falls like Thunder on the prostrate Ace.
The Nymph exulting fills with Shouts the Sky;
The Walls, the Woods, and long Canals reply.   100

    Oh thoughtless Mortals! ever blind to Fate,
Too soon dejected, and too soon elate!
Sudden these Honours shall be snatch'd away,
And curs'd for ever this victorious Day.

    For lo! the Board with Cups and Spoons is crown'd,   105
The Berries crackle, and the Mill turns round;[3]
On shining Altars of *Japan*[4] they raise
The silver Lamp; the fiery Spirits blaze:
From silver Spouts the grateful Liquors glide,
While *China*'s Earth receives the smoking Tide.   110
At once they gratify their Scent and Taste,
And frequent Cups prolong the rich Repast.
Straight hover round the Fair her Airy Band;
Some, as she sipp'd, the fuming Liquor fann'd.
Some o'er her Lap their careful Plumes display'd,   115
Trembling, and conscious of the rich Brocade.
Coffee, (which makes the Politician wise,
And see thro' all Things with his half-shut Eyes)
Sent up in Vapours to the Baron's Brain
New Stratagems the radiant Lock to gain.   120
Ah cease, rash Youth! desist e'er 'tis too late;
Fear the just Gods, and think of *Scylla*'s Fate![5]
Chang'd to a Bird, and sent to flit in Air,
She dearly pays for *Nisus*' injur'd Hair!

    But when to Mischief Mortals bend their Will,   125
How soon they find fit Instruments of Ill?
Just then, *Clarissa* drew with tempting Grace
A two-edg'd Weapon from her shining Case;
So Ladies in Romance assist their Knight,

---

3 Green coffee beans were placed into a mill, ground, and roasted over a fire until they browned.

4 *Shintô* altars and Buddhist altars are made with lacquered dark wood and often painted with gold and silver designs.

5 After falling in love with king Minos of Crete, Scylla cut a magic purple lock of hair from her father Nisus' head. When Minos besieged Nisus' city of Megara, Nisus died and was turned into a sea eagle. Scylla was later transformed into a sea bird and fated to be chased by her father forever.

Present the Spear, and arm him for the Fight.   130
He takes the Gift with Rev'rence, and extends
The little Engine on his Finger's Ends:
This just behind *Belinda*'s Neck he spread,
As o'er the fragrant Steams she bends her Head.
Swift to the Lock a thousand Sprites repair,   135
A thousand Wings by turns, blow back the Hair;
And thrice they twitch'd the Diamond in her Ear;
Thrice she look'd back, and thrice the Foe drew near.
Just in that instant, anxious *Ariel* sought
The close Recesses of the Virgin's Thought;   140
As on the Nosegay in her Breast reclin'd,
He watch'd th' Ideas rising in her Mind,
Sudden he view'd, in spite of all her Art,
An Earthly Lover lurking at her Heart.
Amaz'd, confus'd, he found his Pow'r expir'd,   145
Resign'd to Fate, and with a Sigh retir'd.

From peerage; man w/ a title

The Peer now spreads the glitt'ring *Forfex*[1] wide,
T'inclose the Lock; now joins it, to divide.
Ev'n then, before the fatal Engine clos'd,
A wretched *Sylph* too fondly interpos'd;   150
Fate urg'd the Shears, and cut the *Sylph* in twain,
(But Airy Substance soon unites again)
The meeting Points the sacred Hair dissever
From the fair Head, for ever, and for ever!

Then flash'd the living Lightning from her Eyes,   155
And Screams of Horror rend th' affrighted Skies.
Not louder Shrieks to pitying Heav'n are cast,
When Husbands, or when Lapdogs breath their last;
Or when rich *China* Vessels, fall'n from high,
In glitt'ring Dust, and painted Fragments lie!   160

Let Wreaths of Triumph now my Temples twine,
(The Victor cry'd) the glorious Prize is mine!
While Fish in Streams, or Dirds delight in Air,
Or in a Coach and Six, the *British* Fair,

---

1 Scissors.

As long as *Atalantis*[2] shall be read,   165
Or the small Pillow grace a Lady's Bed,
While Visits shall be paid on solemn Days,
When num'rous Wax-lights in bright Order blaze,
While Nymphs take Treats, or Assignations give,
So long my Honour, Name, and Praise shall live!   170

　　"What Time wou'd spare, from Steel receives its Date,
And Monuments, like Men, submit to Fate!
Steel could the Labour of the Gods destroy,
And strike to dust th' Imperial Tow'rs of *Troy*;
Steel cou'd the Works of mortal Pride confound,   175
And hew Triumphal Arches to the Ground.
What Wonder then, fair Nymph! thy Hairs shou'd feel,
The conqu'ring Force of unresisted steel?"

CANTO IV.

　　But anxious Cares the pensive Nymph opprest,
And secret Passions labour'd in her Breast.
Not youthful Kings in Battle seiz'd alive,
Not scornful Virgins who their Charms survive,
Not ardent Lovers robb'd of all their Bliss,   5
Not ancient Ladies when refus'd a Kiss,
Not Tyrants fierce that unrepenting die,
Not *Cynthia* when her Manteau's[3] pinn'd awry,
E'er felt such Rage, Resentment and Despair,
As thou, sad Virgin! for thy ravish'd Hair.   10

　　For, that sad moment, when the *Sylphs* withdrew
And *Ariel* weeping from *Belinda* flew,
Umbriel, a dusky, melancholy Sprite,
As ever sully'd the fair Face of Light,
Down to the Central Earth, his proper Scene,   15
Repairs to search the gloomy Cave of *Spleen*.[4]

2　*The New Atlantis* (1709) is Delarivier Manley's most well-known piece of scandalous political fiction.

3　A loose-fitting gown.

4　Sometimes called "the English malady," the Cave of Spleen involved low spirits, hypochondria, and hysteria.

Swift on his sooty Pinions flits the *Gnome*,
And in a Vapour reach'd the dismal Dome.
No cheerful Breeze this sullen Region knows,
The dreaded East is all the Wind that blows.   20
Here, in a Grotto, sheltered close from Air,
And screen'd in Shades from Day's detested Glare,
She sighs for ever on her pensive Bed,
Pain at her Side, and *Megrim*[1] at her Head.

Two Handmaids wait the Throne: Alike in Place,   25
But diff'ring far in Figure and in Face.
Here stood *Ill-nature* like an ancient Maid,
Her wrinkled Form in Black and White array'd;
With store of Pray'rs, for Mornings, Nights, and Noons,
Her Hand is fill'd; her Bosom with Lampoons.   30

There *Affectation*, with a sickly Mien,
Shows in her Cheek the Roses of Eighteen,
Practis'd to lisp, and hang the Head aside,
Faints into Airs, and languishes with Pride;
On the rich Quilt, sinks with becoming Woe,   35
Wrapt in a Gown, for Sickness, and for Show.
The Fair ones feel such Maladies as these,
When each new Night-dress gives a new Disease.

A constant Vapour[2] o'er the Palace flies;
Strange Phantoms rising as the Mists arise;   40
Dreadful, as Hermit's Dreams on haunted Shades,
Or bright, as Visions of expiring Maids.
Now glaring Fiends, and Snakes on rolling Spires,
Pale Spectres, gaping Tombs, and purple Fires:
Now Lakes of liquid Gold, *Elysian* Scenes,   45
And Crystal Domes, and Angels in Machines.

Unnumber'd throngs on ev'ry side are seen,
Of Bodies chang'd to various Forms by Spleen.
Here living Tea-pots stand, one Arm held out,

---

1 Migraine.

2 A sudden feeling of nervousness or ill-temperedness.

One bent; the Handle this, and that the Spout: 50
A Pipkin[3] there, like *Homer*'s Tripod[4] walks;
Here sighs a Jar, and there a Goose-pie talks;
Men prove with Child, as pow'rful Fancy works,
And Maids turn'd Bottles, call aloud for Corks.

Safe past the *Gnome* thro' this fantastic Band, 55
A Branch of healing Spleenwort[5] in his Hand.
Then thus address'd the Pow'r—Hail, wayward Queen!
Who rule the Sex to Fifty from Fifteen:
Parent of Vapours and of Female Wit,
Who give th' Hysteric or Poetic Fit, 60
On various Tempers act by various Ways,
Make some take Physic, others scribble Plays;
Who cause the Proud their Visits to delay,
And send the Godly in a Pett, to pray.
A Nymph there is, that all thy Pow'r disdains, 65
And thousands more in equal Mirth maintains.
But oh! if e'er thy *Gnome* could spoil a Grace,
Or raise a Pimple on a beauteous Face;
Like Citron-Waters[6] Matrons Cheeks inflame,
Or change Complexions at a losing Game; 70
If e'er with airy Horns[7] I planted Heads,
Or rumpled Petticoats, or tumbled Beds,
Or caus'd Suspicion when no Soul was rude,
Or discompos'd the Head-dress of a Prude,
Or e'er to costive Lapdog gave Disease, 75
Which not the Tears of brightest Eyes could ease:
Hear me, and touch *Belinda* with Chagrin,
That single Act gives half the World the Spleen.

The Goddess with a discontented Air
Seems to reject him, tho' she grants his Pray'r. 80
A wond'rous Bag with both her Hands she binds,

---

3 An earthenware pot.

4 In the *Iliad*, Vulcan makes special tripods capable of moving on their own.

5 In Virgil's *Aeneid*, Aeneas carries a golden bough into the underworld for protection. Similarly, Umbriel descends into the Cave of Spleen carrying spleenwort, a fern once used to remedy diseases of the spleen, as protection.

6 Brandy or a clear spirit infused with citrus or lemon peels.

7 Horns are the symbol of a cuckold.

Like that where once *Ulysses* held the Winds;[1]
There she collects the Force of Female Lungs,
Sighs, Sobs, and Passions, and the War of Tongues.
A Vial next she fills with fainting Fears,   85
Soft Sorrows, melting Griefs, and flowing Tears.
The *Gnome* rejoicing bears her Gift away,
Spreads his black Wings, and slowly mounts to Day.

    Sunk in *Thalestris*'[2] Arms the Nymph he found,
Her Eyes dejected and her Hair unbound.   90
Full o'er their Heads the swelling Bag he rent,
And all the Furies issu'd at the Vent.
Belinda burns with more than mortal Ire,
And fierce *Thalestris* fans the rising Fire.
"O wretched Maid!" she spread her Hands, and cry'd,   95
(While *Hampton*'s Echoes, "wretched Maid!" reply'd)
"Was it for this you took such constant Care
The Bodkin, Comb, and Essence to prepare?
For this your Locks in Paper-Durance bound,
For this with tort'ring Irons wreath'd around?   100
For this with Fillets strain'd your tender Head,
And bravely bore the double Loads of Lead?
Gods! shall the Ravisher display your Hair,
While the Fops envy, and the Ladies stare!
Honour forbid! at whose unrival'd Shrine,   105
Ease, Pleasure, Virtue, All, our Sex resign.
Methinks already I your Tears survey,
Already hear the horrid Things they say,
Already see you a degraded Toast,
And all your Honour in a Whisper lost!   110
How shall I, then, your helpless Fame defend?
'Twill then be Infamy to seem your Friend!
And shall this Prize, th' inestimable Prize,
Expos'd thro' Crystal to the gazing Eyes,
And heighten'd by the Diamond's circling Rays,   115
On that rapacious Hand for ever blaze?

---

1 Aeolus (later described as a minor god of the winds) provided Ulysses (Odysseus) with favorable winds for his voyage home and restricted all the unfavorable winds in a bag, which he then gave to Ulysses. Ulysses' companions, however, opened the bag. The winds drove them far from their destination.

2 The legendary warrior-queen of the Amazons.

Sooner shall Grass in *Hyde-Park Circus* grow,
And Wits take Lodgings in the Sound of *Bow*;[3]
Sooner let Earth, Air, Sea, to *Chaos* fall,
Men, Monkeys, Lap-dogs, Parrots, perish all!"   120

    She said; then raging to Sir *Plume* repairs,
And bids her Beau demand the precious Hairs:
(Sir *Plume*, of Amber Snuff-Box justly vain,
And the nice Conduct of a Clouded Cane[4])
With earnest Eyes, and round unthinking Face,   125
He first the Snuff-Box open'd, then the Case,
And thus broke out— "My Lord, why, what the Devil?
Z — ds![5] damn the Lock! 'fore Gad, you must be civil!
Plague on't! 'tis past a Jest—nay, prithee, Pox?
Give her the Hair"—he spoke, and rapp'd his Box.   130

    "It grieves me much" (reply'd the Peer again)
"Who speaks so well should ever speak in vain.
But by this Lock, this sacred Lock I swear,
(Which never more shall join its parted Hair;
Which never more its Honours shall renew,   135
Clip'd from the lovely Head where late it grew)
That while my Nostrils draw the vital Air,
This Hand, which won it, shall for ever wear."
He spoke, and speaking, in proud Triumph spread
The long-contended Honours of her Head.   140

    But *Umbriel*, hateful *Gnome!* forbears not so;
He breaks the Vial whence the Sorrow flow.
Then see! the Nymph in beauteous Grief appears,
Her Eyes half languishing, half drown'd in Tears;
On her heav'd Bosom hung her drooping Head,   145
Which, with a Sigh, she rais'd; and thus she said.

    "For ever curs'd be this detested Day,
Which snatch'd my best, my fav'rite Curl away!

---

3 A person born within the sound of the bells of the church of St. Mary-le-Bow, in Cheapside, London, is considered a Cockney.

4 A fashionable cane clouded from age or use.

5 A contraction of "God's wounds," the common oath *Zounds* prevented one from formal swearing but still implied profanity.

Happy! ah ten Times happy, had I been,
If *Hampton-Court* these Eyes had never seen! 150
Yet am not I the first mistaken Maid,
By Love of Courts to num'rous Ills betray'd.
Oh had I rather un-admir'd remain'd
In some lone Isle, or distant *Northern* Land;
Where the gilt Chariot never marks the Way, 155
Where none learn *Ombre*, none e'er taste *Bohea!* [1]
There kept my Charms conceal'd from mortal Eye,
Like Roses, that in Deserts bloom and die.
What mov'd my Mind with youthful Lord to roam?
Oh had I stay'd, and said my Pray'rs at Home! 160
'Twas this, the Morning Omens seem'd to tell;
Thrice from my trembling Hand the Patch-Box fell;
The tort'ring China shook without a Wind,
Nay, *Poll* sat mute, and *Shock* was most unkind!
A *Sylph* too warn'd me of the Threats of Fate, 165
In mystic Visions, now believ'd too late!
See the poor Remnants of these slighted Hairs!
My Hands shall rend what ev'n thy Rapine spares:
These, in two sable Ringlets taught to break,
Once gave new Beauties to the snowy Neck; 170
The Sister-Lock now sits uncouth alone,
And in its Fellow's Fate foresees its own;
Uncurl'd it hangs, the fatal Shears demands;
And tempts once more thy sacrilegious Hands.
Oh hadst thou, Cruel! been content to seize 175
Hairs less in Sight, or any Hairs but these!"

CANTO V.

She said: the pitying Audience melt in Tears.
But Fate and *Jove* had stopp'd the Baron's Ears.
In vain *Thalestris* with Reproach assails,
For who can move when fair *Belinda* fails?
Not half so fix'd the *Trojan* [2] cou'd remain, 5
While *Anna* begg'd and *Dido* rag'd in vain.

---

1 Black tea once esteemed but now considered to be low quality.

2 The Trojan Aenas abandons Carthage at the request of the gods, disregarding arguments from Queen Dido, whom he loves, and entreaties from her sister, Anna (*Aeneid*, IV).

Then grave *Clarissa* graceful wav'd her Fan;
Silence ensu'd, and thus the Nymph began.

"Say, why are Beauties prais'd and honour'd most,
The wise Man's Passion, and the vain Man's Toast? 10
Why deck'd with all that Land and Sea afford,
Why Angels call'd, and Angel-like ador'd?
Why round our Coaches crowd the white-glov'd Beaus,
Why bows the Side-box from its inmost Rows?
How vain are all these Glories, all our Pains, 15
Unless good sense preserve what Beauty gains:
That Men may say, when we the Front-box grace,
'Behold the first in Virtue, as in Face!'
Oh! if to dance all Night, and dress all Day,
Charm'd the Small-pox, or chas'd old Age away; 20
Who would not scorn what Housewife's Cares produce,
Or who would learn one earthly Thing of Use?
To patch, nay ogle, might become a Saint,
Nor could it sure be such a Sin to paint.
But since, alas! frail Beauty must decay, 25
Curl'd or uncurl'd, since Locks will turn to grey,
Since painted, or not painted, all shall fade,
And she who scorns a Man, must die a Maid;
What then remains, but well our Pow'r to use,
And keep good Humour still whate'er we lose? 30
And trust me, Dear! Good Humour can prevail,
When Airs, and Flights, and Screams, and Scolding fail.
Beauties in vain their pretty Eyes may roll;
Charms strike the Sight, but Merit wins the Soul."

So spoke the Dame, but no Applause ensu'd; 35
Belinda frown'd, *Thalestris* call'd her Prude.
"To Arms, to Arms!" the fierce Virago[3] cries,
And swift as Lightning to the Combat flies.
All side in Parties, and begin th' Attack;
Fans clap, Silks rustle, and tough Whalebones crack; 40
Heroes and Heroines Shouts confus'dly rise,
And bass, and treble Voices strike the Skies.

---

3 A female warrior; a woman said to have masculine qualities.

No common Weapons in their Hands are found,
Like Gods they fight, nor dread a mortal Wound.

   So when bold *Homer* makes the Gods engage,   45
And heav'nly Breasts with human Passions rage;
'Gainst *Pallas*, *Mars*; *Latona*, *Hermes*[1] Arms;
And all *Olympus* rings with loud Alarms:
Jove's Thunder roars, Heav'n trembles all around;
Blue *Neptune* storms, the bellowing Deeps resound;   50
Earth shakes her nodding Tow'rs, the Ground gives Way,
And the pale Ghosts start at the Flash of Day!

   Triumphant *Umbriel* on a Sconce's[2] Height
Clap'd his glad Wings, and sate to view the Fight;
Prop'd on their Bodkin Spears, the Sprites survey   55
The growing Combat, or assist the Fray.

   While thro' the Press enrag'd *Thalestris* flies,
And scatters Death around from both her Eyes,
A Beau and Witling perish'd in the Throng,
One died in Metaphor, and one in Song.   60
"O cruel Nymph! a living Death I bear,"
Cry'd *Dapperwit*, and sunk beside his Chair.
A mournful glance Sir *Fopling* upwards cast,
"Those Eyes are made so killing"—was his last:
Thus on *Mæander*'s[3] flow'ry Margin lies   65
Th' expiring *Swan*, and as he sings he dies.

   When bold Sir *Plume* had drawn *Clarissa* down,
Chloe step'd in, and kill'd him with a Frown;
She smil'd to see the doughty Hero slain,
But at her Smile, the Beau reviv'd again.   70

   Now *Jove* suspends his golden Scales in Air,
Weighs the Mens Wits against the Lady's Hair;
The doubtful Beam long nods from side to side;
At length the Wits mount up, the Hairs subside.

---

1 Athena (Minerva), the goddess of war, wisdom, and handicrafts; Ares, the god of war; Leto, the Titan mother of Apollo and Artemis (Diana); and Hermes (Mercury), the messenger of the gods.

2 A candle holder attached to a wall.

3 A winding river in Turkey.

See fierce *Belinda* on the Baron flies,   75
With more than usual Lightning in her Eyes:
Nor fear'd the Chief th' unequal Fight to try,
Who sought no more than on his Foe to die.[4]
But this bold Lord with manly Strength endu'd,
She with one Finger and a Thumb subdu'd: 80
Just where the Breath of Life his Nostrils drew,
A Charge of Snuff the wily Virgin threw;
The *Gnomes* direct, to ev'ry Atom just,
The pungent Grains of titillating Dust.
Sudden, with starting Tears each Eye o'erflows,   85
And the high Dome re-echoes to his Nose.

   "Now meet thy Fate," incens'd *Belinda* cry'd,
And drew a deadly Bodkin from her Side.
(The same, his ancient Personage to deck,
Her great great Grandsire wore about his Neck   90
In three Seal-Rings; which after, melted down,
Form'd a vast Buckle for his Widow's Gown:
Her infant Grandame's Whistle next it grew,
The Bells she jingled, and the Whistle blew;
Then in a Bodkin grac'd her Mother's Hairs,   95
Which long she wore, and now *Belinda* wears.)

   "Boast not my Fall" (he cry'd) "insulting Foe!
Thou by some other shalt be laid as low.
Not think, to die dejects my lofty Mind:
All that I dread is leaving you behind!   100
Rather than so, ah let me still survive,
And burn in *Cupid*'s Flames,— but burn alive."

   "Restore the Lock!" she cries; and all around
"Restore the Lock!" the vaulted Roofs rebound.
Not fierce *Othello* in so loud a Strain,   105
Roar'd for the Handkerchief that caus'd his Pain.
But see how oft' ambitious Aims are cross'd,
And Chiefs contend 'till all the Prize is lost!
The Lock, obtain'd with Guilt, and kept with Pain,

---

4 A sexual euphemism.

In ev'ry Place is sought, but sought in vain: 110
With such a Prize no Mortal must be blest,
So Heav'n decrees! with Heav'n who can contest?

   Some thought it mounted to the Luna Sphere,
Since all Things lost on Earth are treasur'd there.
There Hero's Wits are kept in pond'rous Vases,   115
And Beau's in Snuff-Boxes and Tweezer-Cases.
There broken Vows, and Death-bed Alms are found,
And Lover's Hearts with Ends of Riband bound;
The Courtier's Promises, and Sick Man's Pray'rs,
The Smiles of Harlots, and the Tears of Heirs,   120
Cages for Gnats, and Chains to yoke a Flea;
Dry'd Butterflies, and Tomes of Casuistry.

   But trust the Muse—she saw it upward rise,
Tho' mark'd by none but quick, Poetic Eyes:
(So *Rome*'s great Founder to the Heav'ns withdrew,   125
To *Proculus* alone confess'd in View)[1]
A sudden Star, it shot thro' liquid Air,
And drew behind a radiant Trail of Hair.
Not *Berenice*'s Locks[2] first rose so bright,
The Heav'ns bespangling with dishevel'd Light.   130
The *Sylphs* behold it kindling as it flies,
And pleas'd pursue its Progress thro' the Skies.

   This the *Beau-monde* shall from the Mall[3] survey,
And hail with Music its propitious Ray.
This, the blest Lover shall for *Venus* take,   135
And send up Vows from *Rosamonda*'s Lake.[4]
This *Partridge*[5] soon shall view in cloudless Skies,
When next he looks thro' *Galileo*'s Eyes;

---

1 Romulus, the founder and first king of Rome, died mysteriously. Proculus, a prominent senator, stated that Romulus' spirit appeared before him and told him that he had ascended to heaven.

2 The Egyptian Queen Berenice dedicated a lock of her hair to the gods to ensure the return of her husband Ptolemy II from war. The lock vanished and reappeared as a constellation.

3 A walk in St. James's Park.

4 A pond in St. James's Park frequently alluded to in Restoration comedies. It is linked with ill-fated romantic relationships.

5 John Partridge, an astronomer who published almanacks, despised Pope. Pope, Swift, and other satirists mocked his predictions.

And hence th' Egregious Wizard shall foredoom
The Fate of *Louis*, and the Fall of *Rome*.   140

  Then cease, bright Nymph! to mourn thy ravish'd Hair,
Which adds new Glory to the shining Sphere!
Not all the Tresses that fair Head can boast,
Shall draw such envy as the Lock you lost.
For, after all the Murders of your Eye,   145
When, after Millions slain, yourself shall die;
When those fair Suns shall set, as set they must,
And all those Tresses shall be laid in Dust;
This Lock, the Muse shall consecrate to Fame,
And 'midst the Stars inscribe *Belinda*'s Name!   150

1712, 1714

Lady Mary Wortley Montagu

1689–1762

L ady Mary Pierrepont was the eldest child of aristocratic parents. Her father, Evelyn Pierrepont, became the first Duke of Kingston, and her mother, Lady Mary Fielding, was the daughter of the third Earl of Denbigh. As a child, Montagu was surrounded by affluent acquaintances, but she was discontented with the role prescribed for a young lady. As a teenager, she frequented the library in her father's mansion and covertly taught herself Latin when others assumed she was reading romances. Since she loathed the governess who oversaw her education, she corresponded with two bishops and a circle of literate female peers for additional learning.

In 1712, she eloped with Edward Wortley Montagu against her father's wishes. When Montagu's husband was appointed ambassador to Constantinople in 1716, she eagerly travelled to the Ottoman Empire with him. Political unrest and obligations delayed their arrival until the following year. While abroad, Montagu wrote extensive letters to family and friends back in England. She kept personal copies, intending to rework them into a travel book. A year before her death, she brought a manuscript version of the letters to a Protestant clergyman, trusting they would be printed. Letters Written During Her Travels was published posthumously. The Letters chronicle her experiences, particularly focusing on her stay in regions of the Ottoman Empire.

Prior to her arrival in Turkey, Montagu studied with an Islamic scholar to familiarize herself with Turkish culture. Her fascination deepened into appreciation during her visit. Ottoman women especially enchanted her; she reveled in the power of their veils, their shameless nudity at public baths, and their beauty. She observed elite women as well as harems, carefully noting the rights their culture granted them. Montagu's Letters helped create a reliable account of harems where Western men had failed. Though she applied Western thinking to a non-Western culture, her writings reveal her remarkable ability to make a foreign culture appear familiar and to sympathize with those who differed from her.

While in Turkey, Montagu also witnessed a practice that would have worldwide impacts: smallpox inoculations. She would eventually earn a place in medical history for her efforts related to the procedure, for even though she was not the first Western European to inoculate her child while living in Turkey, she was partially responsible for initiating inoculation in England. Montagu had been deeply afflicted when her only brother lost his life to smallpox, and she had almost died of the same disease in 1715. Smallpox was rampant and deadly in England, yet in Letter XXXI, Montagu reports that the illness was nearly harmless in Turkey due to a procedure termed ingrafting. Alongside Charles Maitland, a surgeon at the embassy, Montagu closely observed a group of old women as they gave weakened strains of the virus to thousands of people who sought treatment. Montagu had her son inoculated, and, later, with Maitland's reluctant assistance, did the same for her daughter. Upon introducing the

practice in Britain, Montagu encountered skepticism and hostility from doctors. She visited sickbeds to reassure others of the procedure's safety and effectiveness, using her daughter as evidence. The media veered between supporting inoculation and attacking it, often slandering Montagu's character in the process.

Montagu was also criticized on the literary front. Her friendship with Alexander Pope, who had corresponded with her for years, inexplicably soured. Although Pope viciously condemned her in his works, Montagu was a powerful writer. She penned numerous poems, essays, and fiction works, and even translated a play. Several of her pieces were printed in her lifetime, notably her anonymous response to Swift's "The Lady's Dressing Room," which she titled "The Reasons that Induced Dr. Swift to Write a Poem Called the Lady's Dressing Room." By injecting traces of feminism into her satirical retort, Montagu effectively defies the patriarchal and misogynistic assertions presented in Swift's poem. She was a fierce supporter of female education and independence; works such as "The Reasons" testify her beliefs.

But Montagu's concerns went beyond literary disputes. The onset of the 1730s marked a series of distressing events in her personal life. In 1728, her only surviving sister went insane. Next, Montagu's son, who had been sent abroad after repeatedly running away from Westminster School, returned to England without permission. Public arguments between them further aggravated their strained relationship. When Montagu's daughter fell in love with a suitor her father disapproved of, Montagu was forced to take sides; she dismissed the suitor her husband preferred and secured a future husband for her daughter. Montagu's own marriage had also eroded by this time. In 1736, the same year as her daughter's wedding, Montagu fell in love with Francesco Algarotti, a young and promising Italian author. Intent on seeing him, she travelled to Italy. Algarotti failed to appear after nearly two years, signifying the end of their relations. Montagu elected to stay abroad, roaming between Avignon, France, and Brescia and Venice, Italy, until shortly before her death.

Montagu's travels frequently informed her writing. Living beyond England's borders empowered her to compare her native culture to the cultures she explored. She treasured diverse places and people, empathizing with those she saw and striving to humanize them in her works. Her letters shocked readers with their wit, candor, audacity, and insight. Montagu resisted traditional domestic womanhood, instead revealing her talents as a spirited, independent, and non-conventional writer.

1689	Lady Mary Pierrepont born 15 May
1712	Elopes with Edward Wortley Montagu
1714	Satirical piece for *The Spectator*
1715	Survives smallpox
1716	*Court Poems*
1717–18	Travels around Turkey
1734	"The Reasons that Induced Dr. Swift to Write a Poem Called the Lady's Dressing Room"
1737–38	*The Nonsense of Common-Sense*
1762	Montagu dies from breast cancer on 21 August
1763	*Letters Written During Her Travels*

THE REASONS THAT INDUCED DR. SWIFT TO WRITE A POEM CALLED "THE LADY'S DRESSING ROOM"

The Doctor, in a clean starch'd-Band,
A Golden Snuff-box in his Hand,
With Care his Diamond Ring displays,
And artful shows its various Rays;
While grave, he stalks down — Street   5
His dearest — to meet.
   Long had he waited for this Hour,
Nor gain'd Admittance to the Bow'r;
Had jok'd and punn'd, and swore, and writ,
Tried all his Gallantry and Wit;   10
Had told her oft what part he bore,
In Oxford's Schemes in Days of yore;
But Bawdy, Politicks, nor Satire,
Could move this dull hard-hearted Creature.
   Jenny, her Maid, could taste a Rhyme,   15
And griev'd to see him lose his time,
Had kindly whispered in his Ear,
"For twice two Pounds you enter here;
My Lady vows without that Sum,
It is in vain you write or come."   20
   The destin'd Off'ring now he brought,
And in a Paradise of Thought;
With a low Bow approach'd the Dame,
Who smiling heard him preach his Flame.
His Gold she took (such Proofs as these   25
Convince most unbelieving Shes)
And in her Trunk rose up to lock it,
(Too wise to trust it in her Pocket)
And then returned with blushing Grace,
Expects the Doctor's warm Embrace.   30
   And now this is the proper Place
Where Morals stare me in the Face;
And for the sake of fine Expression
I'm forc'd to make a small Digression.

Alas! for wretched Human-kind,   35
With Wisdom mad, with Learning blind,
The Ox thinks he's for Saddle fit,
(As long ago Friend *Horace* writ;)
And Men their Talents still mistaking,
The Stutterer fancies his is speaking.   40
    With Admiration oft we see
Hard Features heighten'd by Toupée;
The Beau affects the Politician,
Wit is the Citizen's Ambition;
Poor P— Philosophy displays on,   45
With so much Rhyme and little Reason;
But tho' he preaches ne'er so long,
That *all is right*, his Head is wrong.
None strive to know their proper Merit,
But strain for Wisdom, Beauty, Spirit.   50
    Nature to ev'ry thing alive
Points out the Path to thine or thrive,
But Man, vain Man, who grasps the whole
Shows in all Heads a Touch of Fool;
Who lose the Praise that is their due,   55
While they've th' Impossible in view.
    (So have I seen the injudicious Heir
To add one Window, the whole House impair.)
    Instinct the Hound does better teach,
Who never undertook to preach;   60
The frighted Hare from Dogs does run,
But not attempts to bear a Gun—
    Here many noble Thoughts occur
But I Prolixity abhor;
And will pursue th' instructive Tale,   65
To show the Wise in some things fail.
    The Rev'rend Lover, with surprise,
Peeps in her Bubbies[1] and her Eyes,
And kisses both—and tries—and tries—
The Ev'ning in this hellish Play,   70
Beside his Guineas thrown away;
Provok'd the Priest to that degree,
He swore, "The Fault is not in me.

---

1 Breasts.

Your damn'd Close stool so near my Nose,
Your dirty Smock, and stinking Toes   75
Would make a *Hercules*[2] as tame,
As any Beau that you can name."
   The Nymph grown furious, roar'd, "By God
The Blame lies all in Sixty odd;"
And scornful, pointing to the Door,   80
Sai'd, "Fumbler, see my Face no more."
"With all my Heart I'll go away,
But nothing done, I'll nothing pay;
Give back the Money"—"how," cry'd she,
"Would you palm such a Cheat on me?   85
I've lock'd it in the Trunk stands there,
Go break it open if you dare;
For poor four Pounds to roar and bellow,
Why sure you want some new Prunella?[3]
What if your Verses have not sold,   90
Must therefore I return your Gold?
Perhaps you have no better Luck in
The Knack of Rhyming than of —
I won't give back one single Crown,
To wash your Band, or turn your Gown.   95
   "I'll be reveng'd, you saucy Quean,"
(Replies the disappointed Dean)
"I'll so describe your *Dressing-Room*,
The very *Irish* shall not come;"
She answered short, "I'm glad you'll write.   100
You'll furnish Paper when I Shite."

1734

2 In Greek mythology, Hercules was a hero known primarily for the twelve Labors he performed as punishment for murdering his wife and children.

3 A durable fabric used for gowns and the uppers of shoes.

A RECEIPT TO CURE THE VAPORS

Why will Delia thus retire,
And languish life away,
    While the sighing crowd admire,
'Tis too soon for hartshorn tea.

All these dismal looks and fretting   5
Cannot Damon's life restore;
    Long ago the worms have eat him,
You can never see him more.

Once again consult your toilet,
In the glass your face review;   10
    So much weeping soon will spoil it,
And no spring your charms renew.

I, like you, was born a woman,
Well I know what vapors mean;
    The disease alas is common,   15
Single we have all the spleen.

All the morals that they tell us
Never cured the sorrow yet:
    Choose among the pretty fellows,
One of humor, youth, and wit.   20

Prithee hear him ev'ry morning,
At least an hour or two;
    Once again at night returning,
I believe the dose will do.

1763

Thomas Gray
1716–1771

Born in a milliner's shop that doubled as the family home, Thomas Gray was the fifth of twelve children and the only one to survive infancy. Although Gray's father, a money-scrivener in London, owned the premises of the shop, his mother and aunt kept it. The two women were forced to support themselves and their children off its profits. Gray's parents suffered an unhappy marriage, and at eight years old, the boy was sent to Eton College at his mother's expense. Two maternal uncles, both of whom were assistant masters at Eton, oversaw the boy's education.

The friendships Gray forged at Eton were intimate and enduring. Among those closest to him were Richard West, the son of a Lord Chancellor of Ireland and a fellow poet; Horace Walpole, the son of the prime minister, a writer, and a man of letters; and Thomas Ashton, a preacher. The members of the "Quadruple Alliance," as Walpole declared the group, gave each other literary and mytho-logical nicknames. Dubbed "Orozmades" from Nathaniel Lee's tragedy *The Rival Queens*, Gray proved himself a quiet, serious, and reflective student. He entered the University of Cambridge in 1734, but the prescribed courses displeased him. He preferred to study for personal enjoyment instead. He devoted his time to learning Greek, Latin, French, and Italian, and also immersed himself in natural history, medieval history, and entomology. His studies at Cambridge fortified his love of antiquities and antiquated language, which had developed during his boyhood days at Eton. He left Cambridge in 1738 with a breadth of knowledge but no degree.

Several months after leaving Cambridge, he joined Walpole on a grand tour of Europe. The two travelled extensively in France and Italy, visiting picture-galleries, churches, operas, and plays. Inspired and emboldened by his journeys, Gray's most productive literary period began after the tour. Despite writing constantly, however, most of his compositions remained fragmented and unfinished.

The death of West, Gray's closest friend, affected the poet intensely. Plagued with grief and loneliness, he wrote "Ode on a Distant Prospect of Eton College" in 1742. The poem, which was published anonymously five years later, became Gray's first printed piece. Imbued with nostalgia, "Ode" reflects Gray's increasing desolation. West's death, as well as the death of Gray's aunt in 1749, inspired the poem destined to become Gray's masterpiece. When "Elegy Written in a Country Churchyard" was finally published in 1751, the poem had morphed into an introspective lament for the man of sensibility. A superb juxtaposition of Classicist and Romantic techniques, "Elegy" became the most celebrated and reprinted poem of the century. Samuel Johnson, a prominent man of letters, found the poem deeply relatable and deemed several lines original. Despite its popularity and the encouragement of others, Gray elected to remain anonymous until 1753. He upheld his reclusive lifestyle, resisting pressures to become a public poetic figure and refusing payment for his work. After publishing "The Progress of Poesy" and "The Bard," his stance grew more resolute. The public ridiculed the poems for their obscurity and abstraction, and some critics mocked Gray for the overwrought complexity of his works. Disheartened by the criticism, Gray withdrew from public attention. He stopped writing original poetry almost entirely.

Gray served as Regius Professor of Modern History at Cambridge until his death in 1771. He partook little in university and college business, instead dedicating his efforts to reading, studying, and sending letters to his friends. In writing and everyday life, Gray valued restrained sentiment, emotional exploration, didactic reflection, nature, and the sublime. Though his posthumous published poetry totals fewer than one thousand lines, Gray is distinguished as one of the most influential and admired poets of the mid-eighteenth century. His "Elegy" has never been out of print. It is one of the most widely anthologized pieces ever written.

1716	Thomas Gray born 26 December
1725–34	Attends Eton College
1734–38	Attends the University of Cambridge
1736	"Hymeneal"
1738	Leaves the University of Cambridge with no degree
1739–42	Grand tour of Europe accompanied by Horace Walpole
1747	"Ode on a Distant Prospect of Eton College"
1751	"Elegy Written in a Country Churchyard"
1753	*Designs by Mr. R. Bentley for Six Poems by Mr. T. Gray*
1754	"The Progress of Poesy"
1757	"The Bard"; Declines the post of Poet Laureate
1768	Appointed Regius Professor of Modern History at the University of Cambridge
1771	Gray dies 30 July and is buried beside his mother at St. Giles Churchyard, Stoke Poges, the site of his "Elegy Written in a Country Churchyard"

ODE ON A DISTANT PROSPECT OF ETON COLLEGE

Formal, archaic language

Ye distant spires, ye antique towers,
    That crown the watry glade,
Where grateful Science still adores
    Her Henry's[1] holy shade;
And ye that from the stately brow   5
Of Windsor's heights th' expanse below
    Of grove, of lawn, of mead survey,
Whose turf, whose shade, whose flowers among
Wanders the hoary Thames along
    His silver-winding way.   10

Ah happy hills, ah pleasing shade,
    Ah fields belov'd in vain,
Where once my careless childhood stray'd,
    A stranger yet to pain!
I feel the gales, that from ye blow,   15
A momentary bliss bestow,
    As waving fresh their gladsome wing,
My weary soul they seem to soothe,
And, redolent of joy and youth,
    To breathe a second spring.   20

Say, Father Thames, for thou hast seen
    Full many a sprightly race
Disporting on thy margent green
    The paths of pleasure trace,
Who foremost now delight to cleave   25
With pliant arm thy glassy wave?
    The captive linnet which enthrall?
What idle progeny succeed
To chase the rolling circle's speed,
    Or urge the flying ball?   30

---

1 King Henry the Sixth, founder of the College [Gray].

While some on earnest business bent
    Their murmuring labours ply
'Gainst graver hours, that bring constraint
    To sweeten liberty:
Some bold adventurers disdain   35
The limits of their little reign,
    And unknown regions dare descry:
Still as they run they look behind,
They hear a voice in every wind,
    And snatch a fearful joy.   40

Gay hope is theirs by fancy fed,
    Less pleasing when possess'd;
The tear forgot as soon as shed,
    The sun-shine of the breast,
There's buxom health of rosy hue, 45
Wild wit, invention ever-new,
    And lively cheer of vigour born;
The thoughtless day, the easy night,
The spirits pure, the slumbers light,
    That fly th' approach of morn.   50

Alas, regardless of their doom,
    The little victims play!
No sense have they of ills to come,
    Nor care beyond to-day:
Yet see how all around 'em wait   55
The Ministers of human fate,
    And black Misfortune's baleful train!
Ah, show them where in ambush stand
To seize their prey the murth'rous band!
    Ah, tell them, they are men!   60

These shall the fury Passions tear,
    The vultures of the mind,
Disdainful Anger, pallid Fear,
    And Shame that skulks behind;
Or pining Love shall waste their youth,   65
Or Jealousy with rankling tooth,

That inly gnaws the secret heart,
And Envy wan, and faded Care,
Grim-visag'd comfortless Despair,
    And Sorrow's piercing dart.   70

Ambition this shall tempt to rise,
    Then whirl the wretch from high,
To bitter Scorn a sacrifice,
    And grinning Infamy.
The stings of Falsehood those shall try,   75
And hard Unkindness' alter'd eye,
    That mocks the tear it forc'd to flow;
And keen Remorse with blood defil'd,
And moody Madness laughing wild
    Amid severest woe.   80

Lo, in the vale of years beneath
    A grisly troop are seen,
The painful family of Death,
    More hideous than their Queen:
This racks the joints, this fires the veins,   85
That every labouring sinew strains,
    Those in the deeper vitals rage:
Lo, Poverty, to fill the band,
That numbs the soul with icy hand,
    And slow-consuming Age.   90

To each his suffe'ings: all are men,
    Condemn'd alike to groan;
The tender for another's pain,
    Th' unfeeling for his own.
Yet, ah! why should they know their fate?   95
Since sorrow never comes too late,
    And happiness too swiftly flies.
Thought would destroy their paradise.
No more; where ignorance is bliss,
    'Tis folly to be wise.   100

1747

ODE ON THE DEATH OF A FAVORITE CAT, DROWNED IN A TUB OF GOLDFISHES

'Twas on a lofty vase's side,
Where China's gayest art had dy'd
   The azure flowers, that blow;
Demurest of the tabby kind,
The pensive Selima, reclin'd,   5
   Gaz'd on the lake below.

Her conscious tail her joy declar'd;
The fair round face, the snowy beard,
   The velvet of her paws,
Her coat, that with the tortoise vies,   10
Her ears of jet, and emerald eyes,
   She saw; and purr'd applause.

Still had she gaz'd; but 'midst the tide
Two angel forms were seen to glide,
   The Genii of the stream: 15
Their scaly armour's Tyrian[1] hue
Thro' richest purple to the view
   Betray'd a golden gleam.

The hapless nymph with wonder saw:
A whisker first, and then a claw,   20
   With many an ardent wish,
She stretch'd, in vain, to reach the prize.
What female heart can gold despise?
   What Cat's averse to fish?

Presumptuous maid! with looks intent   25
Again she stretch'd, again she bent,
   Nor knew the gulf between.
(Malignant Fate sat by, and smil'd)

---

1 Crimson or purple color.

The slipp'ry verge her feet beguil'd,
  She tumbled headlong in.   30

Eight times emerging from the flood
She mew'd to ev'ry watery God,
  Some speedy aid to send.
No Dolphin came, no Nereid[1] stirr'd:
Nor cruel *Tom*, nor *Susan* heard;   35
  A fav'rite has no friend!

From hence, ye beauties, undeceiv'd,
Know, one false step is ne'er retriev'd,
  And be with caution bold.
Not all that tempts your wand'ring eyes   40
And heedless hearts is lawful prize,
  Nor all, that glisters, gold.

1749

---

1 In Greek mythology, any of the young, friendly, water-dwelling daughters of the sea god Neseus.

ELEGY WRITTEN IN A COUNTRY CHURCH-YARD

ABAB ryhme

The Curfew tolls the knell of parting day;
    The lowing herd wind slowly o'er the lea;
The ploughman homeward plods his weary way,
    And leaves the world to darkness and to me.

Now fades the glimmering landscape on the sight,   5
    And all the air a solemn stillness holds,
Save where the beetle wheels his droning flight,
    And drowsy tinklings lull the distant folds:

Save that, from yonder ivy-mantled tower
    The moping Owl does to the Moon complain   10
Of such as, wand'ring near her secret bower,
    Molest her ancient solitary reign.

Beneath those rugged elms, that yew-tree's shade,
    Where heaves the turf in many a mouldering heap,
Each in his narrow cell for ever laid,   15
    The rude forefathers of the hamlet sleep.

The breezy call of incense-breathing Morn,
    The swallow twitt'ring from the straw-built shed,
The cock's shrill clarion, or the echoing horn,
    No more shall rouse them from their lowly bed.   20

For them, no more the blazing hearth shall burn,
    Or busy housewife ply her evening care;
No children run to lisp their sire's return,
    Or climb his knees, the envied kiss to share.

Oft did the harvest to their sickle yield;   25
    Their furrow oft the stubborn glebe has broke;
How jocund did they drive their team a-field!
    How bow'd the woods beneath their sturdy stroke!

Let not Ambition mock their useful toil,
    Their homely joys, and destiny obscure;   30

Nor Grandeur hear, with a disdainful smile
    The short and simple annals of the poor.

The boast of heraldry, the pomp of power,
    And all that beauty, all that wealth e'er gave,
Awaits alike th' inevitable hour;—   35
    The paths of glory lead but to the grave.

Nor you, ye proud! impute to these the fault,
    If memory o'er their tomb no trophies raise;
Where, through the long-drawn aisle and fretted vault
    The pealing anthem swells the note of praise.   40

Can storied urn, or animated bust,
    Back to its mansion call the fleeting breath?
Can Honour's voice provoke the silent dust?
    Or Flattery soothe the dull cold ear of Death?

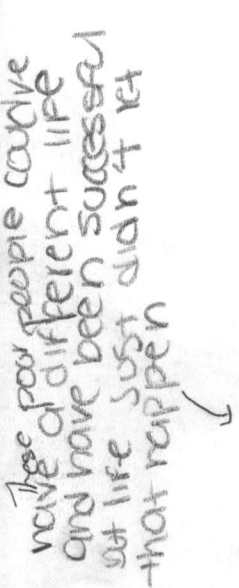

_They're poor people could've
and have been successful
at life just didn't yet
that happen_

Perhaps, in this neglected spot, is laid   45
    Some heart, once pregnant with celestial fire;
Hands, that the rod of empire might have sway'd,
    Or wak'd to ecstasy the living lyre.

But Knowledge, to their eyes, her ample page
    Rich with the spoils of Time, did ne'er unroll;   50
Chill Penury repress'd their noble rage,
    And froze the genial current of the soul.

Full many a gem of purest ray serene
    The dark unfathom'd caves of ocean bear;
Full many a flower is born to blush unseen,   55
    And waste its sweetness on the desert air.

Some village Hampden, that, with dauntless breast,
    The little tyrant of his fields withstood;
Some mute, inglorious Milton,[1]— here may rest;
    Some Cromwell,[2] guiltless of his country's blood.   60

Th' applause of listening senates to command;
    The threats of pain and ruin to despise;

---

1 John Milton (1608–1674), one of the most significant English authors in all history.

2 Oliver Cromwell (1599–1658), a general in the English Civil War, helped overthrow the Stuart monarchy.

To scatter plenty o'er a smiling land,
And read their hist'ry in a nation's eyes,

Their lot forbade: nor circumscrib'd alone 65
Their growing virtues, but their crimes confin'd;
Forbade to wade through slaughter to a throne,
And shut the gates of mercy on mankind.

The struggling pangs of conscious truth to hide;
To quench the blushes of ingenuous shame; 70
Or heap the shrine of Luxury and Pride,
With incense kindled at the Muse's flame.

Far from the madding crowd's ignoble strife,
Their sober wishes never learn'd to stray;
Along the cool, sequester'd vale of life, 75
They kept the noiseless tenor of their way.

Yet ev'n these bones from insult to protect,
Some frail memorial still erected nigh,
With uncouth rhymes and shapeless sculpture deck'd,
Implores the passing tribute of a sigh. 80

Their name, their years, spelt by th' unletter'd Muse,
The place of fame and elegy supply;
And many a holy text around she strews,
That teach the rustic moralist to die.

For who, to dumb Forgetfulness a prey, 85
This pleasing, anxious being e'er resign'd;
Left the warm precincts of the cheerful day,
Nor cast one longing, lingering look behind?

On some fond breast the parting soul relies;
Some pious drops the closing eye requires; 90
Ev'n from the tomb the voice of Nature cries;
Ev'n in our ashes live their wonted fires.

For thee, who mindful of th' unhonour'd dead,
Dost in these lines their artless tale relate;
If 'chance, by lonely Contemplation led, 95
Some kindred spirit shall inquire thy fate;

[handwritten marginalia: the "Thee" is someone who's just like the himself.]

[handwritten marginalia: when your dying someone needs to cry about you'r death in order for your life to have meaning.]

[handwritten note at bottom: Poem glorifies poor, but elegy is really for like-minded poets who can appreciate the poor]

Haply, some hoary-headed swain may say:
  "Oft have we seen him, at the peep of dawn,
Brushing, with hasty steps, the dews away,
  To meet the Sun upon the upland lawn.   100

"There, at the foot of yonder nodding beech,
  That wreathes its old fantastic roots so high,
His listless length, at noontide, would he stretch,
  And pore upon the brook that babbles by.

"Hard by yon wood, now smiling, as in scorn,   105
  Muttering his wayward fancies, he would rove;
Now drooping, woeful wan, like one forlorn,
  Or craz'd with care, or cross'd in hopeless love.

"One morn I miss'd him on the 'custom'd hill,
  Along the heath, and near his fav'rite tree;   110
Another came,—nor yet beside the rill,
  Nor up the lawn, nor at the wood, was he;

"The next, with dirges due, in sad array,
  Slow through the church-way path we saw him borne.
Approach and read (for thou canst read) the lay,   115
  Grav'd on the stone beneath yon aged thorn."

THE EPITAPH

Here rests his head upon the lap of Earth,
  A youth, to fortune and to fame unknown;
Fair Science frown'd not on his humble birth,
  And Melancholy mark'd him for her own.   120

Large was his bounty, and his soul sincere;
  Heaven did a recompense as largely send:
He gave to Mis'ey all he had—a tear;
  He gain'd from Heaven ('twas all he wish'd) a friend.

No farther seek his merits to disclose,   125
  Or draw his frailties from their dread abode:
(There they alike in trembling hope repose,)
  The bosom of his Father and his God.

1751

ROMANTIC PERIOD
1785–1832

ABSTRACT

Economic prosperity, social volatility, and political instability framed the Romantic period. Industrialization, the French Revolution, and the first major British parliamentary reform transformed Britain into a more modernized, democratic nation. Writers reacted to the new social and political consciousness that formed from these ideological and concrete changes. During the Romantic period, the population of women writers eclipsed the number of male ones. The novel dominated as the most financially successful genre of the age, and the Gothic novel gained eminence. However, writers and scholars in the 19th and 20th centuries emphasized the place of poetry, specifically the works of six prominent male writers. The poetic genius was often idealized as a solitary, visionary figure who existed outside of society. In reality, many writers were inspired by contemporary events and sought to capture "the spirit of the age" (as some called it) in their works.

POLITICS

The Romantic period is the only era in British history that is named after a literary movement. The phrases "Romantic movement" and "Romantics," however, were not used until the Victorian age. Scholars then and now contest the dates of the period in respect to its literary and historical framework. Some isolate 1776, the year America declared its independence; others source France's democratic revolution in 1789; still more recognize different political, cultural, and social events as the beginning of the Romantic period. Regardless of the year selected, the incidents that occurred within and around England initiated substantial and formative changes.

The late 1700s and early 1800s saw economic, political, and social revolutions. Britain's agrarian society was gradually overtaken by a more modernized, industrial economy. Large-scale farming accelerated population growth, and by 1801, London had over a million residents. The city's population had almost doubled just thirty years later. Technology affected cotton cloth production early on, inspiring the expansion of textile manufacturing centers. Driven by increased markets and resources, Britain heightened its overseas trade. Port activity provided merchants and manufacturers with money to buy new products, inducing the development of even more industries. Enhanced infrastructure further modernized England. Stagecoaches, though only available to the very wealthy, shortened travel time, and railways, which were more efficient at transporting products than horses and laborers, began appearing in 1825. Although technological advancements often occurred gradually, their impact on society was immediate.

Industrialization was the genesis of a more consumer-based society, but it split the poor from the rich to such an extent that England was commonly called "Two Nations." Those who previously worked in agriculture were increasingly funneled into industrial cities. Workers' efforts fueled the Industrial Revolution, but they saw little of its benefits; the wealthy controlled the means of industrial production. The rich preserved their privilege, leaving workers mostly powerless. As a result, class antagonism festered. But as middle classes formed, they sided themselves with aristocrats rather than the lower classes. Although very wealthy, land-owning people formed only a small portion of Britain's population, they exerted great economic and political influence over the masses. People in the lower echelons observed this power imbalance, and revolutions around the world aimed to establish equaller systems of government.

The spirit of revolution first seized America, then France, and finally took hold in Saint Domingue (modern Haiti). When Britain lost the North American colonies in the 1780s, it indeed lost a vital part of its trade system, but more significantly, British citizens lost confidence in the leading class. Trade wars raised the country's national debt, and Britons faced increased taxation as a consequence. Yet America, by liberating itself from unjust taxation and tyranny, had set a precedent that the people need not obey unchecked monarchical power. Additionally, America was quickly proving that democracy could prosper. Invigorated by America's success, Britons began demanding more civil rights. Perspectives on war shifted, partially due to the influential writer Thomas Paine, who blamed war on the selfish whims of the aristocracy and believed that democracies would not have wars because the population (whose interests are represented in a democracy) would be against unnecessary waste and misery.

Many accepted, however, that war could be justified when people resisted a corrupt and oppressive government. The early stages of the French Revolution were regarded as a cry for democracy and egalitarian principles, thus bolstering widespread English support. Some liberals and radicals even wanted to emulate the Revolution. But France and its revolutionary ideas threatened Britain's extant social structure, and the two nations went to war in 1793. Upon defeating Napoleon at Waterloo, Britain deemed itself "the savior of Europe" and took the victory as divine favor. By the end of the Napoleonic Wars, a distinct British political culture had emerged, bringing a national agenda with it.

Support for the French cause waned after the Revolution because violence and tyranny succeeded it. Still, debates over whether to support some French ideas in Britain infused cultural conversations, and paper wars propagated calls for reform. The government initiated a series of repressive measures in response to these demands. Laws prohibiting seditious writing, treasonous acts, and public meetings were issued in 1795, and the right of habeas corpus (which protects people from unlawful imprisonment) was repeatedly suspended throughout the Romantic period. Even with these measures, appeals for reform could not be quelled permanently.

Slavery—and whether or not to abolish it—was among the first issues to gain national attention. A small group composed mostly of Quakers instigated the end of the Atlantic slave trade. Using the printed word and graphic images to depict the horrors of slavery, abolitionists applied ongoing inquiries about human liberty to propel their mission. The British were painted as violators of human rights since slavery did not correspond with a sensible, modern society. In 1791, slaves in Saint Domingue revolted, further bringing to light doubts about the morality of slavery. Consequently, abolition was viewed as progress against an outdated, cruel system. Since the slave trade fueled Britain's colonial rule and economic wealth, however, early attempts to abolish it had limited success. Many of those in power feared that freedom would foreshadow violence and disorder. The British slave trade nevertheless met its end in 1807, although slaves throughout the empire were not emancipated until 1833. Abolition signified a victory for progressive causes.

Women also sought progress in terms of their legal rights. A woman's education and sexual behavior was already constrained by cultural codes, but attitudes about proper femininity grew even more restrictive. Statements about gender roles proliferated literature and religious services, and women were continuously pressured to accept a life of domesticity. Expected to dedicate their lives to child-rearing and housekeeping, women were tasked with preserving the morality and patriotism of their families. There was little space for poor women in this portrayal of womanhood; the working woman's duty was to industrialists, not to her family. Some, like Mary Wollstonecraft in her 1792 *Vindication of the Rights of Woman*, argued for gender equality by first discussing greater educational rights. But educated women, termed "bluestockings," encountered fierce disdain. Although the fight for women's rights would not gain impetus until the late Victorian age, it became more common in the 1820s for advocates to argue that women could channel their purportedly feminine qualities into social and moral reform projects.

Since most considered women's rights too radical of a cause, reform efforts focused on expanding male liberties, especially in terms of legal representation. Writers, publishers, small landowners, and other middle-class professionals began protesting for voting rights and parliamentary reform. Holding that the right to vote should be attached to person, not property, reformists encouraged people to elect country gentlemen instead of moneyed men. To promote their causes, reformers tried to educate the public through the printed and spoken word. Massive petitioning campaigns aided the fight. Additionally, people began linking inequality and economic oppression with industrialization and unrestricted capitalism. The first Reform Bill, passed in 1832, rearranged the House of Commons. Greater voting privileges were given to populated industrial towns rather than the pocket and rotten boroughs, terms reformers used when discussing areas that had very few voters but equal representative power as larger districts. In many of these boroughs, a single aristocrat or landowning family could bribe and coerce voters into electing their preferred candidate. Consequently, representatives who wanted to please their patrons controlled Parliament. With this bill and subsequent parliamentary reform bills, the British electoral system became better suited to the needs of the people.

LITERATURE

Literature became a formidable agent of social and political change during the Romantic period, illustrating that revolutions and literature often inspire and inform one another. Industrialization benefited the literary market: Improved production methods made printing and distribution easier and cheaper. The first hand-operated iron-frame printing press appeared in 1800, followed soon afterward by machine-made paper. These advancements made books and other publications more widely available. Of course, books were still expensive to buy; borrowing from circulating libraries was an economical option for readers in the lower and middle classes.

Since periodicals reached a large audience, many writers employed them to express political reactions and visions. However, because the government readily charged authors and publishers with sedition and blasphemy, radicals often had to avoid direct statements. Writers also contended with public criticism, popularized by literary magazines and book reviews. Even though the number of readers multiplied during the Romantic period, writing was still not a profitable career for most people. It was an extremely perilous occupation (especially for those who wrote politically), and many writers depended on aristocratic patrons for their livelihood. But because literature infused everyday life, some authors garnered enough recognition to adequately support themselves. The Romantic period marked the first time in British literary history when someone could feasibly earn a living as a writer.

Although passionate essays, prose, and novels burgeoned, later scholars accentuated the poetry of this period over other genres. For many years the Romantic poets were limited to "the big six": William Blake, Samuel Taylor Coleridge, William Wordsworth, Lord Byron, Percy Bysshe Shelley, and John Keats. During their own lifetimes, these authors and others were divided (often derisively) into "schools" or "sects" according to their poetic theories. Coleridge, Wordsworth, and Robert Southey belonged to the "Lake School" because they lived in the Lake District in the north-west of England, exalted nature, enjoyed solitude, and wrote using the language of the common man. The "Cockney School," so named to belittle London-based poets who lacked pedigree, included John Keats and Leigh Hunt. Finally, Byron and Shelley belonged to the so-called "Satanic School" for their unconventional lifestyles. Only in recent decades have scholars seriously studied other genres and women writers from the age.

Several theories of what Romantic poetry should be were imminent, but Wordsworth's 1800 Preface to *Lyrical Ballads* provides his vision for a new type of poetry. As he notes, "poetry is the spontaneous overflow of powerful feelings," prompting an emphasis on emotion and subjective experience. But early Romantics were as equally fascinated with feelings as they were in investigating the relationship between nature and the human mind. Many poets proclaimed that one could only discover their true self when in nature or witnessing the sublime. More often than not, nature provided an external stimulus for internal activities like introspection and self-reflection. Though rife with vivid, ethereal descriptions, a poem's meaning usually resided in its exploration of consciousness or its ability to relate internal sensations. Poets like Wordsworth and Coleridge prized the poet's unique imagination and individuality. Despite Enlightenment claims of a universally-experienced reality, many Romantics believed that every person perceived the world differently. Consequently, the ability to recreate a version of reality with originality and creativity distinguished a true poet from a hack and good poetry from bad poetry.

Like poets, many novelists directed their attention from outer situations to inner conditions. Embracing psychological truths allowed authors to improve character development. Jane Austen's use of free indirect discourse, for example, enabled her to craft characters with believable and complicated minds. Novels were highly popular, especially the Gothic, which gained momentum during the Romantic period. Both Anne Radcliffe and Gregory Lewis expanded on the genre. Radcliffe unnerves readers by implying horror and the supernatural. Lewis emphasizes violence, the supernatural, and graphic descriptions. His novel *The Monk* was best-selling yet condemned for its synthesis of horror, violence, religion, and eroticism. Many novels—especially gothic novels—carry political significance. While works like Wollstonecraft's *Maria* and Godwin's *Caleb Williams* are more overtly political than the works of Radcliffe, Lewis, and other gothic writers, horror often paralleled revolutionary upheaval, and exotic settings marked a reaction against the tameness of mundane existence. Some writers, such as Sir Walter Scott, received praise for liberating readers from probable, familiar events. Scott's *Waverley Novels* submerged readers in historical locales, and he helped popularized the genre. However, many reviewers (usually male) considered novels the lowest literary form because of their loose structure, epistolary and journalistic origin, female readership, and (often) female authorship. Some even claimed that novels negatively affected one's moral wellbeing. As authors began experimenting with content and style, novels gained public interest for their ability to express serious ideas. Romantic period novelists developed new narrative techniques and methods of characterization that would bring the novel to a new high point in the Victorian age.

	CONTEXTS	TEXTS
1785	Edmund Cartwright builds the first power loom	William Cowper, *The Task*
1787	W.A. Mozart, *Don Giovanni* Formation of the Society for Effecting the Abolition of Slaves	
1789	The storming of the Bastille begins the French Revolution Utilitarianism thrives	William Blake, *Songs of Innocence*
1790		Edmund Burke, *Reflections on the Revolution in France*
1791	Revolution in Santo Domingo (modern Haiti) led by Toussaint L'Ouverture	Thomas Paine, *Rights of Man*
1792	September Massacres in Paris renders about 1,200 prisoners dead First commercial use of gas lights in Britain	Mary Wollstonecraft, *A Vindication of the Rights of Woman*
1793	Execution of Louis XVI and Marie Antoinette France and Britain go to war Beginning of the Reign of Terror under Robespierre	William Godwin, *Political Justice*
1794	End of the Reign of Terror Habeas Corpus suspended	Blake, *Songs of Experience* Anne Radcliffe, *The Mysteries of Udolpho*

1795	Passage of the Seditious Meetings Act and the Treasonable Practices Act (the Gagging Acts), suppressing meetings and the freedom of speech	
1796	Edward Jenner gives the first vaccination against smallpox Beginning of Napoleonic Wars	Matthew Gregory Lewis, *The Monk*
1798	Britain quells the Irish Rebellion	Thomas Malthus, *An Essay on the Principle of Population* William Wordsworth and Samuel Taylor Coleridge, *Lyrical Ballads*
1801	Parliament's Act of Union joins Ireland to Great Britain and Scotland	
1802	Treaty of Amiens initiates fourteen months of peace during the Napoleonic Wars *Edinburgh Review* founded	
1804	Napoleon crowned Emperor of France First steam locomotive to run on rails	
1807	Abolition of slave trade in Great Britain	
1809	*Quarterly Review* founded	

1811	Prince of Wales (later George IV) declared regent after George III goes insane	Jane Austen, *Sense and Sensibility*
1812	Britain begins fighting the War of 1812 against the United States of America	Lord Byron, *Childe Harold's Pilgrimage* cantos 1 and 2
1813		Austen, *Pride and Prejudice*
		Percy Bysshe Shelley, *Queen Mab*
1814		Sir Walter Scott, *Waverly*
1815	Napoleon defeated at Waterloo, ending the Napoleonic Wars	
	Passage of Corn Laws, defending the economic interests of land-owning aristocrats	
1816		Byron, *Childe Harold's Pilgrimage* cantos 3 and 4
		Coleridge, *Christabel*, "Kubla Khan"
1817	*Blackwood's Edinburgh Magazine* founded	Coleridge, *Biographia Literaria*
1818		John Keats, *Endymion*
		Mary Shelley, *Frankenstein*
1819	Peterloo Massacre, leaving an estimated 500 injured and 11 killed	Byron, *Don Juan* cantos 1 and 2
1820	Death of George III; Accession of George IV	John Clare, *Poems Descriptive of Rural Life*
		Keats, *Lamia, Isabella, The Eve of St. Agnes, and Other Poems*
		Percy Bysshe Shelley, *Prometheus Unbound*

1821		Thomas De Quincey, *Confessions of an English Opium Eater*
1825	Railways used for product transport	William Hazlitt, *The Spirit of the Age*
1826		Benjamin Disraeli, *Vivian Grey*
1828	Repeal of the Test and Corporation Acts which banned Dissenters from holding public offices	
1829	Catholic Emancipation, freeing Roman Catholics from discrimination	
1830	Death of George IV Accession of William IV July Revolution in France	
1831	Charles Darwin begins his voyage around the world on the *H.M.S. Beagle*	
1832	Passage of the First Reform Bill, transferring voting rights to males owning property worth £10 or more in annual rent	

Anna Laetitia Barbauld
1743–1825

Anna Laetitia (née Aikin) Barbauld was the only daughter born to Presbyterian parents. Her father, a classicist, teacher, and Nonconformist minister named John Aikin, did not normally approve of women receiving advanced educations, but he allowed his daughter to study French, Italian, Greek, and Latin. When Barbauld was fifteen years old, her family relocated to Warrington, Lancashire so that her father could accept a teaching job at Warrington Academy, a school which had recently opened to educate Dissenters who could not attend Oxford or Cambridge. There Barbauld associated with some of Britain's most prominent dissenting intellectuals, namely the liberal theologian Joseph Priestly and the Unitarian minister William Enfield, until she was thirty years old. The friends and colleagues she found at Warrington Academy became her first audience when she began sharing her poetry. Additionally, the debates and political atmosphere of the academy likely portended her future political interests.

At the encouragement of her brother, she published her first volume *Poems* in 1773. The volume revealed her fascination with historical events; she indirectly expressed her views on current politics by evoking the past. Since she claimed to only write about history, she protected herself from criticism and brutal backlash. *Poems* was popular enough that it underwent four editions in its first year. During the same year, Barbauld and her brother jointly wrote and published *Miscellaneous Pieces in Prose*, a collection which also went through several reprints.

In 1774, she married Rochemont Barbauld, the son of Huguenot refugees. Rochemont, who had been a Warrington Academy student, converted to Nonconformity and became an educator and minister after he graduated. The couple moved to Palgrave, Suffolk, where Rochemont opened a school for boys. While Rochemont taught, Barbauld penned educational pieces for young children. Her *Hymns in Prose for Children* achieved such acclaim that it was translated into French, German, and Italian. Barbauld's literary reputation increased, and the academy she helped maintain also improved. Barbauld found like-minded companions in her new environment, and soon the Barbaulds' residence became a rendezvous place for dissenting intellectuals. Rochemont's declining mental health, however, compelled the couple to leave the Palgrave school in 1785 and travel across Europe. Upon their return to England, they relocated to Hampstead. With Rochemont employed as a congregational minister, Barbauld began teaching a group of female students and befriending local literati.

Barbauld's dissenter past emboldened her, and she advocated for greater human liberties. Her publications in the early 1790s address the depths to which she perceived and understood social injustices. Barbauld especially rejected the restrictions placed on non-Anglicans, who could not hold public office, obtain civil service careers, or attend university among a number of other restrictions. In her book *Mr. Gilbert Wakefield's Enquiry*, she asserts that all people should be free to worship as they choose. Barbauld also believed that citizens should be free to criticize the Anglican Church, England, and its constitution. She additionally supported the early French Revolution and denounced the slave trade. Although Barbauld clearly had a passion for expanded and improved human liberties, she avoided stating her views forthrightly in her early political works. She also continued composing pieces for children during this period, notably *Evenings at Home*, a six-volume collection she and her brother wrote and published together.

The Barbaulds moved to Stoke Newington, near Barbauld's brother, after Rochemont's mental and physical health worsened. Rochemont's well-being waned and ultimately collapsed, leaving Barbauld a widow in 1808. She resumed editing a couple years later and began working on *The Female Speaker*, a collection of texts by some of England's distinguished poets and prose writers. One of the selected pieces, Coleridge's mystical ballad *The Rime of the Ancient Mariner*, received Barbauld's criticism because she felt it lacked a clear moral theme. She failed to realize that Coleridge had intentionally deviated from the enlightenment philosophy she was raised to value.

Unfortunately, Barbauld's next blunder essentially ended her career. Unlike her first political pieces, she did not disguise her opinions in her last major work. Rife with scathing criticisms about Britain's declining economic and social conditions, her long satirical poem *Eighteen Hundred and Eleven* condemned Britain's unsuccessful efforts in the Napoleonic Wars. According to Barbauld, Britain, then on the cusp of losing its nearly decade-long war against France, was fated to fall to ruin. Her indictments outraged the public. Her ideas met severely negative reviews; critics' responses evidenced that female writers could not voice the same opinions as male writers without receiving hostility. After the brutal reception of her poem, Barbauld retreated from public attention and wrote minor pieces for family and friends. She continued to associate with intellectuals until her death in 1825. Lucy Aikin, Barbauld's niece, edited and published a compilation of her letters and other works following her death. Both the prolific biblical writer Mary Anne Schimmelpennick and the immensely popular Victorian poet Elizabeth Barrett Browning drew inspiration from Barbauld's writing.

Barbauld wrote boldly in a time when female writers who deviated from specific feminine ideals faced personal castigation. Despite her dissenting beliefs and her upbringing, however, she felt her life was an exception and did not promote an education like hers for young women. She declined an opportunity to start a school for girls because she thought that a practical education—given by fathers or other family members—would create better wives and mothers. Still, the instructional works she published imparted religious values on youths and provided readers with rational as well as emotional interpretations of biblical Scriptures. While Barbauld could be traditional in some senses, she could also speculate on issues of slavery and national politics. She achieved a place among the beloved poets of her age.

1743	Anna Laetitia Aikin born 20 June
1773	*Poems*; *Miscellaneous Pieces in Prose*
1774	Marries Rochemont Barbauld
1781	*Hymns in Prose for Children*; *Early Lessons for Childre*
1790	*An Address to the Opposers of the Repeal of the Corporation and Test Acts*
1791	*Epistle to Mr. Wilberforce on the Rejection of the Bill for Abolishing the Slave Trade*
1792–95	*Evenings at Home; of, The Juvenile Budget Opened: Consisting of a Variety of Miscellaneous Pieces for the Instruction and Amusement of Young Persons* with brother John
1792	*Letter to John Bull; Mr. Gilbert Wakefield's Enquiry into the Expediency and Propriety of Public or Social Worship*
1808	Rochemont dies in London
1810	Edits *The British Novelists: With an Essay and Prefaces, Biographical and Critical*
1811	Edits *The Female Speaker*
1812	*Eighteen Hundred and Eleven*
1825	Barbauld dies 9 March and is buried at St. Mary Churchyard; *Works*

ON A LADY'S WRITING

Her even lines her steady temper show,
Neat as her dress, and polish'd as her brow;
Strong as her judgment, easy as her air;
Correct though free, and regular though fair:
And the same graces o'er her pen preside   5
That form her manners and her footsteps guide.

1773

THE MOUSE'S PETITION[1]

Found in the TRAP where he had been confined all Night.

Parcere subjectis, & debellare superbos.[2]
VIRGIL

Oh! here a pensive prisoner's prayer,
For liberty that sighs;
And never let thine heart be shut
Against the wretch's cries.

For here forlorn and sad I sit,　　　　　　　5
Within the wiry grate;
And tremble at th' approaching morn,
Which brings impending fate.

If e'er thy breast with freedom glow'd,
And spurn'd a tyrant's chain,　　　　　　　10
Let not thy strong oppressive force
A free-born mouse detain.

Oh! do not stain with guiltless blood
Thy hospitable hearth;
Nor triumph that thy wiles betray'd　　　　15
A prize so little worth.

The scatter'd gleanings of a feast
My frugal meals supply;
But if thine unrelenting heart
That slender boon deny,　　　　　　　　20

The cheerful light, the vital air,
Are blessings widely given;

---

1 To Doctor Priestley. The Author is concerned to find, that what was the petition of mercy against justice, has been construed as the plea of humanity against cruelty. She is certain that cruelty could never be apprehended from the Gentleman to whom this is addressed; and the poor animal would have suffered more as the victim of domestic economy, than of philosophical curiosity [Barbauld].

2 From Virgil's *Aeneid*, VI., 854: "To spare the conquered and bring down the haughty."

Let nature's commoners enjoy
The common gifts of heaven.

The well-taught philosophic mind   25
To all compassion gives;
Casts round the world an equal eye,
And feels for all that lives.

If mind,as ancient sages taught,
A never dying flame,   30
Still shifts thro' matter's varying forms,
In every form the same,

Beware, lest in the worm you crush,
A brother's soul you find;
And tremble lest thy luckless hand   35
Dislodge a kindred mind.

Or, if this transient gleam of day
Be *all* of life we share,
Let pity plead within thy breast
That little *all* to spare.   40

So may thy hospitable board
With health and peace be crown'd;
And every charm of heartfelt ease
Beneath thy roof be found.

So, when destruction lurks unseen,   45
Which men like mice may share,
May some kind angel clear thy path,
And break the hidden snare.

1773

EPISTLE TO WILLIAM WILBERFORCE, ESQ.
ON THE REJECTION OF THE BILL FOR ABOLISHING
THE SLAVE TRADE[1]

Cease, Wilberforce, to urge thy generous aim!
Thy Country knows the sin, and stands the shame!
The Preacher, Poet, Senator in vain
Has rattled in her sight the Negro's chain;
With his deep groans assail'd her startled ear,   5
And rent the veil that hid his constant tear;
Forc'd her averted eyes his stripes to scan,
Beneath the bloody scourge laid bare the man,
Claim'd Pity's tear, urged Conscience' strong control,
And flash'd conviction on her shrinking soul.   10
The Muse, too soon awaked, with ready tongue
At Mercy's shrine applausive peans rung;
And Freedom's eager sons, in vain foretold
A new Astrean[2] reign, an age of gold:
She knows and she persists—Still Afric bleeds,   15
Uncheck'd, the human traffic still proceeds;
She stamps her infamy to future time,
And on her hardened forehead seals the crime.

    In vain, to thy white standard gathering round,
Wit, Worth, and Parts and Eloquence are found: 20
In vain, to push to birth thy great design,
Contending chiefs, and hostile virtues join;
All, from conflicting ranks, of power possest
To rouse, to melt, or to inform the breast.
Where seasoned tools of Avarice prevail,   25
A Nation's eloquence, combined, must fail:
Each flimsy sophistry by turns they try;
The plausive argument, the daring lye,

1 William Wilberforce (1759–1833), a British politician and philanthropist, fervently campaigned for abolition. In 1791, he proposed a bill to end the British slave trade. Despite support from the prime minister William Pitt and the Whig leader Charles Fox, the bill was defeated in the House of Commons by a vote of 163 to 88.

2 Astrea, the Greek goddess of justice, resided on Earth during the golden age but returned to heaven after witnessing the immorality of humankind.

The artful gloss, that moral sense confounds,
Th' acknowledged thirst of gain that honour wounds: 30
Bane of ingenuous minds! th' unfeeling sneer,
Which, sudden, turns to stone the falling tear:
They search assiduous, with inverted skill,
For forms of wrong, and precedents of ill;
With impious mockery wrest the sacred page,   35
And glean up crimes from each remoter age:
Wrung Nature's tortures, shuddering, while you tell,
From scoffing fiends bursts forth the laugh of hell;
In Britain's senate, Misery's pangs give birth
To jests unseemly, and to horrid mirth—   40
Forbear!—thy virtues but provoke our doom,
And swell th' account of vengeance yet to come;
For, not unmarked in Heaven's impartial plan,
Shall man, proud worm, contemn his fellow-man?
And injured Afric, by herself redrest,   45
Darts her own serpents at her Tyrant's breast.
Each vice, to minds depraved by bondage known,
With sure contagion fastens on his own;
In sickly languors melts his nerveless frame,
And blows to rage impetuous Passion's flame: 50
Fermenting swift, the fiery venom gains
The milky innocence of infant veins;
There swells the stubborn will, damps learning's fire,
The whirlwind wakes of uncontrolled desire,
Sears the young heart to images of woe,   55
And blasts the buds of Virtue as they blow.

   Lo! where reclin'd, pale Beauty courts the breeze,
Diffus'd on sofas of voluptuous ease;
With anxious awe, her menial train around,
Catch her faint whispers of half-utter'd sound;   60
See her, in monstrous fellowship, unite
At once the Scythian,[1] and the Sybarite;[2]
Blending repugnant vices, misally'd,
Which *frugal* nature purposed to divide;

---

1 Ancient nomadic people known for their war skills, horsemanship, and complex culture.

2 Sybarites, inhabitants of the ancient Greek city of Sybaris, were often famed for their luxuriousness. The term also denotes a self-indulgent person devoted to sensual pleasures.

See her, with indolence to fierceness join'd,   65
Of body delicate, infirm of mind,
With languid tones imperious mandates urge;
With arm recumbent wield the household scourge;
And with unruffled mien, and placid sounds,
Contriving torture, and inflicting wounds.   70

  Nor, in their palmy walks and spicy groves,
The form benign of rural Pleasure roves;
No milk-maid's song, or hum of village talk,
Sooths the lone poet in his evening walk:
No willing arm the flail unwearied plies,   75
Where the mix'd sounds of cheerful labour rise;
No blooming maids and frolic swains are seen
To pay gay homage to their harvest queen:
No heart-expanding scenes their eyes must prove
Of thriving industry, and faithful love: 80
But shrieks and yells disturb the balmy air,
Dumb sullen looks of woe announce despair,
And angry eyes thro' dusky features glare.
Far from the sounding lash the Muses fly,
And sensual riot drowns each finer joy.   85

  Nor less from the gay East, on essenced wings,
Breathing unnamed perfumes, Contagion springs;
The soft luxurious plague alike pervades
The marble palaces, and rural shades;
Hence throng'd Augusta builds her rosy bowers,   90
And decks in summer wreaths her smoky towers;
And hence, in summer bowers, Art's costly hand
Pours courtly splendours o'er the dazzled land:
The manners melt—One undistinguish'd blaze
O'erwhelms the sober pomp of elder days;   95
Corruption follows with gigantic stride,
And scarce vouchsafes his shameless front to hide:
The spreading leprosy[3] taints ev'ry part,
Infects each limb, and sickens at the heart.

---

3 A chronic disease which, at its severest, can lead to skin sores, nerve damage, paralysis, and blindness. For many years, stigmas regarding the contagiousness and disfigurement of leprosy caused patients to be shunned.

Simplicity! most dear of rural maids,   100
Weeping resigns her violated shades:
Stern independence from his glebe retires,
And anxious Freedom eyes her drooping fires;
By foreign wealth are British morals chang'd,
And Afric's sons, and India's smile aveng'd.   105

    For you, whose temper'd ardour long has borne
Untired the labour, and unmoved the scorn;
In Virtue's fasti[1] be inscribed your fame,
And uttered yours with Howard's[2] honour'd name,
Friends of the friendless—Hail, ye generous band   110
Whose efforts yet arrest Heaven's lifted hand,
Around whose steady brows, in union bright,
The civic wreath, and Christian's palm unite:
Your merit stands, no greater and no less,
Without, or with the varnish of success;   115
But seek no more to break a nation's fall,
For ye have sav'd yourselves—and that is all.
Succeeding times your struggles, and their fate,
With mingled shame and triumph shall relate,
While faithful History, in her various page,   120
Marking the features of this motley age,
To shed a glory, and to fix a stain,
Tells how you strove, and that you strove in vain.

1791

---

1 Calendar or historic record.

2 John Howard (1726–1790), a British philanthropist and prison reformer, studied methods of restricting the spread of contagious diseases.

THE RIGHTS OF WOMAN

Yes, injured Woman! rise, assert thy right!
Woman! too long degraded, scorned, opprest;
O born to rule in partial Law's despite,
Resume thy native empire o'er the breast!

Go forth arrayed in panoply divine;   5
That angel pureness which admits no stain;
Go, bid proud Man his boasted rule resign,
And kiss the golden sceptre of thy reign.

Go, gird thyself with grace; collect thy store
Of bright artillery glancing from afar;   10
Soft melting tones thy thundering cannon's roar,
Blushes and fears thy magazine of war.

Thy rights are empire: urge no meaner claim,—
Felt, not defined, and if debated, lost;
Like sacred mysteries, which withheld from fame,   15
Shunning discussion, are revered the most.

Try all that wit and art suggest to bend
Of thy imperial foe the stubborn knee;
Make treacherous Man thy subject, not thy friend;
Thou mayst command, but never canst be free.   20

Awe the licentious, and restrain the rude;
Soften the sullen, clear the cloudy brow:
Be, more than princes' gifts, thy favours sued;—
She hazards all, who will the least allow.

But hope not, courted idol of mankind,   25
On this proud eminence secure to stay;
Subduing and subdued, thou soon shalt find
Thy coldness soften, and thy pride give way.

Then, then, abandon each ambitious thought,
Conquest or rule thy heart shall feebly move,   30
In Nature's school, by her soft maxims taught,
That separate rights are lost in mutual love.

1792

MARY WOLLSTONECRAFT
1759–1797

Mary Wollstonecraft was the eldest daughter born to middle-class parents. Her father Edward inherited his share of the family silk weaving business in 1765, and Edward's aspirations of becoming a gentleman farmer led the family to live at a farm at Epping, Essex. Edward, however, had no talent for farming, and after five subsequent attempts, he had all but squandered his inheritance. Wollstonecraft grew to despise him. He bullied and abused his family, especially his wife Elizabeth. Despite Wollstonecraft's protective interventions, her mother submitted to Edward's violent drunken behavior without objection. The family's financial situation worsened. Since Wollstonecraft's parents had no money to educate either their daughters or sons (excepting Ned, the eldest child), Wollstonecraft assumed responsibility for her studies. She learned how to read and write at a Yorkshire day school, and thereafter, nearly everything she learned—including an array of foreign languages—was self-taught.

Poverty limited her chances of success in the marriage market and withered her employment opportunities. Looking to escape an increasingly bleak situation, Wollstonecraft left her home when she was nineteen years old. She lived with Fanny Blood, a treasured childhood friend, and earned a scant income by doing needlework. In 1784, Wollstonecraft was fetched to help her sister Eliza, whose husband believed she had suffered a nervous breakdown after the birth of a child. Wollstonecraft instead suspected that Eliza's breakdown resulted from marital issues and convinced her to leave her baby and husband. Divorces were not easily available, and while arranging for a legal separation, the sisters struggled to support themselves. Wollstonecraft spent her early twenties despising the handful of occupations available to women. Along with her sisters Eliza and Everina, and her best friend Fanny Blood, Wollstonecraft started a girls' school at Newington Green. In 1785, Wollstonecraft departed for Lisbon after Blood, who had traveled there to accept a marriage proposal earlier that year, implored her to aid with childbirth. When Wollstonecraft arrived, Blood was in premature labor. She died in Wollstonecraft's arms, and the infant died shortly afterward.

Upon arriving back at Newington Green, Wollstonecraft discovered her school was failing. She closed it just two years after it opened. Deprived of a stable income, she found employment as a governess for the wealthy Kingsborough family in County Cork, Ireland. Wollstonecraft at this time also began writing. In 1787, Joseph Johnson, a figure in the rational dissent community who regularly promoted progressive causes, published *Thoughts on the Education of Daughters*, Wollstonecraft's first book. Wollstonecraft's governess job, however, was short-lived; she and Lady Kingsborough had an antagonistic relationship, and Wollstonecraft was dismissed from the position after a year. She returned to England. Desperate to earn money and find work she enjoyed, Wollstonecraft began writing again. Joseph Johnson published her novel *Mary, a Fiction* and her children's book *Original Stories from Real Life* in 1788. By 1790, Wollstonecraft wrote, read manuscripts, and translated works for Joseph Johnson's journal *Analytical Review*. Joseph Johnson proved himself to be a lifelong friend and patron, offering Wollstonecraft advice, encouragement, and financial assistance to ensure her and her sisters' well-being.

Hoping to gather material for her next book, Wollstonecraft traveled to Paris in 1792 to observe the French Revolution. There she met an American named Captain Gilbert Imlay. The two began an affair, and in 1794 Wollstonecraft gave birth to a daughter she named Fanny in honor of her deceased friend. The trio returned to England, but as Imlay became increasingly distant, Wollstonecraft took a suicidal dose of opium. After she recovered, she ventured to Norway at Imlay's request to address one of his business issues. Upon returning to London, Wollstonecraft realized that Imlay had another mistress, and in despair she attempted to jump from Putney Bridge and drown herself in the Thames.

She recuperated, resuming her work for Joseph Johnson and associating with a group of radical writers who nurtured her visionary, progressive ideals. The group included William Blake, Thomas Paine, Thomas Holcroft, and William Godwin. Godwin, like Wollstonecraft, was a writer. He promoted anarchy and personal freedom in his pieces, publishing works about the French Revolution as well as political injustice. Voluble, passionate, and bold, Wollstonecraft and Godwin initially quarreled with each other but quickly transformed into lovers. Though Wollstonecraft and Godwin both rejected the principle of marriage, they married in March 1797 after Wollstonecraft became pregnant. Once married, they maintained their independence as well as their intimacy; they lived together but wrote in separate spaces, and although they shared mutual friends, they often enjoyed solitary visits. At the end of August, Wollstonecraft gave birth to Mary Wollstonecraft Godwin, who would grow up to write the novel *Frankenstein* and marry Percy Bysshe Shelley. Complications with the placenta led to infection, and Wollstonecraft died eleven days later. She was thirty-eight years old.

Deeply aggrieved by her death, Godwin published *Memoirs of the Author of A Vindication of the Rights of Woman* the following year. Conservative critics attacked Wollstonecraft's unconventional lifestyle and used the biography to discourage any attempts to liberate women. Subsequent reviewers were polarized over whether to support or condemn her. Mary Robinson and Mary Hays embraced Wollstone-craft's beliefs, but others ruthlessly criticized Wollstonecraft's personal decisions for years after her death. George Eliot attempted to destigmatize Wollstonecraft's name in her 1855 essay, "Margaret Fuller and Mary Wollstonecraft," but the taint remained. Although women's rights advocates in Victorian England, such as Harriet Taylor, alluded to Wollstonecraft in their works, few dared to mention her directly; for many people, Wollstonecraft was a harbinger of immoral behavior. She did not gain serious followers until the early twentieth century when proto-feminists such as Virginia Woolf applauded her sexual openness and confidence.

Despite its reputation as a radical proto-feminist piece, Wollstonecraft's most famous work, *A Vindication of the Rights of Woman*, sometimes has misogynistic tones and moralizing content. *A Vindication of the Rights of Woman*, however, was trailblazing for its time; Wollstonecraft built her arguments off the then-contested idea that men and women are equal. Drawing on the revolutionary ideals of her day, Wollstonecraft articulated that British society denied women their natural rights. She argued that femininity was a social construct and attacked the popular philosophy of Jean-Jacques Rousseau, who asserted women's inferiority to men. Though British culture emphasized and valued women's sensibility, Wollstonecraft urged women to rely on reason rather than emotions. She additionally remarked that if girls received the same education as boys, they would become outstanding wives and mothers; they would also be able to work in various professions and contribute more to English society. Wollstonecraft experienced firsthand the limited professional opportunities available to women, and she advocated for greater employment prospects, particularly for single women. Her book was an immediate best-seller. Quickly translated into French and German, *A Vindication of the Rights of Woman* permeated cultural conversations, yet it did not inspire any reforms. In the 1840s, however, women's rights movements in Europe and the United States alike employed some of its principles. For instance, Elizabeth Cady Stanton and Margaret Fuller both utilized aspects of Wollstonecraft's argument in their fight for women's liberties.

Wollstonecraft is recognized as England's first major feminist writer. Although women writers were common in the 1790s, Wollstonecraft was one of the few who wrote politically. With an impulse for innovation and self-creation as well as a fierce desire to understand herself, she explored a multitude of literary personae throughout her career. At times an uptight moralist, a blunt philosopher, a satirist, a romantic, and a teacher, Wollstonecraft seemingly tested a range of potential selves and avidly refused to be smothered by conventional womanliness. An intrepid, indefatigable, and formidable individual and writer, Wollstonecraft gained a sig-nificant place in the history of women's rights.

1759	Mary Wollstonecraft born April 27
1787	*Thoughts on the Education of Daughters*
1788	*Mary: A Fiction; Original Stories from Real Life*
1789	*The Female Reader*
1790	*A Vindication of the Rights of Men*
1792	*Vindication of the Rights of Woman: With Strictures on Political and Moral Subjects*
1793–95	Lives in France
1794	Daughter Fanny born; *Historical and Moral View of the French Revolution*
1797	Marries William Godwin 29 March; daughter Mary born; Wollstonecraft dies 10 September due to puerperal infection and is buried in St. Pancras churchyard
1798	Godwin publishes *Memoirs of the Author of A Vindication of the Rights of Woman*
1851	On 15 September, Wollstonecraft's remains, as well as Godwin's, are moved to St. Peter's churchyard, England

A VINDICATION OF THE RIGHTS OF WOMAN

WITH STRICTURES ON POLITICAL AND MORAL SUBJECTS

INTRODUCTION

AFTER CONSIDERING THE HISTORIC PAGE, and viewing the living world with anxious solicitude, the most melancholy emotions of sorrowful indignation have depressed my spirits, and I have sighed when obliged to confess, that either nature has made a great difference between man and man, or that the civilization which has hitherto taken place in the world has been very partial. I have turned over various books written on the subject of education, and patiently observed the conduct of parents and the management of schools; but what has been the result?—a profound conviction that the neglected education of my fellow creatures is the grand source of the misery I deplore; and that women, in particular, are rendered weak and wretched by a variety of concurring causes, originating from one hasty conclusion. The conduct and manners of women, in fact, evidently prove that their minds are not in a healthy state; for, like the flowers that are planted in too rich a soil, strength and usefulness are sacrificed to beauty; and the flaunting leaves, after having pleased a fastidious eye, fade, disregarded on the stalk, long before the season when they ought to have arrived at maturity.—One cause of this barren blooming I attribute to a false system of education, gathered from the books written on this subject by men who, considering females rather as women than human creatures, have been more anxious to make them alluring mistresses than rational wives; and the understanding of the sex has been so bubbled by this specious homage, that the civilized women of the present century, with a few exceptions, are only anxious to inspire love, when they ought to cherish a nobler ambition, and by their abilities and virtues exact respect.

In a treatise, therefore, on female rights and manners, the works which have been particularly written for their improvement must not be overlooked; especially when it is asserted, in direct terms, that the minds of women are enfeebled by false refinement; that the books of instruction, written by men of genius, have had the same tendency as more frivolous productions; and that, in the true style of Mahometanism, they are only considered as females, and not as a part of the human species, when improvable reason is allowed to be the dignified distinction which raises men above the brute creation, and puts a natural sceptre in a feeble hand.

Yet, because I am a woman, I would not lead my readers to suppose that I mean violently to agitate the contested question respecting the equality and inferiority of the sex; but as the subject lies in my way, and I cannot pass it over without subjecting the main tendency of my reasoning to misconstruction, I shall stop a moment to deliver, in a few words, my opinion.—In the government of the physical world it is observable that the female, in general, is inferior to the male. The male pursues, the female yields—this is the law of nature; and it does not appear to be suspended or abrogated in favour of woman. This physical superiority cannot be denied—and it is a noble prerogative! But not content with this natural pre-eminence, men endeavour to sink us still lower, merely to render us alluring objects for a moment; and women, intoxicated by the adoration which men, under the influence of their senses, pay them, do not seek to obtain a durable interest in their hearts, or to become the friends of the fellow creatures who find amusement in their society.

I am aware of an obvious inference:—from every quarter have I heard exclamations against masculine women; but where are they to be found? If by this appellation men mean to inveigh against their ardour in hunting, shooting, and gaming, I shall most cordially join in the cry; but if it be against the imitation of manly virtues, or, more properly speaking, the attainment of those talents and virtues, the exercise of which ennobles the human character, and which raise females in the scale of animal being, when they are comprehensively termed mankind;—all those who view them with a philosophical eye must, I should think, wish with me, that they may every day grow more and more masculine.

This discussion naturally divides the subject. I shall first consider women in the grand light of human creatures, who, in common with men, are placed on this earth to unfold their faculties; and afterwards I shall more particularly point out their peculiar designation.

I wish also to steer clear of an error which many respectable writers have fallen into; for the instruction which has hitherto been addressed to women, has rather been applicable to *ladies*, if the little indirect advice, that is scattered through Sandford and Merton, be excepted; but, addressing my sex in a firmer tone, I pay particular attention to those in the middle class, because they appear to be in the most natural state. Perhaps the seeds of false refinement, immorality, and vanity, have ever been shed by the great. Weak, artificial beings, raised above the common wants and affections of their race, in a premature unnatural manner, undermine the very foundation of virtue, and spread corruption through the whole mass of society! As a class of mankind they have the strongest claim to pity; the education of the rich tends to render them vain and helpless, and the unfolding mind is not strengthened by the practice of those duties which dignify the human character. — They only live to amuse themselves, and by the same law which in nature invariably produces certain effects, they soon only afford barren amusement.

But as I purpose taking a separate view of the different ranks of society, and of the moral character of women, in each, this hint is, for the present, sufficient; and I have only alluded to the subject, because it appears to me to be the very essence of an introduction to give a cursory account of the contents of the work it introduces.

My own sex, I hope, will excuse me, if I treat them like rational creatures, instead of flattering their *fascinating* graces, and viewing them as if they were in a state of perpetual childhood, unable to stand alone. I earnestly wish to point out in what true dignity and human happiness consists—I wish to persuade women to endeavour to acquire strength, both of mind and body, and to convince them, that the soft phrases, susceptibility of heart, delicacy of sentiment, and refinement of taste, are almost synonymous with epithets of weakness, and that those beings who are only the objects of pity and that kind of love, which has been termed its sister, will soon become objects of contempt.

Dismissing then those pretty feminine phrases, which the men condescendingly use to soften our slavish dependence, and despising that weak elegancy of mind, exquisite sensibility, and sweet docility of manners, supposed to be the sexual char-acteristics of the weaker vessel, I wish to show that elegance is inferior to virtue, that the first object of laudable ambition is to obtain a character as a human being, regardless of the distinction of sex; and that secondary views should be brought to this simple touchstone.

This is a rough sketch of my plan; and should I express my conviction with the energetic emotions that I feel whenever I think of the subject, the dictates of experience and reflection will be felt by some of my readers. Animated by this important object, I shall disdain to cull my phrases or polish my style;—I aim at being useful, and sincerity will render me unaffected; for, wishing rather to persuade by the force of my arguments, than dazzle by the elegance of my language, I shall not waste my time in rounding periods, nor in fabricating the turgid bombast of artificial feelings, which, coming from the head, never reach the heart.—I shall be employed about things, not words!—and, anxious to ren-der my sex more respectable members of society, I shall try to avoid that flowery diction which has slided from essays into novels, and from novels into familiar letters and conversation.

These pretty nothings—these caricatures of the real beauty of sensibility, dropping glibly from the tongue, vitiate the taste, and create a kind of sickly delicacy that turns away from simple unadorned truth; and a deluge of false senti-ments and over-stretched feelings, stifling the natural emotions of the heart, render the domestic pleasures insipid, that ought to sweeten the exercise of those severe duties, which educate a rational and immortal being for a nobler field of action.

The education of women has, of late, been more attended to than formerly; yet they are still reckoned a frivolous sex, and ridiculed or pitied by the writers who endeavour by satire or instruction to improve them. It is acknowledged that they spend many of the first years of their lives in acquiring a smattering of accomplishments: meanwhile strength of body and mind are sacrificed to libertine notions of beauty, to the desire of establishing themselves,—the only way women can rise in the world,—by marriage. And this desire making mere animals of them, when they marry they act as such children may be expected to act:—they dress; they paint, and nickname God's creatures.—Surely these weak beings are only fit for the seraglio!—Can they govern a family, or take care of the poor babes whom they bring into the world?

If then it can be fairly deduced from the present conduct of the sex, from the prevalent fondness for pleasure which takes place of ambition and those nobler passions that open and enlarge the soul; that the instruction which women have received has only tended, with the constitution of civil society, to render them insignificant objects of desire—mere propagators of fools!—if it can be proved that in aiming to accomplish them, without cultivating their understandings, they are taken out of their sphere of duties, and made ridiculous and useless when the short-lived bloom of beauty is over,[1] I presume that *rational* men will excuse me for endeavouring to persuade them to become more masculine and respectable.

Indeed the word masculine is only a bugbear: there is little reason to fear that women will acquire too much courage or fortitude; for their apparent inferiority with respect to bodily strength, must render them, in some degree, dependent on men in the various relations of life; but why should it be increased by prejudices that give a sex to virtue, and confound simple truths with sensual reveries?

Women are, in fact, so much degraded by mistaken notions of female excellence, that I do not mean to add a paradox when I assert, that this artificial weakness produces a propensity to tyrannize, and gives birth to cunning, the natural opponent of strength, which leads them to play off those contemptible infantile airs that undermine esteem even whilst they excite desire. Do not foster these prejudices, and they will naturally fall into their subordinate, yet respectable station, in life.

It seems scarcely necessary to say, that I now speak of the sex in general. Many individuals have more sense than their male relatives; and, as nothing preponderates where there is a constant struggle for an equilibrium, without it has naturally more gravity, some women govern their husbands without degrading themselves, because intellect will always govern.

1792

---

1 A lively writer, I cannot recollect his name, asks what business women turned of forty have to do in the world? [Wollstonecraft].

Mary Robinson
1758–1800

After fifteen months at King's Bench Prison, Mary Robinson's husband Tom paid off enough of his debt to obtain his liberty, but—as he never completed the training needed to become a clerk and could not secure financial assistance from his father—he had no means of supporting himself or his wife. Additionally, his pattern of living well beyond his means and entertaining various women largely left Robinson to fend for herself. Desperate and hoping to gain some independence, she pursued literary and theatrical ventures. Despite her enthusiasm, however, writing proved grueling. "At the moment that I write this page," Robinson states in her *Memoirs*, "I feel in every fibre of my brain the fatal conviction that [writing] is a *destroying labour*." Yet even as her physical health rapidly declined, she clung to her pen, her mind too formidable and restless to surrender the practice.

Born Mary Darby in 1758, Mary came from a respectable and wealthy family. Her father, who was born in America, achieved commercial prosperity as a merchant; her mother was a descendant of Richard Seys, Esquire, of Boverton Castle. Once Mary learned how to read, she studied epitaphs and monumental inscriptions. In addition to favoring elegiac literature, she played melancholy melodies on her harpsichord. But the ease of childhood ended when she was nine years old. Determined to start a whale fishery business, her father mortgaged his property and sailed for America, bringing a mistress with him. His scheme failed; Mrs. Darby and the children vacated the house; and after a year, he journeyed to London to announce his decision to return to America and permanently separate from his wife. He sent Mary, who had previously attended a boarding school in Bristol, to Chelsea for her education. Meribah Lorrington, a brilliant but alcoholic woman, taught her literature for just over a year before the school failed and Mary's mother sent her to a seminary at Battersea. Mrs. Darby established her own boarding school in Little Chelsea, where Mary, aged fourteen, taught grammar as well as English prose and poetry.

Mrs. Darby's school had been open for less than a year when Mr. Darby unexpectedly returned, ordered its breakup, and threatened Mrs. Darby to protect their young, attractive, and unmarried daughter from dishonor. While Mary finished her education at Oxford House in Maryleborne, her mother frantically searched for suitors for her. Mary meanwhile dedicated every idle moment to composing poetry. Mr. Hussey, the dancing-master at Oxford House and the ballet-master at Covent Garden Theatre, introduced her to Thomas Hull of the same theatre. Although Hull found her beauty and recitation skills thrilling, Mary's acting career did not begin until she encountered David Garrick, a famous actor and the manager of Drury Lane Theatre, who accepted her as his tutee. She was then fifteen. To her mother's dismay, Mary's training summoned the attention of several men. Only Tom Robinson, Esquire, who boasted of a rich uncle and tended to Mary when she fell ill with smallpox, won Mrs. Darby's favor.

Despite her distaste for the idea of marriage and the fact that she did not love Tom, Mary conceded to her mother's wishes. With only Mrs. Darby, the clerk, and the woman who opened the church pews as witnesses, Mary and Tom wedded in 1774. As acting was not thought a respectable career for a married woman, Robinson relinquished the stage. Several months into her marriage, she realized Tom's dishonesty: He was the illegitimate son of Mr. Harris of Tregunter and heir to no fortune. Still, they lived lavishly and recklessly. Tom introduced her to his wide circle of London acquaintances, including the libertine Lord Lyttelton and the duelist George Robert Fitzgerald. Both men tried unsuccessfully to make Robinson a mistress. Tom increasingly neglected her. He amassed sizable debts, frequently borrowing more money to allay other obligations, and kept mistresses. His debts reached such proportions that the Robinsons fled to Tregunter where Mr. Harris and his family demeaned Mary. She moved into Trevecca House, a secluded mansion at the base of a mountain, where she gave birth to her daughter Maria Elizabeth.

Tom's creditors forced them back to London where the young couple quickly resumed gambling, partying, and other leisure activities. Eager to lessen their ever-growing debt, Robinson published her first volume of poems in 1775. The collection sold but received no recognition, and the Robinsons soon found themselves in King's Bench Prison. For nine months and three weeks, Robinson lived in dismal prison conditions. Tom's licentious friends futilely attempted to seduce her out, but she continued to write, fixated on the theme of captivity, until Georgiana, Duchess of Devonshire, became her literary patron.

By the next year, they were free. As the Robinsons had no viable means of sustaining themselves, Tom finally consented to Robinson's pleas to become an actress. William Brereton, a friend of Tom's, introduced her to Richard Brinsley Sheridan, an actor and the manager of Drury Lane Theatre. Garrick emerged from retirement to tutor Robinson once again, and on December 10, 1776, she made her debut as Juliet to resounding applause. Sheridan cast her in various plays, including her own play, *The Lucky Escape*. She gave birth to a daughter named Sophia later that year, but the infant lived for only six weeks. The loss aggrieved her, but by the following year she had resumed acting. She performed twenty-two different roles, and theatre-goers as well as reviewers praised her until she achieved notable fame. She leased a home for herself while Tom had affairs with two women, one of whom he lived with.

Robinson's admirers multiplied, but her celebrity mutated into notoriety after she acted in a Royal Command performance for King George, Queen Charlotte, and the Prince of Wales (later King George IV). Playing the role of Perdita in Shakespeare's *The Winter's Tale,* Robinson garnered the Prince's special attention, and a written correspondence between them began shortly afterward. Soon he sent her a miniature portrait encircled by diamonds and begged for a meeting. After much refusal and a £20,000 bond the Prince promised to pay her when he came of age, she agreed. By 1780, their relations became public knowledge. The press and public slandered her incessantly. By December, she had accumulated ample debt, her stage career was ruined, and the Prince had abruptly terminated their relationship. She appealed to him but did not receive the bond money; instead, she settled for annuities for herself and her daughter. She then briefly travelled to Paris where she gained widespread adoration as *la belle Anglaise* as well as admiration from Queen Marie Antoinette and numerous men.

Robinson had, however, already begun relations with the man who would become her longest lover. In 1782, she met Colonel Banastre Tarleton, a daring and elegant officer who had returned to England after six years of fighting in the American War of Independence. Tarleton began courting her after Lord Malden, the Prince's messenger, bet him that he could not win Robinson's love. By the end of 1782, Tarleton and Robinson were living together in Windsor. Tarleton's gambling, however, worsened, and his mother refused to assist him unless he left England and Robinson. He departed for France, and Robinson, though pregnant, pursued him. She suffered a miscarriage while traveling and complications led to paralysis. Unable to stand alone or completely flex her fingers, she became helpless at twenty-four years old. They reunited in 1784, settling in France for four years before venturing back to London.

Robinson began writing professionally, often under the pseudonyms "Laura" or "Laura Marie," and established a respectable literary presence. After separating from Tarleton in 1791, she wrote a novel called *Vancenza; or the Dangers of Credulity,* which sold out in a day. After falling ill in 1792, she reunited with Tarleton; their relationship was sporadic until, in 1797, they parted for the final time. Though her health continued to decline, her debt compelled her to write. She penned *Walsingham; or, the Pupil of Nature* in 1797, and then, in response to news of Tarleton's wedding and subsequent inheritance, wrote *The False Friend* in 1798. Both works question and critique gender roles. Autobiographical experiences rendered Robinson painfully aware of the powerlessness women in the late eighteenth century faced. Despite acknowledging male power abuses in English society, Robinson was not known as an activist; only her 1799 essay, *A Letter to the Women of England, on the Cruelties of Mental Subordination,* forthrightly rebukes women's limited position. Robinson, like her friend Mary Wollstonecraft, assaults gender inequalities and criticizes the duties of each gender, especially the notion of males as protectors.

By 1800, Robinson had essentially confined herself to her home. Though extremely ill, her financial distress forced her to work. She undertook the poetical department of *The Morning Post*, various translation projects, and her memoirs. *Lyrical Tales*, a collection of her poems, was her last literary work published during her lifetime. She hoped to return to Bristol, her hometown, and hear once more the poignant choral songs of her childhood. Unable to afford the trip, she died in late December. She was forty-three years old.

The cause of death appeared to be dropsy (edema) in the chest. Two literary friends attended her burial at Old Windsor Churchyard. Remembered chiefly as "Perdita," Robinson's acting career and affair with the Prince of Wales sometimes eclipses her literary accomplishments. However, she created a reputable body of work during her life, penning sentimental novels, plays, and lyric poetry. Robinson obtained inspiration from her environment, minding not only her circumstances, but noting the conditions of the impoverished and societal outcasts as well.

1758	Mary Darby born 27 November
1774	Marries Thomas Robinson; daughter Maria Elizabeth born
1775	*Poems*; the Robinsons are imprisoned for debt at King's Bench Prison for 15 months
1776	10 December Robinson debuts at Drury Lane Theatre
1777	*Captivity, A Poem, and Celadon and Lydia, a Tale*
1778	Performs in *The Lucky Escape, A Comic Opera*, a play she wrote, at Drury Lane Theatre 30 April; daughter Sophia born, but dies six weeks later
1779	Performs Shakespeare's *The Winter's Tale* on 3 December
1790	*Ainsi Va Le Monde, A Poem Inscribed to Robert Merry*, as Laura Maria
1791	*Poems by Mrs. M. Robinson*
1799	*The Natural Daughter, With Portraits of the Leadenhead Family, A Novel; A Letter to the Women of England, on the Cruelties of Mental Subordination* as Anne Frances Randall
1800	*Lyrical Tales*; dies 26 December due to edema and is buried at Old Windsor Churchyard

THE SAVAGE OF AVERYON

'Twas in the mazes of a wood,
　　The lonely wood of Aveyron,
　　I heard a melancholy tone,
　　It seem'd to freeze my blood!
A torrent tear was flowing fast,　　　　　　　　5
And hollow was the midnight blast,
As o'er the leafless woods it past,
　　While terror-fraught I stood!
O! mazy woods of Aveyron!
O! wilds of dreary solitude!　　　　　　　　10
Amid thy thorny alleys rude
　　I thought myself alone!
　　I thought no living thing could be
　　So weary of the world as me,
While on my winding path the pale moon shone.　　15

Sometimes the tone was loud and sad,
And sometimes dulcet, faint and slow;
And then a tone of frantic woe,
　　　It almost made me mad.
The burthen was "alone! alone!"　　　　　　　　20
And then the heart did feebly groan,
Then suddenly a chearful tone
　　Proclaim'd a spirit glad!
"O! mazy woods of Aveyron!
"O! wilds of dreary solitude,　　　　　　　　25
"Amid your thorny alleys rude
"I wish'd myself—a traveller alone!

"Alone!" I heard the wild boy say,
And swift he climb'd a blasted oak;
And there while Morning's herald woke,　　　　　　30
　　He watch'd the opening day;
Yet dark and sunken was his eye,
Like a lorn maniac's, wild and shy,

And scowling like a winter's sky,
    Without one beaming ray! 35
Then mazy woods of Aveyron,
    Then wilds of dreary solitude,
    Amid thy thorny alleys rude,
I sigh'd to be—a traveller alone!

"*Alone! alone!*" I heard him shriek, 40
    'Twas like the shriek of dying man!
    And then to mutter he began,
      But, O! *he could not speak!*
I saw him point to Heav'n, and sigh,
The big drop trembled in his eye, 45
And slowly from the yellow sky,
    I saw the pale moon break:
I saw the woods of Aveyron,
    Their wilds of dreary solitude!
    I mark'd their thorny alleys rude, 50
And wish'd to be a traveller alone!

His hair was long and black, and he
    From infancy *alone* had been!
    For since his fifth year he had seen,
      None mark'd his destiny! 55
No mortal ear had heard his groan,
For him no beam of hope had shone,
While sad he sigh'd—"*alone, alone!*"
      Beneath the blasted tree!
And there, O! woods of Aveyron! 60
    O! wilds of dreary solitude!
    Amid your thorny alleys rude,
I thought myself a traveller alone.

And now upon the blasted tree
    He carv'd *three* notches, broad and long, 65
    And all the while he sang a song
      Of Nature's melody!
And tho' of words he little knew,
And tho' his dulcet tones were few,
Across the yielding bark he drew, 70

   Deep sighing, notches three!
O! mazy woods of Aveyron!
  O! wilds of dreary solitude,
  Amid your thorny alleys rude,
Upon this blasted oak, no sun beam shone!   75

And now he pointed one, two, three,
  Again he shriek'd with wild dismay!
  And now he pac'd the thorny way,
   Quitting the blasted tree.
It was a dark December morn,   80
The dew was frozen on the thorn,
But to a wretch so sad, so lorn,
  All days alike would be!
Yet, mazy woods of Aveyron!
  Yet, wilds of dreary solitude!   85
  Amid your frosty alleys rude,
I wish'd to be—a traveller alone!

I follow'd him along the wood,
  To a small grot his hands had made,
  Deep in a black rock's sullen shade, 90
   Beside a tumbling flood!
Upon the earth I saw him spread
Of wither'd *leaves* a narrow bed,
Yellow as gold, and streak'd with red;
  They look'd like streaks of blood! 95
Fall'n from the woods of Aveyron,
  And scatter'd o'er the solitude
  By midnight whirlwinds, strong and rude,
To pillow the scorch'd brain that throbb'd alone!

Wild berries were his winter food,   100
  With them his sallow lip was dy'd!
  On chesnuts wild he fed beside,
   Steep'd in the foamy flood.
Chequer'd with scars, his breast was seen,
Wounds, streaming fresh with anguish keen! 105
And marks where other wounds had been,
  Torn by the brambles rude.

Such was the boy of Aveyron,
    The tenant of that solitude,
    Where still, by misery unsubdu'd,   110
He wander'd *nine long winters*, all alone!

Before the step of his rude throne
    The *squirrel* sported, tame and gay;
    The *dormouse* slept its life away,
        Nor heard his midnight groan: 115
About his form a garb he wore,
Ragged it was, and mark'd with gore;
And yet, where'er 'twas folded o'er,
      Full many a spangle shone!
Like little stars, O! Aveyron!   120
    They gleam'd amid thy solitude!
    Or like, along thy alleys rude,
The summer dew-drops, sparkling in the sun!

It once had been a lady's vest,
    White as the whitest mountain's snow!   125
    Till ruffian hands had taught to flow
      The fountain of her breast!
Remembrance bade the wild boy trace
Her beauteous form, her angel face,
Her eye that beam'd with heavenly grace,   130
      Her fainting voice that blest!
When in the woods of Aveyron,
    Deep in their deepest solitude,
    Three barb'rous ruffians shed her blood,
And mock'd, with cruel taunts, her dying groan.   135

Remembrance trac'd the summer bright,
    When all the trees were fresh and green,
    When lost the alleys long between,
      The lady pass'd the night;
She past the night bewilder'd wild,   140
She past it with her fearless child,
Who rais'd his little arms, and smiled
      To see the morning light!
While in the woods of Aveyron,

Beneath the broad oak's canopy,   145
   She mark'd aghast the ruffians three,
Waiting to seize the traveller alone!

Beneath the broad oak's canopy
   The lovely lady's bones were laid;
   But since that hour no breeze has play'd   150
     About the blasted tree!
The leaves all wither'd ere the sun
His next day's rapid course had run,
And ere the summer day was done
     It winter seem'd to be!   155
And still, O! woods of Aveyron,
   Amid thy dreary solitude
   The oak, a sapless trunk, has stood,
To mark the spot where murder foul was done!

From her the wild boy learnt "alone:"   160
   She tried to say, *my babe will die*;
   But angels caught her parting sigh,
     The babe her *dying tone!*
And from that hour the boy has been
Lord of the solitary scene,   165
Wandering the dreary shades between,
   Making his dismal moan!
Till, mazy woods of Aveyron!
   Dark wilds of dreary solitude!
   Amid your thorny alleys rude,   170
     I thought myself alone;
   And could a wretch more wretched be,
   More wild or fancy-fraught, than he,
Whose melancholy tale would pierce a heart of stone.

1801

THE POOR SINGING DAME

Beneath an old wall, that went round an old castle,
  For many a year, with brown ivy o'erspread;
A neat little hovel, its lowly roof raising,
  Defied the wild winds that howl'd over its shed:
The turrets, that frown'd on the poor simple dwelling,   5
  Were rock'd to and fro, when the tempest would roar,
And the river, that down the rich valley was swelling,
  Flow'd swiftly beside the green step of its door.

The summer sun gilded the rushy roof slanting,
  The bright dews bespangled its ivy-bound hedge,   10
And above, on the ramparts, the sweet birds were chanting,
  And wild buds thick dappled the clear river's edge,
When the castle's rich chambers were haunted and dreary,
  The poor little hovel was still and secure;
And no robber e'er enter'd, nor goblin nor fairy,   15
  For the splendours of pride had no charms to allure.

The lord of the castle, a proud surly ruler,
  Oft heard the low dwelling with sweet music ring,
For the old dame that lived in the little hut cheerly,
  Would sit at her wheel, and would merrily sing: 20
When with revels the castle's great hall was resounding,
  The old dame was sleeping, not dreaming of fear;
And when over the mountains the huntsmen were bounding
  She would open her lattice, their clamours to hear.

To the merry-toned horn she would dance on the threshold,   25
  And louder, and louder repeat her old song:
And when winter its mantle of frost was displaying,
  She caroll'd, undaunted, the bare woods among:
She would gather dry fern, ever happy and singing,
  With her cake of brown bread, and her jug of brown beer,   30
And would smile when she heard the great castle-bell ringing,

Inviting the proud to their prodigal cheer.

Thus she lived, ever patient and ever contented,
   Till envy the lord of the castle possess'd,
For he hated that poverty should be so cheerful,   35
   While care could the fav'rites of fortune molest;
He sent his bold yeomen with threats to prevent her,
   And still would she carol her sweet roundelay;
At last, an old steward relentless he sent her–
   Who bore her, all trembling, to prison away!   40

Three weeks did she languish, then died broken-hearted,
   Poor dame! how the death-bell did mournfully sound!
And along the green path six young bachelors bore her,
   And laid her for ever beneath the cold ground!
And the primroses pale 'mid the long grass were growing,   45
   The bright dews of twilight bespangled her grave,
And morn heard the breezes of summer soft blowing,
   To bid the fresh flowerets in sympathy wave.

The lord of the castle, from that fatal moment
   When poor singing Mary was laid in her grave,   50
Each night was surrounded by screech-owls appalling,
   Which o'er the black turrets their pinions would wave!
On the ramparts that frown'd on the river, swift flowing,
   They hover'd, still hooting a terrible song,
When his windows would rattle, the winter blast blowing,   55
   They would shriek like a ghost, the dark alleys among!

Wherever he wander'd they followed him crying;
   At dawnlight, at eve, still they haunted his way!
When the moon shone across the wide common they hooted,
   Nor quitted his path till the blazing of day.   60
His bones began wasting, his flesh was decaying,
   And he hung his proud head, and he perish'd with shame;
And the tomb of rich marble, no soft tear displaying,
   O'ershadows the grave of the poor singing dame!

1801

THE HAUNTED BEACH

Upon a lonely desert beach,
　　Where the white foam was scatter'd,
A little shed uprear'd its head,
　　Tho' lofty barks were shatter'd.
The sea-weeds gath'ring near the door,　　　　　5
　　A sombre path display'd;
And, all around the deafening roar
Re-echo'd on the chalky shore,
　　By the green billows made.

Above a jutting cliff was seen,　　　　　10
　　Where sea-birds hover'd, craving;
And all around the craggs were bound
　　With weeds for ever waving.
And here and there a cavern wide
　　Its shad'wy jaws display'd;　　　　　15
And near the sands, at ebb of tide,
A shiver'd mast was seen to ride
　　Where the green billows stray'd.

And often, while the moaning wind
　　Stole o'er the summer ocean;　　　　　20
The moon-light scene was all serene,
　　The waters scarce in motion:
Then while the smoothly slanting sand
　　The tall cliff wrapp'd in shade,
The fisherman beheld a band　　　　　25
Of spectres, gliding hand in hand,
　　Where the green billows play'd.

And pale their faces were as snow,
　　And sullenly they wander'd!
And to the skies with hollow eyes　　　　　30
　　They look'd as tho' they ponder'd.
And sometimes from their hammock shroud

They dismal howlings made,
And while the blast blew strong and loud,
The clear moon mark'd the ghastly crowd,   35
    Where the green billows play'd.

And then above the haunted hut
    The curlews screaming hover'd;
And the low door, with furious roar
    The frothy breakers cover'd.   40
For in the fisherman's lone shed
    A murder'd man was laid,
With ten wide gashes in his head,
And deep was made his sandy bed
    Where the green billows play'd.   45

A shipwreck'd mariner was he,
    Doom'd from his home to sever;
Who swore to be thro' wind and sea
    Firm and undaunted ever!
And when the wave resistless roll'd,   50
    About his arm he made
A packet rich of Spanish gold,
And like a British sailor bold,
    Plung'd where the billows play'd.

The spectre band, his messmates brave   55
    Sunk in the yawning ocean,
While to the mast he lash'd him fast,
    And brav'd the storm's commotion.
The winter moon, upon the sand
    A silv'ry carpet made,   60
And mark'd the sailor reach the land,
And mark'd his murd'rer wash his hand
    Where the green billows play'd.

And since that hour the fisherman
    Has toil'd and toil'd in vain!   65
For all the night the moony light
    Gleams on the specter'd main!
And when the skies are veil'd in gloom,
    The murd'rer's liquid way

Bounds o'er the deeply yawning tomb,   70
And flashing fires the sands illume,
　　Where the green billows play!

Full thirty years his task has been,
　　Day after day more weary;
For Heaven design'd his guilty mind   75
　　Should dwell on prospects dreary.
Bound by a strong and mystic chain,
　　He has not pow'r to stray;
But destin'd mis'ry to sustain,
He wastes in solitude and pain,   80
　　A loathsome life away.

1801

WILLIAM BLAKE
1757–1827

William Blake was determined to publish his poems, but his means were limited. He was too poor to afford a publisher, lacked a public reputation, and had exhausted his few patrons. After months of anxiety, the solution to his predicament arrived. Blake's deceased brother visited him in a dream, and, revealing a strategy that incorporated both Blake's engraving skills and his literary talents, provided the foundation that would help support the Blakes for the rest of their lives. In the morning, Blake's wife, Catherine, went into town with half a crown–all the money they had–to purchase the necessary supplies. Using acid-resistant materials, Blake wrote his text in reverse and added illustrations directly onto small copper plates. When he etched the plates in acid, the untreated copper decayed, leaving his designs in relief. The plates were then painstakingly colored by hand, sometimes matching the colors in the original etching, sometimes varying in hue. Unique variations mark each work. With Catherine's assistance, Blake used "illuminated printing" to write, engrave, and print his works. The first book completed with this process was called *Songs of Innocence*; W. Blake listed himself as author and printer.

It was not atypical for Blake's inspiration to come from uncanny or supernatural places. His brother repeatedly appeared to him in visions, and Blake was frequently visited by otherworldly beings. As a child, fantastic images of angels and spirits materialized before his eyes. When he recounted his perceptions to his parents, they assumed he was lying and threatened to beat him. His visions persisted as he aged, revealing that they were not a child's mysticisms. Blake saw God in everything. His inner spiritual life was a matrix of unshakeable faith and creativity; it had dimension of its own. To him, imagination was more concrete than reality. He preferred to dwell in the lucid corners of his mind, uncovering truths about the human condition and reworking his insights into poetry and art.

Raised in a religious family, Blake absorbed most of his education from lessons of the Bible. When he was ten years old, he briefly attended drawing school, only to be apprenticed due to financial difficulties. Blake's instructor, James Basire, was a respectable, well-known engraver. During Blake's seven-year apprenticeship, Basire dispatched him to London churches and Westminster Abbey to make copies of Gothic tombs and monuments. There, tucked away among vaults and spires,

Blake's study of Gothic architecture developed into fascination. After his apprenticeship, he was admitted to the Royal Academy of Arts, but he rejected artistic and literary trends of his time, instead gravitating towards Renaissance painters and Elizabethan writers. He began sharing his artwork and poetry for the general public to observe, but his pieces encountered only silence or negativity.

To support himself and Catherine (they had married in 1782), Blake eventually began an engraving business of his own. For a short time, his commissions reaped moderate prosperity. Blake illustrated scenes from the works of Milton, Dante, and the Bible. He taught Catherine to read, write, and engrave so that she could assist him with his work. Catherine became Blake's constant pupil and companion, as they had no children of their own. Blake prioritized his work, however, and could be a demanding, difficult husband at times. Although he described Catherine as an ideal wife, their marriage likely suffered from his expectations.

In 1800, William Hayley, a poet, biographer, and literary enthusiast, invited the Blakes to Felpham. Blake, accustomed to the atmosphere of London, relished the natural beauty of the land. Nevertheless, work as Hayley's protégé soon disagreed with Blake. In an effort to multiply Blake's profits and popularity, Hayley had feebly attempted to make the artist more conventional. Blake felt Hayley had trespassed in a sacred artistic, spiritual space; consequently, their relationship withered. Another trespass–this one literal, but just as distressing–occurred in 1803. Blake found John Schofield, a soldier in the Royal Dragoons, in his garden, and insisted that Schofield leave. The man, swearing and uttering threats against Blake and his wife, refused to go. The confrontation escalated until Blake forcibly pushed the soldier from his garden. Schofield charged Blake with assault, and, more dangerously, sedition. Due to the Napoleonic Wars between England and France, statements against the king or country warranted death. Blake was acquitted, but the incident was so harrowing that he left the idyllic seaside.

One of Blake's strengths, however, was his childlike trust in goodness. Even after he returned to London, he fondly recalled the serenity and splendor of Felpham. He sought to evoke a pastoral world of simplicity, beauty, and joy in his works. Innocence, unrestrained, animates many of his poems, especially those in *Songs of Innocence*. In 1794, he added a collection of companion poems to those he had already written, and, representing "two contrary states of the human soul," published *Songs of Innocence and Experience*. While the realm of *Innocence* portrays blissful ignorance, the speakers in *Experience* are conscious of and sometimes complicit in the corruption and oppression in the world. Blake juxtaposes these two perspectives using distinct poetic voices. In *Innocence*, he assumes the voice of the carefree piper; in *Experience*, he embraces the philosophical, disciplined bard. Poems such as "The Chimney-Sweeper" reexamine the same concept or situation, tracing how perception changes from childhood to adulthood, and highlight the differences in both views.

Blake's later works explore human history, innovation, and experience through a mythology of his own invention. Drawing inspiration and insight from biblical events, Blake's prophetic books depict various aspects of creation, the Fall, the fallen world, and redemption. Blake reframes biblical concepts; to him, the Fall he presents in *The Four Zoas* is not the fall of humanity from God as told in the Book of Genesis, but a "fall into Division." In Blake's mythology, the Universal Man sins and splits into separate entities, each representing a component of humanity or the natural world. Only an apocalypse, brought about by the efforts of the Redeemer, will restore the Universal Man to his original form.

Quixotic in character but firmly grounded in his beliefs, Blake refused to compromise the morals of his art. Blake's words, when paired with his designs, are unnerving, enlightening, and thought-provoking. His illustrations magnify the meaning of his poetry, contrasting light and shadow, spontaneity and meditation. His lyrical simplicity leaves much unsaid, inviting readers to engage their own imaginations and embrace his themes.

Unfortunately, Blake's poetry was not widely recognized during his lifetime. A handful of close friends were delighted when they read Blake's work or heard him sing his verses, but aside from these casual praises, he received virtually no attention from critics. Only *Poetical Sketches*, his most conventional work, and *Songs of Innocence and Experience* were discussed while he was alive. These volumes, though deemed original, were also considered wild and utterly incoherent. Even his contemporaries, who found his poetry engaging, admitted that much of it was bizarre. Blake's ideas were too innovative for their time. His engravings also reaped a range of responses, spanning from praise to indifference or hostility. Until the publication of Alexander Gilchrist's book *Life of William Blake, "Pictor Ignotus"* in 1863, Blake's poetry and artwork were essentially dismissed or ignored. Yet even Gilchrist's book could not help Blake's pieces find a wholly receptive audience. The beat poets, however, welcomed his poems, and Blake gained esteem as one of the most remarkable and talented engravers since the Renaissance. The twentieth century brought Blake artistic and literary acclaim.

1757	William Blake born 28 November
1768	Enters Henry Pars's drawing school
1772–79	Apprenticed to the engraver James Basire
1779	Attends Royal Academy School of Arts
1782	Marries Catherine Boucher
1783	*Poetical Sketches*
1788	*There is No Natural Religion; All Religions are One*
1789	*The Book of Thel; Songs of Innocence*
1790	*The Marriage of Heaven and Hell*
1793	*Visions of the Daughters of Albion; America: A Prophecy*
1794	*Europe: A Prophecy; The First Book of Urizen; Songs of Innocence and Experience*
1795	*The Song of Los; The Book of Los; The Book of Ahania*
1827	Blake dies 12 August, likely from gallbladder and liver failure, and is buried in an unmarked common grave in Bunhill Fields Burial Ground, London

SONGS OF INNOCENCE

INTRODUCTION

Piping down the valleys wild,
Piping songs of pleasant glee,
On a cloud I saw a child,
And he laughing said to me:—

"Pipe a song about a lamb:"   5
So I piped with merry cheer.
"Piper, pipe that song again:"
So I piped: he wept to hear.

"Drop thy pipe, thy happy pipe,
Sing thy songs of happy cheer:"   10
So I sung the same again,
While he wept with joy to hear.

"Piper, sit thee down and write
In a book, that all may read—"
So he vanished from my sight;   15
And I pluck'd a hollow reed,

And I made a rural pen,
And I stain'd the water clear,
And I wrote my happy songs
Every child may joy to hear.   20

[handwritten note, right margin] Language & vocab are simple, rhythm is sing-song-y; child-like

[handwritten note, bottom] *look up ingrave poem put picture of it on project*

THE LAMB

Little lamb, who made thee?
Dost thou know who made thee,
Gave thee life, and bid thee feed
By the stream and o'er the mead;
Gave thee clothing of delight,   5
Softest clothing, woolly, bright;
Gave thee such a tender voice
Making all the vales rejoice;
    Little lamb, who made thee?
    Dost thou know who made thee?   10

Little lamb, I'll tell thee,
Little lamb, I'll tell thee.
He is called by thy name,
For He calls himself a Lamb.
He is meek and He is mild,   15
He became a little child.
I a child and thou a lamb,
We are called by His name.
    Little lamb, God bless thee,
    Little lamb, God bless thee.   20

THE LITTLE BLACK BOY

My mother bore me in the southern wild,
And I am black, but oh! my soul is white;
White as an angel is the English child,
But I am black, as if bereaved of light.

My mother taught me underneath a tree, 5
And sitting down before the heat of day,
She took me on her lap and kissed me,
And, pointing to the east, began to say:—

"Look on the rising sun,—there God does live,
And gives His light, and gives His heat away; 10
And flowers, and trees, and beast, and men receive
Comfort in morning, joy in the noon-day.

"And we are put on earth a little space,
That we may learn to bear the beams of love;
And these black bodies and this sun-burnt face 15
Are but a cloud, and like a shady grove.

"For when our souls have learnt the heat to bear,
The clouds will vanish, we shall hear His voice,
Saying, 'Come out from the grove, my love and care,
And round my golden tent like lambs rejoice.'" 20

Thus did my mother say, and kissed me;
And thus I say to little English boy,—
"When I from black, and he from white cloud free,
And round the tent of God like lambs we joy,

"I'll shade him from the heat, till he can bear 25
To lean in joy upon our Father's knee;
And then I'll stand, and stroke his silver hair,
And be like him, and he will then love me."

[Handwritten annotation: negative portrayal of blackness, notion that whiteness is ideal; not questioning or critiquing racism bc of state of innocence]

[Handwritten annotation, left margin: mother + child talking]

[Handwritten annotation, bottom: Even boy's conception of heaven is unequal; even here, he's a servant]

THE CHIMNEY-SWEEPER

When my mother died I was very young,
And my father sold me while yet my tongue
Could scarcely cry "'weep, 'weep, 'weep, 'weep!"
So your chimneys I sweep and in soot I sleep.

There's little Tom Dacre, who cried when his head,   5
That curl'd like a lamb's back, was shaved; so I said:
"Hush, Tom, never mind it, for when your head's bare,
You know that the soot cannot spoil your white hair."

And so he was quiet; and that very night,
As Tom was a-sleeping, he had such a sight;   10
That thousands of sweepers, Dick, Joe, Ned, and Jack,
Were all of them lock'd up in coffins of black.

And by came an angel who had a bright key,
And he open'd the coffins and set them all free;
Then down a green plain, leaping, laughing, they run,   15
And wash in a river and shine in the sun.

Then naked and white, all their bags left behind,
They rise upon clouds and sport in the wind;
And the angel told Tom, if he'd be a good boy,
He'd have God for his father and never want joy.   20

And so Tom awoke; and we rose in the dark,
And got with our bags and our brushes to work.
Though the morning was cold Tom was happy and warm:
So if all do their duty they need not fear harm.

Handwritten annotations:

*The happy kids are in heaven

*This son can't be living in bad conditions

*The kids were all a dream spin in heaven, were actually living in bad conditions

*The tone of the poem doesn't match the true meaning of the poem?

> State of innocence

*The kids died from lung problems

*They used kids as chimney-sweeps because they were small and could fit in the chimney

*Clunk logic

— Included in Songs of innocence bc child, in state of innocence, doesn't understand what's wrong w/ this situation

↳ Innocence ≠ world w/out problems, it = lack of perspective to question & confront problems

HOLY THURSDAY

'Twas on a holy Thursday, their innocent faces clean,
The children walking two and two, in red and blue and green,
Grey-headed beadles walk'd before, with wands as white as snow,
Till into the high dome of Paul's they like Thames' waters flow.
O what a multitude they seem'd, these flowers of London town;   5
Seated in companies, they sit with radiance all their own.
The hum of multitudes was there, but multitudes of lambs,
Thousands of little boys and girls raising their innocent hands.

Now like a mighty wind they raise to heaven the voice of song,
Or like harmonious thunderings the seats of heaven among.   10
Beneath them sit the aged men, wise guardians of the poor;
Then cherish pity, lest you drive an angel from your door.

INFANT JOY

I have no name,
I am but two days old.
What shall I call thee?
I happy am,
Joy is my name.—   5
Sweet joy befall thee!

Pretty joy!
Sweet joy but two days old.
Sweet joy I call thee.
Thou dost smile,   10
I sing the while,
Sweet joy befall thee!

SONGS OF EXPERIENCE

INTRODUCTION

Hear the voice of the Bard,
Who present, past, and future sees;
Whose ears have heard
The Holy Word

That walk'd among the ancient trees.   5
   Calling the lapsed soul,
And weeping in the evening dew;
     That might control
     The starry pole,

And fallen, fallen light renew!   10
   O Earth, O Earth, return!
Arise from out the dewy grass;
     Night is worn;
     And the morn
Rises from the slumbrous mass.   15

   Turn away no more:
Why wilt thou turn away?
     The starry floor,
     The watery shore,
Is given thee till the break of day.   20

INFANT SORROW

My mother groan'd, my father wept,
Into the dangerous world I leapt;
Helpless, naked, piping loud,
Like a fiend hid in a cloud.

Struggling in my father's hands,   5
Striving against my swaddling-bands,
Bound and weary, I thought best
To sulk upon my mother's breast.

*Reality of having a child;
contrasts w/ Infant Joy's
idealism*

THE SICK ROSE

O rose, thou art sick:
The invisible worm,
That flies in the night
In the howling storm,

Has found out thy bed   5
Of crimson joy;
And his dark secret love
Does thy life destroy.

THE TIGER

Tiger, tiger, burning bright
In the forests of the night,
What immortal hand or eye
Could frame thy fearful symmetry?

In what distant deeps or skies   5
Burnt the fire of thine eyes?
On what wings dare he aspire?
What the hand dare seize the fire?

And what shoulder, and what art,
Could twist the sinews of thy heart   10
And when thy heart began to beat,
What dread hand? and what dread feet
 What the hammer? what the chain?

In what furnace was thy brain?
What the anvil? what dread grasp   15
Dare its deadly terrors clasp?

When the stars threw down their spears,
And water'd heaven with their tears,
Did He smile His work to see?
Did He who made the lamb make thee?   20

Tiger, tiger, burning bright
In the forests of the night,
What immortal hand or eye
Dare frame thy fearful symmetry? → *Blake literally does in engravings*

- All questions w/ no overt answers;
contrasts "The Lamb"
- Language evokes hell/hellish imagery

Poem asks who God is, Blake answers w/ "humanity" ← Highlights human capacity for creation, links it w/ the divine

HOLY THURSDAY

Is this a holy thing to see
   In a rich and fruitful land,
Babes reduced to misery,
   Fed with cold and usurous hand?

Is that trembling cry a song? 5
   Can it be a song of joy?
And so many children poor?
   It is a land of poverty!

And their sun does never shine,
   And their fields are bleak and bare. 10
And their ways are filled with thorns:
   It is eternal winter there.

For where'er the sun does shine,
   And where'er the rain does fall,
Babe can never hunger there, 15
   Nor poverty the mind appal.

LONDON

I wander thro' each charter'd street
   Near where the charter'd Thames does flow,
And mark in every face I meet
   Marks of weakness, marks of woe.

In every cry of every man,   5
   In every infant's cry of fear,
In every voice, in every ban,
   The mind-forged manacles I hear.

How the chimney-sweeper's cry
   Every blackening church appals;   10
And the hapless soldier's sigh
   Runs in blood down palace-walls.

But most thro' midnight streets I hear
   How the youthful harlot's curse
Blasts the new-born infant's tear,   15
   And blights with plagues the marriage hearse.

The Child sees the problem of the world

THE CHIMNEY-SWEEPER

A little black thing among the snow,
  Crying, "'weep! 'weep!" in notes of woe:
Where are thy father and mother, say?
—They are both gone up to the church to pray.

Because I was happy upon the heath,   5
  And smiled among the winter's snow,
They clothed me in the clothes of death,
  And taught me to sing the notes of woe.

brings up religion

And because I am happy, and dance and sing,
  They think they have done me no injury,
And are gone to praise God and His Priest and King,   10
  Who make up a heaven of our misery.

The parents caused harm to the child.

Since they Made him work this too.

* Different point of view, from the first Chimney Sweeper.

* This kid is not in the state of innocence

A POISON-TREE

I was angry with my friend;
I told my wrath, my wrath did end.
I was angry with my foe;
I told it not, my wrath did grow.

And I water'd it in fears   5
Night and morning with my tears;
And I sunned it with smiles
And with soft deceitful wiles.

And it grew both day and night,
Till it bore an apple bright;   10
And my foe beheld it shine,
And he knew that it was mine,

And into my garden stole
When the night had veil'd the pole:
In the morning glad I see   15
My foe outstretch'd beneath the tree.

1794

William Wordsworth
1770–1850

William Wordsworth was born in Cockermouth, a village nestled among the rugged hills of the northern English Lake District. Of the five Wordsworth children, only young William concerned his mother; he was inflexible and temperamental. She once told a friend that he "would be remarkable for either good or evil." She died when he was eight years old, and he was sent to a grammar school in Hawkshead along with his three brothers. Well-liked by his peers, his school years passed pleasantly, and he received a respectable education in mathematics and literature. Spending much of his time outdoors, Wordsworth hunted, fished, sailed, and skated as often as he could. He also read constantly and memorized passages of Shakespeare, Spenser, and Milton to later recite to his father.

Wordsworth's father, John Wordsworth, worked as a lawyer for James Lowther, the Earl of Lonsdale and a notoriously harsh nobleman. When John Wordsworth suddenly died in 1783, he left his children the sizeable sum owed to him by Lowther, but the Earl had yet to pay the debt. The family was unable to claim the money for nearly twenty years. At thirteen years old, Wordsworth was orphaned and virtually penniless. He attended St. John's College, University of Cambridge, thanks to the generosity of two uncles, but the university's competitive atmosphere repulsed him. Feeling that he "was not for that hour, nor for that place," Wordsworth graduated without distinction in 1791.

Prior to graduating, Wordsworth and his friend Robert Jones took a walking tour of France before continuing across the Alps. The fall of the Bastille had occurred a year before their visit, and the spirit of the French Revolution impassioned Wordsworth. When he returned to France in November 1791, he once again championed liberty, equality, and other republican principles. While visiting Blois, he fell in love with a Frenchwoman named Annette Vallon, and the two planned to marry. Insufficient funds drove Wordsworth from France in December 1792, forcing him to leave Annette unwed and their baby daughter, Caroline, without her biological father. Once back in London, he faced the stress of his divided loyalties. He felt alienated from both countries: England, for waging war against ideals he supported; France, for failing to bring those ideals to realization. The war also barred him from seeing his family for a decade. Distraught and wrought with turmoil, Wordsworth neared an emotional breakdown.

Wordsworth's life and poetic career were drastically altered in 1795 when he and his sister, Dorothy, first met Samuel Taylor Coleridge. Coleridge had walked some fifty miles to meet the Wordsworths at their house at Racedown, Dorsetshire. They formed an immediate and profound friendship. The Wordsworths relocated to Alfoxden House, Somersetshire, two years later. Since the house was near Coleridge's residence, the poets interacted almost every day. Walking, writing, and talking for hours, Wordsworth and Coleridge flourished in each other's company. Though their styles and work ethics differed, their collaborations proved successful. In 1798, they anonymously published *Lyrical Ballads, with a Few Other Poems*. Despite criticism from reviewers, the book sold out two years later. Wordsworth published a new edition under his name, adding a second volume of poems and the Preface in which he addresses the reasons behind his "experiments": to explain what poetry should be and do, to illustrate the value of nature, and to praise people who lead a simple life close to the natural world.

Wordsworth established a renewed and revolutionary attitude toward nature in his writing. Nature evolved into his metaphor for God and his means of explaining the "growth of a poet's mind," as he did in his long autobiographical poem, *The Prelude*. He usually presented nature as a benevolent force and source of moral goodness. His perspective, however, likely darkened after his favorite brother drowned at sea in 1805. The contrast between nature as compassionate toward human life or cruelly indifferent, as well as a connection between the human mind and the natural world, appears in modern environmentalist works.

Some of Wordsworth's most powerful poetry embodies his turbulent emotions, doubtlessly raised by the joys and afflictions of his later life. Wordsworth had been wracked with guilt for abandoning Annette and Caroline for years, and in 1802, he returned to France to make arrangements for their welfare. Later that year, he married Mary Hutchinson, whom he had known since childhood. They had five children, but only three survived to adulthood; a son and a daughter died in 1812. Wordsworth also lost his friendship with Coleridge. Vicious disputes between the two poets caused their correspondence to dissolve, and animosity between them went unresolved for nearly twenty years. Around the time that Wordsworth and Coleridge made amends, Dorothy was struck with mental and physical illness. Her ailments intensified until she became a senile invalid. Amid these troubles, Wordsworth's reputation prospered. Acknowledged as an illustrious man of letters, he accepted the post of Poet Laureate.

Wordsworth's legacy is not confined to his literary works alone. Cockermouth, as well as the surrounding regions of the English Lake District, was permanently shaped by the Romantic ideals that formed there. The area became a poetic center due to Wordsworth's and Coleridge's efforts. "Poetry," Wordsworth decreed in the Preface to *Lyrical Ballads*, "is the image of man and nature." It is through nature, Wordsworth persisted, that people can better understand themselves. Introspection, emotion, and creativity, as inspired by the natural world, became foundational to Romanticism.

1770	William Wordsworth born 7 April
1787–91	Attends St. John's College, University of Cambridge
1790	Walking tour of France and the Alps with Robert Jones
1793	*The Evening Walk; Descriptive Sketches*
1798	*Lyrical Ballads, with a Few Other Poems*, which included "The Thorn" and "Lines Composed a Few Miles above Tintern Abbey"
1800	"Nutting"
1802	Marries Mary Hutchinson
1812	Two of the Wordsworths' children, a boy and a girl, die
1843	Accepts post of Poet Laureate
1850	Wordsworth dies 23 April due to pleurisy; *The Prelude*

*about death
*Two children have
died. so there is
only 5 of them
but the little
girl keep
saying their
is still 7
of them

*1 girl and
1 boy have
died

*The guy keeps
getting mad
at the girl
for saying that
their is 7
of children

*she wants to
keep her siblings
alive.

WE ARE SEVEN

————A simple Child,
That lightly draws its breath,
And feels its life in every limb,
What should it know of death?

I met a little cottage Girl: 5
She was eight years old, she said;
Her hair was thick with many a curl
That clustered round her head.

She had a rustic, woodland air,
And she was wildly clad: 10
Her eyes were fair, and very fair:
—Her beauty made me glad.

"Sisters and brothers, little Maid,
How many may you be?"
"How many? Seven in all," she said,   15
And wondering looked at me.

"And where are they? I pray you tell."
She answered, "Seven are we;
And two of us at Conway dwell,
And two are gone to sea.   20

"Two of us in the churchyard lie,
My sister and my brother;
And, in the churchyard cottage, I
Dwell near them with my mother."

"You say that two at Conway dwell,   25
And two are gone to sea,
Yet ye are seven! I pray you tell,
Sweet Maid, how this may be."

Then did the little Maid reply,
"Seven boys and girls are we: 30
Two of us in the churchyard lie,
Beneath the churchyard tree."

"You run about, my little Maid,
Your limbs they are alive;
If two are in the churchyard laid,   35
Then ye are only five."

"Their graves are green, they may be seen,"
The little Maid replied,
"Twelve steps or more from my mother's door,
And they are side by side.   40

"My stockings there I often knit,
My kerchief there I hem;
And there upon the ground I sit,
And sing a song to them.

"And often after sunset, sir,   45
When it is light and fair,
I take my little porringer,
And eat my supper there.

"The first that died was sister Jane;
In bed she moaning lay,   50
Till God released her of her pain,
And then she went away.

"So in the churchyard she was laid;
And, when the grass was dry,
Together round her grave we played,   55
My brother John and I.

"And when the ground was white with snow,
And I could run and slide,
My brother John was forced to go,
And he lies by her side."   60

"How many are you then," said I,
"If they two are in heaven?"
Quick was the little Maid's reply,
"O Master! we are seven."

"But they are dead; those two are dead!   65
Their spirits are in heaven!"
'Twas throwing words away; for still
The little Maid would have her will,
And said, "Nay, we are seven!"

1798

THE THORN

⤷ Hawthorn tree

I.

"There is a thorn—it looks so old,
In truth, you'd find it hard to say
How it could ever have been young,
It looks so old and grey.
Not higher than a two-years' child
It stands erect, this aged Thorn;
No leaves it has, no prickly points;
It is a mass of knotted joints,
A wretched thing forlorn.
It stands erect, and like a stone   10
With lichens it is overgrown.

Thorn personified, representative of Martha Ray

✱ She is crazy
✱ Tumor. The baby is buried underneath the thorn

II.

Like rock or stone, it is o'ergrown,
With lichens to the very top,
And hung with heavy tufts of moss,
A melancholy crop: 15

Up from the earth these mosses creep,
And this poor Thorn they clasp it round
So close, you'd say that they were bent
With plain and manifest intent
To drag it to the ground; 20
And all had joined in one endeavor
To bury this poor Thorn for ever.

III.

High on a mountain's highest ridge,
Where oft the stormy winter gale
Cuts like a scythe, while through the clouds 25
It sweeps from vale to vale;
Not five yards from the mountain path,
This Thorn you on your left espy;
And to the left, three yards beyond,
You see a little muddy pond 30
Of water—never dry
Though but of compass small, and bare
To thirsty suns and parching air.

IV.

And, close beside this aged Thorn,
There is a fresh and lovely sight, 35
A beauteous heap, a hill of moss,
Just half a foot in height.
All lovely colours there you see,
All colours that were ever seen;
And mossy network too is there, 40
As if by hand of lady fair
The work had woven been;
And cups, the darlings of the eye,
So deep is their vermilion dye.

V.

Ah me! what lovely tints are there 45
Of olive green and scarlet bright,
In spikes, in branches, and in stars,
Green, red, and pearly white!
This heap of earth o'ergrown with moss,

Which close beside the Thorn you see,   50
So fresh in all its beauteous dyes,
Is like an infant's grave in size
As like as like can be:
But never, never any where,
An infant's grave was half so fair.   55

Foreshadowing (handwritten margin note)

VI.

Now would you see this aged Thorn,
This pond, and beauteous hill of moss,
You must take care and choose your time
The mountain when to cross.
For oft there sits between the heap   60
So like an infant's grave in size,
And that same pond of which I spoke,
A Woman in a scarlet cloak,
And to herself she cries,
'Oh misery! oh misery!   65
Oh woe is me! oh misery!'

VII.

At all times of the day and night
This wretched woman thither goes;
And she is known to every star,
And every wind that blows;   70
And there, beside the Thorn she sits
When the blue daylight's in the skies,
And when the whirlwind's on the hill,
Or frosty air is keen and still,
And to herself she cries,   75
'Oh misery! oh misery!
Oh woe is me! oh misery!'"

VIII.

"Now wherefore, thus, by day and night,
In rain, in tempest, and in snow,
Thus to the dreary mountain-top   80
Does this poor woman go?
And why sits she beside the Thorn
When the blue daylight's in the sky

diff speaker (2) (handwritten margin note)

Or when the whirlwind's on the hill,
Or frosty air is keen and still,   85
And wherefore does she cry?—
O wherefore? wherefore? tell me why
Does she repeat that doleful cry?"

IX.

"I cannot tell; I wish I could;
For the true reason no one knows: 90
But if you'd gladly view the spot,
The spot to which she goes;
The heap that's like an infant's grave,
The pond—and Thorn, so old and grey;
Pass by her door—'tis seldom shut—   95
And, if you see her in her hut—
Then to the spot away!
I never heard of such as dare
Approach the spot when she is there."

X.

"But wherefore to the mountain-top   100
Can this unhappy Woman go,
Whatever star is in the skies,
Whatever wind may blow?"
"Full twenty years are past and gone
Since she (her name is Martha Ray)   105
Gave with a maiden's true good-will
Her company to Stephen Hill;
And she was blithe and gay,
While friends and kindred all approved
Of him whom tenderly she loved.   110

XI.

And they had fix'd the wedding-day,
The morning that must wed them both;
But Stephen to another Maid
Had sworn another oath;
And, with this other Maid to church   115
Unthinking Stephen went—
Poor Martha! On that woeful day

A pang of pitiless dismay
Into her soul was sent;
A fire was kindled in her breast,   120
Whiich might not burn itself to rest.

XII.

They say, full six months after this,
While yet the summer-leaves were green,
She to the mountain-top would go,
And there was often seen.   125
What could she seek?—or wish to hide?
Her state to any eye was plain;
She was with child, and she was mad;
Yet often was she sober sad
From her exceeding pain.   130
O guilty Father—would that death
Had saved him from that breach of faith!

XIII.

Sad case for such a brain to hold
Communion with a stirring child!
Sad case, as you may think, for one   135
Who had a brain so wild!
Last Christmas-eve we talked of this,
And grey-haired Wilfred of the glen
Held that the unborn infant wrought
About its mother's heart, and brought   140
Her senses back again:
And, when at last her time drew near,
Her looks were calm, her senses clear.

XIV.

More know I not, I wish I did,
Andit should all be told to you;   145
For what became of this poor child
No mortal ever knew;
Nay—if a child to her was born
No earthly tongue could ever tell;
And if 'twas born alive or dead,   150
Far less could this with proof be said;

But some remember well,
That Martha Ray about this time
Would up the mountain often climb.

XV.

And all that winter, when at night   155
The wind blew from the mountain-peak,
'Twas worth your while, though in the dark,
The churchyard path to seek:
For many a time and oft were heard
Cries coming from the mountain-head: 160
Some plainly living voices were;
And others, I've heard many swear,
Were voices of the dead:
I cannot think, whate'er they say,
They had to do with Martha Ray.   165

XVI.

But that she goes to this old Thorn,
The Thorn which I described to you,
And there sits in a scarlet cloak,
I will be sworn is true.
For one day with my telescope,   170
To view the ocean wide and bright,
When to this country first I came,
Ere I had heard of Martha's name,
I climbed the mountain's height:—
A storm came on, and I could see   175
No object higher than my knee.

XVII.

'Twas mist and rain, and storm and rain:
No screen, no fence could I discover;
And then the wind! in sooth, it was
A wind full ten times over.   180
I looked around, I thought I saw
A jutting crag,—and off I ran,
Head-foremost, through the driving rain,
The shelter of the crag to gain;
And, as I am a man,   185

Instead of jutting crag, I found
A Woman seated on the ground.

XVIII.

I did not speak—I saw her face;
Her face!—it was enough for me;
I turned about and heard her cry,   190
'Oh misery! oh misery!'
And there she sits, until the moon
Through half the clear blue sky will go;
And, when the little breezes make
The waters of the pond to shake,   195
As all the country know,
She shudders, and you hear her cry,
'Oh misery! oh misery!'"

XIX.

"But what's the Thorn? and what the pond?
And what the hill of moss to her?   200
And what the creeping breeze that comes
The little pond to stir?"
"I cannot tell; but some will say
She hanged her baby on the tree;
Some say she drowned it in the pond,   205
Which is a little step beyond:
But all and each agree,
The little Babe was buried there,
Beneath that hill of moss so fair.

XX.

I've heard, the moss is spotted red   210
With drops of that poor infant's blood;
But kill a new-born infant thus,
I do not think she could!
Some say, if to the pond you go,
And fix on it a steady view,   215
The shadow of a babe you trace,
A baby and a baby's face,
And that it looks at you;
Whene'er you look on it, 'tis plain
The baby looks at you again.   220

XXI.

And some had sworn an oath that she
Should be to public justice brought;
And for the little infant's bones
With spades they would have sought.
But instantly the hill of moss   225
Before their eyes began to stir!
And, for full fifty yards around,
The grass—it shook upon the ground!
But all do still aver
The little Babe lies buried there,   230
Beneath that hill of moss so fair.

XXII.

I cannot tell how this may be
But plain it is the Thorn is bound
With heavy tufts of moss that strive
To drag it to the ground;   235
And this I know, full many a time,
When she was on the mountain high,
By day, and in the silent night,
When all the stars shone clear and bright,
That I have heard her cry,   240
'O misery! oh misery!
'Oh woe is me! oh misery!'"

1798

- Reads like a folk tale (ties into
  themes of rustic life)
- Dead still impact the present
  (same theme of "We are Seven")
- Theme of nature
  ↳ Townsfolk not as connected w/ it,
     but make up many stories about it
- Theme of imagination ←

[handwritten: He is writing in blank verse]

LINES,

COMPOSED A FEW MILES ABOVE TINTERN ABBEY, ON REVISITING THE BANKS OF THE WYE DURING A TOUR

JULY 13, 1798

[handwritten: This section is just setting the setting.]

Five years have passed; five summers, with the length
Of five long winters! and again I hear
These waters, rolling from their mountain-springs
With a soft inland murmur. —Once again
Do I behold these steep and lofty cliffs,   5
That on a wild secluded scene impress
Thoughts of more deep seclusion; and connect
The landscape with the quiet of the sky.
The day is come when I again repose
Here, under this dark sycamore, and view   10
These plots of cottage-ground, these orchard-tufts,
Which at this season, with their unripe fruits,
Are clad in one green hue, and lose themselves
'Mid groves and copses. Once again I see
These hedge-rows, hardly hedge-rows, little lines   15
Of sportive wood run wild: these pastoral farms

[handwritten: He has come back with her and allowing her to enjoy the same place he used to enjoy.]

Green to the very door; and wreaths of smoke
Sent up, in silence, from among the trees!
With some uncertain notice, as might seem,
Of vagrant dwellers in the houseless woods,   20
Or of some Hermit's cave, where by his fire
The Hermit sits alone.

                              These beauteous forms,
Through a long absence, have not been to me
As is a landscape to a blind man's eye:
But oft, in lonely rooms, and 'mid the din   25
Of towns and cities, I have owed to them
In hours of weariness, sensations sweet,
Felt in the blood, and felt along the heart;
And passing even into my purer mind,
With tranquil restoration:—feelings too   30

[handwritten: He can restore those feelings by using his imagination.]

Of unremembered pleasure: such, perhaps,
As have no slight or trivial influence
On that best portion of a good man's life,
His little, nameless, unremembered, acts
Of kindness and of love. Nor less, I trust,   35
To them I may have owed another gift,
Of aspect more sublime; that blessed mood,
In which the burthen of the mystery,
In which the heavy and the weary weight
Of all this unintelligible world   40
Is lightened:—that serene and blessed mood,
In which the affections gently lead us on,—
Until, the breath of this corporeal frame
And even the motion of our human blood
Almost suspended, we are laid asleep   45
In body, and become a living soul:
While with an eye made quiet by the power
Of harmony, and the deep power of joy,
We see into the life of things.

                         If this
Be but a vain belief, yet, oh! how oft—   50
In darkness and amid the many shapes
Of joyless daylight; when the fretful stir
Unprofitable, and the fever of the world,
Have hung upon the beatings of my heart—
How oft, in spirit, have I turned to thee   55
O sylvan Wye! thou wanderer thro' the woods,
How often has my spirit turned to thee!

    And now, with gleams of half-extinguished thought,
With many recognitions dim and faint,
And somewhat of a sad perplexity,   60
The picture of the mind revives again:
While here I stand, not only with the sense
Of present pleasure, but with pleasing thoughts
That in this moment there is life and food
For future years. And so I dare to hope,   65
Though changed, no doubt, from what I was when first
I came among these hills; when like a roe
I bounded o'er the mountains, by the sides

Of the deep rivers, and the lonely streams,
Wherever nature led: more like a man   70
Flying from something that he dreads, than one
Who sought the thing he loved. For nature then
(The coarser pleasures of my boyish days,
And their glad animal movements all gone by)
To me was all in all.—I cannot paint   75
What then I was. The sounding cataract
Haunted me like a passion: the tall rock,
The mountain, and the deep and gloomy wood,
Their colours and their forms, were then to me
An appetite; a feeling and a love,   80
That had no need of a remoter charm,
By thought supplied, or any interest
Unborrowed from the eye.—That time is past,
And all its aching joys are now no more,
And all its dizzy raptures. Not for this   85
Faint I, nor mourn nor murmur; other gifts
Have followed; for such loss, I would believe,
Abundant recompence. For I have learned
To look on nature, not as in the hour
Of thoughtless youth, but hearing oftentimes   90
The still, sad music of humanity,
Not harsh nor grating, though of ample power
To chasten and subdue. And I have felt
A presence that disturbs me with the joy
Of elevated thoughts; a sense sublime   95
Of something far more deeply interfused,
Whose dwelling is the light of setting suns,
And the round ocean and the living air,
And the blue sky, and in the mind of man:
A motion and a spirit, that impels   100
All thinking things, all objects of all thought,
And rolls through all things. Therefore am I still
A lover of the meadows and the woods,
And mountains; and of all that we behold
From this green earth; of all the mighty world   105
Of eye and ear,—both what they half create,
And what perceive; well pleased to recognise
In nature and the language of the sense,
The anchor of my purest thoughts, the nurse,

The guide, the guardian of my heart, and soul   110
Of all my moral being.

                         Nor, perchance,
If I were not thus taught, should I the more
Suffer my genial spirits to decay:
For thou art with me here upon the banks
Of this fair river; thou my dearest Friend,   115
My dear, dear Friend; and in thy voice I catch
The language of my former heart, and read
My former pleasures in the shooting lights
Of thy wild eyes. Oh! yet a little while
May I behold in thee what I was once,   120
My dear, dear Sister! and this prayer I make,
Knowing that Nature never did betray
The heart that loved her; 'tis her privilege,
Through all the years of this our life, to lead
From joy to joy: for she can so inform   125
The mind that is within us, so impress
With quietness and beauty, and so feed
With lofty thoughts, that neither evil tongues,
Rash judgments, nor the sneers of selfish men,
Nor greetings where no kindness is, nor all   130
The dreary intercourse of daily life,
Shall e'er prevail against us, or disturb
Our chearful faith, that all which we behold
Is full of blessings. Therefore let the moon
Shine on thee in thy solitary walk;   135
And let the misty mountain-winds be free
To blow against thee: and, in after years,
When these wild ecstasies shall be matured
Into a sober pleasure; when thy mind
Shall be a mansion for all lovely forms,   140
Thy memory be as a dwelling-place
For all sweet sounds and harmonies; oh! then,
If solitude, or fear, or pain, or grief,
Should be thy portion, with what healing thoughts
Of tender joy wilt thou remember me,   145
And these my exhortations! Nor, perchance—
If I should be where I no more can hear
Thy voice, nor catch from thy wild eyes these gleams

Of past existence—wilt thou then forget
That on the banks of this delightful stream　　　　　150
We stood together; and that I, so long
A worshipper of Nature, hither came
Unwearied in that service: rather say
With warmer love—oh! with far deeper zeal
Of holier love. Nor wilt thou then forget,　　　　　155
That after many wanderings, many years
Of absence, these steep woods and lofty cliffs,
And this green pastoral landscape, were to me
More dear, both for themselves and for thy sake.

1798

it's all about him [handwritten]

Again shows he thinks he's superior, that he's the only one who can fully appreciate nature [handwritten]

Means gathering nuts [handwritten]

NUTTING

————————It seems a day
(I speak of one from many singled out)
One of those heavenly days that cannot die;
When, in the eagerness of boyish hope,
I left our cottage-threshold, sallying forth　　　　　5
With a huge wallet o'er my shoulders slung,
A nutting-crook in hand; and turned my steps
Tow'rd some far-distant wood, a Figure quaint,
Tricked out in proud disguise of cast-off weeds
Which for that service had been husbanded,　　　　　10
By exhortation of my frugal Dame—
Motley accoutrement, of power to smile
At thorns, and brakes, and brambles,—and, in truth,
More ragged than need was! O'er pathless rocks,
Through beds of matted fern, and tangled thickets,　　　　　15
Forcing my way, I came to one dear nook
Unvisited, where not a broken bough

Drooped with its withered leaves, ungracious sign
Of devastation; but the hazels rose
Tall and erect, with tempting clusters hung,   20
A virgin scene!—A little while I stood,
Breathing with such suppression of the heart
As joy delights in; and, with wise restraint
Voluptuous, fearless of a rival, eyed
The banquet;—or beneath the trees I sate   25
Among the flowers, and with the flowers I played;
A temper known to those, who, after long
And weary expectation, have been blest
With sudden happiness beyond all hope.
Perhaps it was a bower beneath whose leaves   30
The violets of five seasons re-appear
And fade, unseen by any human eye;
Where fairy water-breaks do murmur on
For ever; and I saw the sparkling foam,
And—with my cheek on one of those green stones   35
That, fleeced with moss, under the shady trees,
Lay round me, scattered like a flock of sheep—
I heard the murmur and the murmuring sound,
In that sweet mood when pleasure loves to pay
Tribute to ease; and, of its joy secure,   40
The heart luxuriates with indifferent things,
Wasting its kindliness on stocks and stones,
And on the vacant air. Then up I rose,
And dragged to earth both branch and bough, with crash
And merciless ravage: and the shady nook   45
Of hazels, and the green and mossy bower,
Deformed and sullied, patiently gave up
Their quiet being: and, unless I now
Confound my present feelings with the past;
Ere from the mutilated bower I turned   50
Exulting, rich beyond the wealth of kings,
I felt a sense of pain when I beheld
The silent trees, and saw the intruding sky.—
Then, dearest Maiden, move along these shades
In gentleness of heart; with gentle hand   55
Touch—for there is a spirit in the woods.

1799

The emotions are pure

PREFACE TO LYRICAL BALLADS

THE FIRST VOLUME of these Poems has already been submitted to general perusal. It was published as an experiment, which, I hoped, might be of some use to ascertain, how far, by fitting to Metrical arrangement a selection of the real language of men in a state of vivid sensation, that sort of pleasure and that quantity of pleasure may be imparted, which a Poet may rationally endeavour to impart.

I had formed no very inaccurate estimate of the probable effect of those Poems: I flattered myself, that they who should be pleased with them would read them with more than common pleasure; and on the other hand I was well aware, that by those who should dislike them they would be read with more than common dislike. The result has differed from my expectation in this only, that I have pleased a greater number than I ventured to hope I should please.

For the sake of variety, and from a consciousness of my own weakness, I was induced to request the assistance of a friend, who furnished me with the Poems of the ANCIENT MARINER, the FOSTER MOTHER'S TALE, the NIGHTINGALE, the DUNGEON, and the Poem entitled LOVE. I should not however, have requested this assistance, had I not believed, that the Poems of my friend would, in a great measure have the same tendency as my own, and that though there would be found a difference, there would be found no discordance in the colours of our style; as our opinions on the subject of Poetry do almost entirely coincide.

Several of my friends are anxious for the success of these Poems from a belief, that if the views with which they were composed were indeed realized, a Class of Poetry would be produced, well adapted to interest mankind permanently, and not unimportant in the multiplicity, and in the quality of its moral relations; and on this account, they have advised me to prefix a systematic defence of the theory upon which the Poems were written. But I was unwilling to undertake the task, because I knew that on this occasion, the Reader would look coldly upon my arguments, since I might be suspected of having been principally influenced by the selfish, and foolish hope, of *reasoning* him into an approbation of these particular Poems; and I was still more unwilling to undertake the task, because, adequately to display my opinions, and fully to enforce my arguments, would require a space wholly disproportionate to the nature of a Preface. For to treat the subject with the clearness and coherence, of which I believe it susceptible, it would be necessary, to give a full account of the present state of the public taste in this country, and to determine how far this taste is healthy or depraved; which again

Believes his invented this type of poetry / romantic poetry

could not be determined, without pointing out in what manner language and the human mind act and re-act on each other, and without retracing the revolutions, not of literature alone, but likewise of society itself. I have therefore altogether declined to enter regularly upon this defence; yet I am sensible, that there would be some impropriety in abruptly obtruding upon the Public, without a few words of introduction, Poems so materially different from those, upon which general approbation is at present bestowed.

It is supposed, that by the act of writing in Verse, an Author makes a formal engagement that he will gratify certain known habits of association; that he not only thus apprizes the Reader that certain classes of ideas and expressions will be found in his book, but that others will be carefully excluded. This exponent or symbol held forth by Metrical language, must in different eras of literature have excited very different expectations: for example, in the age of Catullus, Terence, and Lucretius, and that of Statius or Claudian, and in our own country in the age of Shakespeare, and Beaumont and Fletcher, and that of Donne and Cowley, or Dryden, or Pope. I will not take upon me to determine the exact import of the promise which, by the act of writing in Verse, an Author in the present day makes to his Reader; but I am certain it will appear to many persons, that I have not fulfilled the terms of an engagement thus voluntarily contracted. I hope therefore the Reader will not censure me, if I attempt to state what I have proposed to myself to perform, and also (as far as the limits of a Preface will permit) to explain some of the chief reasons which have determined me in the choice of my purpose; that at least he may be spared any unpleasant feeling of disappointment, and that I myself may be protected from the most dishonorable accusation which can be brought against an Author, namely, that of an indolence which prevents him from endeavoring to ascertain what is his duty, or when his duty is ascertained, prevents him from performing it.

The principal object then which I proposed to myself in these Poems was, to chuse incidents of common life interesting, by tracing in them, truly, though not ostentatiously, the primary laws of our Nature; chiefly as far as regards the manner in which we associate ideas in a state of excitement. Low and rustic life was generally chosen, because in that condition, the essential passions of the heart find a better soil in which they can attain their maturity, are less under restraint, and speak a plainer and more emphatic language; because, in that situation, our elementary feelings exist in a state of greater simplicity, and consequently, may be more accurately contemplated, and more forcibly communicated; because, the manners of rural life germinate from those elementary feelings; and from the necessary character of rural occupations are more easily comprehended; and are more durable; and lastly, because, in that situation, the passions of men are incorporated with the beautiful and permanent forms of nature. The language too of these men is adopted (purified indeed from what appear to be its real defects, from all lasting

→ Self agrandizing, egotistical, mysoginistic

Believes he's one of very few people who can feel it/ think so deeply →

A true poet (to him) is a man w/ much sensibility who thinks long & hard about it

and rational causes of dislike or disgust) because such men hourly communicate with the best objects from which the best part of language is originally derived; and because, from their rank in society, and the sameness and narrow circle of their intercourse, being less under the action of social vanity, they convey their feelings and notions in simple and unelaborated expressions. Accordingly, such a language arising out of repeated experience and regular feelings is a more permanent, and a far more philosophical language, than that which is frequently substituted for it by Poets, who think that they are conferring honour upon themselves and their art in proportion as they separate themselves from the sympathies of men, and indulge in arbitrary and capricious habits of expression, in order to furnish food for fickle tastes and fickle appetites of their own creation.[1]

I cannot be insensible of the present outcry against the triviality and meanness both of thought and language, which some of my contemporaries have occasionally introduced into their Metrical compositions; and I acknowledge, that this defect where it exists, is more dishonorable to the Writer's own character, than false refinement or arbitrary innovation, though I should contend at the same time that it is far less pernicious in the sum of its consequences. From such Verses, the Poems in these Volumes will be found distinguished at least by one mark of difference, that each of them bas a worthy *purpose*. Not that I mean to say that I always began to write with a distinct purpose formally conceived; but I believe, that my habits of meditation have so formed my feelings, as that my descriptions of such objects as strongly excite those feelings, will be found to carry along with them a *purpose*. If in this opinion I am mistaken, I can have little right to the name of a Poet. For all good Poetry is the spontaneous overflow of powerful feelings; but though this be true, Poems to which any value can be attached, were never produced on any variety of subjects but by a man, who, being possessed of more than usual organic sensibility, had also thought long and deeply. For our continued influxes of feeling are modified and directed by our thoughts, which are indeed the representatives of all our past feelings; and as by contemplating the relation of these general representatives to each other, we discover what is really important to men, so by the repetition and continuance of this act, our feelings connected with important subjects, till at length, if we be originally possessed of much sensibility, such habits of mind will be produced, that by obeying blindly and mechanically the impulses of those habits, we shall describe objects, and utter sentiments of such a nature, and in such connection with each other, that the understanding of the being to whom we address ourselves, if he be in a healthful state of association, must necessarily be in some degree enlightened, his taste exalted, and his affections ameliorated.

---

1 It is worth while here to observe, that the affecting parts of Chaucer are almost always expressed in language pure and universally intelligible even to this day [Wordsworth].

I have said that each of these Poems has a purpose. I have also informed my Reader what this purpose will be found principally to be; namely, to illustrate the manner in which our feelings and ideas are associated in a state of excitement. But speaking in less general language, it is to follow the fluxes and refluxes of the mind when agitated by the great and simple affections of our nature. This object I have endeavoured in these short essays to attain by various means; by tracing the Maternal passion through many of its more subtle windings, as in the Poems of the IDIOT BOY and the MAD MOTHER; by accompanying the last struggles of a human being at the approach of death, cleaving in solitude to life and society, as in the Poem of the FORSAKEN INDIAN; by shewing as in the Stanzas entitled WE ARE SEVEN, the perplexity and obscurity which in childhood attends our notion of death, or rather our utter inability to admit that notion; or by displaying the strength of fraternal, or to speak more philosophically, of moral attachment, when early associated with the great and beautiful objects of Nature, as in the BROTHERS; or, as in the incident of SIMON LEE, by placing my Reader in the way of receiving from ordinary moral sensations, another and more salutary impression than we are accustomed to receive from them. It has also been part of my general purpose to attempt to sketch characters under the influence of less impassioned feelings, as in the OLD MAN TRAVELLING, the TWO THIEVES, &c. characters of which the elements are simple, belonging rather to Nature than to manners, such as exist now, and will probably always exist, and which from their constitution may be distinctly and profitably contemplated. I will not abuse the indulgence of my Reader by dwelling longer upon this subject; but it is proper that I should mention one other circumstance which distinguishes these Poems from the popular Poetry of the day; it is this, that the feeling therein developed gives importance to the action and situation, and not the action and situation to the feeling. My meaning will be rendered perfectly intelligible by referring my Reader to the Poems entitled POOR SUSAN and the CHILDLESS FATHER, particularly to the last stanza of the latter Poem.

I will not suffer a sense of false modesty to prevent me from asserting, that I point my Reader's attention to this mark of distinction far less for the sake of these particular Poems, than from the general importance of the subject. The subject is indeed important! For the human mind is capable of being excited without the application of gross and violent stimulants; and he must have a very faint perception of its beauty and dignity, who does not know this, and who does not further know, that one being is elevated above another, in proportion as he possesses this capability. It has therefore appeared to me, that to endeavour to produce or enlarge this capability is one of the best services, in which, at any period, a Writer can be engaged; but this service, excellent at all times, is especially so at the present day: For a multitude of causes, unknown to former times, are now acting with a combined force to blunt the discriminating powers of the mind, and unfitting it for all voluntary exertion, to reduce it to a state of almost savage torpor. The most effective of these causes are the great National Events[1] which are daily taking place, and the encreasing accumulation of men in cities, where the uniformity of their occupations produces a craving for extraordinary incident, which the rapid communication of intelligence hourly gratifies. To this tendency of life and manners the literature and theatrical exhibitions of the have conformed themselves! The invaluable works of our elder writers, I had almost said the works of Shakespeare and Milton, are driven into neglect by frantic Novels, sickly and stupid German Tragedies, and deluges of idle and extravagant Stories in verse. —When I think upon this degrading thirst after outrageous stimulation, I am almost ashamed to have spoken of the feeble effort with which I have endeavoured to counteract it; and reflecting upon the magnitude of the general evil, I should be oppressed with no dishonorable melancholy, had I not a deep impression of certain inherent and indestructible qualities of the human mind, and likewise of certain powers in the great and permanent objects that act upon it, which are equally inherent and indestructible; and did I not further add to this impression a belief, that the time is approaching, when the evil will be systematically opposed by men of greater powers, and with far more distinguished success.

Having dwelt thus long on the subjects and aim of these Poems, I shall request the Reader's permission to apprise him of a few circumstances relating to their *style*, in order, among other reasons, that I may not be censured for not having performed what I never attempted. Except in a very few instances the Reader will find that personifications of abstract ideas rarely occur in these Volumes, not that I mean to censure such personifications; they may be well fitted for certain sorts of composition, but in these Poems, I propose myself to imitate, and, as far as is possible to adopt, the very language of men; and I do not find that such person-ificiations make any regular or natural part of that language. I wish to keep my Reader in the company of flesh and blood, persuaded, that by so doing, I shall interest him. Not but that I believe, that others who pusue a different track, may interest him likewise: I do not interfere with their claim; I only wish to prefer a different claim of my own. There will also be found in these Volumes little of what is usually called poetic diction; I have taken as much pains to avoid it as others ordinarily take to produce it; this I have done for the reason already alleged, to bring my language near to the language of men, and further, because the pleasure, which I have proposed to myself to impart, is of a kind very different from that which is supposed by many persons to be the proper object of Poetry. I do not know how, without being culpably particular, I can give my Reader a more exact notion of the style in which I wished these Poems to be written, than by informing him,

---

1 England at this time was involved in wars against France as well as industrial urbanization.

that I have at all times endeavoured to look steadily at my subject, consequently, I hope that there is in these Poems little falsehood of description, and that my ideas are expressed in language fitted to their respective importance. Something I must have gained by this practice, as it is friendly to one property of all good Poetry, namely, good sense; but it has necessarily cut me off from a large portion of phrases and figures of speech, which, from father to son have long been regarded as the common inheritance of Poets. I have also thought it expedient to restrict myself still further, having abstained from the use of many expressions, in themselves proper and beautiful, but which have been foolishly repeated by bad Poets, till such feelings of disgust are connected with them as it is scarcely possible by any art of association to overpower.

If in a Poem there should be found a series of lines, or even a single line, in which the language, though naturally arranged, and according to the strict laws of Metre, does not differ from that of Prose, there is a numerous class of critics who, when they stumble upon these Prosaisms, as they call them, imagine that they have made a notable discovery, and exult over the Poet as over a man ignorant of his own profession. Now these men would establish a canon of criticism which the Reader will conclude he must utterly reject if he wishes to be pleased with these Volumes. And it would be a most easy task to prove to him, that not only the language of a large portion of every good Poem, even of the most elevated character, must necessarily, except with reference to the Metre, in no respect differ from that of good Prose, but likewise, that some of the most interesting parts of the best Poems will be found to be strictly the language of Prose, when Prose is well written. The truth of this assertion might be demonstrated by innumerable passages from almost all the Poetical writings even of Milton himself. I have not space for much quotation; but, to illustrate the subject in a general manner, I will here adduce a short composition of Gray, who was at the head of those, who by their reasonings have attempted to widen the space of separation betwixt Prose and Metrical composition, and was more than any other man curiously elaborate in the structure of his own poetic diction.

> In vain to me the smiling mornings shine,
> And reddening Phoebus lifts his golden fire:
> The birds in vain their amorous descant join,
> These ears alas! for other notes repine;
> *A different object do these eyes require;*
> *My lonely anguish melts no heart but mine;*
> *And in my breast the imperfect joys expire;*
> Yet morning smiles the busy race to cheer,
> And new-born pleasure brings to happier men;
> The fields to all their wonted tribute bear;

To warm their little loves the birds complain.
I fruitless mourn to him that cannot hear
And weep the more because I weep in vain.

[Thomas Gray, "Sonnet on the Death of Mr. Richard West," 1742]

It will easily be perceived, that the only part of this Sonnet which is of any value, is the lines printed in Italics: it is equally obvious, that except in the rhyme, and in the use of the single word "fruitless" for fruitlessly, which is so far a defect, the language of these lines does in no respect differ from that of Prose.

Is there then, it will be asked, no essential difference between the language of Prose and Metrical composition? I answer that there neither is nor can be any essential difference. We are fond of tracing the resemblance between Poetry and Painting, and, accordingly, we call them sisters; but where shall we find bonds of connection sufficiently strict to typify the affinity betwixt Metrical and Prose composition? They both speak by and to the same organs; the bodies in which both of them are clothed may be said to be of the same substance, their affections are kindred and almost identical, not necessarily differing even in degree; Poetry[1] sheds no tears "such as Angels weep," but natural and human tears; she can boast of no celestial Ichor[2] that distinguishes her vital juices from those of Prose; the same human blood circulates through the veins of them both.

If it be affirmed that Rhyme and Metrical arrangement, of themselves, constitute a distinction, which overturns what I have been saying on the strict affinity of Metrical language with that of Prose, and paves the way for other distinctions which the mind voluntarily admits, I answer, that the distinction of Rhyme and Metre is regular and uniform, and not, like that which is produced by what isusually called Poetic diction, arbitrary, and subject to infinite caprices, upon which no calculation whatever can be made. In the one case, the Reader is utterly at the mercy of the Poet respecting what imagery or diction he may choose to connect with the passion, whereas in the other, the Metre obeys certain laws, to which the Poet and Reader both willingly submit, because they are certain, and because, no interference is made by them with the passion, but such as the concurring testimony of ages has shewn to heighten and improve the pleasure which co-exists with it.

It will now be proper to answer an obvious question, namely, why, professing these opinions, have I written in Verse? To this in the first place I reply, because,

---

1 I here use the word 'Poetry' (though against my own judgement) as opposed to the word Prose, and synonymous with Metrical composition. But much confusion has been introduced into Criticism by this contradistinction of Poetry and Prose, instead of the more philosophical one of Poetry and Science. The only strict antithesis to Prose is Metre [Wordsworth].

2 The blood-like fluid that flows in the veins of the Greek Gods.

however I may have restricted myself, there is still left open to me, what confessedly constitutes the ost valuable object of all writing, whether in Prose or Verse, the great and universal Passions of men, the most general and interesting of their occupations, and the entire world of Nature, from which I am at liberty to supply myself with endless combinations of form and imagery. Now, granting for a moment, that whatever is interesting in these objects may be as vividly described in Prose, why am I to be condemned if to such description I have endeavored to superadd the charm which, by the consent of all nations, is acknowledged to exist in Metrical language? To this it will be answered that a very small part of the pleasure given by Poetry depends upon the Metre, and that it is injudicious to write in Metre, unless it be accompanied with the other artificial distinctions of style with which Metre is usually accompanied; and that by such deviation more will be lost from the shock which will be thereby given to the Reader's associations, than will be counterbalanced by any pleasure, which he can derive from the general Power of Numbers. In answer to those who thus contend for the necessity of accompanying Metre with certain appropriate colours of style, in order to the accomplishment of its appropriate end, and who, also, in my opinion, greatly under-rate the Power of Metre in itself, it might, perhaps, be almost sufficient to observe, that Poems are extant, written upon more humble subjects, and in a more naked and simple style, than what I have aimed at, which Poems have continued to give pleasure from generation to generation. Now if nakedness and simplicity be a defect, the fact here mentioned affords a strong presumption, that Poems somewhat less naked and simple, are capable of affording pleasure at the present day; and all that I am now attempting is—to justify myself for having written under the impression of this belief.

But I might point out various causes why, when the style is manly, and the subject of some importance, words, Metrically arranged, will long continue to impart such a pleasure to mankind, as he, who is sensible of the extent of that pleasure, will be desirous to impart. The end of Poetry is to produce excitement in co-existence with an overbalance of pleasure. Now, by the supposition, excitement is an unusual and irregular state of the mind; ideas and feelings do not in that state succeed each other in accustomed order. But, if the words by which this excitement is produced are in themselves powerful, or the images and feelings have an undue proportion of pain connected with them, there is some danger, that the excitement may be carried beyond its proper bounds. Now the co-presence of something regular, something to which the mind has been accustomed in an unexcited, or a less excited state, cannot but have great efficacy, in tempering and restraining the passion, by an intertexture of ordinary feeling. This may be illustrated by appealing to the Readers own experience, of the reluctance with which he comes to the re-perusal of the distressful parts of Clarissa Harlowe, or the Gamester.

While Shakespeare's writings, in the most pathetic scenes, never act upon us as pathetic beyond the bounds of pleasure—an effect, which is in a great degree to be ascribed to small, but continual, and regular impulses of pleasurable surprise from the Metrical arrangement—On the other hand (what it must be allowed will much more frequently happen) if the Poet's words should be incommensurate with the passion, and inadequate to raise the Reader to a height of desirable excitement, then (unless the Poet's choice of his Metre has been grossly injudicious) in the feelings of pleasure which the Reader has been accustomed to connect with Metre in general, and in the feeling, whether chearful or melancholy, which he has been accustomed to connect with that particular movement of Metre, there will be found something which will greatly contribute to impart passion to the words, and to effect the complex end which the Poet proposes to himself.

If I had undertaken a systematic defence of the theory upon which these Poems are written, it would have been my duty to develop the various causes upon which the pleasure received from Metrical language depends. Among the chief of these causes is to be reckoned a principle, which must be well known to those who have made any of the Arts the object of accurate reflection; I mean the pleasure which the mind derives from the perception of similitude in dissimilitude. This principle is the great spring of the activity of our minds and their chief feeder. From this principle the direction of the sexual appetite, and all the passions connected with it, take their origin. It is the life of our ordinary conversation; and upon the accuracy with which similitude in dissimilitude, and dissimilitude in similitude are perceived, depend our taste and our moral feelings. It would not have been a useless employment to have applied this principle to the consideration of Metre, and to have shewn, that Metre is hence enabled to afford much pleasure, and to have pointed out in what manner that pleasure is produced. But my limits will not permit me to enter upon this subject, and I must content myself with a general Summary.

I have said that Poetry is the spontaneous overflow of powerful feelings. It takes its origin from emotion recollected in tranquillity; the emotion is contemplated till by a species of reaction the tranquillity gradually disappears, and an emotion, similar to that which was before the subject of contemplation, is gradually produced, and does itself actually exist in the mind. In this mood successful composition generally begins, and in a mood similar to this it is carried on; but the emotion, of whatever kind, and in whatever degree, from various causes is qualified by various pleasures, so that in describing any passions whatsoever, which are voluntarily described, the mind will upon the whole be in a state of enjoyment. Now if Nature be thus cautious in preserving in a state of enjoyment a being thus employed, the Poet ought to profit by the lesson thus held forth to him, and ought especially to take care, that whatever passions he communicates to his Reader, those passions, if his Reader's mind be sound and vigorous, should always be accompanied with an overbalance of pleasure. Now the music of harmonious Metrical language, the sense of difficulty overcome, and the blind association of pleasure which bas been previously received from works of Rhyme or Metre of the same or similar construction, all these imperceptibly make up a complex feeling of delight, which is of the most important use in tempering the painful feeling which will always be found intermingled with powerful descriptions of the deeper passions. This effect is always produced in pathetic and impassioned Poetry; while in lighter compositions the ease and gracefulness with which the Poet manages his numbers are themselves confessedly a principal source of the gratification of the Reader. I might perhaps include all which it is *necessary* to say upon this subject by affirming, what few persons will deny, that of two descriptions either of passions, manners or characters, each of them equally well executed, the one in Prose and the other in Verse, the Verse will be read a hundred times where the Prose is read once. We see that Pope by the power of Verse alone, has contrived to render the plainest common sense interesting, and even frequently to invest it with the appearance of passion. In consequence of these convictions I related in Metre the Tale of GOODY BLAKE AND HARRY GILL, which is one of the rudest of this collection. I wished to draw attention to the truth that the power of the human imagination is sufficient to produce such changes even in our physical nature as might almost appear miraculous. The truth is an important one; the fact (for it is a *fact*) is a valuable illustration of it. And I have the satisfaction of knowing that it has been communicated to many hundreds of people who would never have heard of it, had it not been narrated as a Ballad, and in a more impressive Metre than is usual in Ballads.

Having thus adverted a few of the reasons why I have written in Verse, and why I have chosen subjects from common life, and endeavoured to bring my language near to the real language of men, if I have been too minute in pleading my own cause, I have at the same time been treating a subject of general interest: and it is for this reason that I request the Reader's permission to add a few words with reference solely to these particular Poems, and to some defects which will probably be found in them. I am sensible that my associations must have sometimes been particular instead of general, and that, consequently, giving to things a false importance, sometimes from deceased impulses I may have written upon unworthy subjects; but I am less apprehensive on this account, than that my language may frequently have suffered from those arbitrary connections of feelings and ideas with particular words, from which no man can altogether protect himself. Hence I have no doubt, that in some instances, feelings of the ludicrous may be given to my Readers by expressions which appeared to me tender and pathetic. Such faulty expressions, were I convinced they were faulty at present, and that they must necessarily continue to be so, I would willingly take all reasonable pains to correct. But it is dangerous to make these alterations on the simple authority of a

few individuals, or even of certain classes of men; for where the understanding of
an Author is not convinced, or his feelings altered, this cannot be done without
great injury to himself; for his own feelings are his stay and support, and if he sets
them aside in one instance he may be induced to repeat this act till his mind loses
all confidence in itself and becomes utterly debilitated. To this it may be added,
that the Reader ought never to forget that he is himself exposed to the same errors
as the Poet, and perhaps in a much greater degree; for there can be no presumption
in saying that it is not probable he will be so well acquainted with the various stages
of meaning through which words have passed, or with the fickleness or stability of
the relations of particular ideas to each other and above all, since he is so much less
interested in the subject, he may decide lightly and carelessly.

Long as I have detained my Reader, I hope he will permit me to caution him
against a mode of false criticism which has been applied to Poetry in which the
language closely resembles that of life and nature. Such verses have been triumphed
over in Parodies of which Dr. Johnson's Stanza is a fair specimen.

> "I put my hat upon my bead,
> And walk'd into the Strand,
> And there I met another man
> Whose hat was in his hand."

Immediately under these lines I will place one of the most justly admired
stanzas of the "*Babes* in the Wood."

> "These pretty Babes with hand in hand
> Went wandering up and down;
> But never more they saw the man
> Approaching from the Town."

In both these stanzas the words and the order of the words, in no respect differ
from the most unimpassioned conversation. There are words in both, for example,
"the Strand," and "the Town," connected with none but the most familiar ideas;
yet the one stanza we admit as admirable, and the other as a fair example of the
superlatively contemptible. Whence arises this difference? Not from the Metre,
not from the language, not from the order of the words; but the *matter* expressed
in Dr. Johnson's stanza is contemptible. The proper method of treating trivial
and simple verses, to which Dr. Johnson's stanza would be a fair parallelism, is
not to say, this is a bad kind of Poetry, or this is not Poetry, but, this wants sense;
it is neither interesting in itself, nor can *lead* to any thing interesting; the images
neither originate in that same state of feeling which arises out of thought, nor can
excite thought or feeling in the Reader. This is the only sensible manner of dealing
with such verses: Why trouble yourself about the species till you have previously

decided upon the genus? Why take pains to prove that an Ape is not a Newton when it is self-evident that he is not a man?

I have one request to make of my Reader, which is, that in judging these Poems he would decide by his own feelings genuinely, and not by reflection upon what will probably be the judgment of others. How common is it to hear a person say, "I myself do not object to this style of composition, or this or that expression, but to such and such classes of people it will appear mean or ludicrous." This mode of criticism, so destructive of all sound unadulterated judgment, is almost universal: I have therefore to request that the Reader would abide independently by his own feelings, and that if he finds himself affected he would not suffer such conjectures to interfere with his pleasure.

If an Author by any single composition has impressed us with respect for his talents, it is useful to consider this as affording a presumption, that, on other occasions where we have been displeased, he nevertheless may not have written ill or absurdly; and, further, to give him so much credit for this one composition, as may induce us to review what has displeased us with more care than we should otherwise have bestowed upon it. This is not only an act of justice, but in our decisions, upon Poetry especially, may conduce in a high degree to the improvement of our own taste: for an *accurate* taste in Poetry, and in all the other arts as Sir Joshua Reynolds has observed, is an *acquired* talent, which can only be produced by thought and a long continued intercourse with the best models of composition. This is mentioned not with so ridiculous a purpose as to prevent the most inexperienced Reader from judging for himself (I have already said that I wish him to judge for himself) but merely to temper the rashness of decision, and to suggest that if Poetry be a subject on which much time has not been bestowed, the judgment may be erroneous, and that in many cases it necessarily will be so.

I know that nothing would have so effectually contributed to further the end which I have in view, as to have shewn of what kind the pleasure is, and how the pleasure is produced Metrical composition essentially different from what I have here endeavoured to recommend; for the Reader will say that he has been pleased by such composition, and what can I do more for him? The power of any art is limited and he will suspect, that if I propose to furnish him with new friends it is only upon condition of his abandoning his old friends. Besides as I have said, the Reader is himself conscious of the pleasure which he has received from such composition, composition to which he has peculiarly attached the endearing name of Poetry; and all men feel an habitual gratitude, and something of an honorable bigotry for the objects which have long continued to please them: we not only wish to be pleased, but to be pleased in that particular way in which we have been accustomed to be pleased. There is a host of arguments in these feelings; and I should be the less able to combat them successfully, as I am willing to allow, that, in order entirely to enjoy the Poetry which I am recommending, it would be necessary to give up much of what is ordinarily enjoyed. But would my limits have permitted me to point out how this pleasure is produced, I might have removed many obstacles, and assisted my Reader in perceiving that the powers of language are not so limited as he may suppose; and that it is possible that Poetry may give other enjoyments, of a purer, more lasting, and more exquisite nature. But this part of my subject I have been obliged altogether to omit; as it has been less my present aim to prove that the interest excited by some other kinds of Poetry is less vivid, and less worthy of the nobler powers of the mind, than to offer reasons for presuming, that, if the object which I have proposed to myself were adequately attained, a species of Poetry would be produced, which is genuine Poetry; in its nature well adapted to interest mankind permanently, and likewise important in the multiplicity and quality of its moral relations.

From what has been said, and from a perusal of the Poems, the Reader will be able clearly to perceive the object which I have proposed to myself; he will determine how far I have attained this object; and, what is a much more important question, whether it be worth attaining; and upon the decision of these two questions will rest my claim to the approbation of the Public.

1802

SAMUEL TAYLOR COLERIDGE
1772–1834

Samuel Taylor Coleridge displayed immense potential in his boyhood. Imaginative, eccentric, and industrious, he had a lifelong dedication to learning. After his father's unexpected death, the nine-year-old boy was sent to Christ's Hospital, a charity school in London, where instructors noted his brilliance. His academic efforts reaped a scholarship to the University of Cambridge where he began preparing for a church profession. His diligence soon faltered. Talk of the French Revolution circulated university corridors, heightening the political atmosphere; his relationship with his family was crumbling; his studies disinterested him; and overindulging on alcohol, trips to London theatres, furniture for his dingy college rooms, and other purchases riddled him with debt. In desperation and despair, he enlisted in the Light Dragoons under the alias Silas Tomkyn Comberbache. His brief time in the British army was miserable. Utterly inept at his cavalry duties, he pleaded for his brothers to rescue him. Coleridge returned to Cambridge, but the escapade—in addition to his radical political and religious beliefs—had essentially crippled his chances of university honors. In 1794, he left without a degree.

During that year, Coleridge also encountered an outspoken University of Oxford student named Robert Southey. Zealous republicans and free-thinkers, Southey and Coleridge were infinitely like-minded. Together they devised "Pantisocracy," an ideal community where all members would have equal responsibilities and governing power. Twelve men endeavored to begin the project on the banks of the Susquehanna in Pennsylvania. To ensure the community's continuation and success, each man was required to marry and have children. Although Coleridge loved another woman, he hastily became engaged to Sara Fricker, the sister of Southey's fiancée, to satisfy the conditions of the plan. Coleridge and Southey gained support for their ideas, but they lacked the means to initiate a pantisocratic settlement. Their scheme withered. Coleridge married Sara at Southey's insistence, but disputes eventually engulfed their marriage. Estranged from his wife and children, Coleridge fell hopelessly in love with Sara Hutchinson. Their relationship never reached fruition.

With Pantisocracy extinct, Coleridge's friends developed numerous plans to benefit the talented writer, but Coleridge's creativity did not reach its zenith until 1797. In April of that year, Coleridge began regularly visiting and corresponding with the poet William Wordsworth. Wordsworth and his sister, Dorothy, had settled at Alfoxden House, a mere three miles from where the Coleridges resided. The literary friendship that ensued metamorphosed Coleridge's poetic ambitions. After extensive collaborations, Coleridge and Wordsworth jointly published *Lyrical Ballads, with a Few Other Poems*. The two poets intended to co-write the opening piece, *The Rime of the Ancyent Marinere*, but Wordsworth withdrew from the project after realizing their styles differed too greatly. Coleridge undertook the poem. The poem's original inspiration had come from George Cruikshank, a friend of Coleridge's, who dreamed about a ship manned by ghostly sailors. Though Coleridge wrote most of the ballad, Wordsworth's ideas remained essential to its formation. In addition to contributing lines, Wordsworth recommended the shooting of the albatross and other supernatural elements. Coleridge later stripped *The Ancient Mariner* of its archaic diction, added a Latin epigraph, and incorporated marginal notes, crafting a piece that to this day enchants readers with its mystical storyline.

Following the publication of *Lyrical Ballads* in 1798, Coleridge accompanied the Wordsworths to Germany where he visited the town of Ratzeburg and attended the University of Göttingen. The university lectures, as well as his study of German philosophers and critics, profoundly remolded his thinking. In 1800, Coleridge published his translations of *The Piccolimini* and *The Death of Wallenstein*, both written by the German philosopher Friedrich Schiller. After returning to England, he and the Wordsworths travelled north to the Lake District. Although Coleridge enjoyed the countryside immensely, it physically and mentally debilitated him. In the Lake District, he endured brutal winter weather and suffered the strains of an unhappy marriage. Habitual laudanum usage further aggravated his well-being. Coleridge had been taking laudanum (opium dissolved in water) to alleviate his recurrent physical pains. Laudanum was the conventional medical treatment of that time for pain relief, but for Coleridge, it was ineffectual; he resorted to opium. Coleridge initially marveled at the drug's ability to alter consciousness. Opium had indeed induced the imaginative, passionate vision that led to "Kubla Khan," but the drug's destructive force far exceeded its creative powers. Coleridge fell into irreversible addiction. "Dejection: An Ode" and "The Pains of Sleep" confess his despair. The physician James Gillman tamed Coleridge's addiction, but his condition could not be fully cured. He was tormented by opium addiction until his death in 1834.

Upon Coleridge's death, Wordsworth declared that many men had done wonderful things, but Coleridge was "the only wonderful man" he had ever known. Coleridge generated wonder wherever he went. He had a proclivity for entertaining audiences since childhood, but his need for attention sometimes manifested negatively. Desperate to please, impress, and receive admiration,

Coleridge was driven to incorporate others' works into his own. He often neglected to include citations or allusions of any kind, resulting in repeated accusations of plagiarism. Addiction likely encouraged his behavior. Additionally, longer pieces— such as *Biographia Literaria*—required continuous effort that he could not provide, especially after opium depleted his energy. The fragments of his *Biographia* are stitched together with fillers and plagiarized material. Nevertheless, it is regarded as a critical text of literary criticism in English, and Coleridge is acknowledged as a highly influential philosopher-critic.

In *Biographia Literaria*, he remarks, "The best part of human language, properly so called, is derived from reflection on the acts of the mind itself." His thoughts exemplify a pillar of Romantic philosophy: The power to imagine, create, and communicate resides in one's mind. His potential was recognizable, and, like many of his friends asserted, only idleness abbreviated his success. Most of his pieces arose from sporadic, fleeting bursts of creativity. In these glimpses of poetic genius, Coleridge divulges emotion and introspection—two elements which, for some Romantic writers, constitute human consciousness.

1772	Samuel Taylor Coleridge born 21 October
1778	Enters Ottery Grammar School
1782–89	Enters Christ's Hospital, a charity school
1791	Enters Jesus College, University of Cambridge
1795	Marries Sara Fricker
1796	Launches his periodical, *The Watchman*
1798	*Lyrical Ballads*, including *The Rime of the Ancyent Mariner*, jointly published with Wordsworth; "Frost at Midnight"
1800	Translations of Friedrich Schiller's *The Piccolimini* and *The Death of Wallenstein*
1808	Delivers literary lectures at the Royal Institution
1813	*Remorse* performed at Drury Lane Theatre
1816	*Christabel*; "Kubla Khan"
1817	*Biographia Literaria*
1834	Coleridge dies from pneumonia on 25 July and is buried at Old Highgate Chapel

1834

1797
* Foot injury, kept him from taking the countryside w/ his friends
* He begins to imagination what his friends was doing
* Forced to stay underneath a lime tree

* The lime tree was a physical prison. Not a mental one.

— Blank verse

THIS LIME-TREE BOWER MY PRISON[1]

└ Not a citrus tree, actually a Lindon tree, often ornamental & for shade

Well, they are gone, and here must I remain,
This Lime-tree bower my prison! I have lost
Beauties and feelings, such as would have been
Most sweet to my remembrance, even when age
Had dimm'd mine eyes to blindness! They, meanwhile,   5
Friends, whom I never more may meet again,
On springy heath, along the hill-top edge,
Wander in gladness, and wind down, perchance,
To that still roaring dell, of which I told;
The roaring dell, o'erwooded, narrow, deep,   10
And only speckled by the mid-day sun;
Where its slim trunk the Ash from rock to rock
Flings arching like a bridge;—that branchless Ash,
Unsunn'd and damp, whose few poor yellow leaves
Ne'er tremble in the gale, yet tremble still,   15
Fann'd by the water-fall! and there my friends
Behold the dark green file of long lank weeds,
That all at once (a most fantastic sight!)
Still nod and drip beneath the dripping edge
Of the blue clay-stone.

                 Now, my Friends emerge   20
Beneath the wide wide Heaven–and view again
The many-steepled tract magnificent
Of hilly field and meadows, and the sea,
With some fair bark, perhaps, whose sails light up
The slip of smooth clear blue betwixt two isles   25
Of purple shadow! Yes, they wander on
In gladness all; but thou, methinks, most glad,

---

1 In the June of 1797 some long-expected friends paid a visit to the author's cottage; and on the morning of their arrival, he met with an accident, which disabled him from walking during the whole time of their stay. One evening, when they had left him for a few hours, he composed the following lines in the garden-bower [Coleridge].

My gentle-hearted Charles![2] for thou hast pined
And hunger'd after Nature, many a year,
In the great city pent, winning thy way   30
With sad yet patient soul, through evil and pain
And strange calamity! Ah! slowly sink
Behind the western ridge, thou glorious Sun!
Shine in the slant beams of the sinking orb,
Ye purple heath-flowers! richlier burn, ye clouds!   35
Live in the yellow light, ye distant groves!
And kindle, thou blue Ocean! So my Friend
Struck with deep joy may stand, as I have stood,
Silent with swimming sense; yea, gazing round
On the wide landscape, gaze till all doth seem   40
Less gross than bodily; and of such hues
As veil the Almighty Spirit, when yet he makes
Spirits perceive his presence.

                              A delight
Comes sudden on my heart, and I am glad
As I myself were there! Nor in this bower,   45
This little lime-tree bower, have I not mark'd
Much that has soothed me. Pale beneath the blaze
Hung the transparent foliage; and I watch'd
Some broad and sunny leaf, and loved to see
The shadow of the leaf and stem above   50
Dappling its sunshine! And that Walnut-tree
Was richly tinged, and a deep radiance lay
Full on the ancient Ivy, which usurps
Those fronting elms, and now, with blackest mass
Makes their dark branches gleam a lighter hue   55
Through the late twilight: and though now the Bat
Wheels silent by, and not a Swallow twitters,
Yet still the solitary Humble-Bee
Sings in the bean-flower! Henceforth I shall know
That Nature ne'er deserts the wise and pure;   60
No plot so narrow, be but Nature there,
No waste so vacant, but may well employ
Each faculty of sense, and keep the heart
Awake to Love and Beauty! and sometimes

---

2 Coleridge addressed this poem to his friend Charles Lamb, a Londoner.

'Tis well to be bereft of promised good,   65
That we may lift the soul, and contemplate
With lively joy the joys we cannot share.
My gentle-hearted Charles! when the last Rook
Beat its straight path along the dusky air
Homewards, I blest it! deeming its black wing   70
(Now a dim speck, now vanishing in light)
Had cross'd the mighty Orb's dilated glory,
While thou stood'st gazing; or, when all was still,
Flew creeking o'er thy head, and had a charm
For thee, my gentle-hearted Charles, to whom   80
No sound is dissonant which tells of Life.

1797

*The speaker thinks about his own youth and then turns his hopes for his young child

*The speaker sits up late in a rural cottage, while his baby sleeps at night

*Captures the late-night thoughts of a parent

~ Blank verse

FROST AT MIDNIGHT

The Frost performs its secret ministry,
Unhelp'd by any wind. The owlet's cry
Came loud—and hark, again! loud as before.
The inmates of my cottage, all at rest,
Have left me to that solitude, which suits   5
Abstruser musings: save that at my side
My cradled infant slumbers peacefully.
'Tis calm indeed! so calm, that it disturbs
And vexes meditation with its strange
And extreme silentness. Sea, hill, and wood,   10
This populous village! Sea, and hill, and wood,
With all the numberless goings on of life,
Inaudible as dreams! the thin blue flame
Lies on my low burnt fire, and quivers not;
Only that film, which flutter'd on the grate,   15
Still flutters there, the sole unquiet thing.
Methinks, its motion in this hush of nature

Gives it dim sympathies with me who live,
Making it a companionable form,
Whose puny flaps and freaks the idling Spirit   20
By its own moods interprets, everywhere
Echo or mirror seeking of itself,
And makes a toy of Thought.
                                    But O! how oft,
How oft, at school, with most believing mind,   25
Presageful, have I gazed upon the bars,
To watch that fluttering *stranger!* and as oft
With unclosed lids, already had I dreamt
Of my sweet birth-place, and the old church-tower,
Whose bells, the poor man's only music, rang
From morn to evening, all the hot Fair-day,
So sweetly, that they stirr'd and haunted me
With a wild pleasure, falling on mine ear
Most like articulate sounds of things to come!
So gazed I, till the soothing things, I dreamt,   35
Lull'd me to sleep, and sleep prolong'd my dreams!
And so I brooded all the following morn,
Awed by the stern preceptor's face, mine eye
Fix'd with mock study on my swimming book:
Save if the door half-open'd, and I snatch'd   40
A hasty glance, and still my heart leap'd up,
For still I hoped to see the *stranger's* face,
Townsman, or aunt, or sister more beloved,
My play-mate when we both were clothed alike!

    Dear Babe, that sleepest cradled by my side,   45
Whose gentle breathings, heard in this deep calm,
Fill up the interspersed vacancies
And momentary pauses of the thought!
My babe so beautiful! it thrills my heart
With tender gladness, thus to look at thee,   50
And think that thou shalt learn far other lore,
And in far other scenes! For I was rear'd
In the great city, pent 'mid cloisters dim,
And saw nought lovely but the sky and stars.
But *thou*, my babe! shalt wander like a breeze   55
By lakes and sandy shores, beneath the crags
Of ancient mountain, and beneath the clouds,

[Handwritten marginal note beside lines 26–35:] Bits of ash on grate of fire-place called strangers, said to be a sign of meeting a stranger; memory of seeing this at school brings up thoughts presented in this stanza

Which image in their bulk both lakes and shores
And mountain crags: so shalt thou see and hear
The lovely shapes and sounds intelligible   60
Of that eternal language, which thy God
Utters, who from eternity doth teach
Himself in all, and all things in himself.
Great universal Teacher! he shall mould
Thy spirit, and by giving make it ask.   65

    Therefore all seasons shall be sweet to thee,
Whether the summer clothe the general earth
With greenness, or the redbreast sit and sing
Betwixt the tufts of snow on the bare branch
Of mossy apple-tree, while the nigh thatch   70
Smokes in the sun-thaw; whether the eave-drops fall
Heard only in the trances of the blast,
Or if the secret ministry of frost
Shall hang them up in silent icicles,
Quietly shining to the quiet Moon.   75

1798

shows that a thoughtless/bad acts can have lasting repercussions [handwritten annotation]

THE RIME OF THE ANCIENT MARINER

IN SEVEN PARTS

PART I.

he sins when he kills [handwritten annotation]

It is an ancient Mariner,
And he stoppeth one of three.
"By thy long grey beard and glittering eye,
Now wherefore stopp'st thou me?

An ancient Mariner meeteth three gallants bidden to a wedding-feast, and detaineth one.

"The Bridegroom's doors are opened wide,   5
And I am next of kin;
The guests are met, the feast is set:
May'st hear the merry din."

He holds him with his skinny hand,
"There was a ship," quoth he.   10
"Hold off! unhand me, grey-beard loon!"
Eftsoons his hand dropt he.

He holds him with his glittering eye—
The Wedding-Guest stood still,
And listens like a three years' child: 15
The Mariner hath his will.

The Wedding-Guest is spell-bound by the eye of the old seafaring man, and constrained to hear his tale.

The Wedding-Guest sat on a stone:
He cannot choose but hear;
And thus spake on that ancient man,
The bright-eyed Mariner.   20

"The ship was cheered, the harbour cleared,
Merrily did we drop
Below the kirk, below the hill,
Below the lighthouse top.

"The sun came up upon the left,
Out of the sea came he!
And he shone bright, and on the right
Went down into the sea.

The Mariner tells
how the ship sailed
southward with
a good wind and
fair weather till it
reached the Line.

25

"Higher and higher every day,
Till over the mast at noon—"
The Wedding-Guest here beat his breast,
For he heard the loud bassoon.

30

The Bride hath paced into the hall,
Red as a rose is she;
Nodding their heads before her goes
The merry minstrelsy.

The Wedding-Guest
heareth the bridal
music; but the
Mariner continueth
his tale.

35

The Wedding-Guest he beat his breast,
Yet he cannot choose but hear;
And thus spake on that ancient man,
The bright-eyed Mariner.

40

"And now the storm-blast came, and he
Was tyrannous and strong:
He struck with his o'ertaking wings,
And chased us south along.

The ship drawn by
a storm toward the
south pole.

"With sloping masts and dipping prow,
As who pursued with yell and blow
Still treads the shadow of his foe,
And forward bends his head,
The ship drove fast, loud roared the blast,
And southward aye we fled.

45

50

And now there came both mist and snow,
And it grew wondrous cold:
And ice, mast-high, came floating by,
As green as emerald.

"And through the drifts the snowy clifts
Did send a dismal sheen:
Nor shapes of men nor beasts we ken—
The ice was all between.

*The land of ice, and
of fearful sounds
where no living
thing was to be seen.*   55

"The ice was here, the ice was there,
The ice was all around:
It cracked and growled, and roared and
howled,
Like noises in a swound!

60

"At length did cross an Albatross,
Thorough the fog it came;
As if it had been a Christian soul,
We hailed it in God's name.

*Till a great sea-bird,
called the Albatross,
came through the
snow-fog, and was
received with great
joy and hospitality.*   65

"It ate the food it ne'er had eat,
And round and round it flew.
The ice did split with a thunder-fit;
The helmsman steered us through!

70

"And a good south wind sprung up behind;
The Albatross did follow,
And every day, for food or play,
Came to the mariners' hollo!

*And lo! the Albatross
proveth a bird of
good omen, and fol-
loweth the ship as it
returned northward
through fog and
floating ice.*

"In mist or cloud, on mast or shroud,
It perched for vespers nine;
Whiles all the night, through fog-smoke
    white,
Glimmered the white moon-shine."

75

"God save thee, ancient Mariner!
From the fiends, that plague thee thus!—
Why look'st thou so?"—"With my cross-
    bow
I shot the Albatross."

*The ancient Mariner
inhospitably killeth
the pious bird of
good omen.*   80

PART II.

"The Sun now rose upon the right:
Out of the sea came he,
Still hid in mist, and on the left
Went down into the sea.

"And the good south wind still blew
    behind,   5
But no sweet bird did follow,
Nor any day for food or play
Came to the mariners' hollo!

"And I had done a hellish thing,   His shipmates cry   10
And it would work 'em woe: out against the
For all averred, I had killed the bird   ancient Mariner, for
That made the breeze to blow.   killing the bird of
'Ah wretch!' said they, 'the bird to slay,   good luck.
That made the breeze to blow!'   15

"Nor dim nor red, like God's own head,   But when the fog
The glorious Sun uprist: cleared off, they
Then all averred, I had killed the bird   justify the same, and
That brought the fog and mist.   thus make themselves
"Twas right,' said they, 'such birds to slay,   accomplices in the
That bring the fog and mist.'   crime.   20

"The fair breeze blew, the white foam flew,   The fair breeze
The furrow followed free;   continues; the ship
We were the first that ever burst   enters the Pacific
Into that silent sea.   Ocean, and sails
                                                         northward, even till   25
                                                         it reaches the Line.

"Down dropt the breeze, the sails drop   The ship hath been
    down,   suddenly becalmed.
'Twas sad as sad could be;
And we did speak only to break
The silence of the sea!

"All in a hot and copper sky,   30
The bloody Sun, at noon,
Right up above the mast did stand,
No bigger than the Moon.

"Day after day, day after day,
We stuck, nor breath nor motion;   35
As idle as a painted ship
Upon a painted ocean.

"Water, water, everywhere,   And the Alba-
And all the boards did shrink;   tross begins to be
Water, water, everywhere,   avenged.
Nor any drop to drink.   40

"The very deep did rot: O Christ!
That ever this should be!
Yea, slimy things did crawl with legs
Upon the slimy sea.   45

"About, about, in reel and rout
The death-fires danced at night;
The water, like a witch's oils,
Burnt green, and blue and white.   A spirit had fol-
                                             lowed them; one of
"And some in dreams assured were   the invisible inhab-
Of the spirit that plagued us so;   itants of this planet,   50
Nine fathom deep he had follow'd us   neither departed
From the land of mist and snow.   souls nor angels;
                                             concerning whom
"And every tongue, through utter drought,   the learned Jew,
Was withered at the root;   Josephus, and the
We could not speak, no more than if   Platonic Constanti-
We had been choked with soot.   nopolitan, Michael   55
                                             Psellus, may be
"Ah! well a-day! what evil looks   consulted. They are
Had I from old and young!   very numerous, and
                                             there is no climate
                                             or element without
                                             one or more.

                                             The shipmates, in
                                             their sore distress,
                                             would fain throw the
                                             whole guilt ib the
                                             ancient Mariner:

Instead of the cross, the Albatross
About my neck was hung."

in sign whereof they   60
hang the dead sea-
bird round his neck.

PART III.

"There passed a weary time. Each throat
Was parched, and glazed each eye.
A weary time! a weary time!
How glazed each weary eye,
When looking westward, I beheld   5
A something in the sky.

The ancient Mariner
  beholdeth a sign in
  the element afar off.

"At first it seemed a little speck,
And then it seemed a mist;
It moved and moved, and took at last
A certain shape, I wist.   10

"A speck, a mist, a shape, I wist!
And still it neared and neared:
As if it dodged a water-sprite,
It plunged and tacked and veered.

"With throats unslaked, with black lips
    baked,
We could nor laugh nor wail;
Through utter drought all dumb we stood!
I bit my arm, I sucked the blood,
And cried, A sail! a sail!

As its nearer ap-   15
proach, it seemeth
him to be a ship;
and at a dear ransom
he freeth his speech
from the bonds of
thirst.

"With throats unslaked, with black lips
    baked
Agape they heard me call:
Gramercy! they for joy did grin,
And all at once their breath drew in,
As they were drinking all.

A flash of joy;   20

"See! see! (I cried) she tacks no more!
Hither to work us weal;
Without a breeze, without a tide,
She steadies with upright keel!

"The western wave was all a-flame.
The day was well nigh done!
Almost upon the western wave
Rested the broad bright Sun;
When that strange shape drove suddenly
Betwixt us and the Sun.

"And straight the Sun was flecked with bars,
(Heaven's Mother send us grace!)
As if through a dungeon grate he peered
With broad and burning face.

"Alas! (thought I, and my heart beat loud)
How fast she nears and nears!
Are those her sails that glance in the Sun,
Like restless gossameres?

"Are those her ribs through which the Sun
Did peer, as through a grate?
And is that Woman all her crew?
Is that a Death? and are there two?
Is Death that woman's mate?

"Her lips were red, her looks were free,
Her locks were yellow as gold:
Her skin was as white as leprosy,
The Night-mare Life-in-Death was she,
Who thicks man's blood with cold.

"The naked hulk alongside came,
And the twain were casting dice;
'The game is done! I've won! I've won!'
Quoth she, and whistles thrice.

(marginal glosses)

And horror follows. For can it be a ship that comes onward without wind or tide?   25

It seemeth him but the skeleton of a ship.   35

And its ribs are seen as bars on the face of the setting Sun. The spectre-woman and her death-mate, and no other on board the skeleton ship.   45

Like vessel, like crew!

Death and Life-in-Death have diced for the ship's crew, and she (the latter) winneth the ancient Mariner.   55

30

40

50

"The Sun's rim dips: the stars rush out:
At one stride comes the dark;
With far-heard whisper, o'er the sea,
Off shot the spectre-bark.

"We listened and looked sideways up!
Fear at my heart, as at a cup,
My life-blood seemed to sip!
The stars were dim, and thick the night,
The steersman's face by his lamp gleamed
    white;
From the sails the dew did drip—

Till clomb above the eastern bar
The horned Moon, with one bright star
Within the nether tip.

"One after one, by the star-dogged Moon,
Too quick for groan or sigh,
Each turned his face with a ghastly pang,
And cursed me with his eye.

"Four times fifty living men,
(And I heard nor sigh nor groan,)
With heavy thump, a lifeless lump,
They dropped down one by one.

"The souls did from their bodies fly,—
They fled to bliss or woe!
And every soul, it passed me by,
Like the whizz of my cross-bow!"

Margin glosses:

No twilight within the courts of the Sun. 60

At the rising of the Moon, 65

One after another, 70

His shipmates drop down dead. 75

But Life-in-Death begins her work on the ancient Mariner. 80

PART IV.

"I fear thee, ancient Mariner!
I fear thy skinny hand!
And thou art long, and lank, and brown,
As is the ribbed sea-sand.

The Wedding-Guest
feareth that a Spirit
is talking to him;

"I fear thee and thy glittering eye,
And thy skinny hand, so brown."—
"Fear not, fear not, thou Wedding-Guest!
This body dropt not down.

But the ancient
Mariner assureth
him of his bodily
life, and proceedeth
to relate his horrible
penance.

5

"Alone, alone, all, all alone,
Alone on a wide, wide sea!
And never a saint took pity on
My soul in agony.

10

"The many men, so beautiful!
And they all dead did lie:
And a thousand thousand slimy things
Lived on; and so did I.

He despiseth the
creatures of the
calm.

15

"I looked upon the rotting sea,
And drew my eyes away;
I looked upon the rotting deck,
And there the dead men lay.

And envieth that
they should live, and
so many lie dead.

20

"I looked to heaven, and tried to pray;
But or ever a prayer had gusht,
A wicked whisper came, and made
My heart as dry as dust.

"I closed my lids, and kept them close,
And the balls like pulses beat;
For the sky and the sea, and the sea and
    the sky,
Lay like a load on my weary eye,
And the dead were at my feet.

25

"The cold sweat melted from their limbs,
Nor rot nor reek did they:
The look with which they looked on me
Had never passed away.

But the curse liveth   30
for him in the eye of
the dead men.

"An orphan's curse would drag to hell
A spirit from on high;
But oh! more horrible than that
Is the curse in a dead man's eye!
Seven days, seven nights, I saw that curse,
And yet I could not die.

35

In his loneliness and
fixedness he yearneth

"The moving Moon went up the sky,
And nowhere did abide:
Softly she was going up,
And a star or two beside—

towards the jour-   40
neying Moon, and
the stars that still
sojourn, yet still
move onward; and

"Her beams bemocked the sultry main,
Like April hoar-frost spread;
But where the ship's huge shadow lay,
The charmed water burnt alway
A still and awful red.

everywhere the blue
sky belongs to them,
and is their appoint-
ed rest, and their
native country and
their own natural   45
homes, which they
enter unannounced,
as lords that are cer-
tainly expected and
yet there is a silent
joy at their arrival.

"Beyond the shadow of the ship,
I watched the water-snakes:
They moved in tracks of shining white,
And when they reared, the elfish light
Fell off in hoary flakes.

50

By the light of the
Moon he beholdeth
God's creatures of
the great calm.

"Within the shadow of the ship
I watched their rich attire:
Blue, glossy green, and velvet black,
They coiled and swam; and every track
Was a flash of golden fire.

55

"O happy living things! no tongue
Their beauty might declare:
A spring of love gushed from my heart,

Their beauty and
their happiness.   60

And I blessed them unaware:
Sure my kind saint took pity on me,
And I blessed them unaware.

He blesseth them in
his heart.

"The self-same moment I could pray;
And from my neck so free
The Albatross fell off, and sank
Like lead into the sea."

The spell begins to
break.

65

PART V.

"Oh sleep! it is a gentle thing,
Beloved from pole to pole!
To Mary Queen the praise be given!
She sent the gentle sleep from Heaven,
That slid into my soul.

5

"The silly buckets on the deck,
That had so long remained,
I dreamt that they were filled with dew;
And when I awoke, it rained.

By grace of the holy
Mother, the ancient
Mariner is refreshed
with rain.

"My lips were wet, my throat was cold,
My garments all were dank;
Sure I had drunken in my dreams,
And still my body drank.

10

"I moved, and could not feel my limbs:
I was so light—almost
I thought that I had died in sleep,
And was a blessed ghost.

15

"And soon I heard a roaring wind:
It did not come anear;
But with its sound it shook the sails,
That were so thin and sere.

He heareth sounds
and seeth strange
sights and commo-
tions in the sky and
the elements.

20

"The upper air burst into life!
And a hundred fire-flags sheen,
To and fro they were hurried about!
And to and fro, and in and out,   25
The wan stars danced between.

"And the coming wind did roar more loud,
And the sails did sigh like sedge;
And the rain poured down from one black
    cloud;
The Moon was at its edge.   30

"The thick black cloud was cleft, and still
The Moon was at its side:
Like waters shot from some high crag,
The lightning fell with never a jag,
A river steep and wide.   35

"The loud wind never reached the ship,   The bodies of the
Yet now the ship moved on!   ship's crew are in-
Beneath the lightning and the moon   spired, and the ship
The dead men gave a groan.   moves on;

"They groaned, they stirred, they all uprose,   40
Nor spake, nor moved their eyes;
It had been strange, even in a dream,
To have seen those dead men rise.

The helmsman steered, the ship moved on;
Yet never a breeze up blew;
The mariners all 'gan work the ropes,   45
Where they were wont to do;
They raised their limbs like lifeless tools—
We were a ghastly crew.

"The body of my brother's son   50
Stood by me, knee to knee:
The body and I pulled at one rope,
But he said nought to me."

"I fear thee, ancient Mariner!"
"Be calm, thou Wedding-Guest!
'Twas not those souls that fled in pain,
Which to their corses came again,
But a troop of spirits blest:

For when it dawned—they dropped
    their arms,
And cluster'd round the mast;
Sweet sounds rose slowly through
    their mouths,
And from their bodies passed.

"Around, around, flew each sweet sound,
Then darted to the Sun;
Slowly the sounds came back again,
Now mixed, now one by one.

"Sometimes a-dropping from the sky
I heard the sky-lark sing;
Sometimes all little birds that are,
How they seemed to fill the sea and air
With their sweet jargoning!

"And now 'twas like all instruments,
Now like a lonely flute;
And now it is an angel's song,
That makes the heavens be mute.

"It ceased; yet still the sails made on
A pleasant noise till noon,
A noise like of a hidden brook
In the leafy month of June,
That to the sleeping woods all night
Singeth a quiet tune.

" Till noon we quietly sailed on,
Yet never a breeze did breathe:

But not by the souls
of the men, nor by
dæmons of earth or   55
middle air, but by
a blessed troop of
angelic spirits,

sent down by the
invocation of the
guardian saint.
  60

  65

  70

  75

  80

Slowly and smoothly went the ship,   85
Moved onward from beneath.

"Under the keel nine fathom deep,   The lonesome spirit
From the land of mist and snow,   from the south-pole
The spirit slid: and it was he   carries on the ship
That made the ship to go.   as far as the line,
The sails at noon left off their tune,   in obedience to   90
And the ship stood still also.   the angelic troop,
                                                but still requireth
                                                vengeance.

"The Sun, right up above the mast,
Had fixed her to the ocean:
But in a minute she 'gan stir,   95
With a short uneasy motion—
Backwards and forwards half her length
With a short uneasy motion.

"Then like a pawing horse let go,
She made a sudden bound:
It flung the blood into my head,   100
And I fell down in a swound.

"How long in that same fit I lay,   The Polar Spirit's
I have not to declare;   fellow demons,
But ere my living life returned,   the invisible
I heard, and in my soul discerned   inhabitants of the
Two voices in the air.   element, take part
                                                in his wrong; and   105
                                                two of them relate,
                                                one to the other,

"'Is it he?' quoth one, 'Is this the man?   that penance long
By Him who died on cross,   and heavy for the
With his cruel bow he laid full low   ancient Mariner
The harmless Albatross.   hath been accorded
                                                to the Polar Spirit, 110
                                                who returneth
                                                southward.

"'The spirit who bideth by himself
In the land of mist and snow,
He loved the bird that loved the man
Who shot him with his bow.'

"The other was a softer voice,   115
As soft as honey-dew;
Quoth he, 'The man hath penance done,
And penance more will do.'"

PART VI.

FIRST VOICE

"'But tell me, tell me! speak again,
Thy soft response renewing—
What makes that ship drive on so fast?
What is the ocean doing?'

SECOND VOICE

"'Still as a slave before his lord,   5
The Ocean hath no blast;
His great bright eye most silently
Up to the Moon is cast—

If he may know which way to go;
For she guides him smooth or grim.   10
See, brother, see! how graciously
She looketh down on him.'

FIRST VOICE

"'But why drives on that ship so fast,   The Mariner hath
Without or wave or wind?'   been cast into a
                                              trance; for the an-
                                              gelic power causeth
                                              the vessel to drive
                                              northward faster
                                              than human life can
                                              endure.

SECOND VOICE

"'The air is cut away before,   15
And closes from behind.
"'Fly, brother, fly! more high, more high!
Or we shall be belated:

For slow and slow that ship will go,
When the Mariner's trance is abated.'   20

"I woke, and we were sailing on   The supernatural
As in a gentle weather: motion is retarded;
'Twas night, calm night, the moon   the Mariner awakes,
    was high;   and his penance
The dead men stood together.   begins anew.

"All stood together on the deck,   25
For a charnel-dungeon fitter:
All fixed on me their stony eyes,
That in the Moon did glitter.

"The pang, the curse, with which they died,
Had never passed away: 30
I could not draw my eyes from theirs,
Nor turn them up to pray.

"And now this spell was snapt: once more   The curse is finally
I viewed the ocean green,   expiated.
And looked far forth, yet little saw
Of what had else been seen—   35

"Like one that on a lonesome road
Doth walk in fear and dread,
And having once turned round walks on,   40
And turns no more his head;
Because he knows, a frightful fiend
Doth close behind him tread.

"But soon there breathed a wind on me,
Nor sound nor motion made: 45
Its path was not upon the sea,
In ripple or in shade.

"It raised my hair, it fann'd my cheek
Like a meadow-gale of spring—

It mingled strangely with my fears, 50
Yet it felt like a welcoming.

"Swiftly, swiftly flew the ship,
Yet she sailed softly too:
Sweetly, sweetly blew the breeze—
On me alone it blew.

"Oh! dream of joy! is this indeed
The light-house top I see?
Is this the hill? is this the kirk?
Is this mine own countree?

And the ancient Mariner beholdeth his native country. 55

"We drifted o'er the harbour-bar,
And I with sobs did pray—
O let me be awake, my God!
Or let me sleep alway.

60

"The harbour-bay was clear as glass,
So smoothly it was strewn!
And on the bay the moonlight lay,
And the shadow of the moon.

65

"The rock shone bright, the kirk no less,
That stands above the rock:
The moonlight steeped in silentness,
The steady weathercock.

70

"And the bay was white with silent light,
Till, rising from the same,
Full many shapes, that shadows were,
In crimson colours came.

The angelic spirits leave the dead bodies,

"A little distance from the prow
Those crimson shadows were:
I turned my eyes upon the deck—
Oh, Christ! what saw I there!

And appear in their own forms of light. 75

"Each corse lay flat, lifeless and flat,
And by the holy rood!

80

A man all light, a seraph-man,
On every corse there stood.

"This seraph-band, each waved his hand,
It was a heavenly sight!
They stood as signals to the land,   85
Each one a lovely light;

"This seraph-band, each waved his hand,
No voice did they impart—
No voice; but oh! the silence sank   90
Like music on my heart.

"But soon I heard the dash of oars,
I heard the Pilot's cheer;
My head was turned perforce away,
And I saw a boat appear.

"The Pilot and the Pilot's boy,   95
I heard them coming fast:
Dear Lord in Heaven! it was a joy
The dead men could not blast.

" I saw a third—I heard his voice:
It is the Hermit good!   100
He singeth loud his godly hymns
That he makes in the wood.
He'll shrieve my soul, he'll wash away
The Albatross's blood."

PART VII.

"This Hermit good lives in that wood   The Hermit of the
Which slopes down to the sea.   wood
How loudly his sweet voice he rears!
He loves to talk with mariners
That come from a far countree.   5

"He kneels at morn, and noon, and eve—
He hath a cushion plump:
It is the moss that wholly hides
The rotted old oak stump.

"The skiff-boat neared: I heard them talk,   10
'Why, this is strange, I trow!
Where are those lights so many and fair,
That signal made but now?'

"'Strange, by my faith!' the Hermit said—   Approacheth the
'And they answered not our cheer!   ship with wonder.   15
The planks looked warped! and see
        those sails,
How thin they are and sere!
I never saw aught like to them,
Unless perchance it were

"'Brown skeletons of leaves that lag   20
My forest-brook along;
When the ivy-tod is heavy with snow,
And the owlet whoops to the wolf below,
That eats the she-wolf's young.'

"'Dear Lord! it hath a fiendish look—   25
(The Pilot made reply)
I am a-feared'—'Push on, push on!'
Said the Hermit cheerily.

"The boat came closer to the ship,
But I nor spake nor stirred;   30
The boat came close beneath the ship,
And straight a sound was heard.

"Under the water it rumbled on,   The ship
Still louder and more dread: suddenly sinketh.
It reached the ship, it split the bay;   35
The ship went down like lead.

"Stunned by that loud and dreadful sound,
Which sky and ocean smote,
Like one that hath been seven days drowned
My body lay afloat;   40
But swift as dreams, myself I found
Within the Pilot's boat.

The ancient Mariner
is saved in the Pilot's
boat.

"Upon the whirl, where sank the ship,
The boat spun round and round;   45
And all was still, save that the hill
Was telling of the sound.

"I moved my lips—the Pilot shrieked
And fell down in a fit;
The holy Hermit raised his eyes,   50
And prayed where he did sit.

"I took the oars: the Pilot's boy,
Who now doth crazy go,
Laughed loud and long, and all the while   55
His eyes went to and fro.
'Ha! ha!' quoth he, 'full plain I see.
The Devil knows how to row.'

"And now, all in my own countree,
I stood on the firm land!
The Hermit stepped forth from the boat,   60
And scarcely he could stand.

"'O shrieve me, shrieve me, holy man!'
The Hermit crossed his brow.
'Say quick,' quoth he, 'I bid thee say—
What manner of man art thou?'

The ancient Mariner
earnestly entreateth
the Hermit to
shrieve him; and the
penance of life falls
on him.

"Forthwith this frame of mine was   65
    wrenched
With a woful agony,

Which forced me to begin my tale;
And then it left me free.

"Since then, at an uncertain hour,
That agony returns:
And till my ghastly tale is told,
This heart within me burns.

And ever and anon
throughout his
future life an agony
constraineth him to
travel from land to
land,

70

"I pass, like night, from land to land;
I have strange power of speech;
That moment that his face I see,
I know the man that must hear me:
To him my tale I teach.

75

"What loud uproar bursts from that door!
The wedding-guests are there:
But in the garden-bower the bride
And bride-maids singing are:
And hark the little vesper bell,
Which biddeth me to prayer!

80

"O Wedding-Guest! this soul hath been
Alone on a wide, wide sea:
So lonely 'twas, that God himself
Scarce seemèd there to be.

85

" O sweeter than the marriage-feast,
'Tis sweeter far to me,
To walk together to the kirk
With a goodly company!—

90

"To walk together to the kirk,
And all together pray,
While each to his great Father bends,
Old men, and babes, and loving friends
And youths and maidens gay!

95

"Farewell, farewell! but this I tell
To thee, thou Wedding-Guest!

And to teach, by his
own example, love

He prayeth well, who loveth well
Both man and bird and beast.

"He prayeth best, who loveth best
All things both great and small;
For the dear God who loveth us,
He made and loveth all."

The Mariner, whose eye is bright,
Whose beard with age is hoar,
Is gone: and now the Wedding-Guest
Turned from the Bridegroom's door.

He went like one that hath been stunned,
And is of sense forlorn:
A sadder and a wiser man,
He rose the morrow morn.

1798

and reverence to all things that God made and loveth. 100

105

110

KUBLA KHAN;

OR, A VISION IN A DREAM. A FRAGMENT.

THE FOLLOWING FRAGMENT is here published at the request of a poet of great and deserved celebrity,[1] and, as far as the Author's own opinions are concerned, rather as a psychological curiosity, than on the ground of any supposed *poetic* merits.

In the summer of the year 1797, the Author, then in ill health, had retired to a lonely farm-house between Porlock and Linton, on the Exmoor confines of Somerset and Devonshire. In consequence of a slight indisposition, <u>an anodyne</u> had been prescribed, from the effects of which he fell asleep in his chair at the moment that he was reading the following sentence, or words of the same substance, in "Purchas's Pilgrimage:" "Here the Khan Kubla commanded a palace to be built, and a stately garden thereunto. And thus ten miles of fertile ground were inclosed with a wall."[2] The Author continued for about three hours in a profound sleep, at least of the external senses, during which time he has the most vivid confidence, that he could not have composed less than from two to three hundred lines; if that indeed can be called composition in which all the images rose up before him as *things*, with a parallel production of the correspondent expressions, without any sensation or consciousness of effort. On awaking he appeared to himself to have a distinct recollection of the whole, and taking his pen, ink, and paper, instantly and eagerly wrote down the lines that are here preserved. At this moment he was unfortunately called out by a person on business from Porlock, and detained by him above an hour, and on his return to his room, found to his no small surprise and mortification, that though he still retained some vague and dim recollection of the general purport of the vision, yet, with the exception of some eight or ten scattered lines and images, all the rest had passed away like the images on the surface of a stream into which a stone has been cast, but, alas! without the after restoration of the latter:

> Then all the charm
> Is broken—all that phantom-world so fair

---

1 Lord Byron.

2 From Samuel Purchas's *Purchas his Pilgrimes*: "In Xamdu did Cublai Can build a stately Palace, encompassing sixteene miles of plaine ground with a wall, wherein are fertile Meddowes, pleasant Springs, delightfull Streames, and all sorts of beasts of chase and game, and in the middest thereof a sumptuous house of pleasure."

Vanishes, and a thousand circlets spread,
And each mis-shape[s] the other. Stay awhile,
Poor youth! who scarcely dar'st lift up thine eyes—
The stream will soon renew its smoothness, soon
The visions will return! And lo, he stays,
And soon the fragments dim of lovely forms
Come trembling back, unite, and now once more
The pool becomes a mirror.
[From *The Picture; or, the Lover's Resolution*, II. lines 91-100.]

Yet from the still surviving recollections in his mind, the Author has frequently purposed to finish for himself what had been originally, as it were, given to him. Σαμερον αδιον ασω: but the to-morrow is yet to come.

As a contrast to this vision, I have annexed a fragment of a very different character, describing with equal fidelity the dream of pain and disease.[1]

In Xanadu did Kubla Khan
A stately pleasure-dome decree:
Where Alph, the sacred river, ran
Through caverns measureless to man
Down to a sunless sea.   5
So twice five miles of fertile ground
With walls and towers were girdled round:
And here were gardens bright with sinuous rills,
Where blossom'd many an incense-bearing tree;
And here were forests ancient as the hills,   10
Infolding sunny spots of greenery.

But oh that deep romantic chasm which slanted
Down the green hill athwart a cedarn cover!
A savage place! as holy and inchanted
As e'er beneath a waning moon was haunted   15
By woman wailing for her demon-lover!
And from this chasm, with ceaseless turmoil seething,
As if this earth in fast thick pants were breathing,
A mighty fountain momently was forced:
Amid whose swift half-intermitted Burst   20
Huge fragments vaulted like rebounding hail,
Or chaffy grain beneath the thresher's flail:

---

1 Coleridge references "The Pains of Sleep."

And 'mid these dancing rocks at once and ever
It flung up momently the sacred river.
Five miles meandering with a mazy motion   25
Through wood and dale the sacred river ran,
Then reached the caverns measureless to man,
And sank in tumult to a lifeless ocean:
And 'mid this tumult Kubla heard from far
Ancestral voices prophesying war!   30

     The shadow of the dome of pleasure
     Floated midway on the waves;
     Where was heard the mingled measure
     From the fountain and the caves.
It was a miracle of rare device,   35
A sunny pleasure-dome with caves of ice!

     A damsel with a dulcimer
     In a vision once I saw:
     It was an Abyssinian maid,
     And on her dulcimer she play'd,   40
     Singing of Mount Abora.
     Could I revive within me
     Her symphony and song,
     To such a deep delight 'twould win me,
That with music loud and long,   45
I would build that dome in air,
That sunny dome! those caves of ice!
And all who heard should see them there,
And all should cry, Beware! Beware!
His flashing eyes, his floating hair!   50
Weave a circle round him thrice,
And close your eyes with holy dread:
For he on honey-dew hath fed,
And drunk the milk of Paradise.

1816

George Gordon, Lord Byron
1788–1824

George Gordon was born to Captain John "Mad Jack" Byron, a wild-mannered officer in the British army, and Catherine Gordon, a Scots heiress who Byron claimed was a distant descendent of James I. Captain John squandered Catherine's fortune, and she was soon forced to take the infant George to Scotland. When the Captain died in 1791, Catherine sustained herself and her son on a scant income. Seven years later, however, George inherited the title and estates of his great-uncle, the 5th Baron Byron. He became George Gordon Byron, the 6th Baron Byron, when he was ten years old. He and his mother returned to England where, against the advice of Byron's financial advisor, the two lived in Newstead Abbey, the crumbling mansion that Henry VIII had bestowed upon the Byron family.

Byron enrolled in one of the most prestigious schools in London in 1801, and though he was extremely sensitive about his clubfoot and subsequent lameness, his curiosity remained uninhibited. When he proceeded to Cambridge in 1805, his interests burgeoned. He lived lavishly and extravagantly, keeping a pet bear in his living quarters, engaging in sexually ambivalent behavior, and amassing large debts. After taking a seat in the House of Lords in 1809, Byron and his friend John Cam Hobhouse went on a grand tour of the continent, travelling to Portugal, Spain, Malta, Greece, and Albania before sailing to Constantinople. He also swam the legendary Hellespont strait from Sestos to Abydos, a feat he readily boasted of throughout his life. Byron's journeys reshaped his attitudes toward people, manners, and foreign cultures, and his ventures supplied him with a range of inspirational material.

Byron returned to London in 1811 and continued drafting *Childe Harold's Pilgrimage*, a poem he began while abroad. Upon the publication of the first two cantos in 1812, Byron wrote, "I awoke one morning and found myself famous." The five hundred copies printed sold out in three days; a total 4,500 copies sold in under six months. The poem, like all of Byron's pieces, is autobiographical. Childe Harold, the disillusioned protagonist, takes solitary journeys to foreign lands, yearning to distract himself from his aimless and indulgent existence. While traveling through each location, he portrays significant people, ideas, and events, creating a travelogue that is fitted both with historical and visual elements. Although Childe encounters beautiful and noteworthy places, however, melancholy seeps into his travels. Ambition, as Childe discovers, is vain because perfection can never be found. Pleasure, too, provides only impermanent happiness.

The poem brought Byron literary esteem as well as personal notoriety. His eccentric, unrestrained, promiscuous lifestyle became public. Whisked into social circles, Byron was soon involved in a scandal with the witty and unconventional Lady Caroline Lamb. The two would have eloped had Hobhouse not wisely prevented it. Byron next began an escapade with Lady Oxford before having a relationship with his married half-sister, Augusta Leigh, and flirting with Lady Frances Webster. Hoping to escape a seemingly endless cycle of affairs, Byron proposed to Annabella Milbanke, an intellectual woman, or "bluestocking," in December of 1814. The two married and had a daughter the following year, but by 1816, their marriage was clearly doomed. Byron's sexual and behavioral peculiarities, his explosive and cruel temper, and his financial irresponsibility caused Annabella to seriously question his sanity. Amid rumors of a renewed affair with Augusta Leigh and his suspected bisexuality, Anabella left him, taking their daughter with her. Later that year, Byron went abroad. He never returned to England.

Rather, he traveled to Switzerland with his friend Dr. John Polidori. They settled near Lake Geneva, close to where Percy Bysshe Shelley lived with Mary Godwin (later Mary Shelley) and her half-sister Claire Clairmont. One evening, Byron, the Shelleys, and Polidori challenged one another to write ghost stories. The competition resulted in the eventual publication of Mary Shelley's famous gothic novel, *Frankenstein*, and Polidori's *The Vampyre*, the first English vampire tale. In addition to writing assiduously, Bryon resolved matters with Claire, who was pregnant from their earlier affair. He vouched to care for their child but wanted to remain abroad. Claire gave birth to a daughter named Clara Allegra in Bath, England, in 1817. Also that year Byron reunited with his college companion Hobhouse, and the two left for Italy followed by Greece. Byron continued his pattern of affairs, first with his landlord's wife and then with a baker's wife, as well as his zealous spending habits. He sold Newstead Abbey for £94,500, a sum that cleared his debts and provided sufficient funds to live on, and began *Don Juan*, his next major work.

In Italy, Byron met the nineteen-year-old Countess Teresa Gamba Guiccioli, a woman married to a wealthy man nearly triple her age. Their attraction was mutual, and Byron became her *cavalier servente*, or gentleman-in-waiting. Their affair was his last adulterous act. He befriended her father and brother, the patriotic Counts Ruggero Gamba Ghiselli and Pietro Gamba. The countess's brother eventually initiated Byron into the Carbonari society, a secret organization that aspired to free Italy from Austrian rule. Byron's association with the Gamba family summoned the attention of the Austrian secret police, who began monitoring his activities and reading his mail. The Carbonari revolutionary movement, however, collapsed, and

Teresa and her family were exiled from their home. The Countess, who had obtained a legal separation from her husband, traveled to Pisa along with her father and brother in 1821, and Byron soon followed. While there, he wrote copiously, penning three plays that year as well as continuing work on *Don Juan*. Scathing criticism and disapproval assailed *Don Juan*, which was published anonymously. On a journey abroad, the naïve libertine Don Juan survives a shipwreck that leaves him on a Greek Island. From there, he travels to Constantinople, Russia, and England. Byron's plot veils satirical social commentary; he confronts the hypocrisy of social and sexual conventions, worthless ambitions, and his general frustration with humanity. Though the public condemned *Don Juan*'s indecency and slanders, the poem sold well. Byron completed sixteen cantos total. The seventeenth remained unfinished when he died.

1822 marked a grieving period: Byron's daughter Allegra died, and Shelley, who had become a close friend, drowned at sea. The following year, Byron ventured to Greece and began acting as an agent of the London Greek Committee, a group that formed to help the Greeks gain independence from Turkish rule. In addition to providing financial assistance and medical supplies for the Greek War of Independence, he commanded a brigade. His efforts earned him a title as a Greek national hero.

Despite falling severely ill, Byron voyaged to Missolonghi in February 1824. Unpleasant weather, unreciprocated love from his 15-year-old page boy, and stress and pressure from Greek authorities encumbered his recovery. His fever and aches intensified after being caught in a rainstorm. Byron's health, already weakened, further deteriorated when his physicians bled him. His strength was sapped into non-existence, and after slipping into a comatose state, he died on April 19. When his body was returned to England, he was denied burial at Westminster Abbey for his unconventional lifestyle and negative reputation. His daughter requested his burial in their family vault, and forty-seven carriages (many of them empty) followed his hearse out of London. 145 years passed before Byron got a memorial on the Abbey floor.

Although he was not buried among esteemed and beloved poets, the endurance of the Byronic hero testifies to Byron's impact on English literature. The Byronic hero varies, but the hero is frequently a melancholy man endowed with noble principles and formidable courage. This hero is simultaneously haunted by a dark, mysterious, past wrongdoing. Further, although the hero is proud and passionate, he is alienated from others. Childe Harold was the first Byronic hero, but scores of similar characters have since emerged, such as the monster in Mary Shelley's *Frankenstein*.

Byron differs from his Romantic contemporaries primarily because he adhered to Restoration and Augustan writing styles. Whereas fellow Romantics emphasized emotion, he preferred to explain his ideas through reason, satire, and wit. Nevertheless, as his autobiographical works attest, he observed the trend of enfolding oneself into one's writings. Often brooding, remorseful, and despairing, Byron gleaned the label of "gloomy egoist" for his self-confessional and self-analytical style. At times he grew despondent for the rift between ideals and reality, while at other moments he mocked ambition altogether. Byron's complex, multifaceted personality suffuses his poetry.

1788	George Gordon Byron born 22 January
1798	Becomes Lord Byron, 6th Baron Byron, after inheriting the title and estates of his great-uncle
1805–08	Attends Trinity College, University of Cambridge, and earns a master's degree
1809	Takes seat in House of Lords in March; *English Bards, and Scotch Reviewers*
1809–1811	Takes grand tour of Europe accompanied by John Cam Hobhouse
1812–18	*Childe Harold's Pilgrimage*
1815	*Melodies Ancient and Modern*; Marries Anne Isabella Milbanke; daughter Augusta Ada Byron born 10 December
1816	*Parisina*; *The Siege of Corinth*; legally separates from Annabella; leaves England and never returns
1817	Clara Allegra born to Claire Clairmont on 12 January; travels to Italy and Greece, accompanied by Hobhouse; *Manfred*
1818	*Beppo: A Venetian Story*
1819–24	*Don Juan*
1822	Daughter Allegra dies 20 April in a convent in Bagnacavallo, Italy; his close friend Percy Bysshe Shelley dies 8 July
1824	Dies 19 April in Missolonghi, Greece and is buried in his family vault at Hucknall Torkard Church, near Newstead Abbey, in England

*1815
* compares the woman to a lovely night
* harmonious meeting between
  darkness and light
* representative of inner goodness
and virtue

SHE WALKS IN BEAUTY

She walks in beauty, like the night
  Of cloudless climes and starry skies;
And all that's best of dark and bright
  Meet in her aspect and her eyes:
Thus mellow'd to that tender light   5
  Which heaven to gaudy day denies.

One shade the more, one ray the less,
  Had half impair'd the nameless grace
Which waves in every raven tress,
  Or softly lightens o'er her face;   10
Where thoughts serenely sweet express
  How pure, how dear, their dwelling-place.

And on that cheek, and o'er that brow,
  So soft, so calm, yet eloquent,
The smiles that win, the tints that glow,   15
  But tell of days in goodness spent,
A mind at peace with all below,
  A heart whose love is innocent.

1815

(handwritten, top left: — Iambic pentameter (mostly) — Blank verse)

DARKNESS

*(handwritten, top right: *Human greed and selfishness *Dreams about when the sun burns out and the whole world turns into darkness * about Mercy)*

I had a dream, which was not all a dream.
The bright sun was extinguish'd, and the stars
Did wander darkling in the eternal space,
Rayless, and pathless, and the icy earth
Swung blind and blackening in the moonless air;   5
Morn came and went—and came, and brought no day,
And men forgot their passions in the dread
Of this their desolation; and all hearts
Were chill'd into a selfish prayer for light:
And they did live by watchfires—and the thrones,   10
The palaces of crowned kings—the huts,
The habitations of all things which dwell,
Were burnt for beacons; cities were consumed,
And men were gather'd round their blazing homes
To look once more into each other's face;   15
Happy were those who dwelt within the eye
Of the volcanos, and their mountain-torch:
A fearful hope was all the world contain'd;
Forests were set on fire—but hour by hour
They fell and faded—and the crackling trunks   20
Extinguish'd with a crash—and all was black.
The brows of men by the despairing light
Wore an unearthly aspect, as by fits
The flashes fell upon them; some lay down
And hid their eyes and wept; and some did rest   25
Their chins upon their clenched hands, and smiled;
And others hurried to and fro, and fed
Their funeral piles with fuel, and look'd up
With mad disquietude on the dull sky,
The pall of a past world; and then again   30
With curses cast them down upon the dust,
And gnash'd their teeth and howl'd: the wild birds shriek'd
And, terrified, did flutter on the ground,
And flap their useless wings; the wildest brutes
Came tame and tremulous; and vipers crawl'd   35

(handwritten, right margin: All reference to time disapears after this; shows how sun is only real means of telling time & break down of society; time is a theme in general)

And twined themselves among the multitude,
Hissing, but stingless—they were slain for food:
And War, which for a moment was no more,
Did glut himself again;—a meal was bought
With blood, and each sate sullenly apart   40
Gorging himself in gloom: no love was left;
All earth was but one thought—and that was death
Immediate and inglorious; and the pang
Of famine fed upon all entrails—men
Died, and their bones were tombless as their flesh;   45
The meager by the meager were devour'd,
Even dogs assail'd their masters, all save one,
And he was faithful to a corse, and kept
The birds and beasts and famish'd men at bay,
Till hunger clung them, or the dropping dead   50
Lured their lank jaws; himself sought out no food,
But with a piteous and perpetual moan,
And a quick desolate cry, licking the hand
Which answer'd not with a caress—he died.
The crowd was famish'd by degrees; but two   55
Of an enormous city did survive,
And they were enemies: they met beside
The dying embers of an altar-place
Where had been heap'd a mass of holy things
For an unholy usage; they raked up,   60
And shivering scd with their cold skeleton hands
The feeble ashes, and their feeble breath
Blew for a little life, and made a flame
Which was a mockery; then they lifted up
Their eyes as it grew lighter, and beheld   65
Each other's aspects—saw, and shriek'd, and died—
Even of their mutual hideousness they died,
Unknowing who he was upon whose brow
Famine had written Fiend. The world was void,
The populace and the powerful was a lump,   70
Seasonless, herbless, treeless, manless, lifeless—
A lump of death,—a chaos of hard clay.
The rivers, lakes, and ocean all stood still,
And nothing stirr'd within their silent depths;
Ships sailorless lay rotting on the sea,   75

And their masts fell down piecemeal; as they dropp'd
They slept on the abyss without a surge—
The waves were dead; the tides were in their grave,
The Moon, their mistress, had expired before;
The winds were wither'd in the stagnant air,   80
And the clouds perish'd! Darkness had no need
Of aid from them—She was the Universe.

World ends as it began – in darkness
theme of time

1816 → *"The Year Without a Summer"; volcanic eruption*
in 1815 caused wide-spread climate changes bc of ash cloud;
year marked by famine & unseasonable cold, likely the
inspiration for this poem
⌐ Poem almost romanticizes darkness; terrifying,
dark sort of allure
⌐ Theme of imagination

about adventures

SO, WE'LL GO NO MORE A ROVING

I.
So we'll go no more a roving
  So late into the night,
Though the heart be still as loving,
  And the moon be still as bright.

II.
For the sword outwears its sheath,   5
  And the soul wears out the breast,
And the heart must pause to breathe,
  And love itself have rest.

III.
Though the night was made for loving,
  And the day returns too soon,   10
Yet we'll go no more a roving
  By the light of the moon.

1830

PERCY BYSSHE SHELLEY
1792–1822

Countercultural to his core, nearly every aspect of Percy Bysshe Shelley's life philosophy challenged societal norms. He recognized that established standards propagated economic, social, gender, and political inequality, and he believed that peaceful revolution was the only solution. Oppression and injustice of any kind incensed him, for he truly loved humanity and yearned for a world where all people, irrespective of their religious differences, could live in harmony.

Shelley was born into an aristocratic family. Heir to his grandfather's rich estates, he was expected to uphold conservative values and go into government. Shelley began his education at Syon House Academy, then continued at Eton College, where older and stronger boys terrorized him incessantly. To escape mental and physical bullying, he read, wrote, and drew. When he entered the University of Oxford in 1810, he had already published two Gothic novels and three volumes of verse. He co-authored a pamphlet, *The Necessity of Atheism*, with Thomas Jefferson Hogg, a radical Oxford student and his closest friend. The anonymous pamphlet asserted there was no empirical proof of God's existence. Shelley and Hogg mailed the piece to clergymen, bishops, and the University heads, hoping to incite a response. Shelley refused to admit authorship when questioned, and he was resultantly expelled from Oxford after just six months of attendance.

Shelley did not apologize to his family for the publication. Consequently, his relationship with his father became increasingly strained. After Oxford, Shelley's father and grandfather attempted to use economic means to control the young poet's views. In 1811, Shelley rebelled against their authority and eloped with Harriet Westbrook to Scotland. Though he saw marriage as a misogynistic and degrading institution, he acknowledged the prejudices against unmarried women and united with Harriet. The following year, Shelley, Harriet, and her sister Eliza Westbrook travelled to Ireland to circulate pamphlets. Using his *Address to the Irish People*, Shelley advocated for political rights for Roman Catholics, autonomy for Ireland, and his other freethinking ideals. The trio distributed Shelley's *Address* in pubs, pasted it on walls, dispersed it in the streets, and threw it from their house balcony. Shelley and Harriet journeyed to Lynmouth, Devon, and North Wales to issue more political pamphlets.

The couple partook in political causes and lived on the small allowances given to them by their families. Shelley's philanthropy, however, exceeded his income, and he was driven to moneylenders in London in 1813. During the same year, he privately printed his first major political work, *Queen Mab, A Philosophical Poem* (which was greatly inspired by William Godwin's *Enquiry Concerning Political Justice*) at his own expense. After the fairy Queen Mab reveals the tragedies of the past and present to the spirit of a young woman, the Queen promotes an idealistic future free of the follies of history. Denouncing war, monarchy, marriage, and institutionalized religion, Shelley's work clashed against the ideas of his time. He faithfully defended his poem, even though its revolutionary ideas brought him infamy and he grew dissatisfied by it in his later years. *Queen Mab* went through a dozen editions during the 1830s, many of which (to Shelley's embarrassment) were pirated. The poem eventually reached a working-class readership.

In 1814, Shelley fell in love with Godwin's daughter, Mary Wollstonecraft. His affection infuriated Godwin. Shelley and Mary fled to France, taking Claire Clairmont, Mary's stepsister, with them. By eloping, Shelley had essentially abandoned Harriet. Shelley insisted that his relationship with Harriet was built on friendship, not passion, but he believed in nonexclusive love and invited her to live with them as a sister. In May of 1816, Shelley, Mary, and Claire departed for Geneva, Switzerland, to meet with Claire's lover, Lord Byron. While in Geneva, Shelley composed "Mont Blanc" and Mary began her famous novel, *Frankenstein.* When the Shelleys returned to London, Shelley was shunned by the public, the Godwins, his family, and many of his friends. His unconventional views made him an outcast. Late in 1816, Harriet, pregnant by an unknown lover, drowned herself. Shelley was denied custody of their two children (their daughter had been born in 1813; their son, in 1814), and they were placed in foster care.

Shelley and Mary married in 1816 with Godwin's blessing. The death of Shelley's grandfather in 1815 left the poet with substantial funds, but the couple was forced to live meagerly. In addition to his own obligations, Shelley had generously undertaken Godwin's debts and also assumed the financial needs of his acquaintances. Unable to pay the lenders, the Shelleys, their children, and Mary's stepsister travelled to Italy in the spring of 1818. They migrated between cities and towns until they eventually resided with Lord Byron. Shelley wrote some of his most famous pieces during his stay with Byron, including *Julian and Maddalo*, a poem based on a trip he took with Byron in Venice, and *Prometheus Unbound.* Shelley's visits to Mount Vesuvius, Pompeii, and Herculaneum also inspired his works.

By the summer of 1819, the Shelleys had lost all of their children. Their first child had died in 1815, twelve days after her birth, and their second daughter fell ill and perished shortly after traveling to Venice in 1818. In 1819, their three-and-a-half year old son died in Rome. Mary gave birth to another son in November, but Percy and Mary's marriage had lost its happiness.

Removed from the annoyances of British policy, government, and people, Shelley started his most radical literary endeavors. His prior poems and prose described bloodless revolutions and idealistic protagonists; his next pieces embodied his ideals with renewed vigor and intensity. He wrote his keystone achievements in 1819–1821, beginning with the completion of his closet-drama *Prometheus Unbound*. In it, Shelley reinvents the story of the Titan god Prometheus, who rises above his oppressors and restores human society through the creative arts. Shelley also penned *The Cenci*, a Jacobean-style tragedy of incestuous rape and patricide. *The Mask of Anarchy*, too radical to be printed during Shelley's own lifetime, urges people to follow poetic and artistic virtues, revolt against tyrants, and reform society. Shelley further associated societal reform with poetry, as in his essay "A Defence of Poetry." Shelley asserted that poetry was a means of uncovering beauty; civilization was formed and reformed through beauty. Shelley's other works from this period include those inspired by his literary friends. He drafted *Peter Bell the Third* after Wordsworth's satire on British corruption and discussed Keats's death with the pastoral elegy *Adonais*.

Shelley continued to write radical pieces after he and Mary moved to Pisa in 1820. He also composed a series of longing letters and verses to Jane Williams, with whom he had become irreversibly infatuated. Shelley considered Jane's husband, Edward Williams, among his closest friends. On July 8, 1822, Shelley and Edward sailed to Leghorn to welcome Leigh Hunt, an English essayist, poet, and critic. An unpredicted storm flooded their boat and the men drowned. Their bodies washed ashore several days later. Shelley's ashes were buried in Rome. By 1840, most of his unpublished works had been circulated due to Mary and Hunt's efforts.

Shelley sought to live by the ideals in works like Thomas Paine's *Rights of Man* and Godwin's *Enquiry Concerning Political Justice*. Beyond that, he proposed radical ideas of his own. Though he doubtlessly loved humanity, his idealism has been attributed to gross egotism. In an effort to live by his morals, he brought grim consequences to those closest to him. Shelley's political views were controversial, but they nevertheless empowered generations of radicals, including the Chartists of the mid 1800s, Mahatma Gandhi, and garment worker strikers in the U.S. By infusing politics into poetry, Shelley revealed his vision of what society could become.

1792	Percy Bysshe Shelley born 4 August
1802–04	Attends Syon House Academy
1804–10	Attends Eton College
1810	Enters University College, University of Oxford
1811	*The Necessity of Atheism*; Expelled from Oxford; Elopes with Harriet Westbrook
1813	*Queen Mab, A Philosophical Poem*
1814	Elopes with Mary Wollstonecraft Godwin
1816	Harriet dies; Shelley marries Mary; *Alastor; or, the Spirit of Solitude*
1819	*The Cenci*
1820	*Prometheus Unbound*; "Ode to the West Wind"
1822	Shelley dies 8 July after being shipwrecked, and his ashes are buried in Protestant Cemetery, Rome, Italy
1824	*Posthumous Poems*
1832	*The Mask of Anarchy*
1840	"A Defence of Poetry"

compares the power of the mountain against the power of the human imagination

MONT BLANC

LINES WRITTEN IN THE VALE OF CHAMOUNI

I.

The everlasting universe of things
Flows through the mind, and rolls its rapid waves,
Now dark—now glittering—now reflecting gloom—
Now lending splendor, where from secret springs
The source of human thought its tribute brings   5
Of waters,—with a sound but half its own,
Such as a feeble brook will oft assume
In the wild woods, among the mountains lone,
Where waterfalls around it leap for ever,
Where woods and winds contend, and a vast river   10
Over its rocks ceaselessly bursts and raves.

II.

Thus thou, Ravine of Arve—dark, deep Ravine—
Thou many-colour'd, many-voiced vale,
Over whose pines and crags and caverns sail
Fast clouds, shadows and sunbeams: awful scene,   15
Where Power in likeness of the Arve comes down
From the ice-gulfs that gird his secret throne,
Bursting through these dark mountains like the flame
Of lightning through the tempest; thou dost lie,
Thy giant brood of pines around thee clinging,   20
Children of elder time, in whose devotion
The chainless winds still come and ever came
To drink their odors, and their mighty swinging
To hear—an old and solemn harmony:
Thine earthly rainbows stretch'd across the sweep   25
Of the ethereal waterfall, whose veil
Robes some unsculptured image; the strange sleep
Which, when the voices of the desert fail,
Wraps all in its own deep eternity;—
Thy caverns, echoing to the Arve's commotion,   30
A loud lone sound, no other sound can tame:
Thou art pervaded with that ceaseless motion,

Thou art the path of that unresting sound—
Dizzy Ravine! and when I gaze on thee
I seem as in a trance sublime and strange   35
To muse on my own separate phantasy,
My own, my human mind, which passively
Now renders and receives fast influencings,
Holding an unremitting interchange
With the clear universe of things around;   40
One legion of wild thoughts, whose wandering wings
Now float above thy darkness, and now rest
Where that or thou art no unbidden guest,
In the still cave of the witch Poesy,
Seeking among the shadows that pass by,   45
Ghosts of all things that are, some shade of thee,
Some phantom, some faint image; till the breast
From which they fled recalls them, thou art there!

III.

Some say that gleams of a remoter world
Visit the soul in sleep,—that death is slumber,   50
And that its shapes the busy thoughts outnumber
Of those who wake and live.—I look on high;
Has some unknown omnipotence unfurl'd
The veil of life and death? or do I lie
In dream, and does the mightier world of sleep   55
Spread far around and inaccessibly
Its circles? For the very spirit fails,
Driven like a homeless cloud from steep to steep
That vanishes among the viewless gales!
Far, far above, piercing the infinite sky,   60
Mont Blanc appears,—still, snowy, and serene—
Its subject mountains their unearthly forms
Pile around it, ice and rock; broad vales between
Of frozen floods, unfathomable deeps,
Blue as the overhanging heaven, that spread   65
And wind among the accumulated steeps;
A desert peopled by the storms alone,
Save when the eagle brings some hunter's bone,
And the wolf tracts her there—how hideously
Its shapes are heap'd around! rude, bare, and high,   70
Ghastly, and scarr'd, and riven.—Is this the scene

Where the old Earthquake-demon taught her young
Ruin? Were these their toys? or did a sea
Of fire envelop once this silent snow?
None can reply—all seems eternal now.   75
The wilderness has a mysterious tongue
Which teaches awful doubt, or faith so mild,
So solemn, so serene, that man may be
But for such faith with nature reconciled:
Thou hast a voice, great Mountain, to repeal   80
Large codes of fraud and woe; not understood
By all, but which the wise, and great, and good
Interpret, or make felt, or deeply feel.

         Only those w/ sensibility can fully appreciate the mountain & its sublime nature

The fields, the lakes, the forests, and the streams,
Ocean, and all the living things that dwell   85
Within the daedal earth; lightning, and rain,
Earthquake, and fiery flood, and hurricane,
The torpor of the year when feeble dreams
Visit the hidden buds, or dreamless sleep
Holds every future leaf and flower;—the bound   90
With which from that detested trance they leap;
The works and ways of man, their death and birth,
And that of him and all that his may be;
All things that move and breathe with toil and sound
Are born and die; revolve, subside, and swell.   95
Power dwells apart in its tranquillity,
Remote, serene, and inaccessible:
And *this*, the naked countenance of earth,
On which I gaze, even these primaeval mountains,
Teach the adverting mind. The glaciers creep,   100
Like snakes that watch their prey, from their far fountains,
Slow rolling on; there, many a precipice
Frost and the Sun in scorn of mortal power
Have piled—dome, pyramid, and pinnacle,
A city of death, distinct with many a tower   105
And wall impregnable of beaming ice.
Yet not a city, but a flood of ruin
Is there, that from the boundaries of the sky
Rolls its perpetual stream; vast pines are strewing
Its destined path, or in the mangled soil   110

Branchless and shatter'd stand; the rocks, drawn down
From yon remotest waste, have overthrown
The limits of the dead and living world,
Never to be reclaim'd. The dwelling-place
Of insects, beasts, and birds, becomes its spoil;   115
Their food and their retreat for ever gone,
So much of life and joy is lost. The race
Of man flies far in dread; his work and dwelling
Vanish, like smoke before the tempest's stream,
And their place is not known. Below, vast caves   120
Shine in the rushing torrents' restless gleam,
Which, from those secret chasms in tumult welling
Meet in the vale, and one majestic River,
The breath and blood of distant lands, for ever
Rolls its loud waters to the ocean waves,   125
Breathes its swift vapours to the circling air.

> *Nature itself is powerful, sublime, & worthy of admiration*

V.

Mont Blanc yet gleams on high:—the power is there,
The still and solemn power of many sights
And many sounds, and much of life and death.
In the calm darkness of the moonless nights,
In the lone glare of day, the snows descend   130
Upon that Mountain; none beholds them there,
Nor when the flakes burn in the sinking sun,
Or the star-beams dart through them:—Winds contend
Silently there, and heap the snow with breath   135
Rapid and strong, but silently! Its home
The voiceless lightning in these solitudes
Keeps innocently, and like vapor broods
Over the snow. The secret strength of things
Which governs thought, and to the infinite dome   140
Of heaven is as a law, inhabits thee!
And what were thou, and earth, and stars, and sea,
If to the human mind's imaginings
Silence and solitude were vacancy?

> *Shows power of mind/imagination/contemplation despite its invisibility to others*

> *The mountain can teach us something*

> *Does the mountain mean anything w/out a mind to contemplate its meaning?*

SWITZERLAND, *June* 23, 1816

1817

*shows how
power cquesn't
last forever

* Rhamesses II
(The statue)

OZYMANDIAS[1]

I met a traveller from an antique land,
Who said: Two vast and trunkless legs of stone
Stand in the desert. Near them, on the sand,
Half sunk, a shatter'd visage lies, whose frown,
And wrinkled lip, and sneer of cold command,   5
Tell that its sculptor well those passions read
Which yet survive, stamp'd on these lifeless things,
The hand that mock'd them, and the heart that fed:
And on the pedestal these words appear:
"My name is Ozymandias, king of kings: 10
Look on my works, ye Mighty, and despair!"
Nothing beside remains. Round the decay
Of that colossal wreck, boundless and bare
The lone and level sands stretch far away.

Sculptor/artist's
work lives on
even though the
king does not;
imortality through
art

1818

— Sonnet

---

1 Shelley composed "Ozymandias" after reading an account by the Greek historian Diodorus Siculus, who described remnants of a desert statue. Ozymandias (the Greek name for Ramses II) ruled Egypt in the 13th century B.C.E. The British Museum acquired the ruins in 1817.

*Power of the wind, which can change
in the natural world*

ODE TO THE WEST WIND[2]

I.

O wild West Wind! thou breath of Autumn's being!
Thou, from whose unseen presence the leaves dead
Are driven, like ghosts from an enchanter fleeing,

Yellow, and black, and pale, and hectic red,
Pestilence-stricken multitudes: O, thou,   5
Who chariotest to their dark wintry bed

The winged seeds, where they lie cold and low,
Each like a corpse within its grave, until
Thine azure sister of the spring shall blow

Her clarion o'er the dreaming earth, and fill   10
(Driving sweet buds like flocks to feed in air)
With living hues and odors, plain and hill:

Wild Spirit, which art moving everywhere;
Destroyer and preserver; hear, O, hear!

II.

Thou on whose stream, 'mid the steep sky's commotion,   15
Loose clouds like earth's decaying leaves are shed,
Shook from the tangled boughs of Heaven and Ocean,

Angels of rain and lightning: there are spread
On the blue surface of thine airy surge,
Like the bright hair uplifted from the head   20

---

2 This poem was conceived and chiefly written in a wood that skirts the Arno, near Florence, and on a
day when that tempestuous wind, whose temperature is at once mild and animating, was collecting the
vapors which pour down the autumnal rains. They began, as I foresaw, at sunset with a violent tempest
of hail and rain, attended by that magnificent thunder and lightning peculiar to the Cisalpine regions.
    The phenomenon alluded to at the conclusion of the third stanza is well known to naturalists.
The vegetation at the bottom of the sea, of rivers, and of lakes, sympathizes with that of the land
in the change of seasons, and is consequently influenced by the winds which announce it [Shelley].

Of some fierce Maenad,[1] even from the dim verge
Of the horizon to the zenith's height,
The locks of the approaching storm. Thou dirge

Of the dying year, to which this closing night
Will be the dome of a vast sepulchre,   25
Vaulted with all thy congregated might

Of vapours, from whose solid atmosphere
Black rain, and fire, and hail will burst: O, hear!

III.

Thou who didst waken from his summer dreams
The blue Mediterranean, where he lay,   30
Lull'd by the coil of his crystalline streams,

Beside a pumice isle in Baiae's bay,
And saw in sleep old palaces and towers
Quivering within the wave's intenser day,

All overgrown with azure moss and flowers   35
So sweet, the sense faints picturing them!—Thou,
For whose path the Atlantic's level powers

Cleave themselves into chasms, while far below
The sea blooms and the oozy woods which wear
The sapless foliage of the ocean, know   40

Thy voice, and suddenly grow gray with fear,
And tremble and despoil themselves: O, hear!

IV.

If I were a dead leaf thou mightest bear;
If I were a swift cloud to fly with thee;
A wave to pant beneath thy power, and share   45

---

1 Female followers of Dionysus, the Greek god of wine, roamed the mountains and forests while
dancing.

The impulse of thy strength, only less free
Than thou, O; uncontrollable! If even
I were as in my boyhood, and could be

The comrade of thy wanderings over heaven,
As then, when to outstrip thy skiey speed   50
Scarce seemed a vision; I would ne'er have striven

As thus with thee in prayer in my sore need.
Oh! lift me as a wave, a leaf, a cloud!
I fall upon the thorns of life! I bleed!

A heavy weight of hours has chain'd and bow'd   55
One too like thee: tameless, and swift, and proud.

                        V.

Make me thy lyre, even as the forest is:
What if my leaves are falling like its own!
The tumult of thy mighty harmonies

Will take from both a deep, autumnal tone,   60
Sweet, though in sadness. Be thou, spirit fierce,
My spirit! Be thou me, impetuous one!

Drive my dead thoughts over the universe
Like wither'd leaves, to quicken a new birth!
And, by the incantation of this verse,   65

Scatter, as from an unextinguish'd hearth
Ashes and sparks, my words among mankind!
Be through my lips to unawaken'd earth

The trumpet of a prophecy! O, wind,
If Winter comes, can Spring be far behind?   70

1820

JOHN CLARE
1793–1864

Raised a farm boy, John Clare grew up roaming the sprawling countryside of Helpston, Northamptonshire. His father, a thresher and local wrestler, could read very little; his mother, the daughter of a town shepherd, was completely illiterate. Adamant about his education, his parents sent him to a local school during downtimes in the agricultural year. Intellectually curious and devoted to learning, Clare tirelessly reviewed his lessons. Because of his family's poverty, however, he could not afford paper nor books. To compensate, he wrote on the wrappings from his mother's tea and sugar packages or practiced drawing on dusty barn walls. He also saved prize money he earned from school to purchase books.

Adult responsibilities abbreviated Clare's childhood. Tasks such as tending to sheep and cattle, running errands, and scaring away birds constituted much of his daily life, yet some of his most valuable experiences resulted from working in the fields and interacting with gypsies, vagrants, and people from local fairs. His formal schooling ended when he was apprenticed as a ploughboy at fourteen years old. After stints of work as a gardener, laborer, and lime-burner, he enlisted in the Northamptonshire militia to fight in the Napoleonic wars. A poor soldier, he returned home by May of 1813.

In 1819, Clare fell in love with Mary Joyce, a farmer's daughter who was four years his junior. After she broke off their relationship, Clare began an affair with a milkmaid named Patty Turner whom he married in 1820 after she became pregnant. Clare also published his first volume, *Poems Descriptive of Rural Life and Scenery*, in 1820. Written mostly in his youth, the poems range in topic, theme, and form; he sketches landscapes in vivid detail, channels the folklore he grew up hearing, and discusses social issues, all while portraying his country lifestyle in an unglorified and authentic manner. The collection sold well, allowing Clare to make several excursions to London to foster his reputation.

Though Clare's work was in demand, financial strains somewhat hindered his productivity. To provide for a family of nine, he worked as a manual laborer. Despite limited free time, he managed to publish *The Village Minstrel*, a collection which addressed themes similar to those in his first volume and also depicted consequences of recent parliamentary enclosures. Hoping to capitalize on land, Parliament passed legislation that restructured the Helpston parish, rendering old property lines obsolete. Enclosures privatized common land; after the growing season ended, community members could no longer freely use unworked farmland for their own purposes. Fences, trees, stone walls, and other physical obstructions separated fields, meadows, and pastures that had once been accessible to all. Clare derived his identity from the contours and paths of the land itself, and he was deeply dismayed by enclosures. The poems received respectable reviews, but they failed to attract the same praise as those in *Rural Life.*

His last major publications, *The Shepherd's Calendar* and *The Rural Muse*, did not save his declining reputation. Beset with financial and family burdens, weary of agricultural labor, and fond of alcohol, Clare's physical and mental health weakened. From 1837 to 1841, he became a voluntary patient at Dr. Matthew Allen's asylum. Afflicted with depression, insomnia, and nightmares, he gradually lost his sense of identity. He was often delusional, imagining himself to be Lord Byron or Ben Caunt, the prize-fighter. His poetry and letters, which were composed in code, were frequently addressed to Mary Joyce, who he believed was his first wife. Then, in an experience he powerfully recounts in "Journey out of Essex," he wandered homeward from the asylum, traveling through the woods while drunk and dazed.

Clare was ordered to the Northampton General Lunatic Asylum by doctors five months after his famous excursion. Given considerable freedom, he roamed the Northampton area and continued to write poetry. Poems from this period consist chiefly of love lyrics to various women, but he also composed pieces that resonate with pain. "I Am," written during the mid-1840s, attests to Clare's desolation: "I am–yet what I am none cares or knows; / My friends forsake me like a memory lost." Though his poetry indicates few visible signs of madness, he remained in the asylum until his death in 1864.

Known as the Peasant Poet, much of Clare's novelty as a writer resulted from stylistic deviations from his contemporaries and his lack of formal education. Unlike many of his contemporaries, Clare had first-hand experiences with the land and animals he wrote about. Moreover, for many of his readers and patrons, his spelling and grammatical errors evidenced his capacity for direct, unfiltered expressions of nature that education may have otherwise tainted. "Grammar in learning," Clare once stubbornly declared, "is like Tyranny in government." He refused to restrict his poetry to grammatical conventions and resisted editorial efforts to standardize his verses. An advocate for preserving local dialects and attitudes, he also rejected overly-romanticized portrayals of nature. Originality, simplicity, and beauty flow through his poetry, allowing him to capture the essence of his subject matter. He infuses his work with images and encounters that depict the language and lifestyle of the countryside with startling accuracy.

1793	John Clare born 13 July
1820	*Poems Descriptive of Rural Life and Scenery*; Marries Martha Turner
1821	*The Village Minstrel, and Other Poems*
1827	*The Shepherd's Calendar*
1835	*The Rural Muse*
1864	Clare dies in the Northampton General Lunatic Asylum 20 May after having a stroke and is buried in Helpston
1989	Clare is commemorated by a memorial in Poets' Corner, Westminster Abbey

THE NIGHTINGALE'S NEST

Up this green woodland-ride let's softly rove,
And list the nightingale—she dwells just here.
Hush! let the wood-gate softly clap, for fear
The noise might drive her from her home of love;
For here I've heard her many a merry year—   5
At morn, at eve, nay, all the live-long day,
As though she lived on song. This very spot,
Just where that old-man's-beard all wildly trails
Rude arbours o'er the road, and stops the way—
And where that child its blue-bell flowers hath got,   10
Laughing and creeping through the mossy rails—
There have I hunted like a very boy,
Creeping on hands and knees through matted thorn
To find her nest, and see her feed her young.

And vainly did I many hours employ: 15
All seemed as hidden as a thought unborn.
And where those crimping fern-leaves ramp among
The hazel's under boughs, I've nestled down,
And watched her while she sung; and her renown
Hath made me marvel that so famed a bird   20
Should have no better dress than russet brown.
Her wings would tremble in her ecstasy,
And feathers stand on end, as 'twere with joy,
And mouth wide open to release her heart
Of its out-sobbing songs. The happiest part   25
Of summer's fame she shared, for so to me
Did happy fancies shapen her employ;
But if I touched a bush, or scarcely stirred,
All in a moment stopt. I watched in vain:
The timid bird had left the hazel bush,   30
And at a distance hid to sing again.
Lost in a wilderness of listening leaves,
Rich Ecstasy would pour its luscious strain,
Till envy spurred the emulating thrush
To start less wild and scarce inferior songs;   35
For while of half the year Care him bereaves,
To damp the ardour of his speckled breast;
The nightingale to summer's life belongs,
And naked trees, and winter's nipping wrongs,
Are strangers to her music and her rest.   40
Her joys are evergreen, her world is wide—
Hark! there she is as usual—let's be hush—
For in this black-thorn clump, if rightly guest,
Her curious house is hidden. Part aside
These hazel branches in a gentle way,   45
And stoop right cautious 'neath the rustling boughs,
For we will have another search to day,
And hunt this fern-strewn thorn-clump round and round;
And where this reeded wood-grass idly bows,
We'll wade right through, it is a likely nook: 50
In such like spots, and often on the ground,
They'll build, where rude boys never think to look—
Aye, as I live! her secret nest is here,
Upon this white-thorn stump! I've searched about
For hours in vain. There! put that bramble by—   55

Nay, trample on its branches and get near.
How subtle is the bird! she started out,
And raised a plaintive note of danger nigh,
Ere we were past the brambles; and now, near
Her nest, she sudden stops—as choking fear,   60
That might betray her home. So even now
We'll leave it as we found it: safety's guard
Of pathless solitudes shall keep it still.
See there! she's sitting on the old oak bough,
Mute in her fears; our presence doth retard   65
Her joys, and doubt turns every rapture chill.
Sing on, sweet bird! may no worse hap befall
Thy visions, than the fear that now deceives.
We will not plunder music of its dower,
Nor turn this spot of happiness to thrall;   70
For melody seems hid in every flower,
That blossoms near thy home. These harebells all
Seem bowing with the beautiful in song;
And gaping cuckoo-flower, with spotted leaves,
Seems blushing of the singing it has heard.   75
How curious is the nest; no other bird
Uses such loose materials, or weaves
Its dwelling in such spots: dead oaken leaves
Are placed without, and velvet moss within,
And little scraps of grass, and, scant and spare,   80
What scarcely seem materials, down and hair;
For from men's haunts she nothing seems to win.
Yet Nature is the builder, and contrives
Homes for her children's comfort, even here;
Where Solitude's disciples spend their lives   85
Unseen, save when a wanderer passes near
That loves such pleasant places. Deep adown,
The nest is made a hermit's mossy cell.
Snug lie her curious eggs in number five,
Of deadened green, or rather olive brown;   90
And the old prickly thorn-bush guards them well.
So here we'll leave them, still unknown to wrong,
As the old woodland's legacy of song.

1835

THE PETTICHAP'S NEST

Well! in my many walks I've rarely found
A place less likely for a bird to form
Its nest—close by the rut-gulled waggon-road,
And on the almost bare foot-trodden ground,
With scarce a clump of grass to keep it warm!   5
Where not a thistle spreads its spears abroad,
Or prickly bush, to shield it from harm's way;
And yet so snugly made, that none may spy
It out, save peradventure. You and I
Had surely passed it in our walk to-day,   10
Had chance not led us by it!—Nay, e'en now,
Had not the old bird heard us trampling bye,
And fluttered out, we had not seen it lie,
Brown as the road-way side. Small bits of hay
Plucked from the old propt haystack's pleachy brow,   15
And withered leaves, make up its outward wall,
Which from the gnarl'd oak-dotterel yearly fall,
And in the old hedge-bottom rot away.
Built like an oven, through a little hole,
Scarcely admitting e'en two fingers in,   20
Hard to discern, the birds snug entrance win.
'Tis lined with feathers warm as silken stole,
Softer than seats of down for painless ease,
And full of eggs scarce bigger even than peas!
Here's one most delicate, with spots as small   25
As dust, and of a faint and pinky red.
—Well! let them be, and Safety guard them well;
For Fear's rude paths around are thickly spread,
And they are left to many dangerous ways.
A green grasshopper's jump might break the shells,   30
Yet lowing oxen pass them morn and night,
And restless sheep around them hourly stray;
And no grass springs but hungry horses bite,
That trample past them twenty times a day.
Yet, like a miracle, in Safety's lap,   35

They still abide unhurt, and out of sight.
—Stop! here's the bird—that woodman at the gap
Frightened him from the hedge:—'tis olive green.
Well! I declare it is the Pettichap!
No bigger than the wren, and seldom seen.   40
I've often found her nest in chance's way,
When I in pathless woods did idly roam;
But never did I dream until to-day
A spot like this would be her chosen home.

1835

THE THRUSH'S NEST

Within a thick and spreading hawthorn bush
    That overhung a molehill large and round,
I heard from morn to morn a merry thrush
    Sing hymns to sunrise, and I drank the sound
With joy; and, often an intruding guest,   5
    I watched her secret toil from day to day—
How true she warped the moss, to form a nest,
    And modelled it within with wood and clay;
And by and by, like heath-bells gilt with dew,
    There lay her shining eggs, as bright as flowers,   10
Ink-spotted over shells of greeny blue;
    And there I witnessed, in the sunny hours,
A brood of Nature's minstrels chirp and fly,
Glad as that sunshine and the laughing sky.

1835

THE WRYNECK'S NEST

That summer bird its oft-repeated note
  Chirps from the dottrel ash, and in the hole
The green woodpecker made in years remote,
  It makes its nest. When peeping idlers stroll
In anxious plundering moods, they by and by   5
  The Wryneck's curious eggs, as white as snow,
While squinting in the hollow tree, espy.
  The sitting bird looks up with jetty eye,
And waves her head in terror to and fro,
  Speckled and veined in various shades of brown;   10
  And then a hissing noise assails the clown.
Quickly, with hasty terror in his breast,
  From the tree's knotty trunk he slides adown,
And thinks the strange bird guards a serpent's nest.

1835

BADGER

When midnight comes a host of dogs and men
Go out and track the badger to his den,
And put a sack within the hole, and lie
Till the old grunting badger passes bye.
He comes and hears—they let the strongest loose.   5
The old fox hears the noise and drops the goose.
The poacher shoots and hurries from the cry,
And the old hare half wounded buzzes bye.
They get a forked stick to bear him down
And clap the dogs and take him to the town,   10
And bait him all the day with many dogs,
And laugh and shout and fright the scampering hogs.

He runs along and bites at all he meets:
They shout and hollo down the noisy streets.

He turns about to face the loud uproar   15
And drives the rebels to their very door.
The frequent stone is hurled where eer they go;
When badgers fight, then every one's a foe.
The dogs are clapt and urged to join the fray;
The badger turns and drives them all away.   20
Though scarcely half as big, demure and small,
He fights with dogs for bones and beats them all.
The heavy mastiff, savage in the fray,
Lies down and licks his feet and turns away.
The bulldog knows his match and waxes cold,   25
The badger grins and never leaves his hold.
He drives the crowd and follows at their heels
And bites them through—the drunkard swears and reels.

The frighted women take the boys away,
The blackguard laughs and hurries on the fray.   30
He tries to reach the woods, an awkward race,
But sticks and cudgels quickly stop the chace.
He turns agen and drives the noisy crowd
And beats the many dogs in noises loud.
He drives away and beats them every one,   35
And then they loose them all and set them on.
He falls as dead and kicked by boys and men,
Then starts and grins and drives the crowd agen;
Till kicked and torn and beaten out he lies
And leaves his hold and cackles, groans, and dies. 40

1920

THE FOX

The shepherd on his journey heard when nigh
His dog among the bushes barking high;
The ploughman ran and gave a hearty shout,
He found a weary fox and beat him out.
The ploughman laughed and would have ploughed him in   5
But the old shepherd took him for the skin.
He lay upon the furrow stretched for dead,
The old dog lay and licked the wounds that bled,
The ploughman beat him till his ribs would crack,
And then the shepherd slung him at his back;   10
And when he rested, to his dog's surprise,
The old fox started from his dead disguise;
And while the dog lay panting in the sedge
He up and snapt and bolted through the hedge.

He scampered to the bushes far away;   15
The shepherd called the ploughman to the fray;
The ploughman wished he had a gun to shoot.
The old dog barked and followed the pursuit.
The shepherd threw his hook and tottered past;
The ploughman ran but none could go so fast;   20
The woodman threw his faggot from the way
And ceased to chop and wondered at the fray.
But when he saw the dog and heard the cry
He threw his hatchet—but the fox was bye.
The shepherd broke his hook and lost the skin;   25
He found a badger hole and bolted in.
They tried to dig, but, safe from danger's way,
He lived to chase the hounds another day.

1920

I AM

I am: yet what I am who cares or knows,
   My friends forsake me like a memory lost;
I am the self-consumer of my woes,
   They rise and vanish in oblivious host,
Like shades in love and death's oblivion lost;   5
And yet I am, and live with shadows tost

Into the nothingness of scorn and noise,
   Into the living sea of waking dreams,
Where there is neither sense of life nor joys,
   But the vast shipwreck of my life's esteems;   10
And een the dearest—that I loved the best—
Are strange—nay, they are stranger than the rest.

I long for scenes where man has never trod;
   A place where woman never smiled or wept;
There to abide with my Creator, God,   15
   And sleep as I in childhood sweetly slept:
Untroubling and untroubled where I lie;
The grass below—above the vaulted sky.

1848

John Keats
1795-1821

John Keats was born October 31, 1795. His father, a professional horseman at a London livery stable, died in 1804 after falling off a horse on an early morning ride. Keats's mother remarried about two months later and left Keats, his three brothers, and his sister in the care of their grandmother. Keats had learned of his father's death while at Clarke's Academy, a private school known for its progressive curriculum, where he had been sent in 1803. Keats was a boisterous, unpredictable, and pugnacious boy; despite his stature (as an adult, he was scarcely five feet in height), he fought viciously and skillfully against whomever challenged him. He was gauged "not literary," but under the advisement of Charles Cowden Clarke, the son of the headmaster, Keats began studying Spenser and other poets. Driven by a desire to make his mother proud, Keats submerged himself in literature and writing.

When Keats's mother reentered his life four years later, her second marriage had failed, she was an alcoholic, and she was suffering from tuberculosis. She died of the disease in 1810. The affairs of the Keats children were transferred to the hands of Richard Abbey, a pragmatic businessman. Abbey apprenticed Keats to a surgeon and apothecary named Thomas Hammond. Keats's experience with the local doctor was unpleasant; Hammond apparently regarded him as a servant. A high-spirited youth, Keats resented his treatment and broke off the apprenticeship early. He moved to London in 1815 to work as a junior house surgeon at Guy's and St. Thomas' hospitals. Two years later, he resolved to become a poet.

Keats's poetry is constructed on childhood memories as well as fears of his own fading mortality. He understood that life and the physical world were fleeting; ideals were eternal and transcendental. The suspension of a single moment, sensation, or idea in time became a hallmark of his work. He committed himself to his poetry with unrestricted ardor. Keats existed in emotional extremes, alternating between fierceness and meekness, elation and despair. The conflicting impulses that drove his inner being emerged in his poetry, allowing him to reflect upon youth, beauty, and happiness in relation to the immutability of art. His early poetic endeavors were nurtured by a circle of friends: William Hazlitt, an English writer, social commentator, and philosopher; Percy Bysshe Shelley, a successful poet; Benjamin Robert Haydon, a painter who specialized in historical and religious works; and Leigh Hunt, then editor of *The Examiner.*

Keats composed *Endymion* with Hunt's guidance, but the young poet was dissatisfied with it as soon as it was completed. It received some positive reviews upon its publication, but critics also sniped that Hunt's influence destroyed Keats's talent. Though Keats understood the reviews were motivated by political prejudice (Hunt was radical in his beliefs), he considered *Endymion* "a feverish attempt" and not "a deed accomplished." He hoped to cultivate his skills and revive his creativity before starting his next major work. In the summer of 1818, Keats and his friend Charles Brown took a walking tour of the English Lake District and Scotland. The landscape, historic ruins, cathedrals, and abbeys crystallized in Keats's mind and would later reappear in *The Eve of St. Agnes* and other poems.

The excursion fortified Keats's imagination but annihilated his health. His medical training confirmed what he already feared: He was afflicted with the same disease that had killed his mother and was slowly killing his brother. Upon returning to London, Keats also discovered that ruthless criticisms of his earlier poems had appeared in *Blackwood's Magazine* and *Quarterly Review.* Condescendingly referred to as "poor Keats," rumors circulated that the poet was too fragile and sensitive to bear the reviews. Consequently, he was being killed by them. This was blatantly untrue; Keats reacted calmly and continued writing. Nevertheless, critics and his poetic contemporaries derided his alleged low social origins, medical background, short height, and poetic ambitions. Shelley perpetuated the idea of Keats's weakness in *Adonais*, and Byron sneered that Keats had been "snuffed out by an article." Keats maintained his dignity in public, but the reviews disheartened him.

Financial and family issues simultaneously strained him. His brother George, who had always helped him, had married and travelled to America in the summer of 1818. The George Keatses were swindled out of their money and could no longer supplement Keats's income, pressuring the poet to provide for himself and assist them. He resorted to journalism and play-writing but was haunted by insufficient funds until his death. Keats was also diligently and lovingly nursing his younger brother Tom through the final phases of tuberculosis. Keats's own health was deteriorating; he suffered a persistent ulcerated throat. Tom died in December of 1818, and Keats moved to Wentworth Place. He fell in love with Fanny Brawne, his young neighbor, and became engaged to her. Fanny's widowed mother, however, disapproved of him, and Keats's friends disliked Fanny. Additionally, Keats's financial and physical wellbeing were too unstable to support the couple. Marriage was impractical.

Keats's poetic career, though abbreviated, reached its height amid these misfortunes. The year 1819 signifies the composition and completion of his greatest poetry. Previously, Keats had been susceptible to the influence of other writers in his works (he had abandoned his epic poem *Hyperion* shortly after starting it in 1818 because it was too Miltonic), yet Keats's mature poetic voice is distinctly different from those of his literary idols. He is noted for supporting two separate, contradictory, and entirely valid interpretations of the same event. He frequently presents love ambiguously, portraying it as alluring and fatal or liberating and damning. He pits sentimentality against reality, reveals happiness in melancholy, and exposes violence in peace. When combined with his penchant for fluid verses, graceful movement, and concrete sensory details, Keats's poetry draws in readers with its complexity. His odes (*To Psyche, To a Nightingale, On a Grecian Urn, On Melancholy, To Autumn,* and *On Indolence*), written in the spring of 1819 and

published in 1820, are his enduring accomplishment. In them, he discloses the wanderings of his imagination and depicts his struggle with beauty, love, time, and death. He also completed *The Eve of St. Agnes* and the ballad "La Belle Dame sans Merci" during 1819, both of which explore the ruin that results from idyllic love. Keats additionally penned *Lamia*, sonnets, plays, and extraordinary letters. His poetic genius transcends the Romantic period; the Keatsian style has appeared from the Victorian Age onward.

By 1820, Keats's tuberculosis was undeniable and sustained work became impossible. His weak lungs and frequent blood-spitting permanently confined him to bed. The illness warped his mind until he was misanthropic, paranoid, and volatile. Aware that he could not survive another winter in England, Keats's doctor sent the despairing poet to Italy with his friend, Joseph Severn. Keats's condition continued to decline. In a letter to Brown, Keats recorded a "habitual feeling of my real life having passed, and that I am leading a *posthumous existence.*" Severn diligently tended to him, but Keats experienced a severe relapse in December and died in February of 1821. Since Keats did not want his name on his tomb, only the inscription "Here lies one whose name was writ in water" commemorates his burial place in Rome.

Blackwater's Magazine ruthlessly attacked him after his death. His final inscription was ridiculed and mocked by many. It was not until 1853 that Keats was celebrated in "The Lives of the Illustrious." When he stopped writing at twenty-four years old, he had already displayed incredible talent, but his full brilliance was scarcely acknowledged in his own lifetime. Readers and scholars have since been taunted by the possibilities of what Keats, a clear literary genius, could have written had he been spared a tragic and premature death.

1795	John Keats born 31 October
1803-10	Attends Clarke's Academy
1810	Keats's mother dies of tuberculosis
1817	*Poems*
1818	*Endymion*; Tom Keats dies of tuberculosis
1820	*The Eve of St. Agnes*, "La Belle Dame sans Merci," *Ode to Psyche, Ode to a Nightingale, Ode on a Grecian Urn, Ode on Melancholy, Ode on Indolence, Lamia, Ode to Autumn, The Fall of Hyperion: A Dream* in a single volume
1821	Keats dies from tuberculosis 23 February and is buried with an unmarked headstone in Protestant Cemetery, Rome, Italy

LA BELLE DAME SANS MERCI
A BALLAD

I.

O what can ail thee, knight-at-arms,
    Alone and palely loitering?
The sedge has wither'd from the lake,
    And no birds sing.

II.

O what can ail thee, knight-at-arms!   5
    So haggard and so woe-begone?
The squirrel's granary is full,
    And the harvest's done.

III.

I see a lily on thy brow,
    With anguish moist and fever-dew,   10
And on thy cheeks a fading rose
    Fast withereth too.

IV.

I met a lady in the meads,
    Full beautiful—a faery's child,
Her hair was long, her foot was light,   15
    And her eyes were wild.

V.

I made a garland for her head,
    And bracelets too, and fragrant zone;
She looked at me as she did love,
    And made sweet moan.   20

VI.

I set her on my pacing steed,
    And nothing else saw all day long,

For sidelong would she bend, and sing
    A faery song.

VII.

She found me roots of relish sweet,   25
    And honey wild, and manna dew,
And sure in language strange she said—
    "I love thee true."

VIII.

She took me to her Elfin grot,
    And there she wept, and sigh'd full sore,   30
And there I shut her wild wild eyes
    With kisses four.

IX.

And there she lulled me asleep,
    And there I dream'd—Ah! woe betide!—
The latest dream I ever dream'd   35
    On the cold hill's side.

X.

I saw pale kings and princes too,
    Pale warriors, death-pale were they all;
They cried—"La Belle Dame sans Merci
    Hath thee in thrall!"   40

XI.

I saw their starved lips in the gloam,
    With horrid warning gaped wide,
And I awoke and found me here,
    On the cold hill's side.

XII.

And this is why I sojourn here,   45
    Alone and palely loitering,
Though the sedge is wither'd from the lake,
    And no birds sing.

1819

THE EVE OF ST. AGNES[1]

I.

St. Agnes' Eve—Ah, bitter chill it was!
The owl, for all his feathers, was a-cold;
The hare limp'd trembling through the frozen grass,
And silent was the flock in woolly fold:
Numb were the Beadsman's fingers while he told   5
His rosary, and while his frosted breath,
Like pious incense from a censer old,
Seem'd taking flight for heaven, without a death,
Past the sweet Virgin's picture, while his prayer he saith.

II.

His prayer he saith, this patient, holy man;   10
Then takes his lamp, and riseth from his knees,
And back returneth, meagre, barefoot, wan,
Along the chapel aisle by slow degrees:
The sculptured dead, on each side seem to freeze,
Emprison'd in black, purgatorial rails: 15
Knights, ladies, praying in dumb orat'ries,
He passeth by; and his weak spirit fails
To think how they may ache in icy hoods and mails.

III.

Northward he turneth through a little door,
And scarce three steps, ere Music's golden tongue   20
Flatter'd to tears this aged man and poor;
But no—already had his death-bell rung;
The joys of all his life were said and sung:
His was harsh penance on St. Agnes' Eve:
Another way he went, and soon among   25

---

1 On January 20th, the Eve of St. Agnes, girls and unmarried women wishing to dream of their future husbands would perform rituals prior to going to bed. The tradition is based on St. Agnes, a 4th-century Christian girl who refused to marry a Roman suitor. She was thrown into a brothel as punishment, but heavenly forces preserved her virginity. She was later killed after refusing to renounce her faith.

Rough ashes sat he for his soul's reprieve,
And all night kept awake, for sinner's sake to grieve.

IV.

That ancient Beadsman heard the prelude soft;
And so it chanced, for many a door was wide,
From hurry to and fro. Soon, up aloft,   30
The silver, snarling trumpets 'gan to chide:
The level chambers, ready with their pride,
Were glowing to receive a thousand guests:
The carved angels, ever eager-eyed,
Stared, where upon their heads the cornice rests,   35
With hair blown back, and wings put cross-wise on their breasts.

V.

At length burst in the argent revelry,
With plume, tiara, and all rich array,
Numerous as shadows haunting fairily
The brain, new stuff'd, in youth, with triumphs gay   40
Of old romance. These let us wish away,
And turn, sole-thoughted, to one Lady there,
Whose heart had brooded, all that wintry day,
On love, and wing'd St. Agnes' saintly care,
As she had heard old dames full many times declare.   45

VI.

They told her how, upon St. Agnes' Eve,
Young virgins might have visions of delight,
And soft adorings from their loves receive
Upon the honey'd middle of the night,
If ceremonies due they did aright;   50
As, supperless to bed they must retire,
And couch supine their beauties, lily white;
Nor look behind, nor sideways, but require
Of Heaven with upward eyes for all that they desire.

VII.

Full of this whim was thoughtful Madeline: 55
The music, yearning like a God in pain,
She scarcely heard: her maiden eyes divine,

Fix'd on the floor, saw many a sweeping train
Pass by—she heeded not at all: in vain
Came many a tiptoe, amorous cavalier,   60
And back retired; not cool'd by high disdain,
But she saw not: her heart was otherwhere;
She sigh'd for Agnes' dreams, the sweetest of the year.

VIII.

She danced along with vague, regardless eyes,
Anxious her lips, her breathing quick and short: 65
The hallow'd hour was near at hand: she sighs
Amid the timbrels, and the throng'd resort
Of whisperers in anger, or in sport;
'Mid looks of love, defiance, hate, and scorn,
Hoodwink'd with faery fancy; all amort,   70
Save to St. Agnes and her lambs unshorn,
And all the bliss to be before to-morrow morn.

IX.

So, purposing each moment to retire,
She linger'd still. Meantime, across the moors,
Had come young Porphyro, with heart on fire   75
For Madeline. Beside the portal doors,
Buttress'd from moonlight, stands he, and implores
All saints to give him sight of Madeline,
But for one moment in the tedious hours,
That he might gaze and worship all unseen;   80
Perchance speak, kneel, touch, kiss—in sooth such things have been.

X.

He ventures in: let no buzz'd whisper tell:
All eyes be muffled, or a hundred swords
Will storm his heart, Love's feverous citadel:
For him, those chambers held barbarian hordes,   85
Hyena foemen, and hot-blooded lords,
Whose very dogs would execrations howl
Against his lineage: not one breast affords
Him any mercy, in that mansion foul,
Save one old beldame, weak in body and in soul.   90

XI.

Ah, happy chance! the aged creature came,
   Shuffling along with ivory-headed wand,
   To where he stood, hid from the torch's flame,
   Behind a broad hall-pillar, far beyond
   The sound of merriment and chorus bland: 95
   He startled her; but soon she knew his face,
   And grasp'd his fingers in her palsied hand,
     Saying, "Mercy, Porphyro! hie thee from this place;
They are all here to-night, the whole blood-thirsty race!

XII.

  "Get hence! get hence! there's dwarfish Hildebrand;   100
   He had a fever late, and in the fit
   He cursed thee and thine, both house and land:
   Then there's that old Lord Maurice, not a whit
   More tame for his gray hairs—Alas me! flit!
   Flit like a ghost away."—"Ah, Gossip dear,   105
   We're safe enough; here in this arm-chair sit,
     And tell me how"—"Good Saints! not here, not here;
Follow me, child, or else these stones will be thy bier."

XIII.

He follow'd through a lowly arched way,
   Brushing the cobwebs with his lofty plume;   110
   And as she mutter'd "Well-a—well-a-day!"
   He found him in a little moonlight room,
   Pale, latticed, chill, and silent as a tomb.
   "Now tell me where is Madeline," said he,
   "O tell me, Angela, by the holy loom   115
   Which none but secret sisterhood may see,
When they St. Agnes' wool are weaving piously."

XIV.

  "St. Agnes! Ah! it is St. Agnes' Eve—
   Yet men will murder upon holy days:
   Thou must hold water in a witch's sieve,   120
   And be liege-lord of all the Elves and Fays,
   To venture so: it fills me with amaze
   To see thee, Porphyro!—St. Agnes' Eve!

God's help! my lady fair the conjuror plays
This very night: good angels her deceive! 125
But let me laugh awhile, I've mickle time to grieve."

XV.

Feebly she laugheth in the languid moon,
  While Porphyro upon her face doth look,
Like puzzled urchin on an aged crone
Who keepeth closed a wondrous riddle-book, 130
As spectacled she sits in chimney'd nook.
But soon his eyes grew brilliant, when she told
His lady's purpose; and he scarce could brook
Tears, at the thought of those enchantments cold
And Madeline asleep in lap of legends old. 135

XVI.

Sudden a thought came like a full-blown rose,
Flushing his brow, and in his pained heart
Made purple riot: then doth he propose
A stratagem, that makes the beldame start:
"A cruel man and impious thou art: 140
Sweet lady, let her pray, and sleep and dream
Alone with her good angels, far apart
From wicked men like thee. Go, go! I deem
Thou canst not surely be the same that thou didst seem."

XVII.

"I will not harm her, by all saints I swear," 145
Quoth Porphyro: "O may I ne'er find grace
When my weak voice shall whisper its last prayer,
If one of her soft ringlets I displace,
Or look with ruffian passion in her face:
Good Angela, believe me by these tears; 150
Or I will, even in a moment's space,
Awake, with horrid shout, my foemen's ears,
And beard them, though they be more fang'd than wolves and bears."

XVIII.

"Ah! why wilt thou affright a feeble soul?
A poor, weak, palsy-stricken, churchyard thing, 155
Whose passing-bell may ere the midnight toll;

Whose prayers for thee, each morn and evening,
Were never miss'd." Thus plaining doth she bring
A gentler speech from burning Porphyro;
So woeful, and of such deep sorrowing, 160
That Angela gives promise she will do
Whatever he shall wish, betide her weal or woe.

XIX.

Which was, to lead him, in close secrecy,
Even to Madeline's chamber, and there hide
Him in a closet, of such privacy 165
That he might see her beauty unespied,
And win perhaps that night a peerless bride,
While legion'd fairies paced the coverlet,
And pale enchantment held her sleepy-eyed.
Never on such a night have lovers met, 170
Since Merlin paid his Demon all the monstrous debt.

XX.

"It shall be as thou wishest," said the Dame:
"All cates and dainties shall be stored there
Quickly on this feast-night: by the tambour frame
Her own lute thou wilt see: no time to spare, 175
For I am slow and feeble, and scarce dare
On such a catering trust my dizzy head.
Wait here, my child, with patience kneel in prayer
The while: Ah! thou must needs the lady wed,
Or may I never leave my grave among the dead." 180

XXI.

So saying, she hobbled off with busy fear.
The lover's endless minutes slowly pass'd;
The dame return'd, and whisper'd in his ear
To follow her; with aged eyes aghast
From fright of dim espial. Safe at last, 185
Through many a dusky gallery, they gain
The Maiden's chamber, silken, hush'd, and chaste;
Where Porphyro took covert, pleased amain.
His poor guide hurried back with agues in her brain.

XXII.

Her faltering hand upon the balustrade,   190
Old Angela was feeling for the stair,
When Madeline, St. Agnes' charmed maid,
Rose, like a mission'd spirit, unaware:
With silver taper's light, and pious care,
She turn'd, and down the aged gossip led   195
To a safe level matting. Now prepare,
Young Porphyro, for gazing on that bed;
She comes, she comes again, like ring-dove fray'd and fled.

XXIII.

Out went the taper as she hurried in;
Its little smoke, in pallid moonshine, died: 200
She closed the door, she panted, all akin
To spirits of the air, and visions wide:
No utter'd syllable, or, woe betide!
But to her heart, her heart was voluble,
Paining with eloquence her balmy side;   205
As though a tongueless nightingale should swell
Her throat in vain, and die, heart-stifled, in her dell.

XXIV.

A casement high and triple-arch'd there was,
All garlanded with carven imageries
Of fruits, and flowers, and bunches of knot-grass,   210
And diamonded with panes of quaint device,
Innumerable of stains and splendid dyes,
As are the tiger-moth's deep damask'd wings;
And in the midst, 'mong thousand heraldries,
And twilight saints, and dim emblazonings,   215
A shielded scutcheon blush'd with blood of queens and kings.

XXV.

Full on this casement shone the wintry moon,
And threw warm gules on Madeline's fair breast;
As down she knelt for heaven's grace and boon
Rose-bloom fell on her hands, together prest,   220
And on her silver cross soft amethyst,
And on her hair a glory, like a saint:

She seem'd a splendid angel, newly drest,
  Save wings, for heaven:—Porphyro grew faint:
She knelt, so pure a thing, so free from mortal taint.   225

XXVI.

Anon his heart revives: her vespers done,
  Of all its wreathed pearls her hair she frees;
  Unclasps her warmed jewels one by one;
  Loosens her fragrant boddice; by degrees
  Her rich attire creeps rustling to her knees: 230
  Half-hidden, like a mermaid in sea-weed,
  Pensive awhile she dreams awake, and sees,
  In fancy, fair St. Agnes in her bed,
But dares not look behind, or all the charm is fled.

XXVII.

Soon, trembling in her soft and chilly nest,   235
  In sort of wakeful swoon, perplex'd she lay,
  Until the poppied warmth of sleep oppress'd
  Her soothed limbs, and soul fatigued away;
  Flown, like a thought, until the morrow day;
  Blissfully haven'd both from joy and pain;   240
  Clasp'd like a missal where swart Paynims pray;
  Blinded alike from sunshine and from rain,
As though a rose should shut, and be a bud again.

XXVIII.

Stolen to this paradise, and so entranced,
  Porphyro gazed upon her empty dress,   245
  And listen'd to her breathing, if it chanced
  To wake into a slumberous tenderness;
  Which when he heard, that minute did he bless,
  And breathed himself: then from the closet crept,
  Noiseless as fear in a wide wilderness,   250
  And over the hush'd carpet, silent, stept,
And 'tween the curtains peep'd, where, lo!—how fast she slept.

XXIX.

Then by the bed-side, where the faded moon
  Made a dim, silver twilight, soft he set

A table, and, half anguish'd, threw thereon   255
A cloth of woven crimson, gold, and jet:—
O for some drowsy Morphean amulet!
The boisterous, midnight, festive clarion,
The kettle-drum, and far-heard clarionet,
Affray his ears, though but in dying tone:—   260
The hall-door shuts again, and all the noise is gone.

XXX.

And still she slept an azure-lidded sleep,
In blanched linen, smooth, and lavender'd,
While he from forth the closet brought a heap
Of candied apple, quince, and plum, and gourd;   265
With jellies soother than the creamy curd,
And lucent syrops, tinct with cinnamon;
Manna[1] and dates, in argosy transferr'd
From Fez; and spiced dainties, every one,
From silken Samarcand to cedar'd Lebanon.[2]   270

XXXI.

These delicates he heap'd with glowing hand
On golden dishes and in baskets bright
Of wreathed silver: sumptuous they stand
In the retired quiet of the night,
Filling the chilly room with perfume light.—   275
"And now, my love, my seraph fair, awake!
Thou art my heaven, and I thine eremite:
Open thine eyes, for meek St. Agnes' sake,
Or I shall drowse beside thee, so my soul doth ache."

XXXII.

Thus whispering, his warm, unnerved arm   280
Sank in her pillow. Shaded was her dream
By the dusk curtains:—'twas a midnight charm
Impossible to melt as iced stream:
The lustrous salvers in the moonlight gleam;
Broad golden fringe upon the carpet lies: 285
It seem'd he never, never could redeem

---

1 The food God gave to the Israelites as they wandered through the desert wilderness for forty years.
2 Porphyro brings exotic goods from Morocco, Uzbekistan, and Lebanon, in western Asia.

From such a stedfast spell his lady's eyes;
So mused awhile, entoil'd in woofed phantasies.

XXXIII.

Awakening up, he took her hollow lute,—
Tumultuous,—and, in chords that tenderest be,   290
He play'd an ancient ditty, long since mute,
In Provence call'd "La belle dame sans mercy:"
Close to her ear touching the melody;—
Wherewith disturb'd, she utter'd a soft moan:
He ceased—she panted quick—and suddenly   295
Her blue affrayed eyes wide open shone:
Upon his knees he sank, pale as smooth-sculptured stone.

XXXIV.

Her eyes were open, but she still beheld,
Now wide awake, the vision of her sleep:
There was a painful change, that nigh expell'd   300
The blisses of her dream so pure and deep.
At which fair Madeline began to weep,
And moan forth witless words with many a sigh;
While still her gaze on Porphyro would keep;
Who knelt, with joined hands and piteous eye,   305
Fearing to move or speak, she look'd so dreamingly.

XXXV.

"Ah, Porphyro!" said she, "but even now
Thy voice was at sweet tremble in mine ear,
Made tuneable with every sweetest vow;
And those sad eyes were spiritual and clear: 310
How changed thou art! how pallid, chill, and drear!
Give me that voice again, my Porphyro,
Those looks immortal, those complainings dear!
Oh leave me not in this eternal woe,
For if thou diest, my Love, I know not where to go."   315

XXXVI.

Beyond a mortal man impassion'd far
At these voluptuous accents, he arose,
Ethereal, flush'd, and like a throbbing star
Seen 'mid the sapphire heaven's deep repose;

Into her dream he melted, as the rose   320
Blendeth its odour with the violet,—
Solution sweet: meantime the frost-wind blows
Like Love's alarum, pattering the sharp sleet
Against the window-panes; St. Agnes' moon hath set.

XXXVII.

'Tis dark: quick pattereth the flaw-blown sleet: 325
"This is no dream, my bride, my Madeline!"
'Tis dark: the iced gusts still rave and beat:
"No dream, alas! alas! and woe is mine!
Porphyro will leave me here to fade and pine.—
Cruel! what traitor could thee hither bring?   330
I curse not, for my heart is lost in thine
Though thou forsakest a deceived thing;—
A dove forlorn and lost with sick unpruned wing."

XXXVIII.

"My Madeline! sweet dreamer! lovely bride!
Say, may I be for aye thy vassal blest?   335
Thy beauty's shield, heart-shaped and vermeil dyed?
Ah, silver shrine, here will I take my rest
After so many hours of toil and quest,
A famish'd pilgrim,—saved by miracle.
Though I have found, I will not rob thy nest   340
Saving of thy sweet self; if thou think'st well
To trust, fair Madeline, to no rude infidel."

XXXIX.

"Hark! 'tis an elfin-storm from faery land,
Of haggard seeming, but a boon indeed:
Arise—arise! the morning is at hand;—   345
The bloated wassaillers will never heed:—
Let us away, my love, with happy speed;
There are no ears to hear, or eyes to see,—
Drown'd all in Rhenish[1] and the sleepy mead:
Awake! arise! my love, and fearless be,   350
For o'er the Southern moors I have a home for thee."

---

1 Wine from the river Rhine.

XL.

She hurried at his words, beset with fears,
For there were sleeping dragons all around,
At glaring watch, perhaps, with ready spears—
Down the wide stairs a darkling way they found,   355
In all the house was heard no human sound.
A chain-droop'd lamp was flickering by each door;
The arras, rich with horseman, hawk, and hound,
Flutter'd in the besieging wind's uproar;
And the long carpets rose along the gusty floor.   360

XLI.

They glide, like phantoms, into the wide hall!
Like phantoms, to the iron porch, they glide,
Where lay the Porter, in uneasy sprawl,
With a huge empty flaggon by his side:
The wakeful bloodhound rose, and shook his hide,   365
But his sagacious eye an inmate owns:
By one, and one, the bolts full easy slide:—
The chains lie silent on the footworn stones;
The key turns, and the door upon its hinges groans.

XLII.

And they are gone: ay, ages long ago   370
These lovers fled away into the storm.
That night the Baron dreamt of many a woe,
And all his warrior-guests, with shade and form
Of witch, and demon, and large coffin-worm,
Were long be-nightmared. Angela the old   375
Died palsy-twitch'd, with meagre face deform;
The Beadsman, after thousand aves told,
For aye unsought-for slept among his ashes cold.

1820

 ODE TO A NIGHTINGALE

1.

My heart aches, and a drowsy numbness pains
   My sense, as though of hemlock[1] I had drunk,
Or emptied some dull opiate to the drains
   One minute past, and Lethe-wards[2] had sunk:
'Tis not through envy of thy happy lot,   5
   But being too happy in thine happiness,—
      That thou, light-winged Dryad[3] of the trees,
         In some melodious plot
   Of beechen green, and shadows numberless,
      Singest of summer in full-throated ease.   10

2.

O, for a draught of vintage! that hath been
   Cool'd a long age in the deep-delved earth,
Tasting of Flora and the country green,
   Dance, and Provençal song, and sunburnt mirth!
O for a beaker full of the warm South,   15
   Full of the true, the blushful Hippocrene,[4]
      With beaded bubbles winking at the brim,
         And purple-stained mouth;
   That I might drink, and leave the world unseen,
      And with thee fade away into the forest dim: 20

3.

Fade far away, dissolve, and quite forget
   What thou among the leaves hast never known,
The weariness, the fever, and the fret
   Here, where men sit and hear each other groan;
Where palsy shakes a few, sad, last gray hairs,   25

1 A poisonous plant.

2 If consumed, water from the river Lethe in Hades caused drinkers to forget their past.

3 A forest or tree-dwelling nymph.

4 Sacred to the Muses, the Hippocrene fountain on Mount Helicon inspired poetic and literary activity.

Where youth grows pale, and spectre-thin, and dies;
　　Where but to think is to be full of sorrow
　　　　And leaden-eyed despairs,
　　Where Beauty cannot keep her lustrous eyes,
　　　　Or new Love pine at them beyond to-morrow.　　　30

　　　　　　　　　　　　4.

Mind & imagination are intoxicating, seductive, & dangerous like alcohol

Away! away! for I will fly to thee,
　　Not charioted by Bacchus[1] and his pards,
But on the viewless wings of Poesy,
　　Though the dull brain perplexes and retards:
Already with thee! tender is the night,　　　　　　35
　　And haply the Queen-Moon is on her throne,
　　　　Cluster'd around by all her starry Fays;
　　　　　　But here there is no light,
　　Save what from heaven is with the breezes blown
　　　　Through verdurous glooms and winding mossy ways.　　40

　　　　　　　　　　　　5.

I cannot see what flowers are at my feet,
　　Nor what soft incense hangs upon the boughs,
But, in embalmed darkness, guess each sweet
　　Wherewith the seasonable month endows
The grass, the thicket, and the fruit-tree wild;　　　　45
　　White hawthorn, and the pastoral eglantine;
　　　　Fast fading violets cover'd up in leaves;
　　　　　　And mid-May's eldest child,
　　The coming musk-rose, full of dewy wine,
　　　　The murmurous haunt of flies on summer eves.　　　50

　　　　　　　　　　　　6.

Darkling I listen; and, for many a time
　　I have been half in love with easeful Death,
Call'd him soft names in many a mused rhyme,
　　To take into the air my quiet breath;
　　　Now more than ever seems it rich to die,　　　　55
　　To cease upon the midnight with no pain,
　　　While thou art pouring forth thy soul abroad

Romanticizes death & melancholy, way of thinking feels good in the moment but is dangerous

---

1 The god of wine.

In such an ecstasy!
Still wouldst thou sing, and I have ears in vain—
  To thy high requiem become a sod.   60

7.

Thou wast not born for death, immortal Bird!   — *Bird's song & human*
No hungry generations tread thee down;   *experience of hearing it*
The voice I hear this passing night was heard   *is what's immortal, not*
  In ancient days by emperor and clown: —   *this specific bird; bird's*
Perhaps the self-same song that found a path   *ignorance of its mortality*
  Through the sad heart of Ruth,[2] when, sick for home,   *also makes it "immortal"*
    She stood in tears amid the alien corn;
      The same that oft-times hath
  Charm'd magic casements, opening on the foam
    Of perilous seas, in faery lands forlorn.   70

8.

Forlorn! the very word is like a bell   *Snaps out of this*
  To toll me back from thee to my sole self!   *way of thinking,*
Adieu! the fancy cannot cheat so well   —   *pulls himself back*
  As she is fam'd to do, deceiving elf.   *to reality*
Adieu! adieu! thy plaintive anthem fades   75
  Past the near meadows, over the still stream,
    Up the hill-side; and now 'tis buried deep
      In the next valley-glades:
  Was it a vision, or a waking dream?
    Fled is that music:—Do I wake or sleep?   80

1820   *Power of imagination & consciousness*

---

2 In the Book of Ruth in the Old Testament, the widowed Moabite Ruth chooses to stay with her widowed Isrealite mother-in-law, Noami. Ruth returns to Noami's native land, believes in her God, and works in a field to support them both.

ODE ON A GRECIAN URN

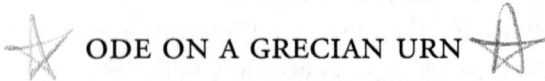

1.

Thou still unravish'd bride of quietness,
Thou foster-child of silence and slow time,
Sylvan[1] historian, who canst thus express
   A flowery tale more sweetly than our rhyme:
What leaf-fring'd legend haunts about thy shape   5
    Of deities or mortals, or of both,
      In Tempe[2] or the dales of Arcady?[3]
    What men or gods are these? What maidens loth?
What mad pursuit? What struggle to escape?
      What pipes and timbrels? What wild ecstasy?   10

2.

Heard melodies are sweet, but those unheard
   Are sweeter; therefore, ye soft pipes, play on;
Not to the sensual ear, but, more endear'd,
   Pipe to the spirit ditties of no tone:
Fair youth, beneath the trees, thou canst not leave   15
   Thy song, nor ever can those trees be bare;
    Bold Lover, never, never canst thou kiss,
Though winning near the goal—yet, do not grieve;
   She cannot fade, though thou hast not thy bliss,
    For ever wilt thou love, and she be fair!   20

3.

Ah, happy, happy boughs! that cannot shed
   Your leaves, nor ever bid the Spring adieu;
And, happy melodist, unwearied,
   For ever piping songs for ever new;
More happy love! more happy, happy love!   25
   For ever warm and still to be enjoy'd,
    For ever panting, and for ever young;

[handwritten annotation:] Immortality through art; Urn is beautiful because it's unchanged by time

---

1 A being that lives in or frequently travels through the woods.

2 The Vale of Tempe in Greece is known for its lush vegetation.

3 A utopic rustic paradise.

All breathing human passion far above,
   That leaves a heart high-sorrowful and cloy'd,
      A burning forehead, and a parching tongue.   30

4.

Who are these coming to the sacrifice?
   To what green altar, O mysterious priest,
Lead'st thou that heifer lowing at the skies,
   And all her silken flanks with garlands drest?
What little town by river or sea shore,   35
   Or mountain-built with peaceful citadel,
      Is emptied of this folk, this pious morn?
And, little town, thy streets for evermore
   Will silent be; and not a soul to tell
      Why thou art desolate, can e'er return.   40

5.

O Attic shape! Fair attitude! with brede   *Shift in language;*
   Of marble men and maidens overwrought,   *more neg., too much*
With forest branches and the trodden weed;
   Thou, silent form, dost tease us out of thought
As doth eternity: Cold Pastoral!   *Art cannot fully*
   When old age shall this generation waste,   *capture the beauty*
      Thou shalt remain, in midst of other woe   *& vibrance of life;*
Than ours, a friend to man, to whom thou say'st,   *cannot answer*
   "Beauty is truth, truth beauty,"—that is all   *questions, only remains*
      Ye know on earth, and all ye need to know.   *a frozen scene*   50

1820   *↳ Alternate ending has quotes around all of*
            last two lines, rather than only
            "beauty is truth, truth beauty"

Final stanza shifts view of urn, keeps w/ Keats' general
themes / tones; push & pull of sentiment/sensability &
rationality / logical mind; intoxicated by imagination &
thoughts about subject & must pull himself back
from that to stay grounded & rational — seeks
balance rather than over-indulgence in the imagination

⭐ ODE TO PSYCHE[1] ⭐

O Goddess! hear these tuneless numbers, wrung
    By sweet enforcement and remembrance dear,
And pardon that thy secrets should be sung
    Even into thine own soft-conched ear:
Surely I dreamt to-day, or did I see   5
    The winged Psyche with awaken'd eyes?
I wander'd in a forest thoughtlessly,
    And, on the sudden, fainting with surprise,
Saw two fair creatures, couched side by side
    In deepest grass, beneath the whisp'ring roof   10
    Of leaves and trembled blossoms, where there ran
        A brooklet, scarce espied:
'Mid hush'd, cool-rooted flowers, fragrant-eyed,
    Blue, silver-white, and budded Tyrian,
They lay calm-breathing on the bedded grass;   15
    Their arms embraced, and their pinions too;
    Their lips touch'd not, but had not bade adieu,
As if disjoined by soft-handed slumber,
And ready still past kisses to outnumber
    At tender eye-dawn of aurorean love: 20
        The winged boy I knew;
    But who wast thou, O happy, happy dove?
        His Psyche true!

O latest born and loveliest vision far
    Of all Olympus' faded hierarchy!   25
Fairer than Phœbe's sapphire-region'd star,
    Or Vesper, amorous glow-worm of the sky;
Fairer than these, though temple thou hast none,
    Nor altar heap'd with flowers;

---

1 The myth of Psyche is one of the newest Greek tales; Apuleius recorded a version of it in the second century A.D. Aphrodite, the goddess of beauty and love, envied the mortal princess Psyche so much that she commanded her son Eros (Cupid in Roman mythology) to make Psyche fall in love with a heinous man. Stunned by Psyche's beauty, Eros instead hid her in his palace and met her at night, forbidding her to see his face. She, however, lit a lamp and saw him. Infuriated, Eros abandoned her. After accomplishing Aphrodite's impossible tasks, Psyche won Eros as her husband. "Psyche" is Greek for "soul."

Nor virgin-choir to make delicious moan 30
    Upon the midnight hours;
No voice, no lute, no pipe, no incense sweet
  From chain-swung censer teeming;
No shrine, no grove, no oracle, no heat
  Of pale-mouth'd prophet dreaming. 35

O brightest! though too late for antique vows,
  Too, too late for the fond believing lyre,
When holy were the haunted forest boughs,
  Holy the air, the water, and the fire;
Yet even in these days so far retir'd 40
  From happy pieties, thy lucent fans,
    Fluttering among the faint Olympians,
I see, and sing, by my own eyes inspired.
So let me be thy choir, and make a moan
    Upon the midnight hours; 45
   Thy voice, thy lute, thy pipe, thy incense sweet
    From swinged censer teeming;
  Thy shrine, thy grove, thy oracle, thy heat
    Of pale-mouth'd prophet dreaming.

Yes, I will be thy priest, and build a fane 50
  In some untrodden region of my mind,
   Where branched thoughts, new grown with pleasant pain,
  Instead of pines shall murmur in the wind:
Far, far around shall those dark-cluster'd trees
  Fledge the wild-ridged mountains steep by steep; 55
And there by zephyrs, streams, and birds, and bees,
  The moss-lain Dryads shall be lull'd to sleep;
And in the midst of this wide quietness
A rosy sanctuary will I dress
With the wreath'd trellis of a working brain, 60
  With buds, and bells, and stars without a name,
With all the gardener Fancy e'er could feign,
  Who breeding flowers, will never breed the same:
And there shall be for thee all soft delight
  That shadowy thought can win, 65
A bright torch, and a casement ope at night,
  To let the warm Love in!

1820

TO AUTUMN

1.

Season of mists and mellow fruitfulness,
   Close bosom-friend of the maturing sun;
Conspiring with him how to load and bless
   With fruit the vines that round the thatch-eves run;
To bend with apples the moss'd cottage-trees,   5
   And fill all fruit with ripeness to the core;
     To swell the gourd, and plump the hazel shells
With a sweet kernel; to set budding more,
   And still more, later flowers for the bees,
   Until they think warm days will never cease,   10
     For summer has o'er-brimm'd their clammy cells.

2.

Who hath not seen thee oft amid thy store?
   Sometimes whoever seeks abroad may find
Thee sitting careless on a granary floor,
   Thy hair soft-lifted by the winnowing wind;   15
Or on a half-reap'd furrow sound asleep,
   Drows'd with the fume of poppies, while thy hook
     Spares the next swath and all its twined flowers:
And sometimes like a gleaner thou dost keep
   Steady thy laden head across a brook;   20
   Or by a cider-press, with patient look,
     Thou watchest the last oozings, hours by hours.

3.

Where are the songs of Spring? Ay, where are they?
   Think not of them, thou hast thy music too,—
While barred clouds bloom the soft-dying day,   25
   And touch the stubble-plains with rosy hue;
Then in a wailful choir the small gnats mourn
   Among the river sallows, borne aloft
     Or sinking as the light wind lives or dies;
And full-grown lambs loud bleat from hilly bourn;   30

Hedge-crickets sing; and now with treble soft
The red-breast whistles from a garden-croft,
    And gathering swallows twitter in the skies.

1820

ODE ON MELANCHOLY

1.

No, no, go not to Lethe, neither twist
    Wolf's-bane,[1] tight-rooted, for its poisonous wine;
Nor suffer thy pale forehead to be kiss'd
    By nightshade, ruby grape of Proserpine;[2]
Make not your rosary of yew-berries,   5
    Nor let the beetle, nor the death-moth be
        Your mournful Psyche, nor the downy owl
A partner in your sorrow's mysteries;
    For shade to shade will come too drowsily,
        And drown the wakeful anguish of the soul.   10

2.

But when the melancholy fit shall fall
    Sudden from heaven like a weeping cloud,
That fosters the droop-headed flowers all,
    And hides the green hill in an April shroud;
Then glut thy sorrow on a morning rose,   15
    Or on the rainbow of the salt sand-wave,
        Or on the wealth of globed peonies;
Or if thy mistress some rich anger shows,
    Emprison her soft hand, and let her rave,
        And feed deep, deep upon her peerless eyes.   20

---

1 A poisonous herb.

2 Persephone, the daughter of Zeus and Demeter, was captured by Hades. Because she ate a pomegranate seed, she was forced to remain in the underworld for part of each year

3.

She dwells with Beauty—Beauty that must die;
   And Joy, whose hand is ever at his lips
Bidding adieu; and aching Pleasure nigh,
   Turning to poison while the bee-mouth sips:
Ay, in the very temple of Delight   25
   Veil'd Melancholy has her sovran shrine,
     Though seen of none save him whose strenuous tongue
Can burst Joy's grape against his palate fine;
   His soul shall taste the sadness of her might,
     And be among her cloudy trophies hung.   30

1820

VICTORIAN AGE
1832–1901

ABSTRACT

Crowned when she was 18 years old, Queen Victoria guided Britain through some of the most transformative, intense, and agonizing years in the nation's history. For many, Britain's national image and social relations with the rest of the world had been unequivocally challenged and changed in the wake of the previous era's revolutions. Now the British Victorians' very conception of the world, one's place in it, and one's place beyond it were uprooted by scientific discoveries. Known as the "Age of Doubt," anxiety about the future, humanity's greater purpose, the necessity of religion, and the value of art troubled the masses during these years. Literature echoed the cries of a society deeply haunted by its own inventions and designs. Though fear saturated the mind, history paints the stereotypical Victorian as a stoic, immovable force—severe in disposition, willful to the core.

POLITICS

Queen Victoria saw Britain become the most powerful nation in the world. By the end of her reign, Britain controlled a quarter of the world's property and a fifth of its population. Called the "empire on which the sun never sets," the nation had some degree of authority in Australia, New Zealand, Hong Kong, Canada, South Africa, Jamaica, and many other territories. Britain had a global reach largely because of its naval prowess. In addition to its quest for resources and markets, the nation had ideological incentives. Ethnocentrism, the belief that one race or culture is superior to another, led many Britons to believe they were doing good by spreading British civilization and values. Holding themselves as the pinnacle of advanced, sophisticated society, imperialists assumed the "White Man's Burden" of educating those they thought lesser than themselves. Christian missionaries

481

flocked abroad, and colonial administrators eagerly implemented their ideals on colonized peoples.

Determined to become the largest empire in the world, Britain attempted a number of imperial enterprises throughout the era. Of course, Britain was not alone in its conquests; France and Russia, two other global powers, contended for territories. From the early-to-mid 1850s, these three nations vied for the "sick man of Europe"—the weakening Ottoman Empire—which presided over much of the Mediterranean and Middle East. Britain feared that if Russia gained control of any of these regions, nearby British colonies (particularly India, the jewel of Britain's imperial crown) would fall prey to foreign influences. After a series of failed political maneuvers, the Crimean War erupted. Many of the casualties in this bloody struggle were not caused by combat injuries. Rather, the death toll rose due to disease, poor medical treatment, and a lack of adequate support from the British government. The Crimean War ended when the Treaty of Paris was signed in 1856. The Treaty solved little; the peace that resulted portended World War I. Many scholars and historians further agree that the Crimean War was unnecessary and avoidable. Nevertheless, the conflict epitomizes the imperial hunger that drove Britain to all corners of the world. Indeed, the struggle for the Ottoman Empire was echoed by the infamous "scramble for Africa" that occurred later in the century.

Colonial wars were often gruesome, and the British military brutally crushed resistances. The Indian Mutiny of 1857 typifies the larger pattern of British imperialism. British officials displaced local aristocrats, upsetting the country's extant societal structure. Missionaries further replaced dominant religions. Traditional Indian culture was increasingly erased by British influences, and conflict eventually broke out. Indian soldiers (called sepoys) serving the British East India Company revolted and shot their British officers. In an act of vengeance, officers bayoneted sepoys and fired cannons against them. After much struggle and unnecessary bloodshed from both sides, direct control of India transferred from the East India Company to the British government, with Queen Victoria taking the title of empress of India in 1877. India's political environment and culture were westernized, and Jamaica and several other imperialized nations that rebelled encountered similar ends. Attempts to thwart foreign influence met limited success at best.

The Opium Wars against China also display the consequences of Britain's influence. The wars, which occurred from 1839 until 1860, were extremely controversial. To justify its attacks, Britain claimed it was defending its national honor and trading rights. The heart of the conflict, however, was China's attempt to suppress drug trafficking. The British imported opium in massive quantities, leaving China with severe addiction and the resulting social and economic problems. Britain's navy overpowered Chinese resistance efforts, and unequal peace negotiations ensued. At Britain's demand, China paid sizable reparations, surrendered Hong Kong, and opened more trading ports. Subsequently, China was prone to foreign commercialism and authority. The effects on Chinese society were irrevocable. Its culture, which was constructed around ruling dynasties, gradually collapsed.

Ireland, too, suffered from the British government's policies. Subjected to English control since 1801, the Irish had long been battling against oppression. Many families had lost their land during earlier English invasions and wars, and most farmers were forced to rent land that was once their own from British landlords. British attitudes toward the Irish increased the distress caused by the Great Famine. From 1845 until 1852, potato crops were blighted, plaguing Ireland with devastating and recurrent starvation. Parliament assumed the Irish would recover from the blight as they had in the past, but as crops continued to fail, action became necessary. By 1847, the British government imported grain to feed the people, but class and political lines rendered distribution unfair. As the blight persisted, the British became less willing to help the Irish. Some even blamed the famine on the purportedly immoral and lazy character of the Irish. Fearful that government handouts would encourage dependency, landlords and officials told agricultural workers to be self-reliant. But the Irish confronted worsening odds. Many were too poor to buy new seeds, forcing them to replant diseased potato tubers. Unsuccessful harvests made it impossible for farmers to afford their rent, and thousands of families faced eviction. When the potato crop finally recovered, the population had been obliterated—from both starvation and emigration—and Ireland's economy lay in ruins.

Agricultural trade hemorrhaged in England as well. Industrialization was still underway, and the mass movement of people toward cities redistributed the population. Rural locations increasingly lost their value as production centers. Instead, the countryside morphed into a vacation destination for those smothered by dismal industrial conditions. Though the era witnessed a rise in philanthropic organizations and missions, relief efforts could scarcely combat capitalist economics. Public institutions known as workhouses provided food and shelter for the destitute in exchange for their work. The workhouse system, however, was notoriously inhumane. It separated families, enacted rigid punishments, and required cruel and unhealthy amounts of physical labor. The working classes demanded democratic representation, and in 1838, William Lovett drafted the "People's Charter," a document outlining workers' request for voting rights. The Chartist movement, as it came to be called, drew attention to the divide between those who owned resources and those who labored. Although the movement had a number of aims, it faded out a decade after its inception. The Ten Hours Act—which limited children to working ten hours a day—showed that Parliament indeed cared somewhat about the wellbeing of the working classes. Parliament eventually conceded to the Chartists' call for voting rights; many working-class males were guaranteed rights when the Third Reform Bill passed in 1884.

Legal rights remained an issue for women. Single women possessed greater rights than married women, but there were very few jobs available. Poor women worked alongside men in factories and mines, but socially acceptable jobs—like governesses and nurses—kept women in subordinate roles. Prostitution was one of the only ways a woman could support herself. Married women were dependent on their husbands, and it was not until the passage of the Married Woman's Property Act in 1870 that women could legally keep the wages they earned. Still, women battled widespread oppression and prejudice. When debating about women and femininity, many men insisted that women were naturally submissive. What is easily recognized as sexism today was a formidable obstacle for Victorian women. The "Woman Question" of the changing professional, economic, social, and political status of women gave rise to feminism. By the 1890s, hundreds of women rebelled against traditional gender roles. Society was largely unkind to the "New Woman." Called "wild women," "social insurgents," and other derogatory terms, women who wanted an education, a career, and suffrage received brutal attacks for challenging tradition. Young women especially acknowledged that raising a family meant sacrificing their personal and intellectual dreams. Some refused to accept their mother's lifestyle. In response to their discontent, colleges provided more opportunities for employment and independence. The press also provided near-constant attention on the women's movement. But unlike Queen Victoria, women did not yet have the power to rule the home and the country.

Both women and men were afflicted by the prevailing intellectual climate of the age: religious doubt. Charles Darwin's theory of evolution and natural selection, as well as other scientists' geological discoveries, seemingly undermined religious doctrines. Natural selection devastated the religious notion that an intelligent being intentionally designed complex biological and physical structures. Developing scientific ideas suggested that chance mutations and undirected processes resulted in these complexities. Fossils further evidenced species development. When Darwin proposed that humans, too, evolved, many Victorians felt degraded and appalled. Science challenged the belief that humankind has a special, privileged role on earth and led many believers to question the meaning of human existence. Some insisted that God had indeed singled out humans, but others were unable to dismiss the existential crises that now tormented them. A religious understanding of the universe—which had long been established and accepted by most of the British population—was irrevocably cast into uncertainty.

Beliefs faltered. The Church of England—already divided into the High Church, Low Church, and Broad Church according to differing doctrinal views—remained the church of the nation, but religion itself was being questioned. Scientific discoveries had polarizing effects on believers: Some turned to doubt while others leaned on religious fervor. Those who lost their attraction to the Church transitioned from Christianity to uncertainty, then from uncertainty to secularism. The Church and state began separating, and religion became a private matter rather than a public one. Still, some tried to reinvigorate religious dogma. The Oxford movement in the High Church is a well-known attempt. Led predominantly by the clergyman John Henry Newman, Catholic leaders tried to steer the Church of England back to the practices of Roman Catholicism instead of popular Protestant customs. Newman preached that doubt was the test of the true believer. He converted to Roman Catholicism and gradually helped followers adopt Roman Catholic beliefs. The Church of England employed greater ceremonial and worship rituals as a result of the movement. The movement alleviated uncertainty for some because it stressed specific ceremonies and strict attendance policies, allowing believers to recover and strengthen their faith.

Even with the Oxford movement, doubt rippled through Victorian society. The Victorians lived in an era of tremendous flux and polarity. Intense moral views about personal conduct and duties on the British homefront validated exploitation abroad; a moneyed middle class hid the abject poverty of the working classes; public and private spheres moved farther apart; discoveries and inventions restructured perceptions of time and space. Victorians recognized their age as a clear break from the past, and everything—whether trivial or significant—merited debate.

LITERATURE

Literacy rates increased substantially and continued to grow throughout the period as basic education became compulsory. With the passage of the Education Act in 1870, poor children aged five to thirteen could attend schools because newly-established school boards paid the necessary fees. By 1880, elementary school was mandatory for all children. Matthew Arnold, a cultural critic and inspector of schools, was a chief promoter and advocate for teaching the masses. Spreading high culture, he believed, would create a literary and philosophical public, which in turn would create a more uniform society. Arnold's ambitions were perhaps idealistic, but greater numbers of adults and children engaged with literature due to ever-evolving printing technology.

As more efficient and cheaper printing methods developed, publishers reached wider audiences. Victorians varied immensely in their opinions and interests, and periodicals addressing all topics circulated the market. Categories ranged between news, religion, science, and literature. Since serial publications allowed writers to keep in contact with their audiences regardless of how regularly their works were printed, serialization became practical and popular. Charles Dickens, William Makepeace Thackeray, and Robert Louis Stevenson gained fame after serializing their stories. With this form, writers had to be especially conscientious about how they organized and developed their pieces. Keeping readers engaged with the plot was essential. It was not unusual for installments to end at moments of suspense; writers lured readers into buying yet another edition to discover how the story unfolded. Serialization greatly affected the style, structure, and sometimes even the content of novels.

Novels were exceptionally popular during the Victorian age, regardless of how they were published. As the dominant genre of the period, the novel developed several subgenres that explored the specialized interests of the reading public. Readers had a wide range of choices, including science fiction, "penny dreadfuls" (cheaply printed crime stories), religious fiction, New Woman fiction (which developed late in the Victorian period), sensation fiction, and many others. Sensation fiction particularly gathered notice because the genre focused around sensational events. Murder, bigamy, drug use, imprisonment, and insanity all made for thrilling, nerve-wracking stories. Mary Elizabeth Braddon's 1862 *Lady Audley's Secret* became one of the most successful sensation novels of its day, and Wilkie Collins preferred to write mystery pieces and detective fiction. Charles Dickens, Collins's friend and mentor, specialized in Condition of England works, or social problem stories, as they were sometimes called. Calling attention to unpleasant or marginalized issues, the most effective agenda-driven novels convinced readers to take action. Stories featuring alcoholism, for example, raised awareness for the mission of temperance societies. Pieces exhibiting class differences were also well-liked as they expounded the necessity of stable relationships between workers and the wealthy for local and national success. Agenda-driven works often contributed to ongoing philanthropic movements. Since philanthropy was a central element of Victorian culture, literature nurtured Victorians' sense of social justice.

Though useful for discussing social change, novels had their weaknesses. Narratives commonly drowned in contextual elements, and it was not uncommon for a book's social mission to overwhelm its characters and plot. Most novels also wove an idealized, moralistic story wherein a disadvantaged protagonist surmounted the challenges they encountered by perseverance and personal virtue. Love and fortune always triumphed, and the protagonist emerged wiser and better off than when they began. Widespread literary idealization is somewhat ironic; not only is Victorian fiction characterized by its realism, but the average Victorian did not live with the boundless optimism embodied by popular stories. Still, in an age of doubt and pessimism, hope surfaced as a concluding message in many pieces.

Doubt was felt, of course, and it was often conveyed with acute devastation and agonizing honesty. People were disoriented, and many were directionless— sent emotionally and intellectually adrift by scientific and religious disputes. Anne Brontë, the youngest of the Brontë sisters, especially anguished over the nature of faith. "What shall I do…if there be no God above…If this be vain delusion all," she lamented in her poem "The Doubter's Prayer." The fear and anxiety of disappearing belief tormented her, and the repercussions of uncertainty were no less severe for many others. Alfred, Lord Tennyson's elegiac poem *In Memoriam*, which was favored by the public and exalted by Queen Victoria herself, relates another distressing cry: "Are God and Nature then at strife?" The struggle to reconcile religious faith after scientific discovery permeated literature as well as daily life. In addition to scientific and religious conflicts, Victorians contended with the prospective loss of art's inherent value.

Some argued that art was only necessary because it had a social responsibility while others believed in "art for art's sake," an idea encapsulated by a minor 1890s literary movement known as the Aesthetic movement. Writers further doubted the morality of the British Empire and took varied stances on its endeavors. A number of people promoted its actions, but others utterly condemned its practices. Amid all the hope presented in Victorian literature, there was indeed a darkness brooding within it.

As people wrestled with external and internal dilemmas, literature continued to echo and communicate contemporary concerns. Whereas Romantics generally focused on injecting the poet's individual experiences into the poem, Victorian writers gravitated toward the nature of identity itself. The question of human nature was not a new one; like early eighteenth-century writers, Victorians took an interest in mannerisms and the complexities of personality. And, as the era was known for its emotionally repressive climate, writers launched narratives that explored psychology and consciousness. Robert Louis Stevenson's *The Strange Case of Dr. Jekyll and Mr. Hyde* is one of the most famous, memorable, and impactful pieces that utilizes the dual nature of humans to propel its plot. As Stevenson relays, people are not simply good or evil, but a composite of both; one constantly grapples against these conflicting impulses. The fluid movement between one's inner, vulnerable self, and the controlled, outward behavior society expects became a favored topic among writers. The concept of a double-life was not purely fictional; the Victorian age witnessed a further solidification of public and private spheres, and men were particularly subjected to conflicting codes of conduct. Required to be ruthless and decisive in public but gentle and moralistic in private, duplicity was a daily reality for many men. Subsequently, literature investigating human nature was an expression and reflection of cultural pressures.

The intimate correlation between literature and societal, cultural, and global phenomena is evidenced by the sheer variety and quantity of publications. Too frequently, history confines Victorian Britain to a dark, rigid form. But despite the stony-faced portraits preserved by the first photographic records, Victorians did not always radiate the coldness that became emblematic of the age. Beneath their inflexible demeanors, many Victorians lived deeply impassioned lives, tending not only to their individual concerns, but greater societal issues as well. In the years to come, Britons would continue to define and understand themselves through the lenses of past times and future possibilities.

CONTEXTS		TEXTS
1832		Sir Charles Lyell, *Principles of Geology*
1833	Passage of the Abolition of Slavery Act Oxford Movement begins	
1836	First train in London	
1837	Death of William IV Succession of Queen Victoria Electric telegraph invented	
1838		Charles Dickens, *Oliver Twist*
1839–60	Opium Wars with China	
1840	Queen Victoria marries Prince Albert	
1843		Dickens, *A Christmas Carol*
1845–52	Irish Potato Famine kills an estimated one million people, and another two million emigrate from Ireland	
1846	Corn Laws repealed, marking a shift toward free trade	
1847	Ten Hours Factory Act passed, limiting the hours children could be employed in British textile factories	Charlotte Brontë, *Jane Eyre* Emily Brontë, *Wuthering Heights*
1848	Pre-Raphaelite Brotherhood founded	Karl Marx and Friedrich Engels, *The Communist Manifesto*

1850		Alfred, Lord Tennyson, *In Memoriam*
		William Wordsworth, *The Prelude*
1851	The Great Exhibition of the Works of Industry of All Nations opens at the Crystal Palace	
1853–56	Crimean War	
1855		Robert Browning, *Men and Women*
1857	Indian Mutiny	
	Matrimonial Causes Act, giving women the legal right to seek divorce or nullity through civil courts	
1859	*Macmillan's Magazine* founded	Charles Darwin, *On the Origin of Species*
		John Stuart Mill, *On Liberty*
1860		Dickens, *Great Expectations*
1861–65	American Civil War	
1861	Death of Prince Albert	
1862		Christina Rossetti, *Goblin Market*
		Mary Elizabeth Braddon, *Lady Audley's Secret*
1865	Jamaica Rebellion	Lewis Carroll, *Alice's Adventures in Wonderland*
1867	Passage of Second Reform Bill, giving voting rights to all householders in the boroughs, some lodgers, and agricultural landowners and tenants who owned small amounts of land	
1868		Wilkie Collins, *The Moonstone*

1869	Suez Canal opens, shortening British trade routes	Matthew Arnold, *Culture and Anarchy*
1870	Married Women's Property Act, allowing women to own and control property for themselves	Dante Gabriel Rossetti, *Poems*
	Elementary Education Act, creating compulsory education for children between ages 5 and 13	
1871		George Eliot, *Middlemarch*
1877	Queen Victoria made empress of India	Henry James, *The American*
1878	Electric street lighting in London	Thomas Hardy, *The Return of the Natives*
1879	Anglo-Zulu War in South Africa	George Meredith, *The Egoist*
1883		Robert Louis Stevenson, *Treasure Island*
1884–85	Berlin Conference begins the "scramble for Africa"	
1884	Passage of the Third Reform Bill, giving voting rights to many working-class British males in rural areas	
1885		Oxford's *Dictionary of National Biography*
1886		Stevenson, *The Strange Case of Dr. Jekyll and Mr. Hyde*
1890	First subway line in London	
1891	Free elementary education	Hardy, *Tess of the D'Urbervilles*
		Oscar Wilde, *The Picture of Dorian Grey*
		Arthur Conan Doyle, *Adventures of Sherlock Holmes*

1893	Independent Labor Party forms	
1894		Rudyard Kipling, *The Jungle Book*
1895	Oscar Wilde arrested and imprisoned for homosexuality	Wilde, *The Importance of Being Earnest*
	Nobel Prizes established	Hardy, *Jude the Obscure*
1897		Bram Stoker, *Dracula*
1898	Marie and Pierre Curie discover radium	Hardy, *Wessex Poems*
		H.G. Wells, *The War of the Worlds*
1899–1902	Anglo-Boer War	
1899	Irish Literary Theatre founded in Dublin	Kipling, "The White Man's Burden"
		Joseph Conrad, *Heart of Darkness*
1900		Conrad, *Lord Jim*
		Sigmund Freud, *The Interpretation of Dreams*
1901	Death of Queen Victoria; Succession of Edward VII	

ALFRED, LORD TENNYSON
1809–1892

Alfred, Lord Tennyson's childhood was not the picturesque and sheltered upbringing many of his colleagues assumed. Tennyson grew up learning fear. While attending Louth Grammar School, he was tormented by stronger boys and beaten by his instructors, who enforced brutality at the headmaster's urging. Tennyson's education largely fell to his father, a knowledgeable but bitter clergyman. After being denied the family inheritance he expected to receive, the Reverend Dr. George Tennyson had turned to alcohol and become violent. The Reverend suffered fits of rage and despondency that terrified young Tennyson so much that Tennyson wished himself dead. Three of Tennyson's brothers also struggled with mental illness or drug addiction. All twelve of the Tennyson children underwent at least one mental breakdown over the course of their lives.

For Tennyson, writing offered an escape from the tensions of daily life. He experimented with the epic form and blank verse poetry prior to entering the University of Cambridge. Along with two of his brothers (Charles and Frederick), he anonymously published *Poems by Two Brothers* in 1827. Though the volume garnered little attention, Tennyson's experience as a published poet pulled him into an elite group of Cambridge students who called themselves "the Apostles." Among the circle of radical and liberal undergraduates was Arthur Hallam, the group's animated and intellectual leader, who would galvanize many of Tennyson's works. The Apostles offered Tennyson stimulating literary and political discussions, encouraged his poetic undertakings, and urged him to venture beyond his limits. In 1830, he and the Apostles travelled to Spain where they supported a revolution to overthrow the Spanish king. Tennyson carried money and secret messages between exiled liberal revolutionaries. The revolution was doomed, but Tennyson's sensations and ideas from the trip electrified his poetry.

The following year, Tennyson's father died and left the family in debt. Tennyson quit Cambridge and returned home to devote himself to poetry. Aside from the gold medal he earned for a prize poem in 1829, he had no distinctions. His 1830 and 1832 volumes of poetry had received contemptuous reviews from *Blackwood's Magazine* and *Quarterly Review*. Upset but undiscouraged, he continued to revise old works and write new pieces. A greater trauma occurred in 1833; Hallam (then engaged to Tennyson's sister Emily) suddenly died while in Vienna. Hallam's death devastated the young poet, yet out of the depths of his grief emerged some of his most characteristic poems, including "Ulysses," "Break, break, break," and "The Two Voices" (which was originally titled "Thoughts of a Suicide"). Tennyson also composed lines for *In Memoriam*, a piece that celebrates Hallam's life and reflects Tennyson's attempts to make sense of loss and search for meaning in life and death. *In Memoriam* embodies a fundamental struggle of the Victorian Age: the need to reconcile traditional beliefs in a world altered by science and technological, political, and social progress.

Tennyson fell in love with Emily Sellwood in 1836, but his poverty made marriage impossible. He broke off their engagement in 1840 and travelled around the London area, mostly living nomadically. In 1842, Tennyson published *Poems*, his first publication in ten years. Eight years later, he achieved significant poetic success when *In Memoriam* reaped positive reviews from critics and the public. During the same year, Tennyson married Emily and became poet laureate. His life stabilized; he, Emily, and their two sons lived comfortably. Queen Victoria offered Tennyson baronetcy four times, but he refused each proposal. His acceptance of a peerage in 1883 marked the first time in history that a title was given to someone for their poetic services.

During his lifetime, he reached such celebrity that he was exalted by Queen Victoria and Prince Albert, followed by admirers in the streets, and hounded by tourists while eating dinner at home. His success, however, is often regarded as destructive. Tennyson loathed attention, and he frequently resorted to outright rudeness to deter it. By the end of his life, he had either outlived his companions or distanced himself from them. Fame also affected his poetic prowess; to maintain elevated language, critics (and Tennyson himself) noted that the descriptions of ordinary objects are overcomplicated. The resulting verses can be confusing or

shallow in meaning. Nevertheless, Tennyson's poetry is esteemed for its melodious phrasing, superb imagery, and melancholy broodings. Several works from his career evoke sentiments of the past, such as the *Idylls of the King* books, which explore the legend of King Arthur, and "The Lotos-Eaters," which is based on an event from the *Odyssey*. History, whether recent or distant, enticed Tennyson, as did contemporary events. "The Charge of the Light Brigade" is among Tennyson's most famous "newspaper verse" poems; it was inspired by a fatal cavalry charge at Balaclava during the Crimean War.

Tennyson wrote during a time when modern discoveries challenged established views. He readily understood the roots of tradition and identified with emblems of the past, but he simultaneously witnessed the wonders of technological advancement. He sometimes used his popularity to influence and inform readers about developing scientific ideas. A Fellow of the Royal Society, he accepted evolution as well as uniformitarianism, a theory that states change on Earth's surface is caused by gradual, continuous processes rather than major catastrophic events, as people previously believed. Further, he was the first major writer to acknowledge and celebrate the expanse of geologic time. As an embodiment of the conflict between past and present, Tennyson became a poetic spokesman for the Victorian Age. He helped people find their place in a world drastically altered by science.

1809	Alfred Tennyson born 6 August
1815–20	Attends Louth Grammar School
1827	"Poems by Two Brothers"; Enters Trinity College, University of Cambridge
1829	Elected member of the Cambridge Conversazione Society (the Apostles)
1830	*Poems: Chiefly Lyrical*; Travels to Spain
1833	Arthur Hallam, Tennyson's closest friend, dies of a hemorrhagic stroke
1842	*Poems*
1850	Marries Emily Sellwood; *In Memoriam*; Appointed poet laureate
1854	"The Charge of the Light Brigade"
1859	*Idylls of the King*
1879	*The Lover's Tale*
1881	*The Nineteenth Century*
1892	Tennyson dies 6 October after falling ill and suffering a recurrence of gout and is buried in Poets' Corner, Westminster Abbey

THE LADY OF SHALOTT

PART I.

On either side the river lie
Long fields of barley and of rye,
That clothe the wold[1] and meet the sky;
And thro' the field the road runs by
   To many-tower'd Camelot;[2]   5
And up and down the people go,
Gazing where the lilies blow
Round an island there below,
   The island of Shalott.

Willows whiten, aspens quiver,   10
Little breezes dusk and shiver
Thro' the wave that runs forever
By the island in the river
   Flowing down to Camelot.
Four gray walls, and four gray towers,   15
Overlook a space of flowers,
And the silent isle imbowers
   The Lady of Shalott.

By the margin, willow-veil'd
Slide the heavy barges trail'd   20
By slow horses; and unhail'd
The shallop[3] flitteth silken-sail'd
   Skimming down to Camelot:
But who hath seen her wave her hand?
Or at the casement seen her stand?   25
Or is she known in all the land,
   The Lady of Shalott?

Only reapers, reaping early
In among the bearded barley,
Hear a song that echoes cheerly   30

---

1 A section of open, uncultivated land.

2 The location of King Arthur's palace and court in Arthurian legend.

3 A type of sailboat.

From the river winding clearly,
  Down to tower'd Camelot:
And by the moon the reaper weary,
Piling sheaves in uplands airy,
Listening, whispers, "'Tis the fairy   35
  Lady of Shalott."

PART II.

There she weaves by night and day
A magic web with colours gay.
She has heard a whisper say,
A curse is on her if she stay   40
  To look down to Camelot.
She knows not what the curse may be,
And so she weaveth steadily,
And little other care hath she,
  The Lady of Shalott.   45

And moving thro' a mirror clear
That hangs before her all the year,
Shadows of the world appear.
There she sees the highway near
  Winding down to Camelot: 50
There the river eddy whirls,
And there the surly village-churls,
And the red cloaks of market girls,
  Pass onward from Shalott.

Sometimes a troop of damsels glad,   55
An abbot on an ambling pad,
Sometimes a curly shepherd-lad,
Or long-hair'd page in crimson clad,
  Goes by to tower'd Camelot;
And sometimes thro' the mirror blue   60
The knights come riding two and two:
She hath no loyal knight and true,
  The Lady of Shalott.

But in her web she still delights
To weave the mirror's magic sights,   65
For often thro' the silent nights
A funeral, with plumes and lights,

And music, went to Camelot:
Or when the moon was overhead,
Came two young lovers lately wed;　　　　　70
"I am half-sick of shadows," said
　　　　The Lady of Shalott.

PART III.

A bow-shot from her bower-eaves,
He rode between the barley sheaves,
The sun came dazzling thro' the leaves,　　　75
And flamed upon the brazen greaves
　　　　Of bold Sir Lancelot.[1]
A redcross knight for ever kneeled
To a lady in his shield,
That sparkled on the yellow field,　　　　80
　　　　Beside remote Shalott.

The gemmy bridle glitter'd free,
Like to some branch of stars we see
Hung in the golden Galaxy.
The bridle bells rang merrily　　　　　85
　　　　As he rode down to Camelot:
And from his blazon'd baldric slung
A mighty silver bugle hung,
And as he rode his armour rung,
　　　　Beside remote Shalott.　　　　90

All in the blue unclouded weather
Thick-jewell'd shone the saddle-leather,
The helmet and the helmet-feather
Burn'd like one burning flame together,
　　　　As he rode down to Camelot.　　　95
As often thro' the purple night,
Below the starry clusters bright,
Some bearded meteor, trailing light,
　　　　Moves over still Shalott.

His broad clear brow in sunlight glow'd;　　100
On burnish'd hooves his war-horse trode;

---

1 One of the greatest knights in Arthurian legend, Sir Lancelot was the lover of Queen Guinevere and symbolized chivalry.

From underneath his helmet flow'd
His coal-black curls as on he rode,
        As he rode down to Camelot.
From the bank and from the river   105
He flashed into the crystal mirror,
"Tirra lirra," by the river
        Sang Sir Lancelot.

She left the web, she left the loom,
She made three paces thro' the room,   110
She saw the water-lily bloom,
She saw the helmet and the plume,
        She look'd down to Camelot.
Out flew the web and floated wide;
The mirror crack'd from side to side;   115
"The curse is come upon me," cried
        The Lady of Shalott.

PART IV.

In the stormy east-wind straining,
The pale yellow woods were waning,
The broad stream in his banks complaining,   120
Heavily the low sky raining
        Over tower'd Camelot;
Down she came and found a boat
Beneath a willow left afloat,
And round about the prow she wrote   125
        The Lady of Shalott.

And down the river's dim expanse—
Like some bold seer in a trance,
Seeing all his own mischance—
With a glassy countenance   130
        Did she look to Camelot.
And at the closing of the day
She loosed the chain, and down she lay;
The broad stream bore her far away,
        The Lady of Shalott.   135

Lying, robed in snowy white
That loosely flew to left and right—
The leaves upon her falling light—

Thro' the noises of the night
      She floated down to Camelot;   140
And as the boat-head wound along
The willowy hills and fields among,
They heard her singing her last song,
      The Lady of Shalott.

Heard a carol, mournful, holy,   145
Chanted loudly, chanted lowly,
Till her blood was frozen slowly,
And her eyes were darken'd wholly,
      Turn'd to tower'd Camelot;
For ere she reach'd upon the tide   150
The first house by the water-side,
Singing in her song she died,
      The Lady of Shalott.

Under tower and balcony,
By garden-wall and gallery,   155
A gleaming shape she floated by,
A corse between the houses high,
      Silent into Camelot,
Out upon the wharfs they came,
Knight and burgher, lord and dame,   160
And round the prow they read her name,
      The Lady of Shalott.

Who is this? and what is here?
And in the lighted palace near
Died the sound of royal cheer: 165
And they cross'd themselves for fear,
      All the knights at Camelot:
But Lancelot mused a little space;
He said, "She has a lovely face:
God in his mercy lend her grace,   170
      The Lady of Shalott."

1833

THE LOTOS-EATERS[1]

"Courage!" he said, and pointed toward the land,
"This mounting wave will roll us shoreward soon."
In the afternoon they came unto a land,
In which it seemed always afternoon.
All round the coast the languid air did swoon,   5
Breathing like one that hath a weary dream.
Full-faced above the valley stood the moon;
And like a downward smoke, the slender stream
Along the cliff to fall and pause and fall did seem.

A land of streams! some, like a downward smoke,   10
Slow-dropping veils of thinnest lawn, did go;
And some thro' wavering lights and shadows broke,
Rolling a slumbrous sheet of foam below.
They saw the gleaming river seaward flow
From the inner land: far off, three mountain-tops,   15
Three silent pinnacles of aged snow,
Stood sunset-flushed: and, dew'd with showery drops,
Up-clomb the shadowy pine above the woven copse.

The charmed sunset linger'd low adown
In the red West: thro' mountain clefts the dale   20
Was seen far inland, and the yellow down
Border'd with palm, and many a winding vale
And meadow, set with slender galingale:[2]
A land where all things always seem'd the same!
And round about the keel with faces pale,   25
Dark faces pale against that rosy flame,
The mild-eyed melancholy Lotos-eaters came.

---

1 In Book IX of Homer's *Odyssey*, the Greek hero Odysseus and his men encounter a tribe of
Lotus-Eaters after being driven off course by a storm. Some of Odysseus' mariners consume the
lotuses and sink into blissful oblivion. Odysseus is forced to drag his men to their ship so they can
voyage back to Ithaca.

2 An herb with strong aromatic rhizomes.

Branches they bore of that enchanted stem,
Laden with flower and fruit, whereof they gave
To each, but whoso did receive of them,   30
And taste, to him the gushing of the wave
Far far away did seem to mourn and rave
On alien shores; and if his fellow spake,
His voice was thin, as voices from the grave;
And deep-asleep he seem'd, yet all awake,   35
And music in his ears his beating heart did make.

They sat them down upon the yellow sand,
Between the sun and moon upon the shore;
And sweet it was to dream of Fatherland,
Of child, and wife, and slave: but evermore   40
Most weary seem'd the sea, weary the oar,
Weary the wandering fields of barren foam.
Then some one said, "We will return no more;"
And all at once they sang, "Our island home
Is far beyond the wave; we will no longer roam."   45

CHORIC SONG

1.

There is sweet music here that softer falls
Than petals from blown roses on the grass,
Or night-dews on still waters between walls
Of shadowy granite, in a gleaming pass;
Music that gentlier on the spirit lies,   50
Than tir'd eyelids upon tir'd eyes:
Music that brings sweet sleep down from the blissful skies.
Here are cool mosses deep,
And thro' the moss the ivies creep,
And in the stream the long-leaved flowers weep,   55
And from the craggy ledge the poppy hangs in sleep.

2.

Why are we weigh'd upon with heaviness,
And utterly consumed with sharp distress,
While all things else have rest from weariness?

All things have rest: why should we toil alone, 60
We only toil, who are the first of things,
And make perpetual moan,
Still from one sorrow to another thrown:
Nor ever fold our wings,
And cease from wanderings, 65
Nor steep our brows in slumber's holy balm:
Nor harken what the inner spirit sings,
"There is no joy but calm!"
Why should we only toil, the roof and crown of things?

3.

Lo! in the middle of the wood, 70
The folded leaf is woo'd from out the bud
With winds upon the branch, and there
Grows green and broad, and takes no care,
Sun-steep'd at noon, and in the moon
Nightly dew-fed; and turning yellow 75
Falls, and floats adown the air.
Lo! sweeten'd with the summer light,
The full-juiced apple, waxing over-mellow,
Drops in a silent autumn night.
All its allotted length of days, 80
The flower ripens in its place,
Ripens and fades, and falls, and hath no toil,
Fast-rooted in the fruitful soil.

4.

Hateful is the dark-blue sky,
Vaulted o'er the dark-blue sea. 85
Death is the end of life; ah, why
Should life all labour be?
Let us alone. Time driveth onward fast,
And in a little while our lips are dumb.
Let us alone. What is it that will last? 90
All things are taken from us, and become
Portions and parcels of the dreadful Past.
Let us alone. What pleasure can we have
To war with evil? Is there any peace
In ever climbing up the climbing wave? 95

All things have rest, and ripen toward the grave
In silence; ripen, fall and cease:
Give us long rest or death, dark death, or dreamful ease.

5.

How sweet it were, hearing the downward stream,
With half-shut eyes ever to seem   100
Falling asleep in a half-dream!
To dream and dream, like yonder amber light,
Which will not leave the myrrh-bush on the height;
To hear each other's whisper'd speech;
Eating the Lotos day by day,   105
To watch the crisping ripples on the beach,
And tender curving lines of creamy spray;
To lend our hearts and spirits wholly
To the influence of mild-minded melancholy;
To muse and brood and live again in memory,   110
With those old faces of our infancy
Heap'd over with a mound of grass,
Two handfuls of white dust, shut in an urn of brass!

6.

Dear is the memory of our wedded lives,
And dear the last embraces of our wives   115
And their warm tears: but all hath suffer'd change;
For surely now our household hearths are cold:
Our sons inherit us: our looks are strange:
And we should come like ghosts to trouble joy.
Or else the island princes over-bold   120
Have eat our substance, and the minstrel sings
Before them of the ten-years' war in Troy,
And our great deeds, as half-forgotten things.
Is there confusion in the little isle?
Let what is broken so remain.   125
The Gods are hard to reconcile:
'Tis hard to settle order once again.
There *is* confusion worse than death,
Trouble on trouble, pain on pain,
Long labor unto aged breath,   130
Sore task to hearts worn out with many wars
And eyes grow dim with gazing on the pilot-stars.

7.

But, propt on beds of amaranth and moly,[1]
How sweet (while warm airs lull us, blowing lowly)
With half-dropt eyelids still,   135
Beneath a heaven dark and holy,
To watch the long bright river drawing slowly
His waters from the purple hill—
To hear the dewy echoes calling
From cave to cave thro' the thick-twined vine—   140
To watch the emerald-colour'd water falling
Thro' many a wov'n acanthus-wreath divine!
Only to hear and see the far-off sparkling brine,
Only to hear were sweet, stretch'd out beneath the pine.

8.

The Lotos blooms below the barren peak: 145
The Lotos blows by every winding creek:
All day the wind breathes low with mellower tone:
Thro' every hollow cave and alley lone
Round and round the spicy downs the yellow Lotos-dust
        is blown.
We have had enough of action, and of motion we,   150
Roll'd to starboard, roll'd to larboard, when the surge was
        seething free,
Where the wallowing monster spouted his foam-fountains
        in the sea.
Let us swear an oath, and keep it with an equal mind,
In the hollow Lotos-land to live and lie reclined
On the hills like Gods together, careless of mankind.   155
For they lie beside their nectar, and the bolts are hurl'd
Far below them in the valleys, and the clouds are lightly curl'd
Round their golden houses, girdled with the gleaming world:
Where they smile in secret, looking over wasted lands,
Blight and famine, plague and earthquake, roaring deeps and 160
        fiery sands,
Clanging fights, and flaming towns, and sinking ships and
        praying hands.
But they smile, they find a music centred in a doleful song

---

1 A mythical herb with magic properties.

Steaming up, a lamentation and an ancient tale of wrong,
Like a tale of little meaning tho' the words are strong;
Chanted from an ill-used race of men that cleave the soil,   165
Sow the seed, and reap the harvest with enduring toil,
Storing yearly little dues of wheat, and wine and oil;
Till they perish and they suffer—some, 'tis whisper'd—
        down in hell
Suffer endless anguish, others in Elysian[1] valleys dwell,
Resting weary limbs at last on beds of asphodel.[2]   170
Surely, surely, slumber is more sweet than toil, the shore
Than labor in the deep mid-ocean, wind and wave and oar;
O rest ye, brother mariners, we will not wander more.

1833, 1842

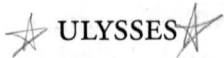

ULYSSES

It little profits that an idle king,
By this still hearth, among these barren crags,
Match'd with an aged wife, I mete and dole
Unequal laws unto a savage race,
That hoard, and sleep, and feed, and know not me.   5
I cannot rest from travel: I will drink
Life to the lees:[3] all times I have enjoy'd
Greatly, have suffer'd greatly, both with those
That loved me, and alone; on shore, and when
Thro' scudding drifts the rainy Hyades[4]   10
Vext the dim sea: I am become a name;
For always roaming with a hungry heart
Much have I seen and known; cities of men
And manners, climates, councils, governments,
Myself not least, but honour'd of them all;   15

---

1 A paradise for heroes in Greek mythology.

2 An undying flower that grows in the Elysian Fields.

3 The sediment of wine at the bottom of the barrel; alternately, the most worthless parts of something

4 Ancient Greeks believed that the five nymphs of the cluster of stars at the head of the constellation Taurus brought rain.

And drunk delight of battle with my peers,
Far on the ringing plains of windy Troy.
I am a part of all that I have met;
Yet all experience is an arch wherethro'
Gleams that untravell'd world, whose margin fades   20
For ever and for ever when I move.
How dull it is to pause, to make an end,
To rust unburnish'd, not to shine in use!
As tho' to breathe were life. Life piled on life
Were all too little, and of one to me   25
Little remains: but every hour is saved
From that eternal silence, something more,
A bringer of new things; and vile it were
For some three suns to store and hoard myself,
And this gray spirit yearning in desire   30
To follow knowledge like a sinking star,
Beyond the utmost bound of human thought.

    This is my son, mine own Telemachus,[5]
To whom I leave the sceptre and the isle—
Well-loved of me, discerning to fulfil   35
This labor, by slow prudence to make mild
A rugged people, and thro' soft degrees
Subdue them to the useful and the good.
Most blameless is he, centred in the sphere
Of common duties, decent not to fail   40
In offices of tenderness, and pay
Meet adoration to my household gods,
When I am gone. He works his work, I mine.

    There lies the port: the vessel puffs her sail:
There gloom the dark broad seas. My mariners,   45
Souls that have toil'd, and wrought, and thought with me—
That ever with a frolic welcome took
The thunder and the sunshine, and opposed
Free hearts, free foreheads—you and I are old;
Old age hath yet his honour and his toil;   50
Death closes all: but something ere the end,

---

5 Telemachus, from Homer's *Odyssey*, is the son of Odysseus. In Roman mythology, Odysseus is called Ulysses.

Some work of noble note, may yet be done,
Not unbecoming men that strove with Gods.
The lights begin to twinkle from the rocks:
The long day wanes: the slow moon climbs: the deep   55
Moans round with many voices. Come, my friends,
'Tis not too late to seek a newer world.
Push off, and sitting well in order smite
The sounding furrows; for my purpose holds
To sail beyond the sunset, and the baths   60
Of all the western stars, until I die.
It may be that the gulfs will wash us down:
It may be we shall touch the Happy Isles,[1]
And see the great Achilles,[2] whom we knew.
Tho' much is taken, much abides; and tho'   65
We are not now that strength which in old days
Moved earth and heaven; that which we are, we are;
One equal temper of heroic hearts,
Made weak by time and fate, but strong in will
To strive, to seek, to find, and not to yield.   70

1842

---

1 The Happy Isles, called the Fortunate Isles or the Isles of the Blessed in Greek and Roman mythologies, are a winterless paradise for deceased heroes. Geographers have determined that the isles are located in the Atlantic Ocean off the west coast of Africa.

2 Achilles was the mightiest and bravest warrior who fought in Agnememnon's army during the Trojan War.

THE CHARGE OF THE LIGHT BRIGADE[3]

I.

Half a league, half a league,
Half a league onward,
All in the valley of Death
   Rode the six hundred.
"Forward, the Light Brigade!"   5
Charge for the guns!" he said:
Into the valley of Death
   Rode the six hundred.

II.

"Forward, the Light Brigade!"
Was there a man dismay'd?   10
Not tho' the soldier knew
   Some one had blunder'd:
Theirs not to make reply,
Theirs not to reason why,
Theirs but to do and die: 15
Into the valley of Death
   Rode the six hundred.

III.

Cannon to right of them,
Cannon to left of them,
Cannon in front of them   20
   Volley'd and thunder'd;
Storm'd at with shot and shell,
Boldly they rode and well,
Into the jaws of Death,
Into the mouth of Hell   25
   Rode the six hundred.

---

3 After a series of blundered commands, approximately 670 members of the British Light Brigade charged the Russian artillery battery. Slaughter ensued; Russian forces fired at the soldiers from three directions, killing about 110 people and wounding an additional 160.

IV.

Flash'd all their sabres bare,
Flash'd as they turn'd in air
Sabring the gunners there,
Charging an army, while   30
   All the world wonder'd:
Plunged in the battery-smoke
Right thro' the line they broke;
Cossack and Russian
Reel'd from the sabre-stroke   35
   Shatter'd and sunder'd.
Then they rode back, but not
   Not the six hundred.

V.

Cannon to right of them,
Cannon to left of them,   40
Cannon behind them
   Volley'd and thunder'd;
Storm'd at with shot and shell,
While horse and hero fell,
They that had fought so well   45
Came thro' the jaws of Death,
Back from the mouth of Hell,
All that was left of them,
   Left of six hundred.

VI.

When can their glory fade?   50
O the wild charge they made!
   All the world wonder'd.
Honour the charge they made!
Honour the Light Brigade,
Noble six hundred!   55

1854

CHARLES DICKENS
1812–1870

After an unadorned, private funeral, Charles Dickens's family and friends emerged from Poets' Corner to find thousands of people waiting outside Westminster Abbey. For the next two days, mourners streamed by Dickens's unfilled grave to pay their respects. The flowers placed on his simple oak coffin accumulated until they cascaded from the edges of the burial site. Those who visited represented a mere fraction of the lives touched by his works and charity.

Dickens transcended his humble beginnings to reach massive literary acclaim. Born in 1812, he was the second child of lower middle-class parents. His father John, a cultured man fond of living beyond his means, was a Navy pay clerk. Because of John's financial irresponsibility and his unpredictable military orders, the family relocated frequently; by age sixteen, Dickens had moved a total of fifteen times. The happiest years of Dickens's childhood passed in Chatham—a busy town brimming with markets, fairs, and annual horse-racing—and Rochester, a quiet and respectable town nearby. In addition to its stunning sixteenth and seventeenth century buildings, Rochester housed a theatre. There Dickens discovered his love for the stage and dreamed of becoming an actor or author. When he was nine years old, however, financial strain drove his family to move. To cope with the loss of his cherished home, his family's mounting debt, and his aunt's imminent marriage to Dr. Lamert (Dickens's Aunt Fanny, who lived with the family, would soon leave the household), he read incessantly. William Giles, his school teacher, recognized and encouraged Dickens's literary talents. Indeed, when Dickens's father was recalled to London about sixteen months after the move, Giles welcomed the boy into his home.

Dickens reunited with his family at their new address in Camden Town, on the outskirts of London, a few months later. His parents, Dr. Lamert's son, six children, and one servant packed into the small house. Tragedy quickly affected the family: Aunt Fanny died just six months after her wedding, and Dickens's younger sister also died, possibly of smallpox. Additionally, the family began selling belongings to reduce debt. Yet Dickens was dismayed for another reason: His older sister attended the Royal Academy of Music, but his parents made no arrangements for his education. In 1824, the twelve-year-old Dickens began working at Warren's Blacking Warehouse. The work was mind-numbing. He pasted labels on shoe polish bottles for ten hours a day, six days a week. Eleven days after he started working, his father was imprisoned for debt. Within half a month, most of the family's belongings, except a few chairs, had been sold or pawned. Dickens's father was released after three months, and Dickens, too, was liberated; his father no longer sent him to work at Warren's Warehouse.

Dickens resumed his education in 1825, three years after his last formal schooling. He attended Wellington House Classical and Commercial Academy. Though reputed as one of the best schools in the area, the head teacher beat the boys—a fate Dickens was fortunately spared from, as he did not board. Dickens received a decent education, but the true value of his schooling resulted from his extracurricular literary activities. The following year, however, Dickens could no longer attend school because his father lost his job and the family was evicted from their home. Dickens took up work for the Gray's Inn offices of Ellis and Blackmore where he ferried legal documents between various public offices, visited law stationers, brought clients into solicitors' offices, and maintained the petty-cash book. He also taught himself shorthand, an invaluable skill for journalism, during

his eighteen months of employment. He acquired a similar position for a solicitor in 1828 before establishing himself as a freelance shorthand writer at Doctors' Commons. He considered a career in law, but, finding the work tedious, never committed.

His first serious romantic interest, Maria Beadnell, caused young Dickens lasting heartache. He hoped to marry her, but she was above his social class, and her parents dissuaded his courting efforts. After two years of torment, Dickens terminated their relationship. To him, she epitomized unattainable love. Only when she briefly reentered his life in 1855, married and much different than he remembered her, did his idealized illusion break.

After his failed courtship, Dickens threw himself into his work. In addition to his job at Doctors' Commons, he found a position as a political journalist for the *Mirror of Parliament* paper. His emotions also fueled his creative writing, and seven months after his breakup with Maria, *Monthly Magazine* published his first sketch, "A Dinner at Poplar Walk." Five more sketches appeared in the *Morning Chronicle,* where he accepted a job as a political journalist in 1834. The journal *Bell's Life in London* published an additional twelve sketches. The innovation of Dickens's stories gathered immediate interest, for no one had written explicitly about the poor, and certainly no one had captured poverty so poignantly. He negotiated the publication of *Sketches by Boz*, a collection of his sketches in a single volume, in 1836.

In April of the same year, he married Catherine Hogarth, the daughter of the *Morning Chronicle*'s editor, and left the paper. Just over a year into the marriage, Catherine's seventeen-year-old sister Mary Hogarth, who lived with the couple, died in Dickens's arms. Mary had been a source of happiness, support, and friendship, and her unexpected death distressed Dickens enough that he postponed forthcoming installments of his work. Mary later inspired Rose Maylie, an angel-like character who appears in *Oliver Twist*.

The publication of *Oliver Twist* in book-form, the first work Dickens attached his name to, improved his spirits. His next serialized novel led him to investigate the abuses of the famed Yorkshire schools. Public response to the cruelties encapsulated in *Nicholas Nickleby* caused the government to shut down the worst schools. Dickens serialized four more works before publishing *A Christmas Carol*. Walking between fifteen and twenty miles a night to work through his thoughts, he completed the novella in six weeks. Its popularity was undeniable; the second print sold out, and by the next year, it was in its seventh edition and had been dramatized on three separate occasions.

Seeking a creative revival, Dickens, his wife, and their five children traveled to Italy. Once there, Dickens found himself mentally exhausted and unable to write. His deceased sister-in-law appeared in a dream and gave him much-needed inspiration. He dashed off *The Chimes*, another Christmas story, in a mere four weeks, and sold some 20,000 copies on the first day. The family then moved to Lausanne, Switzerland, for about six months, where Dickens penned another Christmas story before visiting Paris and returning to London. *David Copperfield*, his heavily autobiographical tenth novel, appeared in book-form in 1850. But from the 1850s onwards, Dickens's novels lost their lighthearted comedy. Though Britain was at its imperial height, Dickens saw only England's interior rot: dehumanization, bureaucracy, materialism, and failing religious agendas. Indeed, the Crimean War distracted from the conditions of England's poor and laboring classes whose plights Dickens reanimated tirelessly in his novels. His final five novels contain more plausible plots than his early stories because he relied less on improvisation and more on deliberate planning. He increased symbolism as well as tragedy, and incorporated darker, harsher satire.

Lost hope and happiness affected his personal life as well. No longer in love with his wife, he proposed an informal separation in May of 1858. Catherine rejected his proposals but conceded to an annual allowance, use of the carriage, and a house he paid for. It was the end of a twenty-two-year marriage. They had raised ten children together, and Catherine had suffered at least three miscarriages. Though she still loved him, Dickens responded with indifference and unwisely publicized their separation. His reputation survived despite the news. He justified his decision, claiming he and Catherine had never been compatible, criticizing her domestic and mothering skills, and finding her eccentricities—namely her purported physical clumsiness and tendency to share her emotions—intolerable. His interests, however, were likely vested elsewhere. Dickens, then forty-six years old, could neither divorce nor marry. He may have carried on a secret relationship with Ellen (Nell) Ternan, an actress whom he had met in 1837. It is speculated that she bore him a son sometime between 1862 and 1865, but the boy did not survive infancy.

A further shock hit Dickens when he, Nell, and her mother almost died in a train accident in 1865. Traveling from Paris to London at 50 mph, they approached a 42-foot gap on the rails. Seven of the eight carriages fell on the riverbank, killing ten people and seriously wounding forty others. Only Dickens and his company, sitting in the eighth carriage, stayed on the tracks. The accident and the possibility of future train travel harrowed Dickens. His literary audience, nonetheless, anxiously awaited his next installment of *Our Mutual Friend*, and he continued writing fervently. As with *A Tale of Two Cities*, *Uncommercial Traveller*, *Great Expectations*, and a number of other works, Dickens serialized *Our Mutual Friend* in his weekly journal, *All the Year Round*.

All the Year Round grew to such acclaim that it surpassed *The Times* in sales three years after its startup. The primary source of Dickens's popularity later in his career, however, resulted from approximately 450 public readings he conducted. Proceeds from Dickens's public speaking events initially went to charitable organizations that benefitted the poor and laboring classes; but in 1858, he commenced a nationwide tour in Britain for financial gain. He achieved astounding success. Crowds packed into his venues, and thousands more waited outside. Invites for tours in Australia and the U.S. ensued. He refused Australia but consented to a reading tour in America in 1867. He received additional requests for private audiences with Queen Victoria; Lord Houghton; Leopold II, King of the Belgians; the Prince of Wales; two British prime ministers; Andrew Johnson, then the American president; and the American Ambassador. Rather than pulling material directly from his books, Dickens composed scripts for himself and delivered extremely manicured readings. His flair for acting emerged, especially in his thrilling rendition of the murder scene in *Oliver Twist*. But the emotional and physical toil of touring proved exhausting, and Dickens relinquished public readings in March of 1870.

In June, Dickens finished the sixth monthly installment of *The Mystery of Edwin Drood*. The latter half of his fifteenth novel would never see completion. Afflicted with a brain hemorrhage, he died at Gad's Place Hill, the home he dreamed of buying since he was five years old. Upon news of his death, public grief reached such intensity that a clergyman proposed a burial at Rochester Cathedral. Though Dickens asked to be buried in the Chatham countryside, his family consented to the offer. However, four days after his death, yet another plan was agreed upon: He would be buried in Poets' Corner, Westminster Abbey, among cherished writers.

When Dickens died, he imparted not only a sizeable and treasured collection of literature, but a legacy of social work as well. He attacked English institutions ferociously, and his motives for writing often revolved around improving the lives of others. Victorian attitudes about the poor, which frequently assumed poverty was ordained by God or caused by alleged immorality, revolted Dickens. He assiduously exposed the failings of the Poor Law System and endeavored to spread consciousness as well as gratitude. Habitually siding with underdogs and the poor, he supported numerous charitable organizations including thirteen hospitals. He also developed a program in conjunction with Angela Burdett Coutts, a socially-conscious and extremely wealthy woman, that educated prostitutes and gave them an opportunity to make a new life in Australia, Canada, or South Africa. Dickens employed his writing to do more than entertain. He hoped to inform others and stimulate change.

What makes Dickens's literary worlds so compelling is his recreation of Victorian London and his grotesque, comical characters. He wielded sentimentality and pathos to maximize the effectiveness of his stories. In some regards, however, his writing is predictable; despite his inventiveness, he succumbs to mechanical and conventional humor. Nonetheless, his contemporaries lionized his work. Dickens's popularity has diminished somewhat since his death, but it has never vanished. He is still regarded as one of the most imaginative and topical English writers, especially in Victorian England and perhaps of all time.

1812	Charles John Huffam Dickens born 7 February
1821	Attends William Giles's School in Clover Lane
1825	Attends Wellington House Academy
1836	*Sketches by Boz*; marries Catherine Hogarth
1838	*The Adventures of Oliver Twist*
1843	*A Christmas Carol*
1852	Tenth child born
1859	First number of weekly journal *All the Year Round*; *A Tale of Two Cities*
1867–68	Completes reading tour in America
1861	*Great Expectations*
1865	*Our Mutual Friend*, Dickens's fourteenth novel
1870	Dies 9 June due to a cerebral hemorrhage and is buried in Poets' Corner, Westminster Abbey

A CHRISTMAS CAROL

STAVE ONE

MARLEY'S GHOST

MARLEY WAS DEAD, to begin with. There is no doubt whatever about that. The register of his burial was signed by the clergyman, the clerk, the undertaker, and the chief mourner. Scrooge signed it. And Scrooge's name was good upon 'Change for anything he chose to put his hand to. Old Marley was as dead as a door-nail.

Mind! I don't mean to say that I know of my own knowledge, what there is particularly dead about a door-nail. I might have been inclined, myself, to regard a coffin-nail as the deadest piece of ironmongery in the trade. But the wisdom of our ancestors is in the simile; and my unhallowed hands shall not disturb it, or the country's done for. You will, therefore, permit me to repeat, emphatically, that Marley was as dead as a door-nail.

Scrooge knew he was dead? Of course he did. How could it be otherwise? Scrooge and he were partners for I don't know how many years. Scrooge was his sole executor, his sole administrator, his sole assign, his sole residuary legatee, his sole friend, and sole mourner. And even Scrooge was not so dreadfully cut up by the sad event but that he was an excellent man of business on the very day of the funeral, and solemnised it with an undoubted bargain.

The mention of Marley's funeral brings me back to the point I started from. There is no doubt that Marley was dead. This must be distinctly understood, or nothing wonderful can come of the story I am going to relate. If we were not perfectly convinced that Hamlet's father died before the play began, there would be nothing more remarkable in his taking a stroll at night, in an easterly wind, upon his own ramparts, than there would be in any other middle-aged gentleman rashly turning out after dark in a breezy spot—say Saint Paul's Churchyard, for instance—literally to astonish his son's weak mind.

Scrooge never painted out Old Marley's name. There it stood, years afterwards, above the warehouse door: Scrooge and Marley. The firm was known as Scrooge and Marley. Sometimes people new to the business called Scrooge Scrooge, and sometimes Marley, but he answered to both names. It was all the same to him.

Oh! but he was a tight-fisted hand at the grindstone, Scrooge! a squeezing, wrenching, grasping, scraping, clutching, covetous, old sinner! Hard and sharp as flint, from which no steel had ever struck out generous fire; secret, and self-contained, and solitary as an oyster. The cold within him froze his old features, nipped his pointed nose, shrivelled his cheek, stiffened his gait; made his eyes red, his thin lips blue; and spoke out shrewdly in his grating voice. A frosty rime was on his head, and on his eyebrows, and his wiry chin. He carried his own low temperature always about with him; he iced his office in the dog-days, and didn't thaw it one degree at Christmas.

External heat and cold had little influence on Scrooge. No warmth could warm, no wintry weather chill him. No wind that blew was bitterer than he, no falling snow was more intent upon its purpose, no pelting rain less open to entreaty. Foul weather didn't know where to have him. The heaviest rain, and snow, and hail, and sleet could boast of the advantage over him in only one respect. They often "came down" handsomely, and Scrooge never did.

Nobody ever stopped him in the street to say, with gladsome looks, "My dear Scrooge, how are you? When will you come to see me?" No beggars implored him to bestow a trifle, no children asked him what it was o'clock, no man or woman ever once in all his life inquired the way to such and such a place, of Scrooge. Even the blind men's dogs appeared to know him; and, when they saw him coming on, would tug their owners into doorways and up courts; and then would wag their tails as though they said, "No eye at all is better than an evil eye, dark master!"

But what did Scrooge care? It was the very thing he liked. To edge his way along the crowded paths of life, warning all human sympathy to keep its distance, was what the knowing ones call "nuts" to Scrooge.

Once upon a time—of all the good days in the year, on Christmas Eve—old Scrooge sat busy in his counting-house. It was cold, bleak, biting weather; foggy withal; and he could hear the people in the court outside go wheezing up and down, beating their hands upon their breasts, and stamping their feet upon the pavement stones to warm them. The City clocks had only just gone three, but it was quite dark already—it had not been light all day—and candles were flaring in the windows of the neighbouring offices, like ruddy smears upon the palpable brown air. The fog came pouring in at every chink and keyhole, and was so dense without, that, although the court was of the narrowest, the houses opposite were mere phantoms. To see the dingy cloud come drooping down, obscuring everything, one might have thought that nature lived hard by, and was brewing on a large scale.

The door of Scrooge's counting-house was open, that he might keep his eye upon his clerk, who in a dismal little cell beyond, a sort of tank, was copying letters. Scrooge had a very small fire, but the clerk's fire was so very much smaller that it looked like one coal. But he couldn't replenish it, for Scrooge kept the coal-box in his own room; and so surely as the clerk came in with the shovel, the master predicted that it would be necessary for them to part. Wherefore the clerk put on his white comforter, and tried to warm himself at the candle; in which effort, not being a man of a strong imagination, he failed.

"A merry Christmas, uncle! God save you!" cried a cheerful voice. It was the voice of Scrooge's nephew, who came upon him so quickly that this was the first intimation he had of his approach.

"Bah!" said Scrooge, "Humbug!"

He had so heated himself with rapid walking in the fog and frost, this nephew of Scrooge's, that he was all in a glow; his face was ruddy and handsome; his eyes sparkled, and his breath smoked again.

"Christmas a humbug, uncle!" said Scrooge's nephew. "You don't mean that, I am sure?"

"I do," said Scrooge. "Merry Christmas! What right have you to be merry? What reason have you to be merry? You're poor enough."

"Come, then," returned the nephew gaily. "What right have you to be dismal? What reason have you to be morose? You're rich enough."

Scrooge, having no better answer ready on the spur of the moment, said, "Bah!" again; and followed it up with "Humbug!"

"Don't be cross, uncle!" said the nephew.

"What else can I be," returned the uncle, "when I live in such a world of fools as this? Merry Christmas! Out upon merry Christmas! What's Christmas-time to you but a time for paying bills without money; a time for finding yourself a year older, but not an hour richer; a time for balancing your books, and having every item in 'em through a round dozen of months presented dead against you? If I could work my will," said Scrooge indignantly, "every idiot who goes about with 'Merry Christmas' on his lips, should be boiled with his own pudding, and buried with a stake of holly through his heart. He should!"

"Uncle!" pleaded the nephew.

"Nephew!" returned the uncle sternly, "keep Christmas in your own way, and let me keep it in mine."

"Keep it!" repeated Scrooge's nephew. "But you don't keep it."

"Let me leave it alone, then," said Scrooge. "Much good may it do you! Much good it has ever done you!"

"There are many things from which I might have derived good, by which I have not profited, I dare say," returned the nephew. "Christmas among the rest. But I am sure I have always thought of Christmas-time, when it has come round— apart from the veneration due to its sacred name and origin, if anything belonging to it can be apart from that—as a good time; a kind, forgiving, charitable, pleasant time; the only time I know of, in the long calendar of the year, when men and women seem by one consent to open their shut-up hearts freely, and to think of people below them as if they really were fellow-passengers to the grave, and not another race of creatures bound on other journeys. And therefore, uncle, though it has never put a scrap of gold or silver in my pocket, I believe that it *has* done me good, and *will* do me good; and I say, God bless it!"

The clerk in the Tank involuntarily applauded. Becoming immediately sensible of the impropriety, he poked the fire, and extinguished the last frail spark for ever.

"Let me hear another sound from *you*," said Scrooge, "and you'll keep your Christmas by losing your situation! You're quite a powerful speaker, sir," he added, turning to his nephew. "I wonder you don't go into Parliament."

"Don't be angry, uncle. Come! Dine with us to-morrow."

Scrooge said that he would see him—Yes, indeed he did. He went the whole length of the expression, and said that he would see him in that extremity first.

"But why?" cried Scrooge's nephew. "Why?"

"Why did you get married?" said Scrooge.

"Because I fell in love."

"Because you fell in love!" growled Scrooge, as if that were the only one thing in the world more ridiculous than a merry Christmas. "Good afternoon!"

"Nay, uncle, but you never came to see me before that happened. Why give it as a reason for not coming now?"

"Good afternoon," said Scrooge.

"I want nothing from you; I ask nothing of you; why cannot we be friends?"

"Good afternoon!" said Scrooge.

"I am sorry, with all my heart, to find you so resolute. We have never had any quarrel to which I have been a party. But I have made the trial in homage to Christmas, and I'll keep my Christmas humour to the last. So A Merry Christmas, uncle!"

"Good afternoon," said Scrooge.

"And A Happy New Year!"

"Good afternoon!" said Scrooge.

His nephew left the room without an angry word, notwithstanding. He stopped at the outer door to bestow the greetings of the season on the clerk, who, cold as he was, was warmer than Scrooge; for he returned them cordially.

"There's another fellow," muttered Scrooge, who overheard him: "my clerk, with fifteen shillings a week, and a wife and family, talking about a merry Christmas. I'll retire to Bedlam."[1]

This lunatic, in letting Scrooge's nephew out, had let two other people in. They were portly gentlemen, pleasant to behold, and now stood, with their hats off, in Scrooge's office. They had books and papers in their hands, and bowed to him.

"Scrooge and Marley's, I believe," said one of the gentlemen, referring to his list. "Have I the pleasure of addressing Mr. Scrooge, or Mr. Marley?"

---

1 An archaic term meaning an institution for the mentally ill.

"Mr. Marley has been dead these seven years," Scrooge replied. "He died seven years ago, this very night."

"We have no doubt his liberality is well represented by his surviving partner," said the gentleman, presenting his credentials.

It certainly was; for they had been two kindred spirits. At the ominous word "liberality" Scrooge frowned, and shook his head, and handed the credentials back.

"At this festive season of the year, Mr. Scrooge," said the gentleman, taking up a pen, "it is more than usually desirable that we should make some slight provision for the poor and destitute, who suffer greatly at the present time. Many thousands are in want of common necessaries; hundreds of thousands are in want of common comforts, sir."

"Are there no prisons?" asked Scrooge.

"Plenty of prisons," said the gentleman, laying down the pen again.

"And the Union workhouses?" demanded Scrooge. "Are they still in operation?"

"They are. Still," returned the gentleman, "I wish I could say they were not."

"The Treadmill[2] and the Poor Law[3] are in full vigour, then?" said Scrooge.

"Both very busy, sir."

"Oh! I was afraid, from what you said at first, that something had occurred to stop them in their useful course," said Scrooge. "I'm very glad to hear it."

"Under the impression that they scarcely furnish Christian cheer of mind or body to the multitude," returned the gentleman, "a few of us are endeavouring to raise a fund to buy the Poor some meat and drink, and means of warmth. We choose this time, because it is a time, of all others, when Want is keenly felt, and Abundance rejoices. What shall I put you down for?"

"Nothing!" Scrooge replied.

"You wish to be anonymous?"

"I wish to be left alone," said Scrooge. "Since you ask me what I wish, gentlemen, that is my answer. I don't make merry myself at Christmas, and I can't afford to make idle people merry. I help to support the establishments I have mentioned—they cost enough: and those who are badly off must go there."

"Many can't go there; and many would rather die."

"If they would rather die," said Scrooge, "they had better do it, and decrease the surplus population. Besides—excuse me—I don't know that."

"But you might know it," observed the gentleman.

---

2 First used in England in 1818, the treadwheel (later named the treadmill) was a gruelling form of physical punishment used to reform prisoners' behavior. The Prisons Act of 1898 abolished the use of penal treadwheels in Britain.

3 Intending to reduce the cost of caring for the poor, the 1843 Poor Law provided housing, clothing, and food for those willing to live and work in the workhouse. Back-breaking labor and atrocious conditions awaited the poor in workhouses.

"It's not my business," Scrooge returned. "It's enough for a man to understand his own business, and not to interfere with other people's. Mine occupies me constantly. Good afternoon, gentlemen!"

Seeing clearly that it would be useless to pursue their point, the gentlemen withdrew. Scrooge resumed his labours with an improved opinion of himself, and in a more facetious temper than was usual with him.

Meanwhile the fog and darkness thickened so, that people ran about with flaring links, proffering their services to go before horses in carriages, and conduct them on their way. The ancient tower of a church, whose gruff old bell was always peeping slily down at Scrooge out of a Gothic window in the wall, became invisible, and struck the hours and quarters in the clouds, with tremulous vibrations afterwards, as if its teeth were chattering in its frozen head up there. The cold became intense. In the main street, at the corner of the court, some labourers were repairing the gas-pipes, and had lighted a great fire in a brazier, round which a party of ragged men and boys were gathered: warming their hands and winking their eyes before the blaze in rapture. The water-plug being left in solitude, its overflowings sullenly congealed, and turned to misanthropic ice. The brightness of the shops, where holly sprigs and berries crackled in the lamp heat of the windows, made pale faces ruddy as they passed. Poulterers' and grocers' trades became a splendid joke: a glorious pageant, with which it was next to impossible to believe that such dull principles as bargain and sale had anything to do. The Lord Mayor, in the stronghold of the mighty Mansion House, gave orders to his fifty cooks and butlers to keep Christmas as a Lord Mayor's household should; and even the little tailor, whom he had fined five shillings on the previous Monday for being drunk and bloodthirsty in the streets, stirred up to-morrow's pudding in his garret, while his lean wife and the baby sallied out to buy the beef.

Foggier yet, and colder! Piercing, searching, biting cold. If the good St. Dunstan had but nipped the Evil Spirit's nose with a touch of such weather as that, instead of using his familiar weapons, then indeed he would have roared to lusty purpose. The owner of one scant young nose, gnawed and mumbled by the hungry cold as bones are gnawed by dogs, stooped down at Scrooge's keyhole to regale him with a Christmas carol; but, at the first sound of

"God bless you, merry gentleman,
May nothing you dismay!"

Scrooge seized the ruler with such energy of action that the singer fled in terror, leaving the keyhole to the fog, and even more congenial frost.

At length the hour of shutting up the counting-house arrived. With an ill-will Scrooge dismounted from his stool, and tacitly admitted the fact to the expectant clerk in the tank, who instantly snuffed his candle out, and put on his hat.

"You'll want all day to-morrow, I suppose?" said Scrooge.

"If quite convenient, sir."

"It's not convenient," said Scrooge, "and it's not fair. If I was to stop half-a-crown for it, you'd think yourself ill-used, I'll be bound?"

The clerk smiled faintly.

"And yet," said Scrooge, "you don't think *me* ill-used when I pay a day's wages for no work."

The clerk observed that it was only once a year.

"A poor excuse for picking a man's pocket every twenty-fifth of December!" said Scrooge, buttoning his greatcoat to the chin. "But I suppose you must have the whole day. Be here all the earlier next morning."

The clerk promised that he would; and Scrooge walked out with a growl. The office was closed in a twinkling, and the clerk, with the long ends of his white comforter dangling below his waist (for he boasted no greatcoat), went down a slide on Cornhill, at the end of a lane of boys, twenty times, in honour of its being Christmas Eve, and then ran home to Camden Town as hard as he could pelt, to play at blindman's-buff.

Scrooge took his melancholy dinner in his usual melancholy tavern; and having read all the newspapers, and beguiled the rest of the evening with his banker's book, went home to bed. He lived in chambers which had once belonged to his deceased partner. They were a gloomy suite of rooms, in a lowering pile of building up a yard, where it had so little business to be, that one could scarcely help fancying it must have run there when it was a young house, playing at hide-and-seek with other houses, and have forgotten the way out again. It was old enough now, and dreary enough; for nobody lived in it but Scrooge, the other rooms being all let out as offices. The yard was so dark that even Scrooge, who knew its every stone, was fain to grope with his hands. The fog and frost so hung about the black old gateway of the house, that it seemed as if the Genius of the Weather sat in mournful meditation on the threshold.

Now, it is a fact that there was nothing at all particular about the knocker on the door, except that it was very large. It is also a fact that Scrooge had seen it, night and morning, during his whole residence in that place; also that Scrooge had as little of what is called fancy about him as any man in the City of London, even including—which is a bold word—the corporation, aldermen, and livery. Let it also be borne in mind that Scrooge had not bestowed one thought on Marley since his last mention of his seven-years'-dead partner that afternoon. And then let any man explain to me, if he can, how it happened that Scrooge, having his key in the lock of the door, saw in the knocker, without its undergoing any intermediate process of change—not a knocker, but Marley's face.

Marley's face. It was not in impenetrable shadow, as the other objects in the yard were, but had a dismal light about it, like a bad lobster in a dark cellar. It was not angry or ferocious, but looked at Scrooge as Marley used to look; with ghostly spectacles turned up on its ghostly forehead. The hair was curiously stirred, as if by breath or hot air; and, though the eyes were wide open, they were perfectly motionless. That, and its livid colour, made it horrible; but its horror seemed to be in spite of the face, and beyond its control, rather than a part of its own expression.

As Scrooge looked fixedly at this phenomenon, it was a knocker again.

To say that he was not startled, or that his blood was not conscious of a terrible sensation to which it had been a stranger from infancy, would be untrue. But he put his hand upon the key he had relinquished, turned it sturdily, walked in, and lighted his candle.

He *did* pause, with a moment's irresolution, before he shut the door; and he *did* look cautiously behind it first, as if he half expected to be terrified with the sight of Marley's pigtail sticking out into the hall. But there was nothing on the back of the door, except the screws and nuts that held the knocker on, so he said "Pooh, pooh!" and closed it with a bang.

The sound resounded through the house like thunder. Every room above, and every cask in the wine-merchant's cellars below, appeared to have a separate peal of echoes of its own. Scrooge was not a man to be frightened by echoes. He fastened the door, and walked across the hall, and up the stairs: slowly too: trimming his candle as he went.

You may talk vaguely about driving a coach and six up a good old flight of stairs, or through a bad young Act of Parliament; but I mean to say you might have got a hearse up that staircase, and taken it broadwise, with the splinter-bar towards the wall, and the door towards the balustrades: and done it easy. There was plenty of width for that, and room to spare; which is perhaps the reason why Scrooge thought he saw a locomotive hearse going on before him in the gloom. Half-a-dozen gas-lamps out of the street wouldn't have lighted the entry too well, so you may suppose that it was pretty dark with Scrooge's dip.

Up Scrooge went, not caring a button for that. Darkness is cheap, and Scrooge liked it. But, before he shut his heavy door, he walked through his rooms to see that all was right. He had just enough recollection of the face to desire to do that.

Sitting-room, bedroom, lumber-room. All as they should be. Nobody under the table, nobody under the sofa; a small fire in the grate; spoon and basin ready; and the little saucepan of gruel (Scrooge had a cold in his head) upon the hob. Nobody under the bed; nobody in the closet; nobody in his dressing-gown, which was hanging up in a suspicious attitude against the wall. Lumber-room as usual. Old fire-guard, old shoes, two fish baskets, washing-stand on three legs, and a poker.

Quite satisfied, he closed his door, and locked himself in; double-locked himself in, which was not his custom. Thus secured against surprise, he took off his cravat; put on his dressing-gown and slippers, and his nightcap; and sat down before the fire to take his gruel.

It was a very low fire indeed; nothing on such a bitter night. He was obliged to sit close to it, and brood over it, before he could extract the least sensation of warmth from such a handful of fuel. The fireplace was an old one, built by some Dutch merchant long ago, and paved all round with quaint Dutch tiles, designed to illustrate the Scriptures. There were Cains and Abels, Pharaoh's daughters, Queens of Sheba, Angelic messengers descending through the air on clouds like feather-beds, Abrahams, Belshazzars, Apostles putting off to sea in butter-boats, hundreds of figures to attract his thoughts; and yet that face of Marley, seven years dead, came like the ancient Prophet's rod, and swallowed up the whole. If each smooth tile had been a blank at first, with power to shape some picture on its surface from the disjointed fragments of his thoughts, there would have been a copy of old Marley's head on every one.

"Humbug!" said Scrooge; and walked across the room.

After several turns he sat down again. As he threw his head back in the chair, his glance happened to rest upon a bell, a disused bell, that hung in the room, and communicated, for some purpose now forgotten, with a chamber in the highest story of the building. It was with great astonishment, and with a strange, inexplicable dread, that, as he looked, he saw this bell begin to swing. It swung so softly in the outset that it scarcely made a sound; but soon it rang out loudly, and so did every bell in the house.

This might have lasted half a minute, or a minute, but it seemed an hour. The bells ceased, as they had begun, together. They were succeeded by a clanking noise deep down below as if some person were dragging a heavy chain over the casks in the wine-merchant's cellar. Scrooge then remembered to have heard that ghosts in haunted houses were described as dragging chains.

The cellar door flew open with a booming sound, and then he heard the noise much louder on the floors below; then coming up the stairs; then coming straight towards his door.

"It's humbug still!" said Scrooge. "I won't believe it."

His colour changed, though, when, without a pause, it came on through the heavy door, and passed into the room before his eyes. Upon its coming in, the dying flame leaped up, as though it cried, "I know him! Marley's Ghost!" and fell again.

The same face: the very same. Marley in his pigtail, usual waistcoat, tights, and boots; the tassels on the latter bristling, like his pigtail, and his coat-skirts, and the hair upon his head. The chain he drew was clasped about his middle. It was long, and wound about him like a tail; and it was made (for Scrooge observed it closely) of cash-boxes, keys, padlocks, ledgers, deeds, and heavy purses wrought in steel. His body was transparent: so that Scrooge, observing him, and looking through his waistcoat, could see the two buttons on his coat behind.

Scrooge had often heard it said that Marley had no bowels, but he had never believed it until now.

No, nor did he believe it even now. Though he looked the phantom through and through, and saw it standing before him; though he felt the chilling influence of its death-cold eyes; and marked the very texture of the folded kerchief bound about its head and chin, which wrapper he had not observed before, he was still incredulous, and fought against his senses.

"How now!" said Scrooge, caustic and cold as ever. "What do you want with me?"

"Much!"—Marley's voice; no doubt about it.

"Who are you?"

"Ask me who I *was*."

"Who *were* you, then?" said Scrooge, raising his voice. "You're particular, for a shade." He was going to say "*to* a shade," but substituted this, as more appropriate.

"In life I was your partner, Jacob Marley."

"Can you—can you sit down?" asked Scrooge, looking doubtfully at him.

"I can."

"Do it, then."

Scrooge asked the question, because he didn't know whether a ghost so transparent might find himself in a condition to take a chair; and felt that in the event of its being impossible, it might involve the necessity of an embarrassing explanation. But the Ghost sat down on the opposite side of the fireplace, as if he were quite used to it.

"You don't believe in me," observed the Ghost.

"I don't," said Scrooge.

"What evidence would you have of my reality beyond that of your own senses?"

"I don't know," said Scrooge.

"Why do you doubt your senses?"

"Because," said Scrooge, "a little thing affects them. A slight disorder of the stomach makes them cheats. You may be an undigested bit of beef, a blot of mustard, a crumb of cheese, a fragment of an underdone potato. There's more of gravy than of grave about you, whatever you are!"

Scrooge was not much in the habit of cracking jokes, nor did he feel in his heart by any means waggish then. The truth is, that he tried to be smart, as a means of distracting his own attention, and keeping down his terror; for the spectre's voice disturbed the very marrow in his bones.

To sit staring at those fixed, glazed eyes in silence for a moment, would play, Scrooge felt, the very deuce with him. There was something very awful, too, in the spectre's being provided with an infernal atmosphere of its own. Scrooge could not feel it himself, but this was clearly the case; for though the Ghost sat perfectly motionless, its hair, and skirts, and tassels, were still agitated as by the hot vapour from an oven.

"You see this toothpick?" said Scrooge, returning quickly to the charge, for the reason just assigned; and wishing, though it were only for a second, to divert the vision's stony gaze from himself.

"I do," replied the Ghost.

"You are not looking at it," said Scrooge.

"But I see it," said the Ghost, "notwithstanding."

"Well!" returned Scrooge, "I have but to swallow this, and be for the rest of my days persecuted by a legion of goblins, all of my own creation. Humbug, I tell you: humbug!"

At this the spirit raised a frightful cry, and shook its chain with such a dismal and appalling noise, that Scrooge held on tight to his chair, to save himself from falling in a swoon. But how much greater was his horror when the phantom, taking off the bandage round its head, as if it were too warm to wear indoors, its lower jaw dropped down upon its breast!

Scrooge fell upon his knees, and clasped his hands before his face.

"Mercy!" he said. "Dreadful apparition, why do you trouble me?"

"Man of the worldly mind!" replied the Ghost, "do you believe in me or not?"

"I do," said Scrooge. "I must. But why do spirits walk the earth, and why do they come to me?"

"It is required of every man," the Ghost returned, "that the spirit within him should walk abroad among his fellow-men, and travel far and wide; and, if that spirit goes not forth in life, it is condemned to do so after death. It is doomed to wander through the world—oh, woe is me!—and witness what it cannot share, but might have shared on earth, and turned to happiness!"

Again the spectre raised a cry, and shook its chain and wrung its shadowy hands.

"You are fettered," said Scrooge, trembling. "Tell me why?"

"I wear the chain I forged in life," replied the Ghost. "I made it link by link, and yard by yard; I girded it on of my own free will, and of my own free will I wore it. Is its pattern strange to *you*?"

Scrooge trembled more and more.

"Or would you know," pursued the Ghost, "the weight and length of the strong coil you bear yourself? It was full as heavy and as long as this seven Christmas Eves ago. You have laboured on it since. It is a ponderous chain!"

Scrooge glanced about him on the floor, in the expectation of finding himself surrounded by some fifty or sixty fathoms of iron cable; but he could see nothing.

"Jacob," he said imploringly. "Old Jacob Marley, tell me more. Speak comfort to me, Jacob!"

"I have none to give," the Ghost replied. "It comes from other regions, Ebenezer Scrooge, and is conveyed by other ministers, to other kinds of men. Nor can I tell you what I would. A very little more is all permitted to me. I cannot rest, I cannot stay, I cannot linger anywhere. My spirit never walked beyond our counting-house—mark me;—in life my spirit never roved beyond the narrow limits of our money-changing hole; and weary journeys lie before me!"

It was a habit with Scrooge, whenever he became thoughtful, to put his hands in his breeches pockets. Pondering on what the Ghost had said, he did so now, but without lifting up his eyes, or getting off his knees.

"You must have been very slow about it, Jacob," Scrooge observed in a business-like manner, though with humility and deference.

"Slow!" the Ghost repeated.

"Seven years dead," mused Scrooge. "And travelling all the time?"

"The whole time," said the Ghost. "No rest, no peace. Incessant torture of remorse."

"You travel fast?" said Scrooge.

"On the wings of the wind," replied the Ghost.

"You might have got over a great quantity of ground in seven years," said Scrooge.

The Ghost, on hearing this, set up another cry, and clanked its chain so hideously in the dead silence of the night, that the Ward would have been justified in indicting it for a nuisance.

"Oh! captive, bound, and double-ironed," cried the phantom, "not to know that ages of incessant labour, by immortal creatures, for this earth must pass into eternity before the good of which it is susceptible is all developed! Not to know that any Christian spirit working kindly in its little sphere, whatever it may be, will find its mortal life too short for its vast means of usefulness! Not to know that no space of regret can make amends for one life's opportunity misused! Yet such was I! Oh, such was I!"

"But you were always a good man of business, Jacob," faltered Scrooge, who now began to apply this to himself.

"Business!" cried the Ghost, wringing its hands again. "Mankind was my business. The common welfare was my business; charity, mercy, forbearance, and benevolence were, all, my business. The dealings of my trade were but a drop of water in the comprehensive ocean of my business!"

It held up its chain at arm's-length, as if that were the cause of all its unavailing grief, and flung it heavily upon the ground again.

"At this time of the rolling year," the spectre said, "I suffer most. Why did I walk through crowds of fellow-beings with my eyes turned down, and never raise them to that blessed Star which led the Wise Men to a poor abode? Were there no poor homes to which its light would have conducted *me*?"

Scrooge was very much dismayed to hear the spectre going on at this rate, and began to quake exceedingly.

"Hear me!" cried the Ghost. "My time is nearly gone."

"I will," said Scrooge. "But don't be hard upon me! Don't be flowery, Jacob! Pray!"

"How it is that I appear before you in a shape that you can see, I may not tell. I have sat invisible beside you many and many a day."

It was not an agreeable idea. Scrooge shivered, and wiped the perspiration from his brow.

"That is no light part of my penance," pursued the Ghost. "I am here to-night to warn you that you have yet a chance and hope of escaping my fate. A chance and hope of my procuring, Ebenezer."

"You were always a good friend to me," said Scrooge. "Thankee!"

"You will be haunted," resumed the Ghost, "by Three Spirits."

Scrooge's countenance fell almost as low as the Ghost's had done.

"Is that the chance and hope you mentioned, Jacob?" he demanded in a faltering voice.

"It is."

"I—I think I'd rather not," said Scrooge.

"Without their visits," said the Ghost, "you cannot hope to shun the path I tread. Expect the first to-morrow, when the bell tolls One."

"Couldn't I take 'em all at once, and have it over, Jacob?" hinted Scrooge.

"Expect the second on the next night at the same hour. The third, upon the next night when the last stroke of Twelve has ceased to vibrate. Look to see me no more; and look that, for your own sake, you remember what has passed between us!"

When it had said these words, the spectre took its wrapper from the table, and bound it round its head as before. Scrooge knew this by the smart sound its teeth made when the jaws were brought together by the bandage. He ventured to raise his eyes again, and found his supernatural visitor confronting him in an erect attitude, with its chain wound over and about its arm.

The apparition walked backward from him; and, at every step it took, the window raised itself a little, so that, when the spectre reached it, it was wide open.

It beckoned Scrooge to approach, which he did. When they were within two paces of each other, Marley's Ghost held up its hand, warning him to come no nearer. Scrooge stopped.

Not so much in obedience as in surprise and fear; for, on the raising of the hand, he became sensible of confused noises in the air; incoherent sounds of lamentation and regret; wailings inexpressibly sorrowful and self-accusatory. The spectre, after listening for a moment, joined in the mournful dirge; and floated out upon the bleak, dark night.

Scrooge followed to the window: desperate in his curiosity. He looked out.

The air was filled with phantoms, wandering hither and thither in restless haste, and moaning as they went. Every one of them wore chains like Marley's Ghost; some few (they might be guilty governments) were linked together; none were free. Many had been personally known to Scrooge in their lives. He had been quite familiar with one old ghost in a white waistcoat, with a monstrous iron safe attached to its ankle, who cried piteously at being unable to assist a wretched woman with an infant, whom it saw below upon a doorstep. The misery with them all was clearly, that they sought to interfere, for good, in human matters, and had lost the power for ever.

Whether these creatures faded into mist, or mist enshrouded them, he could not tell. But they and their spirit voices faded together; and the night became as it had been when he walked home.

Scrooge closed the window, and examined the door by which the Ghost had entered. It was double locked, as he had locked it with his own hands, and the bolts were undisturbed. He tried to say "Humbug!" but stopped at the first syllable. And being, from the emotions he had undergone, or the fatigues of the day, or his glimpse of the Invisible World, or the dull conversation of the Ghost, or the lateness of the hour, much in need of repose, went straight to bed without undressing, and fell asleep upon the instant.

STAVE TWO

THE FIRST OF THE THREE SPIRITS

WHEN SCROOGE AWOKE it was so dark, that, looking out of bed, he could scarcely distinguish the transparent window from the opaque walls of his chamber. He was endeavouring to pierce the darkness with his ferret eyes, when the chimes of a neighbouring church struck the four quarters. So he listened for the hour.

To his great astonishment the heavy bell went on from six to seven, and from seven to eight, and regularly up to twelve; then stopped. Twelve! It was past two when he went to bed. The clock was wrong. An icicle must have got into the works. Twelve!

He touched the spring of his repeater, to correct this most preposterous clock. Its rapid little pulse beat twelve, and stopped.

"Why, it isn't possible," said Scrooge, "that I can have slept through a whole day and far into another night. It isn't possible that anything has happened to the sun, and this is twelve at noon!"

The idea being an alarming one, he scrambled out of bed, and groped his way to the window. He was obliged to rub the frost off with the sleeve of his dressing-gown before he could see anything; and could see very little then. All he could make out was, that it was still very foggy and extremely cold, and that there was no noise of people running to and fro, and making a great stir, as there unquestionably would have been if night had beaten off bright day, and taken possession of the world. This was a great relief, because "Three days after sight of this First of Exchange pay to Mr. Ebenezer Scrooge or his order," and so forth, would have become a mere United States security if there were no days to count by.

Scrooge went to bed again, and thought, and thought, and thought it over and over, and could make nothing of it. The more he thought, the more perplexed he was; and, the more he endeavoured not to think, the more he thought.

Marley's Ghost bothered him exceedingly. Every time he resolved within himself, after mature inquiry, that it was all a dream, his mind flew back again, like a strong spring released, to its first position, and presented the same problem to be worked all through, "Was it a dream or not?"

Scrooge lay in this state until the chime had gone three-quarters more, when he remembered, on a sudden, that the Ghost had warned him of a visitation when the bell tolled one. He resolved to lie awake until the hour was passed; and, considering that he could no more go to sleep than go to heaven, this was, perhaps ,the wisest resolution in his power.

The quarter was so long, that he was more than once convinced he must have sunk into a doze unconsciously, and missed the clock. At length it broke upon his listening ear.

"Ding, dong!"

"A quarter past," said Scrooge, counting.

"Ding, dong!"

"Half-past!" said Scrooge.

"Ding, dong!"

"A quarter to it," said Scrooge.

"Ding, dong!"

"The hour itself," said Scrooge triumphantly, "and nothing else!"

He spoke before the hour bell sounded, which it now did with a deep, dull, hollow, melancholy ONE. Light flashed up in the room upon the instant, and the curtains of his bed were drawn.

The curtains of his bed were drawn aside, I tell you, by a hand. Not the curtains at his feet, nor the curtains at his back, but those to which his face was addressed. The curtains of his bed were drawn aside; and Scrooge, starting up into a half-recumbent attitude, found himself face to face with the unearthly visitor who drew them: as close to it as I am now to you, and I am standing in the spirit at your elbow.

It was a strange figure—like a child: yet not so like a child as like an old man, viewed through some supernatural medium, which gave him the appearance of having receded from the view, and being diminished to a child's proportions. Its hair, which hung about its neck and down its back, was white, as if with age; and yet the face had not a wrinkle in it, and the tenderest bloom was on the skin. The arms were very long and muscular; the hands the same, as if its hold were of uncommon strength. Its legs and feet, most delicately formed, were, like those upper members, bare. It wore a tunic of the purest white; and round its waist was bound a lustrous belt, the sheen of which was beautiful. It held a branch of fresh green holly in its hand; and, in singular contradiction of that wintry emblem, had its dress trimmed with summer flowers. But the strangest thing about it was, that from the crown of its head there sprang a bright clear jet of light, by which all this was visible; and which was doubtless the occasion of its using, in its duller moments, a great extinguisher for a cap, which it now held under its arm.

Even this, though, when Scrooge looked at it with increasing steadiness, was *not* its strangest quality. For, as its belt sparkled and glittered, now in one part and now in another, and what was light one instant, at another time was dark, so the figure itself fluctuated in its distinctness; being now a thing with one arm, now with one leg, now with twenty legs, now a pair of legs without a head, now a head without a body: of which dissolving parts no outline would be visible in the dense gloom wherein they melted away. And, in the very wonder of this, it would be itself again; distinct and clear as ever.

"Are you the Spirit, sir, whose coming was foretold to me?" asked Scrooge.

"I am!"

The voice was soft and gentle. Singularly low, as if, instead of being so close beside him, it were at a distance.

"Who and what are you?" Scrooge demanded.

"I am the Ghost of Christmas Past."

"Long Past?" inquired Scrooge, observant of its dwarfish stature.

"No. Your past."

Perhaps Scrooge could not have told anybody why, if anybody could have asked him; but he had a special desire to see the Spirit in his cap, and begged him to be covered.

"What!" exclaimed the Ghost, "would you so soon put out, with worldly hands, the light I give? Is it not enough that you are one of those whose passions made this cap, and force me through whole trains of years to wear it low upon my brow?"

Scrooge reverently disclaimed all intention to offend or any knowledge of having wilfully "bonneted" the Spirit at any period of his life. He then made bold to inquire what business brought him there.

"Your welfare!" said the Ghost.

Scrooge expressed himself much obliged, but could not help thinking that a night of unbroken rest would have been more conducive to that end. The Spirit must have heard him thinking, for it said immediately—

"Your reclamation, then. Take heed!"

It put out its strong hand as it spoke, and clasped him gently by the arm.

"Rise! and walk with me!"

It would have been in vain for Scrooge to plead that the weather and the hour were not adapted to pedestrian purposes; that bed was warm, and the thermometer a long way below freezing; that he was clad but lightly in his slippers, dressing-gown, and nightcap; and that he had a cold upon him at that time. The grasp, though gentle as a woman's hand, was not to be resisted. He rose; but, finding that the Spirit made towards the window, clasped its robe in supplication.

"I am a mortal," Scrooge remonstrated, "and liable to fall."

"Bear but a touch of my hand *there*," said the Spirit, laying it upon his heart, "and you shall be upheld in more than this!"

As the words were spoken, they passed through the wall, and stood upon an open country road, with fields on either hand. The city had entirely vanished. Not a vestige of it was to be seen. The darkness and the mist had vanished with it, for it was a clear, cold, winter day, with snow upon the ground.

"Good Heaven!" said Scrooge, clasping his hands together, as he looked about him. "I was bred in this place. I was a boy here!"

The Spirit gazed upon him mildly. Its gentle touch, though it had been light and instantaneous, appeared still present to the old man's sense of feeling. He was conscious of a thousand odours floating in the air, each one connected with a thousand thoughts, and hopes, and joys, and cares long, long, forgotten!

"Your lip is trembling," said the Ghost. "And what is that upon your cheek?"

Scrooge muttered, with an unusual catching in his voice, that it was a pimple; and begged the Ghost to lead him where he would.

"You recollect the way?" inquired the Spirit.

"Remember it!" cried Scrooge with fervour; "I could walk it blindfold."

"Strange to have forgotten it for so many years!" observed the Ghost. "Let us go on."

They walked along the road, Scrooge recognising every gate, and post, and tree, until a little market-town appeared in the distance, with its bridge, its church, and winding river. Some shaggy ponies now were seen trotting towards them with boys upon their backs, who called to other boys in country gigs and carts, driven by farmers. All these boys were in great spirits, and shouted to each other, until the broad fields were so full of merry music, that the crisp air laughed to hear it.

"These are but shadows of the things that have been," said the Ghost. "They have no consciousness of us."

The jocund travellers came on; and as they came, Scrooge knew and named them every one. Why was he rejoiced beyond all bounds to see them? Why did his cold eye glisten, and his heart leap up as they went past? Why was he filled with gladness when he heard them give each other merry Christmas, as they parted at cross-roads and by-ways, for their several homes? What was merry Christmas to Scrooge? Out upon merry Christmas! What good had it ever done to him?

"The school is not quite deserted," said the Ghost. "A solitary child, neglected by his friends, is left there still."

Scrooge said he knew it. And he sobbed.

They left the high-road by a well-remembered lane and soon approached a mansion of dull red brick, with a little weather- cock surmounted cupola on the roof, and a bell hanging in it. It was a large house, but one of broken fortunes; for the spacious offices were little used, their walls were damp and mossy, their windows broken, and their gates decayed. Fowls clucked and strutted in the stables; and the coach-houses and sheds were overrun with grass. Nor was it more retentive of its ancient state within; for, entering the dreary hall, and glancing through the open doors of many rooms, they found them poorly furnished, cold, and vast. There was an earthy savour in the air, a chilly bareness in the place, which associated itself somehow with too much getting up by candle light and not too much to eat.

They went, the Ghost and Scrooge, across the hall, to a door at the back of the house. It opened before them, and disclosed a long, bare, melancholy room, made barer still by lines of plain deal forms and desks. At one of these a lonely boy was reading near a feeble fire; and Scrooge sat down upon a form, and wept to see his poor forgotten self as he used to be.

Not a latent echo in the house, not a squeak and scuffle from the mice behind the panelling, not a drip from the half-thawed waterspout in the dull yard behind, not a sigh among the leafless boughs of one despondent poplar, not the idle swinging of an empty storehouse door, no, not a clicking in the fire, but fell upon the heart of Scrooge with a softening influence, and gave a freer passage to his tears.

The Spirit touched him on the arm, and pointed to his younger self, intent upon his reading. Suddenly a man, in foreign garments, wonderfully real and distinct to look at, stood outside the window, with an axe stuck in his belt, and leading by the bridle an ass laden with wood.

"Why, it's Ali Baba!" Scrooge exclaimed in ecstasy. "It's dear old honest Ali

Baba! Yes, yes, I know. One Christmas-time, when yonder solitary child was left here all alone, he *did* come, for the first time, just like that. Poor boy! And Valentine," said Scrooge, "and his wild brother, Orson; there they go! And what's his name, who was put down in his drawers, asleep, at the gate of Damascus; don't you see him? And the Sultan's Groom turned upside down by the Genii; there he is upon his head! Serve him right. I'm glad of it. What business had he to be married to the Princess?"

To hear Scrooge expending all the earnestness of his nature on such subjects, in a most extraordinary voice between laughing and crying; and to see his heightened and excited face; would have been a surprise to his business friends in the City, indeed.

"There's the Parrot!" cried Scrooge. "Green body and yellow tail, with a thing like a lettuce growing out of the top of his head; there he is! Poor Robin Crusoe, he called him, when he came home again after sailing round the island. 'Poor Robin Crusoe, where have you been, Robin Crusoe?' The man thought he was dreaming, but he wasn't. It was the Parrot, you know. There goes Friday, running for his life to the little creek! Halloa! Hoop! Halloo!"

Then, with a rapidity of transition very foreign to his usual character, he said, in pity for his former self, "Poor boy!" and cried again.

"I wish," Scrooge muttered, putting his hand in his pocket, and looking about him, after drying his eyes with his cuff; "but it's too late now."

"What is the matter?" asked the Spirit.

"Nothing," said Scrooge. "Nothing. There was a boy singing a Christmas Carol at my door last night. I should like to have given him something: that's all."

The Ghost smiled thoughtfully, and waved its hand, saying as it did so, "Let us see another Christmas!"

Scrooge's former self grew larger at the words, and the room became a little darker and more dirty. The panels shrunk, the windows cracked; fragments of plaster fell out of the ceiling, and the naked laths were shown instead; but how all this was brought about, Scrooge knew no more than you do. He only knew that it was quite correct; that everything had happened so; that there he was, alone again, when all the other boys had gone home for the jolly holidays.

He was not reading now, but walking up and down despairingly. Scrooge looked at the Ghost, and, with a mournful shaking of his head, glanced anxiously towards the door.

It opened; and a little girl, much younger than the boy, came darting in, and, putting her arms about his neck, and often kissing him, addressed him as her "dear, dear brother."

"I have come to bring you home, dear brother!" said the child, clapping her tiny hands, and bending down to laugh. "To bring you home, home, home!"

"Home, little Fan?" returned the boy.

"Yes!" said the child, brimful of glee. "Home, for good and all. Home for ever and ever. Father is so much kinder than he used to be, that home's like heaven! He spoke so gently to me one dear night when I was going to bed, that I was not afraid to ask him once more if you might come home; and he said Yes, you should; and sent me in a coach to bring you. And you're to be a man!" said the child, opening her eyes; "and are never to come back here; but first we're to be together all the Christmas long, and have the merriest time in all the world."

"You are quite a woman, little Fan!" exclaimed the boy.

She clapped her hands and laughed, and tried to touch his head; but, being too little laughed again, and stood on tiptoe to embrace him. Then she began to drag him, in her childish eagerness, towards the door; and he, nothing loth to go, accompanied her.

A terrible voice in the hall cried, "Bring down Master Scrooge's box, there!" and in the hall appeared the schoolmaster himself, who glared on Master Scrooge with a ferocious condescension, and threw him into a dreadful state of mind by shaking hands with him. He then conveyed him and his sister into the veriest old well of a shivering best parlour that ever was seen, where the maps upon the wall, and the celestial and terrestrial globes in the windows, were waxy with cold. Here he produced a decanter of curiously light wine, and a block of curiously heavy cake, and administered instalments of those dainties to the young people; at the same time sending out a meagre servant to offer a glass of "something" to the postboy, who answered that he thanked the gentleman, but, if it was the same tap as he had tasted before, he had rather not. Master Scrooge's trunk being by this time tied on to the top of the chaise, the children bade the schoolmaster good-bye right willingly; and, getting into it, drove gaily down the garden sweep; the quick wheels dashing the hoar-frost and snow from off the dark leaves of the evergreens like spray.

"Always a delicate creature, whom a breath might have withered," said the Ghost. "But she had a large heart!"

"So she had," cried Scrooge. "You're right. I will not gainsay it, Spirit. God forbid!"

"She died a woman," said the Ghost, "and had, as I think, children."

"One child," Scrooge returned.

"True," said the Ghost. "Your nephew!"

Scrooge seemed uneasy in his mind, and answered briefly, "Yes."

Although they had but that moment left the school behind them, they were now in the busy thoroughfares of a city, where shadowy passengers passed and repassed; where shadowy carts and coaches battled for the way, and all the strife and tumult of a real city were. It was made plain enough, by the dressing of the shops, that here, too, it was Christmas-time again; but it was evening, and the streets were lighted up.

The Ghost stopped at a certain warehouse door, and asked Scrooge if he knew it.

"Know it!" said Scrooge. "Was I apprenticed here?"

They went in. At sight of an old gentleman in a Welsh wig, sitting behind such a high desk, that if he had been two inches taller he must have knocked his head against the ceiling, Scrooge cried in great excitement—

"Why, it's old Fezziwig! Bless his heart, it's Fezziwig alive again!"

Old Fezziwig laid down his pen, and looked up at the clock, which pointed to the hour of seven. He rubbed his hands; adjusted his capacious waistcoat; laughed all over himself, from his shoes to his organ of benevolence; and called out in a comfortable, oily, rich, fat, jovial voice—

"Yo ho, there! Ebenezer! Dick!"

Scrooge's former self, now grown a young man, came briskly in, accompanied by his fellow-'prentice.

"Dick Wilkins, to be sure!" said Scrooge to the Ghost. "Bless me, yes. There he is. He was very much attached to me, was Dick. Poor Dick! Dear, dear!"

"Yo ho, my boys!" said Fezziwig. "No more work to-night. Christmas Eve, Dick. Christmas, Ebenezer! Let's have the shutters up," cried old Fezziwig, with a sharp clap of his hands, "before a man can say Jack Robinson!"

You wouldn't believe how those two fellows went at it! They charged into the street with the shutters—one, two, three—had 'em up in their places—four, five, six—barred 'em and pinned 'em—seven, eight, nine—and came back before you could have got to twelve, panting like racehorses.

"Hilli-ho!" cried old Fezziwig, skipping down from the high desk with wonderful agility. "Clear away, my lads, and let's have lots of room here! Hilli-ho, Dick! Chirrup, Ebenezer!"

Clear away! There was nothing they wouldn't have cleared away, or couldn't have cleared away, with old Fezziwig looking on. It was done in a minute. Every movable was packed off, as if it were dismissed from public life for evermore; the floor was swept and watered, the lamps were trimmed, fuel was heaped upon the fire; and the warehouse was as snug, and warm, and dry, and bright a ball-room, as you would desire to see upon a winter's night.

In came a fiddler with a music-book, and went up to the lofty desk, and made an orchestra of it, and tuned like fifty stomach-aches. In came Mrs. Fezziwig, one vast substantial smile. In came the three Miss Fezziwigs, beaming and lovable. In came the six young followers whose hearts they broke. In came all the young men and women employed in the business. In came the housemaid, with her cousin the baker. In came the cook with her brother's particular friend the milkman. In came the boy from over the way, who was suspected of not having board enough from his master; trying to hide himself behind the girl from next door but one, who was proved to have had her ears pulled by her mistress. In they all came, one after another; some shyly, some boldly, some gracefully, some awkwardly, some pushing, some pulling; in they all came, any how and every how. Away they all went, twenty couple at once; hands half round and back again the other way; down the middle and up again; round and round in various stages of affectionate grouping; old top couple always turning up in the wrong place; new top couple starting off again as soon as they got there; all top couples at last, and not a bottom one to help them! When this result was brought about, old Fezziwig, clapping his hands to stop the dance, cried out, "Well done!" and the fiddler plunged his hot face into a pot of porter, especially provided for that purpose. But, scorning rest upon his reappearance, he instantly began again, though there were no dancers yet, as if the other fiddler had been carried home, exhausted, on a shutter, and he were a bran-new man resolved to beat him out of sight, or perish.

There were more dances, and there were forfeits,[1] and more dances, and there was cake, and there was negus, and there was a great piece of Cold Roast, and there was a great piece of Cold Boiled, and there were mince-pies, and plenty of beer. But the great effect of the evening came after the Roast and Boiled, when the fiddler (an artful dog, mind! The sort of man who knew his business better than you or I could have told it him!) struck up "Sir Roger de Coverley." Then old Fezziwig stood out to dance with Mrs. Fezziwig. Top couple, too; with a good stiff piece of work cut out for them; three or four and twenty pair of partners; people who were not to be trifled with; people who would dance, and had no notion of walking.

But if they had been twice as many—ah! four times—old Fezziwig would have been a match for them, and so would Mrs. Fezziwig. As to *her*, she was worthy to be his partner in every sense of the term. If that's not high praise, tell me higher, and I'll use it. A positive light appeared to issue from Fezziwig's calves. They shone in every part of the dance like moons. You couldn't have predicted, at any given time, what would have become of them next. And when old Fezziwig and Mrs. Fezziwig had gone all through the dance; advance and retire, both hands to your partner, bow and curtsey, cork-screw, thread-the-needle, and back again to your place: Fezziwig "cut"—cut so deftly, that he appeared to wink with his legs, and came upon his feet again without a stagger.

When the clock struck eleven, this domestic ball broke up. Mr. and Mrs. Fezziwig took their stations, one on either side of the door, and, shaking hands

---

1 A game wherein a person must perform a silly or embarrassing act as punishment for losing a game or making a mistake.

with every person individually as he or she went out, wished him or her a merry Christmas. When everybody had retired but the two 'prentices, they did the same to them; and thus the cheerful voices died away, and the lads were left to their beds; which were under a counter in the back-shop.

During the whole of this time Scrooge had acted like a man out of his wits. His heart and soul were in the scene, and with his former self. He corroborated everything, remembered everything, enjoyed everything, and underwent the strangest agitation. It was not until now, when the bright faces of his former self and Dick were turned from them, that he remembered the Ghost, and became conscious that it was looking full upon him, while the light upon its head burnt very clear.

"A small matter," said the Ghost, "to make these silly folks so full of gratitude."

"Small!" echoed Scrooge.

The Spirit signed to him to listen to the two apprentices, who were pouring out their hearts in praise of Fezziwig; and when he had done so, said:

"Why! Is it not? He has spent but a few pounds of your mortal money: three or four, perhaps. Is that so much that he deserves this praise?"

"It isn't that," said Scrooge, heated by the remark, and speaking unconsciously like his former, not his latter self. "It isn't that, Spirit. He has the power to render us happy or unhappy; to make our service light or burdensome; a pleasure or a toil. Say that his power lies in words and looks; in things so slight and insignificant that it is impossible to add and count 'em up: what then? The happiness he gives is quite as great as if it cost a fortune."

He felt the Spirit's glance, and stopped.

"What is the matter?" asked the Ghost.

"Nothing particular," said Scrooge.

"Something, I think?" the Ghost insisted.

"No," said Scrooge, "no. I should like to be able to say a word or two to my clerk just now. That's all."

His former self turned down the lamps as he gave utterance to the wish; and Scrooge and the Ghost again stood side by side in the open air.

"My time grows short," observed the Spirit. "Quick!"

This was not addressed to Scrooge, or to any one whom he could see, but it produced an immediate effect. For again Scrooge saw himself. He was older now; a man in the prime of life. His face had not the harsh and rigid lines of later years; but it had begun to wear the signs of care and avarice. There was an eager, greedy, restless motion in the eye, which showed the passion that had taken root, and where the shadow of the growing tree would fall.

He was not alone, but sat by the side of a fair young girl in a mourning dress: in whose eyes there were tears, which sparkled in the light that shone out of the Ghost of Christmas Past.

"It matters little," she said softly. "To you, very little. Another idol has displaced me; and, if it can cheer and comfort you in time to come as I would have tried to do, I have no just cause to grieve."

"What Idol has displaced you?" he rejoined.

"A golden one."

"This is the even-handed dealing of the world!" he said. "There is nothing on which it is so hard as poverty; and there is nothing it professes to condemn with such severity as the pursuit of wealth!"

"You fear the world too much," she answered gently. "All your other hopes have merged into the hope of being beyond the chance of its sordid reproach. I have seen your nobler aspirations fall off one by one, until the master passion, Gain, engrosses you. Have I not?"

"What then?" he retorted. "Even if I have grown so much wiser, what then? I am not changed towards you."

She shook her head.

"Am I?"

"Our contract is an old one. It was made when we were both poor, and content to be so, until, in good season, we could improve our worldly fortune by our patient industry. You *are* changed. When it was made you were another man."

"I was a boy," he said impatiently.

"Your own feeling tells you that you were not what you are," she returned. "I am. That which promised happiness when we were one in heart is fraught with misery now that we are two. How often and how keenly I have thought of this I will not say. It is enough that I *have* thought of it, and can release you."

"Have I ever sought release?"

"In words. No. Never."

"In what, then?"

"In a changed nature; in an altered spirit; in another atmosphere of life; another Hope as its great end. In everything that made my love of any worth or value in your sight. If this had never been between us," said the girl, looking mildly, but with steadiness, upon him; "tell me, would you seek me out and try to win me now? Ah, no!"

He seemed to yield to the justice of this supposition in spite of himself. But he said, with a struggle, "You think not."

"I would gladly think otherwise if I could," she answered, "Heaven knows! When *I* have learned a Truth like this, I know how strong and irresistible it must be. But if you were free to-day, to-morrow, yesterday, can even I believe that you would choose a dowerless girl—you who, in your very confidence with her, weigh everything by Gain: or, choosing her, if for a moment you were false enough to your one guiding principle to do so, do I not know that your repentance and regret would surely follow? I do; and I release you. With a full heart, for the love of him you once were."

He was about to speak; but, with her head turned from him, she resumed:

"You may—the memory of what is past half makes me hope you will—have pain in this. A very, very brief time, and you will dismiss the recollection of it gladly, as an unprofitable dream, from which it happened well that you awoke. May you be happy in the life you have chosen!"

She left him, and they parted.

"Spirit!" said Scrooge, "show me no more! Conduct me home. Why do you delight to torture me?"

"One shadow more!" exclaimed the Ghost.

"No more!" cried Scrooge. "No more! I don't wish to see it. Show me no more!"

But the relentless Ghost pinioned him in both his arms, and forced him to observe what happened next.

They were in another scene and place; a room, not very large or handsome, but full of comfort. Near to the winter fire sat a beautiful young girl, so like that last that Scrooge believed it was the same, until he saw *her*, now a comely matron, sitting opposite her daughter. The noise in this room was perfectly tumultuous, for there were more children there than Scrooge in his agitated state of mind could count; and, unlike the celebrated herd in the poem, they were not forty children conducting themselves like one, but every child was conducting itself like forty. The consequences were uproarious beyond belief; but no one seemed to care; on the contrary, the mother and daughter laughed heartily, and enjoyed it very much; and the latter, soon beginning to mingle in the sports, got pillaged by the young brigands most ruthlessly. What would I not have given to be one of them! Though I never could have been so rude, no, no! I wouldn't for the wealth of all the world have crushed that braided hair, and torn it down; and for the precious little shoe, I wouldn't have plucked it off, God bless my soul! to save my life. As to measuring her waist in sport, as they did, bold young brood, I couldn't have done it; I should have expected my arm to have grown round it for a punishment, and never come straight again. And yet I should have dearly liked, I own, to have touched her lips; to have questioned her, that she might have opened them; to have looked upon the lashes of her downcast eyes, and never raised a blush; to have let loose waves of hair, an inch of which would be a keepsake beyond price: in short, I should have liked, I do confess, to have had the lightest licence of a child, and yet to have been man enough to know its value.

But now a knocking at the door was heard, and such a rush immediately ensued that she, with laughing face and plundered dress, was borne towards it the centre of a flushed and boisterous group, just in time to greet the father, who came home attended by a man laden with Christmas toys and presents. Then the shouting and the struggling, and the onslaught that was made on the defenceless porter! The scaling him, with chairs for ladders, to dive into his pockets, despoil him of brown-paper parcels, hold on tight by his cravat, hug him round his neck, pommel his back, and kick his legs in irrepressible affection! The shouts of wonder and delight with which the development of every package was received! The terrible announcement that the baby had been taken in the act of putting a doll's frying pan into his mouth, and was more than suspected of having swallowed a fictitious turkey, glued on a wooden platter! The immense relief of finding this a false alarm! The joy, and gratitude, and ecstasy! They are all indescribable alike. It is enough that, by degrees, the children and their emotions got out of the parlour, and, by one stair at a time, up to the top of the house, where they went to bed, and so subsided.

And now Scrooge looked on more attentively than ever, when the master of the house, having his daughter leaning fondly on him, sat down with her and her mother at his own fireside; and when he thought that such another creature, quite as graceful and as full of promise, might have called him father, and been a spring-time in the haggard winter of his life, his sight grew very dim indeed.

"Belle," said the husband, turning to his wife with a smile, "I saw an old friend of yours this afternoon."

"Who was it?"

"Guess!"

"How can I? Tut, don't I know?" she added in the same breath, laughing as he laughed. "Mr. Scrooge."

"Mr. Scrooge it was. I passed his office window; and as it was not shut up, and he had a candle inside, I could scarcely help seeing him. His partner lies upon the point of death, I hear; and there he sat alone. Quite alone in the world, I do believe."

"Spirit!" said Scrooge in a broken voice, "remove me from this place."

"I told you these were shadows of the things that have been," said the Ghost. "That they are what they are do not blame me!"

"Remove me!" Scrooge exclaimed, "I cannot bear it!"

He turned upon the Ghost, and seeing that it looked upon him with a face, in which in some strange way there were fragments of all the faces it had shown him, wrestled with it.

"Leave me! Take me back. Haunt me no longer!"

In the struggle, if that can be called a struggle in which the Ghost with no visible resistance on its own part was undisturbed by any effort of its adversary, Scrooge observed that its light was burning high and bright; and dimly connecting that with its influence over him, he seized the extinguisher-cap, and by a sudden action pressed it down upon its head.

The Spirit dropped beneath it, so that the extinguisher covered its whole form; but though Scrooge pressed it down with all his force, he could not hide the light, which streamed from under it, in an unbroken flood upon the ground.

He was conscious of being exhausted, and overcome by an irresistible drowsiness; and, further, of being in his own bedroom. He gave the cap a parting squeeze, in which his hand relaxed; and had barely time to reel to bed, before he sank into a heavy sleep.

STAVE THREE

THE SECOND OF THE THREE SPIRITS

AWAKING IN THE MIDDLE of a prodigiously tough snore, and sitting up in bed to get his thoughts together, Scrooge had no occasion to be told that the bell was again upon the stroke of One. He felt that he was restored to consciousness in the right nick of time, for the especial purpose of holding a conference with the second messenger despatched to him through Jacob Marley's intervention. But finding that he turned uncomfortably cold when he began to wonder which of his curtains this new spectre would draw back, he put them every one aside with his own hands, and, lying down again, established a sharp look-out all round the bed. For he wished to challenge the Spirit on the moment of its appearance, and did not wish to be taken by surprise and made nervous.

Gentlemen of the free-and-easy sort, who plume themselves on being acquainted with a move or two, and being usually equal to the time of day, express the wide range of their capacity for adventure by observing that they are good for anything from pitch-and-toss to manslaughter; between which opposite extremes, no doubt, there lies a tolerably wide and comprehensive range of subjects. Without venturing for Scrooge quite as hardily as this, I don't mind calling on you to believe that he was ready for a good broad field of strange appearances, and that nothing between a baby and rhinoceros would have astonished him very much.

Now, being prepared for almost anything, he was not by any means prepared for nothing; and consequently, when the bell struck One, and no shape appeared, he was taken with a violent fit of trembling. Five minutes, ten minutes, a quarter of an hour went by, yet nothing came. All this time, he lay upon his bed, the very core and centre of a blaze of ruddy light, which streamed upon it when the clock proclaimed the hour; and which, being only light, was more alarming than a dozen ghosts, as he was powerless to make out what it meant, or would be at; and was sometimes apprehensive that he might be at that very moment an interesting case of spontaneous combustion, without having the consolation of knowing it. At last, however, he began to think—as you or I would have thought at first; for it is always the person not in the predicament who knows what ought to have been done in it, and would unquestionably have done it too—at last, I say, he began to think that the source and secret of this ghostly light might be in the adjoining room, from whence, on further tracing it, it seemed to shine. This idea taking full possession of his mind, he got up softly, and shuffled in his slippers to the door.

The moment Scrooge's hand was on the lock a strange voice called him by his name, and bade him enter. He obeyed.

It was his own room. There was no doubt about that. But it had undergone a surprising transformation. The walls and ceiling were so hung with living green, that it looked a perfect grove; from every part of which bright gleaming berries glistened. The crisp leaves of holly, mistletoe, and ivy reflected back the light, as if so many little mirrors had been scattered there; and such a mighty blaze went roaring up the chimney as that dull petrification of a hearth had never known in Scrooge's time, or Marley's, or for many and many a winter season gone. Heaped up on the floor, to form a kind of throne, were turkeys, geese, game, poultry, brawn, great joints of meat, sucking-pigs, long wreaths of sausages, mince-pies, plum-puddings, barrels of oysters, red-hot chestnuts, cherry-cheeked apples, juicy oranges, luscious pears, immense twelfth-cakes, and seething bowls of punch, that made the chamber dim with their delicious steam. In easy state upon this couch there sat a jolly Giant, glorious to see; who bore a glowing torch, in shape not unlike Plenty's horn, and held it up, high up, to shed its light on Scrooge as he came peeping round the door.

"Come in!" exclaimed the Ghost. "Come in! and know me better, man!"

Scrooge entered timidly, and hung his head before this Spirit. He was not the dogged Scrooge he had been; and though the Spirit's eyes were clear and kind, he did not like to meet them.

"I am the Ghost of Christmas Present," said the Spirit. "Look upon me!"

Scrooge reverently did so. It was clothed in one simple green robe, or mantle, bordered with white fur. This garment hung so loosely on the figure, that its capacious breast was bare, as if disdaining to be warded or concealed by any arti-fice. Its feet, observable beneath the ample folds of the garment, were also bare; and on its head it wore no other covering than a holly wreath, set here and there with shining icicles. Its dark-brown curls were long and free; free as its genial face, its sparkling eye, its open hand, its cheery voice, its unconstrained demeanour, and its joyful air. Girded round its middle was an antique scabbard; but no sword was in it, and the ancient sheath was eaten up with rust.

"You have never seen the like of me before!" exclaimed the Spirit.

"Never," Scrooge made answer to it.

"Have never walked forth with the younger members of my family; meaning (for I am very young) my elder brothers born in these later years?" pursued the Phantom.

"I don't think I have," said Scrooge. "I am afraid I have not. Have you had many brothers, Spirit?"

"More than eighteen hundred," said the Ghost.

"A tremendous family to provide for!" muttered Scrooge.

The Ghost of Christmas Present rose.

"Spirit," said Scrooge submissively, "conduct me where you will. I went forth last night on compulsion, and I learnt a lesson which is working now. To-night if you have aught to teach me, let me profit by it."

"Touch my robe!"

Scrooge did as he was told, and held it fast.

Holly, mistletoe, red berries, ivy, turkeys, geese, game, poultry, brawn, meat, pigs, sausages, oysters, pies, puddings, fruit, and punch, all vanished instantly. So did the room, the fire, the ruddy glow, the hour of night, and they stood in the city streets on Christmas morning, where (for the weather was severe) the people made a rough, but brisk and not unpleasant kind of music, in scraping the snow from the pavement in front of their dwellings, and from the tops of their houses, whence it was mad delight to the boys to see it come plumping down into the road below, and splitting into artificial little snowstorms.

The house-fronts looked black enough, and the windows blacker, contrasting with the smooth white sheet of snow upon the roofs, and with the dirtier snow upon the ground; which last deposit had been ploughed up in deep furrows by the heavy wheels of carts and waggons: furrows that crossed and re-crossed each other hundreds of times where the great streets branched off; and made intricate channels, hard to trace in the thick yellow mud and icy water. The sky was gloomy, and the shortest streets were choked up with a dingy mist, half thawed, half frozen, whose heavier particles descended in a shower of sooty atoms, as if all the chimneys in Great Britain had, by one consent, caught fire, and were blazing away to their dear hearts' content. There was nothing very cheerful in the climate or the town, and yet was there an air of cheerfulness abroad that the clearest summer air and brightest summer sun might have endeavoured to diffuse in vain.

For the people who were shovelling away on the house-tops were jovial and full of glee; calling out to one another from the parapets, and now and then exchanging a facetious snowball—better-natured missile far than many a wordy jest—laughing heartily if it went right, and not less heartily if it went wrong. The poulterers' shops were still half open, and the fruiterers' were radiant in their glory. There were great, round, pot-bellied baskets of chestnuts, shaped like the waistcoats of jolly old gentlemen, lolling at the doors, and tumbling out into the street in their apoplectic opulence. There were ruddy, brown-faced, broad-girthed Spanish Onions, shining in the fatness of their growth like Spanish Friars, and winking from their shelves in wanton slyness at the girls as they went by, and glanced demurely at the hung-up mistletoe. There were pears and apples clustered high in blooming pyramids; there were bunches of grapes, made, in the shopkeepers' benevolence, to dangle from conspicuous hooks that people's mouths might water gratis as they passed; there were piles of filberts, mossy and brown, recalling, in their fragrance, ancient walks among the woods, and pleasant shufflings ankle deep through withered leaves; there were Norfolk Biffins, squat and swarthy, setting off the yellow of the oranges and lemons, and, in the great compactness of their juicy persons, urgently entreating and beseeching to be carried home in paper bags and eaten after dinner. The very gold and silver fish, set forth among these choice fruits in a bowl, though members of a dull and stagnant-blooded race, appeared to know that there was something going on; and, to a fish, went gasping round and round their little world in slow and passionless excitement.

The Grocers'! oh, the Grocers'! nearly closed, with perhaps two shutters down, or one; but through those gaps such glimpses! It was not alone that the scales descending on the counter made a merry sound, or that the twine and roller parted company so briskly, or that the canisters were rattled up and down like juggling tricks, or even that the blended scents of tea and coffee were so grateful to the nose, or even that the raisins were so plentiful and rare, the almonds so extremely white, the sticks of cinnamon so long and straight, the other spices so delicious, the candied fruits so caked and spotted with molten sugar as to make the coldest lookers-on feel faint, and subsequently bilious. Nor was it that the figs were moist and pulpy, or that the French plums blushed in modest tartness from their highly-decorated boxes, or that everything was good to eat and in its Christmas dress; but the customers were all so hurried and so eager in the hopeful promise of the day, that they tumbled up against each other at the door, crashing their wicker baskets wildly, and left their purchases upon the counter, and came running back to fetch them, and committed hundreds of the like mistakes, in the best humour possible; while the grocer and his people were so frank and fresh, that the polished hearts with which they fastened their aprons behind might have been their own, worn outside for general inspection, and for Christmas daws to peck at if they chose.

But soon the steeples called good people all to church and chapel, and away they came, flocking through the streets in their best clothes and with their gayest faces. And at the same time there emerged from scores of by-streets, lanes, and nameless turnings, innumerable people, carrying their dinners to the bakers' shops. The sight of these poor revellers appeared to interest the Spirit very much, for he stood with Scrooge beside him in a baker's doorway, and, taking off the covers as their bearers passed, sprinkled incense on their dinners from his torch. And it was a very uncommon kind of torch, for once or twice, when there were angry words between some dinner-carriers who had jostled each other, he shed a few drops of water on them from it, and their good-humour was restored directly. For they said, it was a shame to quarrel upon Christmas Day. And so it was! God love it, so it was!

In time the bells ceased, and the bakers were shut up; and yet there was a genial shadowing forth of all these dinners, and the progress of their cooking, in the thawed blotch of wet above each baker's oven, where the pavement smoked as if its stones were cooking too.

"Is there a peculiar flavour in what you sprinkle from your torch?" asked Scrooge.

"There is. My own."

"Would it apply to any kind of dinner on this day?" asked Scrooge.

"To any kindly given. To a poor one most."

"Why to a poor one most?" asked Scrooge.

"Because it needs it most."

"Spirit," said Scrooge, after a moment's thought, "I wonder you, of all the beings in the many worlds about us, should desire to cramp these people's opportunities of innocent enjoyment."

"I!" cried the Spirit.

"You would deprive them of their means of dining every seventh day, often the only day on which they can be said to dine at all," said Scrooge; "wouldn't you?"

"I!" cried the Spirit.

"You seek to close these places on the Seventh Day," said Scrooge. "And it comes to the same thing."

"I seek!" exclaimed the Spirit.

"Forgive me if I am wrong. It has been done in your name, or at least in that of your family," said Scrooge.

"There are some upon this earth of yours," returned the Spirit, "who lay claim to know us, and who do their deeds of passion, pride, ill-will, hatred, envy, bigotry, and selfishness in our name, who are as strange to us, and all our kith and kin, as if they had never lived. Remember that, and charge their doings on themselves, not us."

Scrooge promised that he would; and they went on, invisible, as they had been before, into the suburbs of the town. It was a remarkable quality of the Ghost (which Scrooge had observed at the baker's), that notwithstanding his gigantic size, he could accommodate himself to any place with ease; and that he stood beneath a low roof quite as gracefully and like a supernatural creature as it was possible he could have done in any lofty hall.

And perhaps it was the pleasure the good Spirit had in showing off this power of his, or else it was his own kind, generous, hearty nature, and his sympathy with all poor men, that led him straight to Scrooge's clerk's; for there he went, and took Scrooge with him, holding to his robe; and on the threshold of the door the Spirit smiled, and stopped to bless Bob Cratchit's dwelling with the sprinkling of his torch. Think of that! Bob had but fifteen "Bob" a week himself; he pocketed on Saturdays but fifteen copies of his Christian name; and yet the Ghost of Christmas Present blessed his four-roomed house!

Then up rose Mrs. Cratchit, Cratchit's wife, dressed out but poorly in a twice-turned gown, but brave in ribbons, which are cheap, and make a goodly show for sixpence; and she laid the cloth, assisted by Belinda Cratchit, second of her daughters, also brave in ribbons; while Master Peter Cratchit plunged a fork into the saucepan of potatoes, and getting the corners of his monstrous shirt-collar (Bob's private property, conferred upon his son and heir in honour of the day), into his mouth, rejoiced to find himself so gallantly attired, and yearned to show his linen in the fashionable Parks. And now two smaller Cratchits, boy and girl, came tearing in, screaming that outside the baker's they had smelt the goose, and known it for their own; and basking in luxurious thoughts of sage and onion, these young Cratchits danced about the table, and exalted Master Peter Cratchit to the skies, while he (not proud, although his collars nearly choked him) blew the fire, until the slow potatoes, bubbling up, knocked loudly at the saucepan-lid to be let out and peeled.

"What has ever got your precious father, then?" said Mrs. Cratchit. "And your brother, Tiny Tim? And Martha warn't as late last Christmas Day by half an hour!"

"Here's Martha, mother!" said a girl, appearing as she spoke.

"Here's Martha, mother!" cried the two young Cratchits. "Hurrah! There's *such* a goose, Martha!"

"Why, bless your heart alive, my dear, how late you are!" said Mrs. Cratchit, kissing her a dozen times, and taking off her shawl and bonnet for her with officious zeal.

"We'd a deal of work to finish up last night," replied the girl, "and had to clear away this morning, mother!"

"Well! Never mind so long as you are come," said Mrs. Cratchit. "Sit ye down before the fire, my dear, and have a warm, Lord bless ye!"

"No, no! There's father coming," cried the two young Cratchits, who were everywhere at once. "Hide, Martha, hide!"

So Martha hid herself, and in came little Bob, the father, with at least three feet of comforter, exclusive of the fringe, hanging down before him, and his threadbare clothes darned up and brushed to look seasonable, and Tiny Tim upon his shoulder. Alas for Tiny Tim, he bore a little crutch, and had his limbs supported by an iron frame!

"Why, where's our Martha?" cried Bob Cratchit, looking round.

"Not coming," said Mrs. Cratchit.

"Not coming!" said Bob, with a sudden declension in his high spirits; for he had been Tim's blood-horse all the way from church, and had come home rampant. "Not coming upon Christmas Day!"

Martha didn't like to see him disappointed, if it were only in joke; so she came out prematurely from behind the closet door, and ran into his arms, while the two young Cratchits hustled Tiny Tim, and bore him off into the wash-house, that he might hear the pudding singing in the copper.

"And how did little Tim behave?" asked Mrs. Cratchit when she had rallied Bob on his credulity, and Bob had hugged his daughter to his heart's content.

"As good as gold," said Bob, "and better. Somehow, he gets thoughtful, sitting by himself so much, and thinks the strangest things you ever heard. He told me, coming home, that he hoped the people saw him in the church, because he was a cripple, and it might be pleasant to them to remember upon Christmas Day who made lame beggars walk and blind men see."

Bob's voice was tremulous when he told them this, and trembled more when he said that Tiny Tim was growing strong and hearty.

His active little crutch was heard upon the floor, and back came Tiny Tim before another word was spoken, escorted by his brother and sister to his stool before the fire; and while Bob, turning up his cuffs—as if, poor fellow, they were capable of being made more shabby—compounded some hot mixture in a jug with gin and lemons, and stirred it round and round, and put it on the hob to simmer; Master Peter and the two ubiquitous young Cratchits went to fetch the goose, with which they soon returned in high procession.

Such a bustle ensued that you might have thought a goose the rarest of all birds; a feathered phenomenon, to which a black swan was a matter of course—and, in truth, it was something very like it in that house. Mrs. Cratchit made the gravy (ready beforehand in a little saucepan) hissing hot; Master Peter mashed the potatoes with incredible vigour; Miss Belinda sweetened up the apple sauce; Martha dusted the hot plates; Bob took Tiny Tim beside him in a tiny corner at the table; the two young Cratchits set chairs for everybody, not forgetting themselves, and, mounting guard upon their posts, crammed spoons into their mouths, lest they should shriek for goose before their turn came to be helped. At last the dishes were set on, and grace was said. It was succeeded by a breathless pause, as Mrs. Cratchit, looking slowly all along the carving-knife, prepared to plunge it in the breast; but when she did, and when the long-expected gush of stuffing issued forth, one murmur of delight arose all round the board, and even Tiny Tim, excited by the two young Cratchits, beat on the table with the handle of his knife, and feebly cried Hurrah!

There never was such a goose. Bob said he didn't believe there ever was such a goose cooked. Its tenderness and flavour, size and cheapness, were the themes of universal admiration. Eked out by apple sauce and mashed potatoes, it was a sufficient dinner for the whole family; indeed, as Mrs. Cratchit said with great delight (surveying one small atom of a bone upon the dish), they hadn't ate it all at last! Yet every one had had enough, and the youngest Cratchits, in particular, were steeped in sage and onion to the eyebrows! But now, the plates being changed by Miss Belinda, Mrs. Cratchit left the room alone—too nervous to bear witnesses— to take the pudding up, and bring it in.

Suppose it should not be done enough! Suppose it should break in turning out! Suppose somebody should have got over the wall of the back-yard and stolen it, while they were merry with the goose—a supposition at which the two young Cratchits became livid! All sorts of horrors were supposed.

Hallo! A great deal of steam! The pudding was out of the copper. A smell like a washing-day! That was the cloth. A smell like an eating-house and a pastry-cook's next door to each other, with a laundress's next door to that! That was the pudding! In half a minute Mrs. Cratchit entered—flushed, but smiling proudly—with the pudding, like a speckled cannon-ball, so hard and firm, blazing in half of half-a-quartern of ignited brandy, and bedight with Christmas holly stuck into the top.

Oh, a wonderful pudding! Bob Cratchit said, and calmly too, that he regarded it as the greatest success achieved by Mrs. Cratchit since their marriage. Mrs. Cratchit said that, now the weight was off her mind, she would confess she had had her doubts about the quantity of flour. Everybody had something to say about it, but nobody said or thought it was at all a small pudding for a large family. It would have been flat heresy to do so. Any Cratchit would have blushed to hint at such a thing.

At last the dinner was all done, the cloth was cleared, the hearth swept, and the fire made up. The compound in the jug being tasted, and considered perfect, apples and oranges were put upon the table, and a shovel full of chestnuts on the fire. Then all the Cratchit family drew round the hearth in what Bob Cratchit called a circle, meaning half a one; and at Bob Cratchit's elbow stood the family display of glass. Two tumblers and a custard cup without a handle.

These held the hot stuff from the jug, however, as well as golden goblets would have done; and Bob served it out with beaming looks, while the chestnuts on the fire sputtered and cracked noisily. Then Bob proposed:

"A merry Christmas to us all, my dears. God bless us!"

Which all the family re-echoed.

"God bless us every one!" said Tiny Tim, the last of all.

He sat very close to his father's side, upon his little stool. Bob held his withered little hand in his, as if he loved the child, and wished to keep him by his side, and dreaded that he might be taken from him.

"Spirit," said Scrooge, with an interest he had never felt before, "tell me if Tiny Tim will live."

"I see a vacant seat," replied the Ghost, "in the poor chimney corner, and a crutch without an owner, carefully preserved. If these shadows remain unaltered by the Future, the child will die."

"No, no," said Scrooge. "Oh no, kind Spirit! say he will be spared."

"If these shadows remain unaltered by the Future, none other of my race," returned the Ghost, "will find him here. What then? If he be like to die, he had better do it, and decrease the surplus population."

Scrooge hung his head to hear his own words quoted by the Spirit, and was overcome with penitence and grief.

"Man," said the Ghost, "if man you be in heart, not adamant, forbear that wicked cant until you have discovered what the surplus is, and where it is. Will you decide what men shall live, what men shall die? It may be that, in the sight of Heaven, you are more worthless and less fit to live than millions like this poor man's child. O God! to hear the Insect on the leaf pronouncing on the too much life among his hungry brothers in the dust!"

Scrooge bent before the Ghost's rebuke, and, trembling, cast his eyes upon the ground. But he raised them speedily on hearing his own name.

"Mr. Scrooge!" said Bob. "I'll give you Mr. Scrooge, the Founder of the Feast!"

"The Founder of the Feast, indeed!" cried Mrs. Cratchit, reddening. "I wish I had him here. I'd give him a piece of my mind to feast upon, and I hope he'd have a good appetite for it."

"My dear," said Bob, "the children! Christmas Day."

"It should be Christmas Day, I am sure," said she, "on which one drinks the health of such an odious, stingy, hard, unfeeling man as Mr. Scrooge. You know he is, Robert! Nobody knows it better than you do, poor fellow!"

"My dear!" was Bob's mild answer. "Christmas Day."

"I'll drink his health for your sake and the Day's," said Mrs. Cratchit, "not for his. Long life to him! A merry Christmas and a happy New Year! He'll be very merry and very happy, I have no doubt!"

The children drank the toast after her. It was the first of their proceedings which had no heartiness. Tiny Tim drank it last of all, but he didn't care twopence for it. Scrooge was the Ogre of the family. The mention of his name cast a dark shadow on the party, which was not dispelled for full five minutes.

After it had passed away they were ten times merrier than before, from the mere relief of Scrooge the Baleful being done with. Bob Cratchit told them how he had a situation in his eye for Master Peter, which would bring in, if obtained, full five-and-sixpence weekly. The two young Cratchits laughed tremendously at the idea of Peter's being a man of business; and Peter himself looked thoughtfully at the fire from between his collars, as if he were deliberating what particular investments he should favour when he came into the receipt of that bewildering income. Martha, who was a poor apprentice at a milliner's, then told them what kind of work she had to do, and how many hours she worked at a stretch, and how she meant to lie abed to-morrow morning for a good long rest; to-morrow being a holiday she passed at home. Also how she had seen a countess and a lord some days before, and how the lord "was much about as tall as Peter"; at which Peter pulled up his collars so high that you couldn't have seen his head if you had been there. All this time the chestnuts and the jug went round and round; and by-and-bye they had a song, about a lost child travelling in the snow, from Tiny Tim, who had a plaintive little voice, and sang it very well indeed.

There was nothing of high mark in this. They were not a handsome family; they were not well dressed; their shoes were far from being water-proof; their clothes were scanty; and Peter might have known, and very likely did, the inside of a pawnbroker's. But they were happy, grateful, pleased with one another, and contented with the time; and when they faded, and looked happier yet in the bright sprinklings of the Spirit's torch at parting, Scrooge had his eye upon them, and especially on Tiny Tim, until the last.

By this time it was getting dark, and snowing pretty heavily; and as Scrooge and the Spirit went along the streets, the brightness of the roaring fires in kitchens, parlours, and all sorts of rooms was wonderful. Here, the flickering of the blaze showed preparations for a cozy dinner, with hot plates baking through and through before the fire, and deep red curtains, ready to be drawn to shut out cold and darkness. There, all the children of the house were running out into the snow to meet their married sisters, brothers, cousins, uncles, aunts and be the first to greet them. Here, again, were shadows on the window-blinds of guests assembling; and there a group of handsome girls, all hooded and fur-booted, and all chattering at once, tripped lightly off to some near neighbour's house; where, woe upon the single man who saw them enter—artful witches, well they knew it—in a glow!

But, if you had judged from the numbers of people on their way to friendly gatherings, you might have thought that no one was at home to give them welcome when they got there, instead of every house expecting company, and piling up its fires half-chimney high. Blessings on it, how the Ghost exulted! How it bared its breadth of breast, and opened its capacious palm, and floated on, outpouring with a generous hand its bright and harmless mirth on everything within its reach! The very lamplighter, who ran on before, dotting the dusky street with specks of light, and who was dressed to spend the evening somewhere, laughed out loudly as the Spirit passed, though little kenned the lamplighter that he had any company but Christmas.

And now, without a word of warning from the Ghost, they stood upon a bleak and desert moor, where monstrous masses of rude stone were cast about, as though it were the burial-place of giants; and water spread itself wheresoever it listed; or would have done so, but for the frost that held it prisoner; and nothing grew but moss and furze, and coarse, rank grass. Down in the west the setting sun had left a streak of fiery red, which glared upon the desolation for an instant, like a sullen eye, and frowning lower, lower, lower yet, was lost in the thick gloom of darkest night.

"What place is this?" asked Scrooge.

"A place where miners live, who labour in the bowels of the earth," returned the Spirit. "But they know me. See!"

A light shone from the window of a hut, and swiftly they advanced towards it. Passing through the wall of mud and stone, they found a cheerful company assembled round a glowing fire. An old, old man and woman, with their children and their children's children, and another generation beyond that, all decked out gaily in their holiday attire. The old man, in a voice that seldom rose above the howling of the wind upon the barren waste, was singing them a Christmas song; it had been a very old song when he was a boy; and from time to time they all joined in the chorus. So surely as they raised their voices, the old man got quite blithe and loud; and so surely as they stopped, his vigour sank again.

The Spirit did not tarry here, but bade Scrooge hold his robe, and, passing on above the moor, sped whither? Not to sea? To sea. To Scrooge's horror, looking back, he saw the last of the land, a frightful range of rocks, behind them; and his ears were deafened by the thundering of water, as it rolled and roared, and raged among the dreadful caverns it had worn, and fiercely tried to undermine the earth.

Built upon a dismal reef of sunken rocks, some league or so from shore, on which the waters chafed and dashed, the wild year through, there stood a solitary lighthouse. Great heaps of seaweed clung to its base, and storm-birds—born of the wind, one might suppose, as seaweed of the water—rose and fell about it, like the waves they skimmed.

But, even here, two men who watched the light had made a fire, that through the loophole in the thick stone wall shed out a ray of brightness on the awful sea. Joining their horny hands over the rough table at which they sat, they wished each other merry Christmas in their can of grog; and one of them—the elder too, with his face all damaged and scarred with hard weather, as the figure-head of an old ship might be—struck up a sturdy song that was like a gale in itself.

Again the Ghost sped on, above the black and heaving sea—on, on—until being far away, as he told Scrooge, from any shore, they lighted on a ship. They stood beside the helmsman at the wheel, the look-out in the bow, the officers who had the watch; dark, ghostly figures in their several stations; but every man among them hummed a Christmas tune, or had a Christmas thought, or spoke below his breath to his companion of some bygone Christmas Day, with homeward hopes belonging to it. And every man on board, waking or sleeping, good or bad, had had a kinder word for another on that day than on any day in the year; and had shared to some extent in its festivities; and had remembered those he cared for at a distance, and had known that they delighted to remember him.

It was a great surprise to Scrooge, while listening to the moaning of the wind, and thinking what a solemn thing it was to move on through the lonely darkness over an unknown abyss, whose depths were secrets as profound as death: it was a great surprise to Scrooge, while thus engaged, to hear a hearty laugh. It was a much greater surprise to Scrooge to recognise it as his own nephew's and to find himself in a bright, dry, gleaming room, with the Spirit standing smiling by his side, and looking at that same nephew with approving affability!

"Ha, ha!" laughed Scrooge's nephew. "Ha, ha, ha!"

If you should happen, by any unlikely chance, to know a man more blessed in a laugh than Scrooge's nephew, all I can say is, I should like to know him too. Introduce him to me, and I'll cultivate his acquaintance.

It is a fair, even-handed, noble adjustment of things, that while there is infection in disease and sorrow, there is nothing in the world so irresistibly contagious as laughter and good-humour. When Scrooge's nephew laughed in this way—holding his sides, rolling his head, and twisting his face into the most extravagant contortions—Scrooge's niece, by marriage, laughed as heartily as he. And their assembled friends, being not a bit behindhand, roared out lustily.

"Ha, ha! Ha, ha, ha, ha!"

"He said that Christmas was a humbug, as I live!" cried Scrooge's nephew. "He believed it, too!"

"More shame for him, Fred!" said Scrooge's niece indignantly. Bless those women! they never do anything by halves. They are always in earnest.

She was very pretty; exceedingly pretty. With a dimpled, surprised-looking, capital face; a ripe little mouth, that seemed made to be kissed—as no doubt it was; all kinds of good little dots about her chin, that melted into one another when she laughed; and the sunniest pair of eyes you ever saw in any little creature's head. Altogether she was what you would have called provoking, you know; but satisfactory, too. Oh, perfectly satisfactory!

"He's a comical old fellow," said Scrooge's nephew, "that's the truth; and not so pleasant as he might be. However, his offences carry their own punishment, and I have nothing to say against him."

"I'm sure he is very rich, Fred," hinted Scrooge's niece. "At least you always tell *me* so."

"What of that, my dear?" said Scrooge's nephew. "His wealth is of no use to him. He don't do any good with it. He don't make himself comfortable with it. He hasn't the satisfaction of thinking—ha, ha, ha!—that he is ever going to benefit us with it."

"I have no patience with him," observed Scrooge's niece. Scrooge's niece's sisters, and all the other ladies, expressed the same opinion.

"Oh, I have!" said Scrooge's nephew. "I am sorry for him; I couldn't be angry with him if I tried. Who suffers by his ill whims? Himself always. Here he takes it into his head to dislike us, and he won't come and dine with us. What's the consequence? He don't lose much of a dinner."

"Indeed, I think he loses a very good dinner," interrupted Scrooge's niece. Everybody else said the same, and they must be allowed to have been competent judges, because they had just had dinner; and with the dessert upon the table, were clustered round the fire, by lamplight.

"Well! I'm very glad to hear it," said Scrooge's nephew, "because I haven't great faith in these young housekeepers. What do *you* say, Topper?"

Topper had clearly got his eye upon one of Scrooge's niece's sisters, for he answered that a bachelor was a wretched outcast, who had no right to express an opinion on the subject. Whereat Scrooge's niece's sister—the plump one with the lace tucker: not the one with the roses—blushed.

"Do go on, Fred," said Scrooge's niece, clapping her hands. "He never finishes what he begins to say! He is such a ridiculous fellow!"

Scrooge's nephew revelled in another laugh, and as it was impossible to keep the infection off, though the plump sister tried hard to do it with aromatic vinegar, his example was unanimously followed.

"I was only going to say," said Scrooge's nephew, "that the consequence of his taking a dislike to us, and not making merry with us, is, as I think, that he loses some pleasant moments, which could do him no harm. I am sure he loses pleasanter companions than he can find in his own thoughts, either in his mouldy old office or his dusty chambers. I mean to give him the same chance every year, whether he likes it or not, for I pity him. He may rail at Christmas till he dies, but he can't help thinking better of it—I defy him—if he finds me going there, in good temper, year after year, and saying 'Uncle Scrooge, how are you?' If it only puts him in the vein to leave his poor clerk fifty pounds, *that's* something; and I think I shook him yesterday."

It was their turn to laugh now, at the notion of his shaking Scrooge. But being thoroughly good-natured, and not much caring what they laughed at, so that they laughed at any rate, he encouraged them in their merriment, and passed the bottle, joyously.

After tea they had some music. For they were a musical family, and knew what they were about when they sung a Glee or Catch, I can assure you: especially

Topper, who could growl away in the bass like a good one, and never swell the large veins in his forehead, or get red in the face over it. Scrooge's niece played well upon the harp; and played, among other tunes, a simple little air (a mere nothing: you might learn to whistle it in two minutes) which had been familiar to the child who fetched Scrooge from the boarding-school, as he had been reminded by the Ghost of Christmas Past. When this strain of music sounded, all the things that Ghost had shown him came upon his mind; he softened more and more; and thought that if he could have listened to it often, years ago, he might have cultivated the kindnesses of life for his own happiness with his own hands, without resorting to the sexton's spade that buried Jacob Marley.

But they didn't devote the whole evening to music. After a while they played at forfeits[1]; for it is good to be children sometimes, and never better than at Christmas, when its mighty Founder was a child himself. Stop! There was first a game at blindman's buff[2]. Of course there was. And I no more believe Topper was really blind than I believe he had eyes in his boots. My opinion is, that it was a done thing between him and Scrooge's nephew; and that the Ghost of Christmas Present knew it. The way he went after that plump sister in the lace tucker was an outrage on the credulity of human nature. Knocking down the fire-irons, tumbling over the chairs, bumping against the piano, smothering himself amongst the curtains, wherever she went, there went he! He always knew where the plump sister was. He wouldn't catch anybody else. If you had fallen up against him (as some of them did) on purpose, he would have made a feint of endeavouring to seize you, which would have been an affront to your understanding, and would instantly have sidled off in the direction of the plump sister. She often cried out that it wasn't fair; and it really was not. But when, at last, he caught her; when, in spite of all her silken rustlings, and her rapid flutterings past him, he got her into a corner whence there was no escape; then his conduct was the most execrable. For his pretending not to know her; his pretending that it was necessary to touch her head-dress, and further to assure himself of her identity by pressing a certain ring upon her finger, and a certain chain about her neck; was vile, monstrous! No doubt she told him her opinion of it when, another blind man being in office, they were so very confidential together behind the curtains.

Scrooge's niece was not one of the blind-man's bluff[3] party, but was made comfortable with a large chair and a footstool, in a snug corner where the Ghost and Scrooge were close behind her. But she joined in the forfeits, and loved her

1 A person must perform a silly or embarrassing act as punishment for losing a game or making a mistake.

2 A player is blindfolded then spun around. Other players call to the "blind man" but avoid being touched by them. If they are caught by the blind man, they must wear the blindfold.

3 A player is blindfolded then spun around. Other players call to the "blind man" but avoid being touched by them. If they are caught by the blind man, they must wear the blindfold.

love to admiration with all the letters of the alphabet. Likewise at the game of How, When, and Where[4], she was very great, and, to the secret joy of Scrooge's nephew, beat her sisters hollow; though they were sharp girls too, as Topper could have told you. There might have been twenty people there, young and old, but they all played, and so did Scrooge; for wholly forgetting, in the interest he had in what was going on, that his voice made no sound in their ears, he sometimes came out with his guess quite loud, and very often guessed quite right, too; for the sharpest needle, best Whitechapel[5], warranted not to cut in the eye, was not sharper than Scrooge, blunt as he took it in his head to be.

The Ghost was greatly pleased to find him in this mood, and looked upon him with such favour, that he begged like a boy to be allowed to stay until the guests departed. But this the Spirit said could not be done.

"Here is a new game," said Scrooge. "One half hour, Spirit, only one!"

It was a Game called Yes and No, where Scrooge's nephew had to think of something, and the rest must find out what, he only answering to their questions yes or no, as the case was. The brisk fire of questioning to which he was exposed elicited from him that he was thinking of an animal, a live animal, rather a disagreeable animal, a savage animal, an animal that growled and grunted sometimes, and talked sometimes and lived in London, and walked about the streets, and wasn't made a show of, and wasn't led by anybody, and didn't live in a menagerie, and was never killed in a market, and was not a horse, or an ass, or a cow, or a bull, or a tiger, or a dog, or a pig, or a cat, or a bear. At every fresh question that was put to him, this nephew burst into a fresh roar of laughter; and was so inexpressibly tickled, that he was obliged to get up off the sofa and stamp. At last the plump sister, falling into a similar state, cried out:

"I have found it out! I know what it is, Fred! I know what it is!"

"What is it?" cried Fred.

"It's your Uncle Scro-o-o-o-oge."

Which it certainly was. Admiration was the universal sentiment, though some objected that the reply to "Is it a bear?" ought to have been "Yes"; inasmuch as an answer in the negative was sufficient to have diverted their thoughts from Mr. Scrooge, supposing they had ever had any tendency that way.

"He has given us plenty of merriment, I am sure," said Fred, "and it would be ungrateful not to drink his health. Here is a glass of mulled wine ready to our hand at the moment; and I say, 'Uncle Scrooge!'"

---

4 One player leaves the room while the others strategize a word with multiple meanings. Once the player returns, they ask a question beginning with how, when, and where, respectively. The goal is to correctly guess the word after the other players answer these questions.

5 On the East end of London, Whitechapel Street was overpopulated, deeply impoverished, and laden with brothels and crime.

"Well! Uncle Scrooge!" they cried.

"A merry Christmas and a happy New Year to the old man, whatever he is!" said Scrooge's nephew. "He wouldn't take it from me, but may he have it, nevertheless. Uncle Scrooge!"

Uncle Scrooge had imperceptibly become so gay and light of heart, that he would have pledged the unconscious company in return, and thanked them in an inaudible speech, if the Ghost had given him time. But the whole scene passed off in the breath of the last word spoken by his nephew; and he and the Spirit were again upon their travels.

Much they saw, and far they went, and many homes they visited, but always with a happy end. The Spirit stood beside sick-beds, and they were cheerful; on foreign lands, and they were close at home; by struggling men, and they were patient in their greater hope; by poverty, and it was rich. In almshouse, hospital, and gaol, in misery's every refuge, where vain man in his little brief authority had not made fast the door, and barred the Spirit out, he left his blessing and taught Scrooge his precepts.

It was a long night, if it were only a night; but Scrooge had his doubts of this, because the Christmas holidays appeared to be condensed into the space of time they passed together. It was strange, too, that while Scrooge remained unaltered in his outward form, the Ghost grew older, clearly older. Scrooge had observed this change, but never spoke of it until they left a children's-Night[1] party, when, looking at the Spirit as they stood together in an open place, he noticed that its hair was grey.

"Are spirits' lives so short?" asked Scrooge.

"My life upon this globe is very brief," replied the Ghost. "It ends to-night."

"To-night!" cried Scrooge.

"To-night at midnight. Hark! The time is drawing near."

The chimes were ringing the three-quarters past eleven at that moment.

"Forgive me if I am not justified in what I ask," said Scrooge, looking intently at the Spirit's robe, "but I see something strange, and not belonging to yourself, protruding from your skirts. Is it a foot or a claw?"

"It might be a claw, for the flesh there is upon it," was the Spirit's sorrowful reply. "Look here!"

From the foldings of its robe it brought two children, wretched, abject, frightful, hideous, miserable. They knelt down at its feet, and clung upon the outside of its garment.

"O Man! look here. Look, look down here!" exclaimed the Ghost.

---

1 The twelfth evening after Christmas (5 January) marks the eve of the Epiphany. Sometimes Twelfth Night is observed on the twelfth day (6 January) after Christmas. It is the last day of Christmas festivities.

They were a boy and girl. Yellow, meagre, ragged, scowling, wolfish, but prostrate, too, in their humility. Where graceful youth should have filled their features out, and touched them with its freshest tints, a stale and shrivelled hand, like that of age, had pinched and twisted them, and pulled them into shreds. Where angels might have sat enthroned, devils lurked, and glared out menacing. No change, no degradation, no perversion of humanity in any grade, through all the mysteries of wonderful creation, has monsters half so horrible and dread.

Scrooge started back, appalled. Having them shown to him in this way, he tried to say they were fine children, but the words choked themselves, rather than be parties to a lie of such enormous magnitude.

"Spirit! are they yours?" Scrooge could say no more.

"They are Man's," said the Spirit, looking down upon them. "And they cling to me, appealing from their fathers. This boy is Ignorance. This girl is Want. Beware them both, and all of their degree, but most of all beware this boy, for on his brow I see that written which is Doom, unless the writing be erased. Deny it!" cried the Spirit, stretching out its hand towards the city. "Slander those who tell it ye! Admit it for your factious purposes, and make it worse! And bide the end!"

"Have they no refuge or resource?" cried Scrooge.

"Are there no prisons?" said the Spirit, turning on him for the last time with his own words. "Are there no workhouses?"

The bell struck Twelve.

Scrooge looked about him for the Ghost, and saw it not. As the last stroke ceased to vibrate, he remembered the prediction of old Jacob Marley, and, lifting up his eyes, beheld a solemn Phantom, draped and hooded, coming like a mist along the ground, towards him.

STAVE FOUR

THE LAST OF THE SPIRITS

THE PHANTOM SLOWLY, GRAVELY, SILENTLY APPROACHED. When it came near him, Scrooge bent down upon his knee; for in the very air through which this Spirit moved it seemed to scatter gloom and mystery.

It was shrouded in a deep black garment, which concealed its head, its face, its form, and left nothing of it visible, save one outstretched hand. But for this, it would have been difficult to detach its figure from the night, and separate it from the darkness by which it was surrounded.

He felt that it was tall and stately when it came beside him, and that its mysterious presence filled him with a solemn dread. He knew no more, for the Spirit neither spoke nor moved.

"I am in the presence of the Ghost of Christmas Yet To Come?" said Scrooge.

The Spirit answered not, but pointed onward with its hand.

"You are about to show me shadows of the things that have not happened, but will happen in the time before us," Scrooge pursued. "Is that so, Spirit?"

The upper portion of the garment was contracted for an instant in its folds, as if the Spirit had inclined its head. That was the only answer he received.

Although well used to ghostly company by this time, Scrooge feared the silent shape so much that his legs trembled beneath him, and he found that he could hardly stand when he prepared to follow it. The Spirit paused a moment, as observing his condition, and giving him time to recover.

But Scrooge was all the worse for this. It thrilled him with a vague, uncertain horror to know that, behind the dusky shroud, there were ghostly eyes intently fixed upon him, while he, though he stretched his own to the utmost, could see nothing but a spectral hand and one great heap of black.

"Ghost of the Future!" he exclaimed, "I fear you more than any spectre I have seen. But as I know your purpose is to do me good, and as I hope to live to be another man from what I was, I am prepared to bear you company, and do it with a thankful heart. Will you not speak to me?"

It gave him no reply. The hand was pointed straight before them.

"Lead on!" said Scrooge. "Lead on! The night is waning fast, and it is precious time to me, I know. Lead on, Spirit!"

The Phantom moved away as it had come towards him. Scrooge followed in the shadow of its dress, which bore him up, he thought, and carried him along.

They scarcely seemed to enter the City; for the City rather seemed to spring up about them, and encompass them of its own act. But there they were in the heart of it; on 'Change, amongst the merchants, who hurried up and down, and chinked the money in their pockets, and conversed in groups, and looked at their watches, and trifled thoughtfully with their great gold seals, and so forth, as Scrooge had seen them often.

The Spirit stopped beside one little knot of business men. Observing that the hand was pointed to them, Scrooge advanced to listen to their talk.

"No," said a great fat man with a monstrous chin, "I don't know much about it either way. I only know he's dead."

"When did he die?" inquired another.

"Last night, I believe."

"Why, what was the matter with him?" asked a third, taking a vast quantity of snuff out of a very large snuff-box. "I thought he'd never die."

"God knows," said the first, with a yawn.

"What has he done with his money?" asked a red-faced gentleman with a pendulous excrescence on the end of his nose, that shook like the gills of a turkey-cock.

"I haven't heard," said the man with the large chin, yawning again. "Left it to his company, perhaps. He hasn't left it to *me*. That's all I know."

This pleasantry was received with a general laugh.

"It's likely to be a very cheap funeral," said the same speaker; "for, upon my life I don't know of anybody to go to it. Suppose we make up a party, and volunteer?"

"I don't mind going if a lunch is provided," observed the gentleman with the excrescence on his nose. "But I must be fed if I make one."

Another laugh.

"Well, I am the most disinterested among you, after all," said the first speaker, "for I never wear black gloves, and I never eat lunch. But I'll offer to go if anybody else will. When I come to think of it, I'm not at all sure that I wasn't his most particular friend; for we used to stop and speak whenever we met. Bye, bye!"

Speakers and listeners strolled away, and mixed with other groups. Scrooge knew the men, and looked towards the Spirit for an explanation.

The phantom glided on into a street. Its finger pointed to two persons meeting. Scrooge listened again, thinking that the explanation might lie here.

He knew these men, also, perfectly. They were men of business: very wealthy, and of great importance. He had made a point always of standing well in their esteem in a business point of view, that is; strictly in a business point of view.

"How are you?" said one.

"How are you?" returned the other.

"Well!" said the first, "old Scratch has got his own at last, hey?"

"So I am told," returned the second. "Cold, isn't it?"

"Seasonable for Christmas-time. You're not a skater, I suppose?"

"No. No. Something else to think of. Good morning!"

Not another word. That was their meeting, their conversation, and their parting.

Scrooge was at first inclined to be surprised that the Spirit should attach importance to conversations apparently so trivial; but feeling assured that they must have some hidden purpose, he set himself to consider what it was likely to be. They could scarcely be supposed to have any bearing on the death of Jacob, his old partner, for that was Past, and this Ghost's province was the Future. Nor could he think of any one immediately connected with himself to whom he could apply them. But nothing doubting that, to whomsoever they applied, they had some latent moral for his own improvement, he resolved to treasure up every word he heard, and everything he saw; and especially to observe the shadow of himself when it appeared. For he had an expectation that the conduct of his future self would give him the clue he missed, and would render the solution of these riddles easy.

He looked about in that very place for his own image, but another man stood in his accustomed corner; and though the clock pointed to his usual time of day for being there, he saw no likeness of himself among the multitudes that poured in through the Porch. It gave him little surprise, however; for he had been revolving in his mind a change of life, and thought and hoped he saw his new-born resolutions carried out in this.

Quiet and dark, beside him stood the Phantom, with its outstretched hand. When he roused himself from his thoughtful quest, he fancied, from the turn of the hand, and its situation in reference to himself, that the Unseen Eyes were looking at him keenly. It made him shudder, and feel very cold.

They left the busy scene, and went into an obscure part of the town, where Scrooge had never penetrated before, although he recognised its situation, and its bad repute. The ways were foul and narrow; the shops and houses wretched; the people half naked, drunken, slipshod, ugly. Alleys and archways, like so many cesspools, disgorged their offences of smell and dirt, and life upon the straggling streets; and the whole quarter reeked with crime, with filth, and misery.

Far in this den of infamous resort, there was a low-browed, beetling shop, below a penthouse roof, where iron, old rags, bottles, bones, and greasy offal were bought. Upon the floor within, were piled up heaps of rusty keys, nails, chains, hinges, files, scales, weights, and refuse iron of all kinds. Secrets that few would like to scrutinise were bred and hidden in mountains of unseemly rags, masses of corrupted fat, and sepulchres of bones. Sitting in among the wares he dealt in, by a charcoal stove made of old bricks, was a grey-haired rascal, nearly seventy years of age, who had screened himself from the cold air without by a frouzy curtaining of miscellaneous tatters hung upon a line, and smoked his pipe in all the luxury of calm retirement.

Scrooge and the Phantom came into the presence of this man, just as a woman with a heavy bundle slunk into the shop. But she had scarcely entered, when another woman, similarly laden, came in too; and she was closely followed by a man in faded black, who was no less startled by the sight of them, than they had been upon the recognition of each other. After a short period of blank astonishment, in which the old man with the pipe had joined them, they all three burst into a laugh.

"Let the charwoman alone to be the first!" cried she who had entered first. "Let the laundress alone to be the second; and let the undertaker's man alone to be the third. Look here, old Joe, here's a chance! If we haven't all three met here without meaning it!"

"You couldn't have met in a better place," said old Joe, removing his pipe from his mouth. "Come into the parlour. You were made free of it long ago, you know; and the other two an't strangers. Stop till I shut the door of the shop. Ah! How it skreeks! There an't such a rusty bit of metal in the place as its own hinges, I believe; and I'm sure there's no such old bones here as mine. Ha, ha! We're all suitable to our calling, we're well matched. Come into the parlour. Come into the parlour."

The parlour was the space behind the screen of rags. The old man raked the fire together with an old stair-rod, and having trimmed his smoky lamp (for it was night) with the stem of his pipe, put it in his mouth again.

While he did this, the woman who had already spoken threw her bundle on the floor, and sat down in a flaunting manner on a stool, crossing her elbows on her knees, and looking with a bold defiance at the other two.

"What odds, then? What odds, Mrs. Dilber?" said the woman. "Every person has a right to take care of themselves. *He* always did."

"That's true, indeed!" said the laundress. "No man more so."

"Why, then, don't stand staring as if you was afraid, woman! Who's the wiser? We're not going to pick holes in each other's coats, I suppose?"

"No, indeed!" said Mrs. Dilber and the man together. "We should hope not."

"Very well then!" cried the woman. "That's enough. Who's the worse for the loss of a few things like these? Not a dead man, I suppose?"

"No, indeed," said Mrs. Dilber, laughing.

"If he wanted to keep 'em after he was dead, a wicked old screw," pursued the woman, "why wasn't he natural in his lifetime? If he had been, he'd have had somebody to look after him when he was struck with Death, instead of lying gasping out his last there, alone by himself."

"It's the truest word that ever was spoke," said Mrs. Dilber. "It's a judgment on him."

"I wish it was a little heavier judgment," replied the woman: "and it should have been, you may depend upon it, if I could have laid my hands on anything else. Open that bundle, old Joe, and let me know the value of it. Speak out plain. I'm not afraid to be the first, nor afraid for them to see it. We know pretty well that we were helping ourselves before we met here, I believe. It's no sin. Open the bundle, Joe."

But the gallantry of her friends would not allow of this; and the man in faded black, mounting the breach first, produced *his* plunder. It was not extensive. A seal or two, a pencil-case, a pair of sleeve-buttons, and a brooch of no great value, were all. They were severally examined and appraised by old Joe, who chalked the sums he was disposed to give for each, upon the wall, and added them up into a total when he found there was nothing more to come.

"That's your account," said Joe, "and I wouldn't give another sixpence, if I was to be boiled for not doing it. Who's next?"

Mrs. Dilber was next. Sheets and towels, a little wearing apparel, two old-fashioned silver teaspoons, a pair of sugar-tongs, and a few boots. Her account was stated on the wall in the same manner.

"I always give too much to ladies. It's a weakness of mine, and that's the way I ruin myself," said old Joe. "That's your account. If you asked me for another penny, and made it an open question, I'd repent of being so liberal, and knock off half-a-crown."

"And now undo *my* bundle, Joe," said the first woman.

Joe went down on his knees for the greater convenience of opening it, and, having unfastened a great many knots, dragged out a large and heavy roll of some dark stuff.

"What do you call this?" said Joe. "Bed-curtains?"

"Ah!" returned the woman, laughing and leaning forward on her crossed arms. "Bed-curtains!"

"You don't mean to say you took 'em down, rings and all, with him lying there?" said Joe.

"Yes I do," replied the woman. "Why not?"

"You were born to make your fortune," said Joe, "and you'll certainly do it."

"I certainly shan't hold my hand, when I can get anything in it by reaching it out, for the sake of such a man as he was, I promise you, Joe," returned the woman coolly. "Don't drop that oil upon the blankets, now."

"His blankets?" asked Joe.

"Whose else's do you think?" replied the woman. "He isn't likely to take cold without 'em, I dare say."

"I hope he didn't die of anything catching? Eh?" said old Joe, stopping in his work, and looking up.

"Don't you be afraid of that," returned the woman. "I an't so fond of his company that I'd loiter about him for such things, if he did. Ah! you may look through that shirt till your eyes ache, but you won't find a hole in it, nor a thread-bare place. It's the best he had, and a fine one too. They'd have wasted it, if it hadn't been for me."

"What do you call wasting of it?" asked old Joe.

"Putting it on him to be buried in, to be sure," replied the woman, with a laugh. "Somebody was fool enough to do it, but I took it off again. If calico an't good enough for such a purpose, it isn't good enough for anything. It's quite as becoming to the body. He can't look uglier than he did in that one."

Scrooge listened to this dialogue in horror. As they sat grouped about their spoil, in the scanty light afforded by the old man's lamp, he viewed them with a detestation and disgust which could hardly have been greater, though they had been obscene demons marketing the corpse itself.

"Ha, ha!" laughed the same woman when old Joe, producing a flannel bag with money in it, told out their several gains upon the ground. "This is the end of it, you see! He frightened every one away from him when he was alive, to profit us when he was dead! Ha, ha, ha!"

"Spirit!" said Scrooge, shuddering from head to foot. "I see, I see. The case of this unhappy man might be my own. My life tends that way now. Merciful Heaven, what is this?"

He recoiled in terror, for the scene had changed, and now he almost touched a bed—a bare, uncurtained bed—on which, beneath a ragged sheet, there lay a some-thing covered up, which, though it was dumb, announced itself in awful language.

The room was very dark, too dark to be observed with any accuracy, though Scrooge glanced round it in obedience to a secret impulse, anxious to know what kind of room it was. A pale light, rising in the outer air, fell straight upon the bed; and on it, plundered and bereft, unwatched, unwept, uncared for, was the body of this man.

Scrooge glanced towards the Phantom. Its steady hand was pointed to the head. The cover was so carelessly adjusted that the slightest raising of it, the motion of a finger upon Scrooge's part, would have disclosed the face. He thought of it, felt how easy it would be to do, and longed to do it; but had no more power to withdraw the veil than to dismiss the spectre at his side.

Oh cold, cold, rigid, dreadful Death, set up thine altar here, and dress it with such terrors as thou hast at thy command; for this is thy dominion! But of the loved, revered, and honoured head thou canst not turn one hair to thy dread purposes, or make one feature odious. It is not that the hand is heavy, and will fall down when released; it is not that the heart and pulse are still; but that the hand was open, generous, and true; the heart brave, warm, and tender, and the pulse a man's. Strike, Shadow, strike! And see his good deeds springing from the wound, to sow the world with life immortal!

No voice pronounced these words in Scrooge's ears, and yet he heard them when he looked upon the bed. He thought, if this man could be raised up now, what would be his foremost thoughts? Avarice, hard dealing, griping cares? They have brought him to a rich end, truly!

He lay in the dark empty house, with not a man, a woman, or a child to say that he was kind to me in this or that, and for the memory of one kind word I will be kind to him. A cat was tearing at the door, and there was a sound of gnawing rats beneath the hearthstone. What *they* wanted in the room of death, and why they were so restless and disturbed, Scrooge did not dare to think.

"Spirit!" he said, "this is a fearful place. In leaving it, I shall not leave its lesson, trust me. Let us go!"

Still the Ghost pointed with an unmoved finger to the head.

"I understand you," Scrooge returned, "and I would do it if I could. But I have not the power, Spirit. I have not the power."

Again it seemed to look upon him.

"If there is any person in the town, who feels emotion caused by this man's death," said Scrooge, quite agonised, "show that person to me, Spirit, I beseech you!"

The Phantom spread its dark robe before him for a moment, like a wing; and, withdrawing it, revealed a room by daylight, where a mother and her children were.

She was expecting some one, and with anxious eagerness; for she walked up and down the room, started at every sound, looked out from the window, glanced at the clock, tried, but in vain, to work with her needle, and could hardly bear the voices of the children in their play.

At length the long-expected knock was heard. She hurried to the door, and met her husband; a man whose face was careworn and depressed, though he was young. There was a remarkable expression in it now; a kind of serious delight of which he felt ashamed, and which he struggled to repress.

He sat down to the dinner that had been hoarding for him by the fire, and when she asked him faintly what news (which was not until after a long silence), he appeared embarrassed how to answer.

"Is it good?" she said, "or bad?"to help him.

"Bad," he answered.

"We are quite ruined?"

"No. There is hope yet, Caroline."

"If *he* relents," she said, amazed, "there is! Nothing is past hope, if such a miracle has happened."

"He is past relenting," said her husband. "He is dead."

She was a mild and patient creature, if her face spoke truth; but she was thankful in her soul to hear it, and she said so with clasped hands. She prayed forgiveness the next moment, and was sorry; but the first was the emotion of her heart.

"What the half-drunken woman, whom I told you of last night, said to me when I tried to see him and obtain a week's delay—and what I thought was a mere excuse to avoid me—turns out to have been quite true. He was not only very ill, but dying, then."

"To whom will our debt be transferred?"

"I don't know. But, before that time, we shall be ready with the money; and even though we were not, it would be a bad fortune indeed to find so merciless a creditor in his successor. We may sleep to-night with light hearts, Caroline!"

Yes. Soften it as they would, their hearts were lighter. The children's faces, hushed and clustered round to hear what they so little understood, were brighter; and it was a happier house for this man's death! The only emotion that the Ghost could show him, caused by the event, was one of pleasure.

"Let me see some tenderness connected with a death," said Scrooge; "or that dark chamber, Spirit, which we left just now, will be for ever present to me."

The Ghost conducted him through several streets familiar to his feet; and as they went along, Scrooge looked here and there to find himself, but nowhere was he to be seen. They entered poor Bob Cratchit's house; the dwelling he had visited before; and found the mother and the children seated round the fire.

Quiet. Very quiet. The noisy little Cratchits were as still as statues in one corner, and sat looking up at Peter, who had a book before him. The mother and her daughters were engaged in sewing. But surely they were very quiet!

"'And he took a child, and set him in the midst of them.'"

Where had Scrooge heard those words? He had not dreamed them. The boy must have read them out as he and the Spirit crossed the threshold. Why did he not go on?

The mother laid her work upon the table, and put her hand up to her face.

"The colour hurts my eyes," she said.

The colour? Ah, poor Tiny Tim!

"They're better now again," said Cratchit's wife. "It makes them weak by candle-light; and I wouldn't show weak eyes to your father when he comes home for the world. It must be near his time."

"Past it rather," Peter answered, shutting up his book. "But I think he has walked a little slower than he used, these few last evenings, mother."

They were very quiet again. At last she said, and in a steady, cheerful voice, that only faltered once:

"I have known him walk with—I have known him walk with Tiny Tim upon his shoulder very fast indeed."

"And so have I," cried Peter. "Often."

"And so have I," exclaimed another. So had all.

"But he was very light to carry," she resumed, intent upon her work, "and his father loved him so, that it was no trouble, no trouble. And there is your father at the door!"

She hurried out to meet him; and little Bob in his comforter—he had need of it, poor fellow—came in. His tea was ready for him on the hob, and they all tried who should help him to it most. Then the two young Cratchits got upon his knees, and laid, each child, a little cheek against his face, as if they said, "Don't mind it, father. Don't be grieved!"

Bob was very cheerful with them, and spoke pleasantly to all the family. He looked at the work upon the table, and praised the industry and speed of Mrs. Cratchit and the girls. They would be done long before Sunday, he said.

"Sunday! You went to-day, then, Robert?" said his wife.

"Yes, my dear," returned Bob. "I wish you could have gone. It would have done you good to see how green a place it is. But you'll see it often. I promised him that I would walk there on a Sunday. My little, little child!" cried Bob. "My little child!"

He broke down all at once. He couldn't help it. If he could have helped it, he and his child would have been farther apart, perhaps, than they were.

He left the room, and went upstairs into the room above, which was lighted cheerfully, and hung with Christmas. There was a chair set close beside the child, and there were signs of some one having been there, lately. Poor Bob sat down in it, and when he had thought a little and composed himself, he kissed the little face. He was reconciled to what had happened, and went down again quite happy.

They drew about the fire, and talked, the girls and mother working still. Bob told them of the extraordinary kindness of Mr. Scrooge's nephew, whom he had scarcely seen but once, and who, meeting him in the street that day, and seeing that he looked a little—"just a little down, you know," said Bob, inquired what had happened to distress him. "On which," said Bob, "for he is the pleasantest-spoken gentleman you ever heard, I told him. 'I am heartily sorry for it, Mr. Cratchit,' he said, 'and heartily sorry for your good wife.' By-the-bye, how he ever knew *that* I don't know."

"Knew what, my dear?"

"Why, that you were a good wife," replied Bob.

"Everybody knows that," said Peter.

"Very well observed, my boy!" cried Bob. "I hope they do. 'Heartily sorry,' he said, 'for your good wife. If I can be of service to you in any way,' he said, giving me his card, 'that's where I live. Pray come to me.' Now, it wasn't," cried Bob, "for the sake of anything he might be able to do for us, so much as for his kind way, that this was quite delightful. It really seemed as if he had known our Tiny Tim, and felt with us."

"I'm sure he's a good soul!" said Mrs. Cratchit.

"You would be surer of it, my dear," returned Bob, "if you saw and spoke to him. I shouldn't be at all surprised—mark what I say!—if he got Peter a better situation."

"Only hear that, Peter," said Mrs. Cratchit.

"And then," cried one of the girls, "Peter will be keeping company with some one, and setting up for himself."

"Get along with you!" retorted Peter, grinning.

"It's just as likely as not," said Bob, "one of these days; though there's plenty of time for that, my dear. But, however and whenever we part from one another, I am sure we shall none of us forget poor Tiny Tim—shall we—or this first parting that there was among us?"

"Never, father!" cried they all.

"And I know," said Bob, "I know, my dears, that when we recollect how patient and how mild he was; although he was a little, little child; we shall not quarrel easily among ourselves, and forget poor Tiny Tim in doing it."

"No, never, father!" they all cried again.

"I am very happy," said little Bob, "I am very happy!"

Mrs. Cratchit kissed him, his daughters kissed him, the two young Cratchits kissed him, and Peter and himself shook hands. Spirit of Tiny Tim, thy childish essence was from God!

"Spectre," said Scrooge, "something informs me that our parting moment is at hand. I know it but I know not how. Tell me what man that was whom we saw lying dead?"

The Ghost of Christmas Yet To Come conveyed him, as before—though at a different time, he thought: indeed there seemed no order in these latter visions, save that they were in the Future—into the resorts of business men, but showed him not himself. Indeed, the Spirit did not stay for anything, but went straight on, as to the end just now desired, until besought by Scrooge to tarry for a moment.

"This court," said Scrooge, "through which we hurry now, is where my place of occupation is, and has been for a length of time. I see the house. Let me behold what I shall be in days to come."

The Spirit stopped; the hand was pointed elsewhere.

"The house is yonder," Scrooge exclaimed. "Why do you point away?"

The inexorable finger underwent no change.

Scrooge hastened to the window of his office, and looked in. It was an office still, but not his. The furniture was not the same, and the figure in the chair was not himself. The Phantom pointed as before.

He joined it once again, and, wondering why and whither he had gone, accompanied it until they reached an iron gate. He paused to look round before entering.

A churchyard. Here, then, the wretched man, whose name he had now to learn, lay underneath the ground. It was a worthy place. Walled in by houses;

overrun by grass and weeds, the growth of vegetation's death, not life; choked up with too much burying; fat with repleted appetite. A worthy place!

The Spirit stood among the graves, and pointed down to One. He advanced towards it trembling. The Phantom was exactly as it had been, but he dreaded that he saw new meaning in its solemn shape.

"Before I draw nearer to that stone to which you point," said Scrooge, "answer me one question. Are these the shadows of the things that Will be, or are they shadows of things that May be only?"

Still the Ghost pointed downward to the grave by which it stood.

"Men's courses will foreshadow certain ends, to which, if persevered in, they must lead," said Scrooge. "But if the courses be departed from, the ends will change. Say it is thus with what you show me!"

The Spirit was immovable as ever.

Scrooge crept towards it, trembling as he went; and, following the finger, read upon the stone of the neglected grave his own name, EBENEZER SCROOGE.

"Am *I* that man who lay upon the bed?" he cried upon his knees.

The finger pointed from the grave to him, and back again.

"No, Spirit! Oh no, no!"

The finger still was there.

"Spirit!" he cried, tight clutching at its robe, "hear me! I am not the man I was. I will not be the man I must have been but for this intercourse. Why show me this, if I am past all hope?"

For the first time the hand appeared to shake.

"Good Spirit," he pursued, as down upon the ground he fell before it, "your nature intercedes for me, and pities me. Assure me that I yet may change these shadows you have shown me by an altered life?"

The kind hand trembled.

"I will honour Christmas in my heart, and try to keep it all the year. I will live in the Past, the Present, and the Future. The Spirits of all Three shall strive within me. I will not shut out the lessons that they teach. Oh, tell me I may sponge away the writing on this stone!"

In his agony he caught the spectral hand. It sought to free itself, but he was strong in his entreaty, and detained it. The Spirit stronger yet, repulsed him.

Holding up his hands in a last prayer to have his fate reversed, he saw an alteration in the Phantom's hood and dress. It shrunk, collapsed, and dwindled down into a bed-post.

STAVE FIVE

THE END OF IT

Yes! and the bedpost was his own. The bed was his own, the room was his own. Best and happiest of all, the Time before him was his own, to make amends in!

"I will live in the Past, the Present, and the Future!" Scrooge repeated as he scrambled out of bed. "The Spirits of all Three shall strive within me. Oh Jacob Marley! Heaven, and the Christmas Time be praised for this! I say it on my knees, old Jacob; on my knees!"

He was so fluttered and so glowing with his good intentions, that his broken voice would scarcely answer to his call. He had been sobbing violently in his conflict with the Spirit, and his face was wet with tears.

"They are not torn down," cried Scrooge, folding one of his bed-curtains in his arms, "they are not torn down, rings and all. They are here—I am here—the shadows of the things that would have been may be dispelled. They will be. I know they will!"

His hands were busy with his garments all this time: turning them inside out, putting them on upside down, tearing them, mislaying them, making them parties to every kind of extravagance.

"I don't know what to do!" cried Scrooge, laughing and crying in the same breath, and making a perfect Laocoön[1] of himself with his stockings. "I am as light as a feather, I am as happy as an angel, I am as merry as a schoolboy, I am as giddy as a drunken man. A merry Christmas to everybody! A happy New Year to all the world! Hallo here! Whoop! Hallo!"

He had frisked into the sitting-room, and was now standing there, perfectly winded.

"There's the saucepan that the gruel was in!" cried Scrooge, starting off again, and going round the fireplace. "There's the door by which the Ghost of Jacob Marley entered! There's the corner where the Ghost of Christmas Present sat! There's the window where I saw the wandering Spirits! It's all right, it's all true, it all happened. Ha ha ha!"

Really, for a man who had been out of practice for so many years, it was a splendid laugh, a most illustrious laugh. The father of a long, long line of brilliant laughs!

---

1 After warning the Trojans about the Trojan Horse, a priest named Laocoön was killed, along with his two sons, by two monstrous serpents sent by the Greek gods. Dickens is likely alluding to the statue *Laocoön and His Sons*, which shows Laocoön in agony.

"I don't know what day of the month it is," said Scrooge. "I don't know how long I've been among the Spirits. I don't know anything. I'm quite a baby. Never mind. I don't care. I'd rather be a baby. Hallo! Whoop! Hallo here!"

He was checked in his transports by the churches ringing out the lustiest peals he had ever heard. Clash, clash, hammer; ding, dong, bell! Bell, dong, ding; hammer, clang, clash! Oh, glorious, glorious!

Running to the window, he opened it, and put out his head. No fog, no mist; clear, bright, jovial, stirring, cold; cold, piping for the blood to dance to; golden sunlight; heavenly sky; sweet fresh air; merry bells. Oh, glorious! Glorious!

"What's to-day!" cried Scrooge, calling downward to a boy in Sunday clothes, who perhaps had loitered in to look about him.

"Eh?" returned the boy with all his might of wonder.

"What's to-day, my fine fellow?" said Scrooge.

"To-day!" replied the boy. "Why, Christmas Day."

"It's Christmas Day!" said Scrooge to himself. "I haven't missed it. The Spirits have done it all in one night. They can do anything they like. Of course they can. Of course they can. Hallo, my fine fellow!"

"Hallo!" returned the boy.

"Do you know the poulterer's, in the next street but one, at the corner?" Scrooge inquired.

"I should hope I did," replied the lad.

"An intelligent boy!" said Scrooge. "A remarkable boy! Do you know whether they've sold the prize turkey that was hanging up there?—Not the little prize turkey: the big one?"

"What! the one as big as me?" returned the boy.

"What a delightful boy!" said Scrooge. "It's a pleasure to talk to him. Yes, my buck!"

"It's hanging there now," replied the boy.

"Is it?" said Scrooge. "Go and buy it."

"Walk-er!" exclaimed the boy.

"No, no," said Scrooge, "I am in earnest. Go and buy it, and tell 'em to bring it here, that I may give them the direction where to take it. Come back with the man, and I'll give you a shilling. Come back with him in less than five minutes, and I'll give you half-a-crown!"

The boy was off like a shot. He must have had a steady hand at a trigger who could have got a shot off half as fast.

"I'll send it to Bob Cratchit's," whispered Scrooge, rubbing his hands, and splitting with a laugh. "He sha'n't know who sends it. It's twice the size of Tiny Tim. Joe Miller never made such a joke as sending it to Bob's will be!"

The hand in which he wrote the address was not a steady one; but write it he did, somehow, and went downstairs to open the street-door, ready for the coming of the poulterer's man. As he stood there, waiting his arrival, the knocker caught his eye.

"I shall love it as long as I live!" cried Scrooge, patting it with his hand. "I scarcely ever looked at it before. What an honest expression it has in its face! It's a wonderful knocker!—Here's the turkey! Hallo! Whoop! How are you! Merry Christmas!"

It *was* a turkey! He never could have stood upon his legs, that bird. He would have snapped 'em short off in a minute, like sticks of sealing-wax.

"Why, it's impossible to carry that to Camden Town," said Scrooge. "You must have a cab."

The chuckle with which he said this, and the chuckle with which he paid for the turkey, and the chuckle with which he paid for the cab, and the chuckle with which he recompensed the boy, were only to be exceeded by the chuckle with which he sat down breathless in his chair again, and chuckled till he cried.

Shaving was not an easy task, for his hand continued to shake very much; and shaving requires attention, even when you don't dance while you are at it. But if he had cut the end of his nose off, he would have put a piece of sticking-plaster over it, and been quite satisfied.

He dressed himself "all in his best," and at last got out into the streets. The people were by this time pouring forth, as he had seen them with the Ghost of Christmas Present; and, walking with his hands behind him, Scrooge regarded every one with a delighted smile. He looked so irresistibly pleasant, in a word, that three or four good-humoured fellows said, "Good morning, sir! A merry Christmas to you!" And Scrooge said often afterwards that, of all the blithe sounds he had ever heard, those were the blithest in his ears.

He had not gone far when, coming on towards him, he beheld the portly gentleman who had walked into his counting-house the day before, and said, "Scrooge and Marley's, I believe?" It sent a pang across his heart to think how this old gentleman would look upon him when they met; but he knew what path lay straight before him, and he took it.

"My dear sir," said Scrooge, quickening his pace, and taking the old gentleman by both his hands, "how do you do? I hope you succeeded yesterday. It was very kind of you. A merry Christmas to you, sir!"

"Mr. Scrooge?"

"Yes," said Scrooge. "That is my name, and I fear it may not be pleasant to you. Allow me to ask your pardon. And will you have the goodness—" Here Scrooge whispered in his ear.

"Lord bless me!" cried the gentleman, as if his breath were taken away. "My dear Mr. Scrooge, are you serious?"

"If you please," said Scrooge. "Not a farthing less. A great many back-payments are included in it, I assure you. Will you do me that favour?"

"My dear sir," said the other, shaking hands with him. "I don't know what to say to such munifi—"

"Don't say anything, please," retorted Scrooge. "Come and see me. Will you come and see me?"

"I will!" cried the old gentleman. And it was clear he meant to do it.

"Thankee," said Scrooge. "I am much obliged to you. I thank you fifty times. Bless you!"

He went to church, and walked about the streets, and watched the people hurrying to and fro, and patted children on the head, and questioned beggars, and looked down into the kitchens of houses, and up to the windows; and found that everything could yield him pleasure. He had never dreamed that any walk—that anything—could give him so much happiness. In the afternoon he turned his steps towards his nephew's house.

He passed the door a dozen times before he had the courage to go up and knock. But he made a dash and did it.

"Is your master at home, my dear?" said Scrooge to the girl. "Nice girl! Very."

"Yes, sir."

"Where is he, my love?" said Scrooge.

"He's in the dining-room, sir, along with mistress. I'll show you upstairs, if you please."

"Thankee. He knows me," said Scrooge, with his hand already on the dining-room lock. "I'll go in here, my dear."

He turned it gently, and sidled his face in round the door. They were looking at the table (which was spread out in great array); for these young housekeepers are always nervous on such points, and like to see that everything is right.

"Fred!" said Scrooge.

Dear heart alive, how his niece by marriage started! Scrooge had forgotten, for the moment, about her sitting in the corner with the footstool, or he wouldn't have done it on any account.

"Why, bless my soul!" cried Fred, "who's that?"

"It's I. Your uncle Scrooge. I have come to dinner. Will you let me in, Fred?"

Let him in! It is a mercy he didn't shake his arm off. He was at home in five minutes. Nothing could be heartier. His niece looked just the same. So did Topper when *he* came. So did the plump sister when *she* came. So did every one when *they* came. Wonderful party, wonderful games, wonderful unanimity, won-der-ful happiness!

But he was early at the office next morning. Oh, he was early there! If he could only be there first, and catch Bob Cratchit coming late! That was the thing he had set his heart upon.

And he did it; yes, he did! The clock struck nine. No Bob. A quarter past. No

Bob. He was full eighteen minutes and a half behind his time. Scrooge sat with his door wide open, that he might see him come into the tank.

His hat was off before he opened the door; his comforter too. He was on his stool in a jiffy, driving away with his pen, as if he were trying to overtake nine o'clock.

"Hallo!" growled Scrooge in his accustomed voice as near as he could feign it. "What do you mean by coming here at this time of day?"

"I am very sorry, sir," said Bob. "I *am* behind my time."

"You are!" repeated Scrooge. "Yes, I think you are. Step this way, sir, if you please."

"It's only once a year, sir," pleaded Bob, appearing from the tank. "It shall not be repeated. I was making rather merry yesterday, sir."

"Now, I'll tell you what, my friend," said Scrooge. "I am not going to stand this sort of thing any longer. And therefore," he continued, leaping from his stool, and giving Bob such a dig in the waistcoat that he staggered back into the tank again—"and therefore I am about to raise your salary!"

Bob trembled, and got a little nearer to the ruler. He had a momentary idea of knocking Scrooge down with it, holding him, and calling to the people in the court for help and a strait-waistcoat.

"A merry Christmas, Bob!" said Scrooge, with an earnestness that could not be mistaken, as he clapped him on the back. "A merrier Christmas, Bob, my good fellow, than I have given you, for many a year! I'll raise your salary, and endeavour to assist your struggling family, and we will discuss your affairs this very afternoon, over a Christmas bowl of smoking bishop, Bob! Make up the fires and buy another coal-scuttle before you dot another i, Bob Cratchit!"

Scrooge was better than his word. He did it all, and infinitely more; and to Tiny Tim, who did not die, he was a second father. He became as good a friend, as good a master, and as good a man as the good old City knew, or any other good old city, town, or borough in the good old world. Some people laughed to see the alteration in him, but he let them laugh, and little heeded them; for he was wise enough to know that nothing ever happened on this globe, for good, at which some people did not have their fill of laughter in the outset; and knowing that such as these would be blind anyway, he thought it quite as well that they should wrinkle up their eyes in grins as have the malady in less attractive forms. His own heart laughed, and that was quite enough for him.

He had no further intercourse with Spirits, but lived upon the Total-Abstinence Principle ever afterwards; and it was always said of him that he knew how to keep Christmas well, if any man alive possessed the knowledge. May that be truly said of us, and all of us! And so, as Tiny Tim observed, God bless Us, Every One!

1843

ROBERT BROWNING
1812–1889

Robert Browning was born to a modest family in Camberwall, a London suburb. His mother's gentle, quiet ways guided the household. His father, a scholarly and artistic man, served as a clerk at the Bank of England. Browning's early education began at his father's personal library, a collection that numbered some six thousand books. Browning's formal schooling was sporadic, but he displayed remarkable precocity as a child. Shortly after entering his first school, he was sent home because his abilities far exceeded those of his peers. At his next school, his classmates resented his intellect and cruelly bullied him. Between the ages of fourteen and sixteen, Browning received a "gentleman's education" at home: He learned how to box, ride horses, dance, and play numerous musical instruments. He yearned to attend college, but he was barred from most universities because he was a conscientious nonconformist, a person who refused to conform to the established Church of England. In 1828, however, he was accepted by the University of London, a newly-founded secular institution. Bored by the perfunctory lessons, Browning withdrew after his first year. His linguistic ambitions differed from those of his colleagues; poetry interested him, not law, medicine, or mercantile affairs.

Browning's father reluctantly consented to his son's wishes of becoming a poet. For several years, Browning self-educated by studying foreign languages, examining art, and reading the works of Romantic writers. Percy Bysshe Shelley's influence on the fledgling poet is especially evident; Browning's first published poem, *Pauline*, is a confessional piece that exhibits the deeply personal style that characterizes Shelley's work. *Pauline* received mixed reviews, but critics assessed Browning's next poem, *Paracelsus,* positively. John Forster, a theatrical critic for the *Examiner*, hailed it "a true poem" and predicted Browning would have a propitious career.

In 1836, William Charles Macready, a talented actor and play producer, implored Browning to compose a historical tragedy. *Strafford*, as Browning initially presented it to Macready and Forster, was a dramatic failure; the play underwent extensive revisions before Macready hesitantly agreed to produce it. Browning earned his first money from the play, but his tendency to reveal "Action in Character rather than Character in Action," as he stated in the preface to *Strafford*, did not translate well on stage. He struggled as a playwright for ten years, and his plays never achieved critical success.

In 1840, Browning published *Sordello* at his father's expense. He hoped the poem would enhance his reputation. Instead, it bewildered readers. Critics and readers lambasted *Sordello* for its unreadability, condemning it as the most notorious poem of the nineteenth century. Not only did Browning include obscure references and unusual language, but he also omitted entire lines of his poem in the published version. Many considered *Sordello* an unfinished failure or regarded it as an unintelligible, nonsensical work. In an effort to recover his status, Browning published *Bells and Pomegranates*, a series of eight paper-bound pamphlets that contained plays as well as poems. Some of

Browning's most acclaimed poetry appeared in the third and seventh pamphlets, including "My Last Duchess," "Porphyria's Lover," and "The Bishop Orders His Tomb at Saint Praxed's Church." Browning popularized the dramatic monologue, a type of poem wherein a character shares their side of a dialogue; the character unconsciously exposes their true personality or suspect motives through their description of a situation or several events. The character addresses a silent listener or listeners; alternately, they may speak to themselves in the form of a soliloquy. Since the character is distinctly separate from the poet, he or she does not necessarily reflect the poet's opinions.

Browning used the dramatic monologue to develop characters with exceptional psychological depth while simultaneously economizing space. He further distinguished his writing by focusing on obscure individuals and subject matters. As he declared in *Sordello*, he wanted to be one of the "setters-forth of unexampled themes, / Makers of quite new men." At times, readers denounced Browning for his shocking, unfashionable, and repulsive topics. Other reviewers critiqued his seemingly-careless language and syntax. His frequent usage of unnaturally stressed rhymes, awkward diction, and enjambed lines frustrate some readers, but these imperfections are symptoms of a desire to mirror reality. Unlike many of his contemporaries, Browning did not depict an idealized world. Those who appreciated the deliberate incongruities of his work remarked that he was fresh, original, and daring.

Browning's poetry can scarcely be examined without considering his relationship with Elizabeth Barrett, a famous poet who greatly admired his works. When they met in 1845, they forged a literary friendship. Browning, however, fell in love with her almost immediately. Barrett resisted his affections and denied her own feelings towards him; she was six years older than him, a semi-invalid, and had been forbidden to marry by her domineering, egotistical, and possessive father. The couple's love prevailed; they eloped to Italy under intense secrecy. Their married life was joyous, and the writers flourished together until 1861 when Barrett died.

After her death, Browning reorganized his life almost immediately. He and his son returned to London, where Browning remained for the next twenty-five years. He wrote copiously and published *Dramatis Personae*, a series of monologues concerned with contemporary issues, in 1864. Its popularity revolutionized Browning's reputation. He became increasingly fond of social life and regularly dined out with friends. Shortly after his success, Browning lost his father, and Barrett's only surviving sister died in his arms. To abate his grief, he delved into "the Old Yellow Book," a collection of pamphlets, legal documents, and manuscript letters he had purchased in Florence. The papers concerned Count Guido Franceschini, who was found guilty of multiple murders in seventeenth-century Rome. Franceschini accused his young wife, Pompilia, of having an adulterous affair with a priest; he then killed her parents and stabbed her to death. In *The Ring and the Book*, Browning presents the perspectives of the various figures involved, effectively recrafting the case across twelve books. Totaling over twenty thousand lines, the work became Browning's longest and most significant poem.

Browning achieved his dream of public fame. He was awarded honorary degrees from the University of Cambridge and the University of Oxford. Browning societies formed in England and America, and he began addressing philosophical and religious topics to appease his admirers. His later works were either lauded or condemned by reviewers, but he was nevertheless appreciated as a philosopher and scholar. Browning's aggressive optimism sometimes alienates him from other mid-Victorian writers who suffered from doubts brought about by a modernizing world. Although Browning asserted that life is inherently good, his work is rife with villainous characters and grotesque circumstances, both of which evidence his awareness of a morally polarized world.

1812	Robert Browning born 7 May
1828–29	Attends London University
1833	*Pauline: A Fragment of a Confession*
1835	*Paracelsus*
1836	"Porphyria" (now known as "Porphyria's Lover") and companion poem "Johannes Agricola"
1837	*Strafford* staged at Covent Garden
1840	*Sordello*
1841–46	*Bells and Pomegranates*
1842	*Dramatic Lyrics* (included "My Last Duchess," then titled "Italy")
1846	Marries Elizabeth Barrett
1861	Barrett dies from a mysterious illness, likely tuberculosis but possibly poliomyelitis
1868	*The Ring and the Book*
1887	*Parleyings with Certain People in their Day*
1889	Browning dies 12 December due to bronchitis and a weakened heart and is buried in Poets' Corner, Westminster Abbey

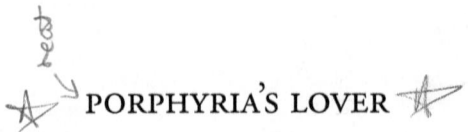

PORPHYRIA'S LOVER

The rain set early in to-night,
   The sullen wind was soon awake,
It tore the elm-tops down for spite,
   And did its worst to vex the lake:
I listened with heart fit to break.   5
When glided in Porphyria; straight
   She shut the cold out and the storm,
And kneeled and made the cheerless grate
   Blaze up, and all the cottage warm;
Which done, she rose, and from her form   10
Withdrew the dripping cloak and shawl,
   And laid her soiled gloves by, untied
Her hat and let the damp hair fall,
   And, last, she sat down by my side
And called me. When no voice replied,   15
She put my arm about her waist,
   And made her smooth white shoulder bare
And all her yellow hair displaced,
   And, stooping, made my cheek lie there,
And spread, o'er all, her yellow hair,   20
Murmuring how she loved me—she
   Too weak, for all her heart's endeavor,
To set its struggling passion free
   From pride, and vainer ties dissever,
And give herself to me forever.   25
But passion sometimes would prevail,
   Nor could to-night's gay feast restrain
A sudden thought of one so pale
   For love of her, and all in vain:
So, she was come through wind and rain.   30
Be sure I looked up at her eyes
   Happy and proud; at last I knew
Porphyria worshipped me; surprise
   Made my heart swell, and still it grew
While I debated what to do.   35

That moment she was mine, mine, fair,
   Perfectly pure and good: I found
A thing to do, and all her hair
   In one long yellow string I wound
Three times her little throat around,
And strangled her. No pain felt she;
   I am quite sure she felt no pain.   —
As a shut bud that holds a bee,
   I warily oped her lids: again
Laughed the blue eyes without a stain.
And I untightened next the tress
   About her neck; her cheek once more
Blushed bright beneath my burning kiss:
   I propped her head up as before,
Only, this time my shoulder bore
Her head, which droops upon it still:
   The smiling rosy little head,
So glad it has its utmost will,
   That all it scorned at once is fled,
And I, its love, am gained instead!
Porphyria's love: she guessed not how
   Her darling one wish would be heard.
And thus we sit together now,
   And all night long we have not stirred,
And yet God has not said a word!

1836

[handwritten annotation:] Repitition shows he's trying to convince himself

[handwritten marginal note:] Dramatic Monologue

[line numbers in margin: 40, 45, 50, 55, 60]

⭐MY LAST DUCHESS⭐

Ferrara

That's my last Duchess painted on the wall,
Looking as if she were alive. I call
That piece a wonder, now: Frà Pandolf's hands
Worked busily a day, and there she stands.
Will 't please you sit and look at her? I said   5
"Frà Pandolf" by design, for never read
Strangers like you that pictured countenance,
The depth and passion of its earnest glance,
But to myself they turned (since none puts by
the curtain I have drawn for you, but I)   10
And seemed as they would ask me, if they durst,
How such a glance came there; so, not the first
Are you to turn and ask thus. Sir, 'twas not
Her husband's presence only, called that spot
Of joy into the Duchess' cheek: perhaps   15
Frà Pandolf chanced to say "Her mantle laps
Over my lady's wrist too much," or "Paint
Must never hope to reproduce the faint
Half-flush that dies along her throat;" such stuff
Was courtesy, she thought, and cause enough   20
For calling up that spot of joy. She had
A heart—how shall I say—too soon made glad,
Too easily impressed; she liked whate'er
She looked on, and her looks went everywhere.
Sir, 'twas all one! My favour at her breast,   25
The dropping of the daylight in the West,
The bough of cherries some officious fool
Broke in the orchard for her, the white mule
She rode with round the terrace—all and each
Would draw from her alike the approving speech,   30
Or blush, at least. She thanked men—good! but thanked
Somehow—I know not how—as if she ranked
My gift of a nine-hundred-years-old name
With anybody's gift. Who'd stoop to blame

This sort of trifling? Even had you skill   35
In speech—(which I have not)—to make your will
Quite clear to such an one, and say, "Just this
Or that in you disgusts me; here you miss,
Or there exceed the mark"—and if she let
Herself be lessoned so, nor plainly set   40
Her wits to yours, forsooth, and made excuse,
—E'en that would be some stooping; and I choose
Never to stoop. Oh sir, she smiled, no doubt,
Whene'er I passed her; but who passed without
Much the same smile? This grew; I gave commands;   45
Then all smiles stopped together. There she stands
As if alive. Will 't please you rise? We'll meet
The company below, then. I repeat,
The Count your master's known munificence
Is ample warrant that no just pretence   50
Of mine for dowry will be disallowed;
Though his fair daughter's self, as I avowed
At starting, is my object. Nay, we'll go
Together down, sir. Notice Neptune,[1] though,
Taming a sea-horse, thought a rarity,   55
Which Claus of Innsbruck cast in bronze for me!

1842

---

1 The Roman god of the sea.

⚝ THE BISHOP ORDERS HIS TOMB ⚝ AT ST. PRAXED'S CHURCH

[Rome, 15—]

Vanity, saith the preacher, vanity!
Draw round my bed: is Anselm keeping back?
Nephews—sons mine...ah God, I know not! Well—
She, men would have to be your mother once,
Old Gandolf envied me, so fair she was!   5
What's done is done, and she is dead beside,
Dead long ago, and I am Bishop since,
And as she died so must we die ourselves,
And thence ye may perceive the world's a dream.
Life, how and what is it? As here I lie   10
In this state-chamber, dying by degrees,
Hours and long hours in the dead night, I ask
"Do I live, am I dead?" Peace, peace seems all.
Saint Praxed's ever was the church for peace;
And so, about this tomb of mine. I fought   15
With tooth and nail to save my niche, ye know:
—Old Gandolf cozened me, despite my care;
Shrewd was that snatch from out the corner South
He graced his carrion with, God curse the same!
Yet still my niche is not so cramped but thence   20
One sees the pulpit o' the epistle-side,
And somewhat of the choir, those silent seats,
And up into the aery dome where live
The angels, and a sunbeam's sure to lurk:
And I shall fill my slab of basalt there,   25
And 'neath my tabernacle take my rest,
With those nine columns round me, two and two,
The odd one at my feet where Anselm stands:
Peach-blossom marble all, the rare, the ripe
As fresh-poured red wine of a mighty pulse.   30
—Old Gandolf with his paltry onion-stone,[1]
Put me where I may look at him! True peach,

---

1 Cipollino marble splits into layers like an onion.

Rosy and flawless: how I earned the prize!
Draw close: that conflagration of my church
—What then? So much was saved if aught were missed!   35
My sons, ye would not be my death? Go dig
The white-grape vineyard where the oil-press stood,
Drop water gently till the surface sinks,
And if ye find...Ah, God I know not, I!...
Bedded in store of rotten figleaves soft,   40
And corded up in a tight olive-frail,[2]
Some lump, ah God, of *lapis lazuli*,[3]
Big as a Jew's head cut off at the nape,
Blue as a vein o'er the Madonna's breast...
Sons, all have I bequeathed you, villas, all,   45
That brave Frascati villa with its bath,
So, let the blue lump poise between my knees,
Like God the Father's globe on both his hands
Ye worship in the Jesu Church so gay,
For Gandolf shall not choose but see and burst!   50
Swift as a weaver's shuttle fleet our years:
Man goeth to the grave, and where is he?
Did I say, basalt for my slab, sons? Black—
'Twas ever antique-black I meant! How else
Shall ye contrast my frieze to come beneath?   55
The bas-relief in bronze ye promised me,
Those Pans and Nymphs[4] ye wot of, and perchance
Some tripod, thyrsus,[5] with a vase or so,
The Saviour at his sermon on the mount,
Saint Praxed in a glory, and one Pan   60
Ready to twitch the Nymph's last garment off,
And Moses with the tables[6]...but I know
Ye mark me not! What do they whisper thee,
Child of my bowels, Anselm? Ah, ye hope
To revel down my villas while I gasp   65
Bricked o'er with beggar's mouldy travertine[7]

2 A basket used to pack olives.

3 A semiprecious bright blue stone.

4 Nature and fertility deities in Greek mythology.

5 A staff or spear topped with a pine-cone, held by Bacchus, the god of wine.

6 The Ten Commandments, written on two stone tablets, were divinely revealed to Moses.

7 White rock.

Which Gandolf from his tomb-top chuckles at!
Nay, boys, ye love me—all of jasper, then!
'Tis jasper ye stand pledged to, lest I grieve
My bath must needs be left behind, alas!   70
One block, pure green as a pistachio-nut,
There's plenty jasper somewhere in the world—
And have I not Saint Praxed's ear to pray
Horses for ye, and brown Greek manuscripts,
And mistresses with great smooth marbly limbs?   75
—That's if ye carve my epitaph aright,
Choice Latin, picked phrase, Tully's[1] every word,
No gaudy ware like Gandolf's second line—
Tully, my masters? Ulpian[2] serves his need!
And then how I shall lie through centuries,   80
And hear the blessed mutter of the mass,
And see God made and eaten all day long,
And feel the steady candle-flame, and taste
Good strong thick stupefying incense-smoke!
For as I lie here, hours of the dead night,   85
Dying in state and by such slow degrees,
I fold my arms as if they clasped a crook,
And stretch my feet forth straight as stone can point,
And let the bedclothes for a mortcloth[3] drop
Into great laps and folds of sculptor's work: 90
And as yon tapers dwindle, and strange thoughts
Grow, with a certain humming in my ears,
About the life before I lived this life,
And this life too, Popes, Cardinals and Priests,
St. Praxed at his sermon on the mount,   95
Your tall pale mother with her talking eyes,
And new-found agate urns as fresh as day,
And marble's language, Latin pure, discreet,
—Aha, ELUCESCEBAT[4] quoth our friend?
No Tully, said I, Ulpian at the best!   100
Evil and brief hath been my pilgrimage.

---

1 Marcus Tullius Cicero (106–43 BC), a Roman statesman, orator, and writer who is lauded for his mastery of Latin prose.

2 A third-century Roman jurist and writer.

3 A funeral cloth; pall.

4 From the verb "elucere," meaning "to be notable."

All *lapis*, all, sons! Else I give the Pope
My villas: will ye ever eat my heart?
Ever your eyes were as a lizard's quick,
They glitter like your mother's for my soul,   105
Or ye would heighten my impoverished frieze,
Piece out its starved design, and fill my vase
With grapes, and add a vizor and a Term,
And to the tripod ye would tie a lynx
That in his struggle throws the thyrsus down,   110
To comfort me on my entablature
Whereon I am to lie till I must ask
"Do I live, am I dead?" There, leave me, there!
For ye have stabbed me with ingratitude
To death—ye wish it—God, ye wish it! Stone—   115
Gritstone, a-crumble! Clammy squares which sweat
As if the corpse they keep were oozing through—
And no more *lapis* to delight the world!
Well go! I bless ye. Fewer tapers there,
But in a row: and, going, turn your backs   120
—Ay, like departing altar-ministrants,
And leave me in my church, the church for peace,
That I may watch at leisure if he leers—
Old Gandolf, at me, from his onion-stone,
As still he envied me, so fair she was!   125

1845

FRA LIPPO LIPPI[1]

I am poor brother Lippo, by your leave!
You need not clap your torches to my face.
Zooks,[2] what's to blame? you think you see a monk!
What, 'tis past midnight, and you go the rounds,
And here you catch me at an alley's end   5
Where sportive ladies leave their doors ajar?
The Carmine's[3] my cloister: hunt it up,
Do,—harry out, if you must show your zeal,
Whatever rat, there, haps on his wrong hole,
And nip each softling of a wee white mouse,   10
Weke, weke, that's crept to keep him company!
Aha, you know your betters! Then, you'll take
Your hand away that's fiddling on my throat,
And please to know me likewise. Who am I?
 Why, one, sir, who is lodging with a friend   15
Three streets off—he's a certain...how d'ye call?
Master—a...Cosimo of the Medici,[4]
I' the house that caps the corner. Boh! you were best!
Remember and tell me, the day you're hanged,
How you affected such a gullet's-gripe!   20
But you, sir, it concerns you that your knaves
Pick up a manner nor discredit you:
Zooks, are we pilchards, that they sweep the streets
And count fair price what comes into their net?
He's Judas[5] to a tittle, that man is!   25
Just such a face! Why, sir, you make amends.
Lord, I'm not angry! Bid your hangdogs[6] go

---

1 Browning's poem is based on Giorgio Vasari's biography of the Florentine painter Fra Lippo Lippi (1406–1469). Orphaned as a boy, Lippi was placed in a convent by his aunt, Mona Lapaccia, when he was eight years old.

2 A mild oath or exclamation of surprise.

3 Santa Maria del Carmine, where Lippi was raised.

4 In addition to his extreme wealth and political influence, Cosimo de' Medici (1389–1464) began the Medici family's one-hundred-year rule over Florence.

5 Judas Iscariot betrayed Jesus for thirty pieces of silver; alternately, a term for a traitor or deceiver.

6 Miserable or contemptible people.

Drink out this quarter-florin to the health
Of the munificent House that harbours me
(And many more beside, lads! more beside!)   30
And all's come square again. I'd like his face—
His, elbowing on his comrade in the door
With the pike and lantern,—for the slave that holds
John Baptist's head[7] a-dangle by the hair
With one hand ("Look you, now," as who should say)   35
And his weapon in the other, yet unwiped!
It's not your chance to have a bit of chalk,
A wood-coal or the like? or you should see!
Yes, I'm the painter, since you style me so.
What, brother Lippo's doings, up and down,   40
You know them and they take you? like enough!
I saw the proper twinkle in your eye—
'Tell you, I liked your looks at very first.
Let's sit and set things straight now, hip to haunch.
Here's spring come, and the nights one makes up bands   45
To roam the town and sing out carnival,
And I've been three weeks shut within my mew,
A-painting for the great man, saints and saints
And saints again. I could not paint all night—
Ouf! I leaned out of window for fresh air.   50
There came a hurry of feet and little feet,
A sweep of lute-strings, laughs, and whifts of song,—
Flower o' the broom,
Take away love, and our earth is a tomb!
Flower o' the quince,   55
I let Lisa go, and what good in life since?
Flower o' the thyme—and so on. Round they went.
Scarce had they turned the corner when a titter
Like the skipping of rabbits by moonlight,—three slim shapes,
And a face that looked up...zooks, sir, flesh and blood,   60
That's all I'm made of! Into shreds it went,
Curtain and counterpane and coverlet,
All the bed-furniture—a dozen knots,
There was a ladder! Down I let myself,

---

7 The Jewish prophet John the Baptist denounced a marriage between Herod and Herodias (the
nature of which was illegitimate according to Jewish Law). Enraged, Herodias demanded that John
the Baptist's head be brought to her on a silver platter. The Roman Catholic Church recognizes him
as a saint.

Hands and feet, scrambling somehow, and so dropped,   65
And after them. I came up with the fun
Hard by Saint Laurence,[1] hail fellow, well met,—
Flower o' the rose,
If I've been merry, what matter who knows?
And so as I was stealing back again   70
To get to bed and have a bit of sleep
Ere I rise up to-morrow and go work
On Jerome[2] knocking at his poor old breast
With his great round stone to subdue the flesh,
You snap me of the sudden. Ah, I see!   75
Though your eye twinkles still, you shake your head—
Mine's shaved—a monk, you say—the sting's in that!
If Master Cosimo announced himself,
Mum's the word naturally; but a monk!
Come, what am I a beast for? tell us, now!   80
I was a baby when my mother died
And father died and left me in the street.
I starved there, God knows how, a year or two
On fig-skins, melon-parings, rinds and shucks,
Refuse and rubbish. One fine frosty day,   85
My stomach being empty as your hat,
The wind doubled me up and down I went.
Old Aunt Lapaccia trussed me with one hand,
(Its fellow was a stinger as I knew)
And so along the wall, over the bridge,   90
By the straight cut to the convent. Six words there,
While I stood munching my first bread that month:
"So, boy, you're minded," quoth the good fat father
Wiping his own mouth, 'twas refection-time,—
"To quit this very miserable world?   95
Will you renounce"..."the mouthful of bread?" thought I;
By no means! Brief, they made a monk of me;
I did renounce the world, its pride and greed,
Palace, farm, villa, shop and banking-house,
Trash, such as these poor devils of Medici   100
Have given their hearts to—all at eight years old.
Well, sir, I found in time, you may be sure,

---

1 Lippi painted *Saint Laurence Enthroned with Saints and Donors.*

2 St. Jerome is revered as a learned scholar, biblical translator, and monastic leader.

'Twas not for nothing—the good bellyful,
The warm serge and the rope that goes all round,
And day-long blessed idleness beside!   105
"Let's see what the urchin's fit for"—that came next.
Not overmuch their way, I must confess.
Such a to-do! They tried me with their books:
Lord, they'd have taught me Latin in pure waste!
Flower o' the clove,   110
All the Latin I construe is, "amo" I love!
But, mind you, when a boy starves in the streets
Eight years together, as my fortune was,
Watching folk's faces to know who will fling
The bit of half-stripped grape-bunch he desires,   115
And who will curse or kick him for his pains,—
Which gentleman processional and fine,
Holding a candle to the Sacrament,
Will wink and let him lift a plate and catch
The droppings of the wax to sell again,   120
Or holla for the Eight and have him whipped,—
How say I?—nay, which dog bites, which lets drop
His bone from the heap of offal in the street,—
Why, soul and sense of him grow sharp alike,
He learns the look of things, and none the less   125
For admonition from the hunger-pinch.
I had a store of such remarks, be sure,
Which, after I found leisure, turned to use.
I drew men's faces on my copy-books,
Scrawled them within the antiphonary's marge,   130
Joined legs and arms to the long music-notes,
Found eyes and nose and chin for A's and B's,
And made a string of pictures of the world
Betwixt the ins and outs of verb and noun,
On the wall, the bench, the door. The monks looked black. 135
"Nay," quoth the Prior, "turn him out, d'ye say?
In no wise. Lose a crow and catch a lark.
What if at last we get our man of parts,
We Carmelites,[3] like those Camaldolese[4]

---

3 A mendicant order of the Roman Catholic Church.

4 A member of the Congregation of Monk Hermits of Camaldoli, which combines the solitary
lifestyle of the hermit with the community life of the monk.

And Preaching Friars,[1] to do our church up fine   140
And put the front on it that ought to be!"
And hereupon he bade me daub away.
Thank you! my head being crammed, the walls a blank,
Never was such prompt disemburdening.
First, every sort of monk, the black and white,[2]   145
I drew them, fat and lean: then, folk at church,
From good old gossips waiting to confess
Their cribs of barrel-droppings, candle-ends,—
To the breathless fellow at the altar-foot,
Fresh from his murder, safe and sitting there   150
With the little children round him in a row
Of admiration, half for his beard and half
For that white anger of his victim's son
Shaking a fist at him with one fierce arm,
Signing himself with the other because of Christ   155
(Whose sad face on the cross sees only this
After the passion of a thousand years)
Till some poor girl, her apron o'er her head,
(Which the intense eyes looked through) came at eve
On tiptoe, said a word, dropped in a loaf,   160
Her pair of earrings and a bunch of flowers
(The brute took growling), prayed, and so was gone.
I painted all, then cried "'Tis ask and have;
Choose, for more's ready!"—laid the ladder flat,
And showed my covered bit of cloister-wall.   165
The monks closed in a circle and praised loud
Till checked, taught what to see and not to see,
Being simple bodies,—"That's the very man!
Look at the boy who stoops to pat the dog!
That woman's like the Prior's niece who comes   170
To care about his asthma: it's the life!"
But there my triumph's straw-fire flared and funked;
Their betters took their turn to see and say:
The Prior and the learned pulled a face
And stopped all that in no time. "How? what's here?   175
Quite from the mark of painting, bless us all!
Faces, arms, legs, and bodies like the true

---

1 Dominican mendicant order of the Roman Catholic Church.

2 Dominicans (Black Friars) and Carmelites (White Friars).

As much as pea and pea! it's devil's-game!
Your business is not to catch men with show,
With homage to the perishable clay, 180
But lift them over it, ignore it all,
Make them forget there's such a thing as flesh.
Your business is to paint the souls of men—
Man's soul, and it's a fire, smoke...no, it's not...
It's vapor done up like a new-born babe— 185
(In that shape when you die it leaves your mouth)
It's...well, what matters talking, it's the soul!
Give us no more of body than shows soul!
Here's Giotto,[3] with his Saint a-praising God,
That sets us praising,—why not stop with him? 190
Why put all thoughts of praise out of our head
With wonder at lines, colors, and what not?
Paint the soul, never mind the legs and arms!
Rub all out, try at it a second time.
Oh, that white smallish female with the breasts, 195
She's just my niece...Herodias, I would say,—
Who went and danced and got men's heads cut off!
Have it all out!" Now, is this sense, I ask?
A fine way to paint soul, by painting body
So ill, the eye can't stop there, must go further 200
And can't fare worse! Thus, yellow does for white
When what you put for yellow's simply black,
And any sort of meaning looks intense
When all beside itself means and looks nought.
Why can't a painter lift each foot in turn, 205
Left foot and right foot, go a double step,
Make his flesh liker and his soul more like,
Both in their order? Take the prettiest face,
The Prior's niece...patron-saint—is it so pretty
You can't discover if it means hope, fear, 210
Sorrow or joy? won't beauty go with these?
Suppose I've made her eyes all right and blue,
Can't I take breath and try to add life's flash,
And then add soul and heighten them threefold?
Or say there's beauty with no soul at all— 215

---

3 The 14th century Florentine painter and architect Giotto di Bondone (1266/67–1337) is often praised as the father of European painting; his works portend the Renaissance style.

(I never saw it—put the case the same—)
If you get simple beauty and nought else,
You get about the best thing God invents:
That's somewhat: and you'll find the soul you have missed,
Within yourself, when you return him thanks.   220
"Rub all out!" Well, well, there's my life, in short,
And so the thing has gone on ever since.
I'm grown a man no doubt, I've broken bounds:
You should not take a fellow eight years old
And make him swear to never kiss the girls.   225
I'm my own master, paint now as I please—
Having a friend, you see, in the Corner-house!
Lord, it's fast holding by the rings in front—
Those great rings serve more purposes than just
To plant a flag in, or tie up a horse!   230
And yet the old schooling sticks, the old grave eyes
Are peeping o'er my shoulder as I work,
The heads shake still—"It's art's decline, my son!
You're not of the true painters, great and old;
Brother Angelico's[1] the man, you'll find;   235
Brother Lorenzo[2] stands his single peer:
Fag on at flesh, you'll never make the third!"
Flower o' the pine,
You keep your mistr...manners, and I'll stick to mine!
I'm not the third, then: bless us, they must know!   240
Don't you think they're the likeliest to know,
They with their Latin? So, I swallow my rage,
Clench my teeth, suck my lips in tight, and paint
To please them—sometimes do and sometimes don't;
For, doing most, there's pretty sure to come   245
A turn, some warm eve finds me at my saints—
A laugh, a cry, the business of the world—
(*Flower o' the peach*
Death for us all, and his own life for each!)
And my whole soul revolves, the cup runs over,   250
The world and life's too big to pass for a dream,
And I do these wild things in sheer despite,

---

1 Fra Angelico (1400–1455) was one of the great 15th century Italian painters.

2 Lorenzo Monaco (1372–1424), a Florentine painter and member of the Camaldolese monastery of Santa Maria degli Angeli.

And play the fooleries you catch me at,
In pure rage! The old mill-horse, out at grass
After hard years, throws up his stiff heels so,   255
Although the miller does not preach to him
The only good of grass is to make chaff.
What would men have? Do they like grass or no—
May they or mayn't they? all I want's the thing
Settled for ever one way. As it is,   260
You tell too many lies and hurt yourself:
You don't like what you only like too much,
You do like what, if given you at your word,
You find abundantly detestable.
For me, I think I speak as I was taught;   265
I always see the garden and God there
A-making man's wife: and, my lesson learned,
The value and significance of flesh,
I can't unlearn ten minutes afterwards.

    You understand me: I'm a beast, I know.   270
But see, now—why, I see as certainly
As that the morning-star's about to shine,
What will hap some day. We've a youngster here
Comes to our convent, studies what I do,
Slouches and stares and lets no atom drop: 275
His name is Guidi[3]—he'll not mind the monks—
They call him Hulking Tom, he lets them talk—
He picks my practice up—he'll paint apace,
I hope so—though I never live so long,
I know what's sure to follow. You be judge!   280
You speak no Latin more than I, belike;
However, you're my man, you've seen the world
—The beauty and the wonder and the power,
The shapes of things, their colors, lights and shades,
Changes, surprises,—and God made it all!   285
—For what? Do you feel thankful, ay or no,
For this fair town's face, yonder river's line,
The mountain round it and the sky above,
Much more the figures of man, woman, child,

3 Masaccio, byname of Tommaso di Giovanni di Simone Guidi (1401–1428), was an early Renais-
sance painter who drastically changed Florentine painting.

These are the frame to? What's it all about? 290
To be passed over, despised? or dwelt upon,
Wondered at? oh, this last of course!—you say.
But why not do as well as say,—paint these
Just as they are, careless what comes of it?
God's works—paint any one, and count it crime 295
To let a truth slip. Don't object, "His works
Are here already; nature is complete:
Suppose you reproduce her—(which you can't)
There's no advantage! you must beat her, then."
For, don't you mark? we're made so that we love 300
First when we see them painted, things we have passed
Perhaps a hundred times nor cared to see;
And so they are better, painted—better to us,
Which is the same thing. Art was given for that;
God uses us to help each other so, 305
Lending our minds out. Have you noticed, now,
Your cullion's[1] hanging face? A bit of chalk,
And trust me but you should, though! How much more,
If I drew higher things with the same truth!
That were to take the Prior's pulpit-place, 310
Interpret God to all of you! Oh, oh,
It makes me mad to see what men shall do
And we in our graves! This world's no blot for us,
Nor blank; it means intensely, and means good:
To find its meaning is my meat and drink. 315
"Ay, but you don't so instigate to prayer!"
Strikes in the Prior: "when your meaning's plain
It does not say to folk—remember matins,[2]
Or, mind you fast next Friday!" Why, for this
What need of art at all? A skull and bones, 320
Two bits of stick nailed crosswise, or, what's best,
A bell to chime the hour with, does as well.
I painted a Saint Laurence six months since
At Prato,[3] splashed the fresco in fine style:
"How looks my painting, now the scaffold's down?" 325
I ask a brother: "Hugely," he returns—

---

1 A low, mischievous person.

2 Morning prayer service.

3 Lippi painted frescoes in Prato Cathedral near Florence.

"Already not one phiz of your three slaves
Who turn the Deacon off his toasted side,
But's scratched and prodded to our heart's content,
The pious people have so eased their own   330
With coming to say prayers there in a rage:
We get on fast to see the bricks beneath.
Expect another job this time next year,
For pity and religion grow i' the crowd—
Your painting serves its purpose!" Hang the fools!   335

   —That is—you'll not mistake an idle word
Spoke in a huff by a poor monk, God wot,
Tasting the air this spicy night which turns
The unaccustomed head like Chianti wine!
Oh, the church knows! don't misreport me, now!   340
It's natural a poor monk out of bounds
Should have his apt word to excuse himself:
And hearken how I plot to make amends.
I have bethought me: I shall paint a piece
...There's for you! Give me six months, then go, see   345
Something in Sant'Ambrogio's![4] Bless the nuns!
They want a cast o' my office. I shall paint
God in the midst, Madonna and her babe,
Ringed by a bowery flowery angel-brood,
Lilies and vestments and white faces, sweet   350
As puff on puff of grated orris-root[5]
When ladies crowd to Church at midsummer.
And then i' the front, of course a saint or two—
Saint John,[6] because he saves the Florentines,
Saint Ambrose,[7] who puts down in black and white   355
The convent's friends and gives them a long day,
And Job, I must have him there past mistake,
The man of Uz[8] (and Us without the z,
Painters who need his patience). Well, all these

---

4 Sant'Ambrogio Basilica in Milan, Italy, is noted for its architecture.

5 A plant used in perfumes and medicines.

6 John the Baptist baptized Jesus. He is the patron saint of Florence.

7 Ambrose of Camaldoli (1386–1439), a patristic translator and member of the Camaldolese Order; or Saint Ambrose (339–397), bishop of Milan.

8 Job, from The Book of Job in the Hebrew Bible, lived in Uz. The book documents Job's attempt to understand his own undeserved suffering as well as the unmerited suffering of humankind.

Secured at their devotion, up shall come   360
Out of a corner when you least expect,
As one by a dark stair into a great light,
Music and talking, who but Lippo! I!—
Mazed, motionless and moonstruck—I'm the man!
Back I shrink—what is this I see and hear?   365
I, caught up with my monk's-things by mistake,
My old serge gown and rope that goes all round,
I, in this presence, this pure company!
Where's a hole, where's a corner for escape?
Then steps a sweet angelic slip of a thing   370
Forward, puts out a soft palm—"Not so fast!"
—Addresses the celestial presence, "nay—
He made you and devised you, after all,
Though he's none of you! Could Saint John there draw—
His camel-hair make up a painting-brush?   375
We come to brother Lippo for all that,
Iste perfecit opus!"[1] So, all smile—
I shuffle sideways with my blushing face
Under the cover of a hundred wings
Thrown like a spread of kirtles[2] when you're gay   380
And play hot cockles,[3] all the doors being shut,
Till, wholly unexpected, in there pops
The hothead husband! Thus I scuttle off
To some safe bench behind, not letting go
The palm of her, the little lily thing   385
That spoke the good word for me in the nick,
Like the Prior's niece...Saint Lucy,[4] I would say.
And so all's saved for me, and for the church
A pretty picture gained. Go, six months hence!
Your hand, sir, and good-bye: no lights, no lights!   390
The street's hushed, and I know my own way back,
Don't fear me! There's the grey beginning. Zooks!

1855

---

1 From the Latin, "This one painted the picture!"

2 A woman's gown or a man's tunic.

3 A euphemism for having sex with married women.

4 A virgin, martyr, and the patron of sight, Saint Lucy is also the patron saint of Sicily.

MATTHEW ARNOLD
1822–1888

Although it was Matthew Arnold's work as a critic that earned him a spott among the great literary figures, his name is closely linked to education reforms as well. The writer's father had an unmistakable impact on him; the Reverend Dr. Thomas Arnold became famous for transforming English school systems. Dr. Arnold had been appointed headmaster at Rugby School where young Arnold was sent when he was six years old. The boy experienced his father's magnetism first-hand. Both awed and disgusted by the Reverend's power as a reformer, Arnold rebelled against the teachings instilled in him. To counteract the parental control he endured at home and at school, Arnold refused to be serious. When he entered Oxford University, he adopted the fashionable, colorful attire of a dandy and rankled many of his peers with excessively jolly or slothful behavior.

Arnold idled away his time on frivolous activities, but he proved his ambition by winning a fellowship at Oriel College in 1845. Two years later, he accepted the post of private secretary to Lord Lansdowne, an important politician. His job provided ample time for travel and poetry. Arnold became deeply conscious of literature's ability to shape national life after he journeyed to Paris during the Revolution of 1848. France's political and cultural atmosphere remained a model for Arnold's later criticisms of British life. His travels to France and Switzerland also stimulated his first volume, *The Strayed Reveler and Other Poems*, which he published under the pseudonym A in 1849. Darkly philosophical and surprisingly solemn, Arnold displayed an early understanding of the significance and value of English literature.

He married Frances Lucy Wightman in 1851, and though they enjoyed an affable marriage, Arnold's cheerfulness was blighted by the early deaths of three sons. His profession was also physically and spiritually taxing. As a government school inspector (he had been appointed to the position shortly before his marriage), he constantly travelled, worked long hours, and performed monotonous duties. More importantly, he witnessed the aftermath of a modern industrial society–cities saturated with pollution and brimming with garbage, children diseased and starving in the streets–and the intellectual and emotional emptiness that resulted from it. Haunted by his observations, Arnold questioned how people could achieve meaningful lives in the midst of abject suffering. Writing became his vessel for edifying the public. Intense occupational demands deprived him of writing time, but he nevertheless recognized the importance of his work and held the post for thirty-five years. His experiences shaped his publications; since he trekked across England and the Continent extensively, Arnold drew cross-cultural comparisons and had continuous sources of information for poetry and prose.

Modern poetry, Arnold remarked, is "the dialogue of the mind with itself." He wrote relatively few poems, but his compositions reflect his own internal struggles. His style is elegiac and nostalgic despite his attempts to avoid the introspective laments of the Romantic poets. Arnold was skeptical of his predecessors' beliefs on creativity and nature; he treated the natural world scientifically, but he did not reduce it to an idyllic backdrop. Rather, he bonded the landscapes in his poems with the meaning he attempted to convey, as exemplified in his most famous poem, "Dover Beach":

> Sophocles long ago
> Heard it on the Aegean, and it brought
> Into his mind the turbid ebb and flow
> Of human misery; we
> Find also in the sound a thought,
> Hearing it by this distant northern sea.

Beneath his cheerful demeanor, Arnold brooded over the same agonies that afflicted his contemporaries. He echoed the cries of his age by illustrating the apparent weakness of nature, the deterioration of traditional faith, and a human need to make the outer world conform to one's inner feelings.

Arnold was elected professor of poetry at Oxford in honor of his accomplishments. His professorship concluded after ten years, at which point he began the second phase of his literary career. With the support of some and the disapproval of others, Arnold turned from poetry to prose. Feeling that prose would better serve the public, Arnold dedicated himself to criticizing English national life, beliefs, and tastes until his death in 1888. Criticism, he asserted, provided a means of awakening greater intelligence because it provoked new ideas. His exposure to other European cultures made him cognizant of the areas where England lagged behind. Spreading a sense of culture–beyond the learned and elite–became his antidote. As Arnold states in *Culture and Anarchy*, culture is "the best that has been thought and said" in the world; culture can remedy the moral chaos, physical misery, and anarchy in society. He elaborated on his views in numerous essays, all of which can be divided into four categories: literary, social, political, and religious.

Arnold's reputation as a critic and controversialist developed during the 1860s when he began writing literary criticism. His preliminary ideas are outlined in *Essays in Criticism*, which has remained a benchmark of the tradition of English literary criticism since its first publication in 1865. As he predicted in "The Study of Poetry," people will increasingly "turn to poetry to interpret life for us, to console us, to sustain us" as traditional religion crumbles. He urged Britons to view poetry as a source of moral support and clarity. He claimed the future of poetry was immense and profound; therefore, he argued for a separation of good poetry from great poetry. He references "touchstones"–passages from recognized masters that are distinguished for their seriousness, diction, and impersonality–to determine the relative merit of literature. Arnold further asserted that British readers must familiarize themselves with literature outside the English canon to better educate themselves.

Arnold insisted that education was too vital to be left to private provision. After Essays in Criticism, he shifted his attention to social and political criticism. His most important social essay, *Culture and Anarchy*, examines the features Victorian society emphasizes: complacency, moralism, and practicality. Using culture as a lens, he crafts an ideal of human life centered on aesthetic, intellectual, and moral enrichment. He isolates individualism as a root of Britain's faltering civilization; individualism, he declares, prohibits the formation of a collective national community. He further questions democracy as a solution to the lawless impulses of society. In his own lifetime and after, Arnold was attacked as conservative, authoritarian, and elitist for his views.

Constant demands to write and speak evidenced Arnold's authority as a public figure. By the 1870s, he addressed a wide readership, but he received severe criticism for his religious writings. Arnold held that religious narrowness was a primary obstacle to culture. Consequently, he scorned theology that was constructed on the shifting beliefs of present times. He also waged forthright attacks on the literalist interpretation of the Bible; he incensed some believers after effectively accusing them of poor literary analysis and misinterpretation. Arnold did not discredit religion. Though his other writings note its decay, he regarded religion highly and emphasized its role in a full life.

Arnold's reputation was not limited to Britain; he made two lecture tours to the United States. He revealed several identities through different kinds of publication. At times, he showed a frigid moral and intellectual temper; alternately, he displayed amicability. Regardless of his external behavior, he possessed a genuine consciousness of English society and life. His legacy endures because he served not only as a literary critic, but a social, political, and religious one as well.

1822	Matthew Arnold born 24 December
1841–44	Attends Balliol College, Oxford University
1849	*The Strayed Reveler and Other Poems*
1851	Appointed government school inspector; Marries Frances Lucy Wightman
1857–67	Serves as professor of poetry at Oxford University
1865	*Essays in Criticism*
1867	*New Poems* (including "Dover Beach")
1869	*Culture and Anarchy*
1871	*Friendship's Garland*
1875	*God and the Bible*
1880	"The Study of Poetry
1888	Arnold dies of congestive heart failure 15 April and is buried at All Saints church, Laleham

MEMORIAL VERSES

Goethe[1] in Weimar sleeps, and Greece,
Long since, saw Byron's struggle cease.
But one such death remain'd to come;
The last poetic voice is dumb—
We stand to-day by Wordsworth's tomb   5
When Byron's eyes were shut in death,

We bow'd our head, and held our breath.
He taught us little; but our soul
Had *felt* him like the thunder's roll.
With shivering heart the strife we saw   10
Of passion with eternal law;
And yet with reverential awe
We watch'd the fount of fiery life
Which served for that Titanic strife.

When Goethe's death was told, we said: 15
Sunk, then, is Europe's sagest head.
Physician of the iron age,
Goethe has done his pilgrimage.
He took the suffering human race,
He read each wound, each weakness clear;   20
And struck his finger on the place,
And said: *Thou ailest here, and here!*
He look'd on Europe's dying hour
Of fitful dream and feverish power;
His eye plunged down the weltering strife,   25
The turmoil of expiring life—
He said: *The end is everywhere,*
Art still has truth, take refuge there!
And he was happy, if to know
Causes of things, and far below   30
His feet to see the lurid flow

---

1 The German poet, playwright, novelist, and theatre director Johann Wolfgang von Goethe
(1749–1832) adopted Weimar as his homeland and conducted most of his writing and work there.

Of terror, and insane distress,
And headlong fate be happiness.

And Wordsworth!—Ah, pale ghosts, rejoice!
For never has such soothing voice   35
Been to your shadowy world convey'd,
Since erst, at morn, some wandering shade
Heard the clear song of Orpheus[1] come
Through Hades and the mournful gloom.
Wordsworth has gone from us—and ye,   40
Ah, may ye feel his voice as we!
He too upon a wintry clime
Had fallen—on this iron time
Of doubts, disputes, distractions, fears.
He found us when the age had bound   45
Our souls in its benumbing round;
He spoke, and loosed our heart in tears.
He laid us as we lay at birth
On the cool flowery lap of earth,
Smiles broke from us, and we had ease;   50
The hills were round us, and the breeze
Went o'er the sun-lit fields again;
Our foreheads felt the wind and rain.
Our youth return'd; for there was shed
On spirits that had long been dead,   55
Spirits dried up and closely furl'd,
The freshness of the early world.

Ah! since dark days still bring to light
Man's prudence and man's fiery might,
Time may restore us in his course   60
Goethe's sage mind and Byron's force;
But where will Europe's latter hour
Again find Wordsworth's healing power?
Others will teach us how to dare,
And against fear our breast to steel;   65
Others will strengthen us to bear—
But who, ah! who will make us feel?

---

1 The Greek hero Orpheus descended into the underworld and used his superhuman musical abilities
to persuade Hades to free Eurydice, Orpheus's wife.

The cloud of mortal destiny,
Others will front it fearlessly—
But who, like him, will put it by? 70
Keep fresh the grass upon his grave,
O Rotha,[2] with thy living wave!
Sing him thy best! for few or none
Hear thy voice right, now he is gone.

1850

DOVER BEACH

The sea is calm to-night.
The tide is full, the moon lies fair
Upon the straits;—on the French coast the light
Gleams and is gone; the cliffs of England stand,
Glimmering and vast, out in the tranquil bay. 5
Come to the window, sweet is the night-air!
Only, from the long line of spray
Where the sea meets the moon-blanch'd sand,
Listen! you hear the grating roar
Of pebbles which the waves draw back, and fling, 10
At their return, up the high strand,
Begin and cease, and then again begin,
With tremulous cadence slow, and bring
The eternal note of sadness in.

Sophocles[3] long ago 15
Heard it on the Ægean,[4] and it brought
Into his mind the turbid ebb and flow
Of human misery; we
Find also in the sound a thought,
Hearing it by this distant northern sea. 20

---

2 The Rotha River in England.
3 The Grecian Sophocles (c. 496 BCE–406) was a tragic playwright.
4 The Aegean Sea is located between the Greek peninsula and Turkey.

    The Sea of Faith
Was once, too, at the full, and round earth's shore
Lay like the folds of a bright girdle furl'd.
But now I only hear
Its melancholy, long, withdrawing roar,   25
Retreating, to the breath
Of the night-wind, down the vast edges drear
And naked shingles of the world.

Ah, love, let us be true
To one another! for the world, which seems   30
To lie before us like a land of dreams,
So various, so beautiful, so new,
Hath really neither joy, nor love, nor light,
Nor certitude, nor peace, nor help for pain;
And we are here as on a darkling plain   35
Swept with confused alarms of struggle and flight,
Where ignorant armies clash by night.

1850

CHRISTINA ROSSETTI
1830–1894

Christina Rossetti's father, an exiled Italian patriot and Dante scholar, classified his four children as two calms and two storms. Energetic, spirited, and short-tempered, young Christina was undoubtedly a storm. Her childhood was filled with family visits to the zoo, chess matches, and bouts-rimés, a sonnet rhyming game. Like her siblings, she cultivated an early love for literature and art. She was encouraged to draw and write, and she excelled in composing verses. Rossetti's earliest poems were addressed to her mother, a former governess who educated all her children. As a tribute to their intimate relationship, Rossetti dedicated her first privately-printed volume of poems, *Verses*, and all but two of her later books to her mother.

The family's stability ruptured permanently when Rossetti's father fell too ill to continue teaching. While the rest of her family found employment outside the home, Rossetti tended to her father and stabilized her own condition. When she was about fifteen years old, her health collapsed. Afterward, her wellbeing was never as strong as it had once been, nor was her disposition ever the same. In his memoir of his sister, William Michael noted that Rossetti's personality was wholly altered after her illness and treatment: "Her temperament and character, naturally warm and free, became 'a fountain sealed'." William Michael's biblical allusion to a fountain sealed, as well as other documents referencing this period of Rossetti's life, has allowed scholars to extrapolate connections between Rossetti's apparent transformation and her submersion into the Church of England. An earnest and devout Anglican since girlhood, she became deeply involved with the Anglo-Catholic movement in the Church, which occurred at approximately the same time as her collapse. Valuing religion above her desires and emotions, she adhered to strict behavioral codes and practiced self-denial. She became obsessively self-aware and hyperconscious of vanity, idleness, and sin, all themes which would color her work.

Rossetti rejected both of her suitors on religious grounds alone. Her first suitor, a member of her brother Dante Gabriel's Pre-Raphaelite painting group, proposed to marry her in 1849. Their engagement was broken off after he reverted to Roman Catholicism. She refused to marry Charles Cayley, a former student of her father's, after discovering that his beliefs were not as firm as her own. Cayley remained a friend until his death in 1883. With no further proposals forthcoming, she devoted her life to her religious beliefs, cared for her family, volunteered at a penitentiary for "fallen" women, and wrote poetry.

Rossetti published numerous poems in ladies' annuals and magazines under the pseudonym Ellen Alleyn, but it was *Goblin Market and Other Poems*, her first collection published under her own name, that spurred her career. The volume earned universal praise. Reviewers commended the heartfelt emotion, lucidity, and piety that characterized her writing. *Goblin Market*, the title poem, is her most discussed work and a major contributor to the survival of her posthumous reputation. As a critic from the *London Quarterly Review* stated, "[t]he narrative has so matter-of-fact, and at the same time so fantastic and bewildering an air, that we are fairly puzzled into acceptance of everything." The poem's naiveté fooled some readers into accepting *Goblin Market* as a moral fable for children. It is more than an anecdote about sisterly love; closer inspection discloses the sensuousness of the goblin fruit and underlying religious themes of temptation, sin, and redemption.

Nearly all of Rossetti's work after 1866 is devotional. Emphasizing the virtuous path, the insufficiency of mortal love, and the transitory nature of life, her religious works are notable for their fervor and sincerity. In her later years, Rossetti frequently delved into a line-by-line study of the books of the Bible. In her late work *The Face of the Deep*, she provides detailed commentary on the Apocalypse as predicted in the book of Revelation. Nineteenth-century admirers promoted her as a wholly Christian writer, but twentieth-century biographers have since reconsidered her work through the lens of her life experiences. Critics, for example, generally trace the recurrent theme of unfulfilled love to Rossetti's failed romantic relationship with Cayley. Similarly, the conflict between public and private selves that appears in *Maude* is paralleled by Rossetti's external apologetic behavior but her inward confidence.

As a female poet, Rossetti was conscious of the prejudices she faced; in writing about religion, she additionally encroached into traditionally-male territory. She nevertheless defended the female poet's right to explore indelicate issues. Rossetti has been criticized and praised for her assessment of gender relations and exploration of traditional gender roles. While she encourages submission and obedience to divinity and authority in some poems, her work is dually assertive, confrontational, and subversive. Her views waver. For example, in *Goblin Market*, female solidarity and loyalty triumph over the possessive and predatory goblin men. The dramatic monologue "Cousin Kate," however, defies sisterly bonds; the speaker feels betrayed when her cousin marries the lord with whom she has a child. The speaker loves the lord, yet she is shunned and reduced to his "plaything" while her cousin is prized as his wife. Rossetti does not simplify gender issues in her poetry; rather, she offers a range of ambiguous motives and meanings.

Early in the 1860s, Rossetti came into contact with female artists and poets, but despite her growing reputation, she refrained from joining literary circles. Her health continued to deteriorate, and in 1872, her recurrent illness was finally diagnosed as Graves' disease, a rare autoimmune disease that weakened her physically and permanently altered her looks. Her habits became more reclusive. She continued to write occasional pieces and often donated her works to Christian charities she supported, such as the Society for Promoting Christian Knowledge and the Anti-Vivisectionist League. At the time of her death in 1895, her status as a female poet rivaled Elizabeth Barret Browning's. Her posthumous reputation has since superseded those of her popular contemporaries.

1830	Christina Rossetti born 5 December
1847	*Verses*
1862	*Goblin Market and Other Poems*
1866	*The Prince's Progress and Other Poems*
1870	*Commonplace and Other Short Stories*
1872	Diagnosed with Graves' disease; *Sing-Song: A Nursery Rhyme Book*
1874	*Speaking Likenesses; Annus Domini*
1881	*Monna Innominata*
1885	*Time Flies: A Reading Diary*
1892	*The Face of the Deep*
1894	Rossetti dies 2 January due to breast cancer and is buried in her family plot at Highgate Cemetery, London

GOBLIN MARKET

Morning and evening
Maids heard the goblins cry: [Temptation of women/girls specifically]
"Come buy our orchard fruits,
Come buy, come buy:
Apples and quinces,   5
Lemons and oranges,
Plump unpecked cherries,
Melons and raspberries,
Bloom-down-cheeked peaches,
Swart-headed mulberries,   10
Wild free-born cranberries,
Crab-apples, dewberries,
Pine-apples, blackberries,
Apricots, strawberries;—
All ripe together   15
In summer weather,—   [abundance]
Morns that pass by,
Fair eves that fly;
Come buy, come buy:
Our grapes fresh from the vine,   20
Pomegranates full and fine,
Dates and sharp bullaces,
Rare pears and greengages,
Damsons and bilberries,
Taste them and try: 25
Currants and gooseberries,
Bright-fire-like barberries,
Figs to fill your mouth,
Citrons from the South,
Sweet to tongue and sound to eye;   30
Come buy, come buy."

　Evening by evening
Among the brookside rushes,
Laura bowed her head to hear,
Lizzie veiled her blushes: 35

Crouching close together
In the cooling weather,
With clasping arms and cautioning lips,
With tingling cheeks and finger tips.
"Lie close," Laura said,   40
Pricking up her golden head:
"We must not look at goblin men,
We must not buy their fruits:
Who knows upon what soil they fed
Their hungry thirsty roots?"   45
"Come buy," call the goblins
Hobbling down the glen.
"Oh," cried Lizzie, "Laura, Laura,
You should not peep at goblin men."
Lizzie covered up her eyes,   50
Covered close lest they should look;
Laura reared her glossy head,
And whispered like the restless brook:
"Look, Lizzie, look, Lizzie,
Down the glen tramp little men.   55
One hauls a basket,
One bears a plate,
One lugs a golden dish
Of many pounds weight.
How fair the vine must grow   60
Whose grapes are so luscious;
How warm the wind must blow
Through those fruit bushes."
"No," said Lizzie "No, no, no;
Their offers should not charm us, — *Deceptive, evil,*   65
Their evil gifts would harm us." *harmful nature;*
She thrust a dimpled finger   *temptation*
In each ear, shut eyes and ran:
Curious Laura chose to linger — *Eve also driven*
Wondering at each merchant man. *by curiosity*   70
One had a cat's face,
One whisked a tail,
One tramped at a rat's pace,
One crawled like a snail,
One like a wombat prowled obtuse and furry,   75
One like a ratel tumbled hurry skurry.

She heard a voice like voice of doves
Cooing all together:
They sounded kind and full of loves — Temptation /
In the pleasant weather.   deception   80

   Laura stretched her gleaming neck
Like a rush-imbedded swan,
Like a lily from the beck,
Like a moonlit poplar branch,
Like a vessel at the launch   85
When its last restraint is gone.

   Backwards up the mossy glen
Turned and trooped the goblin men,
With their shrill repeated cry,
"Come buy, come buy."   90
When they reached where Laura was
They stood stock still upon the moss,
Leering at each other,
Brother with queer brother;
Signalling each other,   95
Brother with sly brother.
One set his basket down,
One reared his plate;
One began to weave a crown
Of tendrils, leaves and rough nuts brown   100
(Men sell not such in any town);
One heaved the golden weight
Of dish and fruit to offer her:
"Come buy, come buy," was still their cry.
Laura stared but did not stir,   105
Longed but had no money:
The whisk-tailed merchant bade her taste — Temptation /
In tones as smooth as honey,   deception
The cat-faced purr'd,
The rat-faced spoke a word   110
Of welcome, and the snail-paced even was heard;
One parrot-voiced and jolly
Cried "Pretty Goblin" still for "Pretty Polly;"—
One whistled like a bird.

But sweet-tooth Laura spoke in haste: 115
"Good folk, I have no coin;
To take were to purloin:
I have no copper in my purse,
I have no silver either,
And all my gold is on the furze   120
That shakes in windy weather
Above the rusty heather."
"You have much gold upon your head,"
They answered all together:
"Buy from us with a golden curl."   125
She clipped a precious golden lock,
She dropped a tear more rare than pearl,
Then sucked their fruit globes fair or red:
Sweeter than honey from the rock,
Stronger than man-rejoicing wine,   130
Clearer than water flowed that juice;
She never tasted such before,
How should it cloy with length of use?
She sucked and sucked and sucked the more
Fruits which that unknown orchard bore;   135
She sucked until her lips were sore;
Then flung the emptied rinds away
But gathered up one kernel stone,
And knew not was it night or day
As she turned home alone.   140

    Lizzie met her at the gate
Full of wise upbraidings:
"Dear, you should not stay so late,
Twilight is not good for maidens;
Should not loiter in the glen   145
In the haunts of goblin men.
Do you not remember Jeanie,
How she met them in the moonlight,
Took their gifts both choice and many,
Ate their fruits and wore their flowers   150
Plucked from bowers
Where summer ripens at all hours?

But ever in the noonlight
She pined and pined away;
Sought them by night and day,   155
Found them no more, but dwindled and grew grey;
Then fell with the first snow,
While to this day no grass will grow
Where she lies low:
I planted daisies there a year ago   160
That never blow.
You should not loiter so."
"Nay, hush," said Laura:
"Nay, hush, my sister:
I ate and ate my fill,   165
Yet my mouth waters still;
To-morrow night I will
Buy more:" and kissed her:
"Have done with sorrow;
I'll bring you plums to-morrow   170
Fresh on their mother twigs,
Cherries worth getting;
You cannot think what figs
My teeth have met in,
What melons icy-cold   175
Piled on a dish of gold
Too huge for me to hold,
What peaches with a velvet nap,
Pellucid grapes without one seed:
Odorous indeed must be the mead   180
Whereon they grow, and pure the wave they drink
With lilies at the brink,
And sugar-sweet their sap."

   Golden head by golden head,
Like two pigeons in one nest   185
Folded in each other's wings,
They lay down in their curtained bed:
Like two blossoms on one stem,
Like two flakes of new-fall'n snow,
Like two wands of ivory   190
Tipped with gold for awful kings.
Moon and stars gazed in at them,

Wind sang to them lullaby,
Lumbering owls forbore to fly,
Not a bat flapped to and fro   195
Round their rest:
Cheek to cheek and breast to breast
Locked together in one nest.

   Early in the morning
When the first cock crowed his warning,   200
Neat like bees, as sweet and busy,
Laura rose with Lizzie:
Fetched in honey, milked the cows,
Aired and set to rights the house,
Kneaded cakes of whitest wheat,   205
Cakes for dainty mouths to eat,
Next churned butter, whipped up cream,
Fed their poultry, sat and sewed;
Talked as modest maidens should:
Lizzie with an open heart,   210
Laura in an absent dream,
One content, one sick in part;
One warbling for the mere bright day's delight,
One longing for the night.

   At length slow evening came: 215
They went with pitchers to the reedy brook;
Lizzie most placid in her look,
Laura most like a leaping flame.
They drew the gurgling water from its deep;
Lizzie plucked purple and rich golden flags,   220
Then turning homeward said: "The sunset flushes
Those furthest loftiest crags;
Come, Laura, not another maiden lags,
No wilful squirrel wags,
The beasts and birds are fast asleep."   225
But Laura loitered still among the rushes
And said the bank was steep.

   And said the hour was early still
The dew not fall'n, the wind not chill:
Listening ever, but not catching   230

The customary cry,
"Come buy, come buy,"
With its iterated jingle
Of sugar-baited words: — *Temptation / deception*
Not for all her watching   235
Once discerning even one goblin
Racing, whisking, tumbling, hobbling;
Let alone the herds
That used to tramp along the glen,
In groups or single,   240
Of brisk fruit-merchant men.

Till Lizzie urged, "O Laura, come;
I hear the fruit-call but I dare not look:
You should not loiter longer at this brook:
Come with me home.   245
The stars rise, the moon bends her arc,
Each glowworm winks her spark,
Let us get home before the night grows dark:
For clouds may gather
Though this is summer weather,   250
Put out the lights and drench us through;
Then if we lost our way what should we do?"

  Laura turned cold as stone
To find her sister heard that cry alone,
That goblin cry,   255
"Come buy our fruits, come buy."
Must she then buy no more such dainty fruit?
Must she no more such succous pasture find,
Gone deaf and blind? — *fruit of knowledge is "eye-opening";*
Tree of knowledge vs. tree of life Her tree of life drooped from the root: *contrast*   260
She said not one word in her heart's sore ache;
But peering thro' the dimness, nought discerning,
Trudged home, her pitcher dripping all the way;
So crept to bed, and lay
Silent till Lizzie slept;   265
Then sat up in a passionate yearning,
And gnashed her teeth for baulked desire, and wept
As if her heart would break.

Day after day, night after night,
Laura kept watch in vain   270
In sullen silence of exceeding pain.
She never caught again the goblin cry:
"Come buy, come buy;"—
She never spied the goblin men
Hawking their fruits along the glen: 275
But when the noon waxed bright   — *Aging quickens; now knows*
Her hair grew thin and grey;   *suffering*
She dwindled, as the fair full moon doth turn
To swift decay and burn
Her fire away.   280

One day remembering her kernel-stone __ *seed motif?*
She set it by a wall that faced the south;
Dewed it with tears, hoped for a root,
Watched for a waxing shoot,
But there came none;   285
It never saw the sun,
It never felt the trickling moisture run:
While with sunk eyes and faded mouth
She dreamed of melons, as a traveller sees
False waves in desert drouth   290
With shade of leaf-crowned trees,
And burns the thirstier in the sandful breeze.

She no more swept the house,
Tended the fowls or cows,
Fetched honey, kneaded cakes of wheat,   295
Brought water from the brook:
But sat down listless in the chimney-nook
And would not eat.

Tender Lizzie could not bear
To watch her sister's cankerous care   300
Yet not to share.
She night and morning
Caught the goblins' cry:
"Come buy our orchard fruits,
Come buy, come buy:"—   305

Beside the brook, along the glen,
She heard the tramp of goblin men,
The voice and stir
Poor Laura could not hear;
Longed to buy fruit to comfort her,   310
But feared to pay too dear.
She thought of Jeanie in her grave,
Who should have been a bride;
But who for joys brides hope to have
Fell sick and died   315
In her gay prime,
In earliest Winter time,
With the first glazing rime,
With the first snow-fall of crisp Winter time.

    Till Laura dwindling   320
Seemed knocking at Death's door:
Then Lizzie weighed no more
Better and worse;
But put a silver penny in her purse,
Kissed Laura, crossed the heath with clumps of furze   325
At twilight, halted by the brook:
And for the first time in her life
Began to listen and look.

    Laughed every goblin
When they spied her peeping: 330
Came towards her hobbling,
Flying, running, leaping,
Puffing and blowing,
Chuckling, clapping, crowing,
Clucking and gobbling,   335
Mopping and mowing,
Full of airs and graces,
Pulling wry faces,
Demure grimaces,
Cat-like and rat-like,   340
Ratel- and wombat-like,
Snail-paced in a hurry,
Parrot-voiced and whistler,
Helter skelter, hurry skurry,

Chattering like magpies,   345
Fluttering like pigeons,
Gliding like fishes,—
Hugged her and kissed her,
Squeezed and caressed her:
Stretched up their dishes,   350
Panniers, and plates:
"Look at our apples
Russet and dun,
Bob at our cherries,
Bite at our peaches,   355
Citrons and dates,
Grapes for the asking,
Pears red with basking
Out in the sun,
Plums on their twigs;   360
Pluck them and suck them,
Pomegranates, figs."—

    "Good folk," said Lizzie,
Mindful of Jeanie:
"Give me much and many:"—   365
Held out her apron,
Tossed them her penny.
"Nay, take a seat with us,
Honour and eat with us,"
They answered grinning: 370
"Our feast is but beginning.
Night yet is early,
Warm and dew-pearly,
Wakeful and starry:
Such fruits as these   375
No man can carry;
Half their bloom would fly,
Half their dew would dry,
Half their flavour would pass by.
Sit down and feast with us,   380
Be welcome guest with us,
Cheer you and rest with us."—
"Thank you," said Lizzie: "But one waits
At home alone for me:

So without further parleying,   385
If you will not sell me any
Of your fruits though much and many,
Give me back my silver penny
I tossed you for a fee."—
They began to scratch their pates,   390
No longer wagging, purring,
But visibly demurring,
Grunting and snarling.
One called her proud,
Cross-grained, uncivil;   395
Their tones waxed loud,
Their looks were evil.
Lashing their tails
They trod and hustled her,
Elbowed and jostled her,   400
Clawed with their nails,
Barking, mewing, hissing, mocking,
Tore her gown and soiled her stocking,
Twitched her hair out by the roots,
Stamped upon her tender feet,   405
Held her hands and squeezed their fruits
Against her mouth to make her eat.

    White and golden Lizzie stood,   — Colors associated
Like a lily in a flood,—   w/ purity
Like a rock of blue-veined stone   410
Lashed by tides obstreperously,—
Like a beacon left alone
In a hoary roaring sea,
Sending up a golden fire,—
Like a fruit-crowned orange-tree   415
White with blossoms honey-sweet
Sore beset by wasp and bee,—
Like a royal virgin town
Topped with gilded dome and spire
Close beleaguered by a fleet   420
Mad to tug her standard down.

One may lead a horse to water,
Twenty cannot make him drink.
Though the goblins cuffed and caught her,
Coaxed and fought her,   425
Bullied and besought her,
Scratched her, pinched her black as ink,
Kicked and knocked her,
Mauled and mocked her,
Lizzie uttered not a word;   430
Would not open lip from lip
Lest they should cram a mouthful in:
But laughed in heart to feel the drip
Of juice that syrupped all her face,
And lodged in dimples of her chin,   435
And streaked her neck which quaked like curd.
At last the evil people,
Worn out by her resistance,
Flung back her penny, kicked their fruit
Along whichever road they took,   440
Not leaving root or stone or shoot;
Some writhed into the ground,
Some dived into the brook
With ring and ripple,
Some scudded on the gale without a sound,   445
Some vanished in the distance.

In a smart, ache, tingle,
Lizzie went her way;
Knew not was it night or day;
Sprang up the bank, tore thro' the furze,   450
Threaded copse and dingle,
And heard her penny jingle
Bouncing in her purse,—
Its bounce was music to her ear.
She ran and ran   455
As if she feared some goblin man
Dogged her with gibe or curse
Or something worse:
But not one goblin skurried after,

Nor was she pricked by fear;   460
The kind heart made her windy-paced
That urged her home quite out of breath with haste
And inward laughter.

   She cried "Laura," up the garden,
"Did you miss me?   465
Come and kiss me.
Never mind my bruises,
Hug me, kiss me, suck my juices
Squeezed from goblin fruits for you,
Goblin pulp and goblin dew.   470
Eat me, drink me, love me;
Laura, make much of me:
For your sake I have braved the glen
And had to do with goblin merchant men."

   Laura started from her chair,   475
Flung her arms up in the air,
Clutched her hair:
"Lizzie, Lizzie, have you tasted
For my sake the fruit forbidden?
Must your light like mine be hidden,   480
Your young life like mine be wasted,
Undone in mine undoing,
And ruined in my ruin,
Thirsty, cankered, goblin-ridden?"—
She clung about her sister,   485
Kissed and kissed and kissed her:
Tears once again
Refreshed her shrunken eyes,
Dropping like rain
After long sultry drouth;   490
Shaking with aguish fear, and pain,
She kissed and kissed her with a hungry mouth.

   Her lips began to scorch,
That juice was wormwood to her tongue,
She loathed the feast: 495
Writhing as one possessed she leaped and sung,
Rent all her robe, and wrung

Her hands in lamentable haste,
And beat her breast.
Her locks streamed like the torch   500
Borne by a racer at full speed,
Or like the mane of horses in their flight,
Or like an eagle when she stems the light
Straight toward the sun,
Or like a caged thing freed,   505
Or like a flying flag when armies run.

   Swift fire spread through her veins, knocked at her heart,
Met the fire smouldering there
And overbore its lesser flame;
She gorged on bitterness without a name: 510
Ah! fool, to choose such part
Of soul-consuming care!
Sense failed in the mortal strife:
Like the watch-tower of a town
Which an earthquake shatters down,   515
Like a lightning-stricken mast,
Like a wind-uprooted tree
Spun about,
Like a foam-topped waterspout
Cast down headlong in the sea,   520
She fell at last;
Pleasure past and anguish past,
Is it death or is it life?

   Life out of death.   / Christ - like
That night long Lizzie watched by her,   525
Counted her pulse's flagging stir,
Felt for her breath,
Held water to her lips, and cooled her face
With tears and fanning leaves:
But when the first birds chirped about their eaves, 530
And early reapers plodded to the place
Of golden sheaves,
And dew-wet grass
Bowed in the morning winds so brisk to pass,
And new buds with new day   535
Opened of cup-like lilies on the stream,

Laura awoke as from a dream,
Laughed in the innocent old way, —
Hugged Lizzie but not twice or thrice;
Her gleaming locks showed not one thread of grey,   540
Her breath was sweet as May
And light danced in her eyes.

   Days, weeks, months, years
Afterwards, when both were wives
With children of their own;   545
Their mother-hearts beset with fears,
Their lives bound up in tender lives;
Laura would call the little ones
And tell them of her early prime,
Those pleasant days long gone   550
Of not-returning time:
Would talk about the haunted glen,
The wicked, quaint fruit-merchant men,
Their fruits like honey to the throat
But poison in the blood;   555
(Men sell not such in any town:)
Would tell them how her sister stood
In deadly peril to do her good,
And win the fiery antidote:
Then joining hands to little hands   560
Would bid them cling together,
"For there is no friend like a sister
In calm or stormy weather;
To cheer one on the tedious way,
To fetch one if one goes astray,   565
To lift one if one totters down,
To strengthen whilst one stands."

1862

UP-HILL

"Does the road wind up-hill all the way?"
  "Yes, to the very end."
"Will the day's journey take the whole long day?"
  "From morn to night, my friend."

"But is there for the night a resting-place?"   5
  "A roof for when the slow dark hours begin."
"May not the darkness hide it from my face?"
  "You cannot miss that inn."

"Shall I meet other wayfarers at night?"
  "Those who have gone before."   10
"Then must I knock, or call when just in sight?"
  "They will not keep you standing at that door."

"Shall I find comfort, travel-sore and weak?"
  "Of labor you shall find the sum."
"Will there be beds for me and all who seek?"   15
  "Yea, beds for all who come."

1862

COBWEBS

It is a land with neither night nor day,
   Nor heat nor cold, nor any wind nor rain,
   Nor hills nor valleys: but one even plain
Stretches through long unbroken miles away,
While through the sluggish air a twilight grey   5
   Broodeth: no moons or seasons wax and wane,
   No ebb and flow are there among the main,
No bud-time, no leaf-falling, there for aye:—
No ripple on the sea, no shifting sand,
   No beat of wings to stir the stagnant space: 10
No pulse of life through all the loveless land
And loveless sea; no trace of days before,
   No guarded home, no toil-worn resting-place
No future hope, no fear for evermore.

1904

GERARD MANLEY HOPKINS
1844–1889

Gerard Manley Hopkins was the first of nine children born to a Protestant family. An adept student, he won a poetry prize at Highgate School in 1860 and exhibited his intellect at Balliol College, Oxford, where he graduated with first-class honors. Intending to be a professional painter but fascinated with language, Hopkins's time at the University of Oxford was characterized by an exuberant social life and prolific writing; he penned poems, dramatic fragments, and other compositions so rapidly and in such great quantities that he began to regard his activity as promiscuity. To tame his self-indulgent lifestyle, he familiarized himself with the disciplines and doctrines of Roman Catholicism. He was received into the Roman Catholic Church in 1866—a decision that anguished his parents—and later decided to become a priest.

In an act he referred to as "slaughter of the innocents," Hopkins methodically burned his poetry after determining "to write no more, as not belonging to my profession." He became a Jesuit, entering one of the most severely-disciplined and structured orders with the hope of regulating his life. With the exception of a journal containing his responses to nature and philosophy, he forsook writing until 1875. He ended his hiatus after reading a newspaper report about five Franciscan nuns who drowned in a shipwreck. Moved by the event, he composed the long narrative ode "The Wreck of the Deutschland." He submitted the poem for publication in a Jesuit periodical, but after repeated delays, Hopkins claimed that the editor "dared not print it." He was left with an enduring feeling of rejection from his own community and rarely submitted his work for publication.

Hopkins nevertheless continued to write, electing to compose sonnets because he felt guilty for devoting extensive time to his poetry. During the spring of 1877, he wrote a series of lyrical sonnets, among which are "God's Grandeur," "The Windhover," "Pied Beauty," and some of his other well-known poems. Sonnets from this year largely celebrate Hopkins's appreciation of the natural beauty that surrounded him. His poetry reflects the ideas of Duns Scotus, a medieval theologian whose writings stimulated Hopkins's personal philosophy. Hopkins viewed his surroundings through the lenses of inscape and instress. *Inscape*, according to Hopkins, is the essential inner nature of a person or object—its selfness. Human beings are the most highly selved beings in the universe. In an act called *instress*, the viewer recognizes the inscape of what they are viewing. The instress of inscape leads one to Christ because individual identity is the hallmark of God's creation; "capturing" identity is a celebration of the divine.

Hopkins's poetic distinctiveness is further evidenced by his use of *sprung rhythm*, a metrical system he devised to mimic the natural rhythm of common speech. In sprung rhythm, each line consists of a given number of stressed syllables followed by varying numbers of unstressed syllables. The stress can appear at any point in the foot, but it is often most convenient to place it on the first syllable. Sprung rhythm involves scanning a line by accents or stresses alone rather than limiting a line to a regular number of syllables, as in traditional meter. Hopkins insisted that his poetry must be read aloud, remarking that poetry is not a written word, but a sound. He violates and exploits the norms of the English language; his works are rife with compressed syntax, alliteration, internal and half-rhymes, compound adjectives, omitted or displaced prepositions, and repetition. His resulting poems are as unique as the objects and phenomena which he describes.

Hopkins was ordained a priest in 1877. Over the course of eight years, he held eleven postings in four countries, alternately working as a missioner, preacher, and parish priest. He was eventually appointed as a professor at University College in Dublin. Overworked and weary in body and mind, he began his "terrible sonnets." Poems belonging to this period are filled with artistic frustration and overwhelming desolation. "No worst, there is none" and "I wake and feel the fell of dark, not day," both written in 1885, echo Hopkins's despairing cries and sense of spiritual darkness. Whereas he formerly praised the God who fashioned each being with a distinctive identity, Hopkins's later poems lament his own isolating individuality.

Despite urgings from his friends and superiors, Hopkins feared his poetry would be misconstrued or misunderstood by his audience. As a result, he resisted publishing during his own lifetime. The first collection of his work was not published until 1918, twenty-nine years after his death. His literary executor Robert Bridges delayed printing Hopkins's letters and poems due to their private content; he also believed Hopkins's melancholy should not be publicly exposed. Nevertheless, as readers demanded new poetic voices in the early twentieth century, Hopkins's unorthodox meter and diction gathered attention. He was mainly disassociated from his fellow Victorian poets and instead prized as a modern poet. Discussions regarding his place in each era's canon have endured; his poems are reminiscent of Victorian themes, yet his ruminations on inner divisions and conflicts foreshadow modern literature. Although he has since been reclassified in the Victorian age, his work bridges two markedly different periods.

1844	Gerard Manley Hopkins born 28 July
1863–67	Attends Balliol College, the University of Oxford
1866	Received into the Roman Catholic Church
1868	Joins Jesuit order
1874–77	Attends St. Beuno's College, Wales
1884	Appointed professor at University College, Dublin
1889	Hopkins dies of typhoid fever 8 June and is buried in Glasnevin Cemetery, Dublin, Ireland
1918	*Poems of Gerard Manley Hopkins*

SPRING AND FALL
to a young child

Márgarét, áre you gríeving
Over Goldengrove unleaving?
Leáves like the things of man you
With your fresh thoughts care for, can you?
Áh! ás the heart grows older   5
It will come to such sights colder
By and by, nor spare a sigh
Though worlds of wanwood leafmeal lie;
And yet you wíll weep and know why.
    Now no matter, child, the name: 10
Sórrow's spríngs áre the same.
Nor mouth had, no, nor mind, expressed
What heart heard of, ghost guessed:
It is the blight man was born for,
It is Margaret you mourn for.   15

1918

BINSEY POPLARS
felled 1879

My aspens dear, whose airy cages quelled,
Quelled or quenched in leaves the leaping sun,
All felled, felled, are all felled;
  Of a fresh and following folded rank
     Not spared, not one   5
     That dandled a sandalled
Shadow that swam or sank
On meadow and river and wind-wandering weed-winding
     bank.

O, if we but knew what we do
    When we delve or hew—   10
Hack and rack the growing green!
    Since country is so tender
To touch, her being só slender
That, like this sleek and seeing ball
But a prick will make no eye at all,   15
Where we, even where we mean
    To mend her we end her,
    When we hew or delve:
After-comers cannot guess the beauty been.
Ten or twelve, only ten or twelve   20
    Strokes of havoc únselve
    The sweet especial scene,
Rural scene, a rural scene,
Sweet especial rural scene.

1918

PIED BEAUTY

Glory be to God for dappled things—
    For skies of couple-colour as a brinded cow;
        For rose-moles all in stipple upon trout that swim:
Fresh-firecoal chestnut-falls; finches' wings;
    Landscape plotted and pieced—fold, fallow, and plough;   5
        And àll tràdes, their gear and tackle and trim.
All things counter, original, spare, strange;
    Whatever is fickle, freckled (who knows how?)
        With swift, slow; sweet, sour; adazzle, dim;
He fathers-forth whose beauty is past change: 10
        Praise him.

1918

GOD'S GRANDEUR

The world is charged with the grandeur of God.
    It will flame out, like shining from shook foil;
    It gathers to a greatness, like the ooze of oil
Crushed.[1] Why do men then now not reck His rod?
Generations have trod, have trod, have trod;
    And all is seared with trade; bleared, smeared with toil;
    And wears man's smudge and shares man's smell: the soil
Is bare now, nor can foot feel, being shod.
And for all this, nature is never spent;
    There lives the dearest freshness deep down things;
And though the last lights off the black West went,
    Oh, morning, at the brown brink eastward, springs—
Because the Holy Ghost over the bent
    World broods with warm breast and with ah! bright wings.

1918

---

1 Olive oil is obtained by pressing olives. Biblically, people used olive oil to anoint priests and mon-
archs. The olive tree is also a symbol of peace in Christianity; for example, a dove with an olive leaf
in its beak returned to Noah's ark after the flood (Genesis 8:11).

THE WINDHOVER
To Christ our Lord

I caught this morning morning's minion,[2] kingdom of daylight's
        dauphin,[3] dapple-dawn-drawn Falcon, in his riding
  Of the rolling level underneath him steady air, and striding
High there, how he rung upon the rein of a wimpling wing
In his ecstacy! then off, off forth on swing,   5
    As a skate's heel sweeps smooth on a bow-bend: the hurl
        and gliding
  Rebuffed the big wind. My heart in hiding
Stirred for a bird,—the achieve of, the mastery of the thing!

Brute beauty and valour and act, oh, air, pride, plume, here
    Buckle![4] AND the fire that breaks from thee then, a billion   10
Times told lovelier, more dangerous, O my chevalier![5]

    No wonder of it: shéer plód makes plough down sillion[6]
Shine, and blue-bleak embers, ah my dear,
    Fall, gall themselves, and gash gold-vermillion.

1918

2 A servile follower; alternately, one who is favored or highly esteemed.
3 Historically, the title given to the eldest son of the King of France.
4 To bend; alternately, to prepare oneself.
5 In French history, a knight.
6 The fresh soil overturned by a plow.

ROBERT LOUIS STEVENSON
1850–1894

R obert Louis Stevenson (born Robert Lewis Balfour Stevenson) often recounted his childhood as a golden age of glee and imagination. In reality, he was habitually bedridden with various illnesses, frequently too sick to attend school or play with friends. He was diligently cared for by his nurse, a devout woman who curated his "high-strung religious ecstasies and terrors," as he later quipped. He paid homage to her in the dedication of *A Child's Garden of Verses*, a collection of poems reminiscent of the joys and pains of his early years.

Stevenson's family was of the Scottish middle class. Margaret Isabella Balfour, his mother, was the youngest daughter of a reverend at the Church of Scotland at Colinton, and Thomas Stevenson, his father, was a marine engineer and designer of lighthouses. When Stevenson entered Edinburgh University in 1867, people assumed he would find a profession in lighthouse engineering like his father. Although he loved seafaring, he loathed office work. After confessing to his father that he cared for nothing but literature, the two compromised on a profession in law. Stevenson was called to the Scottish bar in 1875 but abandoned the practice.

Throughout college, he avoided his formal studies and instead read widely. Stevenson taught himself how to write well by composing descriptive passages and mimicking the style of authors whom he admired. To his father's distress, he became a socialist and agnostic. He also visited cheap bars and brothels, wore his hair long, and donned a velvet jacket. His eccentric style and thin, towering stature summoned constant attention, as did his intellect. A dazzling conversationalist, Stevenson entranced people with his expressive gestures and restless energy.

Compelled by insatiable wanderlust and in a quest for better health, Stevenson mostly spent his life traveling between the far-flung reaches of the world. After a trip to France in 1876, he published his first book, a travelogue titled *An Inland Voyage*. He reinforced his developing reputation with *Travels with a Donkey in the Cévennes*, in which he relates his famous journey across the mountains of south-central France. While abroad, Stevenson also met Frances (Fanny) Van de Grift Osborne, an American who had left her husband and journeyed to Europe with her two children. She and Stevenson became lovers in 1877, and Stevenson spent much of the next year and a half visiting her.

In 1879, Stevenson made an excursion that nearly killed him. After sailing to New York, he took a nightmarish trip on an emigrant train to California, where Fanny had returned after their affair in France. While Fanny awaited the finalization of her divorce, Stevenson struggled as a writer and half-starved himself to save money. The combined stress of the trip and his impoverished lifestyle aggravated his health, and he began suffering from the lung hemorrhages that haunted him for the rest of his life. He married Fanny in 1880, and the two spent their honeymoon in a deserted mining camp, a venture that later inspired *The Silverado Squatters*.

Travel journals comprise a fraction of Stevenson's writing. He was also an enthusiastic essayist and fiction writer. Faring across seas and lands suited Stevenson's spirit, and his first major success was *Treasure Island*, a coming-of-age and adventure story about a cabin boy named Jim Hawkins. The tale, which began as an amusement for Stevenson's stepson, was serialized in a boys' magazine from 1881 to 1882 under the pseudonym Captain George North. It appeared as a book in 1883 and has never been out of print since. Its popularity is widespread; *Treasure Island* has been modified into plays, films, television shows, musicals, and has been reprinted in illustrated editions.

Stevenson further secured his popularity with *The Strange Case of Dr. Jekyll and Mr. Hyde*. Published in 1886, the novella shocked and unsettled readers in Britain and America alike. Representing the two moral extremes of human nature, the characters Dr. Jekyll and Mr. Hyde present allegorical evidence of the divided self. The depth of the story, however, cannot be reduced to the separation of good from evil, but an understanding of their coexistence within one body. Stevenson questions what identity is, how it evolves, and how it shapes morals. He deprives his readers of definitive answers. *Jekyll and Hyde* is largely integrated into popular culture, and though the basic plot is familiar to many, the story has continued to inspire new adaptations and interpretations since its original publication.

Despite his chronic lung disease, Stevenson wrote rigorously for many hours per day and embarked on numerous trips. He and his family spent extensive time sailing between islands in the South Seas. After purchasing an estate in Samoa, he became involved in local politics. In honor of his peacemaking efforts, several minor chiefs built the Road of Gratitude to connect his home to the main highway in October of 1894. In December of the same year, still feverishly at work on *Weir of Hermiston*, Stevenson died of a cerebral hemorrhage. Over forty Samoans cut a path through the untamed jungle leading up to Mount Vaea, a nearby mountain, and buried him at the summit.

To the local Samoans, Stevenson was known as Tusitala, or the "writer of tales." In his own words, Stevenson used fiction "to get out the facts of life as clean and naked and sharp as I could manage it." His emotional vitality and passion for writing were palpable, as was his desire to venture to distant lands. At the time of his death, he had moved across Europe, North America, Australia, and numerous islands in the Pacific, distinguishing himself as the most widely-traveled prominent Victorian writer.

1850	Robert Lewis Balfour Stevenson born 13 November
1866	*The Pentland Rising: a Page of History, 1666*
1867–75	Attends Edinburgh University
1875	Called to the Scottish bar
1878	*An Inland Voyage; Edinburgh: Picturesque Notes*
1879	*Travels with a Donkey in the Cévennes*
1880	Marries Frances Osborne
1883	*Treasure Island; The Silverado Squatters*
1885	*A Child's Garden of Verses*
1886	*The Strange Case of Dr. Jekyll and Mr. Hyde; Kidnapped*
1894	Stevenson dies 3 December due to a cerebral hemorrhage and is buried at the summit of Mount Vaea, Samoa
1896	*Weir of Hermiston*

THE STRANGE CASE OF DR. JEKYLL AND MR. HYDE

STORY OF THE DOOR

MR. UTTERSON THE LAWYER was a man of a rugged countenance, that was never lighted by a smile; cold, scanty and embarrassed in discourse; backward in sentiment; lean, long, dusty, dreary and yet somehow lovable. At friendly meetings, and when the wine was to his taste, something eminently human beaconed from his eye; something indeed which never found its way into his talk, but which spoke not only in these silent symbols of the after-dinner face, but more often and loudly in the acts of his life. He was austere with himself; drank gin when he was alone, to mortify a taste for vintages; and though he enjoyed the theatre, had not crossed the doors of one for twenty years. But he had an approved tolerance for others; sometimes wondering, almost with envy, at the high pressure of spirits involved in their misdeeds; and in any extremity inclined to help rather than to reprove. "I incline to Cain's heresy,"[1] he used to say quaintly: "I let my brother go to the devil in his own way." In this character, it was frequently his fortune to be the last reputable acquaintance and the last good influence in the lives of downgoing men. And to such as these, so long as they came about his chambers, he never marked a shade of change in his demeanour.

No doubt the feat was easy to Mr. Utterson; for he was undemonstrative at the best, and even his friendship seemed to be founded in a similar catholicity of good-nature. It is the mark of a modest man to accept his friendly circle ready-made from the hands of opportunity; and that was the lawyer's way. His friends were those of his own blood or those whom he had known the longest; his affections, like ivy, were the growth of time, they implied no aptness in the object. Hence, no doubt, the bond that united him to Mr. Richard Enfield, his distant kinsman, the well-known man about town. It was a nut to crack for many, what these two could see in each other, or what subject they could find in common. It was reported by those who encountered them in their Sunday walks, that they said nothing, looked singularly dull and would hail with obvious relief the appearance of a friend. For all that, the two men put the greatest store by these

---

1 Cain murders his brother Abel in Genesis 4:8. When God asks Cain where Abel is, Cain claims not to know and tries to reject responsibility (Genesis 4:9). Utterson does not meddle in others' personal affairs.

excursions, counted them the chief jewel of each week, and not only set aside occasions of pleasure, but even resisted the calls of business, that they might enjoy them uninterrupted.

It chanced on one of these rambles that their way led them down a by-street in a busy quarter of London. The street was small and what is called quiet, but it drove a thriving trade on the weekdays. The inhabitants were all doing well, it seemed, and all emulously hoping to do better still, and laying out the surplus of their grains in coquetry; so that the shop fronts stood along that thoroughfare with an air of invitation, like rows of smiling saleswomen. Even on Sunday, when it veiled its more florid charms and lay comparatively empty of passage, the street shone out in contrast to its dingy neighbourhood, like a fire in a forest; and with its freshly painted shutters, well-polished brasses, and general cleanliness and gaiety of note, instantly caught and pleased the eye of the passenger.

Two doors from one corner, on the left hand going east, the line was broken by the entry of a court; and just at that point, a certain sinister block of building thrust forward its gable on the street. It was two storys high; showed no window, nothing but a door on the lower story and a blind forehead of discoloured wall on the upper; and bore in every feature, the marks of prolonged and sordid negligence. The door, which was equipped with neither bell nor knocker, was blistered and distained. Tramps slouched into the recess and struck matches on the panels; children kept shop upon the steps; the schoolboy had tried his knife on the mouldings; and for close on a generation, no one had appeared to drive away these random visitors or to repair their ravages.

Mr. Enfield and the lawyer were on the other side of the by-street; but when they came abreast of the entry, the former lifted up his cane and pointed.

"Did you ever remark that door?" he asked; and when his companion had replied in the affirmative, "It is connected in my mind," added he, "with a very odd story."

"Indeed?" said Mr. Utterson, with a slight change of voice, "and what was that?"

"Well, it was this way," returned Mr. Enfield: "I was coming home from some place at the end of the world, about three o'clock of a black winter morning, and my way lay through a part of town where there was literally nothing to be seen but lamps. Street after street, and all the folks asleep—street after street, all lighted up as if for a procession and all as empty as a church—till at last I got into that state of mind when a man listens and listens and begins to long for the sight of a policeman. All at once, I saw two figures: one a little man who was stumping along eastward at a good walk, and the other a girl of maybe eight or ten who was running as hard as she was able down a cross street. Well, sir, the two ran into one another naturally enough at the corner; and then came the horrible part of the thing; for the man trampled calmly over the child's body and left her screaming on the ground. It sounds nothing to hear, but it was hellish to see. It wasn't like a man; it was like some damned Juggernaut. I gave a few halloa, took to my heels, collared my gentleman, and brought him back to where there was already quite a group about the screaming child. He was perfectly cool and made no resistance, but gave me one look, so ugly that it brought out the sweat on me like running. The people who had turned out were the girl's own family; and pretty soon, the doctor, for whom she had been sent put in his appearance. Well, the child was not much the worse, more frightened, according to the Sawbones;[1] and there you might have supposed would be an end to it. But there was one curious circumstance. I had taken a loathing to my gentleman at first sight. So had the child's family, which was only natural. But the doctor's case was what struck me. He was the usual cut and dry apothecary, of no particular age and colour, with a strong Edinburgh accent, and about as emotional as a bagpipe. Well, sir, he was like the rest of us; every time he looked at my prisoner, I saw that Sawbones turn sick and white with the desire to kill him. I knew what was in his mind, just as he knew what was in mine; and killing being out of the question, we did the next best. We told the man we could and would make such a scandal out of this, as should make his name stink from one end of London to the other. If he had any friends or any credit, we undertook that he should lose them. And all the time, as we were pitching it in red hot, we were keeping the women off him as best we could, for they were as wild as harpies. I never saw a circle of such hateful faces; and there was the man in the middle, with a kind of black sneering coolness—frightened too, I could see that—but carrying it off, sir, really like Satan. 'If you choose to make capital out of this accident,' said he, 'I am naturally helpless. No gentleman but wishes to avoid a scene,' says he. 'Name your figure.' Well, we screwed him up to a hundred pounds for the child's family; he would have clearly liked to stick out; but there was something about the lot of us that meant mischief, and at last he struck. The next thing was to get the money; and where do you think he carried us but to that place with the door?—whipped out a key, went in, and presently came back with the matter of ten pounds in gold and a cheque for the balance on Coutts's,[2] drawn payable to bearer and signed with a name that I can't mention, though it's one of the points of my story, but it was a name at least very well known and often printed. The figure was stiff; but the signature was good for more than that, if it was only genuine. I took the liberty of pointing out to my gentleman that the whole business looked apocryphal, and that a man does not, in real life, walk into a cellar door at four in the morning and come out with another man's cheque for close upon a hundred pounds. But he was quite easy and sneering. 'Set your mind at rest,' says he, 'I will stay with you till the banks open and cash the cheque myself.' So we all set off, the

---

1 Doctor.

2 A highly respected bank in London that services extremely wealthy customers.

doctor, and the child's father, and our friend and myself, and passed the rest of the night in my chambers; and next day, when we had breakfasted, went in a body to the bank. I gave in the cheque myself, and said I had every reason to believe it was a forgery. Not a bit of it. The cheque was genuine."

"Tut-tut!" said Mr. Utterson.

"I see you feel as I do," said Mr. Enfield. "Yes, it's a bad story. For my man was a fellow that nobody could have to do with, a really damnable man; and the person that drew the cheque is the very pink of the proprieties, celebrated too, and (what makes it worse) one of your fellows who do what they call good. Blackmail, I suppose; an honest man paying through the nose for some of the capers of his youth. Black Mail House is what I call the place with the door, in consequence. Though even that, you know, is far from explaining all," he added, and with the words fell into a vein of musing.

From this he was recalled by Mr. Utterson asking rather suddenly: "And you don't know if the drawer of the cheque lives there?"

"A likely place, isn't it?" returned Mr. Enfield. "But I happen to have noticed his address; he lives in some square or other."

"And you never asked about the—place with the door?" said Mr. Utterson.

"No, sir: I had a delicacy," was the reply. "I feel very strongly about putting questions; it partakes too much of the style of the day of judgment. You start a question, and it's like starting a stone. You sit quietly on the top of a hill; and away the stone goes, starting others; and presently some bland old bird (the last you would have thought of) is knocked on the head in his own back garden and the family have to change their name. No sir, I make it a rule of mine: the more it looks like Queer Street,[1] the less I ask."

"A very good rule, too," said the lawyer.

"But I have studied the place for myself," continued Mr. Enfield. "It seems scarcely a house. There is no other door, and nobody goes in or out of that one but, once in a great while, the gentleman of my adventure. There are three windows looking on the court on the first floor; none below; the windows are always shut but they're clean. And then there is a chimney which is generally smoking; so somebody must live there. And yet it's not so sure; for the buildings are so packed together about the court, that it's hard to say where one ends and another begins."

The pair walked on again for a while in silence; and then "Enfield," said Mr. Utterson, "that's a good rule of yours."

"Yes, I think it is," returned Enfield.

"But for all that," continued the lawyer, "there's one point I want to ask: I want to ask the name of that man who walked over the child."

---

1 A colloquial term meaning a difficult situation, typically financial in nature (such as debt or bankruptcy).

"Well," said Mr. Enfield, "I can't see what harm it would do. It was a man of the name of Hyde."

"H'm," said Mr. Utterson. "What sort of a man is he to see?"

"He is not easy to describe. There is something wrong with his appearance; something displeasing, something downright detestable. I never saw a man I so disliked, and yet I scarce know why. He must be deformed somewhere; he gives a strong feeling of deformity, although I couldn't specify the point. He's an extraordinary looking man, and yet I really can name nothing out of the way. No, sir; I can make no hand of it; I can't describe him. And it's not want of memory; for I declare I can see him this moment."

Mr. Utterson again walked some way in silence and obviously under a weight of consideration. "You are sure he used a key?" he inquired at last.

"My dear sir..." began Enfield, surprised out of himself.

"Yes, I know," said Utterson; "I know it must seem strange. The fact is, if I do not ask you the name of the other party, it is because I know it already. You see, Richard, your tale has gone home. If you have been inexact in any point you had better correct it."

"I think you might have warned me," returned the other with a touch of sullenness. "But I have been pedantically exact, as you call it. The fellow had a key; and what's more, he has it still. I saw him use it not a week ago."

Mr. Utterson sighed deeply but said never a word; and the young man presently resumed. "Here is another lesson to say nothing," said he. "I am ashamed of my long tongue. Let us make a bargain never to refer to this again."

"With all my heart," said the lawyer. "I shake hands on that, Richard."

SEARCH FOR MR. HYDE

THAT EVENING MR. UTTERSON CAME HOME to his bachelor house in sombre spirits and sat down to dinner without relish. It was his custom of a Sunday, when this meal was over, to sit close by the fire, a volume of some dry divinity on his reading desk, until the clock of the neighbouring church rang out the hour of twelve, when he would go soberly and gratefully to bed. On this night, however, as soon as the cloth was taken away, he took up a candle and went into his business room. There he opened his safe, took from the most private part of it a document endorsed on the envelope as Dr. Jekyll's Will, and sat down with a clouded brow to study its contents. The will was holograph, for Mr. Utterson, though he took charge of it now that it was made, had refused to lend the least assistance in the making of it; it provided not only that, in case of the decease of Henry Jekyll, M.D., D.C.L., L.L.D., F.R.S., etc., all his possessions were to pass into the hands of his "friend and benefactor Edward Hyde," but that in case of Dr. Jekyll's "disappearance or unexplained absence for any period exceeding three calendar months," the said Edward Hyde should step into the said Henry Jekyll's shoes without further delay and free from any burthen or obligation, beyond the payment of a few small sums to the members of the doctor's household. This document had long been the lawyer's eyesore. It offended him both as a lawyer and as a lover of the sane and customary sides of life, to whom the fanciful was the immodest. And hitherto it was his ignorance of Mr. Hyde that had swelled his indignation; now, by a sudden turn, it was his knowledge. It was already bad enough when the name was but a name of which he could learn no more. It was worse when it began to be clothed upon with detestable attributes; and out of the shifting, insubstantial mists that had so long baffled his eye, there leaped up the sudden, definite presentment of a fiend.

"I thought it was madness," he said, as he replaced the obnoxious paper in the safe, "and now I begin to fear it is disgrace."

With that he blew out his candle, put on a greatcoat, and set forth in the direction of Cavendish Square, that citadel of medicine, where his friend, the great Dr. Lanyon, had his house and received his crowding patients. "If anyone knows, it will be Lanyon," he had thought.

The solemn butler knew and welcomed him; he was subjected to no stage of delay, but ushered direct from the door to the dining-room where Dr. Lanyon sat alone over his wine. This was a hearty, healthy, dapper, red-faced gentleman, with a shock of hair prematurely white, and a boisterous and decided manner. At sight of Mr. Utterson, he sprang up from his chair and welcomed him with both hands. The geniality, as was the way of the man, was somewhat theatrical to the eye; but it reposed on genuine feeling. For these two were old friends, old mates both at school and college, both thorough respectors of themselves and of each other, and, what does not always follow, men who thoroughly enjoyed each other's company.

After a little rambling talk, the lawyer led up to the subject which so disagreeably preoccupied his mind.

"I suppose, Lanyon," said he, "you and I must be the two oldest friends that Henry Jekyll has?"

"I wish the friends were younger," chuckled Dr. Lanyon. "But I suppose we are. And what of that? I see little of him now."

"Indeed?" said Utterson. "I thought you had a bond of common interest."

"We had," was the reply. "But it is more than ten years since Henry Jekyll became too fanciful for me. He began to go wrong, wrong in mind; and though of course I continue to take an interest in him for old sake's sake, as they say, I see and I have seen devilish little of the man. Such unscientific balderdash," added the doctor, flushing suddenly purple, "would have estranged Damon and Pythias."[1]

This little spirit of temper was somewhat of a relief to Mr. Utterson. "They have only differed on some point of science," he thought; and being a man of no scientific passions (except in the matter of conveyancing), he even added: "It is nothing worse than that!" He gave his friend a few seconds to recover his composure, and then approached the question he had come to put. "Did you ever come across a *protégé* of his—one Hyde?" he asked.

"Hyde?" repeated Lanyon. "No. Never heard of him. Since my time."

That was the amount of information that the lawyer carried back with him to the great, dark bed on which he tossed to and fro, until the small hours of the morning began to grow large. It was a night of little ease to his toiling mind, toiling in mere darkness and besieged by questions.

Six o'clock struck on the bells of the church that was so conveniently near to Mr. Utterson's dwelling, and still he was digging at the problem. Hitherto it had touched him on the intellectual side alone; but now his imagination also was engaged, or rather enslaved; and as he lay and tossed in the gross darkness of the night and the curtained room, Mr. Enfield's tale went by before his mind in a scroll of lighted pictures. He would be aware of the great field of lamps of a nocturnal city; then of the figure of a man walking swiftly; then of a child running from the doctor's; and then these met, and that human Juggernaut trod the child down and passed on regardless of her screams. Or else he would see a room in a rich house, where his friend lay asleep, dreaming and smiling at his dreams; and then the door of that room would be opened, the curtains of the bed plucked apart, the sleeper recalled, and lo! there would stand by his side a figure to whom power was given, and even at that dead hour, he must rise and do its bidding. The figure in these two phases haunted the lawyer all night; and if at any time he dozed over, it was but to see it glide more stealthily through sleeping houses, or move the more swiftly and still the more ly, even to dizziness, through wider labyrinths of lamplighted city, and at every street corner crush a child and leave her screaming. And still the figure had no face by which he might know it even in his dreams, it had no face, or one that baffled him and melted before his eyes; and thus it was that there sprang up and grew apace in the lawyer's mind a singularly strong, almost an inordinate, curiosity to behold the features of the real Mr. Hyde. If he could but once set eyes on him, he thought the mystery would lighten and perhaps roll altogether away, as was the habit of mysterious things when well examined. He might see a reason for his friend's strange preference or bondage (call it which

---

1 The Greek legend of Damon and Pythias epitomizes true friendship; their loyalty to each other is so strong that one willingly sacrifices his life for the other.

you please) and even for the startling clause of the will. At least it would be a face worth seeing: the face of a man who was without bowels of mercy: a face which had but to show itself to raise up, in the mind of the unimpressionable Enfield, a spirit of enduring hatred.

From that time forward, Mr. Utterson began to haunt the door in the by-street of shops. In the morning before office hours, at noon when business was plenty, and time scarce, at night under the face of the fogged city moon, by all lights and at all hours of solitude or concourse, the lawyer was to be found on his chosen post.

"If he be Mr. Hyde," he had thought, "I shall be Mr. Seek."

And at last his patience was rewarded. It was a fine dry night; frost in the air; the streets as clean as a ballroom floor; the lamps, unshaken by any wind, drawing a regular pattern of light and shadow. By ten o'clock, when the shops were closed, the by-street was very solitary and, in spite of the low growl of London from all round, very silent. Small sounds carried far; domestic sounds out of the houses were clearly audible on either side of the roadway; and the rumour of the approach of any passenger preceded him by a long time. Mr. Utterson had been some minutes at his post, when he was aware of an odd, light footstep drawing near. In the course of his nightly patrols, he had long grown accustomed to the quaint effect with which the footfalls of a single person, while he is still a great way off, suddenly spring out distinct from the vast hum and clatter of the city. Yet his attention had never before been so sharply and decisively arrested; and it was with a strong, superstitious prevision of success that he withdrew into the entry of the court.

The steps drew swiftly nearer, and swelled out suddenly louder as they turned the end of the street. The lawyer, looking forth from the entry, could soon see what manner of man he had to deal with. He was small and very plainly dressed, and the look of him, even at that distance, went somehow strongly against the watcher's inclination. But he made straight for the door, crossing the roadway to save time; and as he came, he drew a key from his pocket like one approaching home.

Mr. Utterson stepped out and touched him on the shoulder as he passed. "Mr. Hyde, I think?"

Mr. Hyde shrank back with a hissing intake of the breath. But his fear was only momentary; and though he did not look the lawyer in the face, he answered coolly enough: "That is my name. What do you want?"

"I see you are going in," returned the lawyer. "I am an old friend of Dr. Jekyll's—Mr. Utterson of Gaunt Street—you must have heard of my name; and meeting you so conveniently, I thought you might admit me."

"You will not find Dr. Jekyll; he is from home," replied Mr. Hyde, blowing in the key. And then suddenly, but still without looking up, "How did you know me?" he asked.

"On your side," said Mr. Utterson "will you do me a favour?"

"With pleasure," replied the other. "What shall it be?"

"Will you let me see your face?" asked the lawyer.

Mr. Hyde appeared to hesitate, and then, as if upon some sudden reflection, fronted about with an air of defiance; and the pair stared at each other pretty fixedly for a few seconds. "Now I shall know you again," said Mr. Utterson. "It may be useful."

"Yes," returned Mr. Hyde, "It is as well we have met; and *à propos*, you should have my address." And he gave a number of a street in Soho.

"Good God!" thought Mr. Utterson, "can he, too, have been thinking of the will?" But he kept his feelings to himself and only grunted in acknowledgment of the address.

"And now," said the other, "how did you know me?"

"By description," was the reply.

"Whose description?"

"We have common friends," said Mr. Utterson.

"Common friends," echoed Mr. Hyde, a little hoarsely. "Who are they?"

"Jekyll, for instance," said the lawyer.

"He never told you," cried Mr. Hyde, with a flush of anger. "I did not think you would have lied."

"Come," said Mr. Utterson, "that is not fitting language."

The other snarled aloud into a savage laugh; and the next moment, with extraordinary quickness, he had unlocked the door and disappeared into the house.

The lawyer stood awhile when Mr. Hyde had left him, the picture of disquietude. Then he began slowly to mount the street, pausing every step or two and putting his hand to his brow like a man in mental perplexity. The problem he was thus debating as he walked, was one of a class that is rarely solved. Mr. Hyde was pale and dwarfish, he gave an impression of deformity without any nameable malformation, he had a displeasing smile, he had borne himself to the lawyer with a sort of murderous mixture of timidity and boldness, and he spoke with a husky, whispering and somewhat broken voice; all these were points against him, but not all of these together could explain the hitherto unknown disgust, loathing and fear with which Mr. Utterson regarded him. "There must be something else," said the perplexed gentleman. "There *is* something more, if I could find a name for it. God bless me, the man seems hardly human! Something troglodytic, shall we say? or can it be the old story of Dr. Fell?[1] or is it the mere radiance of a foul soul that thus transpires through, and transfigures, its clay continent? The last, I think; for,

---

1 A Nursery Rhyme about Dr. John Fell, Bishop of Oxford, that was written by the poet Tom Brown in 1680. The name Dr. Fell is sometimes evoked to indicate an inexplicable repulsion toward someone.

O my poor old Harry Jekyll, if ever I read Satan's signature upon a face, it is on that of your new friend."

Round the corner from the by-street, there was a square of ancient, handsome houses, now for the most part decayed from their high estate and let in flats and chambers to all sorts and conditions of men; map-engravers, architects, shady lawyers and the agents of obscure enterprises. One house, however, second from the corner, was still occupied entire; and at the door of this, which wore a great air of wealth and comfort, though it was now plunged in darkness except for the fanlight, Mr. Utterson stopped and knocked. A well-dressed, elderly servant opened the door.

"Is Dr. Jekyll at home, Poole?" asked the lawyer.

"I will see, Mr. Utterson," said Poole, admitting the visitor, as he spoke, into a large, low-roofed, comfortable hall, paved with flags, warmed (after the fashion of a country house) by a bright, open fire, and furnished with costly cabinets of oak. "Will you wait here by the fire, sir? or shall I give you a light in the dining-room?"

"Here, thank you," said the lawyer, and he drew near and leaned on the tall fender. This hall, in which he was now left alone, was a pet fancy of his friend the doctor's; and Utterson himself was wont to speak of it as the pleasantest room in London. But to-night there was a shudder in his blood; the face of Hyde sat heavy on his memory; he felt (what was rare with him) a nausea and distaste of life; and in the gloom of his spirits, he seemed to read a menace in the flickering of the firelight on the polished cabinets and the uneasy starting of the shadow on the roof. He was ashamed of his relief, when Poole presently returned to announce that Dr. Jekyll was gone out.

"I saw Mr. Hyde go in by the old dissecting room, Poole," he said. "Is that right, when Dr. Jekyll is from home?"

"Quite right, Mr. Utterson, sir," replied the servant. "Mr. Hyde has a key."

"Your master seems to repose a great deal of trust in that young man, Poole," resumed the other musingly.

"Yes, sir, he do indeed," said Poole. "We have all orders to obey him."

"I do not think I ever met Mr. Hyde?" asked Utterson.

"O, dear no, sir. He never *dines* here," replied the butler. "Indeed we see very little of him on this side of the house; he mostly comes and goes by the laboratory."

"Well, good-night, Poole."

"Good-night, Mr. Utterson."

And the lawyer set out homeward with a very heavy heart. "Poor Harry Jekyll," he thought, "my mind misgives me he is in deep waters! He was wild when he was young; a long while ago to be sure; but in the law of God, there is no statute of limitations. Ay, it must be that; the ghost of some old sin, the cancer of some concealed disgrace: punishment coming, *pede claudo*,[1] years after memory has forgotten and self-love condoned the fault." And the lawyer, scared by the thought, brooded awhile on his own past, groping in all the corners of memory, least by chance some Jack-in-the-Box of an old iniquity should leap to light there. His past was fairly blameless; few men could read the rolls of their life with less apprehension; yet he was humbled to the dust by the many ill things he had done, and raised up again into a sober and fearful gratitude by the many he had come so near to doing, yet avoided. And then by a return on his former subject, he conceived a spark of hope. "This Master Hyde, if he were studied," thought he, "must have secrets of his own; black secrets, by the look of him; secrets compared to which poor Jekyll's worst would be like sunshine. Things cannot continue as they are. It turns me cold to think of this creature stealing like a thief to Harry's bedside; poor Harry, what a wakening! And the danger of it; for if this Hyde suspects the existence of the will, he may grow impatient to inherit. Ay, I must put my shoulders to the wheel—if Jekyll will but let me," he added, "if Jekyll will only let me." For once more he saw before his mind's eye, as clear as transparency, the strange clauses of the will.

DR. JEKYLL WAS QUITE AT EASE

A FORTNIGHT LATER, by excellent good fortune, the doctor gave one of his pleasant dinners to some five or six old cronies, all intelligent, reputable men and all judges of good wine; and Mr. Utterson so contrived that he remained behind after the others had departed. This was no new arrangement, but a thing that had befallen many scores of times. Where Utterson was liked, he was liked well. Hosts loved to detain the dry lawyer, when the light-hearted and loose-tongued had already their foot on the threshold; they liked to sit a while in his unobtrusive company, practising for solitude, sobering their minds in the man's rich silence after the expense and strain of gaiety. To this rule, Dr. Jekyll was no exception; and as he now sat on the opposite side of the fire—a large, well-made, smooth-faced man of fifty, with something of a slyish cast perhaps, but every mark of capacity and kindness—you could see by his looks that he cherished for Mr. Utterson a sincere and warm affection.

---

1 Horace, *Odes* 3.2.32. The Latin phrase *pede claudo* signifies the inevitability of punishment.

"I have been wanting to speak to you, Jekyll," began the latter. "You know that will of yours?"

A close observer might have gathered that the topic was distasteful; but the doctor carried it off gaily. "My poor Utterson," said he, "you are unfortunate in such a client. I never saw a man so distressed as you were by my will; unless it were that hide-bound pedant, Lanyon, at what he called my scientific heresies. O, I know he's a good fellow—you needn't frown—an excellent fellow, and I always mean to see more of him; but a hide-bound pedant for all that; an ignorant, blatant pedant. I was never more disappointed in any man than Lanyon."

"You know I never approved of it," pursued Utterson, ruthlessly disregarding the fresh topic.

"My will? Yes, certainly, I know that," said the doctor, a trifle sharply. "You have told me so."

"Well, I tell you so again," continued the lawyer. "I have been learning something of young Hyde."

The large handsome face of Dr. Jekyll grew pale to the very lips, and there came a blackness about his eyes. "I do not care to hear more," said he. "This is a matter I thought we had agreed to drop."

"What I heard was abominable," said Utterson.

"It can make no change. You do not understand my position," returned the doctor, with a certain incoherency of manner. "I am painfully situated, Utterson; my position is a very strange—a very strange one. It is one of those affairs that cannot be mended by talking."

"Jekyll," said Utterson, "you know me: I am a man to be trusted. Make a clean breast of this in confidence; and I make no doubt I can get you out of it."

"My good Utterson," said the doctor, "this is very good of you, this is down-right good of you, and I cannot find words to thank you in. I believe you fully; I would trust you before any man alive, ay, before myself, if I could make the choice; but indeed it isn't what you fancy; it is not as bad as that; and just to put your good heart at rest, I will tell you one thing: the moment I choose, I can be rid of Mr. Hyde. I give you my hand upon that; and I thank you again and again; and I will just add one little word, Utterson, that I'm sure you'll take in good part: this is a private matter, and I beg of you to let it sleep."

Utterson reflected a little, looking in the fire.

"I have no doubt you are perfectly right," he said at last, getting to his feet.

"Well, but since we have touched upon this business, and for the last time I hope," continued the doctor, "there is one point I should like you to understand. I have really a very great interest in poor Hyde. I know you have seen him; he told me so; and I fear he was rude. But I do sincerely take a great, a very great interest in that young man; and if I am taken away, Utterson, I wish you to promise me that you will bear with him and get his rights for him. I think you would, if you knew all; and it would be a weight off my mind if you would promise."

"I can't pretend that I shall ever like him," said the lawyer.

"I don't ask that," pleaded Jekyll, laying his hand upon the other's arm; "I only ask for justice; I only ask you to help him for my sake, when I am no longer here."

Utterson heaved an irrepressible sigh. "Well," said he, "I promise."

THE CAREW MURDER CASE

NEARLY A YEAR LATER, in the month of October, 18—, London was startled by a crime of singular ferocity and rendered all the more notable by the high position of the victim. The details were few and startling. A maid servant living alone in a house not far from the river, had gone upstairs to bed about eleven. Although a fog rolled over the city in the small hours, the early part of the night was cloudless, and the lane, which the maid's window overlooked, was brilliantly lit by the full moon. It seems she was romantically given, for she sat down upon her box, which stood immediately under the window, and fell into a dream of musing. Never (she used to say, with streaming tears, when she narrated that experience), never had she felt more at peace with all men or thought more kindly of the world. And as she so sat she became aware of an aged beautiful gentleman with white hair, drawing near along the lane; and advancing to meet him, another and very small gentleman, to whom at first she paid less attention. When they had come within speech (which was just under the maid's eyes) the older man bowed and accosted the other with a very pretty manner of politeness. It did not seem as if the subject of his address were of great importance; indeed, from his pointing, it sometimes appeared as if he were only inquiring his way; but the moon shone on his face as he spoke, and the girl was pleased to watch it, it seemed to breathe such an innocent and old-world kindness of disposition, yet with something high too, as of a well-founded self-content. Presently her eye wandered to the other, and she was surprised to recognise in him a certain Mr. Hyde, who had once visited her master and for whom she had conceived a dislike. He had in his hand a heavy cane, with which he was trifling; but he answered never a word, and seemed to listen with an ill-contained impatience. And then all of a sudden he broke out in a great flame of anger, stamping with his foot, brandishing the cane, and carrying on (as the maid described it) like a madman. The old gentleman took a step back, with the air of one very much surprised and a trifle hurt; and at that Mr. Hyde broke out of all bounds and clubbed him to the earth. And next moment, with ape-like fury, he was trampling his victim under foot and hailing down a storm of blows, under which the bones were audibly shattered and the body jumped upon the roadway. At the horror of these sights and sounds, the maid fainted.

It was two o'clock when she came to herself and called for the police. The murderer was gone long ago; but there lay his victim in the middle of the lane, incredibly mangled. The stick with which the deed had been done, although it was of some rare and very tough and heavy wood, had broken in the middle under the stress of this insensate cruelty; and one splintered half had rolled in the neighbouring gutter—the other, without doubt, had been carried away by the murderer. A purse and gold watch were found upon the victim: but no cards or papers, except a sealed and stamped envelope, which he had been probably carrying to the post, and which bore the name and address of Mr. Utterson.

This was brought to the lawyer the next morning, before he was out of bed; and he had no sooner seen it and been told the circumstances, than he shot out a solemn lip. "I shall say nothing till I have seen the body," said he; "this may be very serious. Have the kindness to wait while I dress." And with the same grave countenance he hurried through his breakfast and drove to the police station, whither the body had been carried. As soon as he came into the cell, he nodded.

"Yes," said he, "I recognise him. I am sorry to say that this is Sir Danvers Carew."

"Good God, sir," exclaimed the officer, "is it possible?" And the next moment his eye lighted up with professional ambition. "This will make a deal of noise," he said. "And perhaps you can help us to the man." And he briefly narrated what the maid had seen, and showed the broken stick.

Mr. Utterson had already quailed at the name of Hyde; but when the stick was laid before him, he could doubt no longer; broken and battered as it was, he recognised it for one that he had himself presented many years before to Henry Jekyll.

"Is this Mr. Hyde a person of small stature?" he inquired.

"Particularly small and particularly wicked-looking, is what the maid calls him," said the officer.

Mr. Utterson reflected; and then, raising his head, "If you will come with me in my cab," he said, "I think I can take you to his house."

It was by this time about nine in the morning, and the first fog of the season. A great chocolate-coloured pall lowered over heaven, but the wind was continually charging and routing these embattled vapours; so that as the cab crawled from street to street, Mr. Utterson beheld a marvelous number of degrees and hues of twilight; for here it would be dark like the back-end of evening; and there would be a glow of a rich, lurid brown, like the light of some strange conflagration; and here, for a moment, the fog would be quite broken up, and a haggard shaft of daylight would glance in between the swirling wreaths. The dismal quarter of Soho seen under these changing glimpses, with its muddy ways, and slatternly passengers, and its lamps, which had never been extinguished or had been kindled afresh to combat this mournful reinvasion of darkness, seemed, in the lawyer's eyes, like a district of some city in a nightmare. The thoughts of his mind, besides, were of the gloomiest dye; and when he glanced at the companion of his drive, he was conscious of some touch of that terror of the law and the law's officers, which may at times assail the most honest.

As the cab drew up before the address indicated, the fog lifted a little and showed him a dingy street, a gin palace, a low French eating house, a shop for the retail of penny numbers and twopenny salads, many ragged children huddled in the doorways, and many women of many different nationalities passing out, key in hand, to have a morning glass; and the next moment the fog settled down again upon that part, as brown as umber, and cut him off from his blackguardly surroundings. This was the home of Henry Jekyll's favourite; of a man who was heir to a quarter of a million sterling.

An ivory-faced and silvery-haired old woman opened the door. She had an evil face, smoothed by hypocrisy: but her manners were excellent. Yes, she said, this was Mr. Hyde's, but he was not at home; he had been in that night very late, but he had gone away again in less than an hour; there was nothing strange in that; his habits were very irregular, and he was often absent; for instance, it was nearly two months since she had seen him till yesterday.

"Very well, then, we wish to see his rooms," said the lawyer; and when the woman began to declare it was impossible, "I had better tell you who this person is," he added. "This is Inspector Newcomen of Scotland Yard."

A flash of odious joy appeared upon the woman's face. "Ah!" said she, "he is in trouble! What has he done?"

Mr. Utterson and the inspector exchanged glances. "He don't seem a very popular character," observed the latter. "And now, my good woman, just let me and this gentleman have a look about us."

In the whole extent of the house, which but for the old woman remained otherwise empty, Mr. Hyde had only used a couple of rooms; but these were furnished with luxury and good taste. A closet was filled with wine; the plate was of silver, the napery elegant; a good picture hung upon the walls, a gift (as Utterson supposed) from Henry Jekyll, who was much of a connoisseur; and the carpets were of many plies and agreeable in colour. At this moment, however, the rooms bore every mark of having been recently and hurriedly ransacked; clothes lay about the floor, with their pockets inside out; lock-fast drawers stood open; and on the hearth there lay a pile of grey ashes, as though many papers had been burned. From these embers the inspector disinterred the butt end of a green cheque book, which had resisted the action of the fire; the other half of the stick was found behind the door; and as this clinched his suspicions, the officer declared himself delighted. A visit to the bank, where several thousand pounds were found to be lying to the murderer's credit, completed his gratification.

"You may depend upon it, sir," he told Mr. Utterson: "I have him in my hand. He must have lost his head, or he never would have left the stick or, above all, burned the cheque book. Why, money's life to the man. We have nothing to do but wait for him at the bank, and get out the handbills."

This last, however, was not so easy of accomplishment; for Mr. Hyde had numbered few familiars—even the master of the servant maid had only seen him twice; his family could nowhere be traced; he had never been photographed; and the few who could describe him differed widely, as common observers will. Only on one point, were they agreed; and that was the haunting sense of unexpressed deformity with which the fugitive impressed his beholders.

INCIDENT OF THE LETTER

IT WAS LATE in the afternoon, when Mr. Utterson found his way to Dr. Jekyll's door, where he was at once admitted by Poole, and carried down by the kitchen offices and across a yard which had once been a garden, to the building which was indifferently known as the laboratory or dissecting rooms. The doctor had bought the house from the heirs of a celebrated surgeon; and his own tastes being rather chemical than anatomical, had changed the destination of the block at the bottom of the garden. It was the first time that the lawyer had been received in that part of his friend's quarters; and he eyed the dingy, windowless structure with curiosity, and gazed round with a distasteful sense of strangeness as he crossed the theatre, once crowded with eager students and now lying gaunt and silent, the tables laden with chemical apparatus, the floor strewn with crates and littered with packing straw, and the light falling dimly through the foggy cupola. At the further end, a flight of stairs mounted to a door covered with red baize; and through this, Mr. Utterson was at last received into the doctor's cabinet. It was a large room, fitted round with glass presses, furnished, among other things, with a cheval-glass and a business table, and looking out upon the court by three dusty windows barred with iron. A fire burned in the grate; a lamp was set lighted on the chimney shelf, for even in the houses the fog began to lie thickly; and there, close up to the warmth, sat Dr. Jekyll, looking deathly sick. He did not rise to meet his visitor, but held out a cold hand and bade him welcome in a changed voice.

"And now," said Mr. Utterson, as soon as Poole had left them, "you have heard the news?"

The doctor shuddered. "They were crying it in the square," he said. "I heard them in my dining-room."

"One word," said the lawyer. "Carew was my client, but so are you, and I want to know what I am doing. You have not been mad enough to hide this fellow?"

"Utterson, I swear to God," cried the doctor, "I swear to God I will never set eyes on him again. I bind my honour to you that I am done with him in this world. It is all at an end. And indeed he does not want my help; you do not know him as I do; he is safe, he is quite safe; mark my words, he will never more be heard of."

The lawyer listened gloomily; he did not like his friend's feverish manner. "You seem pretty sure of him," said he; "and for your sake, I hope you may be right. If it came to a trial, your name might appear."

"I am quite sure of him," replied Jekyll; "I have grounds for certainty that I cannot share with any one. But there is one thing on which you may advise me. I have—I have received a letter; and I am at a loss whether I should show it to the police. I should like to leave it in your hands, Utterson; you would judge wisely, I am sure; I have so great a trust in you."

"You fear, I suppose, that it might lead to his detection?" asked the lawyer.

"No," said the other. "I cannot say that I care what becomes of Hyde; I am quite done with him. I was thinking of my own character, which this hateful business has rather exposed."

Utterson ruminated awhile; he was surprised at his friend's selfishness, and yet relieved by it. "Well," said he, at last, "let me see the letter."

The letter was written in an odd, upright hand and signed "Edward Hyde": and it signified, briefly enough, that the writer's benefactor, Dr. Jekyll, whom he had long so unworthily repaid for a thousand generosities, need labour under no alarm for his safety, as he had means of escape on which he placed a sure dependence. The lawyer liked this letter well enough; it put a better colour on the intimacy than he had looked for; and he blamed himself for some of his past suspicions.

"Have you the envelope?" he asked.

"I burned it," replied Jekyll, "before I thought what I was about. But it bore no postmark. The note was handed in."

"Shall I keep this and sleep upon it?" asked Utterson.

"I wish you to judge for me entirely," was the reply. "I have lost confidence in myself."

"Well, I shall consider," returned the lawyer. "And now one word more: it was Hyde who dictated the terms in your will about that disappearance?"

The doctor seemed seized with a qualm of faintness; he shut his mouth tight and nodded.

"I knew it," said Utterson. "He meant to murder you. You had a fine escape."

"I have had what is far more to the purpose," returned the doctor solemnly: "I have had a lesson—O God, Utterson, what a lesson I have had!" And he covered his face for a moment with his hands.

On his way out, the lawyer stopped and had a word or two with Poole. "By the bye," said he, "there was a letter handed in to-day: what was the messenger like?" But Poole was positive nothing had come except by post; "and only circulars by that," he added.

This news sent off the visitor with his fears renewed. Plainly the letter had come by the laboratory door; possibly, indeed, it had been written in the cabinet; and if that were so, it must be differently judged, and handled with the more caution. The newsboys, as he went, were crying themselves hoarse along the footways: "Special edition. Shocking murder of an M.P." That was the funeral oration of one friend and client; and he could not help a certain apprehension lest the good name of another should be sucked down in the eddy of the scandal. It was, at least, a ticklish decision that he had to make; and self-reliant as he was by habit, he began to cherish a longing for advice. It was not to be had directly; but perhaps, he thought, it might be fished for.

Presently after, he sat on one side of his own hearth, with Mr. Guest, his head clerk, upon the other, and midway between, at a nicely calculated distance from the fire, a bottle of a particular old wine that had long dwelt unsunned in the foundations of his house. The fog still slept on the wing above the drowned city, where the lamps glimmered like carbuncles; and through the muffle and smother of these fallen clouds, the procession of the town's life was still rolling in through the great arteries with a sound as of a mighty wind. But the room was gay with firelight. In the bottle the acids were long ago resolved; the imperial dye had softened with time, as the colour grows richer in stained windows; and the glow of hot autumn afternoons on hillside vineyards, was ready to be set free and to disperse the fogs of London. Insensibly the lawyer melted. There was no man from whom he kept fewer secrets than Mr. Guest; and he was not always sure that he kept as many as he meant. Guest had often been on business to the doctor's; he knew Poole; he could scarce have failed to hear of Mr. Hyde's familiarity about the house; he might draw conclusions: was it not as well, then, that he should see a letter which put that mystery to rights? and above all since Guest, being a great student and critic of handwriting, would consider the step natural and obliging? The clerk, besides, was a man of counsel; he could scarce read so strange a document without dropping a remark; and by that remark Mr. Utterson might shape his future course.

"This is a sad business about Sir Danvers," he said.

"Yes, sir, indeed. It has elicited a great deal of public feeling," returned Guest. "The man, of course, was mad."

"I should like to hear your views on that," replied Utterson. "I have a document here in his handwriting; it is between ourselves, for I scarce know what to do about it; it is an ugly business at the best. But there it is; quite in your way: a murderer's autograph."

Guest's eyes brightened, and he sat down at once and studied it with passion. "No sir," he said: "not mad; but it is an odd hand."

"And by all accounts a very odd writer," added the lawyer.

Just then the servant entered with a note.

"Is that from Dr. Jekyll, sir?" inquired the clerk. "I thought I knew the writing. Anything private, Mr. Utterson?"

"Only an invitation to dinner. Why? Do you want to see it?"

"One moment. I thank you, sir;" and the clerk laid the two sheets of paper alongside and sedulously compared their contents. "Thank you, sir," he said at last, returning both; "it's a very interesting autograph."

There was a pause, during which Mr. Utterson struggled with himself. "Why did you compare them, Guest?" he inquired suddenly.

"Well, sir," returned the clerk, "there's a rather singular resemblance; the two hands are in many points identical: only differently sloped."

"Rather quaint," said Utterson.

"It is, as you say, rather quaint," returned Guest.

"I wouldn't speak of this note, you know," said the master.

"No, sir," said the clerk. "I understand."

But no sooner was Mr. Utterson alone that night than he locked the note into his safe, where it reposed from that time forward. "What!" he thought. "Henry Jekyll forge for a murderer!" And his blood ran cold in his veins.

REMARKABLE INCIDENT OF DR. LANYON

TIME RAN ON; thousands of pounds were offered in reward, for the death of Sir Danvers was resented as a public injury; but Mr. Hyde had disappeared out of the ken of the police as though he had never existed. Much of his past was unearthed, indeed, and all disreputable: tales came out of the man's cruelty, at once so callous and violent; of his vile life, of his strange associates, of the hatred that seemed to have surrounded his career; but of his present whereabouts, not a whisper. From the time he had left the house in Soho on the morning of the murder, he was simply blotted out; and gradually, as time drew on, Mr. Utterson began to recover from the hotness of his alarm, and to grow more at quiet with himself. The death of Sir Danvers was, to his way of thinking, more than paid for by the disappearance of Mr. Hyde. Now that that evil influence had been withdrawn, a new life began for Dr. Jekyll. He came out of his seclusion, renewed relations with his friends, became once more their familiar guest and entertainer; and whilst he had always been known for charities, he was now no less distinguished for religion. He was busy, he was much in the open air, he did good; his face seemed to open and brighten, as if with an inward consciousness of service; and for more than two months, the doctor was at peace.

On the 8th of January Utterson had dined at the doctor's with a small party; Lanyon had been there; and the face of the host had looked from one to the other as in the old days when the trio were inseparable friends. On the 12th, and again on the 14th, the door was shut against the lawyer. "The doctor was confined to the house," Poole said, "and saw no one." On the 15th, he tried again, and was again refused; and having now been used for the last two months to see his friend almost daily, he found this return of solitude to weigh upon his spirits. The fifth night he had in Guest to dine with him; and the sixth he betook himself to Dr. Lanyon's.

There at least he was not denied admittance; but when he came in, he was shocked at the change which had taken place in the doctor's appearance. He had his death-warrant written legibly upon his face. The rosy man had grown pale; his flesh had fallen away; he was visibly balder and older; and yet it was not so much these tokens of a swift physical decay that arrested the lawyer's notice, as a look in the eye and quality of manner that seemed to testify to some deep-seated terror of the mind. It was unlikely that the doctor should fear death; and yet that was what Utterson was tempted to suspect. "Yes," he thought; "he is a doctor, he must know his own state and that his days are counted; and the knowledge is more than he can bear." And yet when Utterson remarked on his ill looks, it was with an air of great firmness that Lanyon declared himself a doomed man.

"I have had a shock," he said, "and I shall never recover. It is a question of weeks. Well, life has been pleasant; I liked it; yes, sir, I used to like it. I sometimes think if we knew all, we should be more glad to get away."

"Jekyll is ill, too," observed Utterson. "Have you seen him?"

But Lanyon's face changed, and he held up a trembling hand. "I wish to see or hear no more of Dr. Jekyll," he said in a loud, unsteady voice. "I am quite done with that person; and I beg that you will spare me any allusion to one whom I regard as dead."

"Tut, tut!" said Mr. Utterson; and then after a considerable pause, "Can't I do anything?" he inquired. "We are three very old friends, Lanyon; we shall not live to make others."

"Nothing can be done," returned Lanyon; "ask himself."

"He will not see me," said the lawyer.

"I am not surprised at that," was the reply. "Some day, Utterson, after I am dead, you may perhaps come to learn the right and wrong of this. I cannot tell you. And in the meantime, if you can sit and talk with me of other things, for God's sake, stay and do so; but if you cannot keep clear of this accursed topic, then, in God's name, go, for I cannot bear it."

As soon as he got home, Utterson sat down and wrote to Jekyll, complaining of his exclusion from the house, and asking the cause of this unhappy break with Lanyon; and the next day brought him a long answer, often very pathetically worded, and sometimes darkly mysterious in drift. The quarrel with Lanyon was incurable. "I do not blame our old friend," Jekyll wrote, "but I share his view that we must never meet. I mean from henceforth to lead a life of extreme seclusion; you must not be surprised, nor must you doubt my friendship, if my door is often shut even to you. You must suffer me to go my own dark way. I have brought on myself a punishment and a danger that I cannot name. If I am the chief of sinners, I am the chief of sufferers also. I could not think that this earth contained a place for sufferings and terrors so unmanning; and you can do but one thing, Utterson, to lighten this destiny, and that is to respect my silence." Utterson was amazed; the dark influence of Hyde had been withdrawn, the doctor had returned to his old tasks and amities; a week ago, the prospect had smiled with every promise of a cheerful and an honoured age; and now in a moment, friendship, and peace of mind, and the whole tenor of his life were wrecked. So great and unprepared a change pointed to madness; but in view of Lanyon's manner and words, there must lie for it some deeper ground.

A week afterwards Dr. Lanyon took to his bed, and in something less than a fortnight he was dead. The night after the funeral, at which he had been sadly affected, Utterson locked the door of his business room, and sitting there by the light of a melancholy candle, drew out and set before him an envelope addressed by the hand and sealed with the seal of his dead friend. "PRIVATE: for the hands of G. J. Utterson ALONE, and in case of his predecease *to be destroyed unread*," so it was emphatically superscribed; and the lawyer dreaded to behold the contents. "I have buried one friend to-day," he thought: "what if this should cost me another?" And then he condemned the fear as a disloyalty, and broke the seal. Within there was another enclosure, likewise sealed, and marked upon the cover as "not to be opened till the death or disappearance of Dr. Henry Jekyll." Utterson could not trust his eyes. Yes, it was disappearance; here again, as in the mad will which he had long ago restored to its author, here again were the idea of a disappearance and the name of Henry Jekyll bracketted. But in the will, that idea had sprung from the sinister suggestion of the man Hyde; it was set there with a purpose all too plain and horrible. Written by the hand of Lanyon, what should it mean? A great curiosity came on the trustee, to disregard the prohibition and dive at once to the bottom of these mysteries; but professional honour and faith to his dead friend were stringent obligations; and the packet slept in the inmost corner of his private safe.

It is one thing to mortify curiosity, another to conquer it; and it may be doubted if, from that day forth, Utterson desired the society of his surviving friend with the same eagerness. He thought of him kindly; but his thoughts were disquieted and fearful. He went to call indeed; but he was perhaps relieved to be denied admittance; perhaps, in his heart, he preferred to speak with Poole upon the doorstep and surrounded by the air and sounds of the open city, rather than to be admitted into that house of voluntary bondage, and to sit and speak with its inscrutable recluse. Poole had, indeed, no very pleasant news to communicate. The doctor, it appeared, now more than ever confined himself to the cabinet over the laboratory, where he would sometimes even sleep; he was out of spirits, he had grown very silent, he did not read; it seemed as if he had something on his mind. Utterson became so used to the unvarying character of these reports, that he fell off little by little in the frequency of his visits.

INCIDENT AT THE WINDOW

IT CHANCED ON SUNDAY, when Mr. Utterson was on his usual walk with Mr. Enfield, that their way lay once again through the by-street; and that when they came in front of the door, both stopped to gaze on it.

"Well," said Enfield, "that story's at an end at least. We shall never see more of Mr. Hyde."

"I hope not," said Utterson. "Did I ever tell you that I once saw him, and shared your feeling of repulsion?"

"It was impossible to do the one without the other," returned Enfield. "And by the way, what an ass you must have thought me, not to know that this was a back way to Dr. Jekyll's! It was partly your own fault that I found it out, even when I did."

"So you found it out, did you?" said Utterson. "But if that be so, we may step into the court and take a look at the windows. To tell you the truth, I am uneasy about poor Jekyll; and even outside, I feel as if the presence of a friend might do him good."

The court was very cool and a little damp, and full of premature twilight, although the sky, high up overhead, was still bright with sunset. The middle one of the three windows was half-way open; and sitting close beside it, taking the air with an infinite sadness of mien, like some disconsolate prisoner, Utterson saw Dr. Jekyll.

"What! Jekyll!" he cried. "I trust you are better."

"I am very low, Utterson," replied the doctor drearily, "very low. It will not last long, thank God."

"You stay too much indoors," said the lawyer. "You should be out, whipping up the circulation like Mr. Enfield and me. (This is my cousin—Mr. Enfield—Dr. Jekyll.) Come now; get your hat and take a quick turn with us."

"You are very good," sighed the other. "I should like to very much; but no, no, no, it is quite impossible; I dare not. But indeed, Utterson, I am very glad to see you; this is really a great pleasure; I would ask you and Mr. Enfield up, but the place is really not fit."

"Why, then," said the lawyer, good-naturedly, "the best thing we can do is to stay down here and speak with you from where we are."

"That is just what I was about to venture to propose," returned the doctor with a smile. But the words were hardly uttered, before the smile was struck out of his face and succeeded by an expression of such abject terror and despair, as froze the very blood of the two gentlemen below. They saw it but for a glimpse, for the window was instantly thrust down; but that glimpse had been sufficient, and they turned and left the court without a word. In silence, too, they traversed the by-street; and it was not until they had come into a neighbouring thoroughfare, where even upon a Sunday there were still some stirrings of life, that Mr. Utterson at last turned and looked at his companion. They were both pale; and there was an answering horror in their eyes.

"God forgive us, God forgive us," said Mr. Utterson.

But Mr. Enfield only nodded his head very seriously, and walked on once more in silence.

THE LAST NIGHT

MR. UTTERSON WAS SITTING by his fireside one evening after dinner, when he was surprised to receive a visit from Poole.

"Bless me, Poole, what brings you here?" he cried; and then taking a second look at him, "What ails you?" he added; "is the doctor ill?"

"Mr. Utterson," said the man, "there is something wrong."

"Take a seat, and here is a glass of wine for you," said the lawyer. "Now, take your time, and tell me plainly what you want."

"You know the doctor's ways, sir," replied Poole, "and how he shuts himself up. Well, he's shut up again in the cabinet; and I don't like it, sir—I wish I may die if I like it. Mr. Utterson, sir, I'm afraid."

"Now, my good man," said the lawyer, "be explicit. What are you afraid of?"

"I've been afraid for about a week," returned Poole, doggedly disregarding the question, "and I can bear it no more."

The man's appearance amply bore out his words; his manner was altered for the worse; and except for the moment when he had first announced his terror, he had not once looked the lawyer in the face. Even now, he sat with the glass of wine untasted on his knee, and his eyes directed to a corner of the floor. "I can bear it no more," he repeated.

"Come," said the lawyer, "I see you have some good reason, Poole; I see there is something seriously amiss. Try to tell me what it is."

"I think there's been foul play," said Poole, hoarsely.

"Foul play!" cried the lawyer, a good deal frightened and rather inclined to be irritated in consequence. "What foul play? What does the man mean?"

"I daren't say, sir," was the answer; "but will you come along with me and see for yourself?"

Mr. Utterson's only answer was to rise and get his hat and great coat; but he observed with wonder the greatness of the relief that appeared upon the butler's face, and perhaps with no less, that the wine was still untasted when he set it down to follow.

It was a wild, cold, seasonable night of March, with a pale moon, lying on her back as though the wind had tilted her, and flying wrack of the most diaphanous and lawny texture. The wind made talking difficult, and flecked the blood into the face. It seemed to have swept the streets unusually bare of passengers, besides; for Mr. Utterson thought he had never seen that part of London so deserted. He could have wished it otherwise; never in his life had he been conscious of so sharp a wish to see and touch his fellow-creatures; for struggle as he might, there was borne in upon his mind a crushing anticipation of calamity. The square, when they got there, was full of wind and dust, and the thin trees in the garden were lashing themselves along the railing. Poole, who had kept all the way a pace or two ahead, now pulled up in the middle of the pavement, and in spite of the biting weather, took off his hat and mopped his brow with a red pocket-handkerchief. But for all the hurry of his coming, these were not the dews of exertion that he wiped away, but the moisture of some strangling anguish; for his face was white and his voice, when he spoke, harsh and broken.

"Well, sir," he said, "here we are, and God grant there be nothing wrong."

"Amen, Poole," said the lawyer.

Thereupon the servant knocked in a very guarded manner; the door was opened on the chain; and a voice asked from within, "Is that you, Poole?"

"It's all right," said Poole. "Open the door."

The hall, when they entered it, was brightly lighted up; the fire was built high; and about the hearth the whole of the servants, men and women, stood huddled together like a flock of sheep. At the sight of Mr. Utterson, the housemaid broke into hysterical whimpering; and the cook, crying out "Bless God! it's Mr. Utterson," ran forward as if to take him in her arms.

"What, what? Are you all here?" said the lawyer peevishly. "Very irregular, very unseemly; your master would be far from pleased."

"They're all afraid," said Poole.

Blank silence followed, no one protesting; only the maid lifted her voice and now wept loudly.

"Hold your tongue!" Poole said to her, with a ferocity of accent that testified to his own jangled nerves; and indeed, when the girl had so suddenly raised the note of her lamentation, they had all started and turned towards the inner door with faces of dreadful expectation. "And now," continued the butler, addressing the knife-boy, "reach me a candle, and we'll get this through hands at once." And then he begged Mr. Utterson to follow him, and led the way to the back garden.

"Now, sir," said he, "you come as gently as you can. I want you to hear, and I don't want you to be heard. And see here, sir, if by any chance he was to ask you in, don't go."

Mr. Utterson's nerves, at this unlooked-for termination, gave a jerk that nearly threw him from his balance; but he recollected his courage and followed the butler into the laboratory building through the surgical theatre, with its lumber of crates and bottles, to the foot of the stair. Here Poole motioned him to stand on one side and listen; while he himself, setting down the candle and making a great and obvious call on his resolution, mounted the steps and knocked with a somewhat uncertain hand on the red baize of the cabinet door.

"Mr. Utterson, sir, asking to see you," he called; and even as he did so, once more violently signed to the lawyer to give ear.

A voice answered from within: "Tell him I cannot see anyone," it said complainingly.

"Thank you, sir," said Poole, with a note of something like triumph in his voice; and taking up his candle, he led Mr. Utterson back across the yard and into the great kitchen, where the fire was out and the beetles were leaping on the floor.

"Sir," he said, looking Mr. Utterson in the eyes, "was that my master's voice?"

"It seems much changed," replied the lawyer, very pale, but giving look for look.

"Changed? Well, yes, I think so," said the butler. "Have I been twenty years in this man's house, to be deceived about his voice? No, sir; master's made away with; he was made away with, eight days ago, when we heard him cry out upon the name of God; and *who's* in there instead of him, and *why* it stays there, is a thing that cries to Heaven, Mr. Utterson!"

"This is a very strange tale, Poole; this is rather a wild tale, my man," said Mr. Utterson, biting his finger. "Suppose it were as you suppose, supposing Dr. Jekyll to have been—well, murdered, what could induce the murderer to stay? That won't hold water; it doesn't commend itself to reason."

"Well, Mr. Utterson, you are a hard man to satisfy, but I'll do it yet," said Poole. "All this last week (you must know) him, or it, whatever it is that lives in that cabinet, has been crying night and day for some sort of medicine and cannot get it to his mind. It was sometimes his way—the master's, that is—to write his orders on a sheet of paper and throw it on the stair. We've had nothing else this week back; nothing but papers, and a closed door, and the very meals left there to be smuggled in when nobody was looking. Well, sir, every day, ay, and twice and thrice in the same day, there have been orders and complaints, and I have been sent flying to all the wholesale chemists in town. Every time I brought the stuff back, there would be another paper telling me to return it, because it was not pure, and another order to a different firm. This drug is wanted bitter bad, sir, whatever for."

"Have you any of these papers?" asked Mr. Utterson.

Poole felt in his pocket and handed out a crumpled note, which the lawyer, bending nearer to the candle, carefully examined. Its contents ran thus: "Dr. Jekyll presents his compliments to Messrs. Maw. He assures them that their last sample is impure and quite useless for his present purpose. In the year 18—, Dr. J. purchased a somewhat large quantity from Messrs. M. He now begs them to search with most sedulous care, and should any of the same quality be left, to forward it to him at once. Expense is no consideration. The importance of this to Dr. J. can hardly be exaggerated." So far the letter had run composedly enough, but here with a sudden splutter of the pen, the writer's emotion had broken loose. "For God's sake," he added, "find me some of the old."

"This is a strange note," said Mr. Utterson; and then sharply, "How do you come to have it open?"

"The man at Maw's was main angry, sir, and he threw it back to me like so much dirt," returned Poole.

"This is unquestionably the doctor's hand, do you know?" resumed the lawyer.

"I thought it looked like it," said the servant rather sulkily; and then, with another voice, "But what matters hand of write?" he said. "I've seen him!"

"Seen him?" repeated Mr. Utterson. "Well?"

"That's it!" said Poole. "It was this way. I came suddenly into the theatre from the garden. It seems he had slipped out to look for this drug or whatever it is; for the cabinet door was open, and there he was at the far end of the room digging among the crates. He looked up when I came in, gave a kind of cry, and whipped upstairs into the cabinet. It was but for one minute that I saw him, but the hair stood upon my head like quills. Sir, if that was my master, why had he a mask upon his face? If it was my master, why did he cry out like a rat, and run from me? I have served him long enough. And then..." The man paused and passed his hand over his face.

"These are all very strange circumstances," said Mr. Utterson, "but I think I begin to see daylight. Your master, Poole, is plainly seized with one of those maladies that both torture and deform the sufferer; hence, for aught I know, the alteration of his voice; hence the mask and the avoidance of his friends; hence his eagerness to find this drug, by means of which the poor soul retains some hope of ultimate recovery—God grant that he be not deceived! There is my explanation; it is sad enough, Poole, ay, and appalling to consider; but it is plain and natural, hangs well together, and delivers us from all exorbitant alarms."

"Sir," said the butler, turning to a sort of mottled pallor, "that thing was not my master, and there's the truth. My master"—here he looked round him and began to whisper—"is a tall, fine build of a man, and this was more of a dwarf." Utterson attempted to protest. "O, sir," cried Poole, "do you think I do not know my master after twenty years? Do you think I do not know where his head comes to in the cabinet door, where I saw him every morning of my life? No, sir, that thing in the mask was never Dr. Jekyll—God knows what it was, but it was never Dr. Jekyll; and it is the belief of my heart that there was murder done."

"Poole," replied the lawyer, "if you say that, it will become my duty to make certain. Much as I desire to spare your master's feelings, much as I am puzzled by this note which seems to prove him to be still alive, I shall consider it my duty to break in that door."

"Ah, Mr. Utterson, that's talking!" cried the butler.

"And now comes the second question," resumed Utterson: "Who is going to do it?"

"Why, you and me," was the undaunted reply.

"That's very well said," returned the lawyer; "and whatever comes of it, I shall make it my business to see you are no loser."

"There is an axe in the theatre," continued Poole; "and you might take the kitchen poker for yourself."

The lawyer took that rude but weighty instrument into his hand, and balanced it. "Do you know, Poole," he said, looking up, "that you and I are about to place ourselves in a position of some peril?"

"You may say so, sir, indeed," returned the butler.

"It is well, then that we should be frank," said the other. "We both think more than we have said; let us make a clean breast. This masked figure that you saw, did you recognise it?"

"Well, sir, it went so quick, and the creature was so doubled up, that I could hardly swear to that," was the answer. "But if you mean, was it Mr. Hyde?—why, yes, I think it was! You see, it was much of the same bigness; and it had the same quick, light way with it; and then who else could have got in by the laboratory door? You have not forgot, sir, that at the time of the murder he had still the key with him? But that's not all. I don't know, Mr. Utterson, if ever you met this Mr. Hyde?"

"Yes," said the lawyer, "I once spoke with him."

"Then you must know as well as the rest of us that there was something queer about that gentleman—something that gave a man a turn—I don't know rightly how to say it, sir, beyond this: that you felt in your marrow kind of cold and thin."

"I own I felt something of what you describe," said Mr. Utterson.

"Quite so, sir," returned Poole. "Well, when that masked thing like a monkey jumped from among the chemicals and whipped into the cabinet, it went down my spine like ice. O, I know it's not evidence, Mr. Utterson; I'm book-learned enough for that; but a man has his feelings, and I give you my bible-word it was Mr. Hyde!"

"Ay, ay," said the lawyer. "My fears incline to the same point. Evil, I fear, founded—evil was sure to come—of that connection. Ay truly, I believe you; I believe poor Harry is killed; and I believe his murderer (for what purpose, God alone can tell) is still lurking in his victim's room. Well, let our name be vengeance. Call Bradshaw."

The footman came at the summons, very white and nervous.

"Pull yourself together, Bradshaw," said the lawyer. "This suspense, I know, is telling upon all of you; but it is now our intention to make an end of it. Poole, here, and I are going to force our way into the cabinet. If all is well, my shoulders are broad enough to bear the blame. Meanwhile, lest anything should really be amiss, or any malefactor seek to escape by the back, you and the boy must go round the corner with a pair of good sticks and take your post at the laboratory door. We give you ten minutes to get to your stations."

As Bradshaw left, the lawyer looked at his watch. "And now, Poole, let us get to ours," he said; and taking the poker under his arm, led the way into the yard. The scud had banked over the moon, and it was now quite dark. The wind, which only broke in puffs and draughts into that deep well of building, tossed the light of the candle to and fro about their steps, until they came into the shelter of the theatre, where they sat down silently to wait. London hummed solemnly all around; but nearer at hand, the stillness was only broken by the sounds of a footfall moving to and fro along the cabinet floor.

"So it will walk all day, sir," whispered Poole; "ay, and the better part of the night. Only when a new sample comes from the chemist, there's a bit of a break. Ah, it's an ill-conscience that's such an enemy to rest! Ah, sir, there's blood foully shed in every step of it! But hark again, a little closer—put your heart in your ears, Mr. Utterson, and tell me, is that the doctor's foot?"

The steps fell lightly and oddly, with a certain swing, for all they went so slowly; it was different indeed from the heavy creaking tread of Henry Jekyll. Utterson sighed. "Is there never anything else?" he asked.

Poole nodded. "Once," he said. "Once I heard it weeping!"

"Weeping? how that?" said the lawyer, conscious of a sudden chill of horror.

"Weeping like a woman or a lost soul," said the butler. "I came away with that upon my heart, that I could have wept too."

But now the ten minutes drew to an end. Poole disinterred the axe from under a stack of packing straw; the candle was set upon the nearest table to light them to the attack; and they drew near with bated breath to where that patient foot was still going up and down, up and down, in the quiet of the night.

"Jekyll," cried Utterson, with a loud voice, "I demand to see you." He paused a moment, but there came no reply. "I give you fair warning, our suspicions are aroused, and I must and shall see you," he resumed; "if not by fair means, then by foul—if not of your consent, then by brute force!"

"Utterson," said the voice, "for God's sake, have mercy!"

"Ah, that's not Jekyll's voice—it's Hyde's!" cried Utterson. "Down with the door, Poole!"

Poole swung the axe over his shoulder; the blow shook the building, and the red baize door leaped against the lock and hinges. A dismal screech, as of mere animal terror, rang from the cabinet. Up went the axe again, and again the panels crashed and the frame bounded; four times the blow fell; but the wood was tough and the fittings were of excellent workmanship; and it was not until the fifth, that the lock burst and the wreck of the door fell inwards on the carpet.

The besiegers, appalled by their own riot and the stillness that had succeeded, stood back a little and peered in. There lay the cabinet before their eyes in the quiet lamplight, a good fire glowing and chattering on the hearth, the kettle singing its thin strain, a drawer or two open, papers neatly set forth on the business table, and nearer the fire, the things laid out for tea: the quietest room, you would have said, and, but for the glazed presses full of chemicals, the most commonplace that night in London.

Right in the midst there lay the body of a man sorely contorted and still twitching. They drew near on tiptoe, turned it on its back and beheld the face of Edward Hyde. He was dressed in clothes far too large for him, clothes of the doctor's bigness; the cords of his face still moved with a semblance of life, but life was quite gone; and by the crushed phial in the hand and the strong smell of kernels that hung upon the air, Utterson knew that he was looking on the body of a self-destroyer.

"We have come too late," he said sternly, "whether to save or punish. Hyde is gone to his account; and it only remains for us to find the body of your master."

The far greater proportion of the building was occupied by the theatre, which filled almost the whole ground story and was lighted from above, and by the cabinet, which formed an upper story at one end and looked upon the court. A corridor joined the theatre to the door on the by-street; and with this the cabinet communicated separately by a second flight of stairs. There were besides a few dark closets and a spacious cellar. All these they now thoroughly examined. Each closet needed but a glance, for all were empty, and all, by the dust that fell from their doors, had stood long unopened. The cellar, indeed, was filled with crazy lumber, mostly dating from the times of the surgeon who was Jekyll's predecessor; but even as they opened the door they were advertised of the uselessness of further search, by the fall of a perfect mat of cobweb which had for years sealed up the entrance. Nowhere was there any trace of Henry Jekyll, dead or alive.

Poole stamped on the flags of the corridor. "He must be buried here," he said, hearkening to the sound.

"Or he may have fled," said Utterson, and he turned to examine the door in the by-street. It was locked; and lying near by on the flags, they found the key, already stained with rust.

"This does not look like use," observed the lawyer.

"Use!" echoed Poole. "Do you not see, sir, it is broken? much as if a man had stamped on it."

"Ay," continued Utterson, "and the fractures, too, are rusty." The two men looked at each other with a scare. "This is beyond me, Poole," said the lawyer. "Let us go back to the cabinet."

They mounted the stair in silence, and still with an occasional awestruck glance at the dead body, proceeded more thoroughly to examine the contents of the cabinet. At one table, there were traces of chemical work, various measured heaps of some white salt being laid on glass saucers, as though for an experiment in which the unhappy man had been prevented.

"That is the same drug that I was always bringing him," said Poole; and even as he spoke, the kettle with a startling noise boiled over.

This brought them to the fireside, where the easy-chair was drawn cosily up, and the tea things stood ready to the sitter's elbow, the very sugar in the cup. There were several books on a shelf; one lay beside the tea things open, and Utterson was amazed to find it a copy of a pious work, for which Jekyll had several times expressed a great esteem, annotated, in his own hand, with startling blasphemies.

Next, in the course of their review of the chamber, the searchers came to the cheval-glass, into whose depths they looked with an involuntary horror. But it was so turned as to show them nothing but the rosy glow playing on the roof, the fire sparkling in a hundred repetitions along the glazed front of the presses, and their own pale and fearful countenances stooping to look in.

"This glass has seen some strange things, sir," whispered Poole.

"And surely none stranger than itself," echoed the lawyer in the same tones. "For what did Jekyll"—he caught himself up at the word with a start, and then conquering the weakness—"what could Jekyll want with it?" he said.

"You may say that!" said Poole.

Next they turned to the business table. On the desk, among the neat array of papers, a large envelope was uppermost, and bore, in the doctor's hand, the name of Mr. Utterson. The lawyer unsealed it, and several enclosures fell to the floor. The first was a will, drawn in the same eccentric terms as the one which he had returned six months before, to serve as a testament in case of death and as a deed of gift in case of disappearance; but in place of the name of Edward Hyde, the lawyer, with indescribable amazement, read the name of Gabriel John Utterson. He looked at Poole, and then back at the paper, and last of all at the dead malefactor stretched upon the carpet.

"My head goes round," he said. "He has been all these days in possession; he had no cause to like me; he must have raged to see himself displaced; and he has not destroyed this document."

He caught up the next paper; it was a brief note in the doctor's hand and dated at the top. "O Poole!" the lawyer cried, "he was alive and here this day. He cannot have been disposed of in so short a space; he must be still alive, he must have fled! And then, why fled? and how? and in that case, can we venture to declare this suicide? O, we must be careful. I foresee that we may yet involve your master in some dire catastrophe."

"Why don't you read it, sir?" asked Poole.

"Because I fear," replied the lawyer solemnly. "God grant I have no cause for it!" And with that he brought the paper to his eyes and read as follows:

"MY DEAR UTTERSON,—When this shall fall into your hands, I shall have disappeared, under what circumstances I have not the penetration to foresee, but my instinct and all the circumstances of my nameless situation tell me that the end is sure and must be early. Go then, and first read the narrative which Lanyon warned me he was to place in your hands; and if you care to hear more, turn to the confession of

"Your unworthy and unhappy friend,

"HENRY JEKYLL."

"There was a third enclosure?" asked Utterson.

"Here, sir," said Poole, and gave into his hands a considerable packet sealed in several places.

The lawyer put it in his pocket. "I would say nothing of this paper. If your master has fled or is dead, we may at least save his credit. It is now ten; I must go home and read these documents in quiet; but I shall be back before midnight, when we shall send for the police."

They went out, locking the door of the theatre behind them; and Utterson, once more leaving the servants gathered about the fire in the hall, trudged back to his office to read the two narratives in which this mystery was now to be explained.

DR. LANYON'S NARRATIVE

ON THE NINTH OF JANUARY, now four days ago, I received by the evening delivery a registered envelope, addressed in the hand of my colleague and old school companion, Henry Jekyll. I was a good deal surprised by this; for we were by no means in the habit of correspondence; I had seen the man, dined with him, indeed, the night before; and I could imagine nothing in our intercourse that should justify formality of registration. The contents increased my wonder; for this is how the letter ran:

"10th December, 18—

"DEAR LANYON,—You are one of my oldest friends; and although we may have differed at times on scientific questions, I cannot remember, at least on my side, any break in our affection. There was never a day when, if you had said to me, 'Jekyll, my life, my honour, my reason, depend upon you,' I would not have sacrificed my left hand to help you. Lanyon, my life, my honour, my reason, are all at your mercy; if you fail me to-night, I am lost. You might suppose, after this preface, that I am going to ask you for something dishonourable to grant. Judge for yourself.

"I want you to postpone all other engagements for to-night—ay, even if you were summoned to the bedside of an emperor; to take a cab, unless your carriage should be actually at the door; and with this letter in your hand for consultation, to drive straight to my house. Poole, my butler, has his orders; you will find him waiting your arrival with a locksmith. The door of my cabinet is then to be forced: and you are to go in alone; to open the glazed press (letter E) on the left hand, breaking the lock if it be shut; and to draw out, *with all its contents as they stand*, the fourth drawer from the top or (which is the same thing) the third from the bottom. In my extreme distress of mind, I have a morbid fear of misdirecting you; but even if I am in error, you may know the right drawer by its contents: some powders, a phial and a paper book. This drawer I beg of you to carry back with you to Cavendish Square exactly as it stands.

"That is the first part of the service: now for the second. You should be back, if you set out at once on the receipt of this, long before midnight; but I will leave you that amount of margin, not only in the fear of one of those obstacles that can neither be prevented nor foreseen, but because an hour when your servants are in bed is to be preferred for what will then remain to do. At midnight, then, I have to ask you to be alone in your consulting room, to admit with your own hand into the house a man who will present himself in my name, and to place in his hands the drawer that you will have brought with you from my cabinet. Then you will have played your part and earned my gratitude completely. Five minutes afterwards, if you insist upon an explanation, you will have understood that these arrangements are of capital importance; and that by the neglect of one of them, fantastic as they must appear, you might have charged your conscience with my death or the ship-wreck of my reason.

"Confident as I am that you will not trifle with this appeal, my heart sinks and my hand trembles at the bare thought of such a possibility. Think of me at this hour, in a strange place, labouring under a blackness of distress that no fancy can exaggerate, and yet well aware that, if you will but punctually serve me, my troubles will roll away like a story that is told. Serve me, my dear Lanyon and save

"Your friend,

"H.J.

"P.S.—I had already sealed this up when a fresh terror struck upon my soul. It is possible that the post-office may fail me, and this letter not come into your hands until to-morrow morning. In that case, dear Lanyon, do my errand when it shall be most convenient for you in the course of the day; and once more expect my messenger at midnight. It may then already be too late; and if that night passes without event, you will know that you have seen the last of Henry Jekyll."

Upon the reading of this letter, I made sure my colleague was insane; but till that was proved beyond the possibility of doubt, I felt bound to do as he requested. The less I understood of this farrago, the less I was in a position to judge of its importance; and an appeal so worded could not be set aside without a grave responsibility. I rose accordingly from table, got into a hansom, and drove straight to Jekyll's house. The butler was awaiting my arrival; he had received by the same post as mine a registered letter of instruction, and had sent at once for a locksmith and a carpenter. The tradesmen came while we were yet speaking; and we moved in a body to old Dr. Denman's surgical theatre, from which (as you are doubtless aware) Jekyll's private cabinet is most conveniently entered. The door was very strong, the lock excellent; the carpenter avowed he would have great trouble and have to do much damage, if force were to be used; and the locksmith was near despair. But this last was a handy fellow, and after two hours' work, the door stood open. The press marked E was unlocked; and I took out the drawer, had it filled up with straw and tied in a sheet, and returned with it to Cavendish Square.

Here I proceeded to examine its contents. The powders were neatly enough made up, but not with the nicety of the dispensing chemist; so that it was plain they were of Jekyll's private manufacture: and when I opened one of the wrappers I found what seemed to me a simple crystalline salt of a white colour. The phial, to which I next turned my attention, might have been about half full of a blood-red liquor, which was highly pungent to the sense of smell and seemed to me to contain phosphorus and some volatile ether. At the other ingredients I could make no guess. The book was an ordinary version book and contained little but a series of dates. These covered a period of many years, but I observed that the entries ceased nearly a year ago and quite abruptly. Here and there a brief remark was appended to a date, usually no more than a single word: "double" occurring perhaps six times in a total of several hundred entries; and once very early in the list and followed by several marks of exclamation, "total failure!!!" All this, though it whetted my curiosity, told me little that was definite. Here were a phial of some tincture, a paper of some salt, and the record of a series of experiments that had led (like too many of Jekyll's investigations) to no end of practical usefulness. How could the presence of these articles in my house affect either the honour, the sanity, or the life of my flighty colleague? If his messenger could go to one place, why could he not go to another? And even granting some impediment, why was this gentleman to be received by me in secret? The more I reflected the more convinced I grew that I was dealing with a case of cerebral disease; and though I dismissed my servants to bed, I loaded an old revolver, that I might be found in some posture of self-defence.

Twelve o'clock had scarce rung out over London, ere the knocker sounded very gently on the door. I went myself at the summons, and found a small man crouching against the pillars of the portico.

"Are you come from Dr. Jekyll?" I asked.

He told me "yes" by a constrained gesture; and when I had bidden him enter, he did not obey me without a searching backward glance into the darkness of the square. There was a policeman not far off, advancing with his bull's eye open; and at the sight, I thought my visitor started and made greater haste.

These particulars struck me, I confess, disagreeably; and as I followed him into the bright light of the consulting room, I kept my hand ready on my weapon. Here, at last, I had a chance of clearly seeing him. I had never set eyes on him before, so much was certain. He was small, as I have said; I was struck besides with the shocking expression of his face, with his remarkable combination of great muscular activity and great apparent debility of constitution, and—last but not least—with the odd, subjective disturbance caused by his neighbourhood. This bore some resemblance to incipient rigour, and was accompanied by a marked sinking of the pulse. At the time, I set it down to some idiosyncratic, personal distaste, and merely wondered at the acuteness of the symptoms; but I have since had reason to believe the cause to lie much deeper in the nature of man, and to turn on some nobler hinge than the principle of hatred.

This person (who had thus, from the first moment of his entrance, struck in me what I can only describe as a disgustful curiosity) was dressed in a fashion that would have made an ordinary person laughable; his clothes, that is to say, although they were of rich and sober fabric, were enormously too large for him in every measurement—the trousers hanging on his legs and rolled up to keep them from the ground, the waist of the coat below his haunches, and the collar sprawling wide upon his shoulders. Strange to relate, this ludicrous accoutrement was far from moving me to laughter. Rather, as there was something abnormal and misbegotten in the very essence of the creature that now faced me—something seizing, surprising and revolting—this fresh disparity seemed but to fit in with and to reinforce it; so that to my interest in the man's nature and character, there was added a curiosity as to his origin, his life, his fortune and status in the world.

These observations, though they have taken so great a space to be set down in, were yet the work of a few seconds. My visitor was, indeed, on fire with sombre excitement.

"Have you got it?" he cried. "Have you got it?" And so lively was his impatience that he even laid his hand upon my arm and sought to shake me.

I put him back, conscious at his touch of a certain icy pang along my blood. "Come, sir," said I. "You forget that I have not yet the pleasure of your acquaintance. Be seated, if you please." And I showed him an example, and sat down myself in my customary seat and with as fair an imitation of my ordinary manner to a patient, as the lateness of the hour, the nature of my preoccupations, and the horror I had of my visitor, would suffer me to muster.

"I beg your pardon, Dr. Lanyon," he replied civilly enough. "What you say is very well founded; and my impatience has shown its heels to my politeness. I come here at the instance of your colleague, Dr. Henry Jekyll, on a piece of business of some moment; and I understood..." He paused and put his hand to his throat, and I could see, in spite of his collected manner, that he was wrestling against the approaches of the hysteria—"I understood, a drawer..."

But here I took pity on my visitor's suspense, and some perhaps on my own growing curiosity.

"There it is, sir," said I, pointing to the drawer, where it lay on the floor behind a table and still covered with the sheet.

He sprang to it, and then paused, and laid his hand upon his heart: I could hear his teeth grate with the convulsive action of his jaws; and his face was so ghastly to see that I grew alarmed both for his life and reason.

"Compose yourself," said I.

He turned a dreadful smile to me, and as if with the decision of despair, plucked away the sheet. At sight of the contents, he uttered one loud sob of such immense relief that I sat petrified. And the next moment, in a voice that was already fairly well under control, "Have you a graduated glass?" he asked.

I rose from my place with something of an effort and gave him what he asked.

He thanked me with a smiling nod, measured out a few minims of the red tincture and added one of the powders. The mixture, which was at first of a reddish hue, began, in proportion as the crystals melted, to brighten in colour, to effervesce audibly, and to throw off small fumes of vapour. Suddenly and at the same moment, the ebullition ceased and the compound changed to a dark purple, which faded again more slowly to a watery green. My visitor, who had watched these metamorphoses with a keen eye, smiled, set down the glass upon the table, and then turned and looked upon me with an air of scrutiny.

"And now," said he, "to settle what remains. Will you be wise? will you be guided? will you suffer me to take this glass in my hand and to go forth from your house without further parley? or has the greed of curiosity too much command of you? Think before you answer, for it shall be done as you decide. As you decide, you shall be left as you were before, and neither richer nor wiser, unless the sense of service rendered to a man in mortal distress may be counted as a kind of riches of the soul. Or, if you shall so prefer to choose, a new province of knowledge and new avenues to fame and power shall be laid open to you, here, in this room, upon the instant; and your sight shall be blasted by a prodigy to stagger the unbelief of Satan."

"Sir," said I, affecting a coolness that I was far from truly possessing, "you speak enigmas, and you will perhaps not wonder that I hear you with no very strong impression of belief. But I have gone too far in the way of inexplicable services to pause before I see the end."

"It is well," replied my visitor. "Lanyon, you remember your vows: what follows is under the seal of our profession. And now, you who have so long been bound to the most narrow and material views, you who have denied the virtue of transcendental medicine, you who have derided your superiors—behold!"

He put the glass to his lips and drank at one gulp. A cry followed; he reeled, staggered, clutched at the table and held on, staring with injected eyes, gasping with open mouth; and as I looked there came, I thought, a change—he seemed to swell—his face became suddenly black and the features seemed to melt and alter—and the next moment, I had sprung to my feet and leaped back against the wall, my arms raised to shield me from that prodigy, my mind submerged in terror.

"O God!" I screamed, and "O God!" again and again; for there before my eyes—pale and shaken, and half fainting, and groping before him with his hands, like a man restored from death—there stood Henry Jekyll!

What he told me in the next hour, I cannot bring my mind to set on paper. I saw what I saw, I heard what I heard, and my soul sickened at it; and yet now when that sight has faded from my eyes, I ask myself if I believe it, and I cannot answer. My life is shaken to its roots; sleep has left me; the deadliest terror sits by me at all hours of the day and night; and I feel that my days are numbered, and that I must die; and yet I shall die incredulous. As for the moral turpitude that man unveiled to me, even with tears of penitence, I cannot, even in memory, dwell on it without a start of horror. I will say but one thing, Utterson, and that (if you can bring your mind to credit it) will be more than enough. The creature who crept into my house that night was, on Jekyll's own confession, known by the name of Hyde and hunted for in every corner of the land as the murderer of Carew.

HASTIE LANYON.

HENRY JEKYLL'S FULL STATEMENT OF THE CASE

I WAS BORN in the year 18— to a large fortune, endowed besides with excellent parts, inclined by nature to industry, fond of the respect of the wise and good among my fellow-men, and thus, as might have been supposed, with every guarantee of an honourable and distinguished future. And indeed the worst of my faults was a certain impatient gaiety of disposition, such as has made the happiness of many, but such as I found it hard to reconcile with my imperious desire to carry my head high, and wear a more than commonly grave countenance before the public. Hence it came about that I concealed my pleasures; and that when I reached years of reflection, and began to look round me and take stock of my progress and position in the world, I stood already committed to a profound duplicity of life. Many a man would have even blazoned such irregularities as I was guilty of; but from the high views that I had set before me, I regarded and hid them with an almost morbid sense of shame. It was thus rather the exacting nature of my aspirations than any particular degradation in my faults, that made me what I was, and, with even a deeper trench than in the majority of men, severed in me those provinces of good and ill which divide and compound man's dual nature. In this case, I was driven to reflect deeply and inveterately on that hard law of life, which lies at the root of religion and is one of the most plentiful springs of distress. Though so profound a double-dealer, I was in no sense a hypocrite; both sides of me were in dead earnest; I was no more myself when I laid aside restraint and plunged in shame, than when I laboured, in the eye of day, at the furtherance of knowledge or the relief of sorrow and suffering. And it chanced that the direction of my scientific studies, which led wholly towards the mystic and the transcendental, reacted and shed a strong light on this consciousness of the perennial war among my members. With every day, and from both sides of my intelligence, the moral and the intellectual, I thus drew steadily nearer to that truth, by whose partial discovery I have been doomed to such a dreadful ship-wreck: that man is not truly one, but truly two. I say two, because the state of my own knowledge does not pass beyond that point. Others will follow, others will outstrip me on the same lines; and I hazard the guess that man will be ultimately known for a mere polity of multifarious, incongruous and independent denizens. I, for my part, from the nature of my life, advanced infallibly in one direction and in one direction only. It was on the moral side, and in my own person, that I learned to recognise the thorough and primitive duality of man; I saw that, of the two natures that contended in the field of my consciousness, even if I could rightly be said to be either, it was only because I was radically both; and from an early date, even before the course of my scientific discoveries had begun to suggest the most naked possibility of such a miracle, I had learned to dwell with pleasure, as a be-loved day-dream, on the thought of the separation of these elements. If each, I told myself, could be housed in separate identities, life would be relieved of all that was unbearable; the unjust might go his way, delivered from the aspirations and remorse of his more upright twin; and the just could walk steadfastly and securely on his upward path, doing the good things in which he found his pleasure, and no longer exposed to disgrace and penitence by the hands of this extraneous evil. It was the curse of mankind that these incongruous faggots were thus bound together—that in the agonised womb of consciousness, these polar twins should be continuously struggling. How, then, were they dissociated?

I was so far in my reflections when, as I have said, a side light began to shine upon the subject from the laboratory table. I began to perceive more deeply than it has ever yet been stated, the trembling immateriality, the mist-like transience, of this seemingly so solid body in which we walk attired. Certain agents I found to have the power to shake and pluck back that fleshly vestment, even as a wind might toss the curtains of a pavilion. For two good reasons, I will not enter deeply into this scientific branch of my confession. First, because I have been made to learn that the doom and burthen of our life is bound for ever on man's shoulders, and when the attempt is made to cast it off, it but returns upon us with more unfamiliar and more awful pressure. Second, because, as my narrative will make, alas! too evident, my discoveries were incomplete. Enough then, that I not only recognised my natural body from the mere aura and effulgence of certain of the powers that made up my spirit, but managed to compound a drug by which these powers should be dethroned from their supremacy, and a second form and countenance substituted, none the less natural to me because they were the expression, and bore the stamp, of lower elements in my soul.

I hesitated long before I put this theory to the test of practice. I knew well that I risked death; for any drug that so potently controlled and shook the very fortress of identity, might by the least scruple of an overdose or at the least inopportunity in the moment of exhibition, utterly blot out that immaterial tabernacle which I looked to it to change. But the temptation of a discovery so singular and profound, at last overcame the suggestions of alarm. I had long since prepared my tincture; I purchased at once, from a firm of wholesale chemists, a large quantity of a particular salt which I knew, from my experiments, to be the last ingredient required; and late one accursed night, I compounded the elements, watched them boil and smoke together in the glass, and when the ebullition had subsided, with a strong glow of courage, drank off the potion.

The most racking pangs succeeded: a grinding in the bones, deadly nausea, and a horror of the spirit that cannot be exceeded at the hour of birth or death. Then these agonies began swiftly to subside, and I came to myself as if out of a great sickness. There was something strange in my sensations, something indescribably new and, from its very novelty, incredibly sweet. I felt younger, lighter, happier in body; within I was conscious of a heady recklessness, a current of disordered sensual images running like a mill race in my fancy, a solution of the bonds of obligation, an unknown but not an innocent freedom of the soul. I knew myself, at the first breath of this new life, to be more wicked, tenfold more wicked, sold a slave to my original evil; and the thought, in that moment, braced and delighted me like wine. I stretched out my hands, exulting in the freshness of these sensations; and in the act, I was suddenly aware that I had lost in stature.

There was no mirror, at that date, in my room; that which stands beside me as I write, was brought there later on and for the very purpose of these transformations. The night however, was far gone into the morning—the morning, black as it was,

was nearly ripe for the conception of the day—the inmates of my house were locked in the most rigorous hours of slumber; and I determined, flushed as I was with hope and triumph, to venture in my new shape as far as to my bedroom. I crossed the yard, wherein the constellations looked down upon me, I could have thought, with wonder, the first creature of that sort that their unsleeping vigilance had yet disclosed to them; I stole through the corridors, a stranger in my own house; and coming to my room, I saw for the first time the appearance of Edward Hyde.

I must here speak by theory alone, saying not that which I know, but that which I suppose to be most probable. The evil side of my nature, to which I had now transferred the stamping efficacy, was less robust and less developed than the good which I had just deposed. Again, in the course of my life, which had been, after all, nine tenths a life of effort, virtue and control, it had been much less exercised and much less exhausted. And hence, as I think, it came about that Edward Hyde was so much smaller, slighter and younger than Henry Jekyll. Even as good shone upon the countenance of the one, evil was written broadly and plainly on the face of the other. Evil besides (which I must still believe to be the lethal side of man) had left on that body an imprint of deformity and decay. And yet when I looked upon that ugly idol in the glass, I was conscious of no repugnance, rather of a leap of welcome. This, too, was myself. It seemed natural and human. In my eyes it bore a livelier image of the spirit, it seemed more express and single, than the imperfect and divided countenance I had been hitherto accustomed to call mine. And in so far I was doubtless right. I have observed that when I wore the semblance of Edward Hyde, none could come near to me at first without a visible misgiving of the flesh. This, as I take it, was because all human beings, as we meet them, are commingled out of good and evil: and Edward Hyde, alone in the ranks of mankind, was pure evil.

I lingered but a moment at the mirror: the second and conclusive experiment had yet to be attempted; it yet remained to be seen if I had lost my identity beyond redemption and must flee before daylight from a house that was no longer mine; and hurrying back to my cabinet, I once more prepared and drank the cup, once more suffered the pangs of dissolution, and came to myself once more with the character, the stature and the face of Henry Jekyll.

That night I had come to the fatal cross-roads. Had I approached my discovery in a more noble spirit, had I risked the experiment while under the empire of generous or pious aspirations, all must have been otherwise, and from these agonies of death and birth, I had come forth an angel instead of a fiend. The drug had no discriminating action; it was neither diabolical nor divine; it but shook the doors of the prison-house of my disposition; and like the captives of Philippi,[1]

---

1 Paul's account in Acts 16:26 tells of an earthquake that opens the doors of the Philippian jail cells and loosens the prisoners' bonds, setting them free.

that which stood within ran forth. At that time my virtue slumbered; my evil, kept awake by ambition, was alert and swift to seize the occasion; and the thing that was projected was Edward Hyde. Hence, although I had now two characters as well as two appearances, one was wholly evil, and the other was still the old Henry Jekyll, that incongruous compound of whose reformation and improvement I had already learned to despair. The movement was thus wholly toward the worse.

Even at that time, I had not conquered my aversions to the dryness of a life of study. I would still be merrily disposed at times; and as my pleasures were (to say the least) undignified, and I was not only well known and highly considered, but growing towards the elderly man, this incoherency of my life was daily growing more unwelcome. It was on this side that my new power tempted me until I fell in slavery. I had but to drink the cup, to doff at once the body of the noted professor, and to assume, like a thick cloak, that of Edward Hyde. I smiled at the notion; it seemed to me at the time to be humourous; and I made my preparations with the most studious care. I took and furnished that house in Soho, to which Hyde was tracked by the police; and engaged as a housekeeper a creature whom I knew well to be silent and unscrupulous. On the other side, I announced to my servants that a Mr. Hyde (whom I described) was to have full liberty and power about my house in the square; and to parry mishaps, I even called and made myself a familiar object, in my second character. I next drew up that will to which you so much objected; so that if anything befell me in the person of Dr. Jekyll, I could enter on that of Edward Hyde without pecuniary loss. And thus fortified, as I supposed, on every side, I began to profit by the strange immunities of my position.

Men have before hired bravos to transact their crimes, while their own person and reputation sat under shelter. I was the first that ever did so for his pleasures. I was the first that could plod in the public eye with a load of genial respectability, and in a moment, like a schoolboy, strip off these lendings and spring headlong into the sea of liberty. But for me, in my impenetrable mantle, the safety was complete. Think of it—I did not even exist! Let me but escape into my laboratory door, give me but a second or two to mix and swallow the draught that I had always standing ready; and whatever he had done, Edward Hyde would pass away like the stain of breath upon a mirror; and there in his stead, quietly at home, trimming the midnight lamp in his study, a man who could afford to laugh at suspicion, would be Henry Jekyll.

The pleasures which I made haste to seek in my disguise were, as I have said, undignified; I would scarce use a harder term. But in the hands of Edward Hyde, they soon began to turn toward the monstrous. When I would come back from these excursions, I was often plunged into a kind of wonder at my vicarious depravity. This familiar that I called out of my own soul, and sent forth alone to do his good pleasure, was a being inherently malign and villainous; his every act and thought centered on self; drinking pleasure with bestial avidity from any degree of torture to another; relentless like a man of stone. Henry Jekyll stood at times aghast before the acts of Edward Hyde; but the situation was apart from ordinary laws, and insidiously relaxed the grasp of conscience. It was Hyde, after all, and Hyde alone, that was guilty. Jekyll was no worse; he woke again to his good qualities seemingly unimpaired; he would even make haste, where it was possible, to undo the evil done by Hyde. And thus his conscience slumbered.

Into the details of the infamy at which I thus connived (for even now I can scarce grant that I committed it) I have no design of entering; I mean but to point out the warnings and the successive steps with which my chastisement approached. I met with one accident which, as it brought on no consequence, I shall no more than mention. An act of cruelty to a child aroused against me the anger of a passer-by, whom I recognised the other day in the person of your kinsman; the doctor and the child's family joined him; there were moments when I feared for my life; and at last, in order to pacify their too just resentment, Edward Hyde had to bring them to the door, and pay them in a cheque drawn in the name of Henry Jekyll. But this danger was easily eliminated from the future, by opening an account at another bank in the name of Edward Hyde himself; and when, by sloping my own hand backward, I had supplied my double with a signature, I thought I sat beyond the reach of fate.

Some two months before the murder of Sir Danvers, I had been out for one of my adventures, had returned at a late hour, and woke the next day in bed with somewhat odd sensations. It was in vain I looked about me; in vain I saw the decent furniture and tall proportions of my room in the square; in vain that I recognised the pattern of the bed curtains and the design of the mahogany frame; something still kept insisting that I was not where I was, that I had not wakened where I seemed to be, but in the little room in Soho where I was accustomed to sleep in the body of Edward Hyde. I smiled to myself, and in my psychological way began lazily to inquire into the elements of this illusion, occasionally, even as I did so, dropping back into a comfortable morning doze. I was still so engaged when, in one of my more wakeful moments, my eyes fell upon my hand. Now the hand of Henry Jekyll (as you have often remarked) was professional in shape and size: it was large, firm, white and comely. But the hand which I now saw, clearly enough, in the yellow light of a mid-London morning, lying half shut on the bed clothes, was lean, corded, knuckly, of a dusky pallor and thickly shaded with a swart growth of hair. It was the hand of Edward Hyde.

I must have stared upon it for near half a minute, sunk as I was in the mere stupidity of wonder, before terror woke up in my breast as sudden and startling as the crash of cymbals; and bounding from my bed, I rushed to the mirror. At the sight that met my eyes, my blood was changed into something exquisitely thin and icy. Yes, I had gone to bed Henry Jekyll, I had awakened Edward Hyde. How was this to be explained? I asked myself; and then, with another bound of terror—how was it to be remedied? It was well on in the morning; the servants were up; all my drugs were in the cabinet—a long journey down two pairs of stairs, through the back passage, across the open court and through the anatomical theatre, from where I was then standing horror-struck. It might indeed be possible to cover my face; but of what use was that, when I was unable to conceal the alteration in my stature? And then with an overpowering sweetness of relief, it came back upon my mind that the servants were already used to the coming and going of my second self. I had soon dressed, as well as I was able, in clothes of my own size: had soon passed through the house, where Bradshaw stared and drew back at seeing Mr. Hyde at such an hour and in such a strange array; and ten minutes later, Dr. Jekyll had returned to his own shape and was sitting down, with a darkened brow, to make a feint of breakfasting.

Small indeed was my appetite. This inexplicable incident, this reversal of my previous experience, seemed, like the Babylonian finger on the wall, to be spelling out the letters of my judgment;[1] and I began to reflect more seriously than ever before on the issues and possibilities of my double existence. That part of me which I had the power of projecting, had lately been much exercised and nourished; it had seemed to me of late as though the body of Edward Hyde had grown in stature, as though (when I wore that form) I were conscious of a more generous tide of blood; and I began to spy a danger that, if this were much prolonged, the balance of my nature might be permanently overthrown, the power of voluntary change be forfeited, and the character of Edward Hyde become irrevocably mine. The power of the drug had not been always equally displayed. Once, very early in my career, it had totally failed me; since then I had been obliged on more than one occasion to double, and once, with infinite risk of death, to treble the amount; and these rare uncertainties had cast hitherto the sole shadow on my contentment. Now, however, and in the light of that morning's accident, I was led to remark that whereas, in the beginning, the difficulty had been to throw off the body of Jekyll, it had of late gradually but decidedly transferred itself to the other side. All things therefore seemed to point to this; that I was slowly losing hold of my original and better self, and becoming slowly incorporated with my second and worse.

Between these two, I now felt I had to choose. My two natures had memory in common, but all other faculties were most unequally shared between them. Jekyll (who was composite) now with the most sensitive apprehensions, now with a greedy gusto, projected and shared in the pleasures and adventures of Hyde;

---

1 King Belshazzar of Babylon observes a human hand writing on the wall. As he cannot read it, he summons Daniel; Daniel reads the message and tells the king that he will be punished because he did not honor God (Daniel 5:5-28).

but Hyde was indifferent to Jekyll, or but remembered him as the mountain bandit remembers the cavern in which he conceals himself from pursuit. Jekyll had more than a father's interest; Hyde had more than a son's indifference. To cast in my lot with Jekyll, was to die to those appetites which I had long secretly indulged and had of late begun to pamper. To cast it in with Hyde, was to die to a thousand interests and aspirations, and to become, at a blow and forever, despised and friendless. The bargain might appear unequal; but there was still another consideration in the scales; for while Jekyll would suffer smartingly in the fires of abstinence, Hyde would be not even conscious of all that he had lost. Strange as my circumstances were, the terms of this debate are as old and commonplace as man; much the same inducements and alarms cast the die for any tempted and trembling sinner; and it fell out with me, as it falls with so vast a majority of my fellows, that I chose the better part and was found wanting in the strength to keep to it.

Yes, I preferred the elderly and discontented doctor, surrounded by friends and cherishing honest hopes; and bade a resolute farewell to the liberty, the comparative youth, the light step, leaping impulses and secret pleasures, that I had enjoyed in the disguise of Hyde. I made this choice perhaps with some unconscious reservation, for I neither gave up the house in Soho, nor destroyed the clothes of Edward Hyde, which still lay ready in my cabinet. For two months, however, I was true to my determination; for two months I led a life of such severity as I had never before attained to, and enjoyed the compensations of an approving conscience. But time began at last to obliterate the freshness of my alarm; the praises of conscience began to grow into a thing of course; I began to be tortured with throes and longings, as of Hyde struggling after freedom; and at last, in an hour of moral weakness, I once again compounded and swallowed the transforming draught.

I do not suppose that, when a drunkard reasons with himself upon his vice, he is once out of five hundred times affected by the dangers that he runs through his brutish, physical insensibility; neither had I, long as I had considered my position, made enough allowance for the complete moral insensibility and insensate readiness to evil, which were the leading characters of Edward Hyde. Yet it was by these that I was punished. My devil had been long caged, he came out roaring. I was conscious, even when I took the draught, of a more unbridled, a more furious propensity to ill. It must have been this, I suppose, that stirred in my soul that tempest of impatience with which I listened to the civilities of my unhappy victim; I declare, at least, before God, no man morally sane could have been guilty of that crime upon so pitiful a provocation; and that I struck in no more reasonable spirit than that in which a sick child may break a plaything. But I had voluntarily stripped myself of all those balancing instincts by which even the worst of us continues to walk with some degree of steadiness among temptations; and in my case, to be tempted, however slightly, was to fall.

Instantly the spirit of hell awoke in me and raged. With a transport of glee, I mauled the unresisting body, tasting delight from every blow; and it was not till weariness had begun to succeed, that I was suddenly, in the top fit of my delirium, struck through the heart by a cold thrill of terror. A mist dispersed; I saw my life to be forfeit; and fled from the scene of these excesses, at once glorying and trembling, my lust of evil gratified and stimulated, my love of life screwed to the topmost peg. I ran to the house in Soho, and (to make assurance doubly sure) destroyed my papers; thence I set out through the lamplit streets, in the same divided ecstasy of mind, gloating on my crime, light-headedly devising others in the future, and yet still hastening and still hearkening in my wake for the steps of the avenger. Hyde had a song upon his lips as he compounded the draught, and as he drank it, pledged the dead man. The pangs of transformation had not done tearing him, before Henry Jekyll, with streaming tears of gratitude and remorse, had fallen upon his knees and lifted his clasped hands to God. The veil of self-indulgence was rent from head to foot. I saw my life as a whole: I followed it up from the days of childhood, when I had walked with my father's hand, and through the self-denying toils of my professional life, to arrive again and again, with the same sense of unreality, at the damned horrors of the evening. I could have screamed aloud; I sought with tears and prayers to smother down the crowd of hideous images and sounds with which my memory swarmed against me; and still, between the petitions, the ugly face of my iniquity stared into my soul. As the acuteness of this remorse began to die away, it was succeeded by a sense of joy. The problem of my conduct was solved. Hyde was thenceforth impossible; whether I would or not, I was now confined to the better part of my existence; and O, how I rejoiced to think of it! with what willing humility, I embraced anew the restrictions of natural life! with what sincere renunciation I locked the door by which I had so often gone and come, and ground the key under my heel!

The next day, came the news that the murder had been overlooked, that the guilt of Hyde was patent to the world, and that the victim was a man high in public estimation. It was not only a crime, it had been a tragic folly. I think I was glad to know it; I think I was glad to have my better impulses thus buttressed and guarded by the terrors of the scaffold. Jekyll was now my city of refuge; let but Hyde peep out an instant, and the hands of all men would be raised to take and slay him.

I resolved in my future conduct to redeem the past; and I can say with honesty that my resolve was fruitful of some good. You know yourself how earnestly in the last months of the last year, I laboured to relieve suffering; you know that much was done for others, and that the days passed quietly, almost happily for myself. Nor can I truly say that I wearied of this beneficent and innocent life; I think instead that I daily enjoyed it more completely; but I was still cursed with my duality of purpose; and as the first edge of my penitence wore off, the lower side of me, so long indulged, so recently chained down, began to growl for licence. Not that I dreamed of resuscitating Hyde; the bare idea of that would startle me to frenzy: no, it was in my own person, that I was once more tempted to trifle with my conscience; and it was as an ordinary secret sinner, that I at last fell before the assaults of temptation.

There comes an end to all things; the most capacious measure is filled at last; and this brief condescension to my evil finally destroyed the balance of my soul. And yet I was not alarmed; the fall seemed natural, like a return to the old days before I had made my discovery. It was a fine, clear, January day, wet under foot where the frost had melted, but cloudless overhead; and the Regent's Park was full of winter chirrupings and sweet with spring odours. I sat in the sun on a bench; the animal within me licking the chops of memory; the spiritual side a little drowsed, promising subsequent penitence, but not yet moved to begin. After all, I reflected, I was like my neighbours; and then I smiled, comparing myself with other men, comparing my active goodwill with the lazy cruelty of their neglect. And at the very moment of that vain-glorious thought, a qualm came over me, a horrid nausea and the most deadly shuddering. These passed away, and left me faint; and then as in its turn faintness subsided, I began to be aware of a change in the temper of my thoughts, a greater boldness, a contempt of danger, a solution of the bonds of obligation. I looked down; my clothes hung formlessly on my shrunken limbs; the hand that lay on my knee was corded and hairy. I was once more Edward Hyde. A moment before I had been safe of all men's respect, wealthy, beloved—the cloth laying for me in the dining-room at home; and now I was the common quarry of mankind, hunted, houseless, a known murderer, thrall to the gallows.

My reason wavered, but it did not fail me utterly. I have more than once observed that, in my second character, my faculties seemed sharpened to a point and my spirits more tensely elastic; thus it came about that, where Jekyll perhaps might have succumbed, Hyde rose to the importance of the moment. My drugs were in one of the presses of my cabinet; how was I to reach them? That was the problem that (crushing my temples in my hands) I set myself to solve. The laboratory door I had closed. If I sought to enter by the house, my own servants would consign me to the gallows. I saw I must employ another hand, and thought of Lanyon. How was he to be reached? how persuaded? Supposing that I escaped capture in the streets, how was I to make my way into his presence? and how should I, an unknown and displeasing visitor, prevail on the famous physician to rifle the study of his colleague, Dr. Jekyll? Then I remembered that of my original character, one part remained to me: I could write my own hand; and once I had conceived that kindling spark, the way that I must follow became lighted up from end to end.

Thereupon, I arranged my clothes as best I could, and summoning a passing hansom, drove to an hotel in Portland Street, the name of which I chanced to remember. At my appearance (which was indeed comical enough, however tragic a fate these garments covered) the driver could not conceal his mirth. I gnashed my teeth upon him with a gust of devilish fury; and the smile withered from his face—happily for him—yet more happily for myself, for in another instant I had certainly dragged him from his perch. At the inn, as I entered, I looked about me with so black a countenance as made the attendants tremble; not a look did they exchange in my presence; but obsequiously took my orders, led me to a private room, and brought me wherewithal to write. Hyde in danger of his life was a creature new to me; shaken with inordinate anger, strung to the pitch of murder, lusting to inflict pain. Yet the creature was astute; mastered his fury with a great effort of the will; composed his two important letters, one to Lanyon and one to Poole; and that he might receive actual evidence of their being posted, sent them out with directions that they should be registered.

Thenceforward, he sat all day over the fire in the private room, gnawing his nails; there he dined, sitting alone with his fears, the waiter visibly quailing before his eye; and thence, when the night was fully come, he set forth in the corner of a closed cab, and was driven to and fro about the streets of the city. He, I say—I cannot say, I. That child of Hell had nothing human; nothing lived in him but fear and hatred. And when at last, thinking the driver had begun to grow suspicious, he discharged the cab and ventured on foot, attired in his misfitting clothes, an object marked out for observation, into the midst of the nocturnal passengers, these two base passions raged within him like a tempest. He walked fast, hunted by his fears, chattering to himself, skulking through the less frequented thoroughfares, counting the minutes that still divided him from midnight. Once a woman spoke to him, offering, I think, a box of lights. He smote her in the face, and she fled.

When I came to myself at Lanyon's, the horror of my old friend perhaps affected me somewhat: I do not know; it was at least but a drop in the sea to the abhorrence with which I looked back upon these hours. A change had come over me. It was no longer the fear of the gallows, it was the horror of being Hyde that racked me. I received Lanyon's condemnation partly in a dream; it was partly in a dream that I came home to my own house and got into bed. I slept after the prostration of the day, with a stringent and profound slumber which not even the nightmares that wrung me could avail to break. I awoke in the morning shaken, weakened, but refreshed. I still hated and feared the thought of the brute that slept within me, and I had not of course forgotten the appalling dangers of the day before; but I was once more at home, in my own house and close to my drugs;

and gratitude for my escape shone so strong in my soul that it almost rivalled the brightness of hope.

I was stepping leisurely across the court after breakfast, drinking the chill of the air with pleasure, when I was seized again with those indescribable sensations that heralded the change; and I had but the time to gain the shelter of my cabinet, before I was once again raging and freezing with the passions of Hyde. It took on this occasion a double dose to recall me to myself; and alas! six hours after, as I sat looking sadly in the fire, the pangs returned, and the drug had to be re-administered. In short, from that day forth it seemed only by a great effort as of gymnastics, and only under the immediate stimulation of the drug, that I was able to wear the countenance of Jekyll. At all hours of the day and night, I would be taken with the premonitory shudder; above all, if I slept, or even dozed for a moment in my chair, it was always as Hyde that I awakened. Under the strain of this continually impending doom and by the sleeplessness to which I now condemned myself, ay, even beyond what I had thought possible to man, I became, in my own person, a creature eaten up and emptied by fever, languidly weak both in body and mind, and solely occupied by one thought: the horror of my other self. But when I slept, or when the virtue of the medicine wore off, I would leap almost without transition (for the pangs of transformation grew daily less marked) into the possession of a fancy brimming with images of terror, a soul boiling with causeless hatreds, and a body that seemed not strong enough to contain the raging energies of life. The powers of Hyde seemed to have grown with the sickliness of Jekyll. And certainly the hate that now divided them was equal on each side. With Jekyll, it was a thing of vital instinct. He had now seen the full deformity of that creature that shared with him some of the phenomena of consciousness, and was co-heir with him to death: and beyond these links of community, which in themselves made the most poignant part of his distress, he thought of Hyde, for all his energy of life, as of something not only hellish but inorganic. This was the shocking thing; that the slime of the pit seemed to utter cries and voices; that the amorphous dust gesticulated and sinned; that what was dead, and had no shape, should usurp the offices of life. And this again, that that insurgent horror was knit to him closer than a wife, closer than an eye; lay caged in his flesh, where he heard it mutter and felt it struggle to be born; and at every hour of weakness, and in the confidence of slumber, prevailed against him, and deposed him out of life. The hatred of Hyde for Jekyll, was of a different order. His terror of the gallows drove him continually to commit temporary suicide, and return to his subordinate station of a part instead of a person; but he loathed the necessity, he loathed the despondency into which Jekyll was now fallen, and he resented the dislike with which he was himself regarded. Hence the ape-like tricks that he would play me, scrawling in my own hand blasphemies on the pages of my books, burning the letters and destroying the portrait of my father; and indeed, had it not been for his fear of death, he would long ago have ruined himself in order to involve me in the ruin. But his love of life is wonderful; I go further: I, who sicken and freeze at the mere thought of him, when I recall the abjection and passion of this attachment, and when I know how he fears my power to cut him off by suicide, I find it in my heart to pity him.

It is useless, and the time awfully fails me, to prolong this description; no one has ever suffered such torments, let that suffice; and yet even to these, habit brough—no, not alleviation—but a certain callousness of soul, a certain acquiescence of despair; and my punishment might have gone on for years, but for the last calamity which has now fallen, and which has finally severed me from my own face and nature. My provision of the salt, which had never been renewed since the date of the first experiment, began to run low. I sent out for a fresh supply, and mixed the draught; the ebullition followed, and the first change of colour, not the second; I drank it and it was without efficiency. You will learn from Poole how I have had London ransacked; it was in vain; and I am now persuaded that my first supply was impure, and that it was that unknown impurity which lent efficacy to the draught.

About a week has passed, and I am now finishing this statement under the influence of the last of the old powders. This, then, is the last time, short of a miracle, that Henry Jekyll can think his own thoughts or see his own face (now how sadly altered!) in the glass. Nor must I delay too long to bring my writing to an end; for if my narrative has hitherto escaped destruction, it has been by a combination of great prudence and great good luck. Should the throes of change take me in the act of writing it, Hyde will tear it in pieces; but if some time shall have elapsed after I have laid it by, his wonderful selfishness and circumscription to the moment will probably save it once again from the action of his ape-like spite. And indeed the doom that is closing on us both, has already changed and crushed him. Half an hour from now, when I shall again and forever reindue that hated personality, I know how I shall sit shuddering and weeping in my chair, or continue, with the most strained and fearstruck ecstasy of listening, to pace up and down this room (my last earthly refuge) and give ear to every sound of menace. Will Hyde die upon the scaffold? or will he find courage to release himself at the last moment? God knows; I am careless; this is my true hour of death, and what is to follow concerns another than myself. Here then, as I lay down the pen and proceed to seal up my confession, I bring the life of that unhappy Henry Jekyll to an end.

1886

T WENTIETH CENTURY AND THE MODERNISTS

1901–1945

ABSTRACT

Little of the Victorians' belief in British exceptionalism survived beyond the first decade of the twentieth century. World War I further shattered any lingering sense of stability. The norms of daily life clearly had evolved and were evolving yet: trains and cars affected travel time; radio transformed communication; television and films opened new venues of entertainment; Albert Einstein's theories of relativity revolutionized human understanding of the universe. Views about the purpose of art also changed, inspiring many artists and writers to forgo the utilitarian, social duty of art and create "art for art's sake." Modernism—a movement in the fine arts and literature dedicated to innovation and experimentation—echoed feelings of anxiety, fragmentation, and disorientation that resulted from living in a modern, fragile, violent world. Loss, death, and destruction caused by global depression and World War II stirred writers to capture the reality of existence. The events in the first half of the twentieth century reshaped global relations as well as artistic expression.

POLITICS

Although Queen Victoria's death in 1901 clearly marked the end of the Victorian age, little radically changed at the turn of the century. Her death marked no transition in political power groups; conservatives initially dominated the political atmosphere. But in 1906, about halfway through the reign of King Edward VII, conservatives lost favor to the Liberal party. Their downfall chiefly resulted from proposed changes to Britain's free trade policy. To increase Britain's revenue, tariffs would be applied to competitors' goods. Theoretically, consumers would purchase colonial goods because they had lower tariffs than those from other countries, a policy known as "imperial preference." But the public, and especially those in the working classes, feared tariffs would raise prices. The Conservative party failed to soothe Britons' panic, and the Liberal platform, which supported free trade, won favor.

Once in power, Liberals endorsed numerous other acts of legislation including several social reforms. Many policies focused on education. Schools provided children with free meals starting in 1906, though supplying food did not become compulsory until 1914. Schools also received grants for medical clinics. Finally, the government required secondary schools to set aside twenty-five percent of their space for deserving but financially underprivileged children. These students attended for free. Lawmakers further turned their attention to improving the wellbeing of workers and those in retirement. Parliament established old-age pensions in 1908 and enforced the National Insurance Act three years later. Requests for unemployment insurance generated some controversy, but health insurance caused much greater debate. Although conservatives insisted that the government could not force workers to pay from their wages, the act passed. Other notable legislature from the Edwardian Age contended with restricting immigration. From the mid-nineteenth century until after the second World War, immigrants funneled into British territory. The Aliens Act of 1905 sought to temper the influx of Irish, German, Russian, Polish, Indian, Japanese, and other migrant groups. The act permitted the Home Secretary to deny any migrant's entrance if they could not support themselves. As a result, migrants typically worked for lower wages, leading many British workers to feel threatened that they may lose their jobs.

Britain not only struggled to control immigration; the sheer geographical distance between its imperial colonies made it challenging to control its empire. Until the early twentieth century, Britain followed "splendid isolation," a policy that prevented it from entering permanent European alliances. Britain's struggle to win the Boer War in South Africa, however, made the nation painfully conscious of its defensive inadequacies. Boers, the largely-farming population of South Africans of Dutch, German, and Hugeonot descent, resisted the British government's attempt to control their resources. Britain's utter mismanagement of the war caused 20,000 to 40,000 Boers to die of unsanitary conditions while placed in British camps. Moreover, mounting colonial rivalries and fears of foreign aggression convinced Britain to ally itself with other countries. British officials especially considered the German Reich a threat. Wilhelm II, the notoriously unpredictable Kaiser, was building a navy fleet for the alleged purpose of contesting Britain's authority. Britain turned to France, its closest European ally, for arms support. But Germany targeted France, and Britain, duty-bound to assist its ally, began strategizing military attacks. The Edwardian age of peace had met its decisive end.

In June 1914, Serbian terrorists assassinated Archduke Franz Ferdinand, the heir to Austria-Hungary's throne. Austria-Hungary, supported by the German military, declared war on Serbia. Though Britain attempted to quell the war, Germany's subsequent invasion of Belgium caused Britain to join the fight. When the British Expeditionary Force (BEF) travelled abroad to assist the French army, however, it suffered such great casualties that mass recruitment became necessary. The lack of anti-war sentiment made propaganda extremely effective. Stories about German atrocities proliferated. Though the British media exaggerated success and suppressed negative aspects of the fight, Britain's participation certainly came with a price. Huge battles brought the nation to the brink of bankruptcy. In spite of Britain's long-term strengths—its navy, widespread empire, and trade routes to Japan, the U.S., and the Commonwealth—its industries were not suited for warfare. Since Britain's industrial base consisted of textiles, coal, iron, shipbuilding, and engineering businesses, it initially floundered to supply the massive amounts of artillery needed for trench warfare.

With so many men fighting, greater numbers of women entered and mobilized the workforce. Nonetheless, socially acceptable employment for women remained extremely limited during the first decade of the twentieth century. Working-class girls received schooling in domestic fields such as cookery and needlework, and the handful of non-domestic occupations included secretarial positions in banking and other businesses. Some middle-class girls studied math and science in order to pursue a higher education. For middle-class women who worked, available occupations involved teaching or nursing. Most women employed during war-time worked in munitions, a dangerous and exacting job. Others became laborers, clerks, and policewomen. Still, the majority of women stayed home. In fact, women experienced increased pressures to raise children and make do with what they had. The cultural relationship between women and men did not change much, and most of those women who found war-time employment were forced back into the home once men returned. But champions of women's rights claimed some victories in 1918. In October, legislature allowing women to become Members of Parliament passed. With the passage of the Sex Disqualification Act in December, women could become magistrates, barristers, senior civil servants, and serve on juries. The war also stimulated increased suffrage rights. The Representation of the People Act assured all men over twenty-one years old the right to vote, and women over thirty—provided they or their husband met a property qualification—could also vote. Complete women's suffrage arrived ten years later, in 1928, and established Britain as a full democracy.

The British government also delayed answering Ireland's appeals. Yearning for independence, the Irish demanded Home Rule for complying with Britain's control of domestic Irish affairs. In preparation for self-rule, Ireland underwent cultural revivals that aimed to form a distinct Irish identity. In 1914, shortly after the beginning of the Great War, Parliament assured Ireland self-government through the Irish Home Rule Act. Parliament refused to enact the legislature during the war, however. Incensed, a group of revolutionary Irish nationalists known as the Irish Republican Brotherhood (IRB) plotted against the British government. On Easter Sunday of 1916, the IRB seized strategic buildings throughout Dublin and proclaimed the formation of an Irish republic. British troops successfully suppressed the rebellion after nearly a week of fighting. The Easter Rising resulted in the execution of fifteen IRB leaders, the implementation of martial law, mass arrests, and a reignition of widespread Irish animosity towards the British. Ireland's War of Independence resumed after World War I. In 1919, the Irish Republican Army (IRA) launched guerrilla attacks against the British government until a cease-fire resulted in the formation of the Irish Free State in 1922. But by that time, Ireland's faltering agrarian economy had already caused extensive poverty and had driven many people to migrate to Britain and the U.S. in the pursuit of more stable lives.

In August of 1918, Germany's military fortitude began to fail. The Bulgarians asked for peace, followed successively by surrenders from Turkey and Austria-Hungary. On November 11, 1918, Britain and the Allied Powers emerged victorious over the Central Powers. The Treaty of Versailles dealt with war reparations, and the formation of the League of Nations in 1920 pledged to maintain world peace, but the Great War inflicted immense damage across the world. The Lost Generation of young men who died in combat totaled over 8.5 million with an additional 20 million wounded. The war debilitated Britain's wellbeing. It owed sizeable debts (mostly to the U.S.) and suffered a severely weakened economy. Domestic production and cheap foreign competitors eliminated its overseas markets. The government hoped returning to the gold standard would generate investment in British businesses which in turn would lower unemployment and stimulate internal demands for British products. Instead, prices skyrocketed, employers slashed wages, and goods were uncompetitive in the global market.

The Great Depression had a severe, worldwide impact. Beginning in the U.S., it soon spread to Europe. In December of 1930, 2.5 million Britons were unemployed, and the nation spent £125 million annually on unemployment benefits. Between 1932 and 1933, unemployed reached its peak at 3 million. Poverty reigned. Areas that relied most heavily upon the "stable" manufacturing industries—such as shipbuilding, coal-mining, heavy equipment manufacturing, and textiles—suffered greatly. Already downscaled from the war, these industries experienced little growth until new trades stimulated their revival. Starting in 1934, development in chemicals, electrical goods, cars, processed foods, and aircraft industries improved Britain's economy. Some trades, however, endured the pangs of the Great Depression until about 1940.

When Britain declared war on Germany on September 3, 1939, Britons met World War II with dread. The country lacked war aims. Mostly it sought to defend its reputation as a global power and protect its European trading interests. Still feeling the fragility of the economy after the Great Depression, the government elected to appease rather than confront the Italian ruler Benito Mussolini and the German Kaiser Adolf Hitler. Still, blackouts and evacuations began almost immediately. Civil liberties were temporarily suspended, and the government encouraged civilians to assist in war efforts by adopting a do-it-yourself mentality. But new hardships began in 1940. Germany invaded France in May, and British forces in France, under the direction of the Prime Minister Winston Churchill, turned and fled. Though Churchill sought a more aggressive, offensive approach, Britain was slow to militarize. Concrete forts, gun emplacements, anti-tank obstacles, barbed wire, and minefields lined England's coast to prevent potential invasion.

Despite its defensive provisions, Britain was ill-equipped to resist Germany's intense Blitzkrieg attacks. The 1940 Battle of Britain and the Blitz resulted in devastation. The Nazis bombed London and other civilian cities nightly. Bombs that landed in working-class neighborhoods decimated entire streets and demolished one-fifth of England's schools. By the end of the war, some 60,000 civilians died during air raids and another 100,000 acquired serious injuries. Lacking fighter planes, Britain won the Battle largely because of Germany's tactical blunders.

The following year, Germany invaded the Soviet Union and Japanese forces attacked Britain's Eastern colonies, including Malaya and Hong Kong. Late in 1941, the Japanese also fired on Pearl Harbor, bringing the U.S. into the fight. After Japan's strikes, the Allies no longer tolerated the idea of ending the war by negotiating for an armistice. Instead, they were determined to force the Axis powers into unconditional surrender. Britain's darkest day loomed ahead, however. On February 15, 1942, Japanese forces invaded Singapore and captured 100,000 British, Australian, New Zealand, and Indian troops. Retaliation ensued. By 1943, Germany shifted to defensive maneuvers. Evidence of its defeat came on D-Day when Allied forces landed in Normandy, France. In addition to destroying the German V-1 and V-2 rocket launch sites, British and ally soldiers discovered concentration camps. News of the human cruelties Hitler and the Nazis committed incensed British civilians. In February of 1945, British and American bombers attacked Dresden, Germany, and killed 135,000 civilians in a single night. The Allied forces claimed V-E Day (Victory in Europe) on May 8, 1945, and V-J Day

(Victory in Japan) on August 14, 1945, following the dropping of atomic bombs on Hiroshima and Nagasaki by the U.S. World War II had become symbolic and ideological—a war of democracy against dictatorship, with democracy prevailing.

World War II rendered Britain bankrupt and financially dependent on the U.S. Moreover, humiliating military defeats obliterated Britain's image of superiority. Indeed, some of Britain's empire had already dissolved during the inter-war years, and the loss of the Asian colonies to Japan evidenced Britain's decreasing power. As waves of anti-colonial sentiment arose, the British government faced renewed pressures to allow territories self-rule. Though it granted India independence in 1947, it prolonged restoring self-government to many of its African colonies. Most African colonies gained independence throughout the 1960s, but Zimbabwe, the last to be liberated, remained under British power until 1980. The majority of Britain's former colonies became part of the British Commonwealth, an international association symbolically guided by the British monarch.

Though still an influential nation, Britain lost global power to the U.S. and the U.S.S.R. after the war. Britain did, however, dedicate itself to managing future humanitarian world crises by joining the United Nations in 1945. Though the British Empire met its end in the years following World War II, the impacts of its control and ideas influenced nations worldwide. The empire is perhaps most known for its efforts to spread the English language, democracy, and Christianity, although it also expanded educational opportunities and technological resources. But for many people, the empire equally provoked discrimination, prejudice, and violence. From the sixteenth century to the twenty-first, the British Empire greatly directed the course of world history.

LITERATURE

Artistic and literary culture struggled to find new direction at the turn of the century. Movements in the fine arts challenged accepted patterns of aesthetic expression well before literature did. The 1910 London art exhibition "Manet and the Post-Impressionists" evidenced the emergence of cubism, art deco, and expressionism, yet literature continued to echo trends of the past. Conservative, imperialistic, and patriotic in nature, Edwardian literature was dominated by male writers and characters. Underlying turmoil about gender, however, materialized. Male writers sought to portray the "unrepresented life" of women, but sexist attitudes infuse nearly all these attempts. New Woman fiction, as written by women, faced a decline, and women writers only gained acknowledgement in lower-status genres, namely children's literature and romance.

Edwardian literature, named after King Edward VII, who reigned from 1901 until 1910, is often colored by themes of melancholy, nostalgia, and idealization of the past. J.M. Barrie's 1904 play *Peter Pan*, for example, is underscored by death, and Peter laments the loss of childhood. Some fictional works noted that the military blunders in the previous era led to a crisis of imperial destiny, as in Joseph Conrad's 1902 novella *Heart of Darkness*. Other writers celebrated the end of Victorian culture. Generational revolt, wherein a young protagonist rejects oppressive Victorian rules and symbols, became a common theme, as did the liberation of the younger generation through the death of their parents.

Writers of Edwardian literature belong in the Modernist period, but their beliefs frequently differ from those of later Modernist writers. Edwardian literature often focuses on external events rather than internal action and is laden with material details. The Edwardian giants—such as John Galsworthy, H.G. Wells, and the highly-respected novelist Arnold Bennet—tend to define their characters in relation to markers such as wealth, clothing, and property. The next generation of writers, which emerged in 1910 when George V ascended to the throne, scrutinized Edwardians for failing to reveal the value or significance of concrete, physical details. The younger generation further accused them of creating unbelievable characters. The Edwardian literary realm of logic and science seemingly shattered with World War I, and upcoming writers began experimenting with how characters are presented, focusing not on external details, but on internal feelings.

Modernists shifted from describing the world to exploring how it is depicted through narration, form, perspective, and diction. Characterized by experimentation, innovation, and self-awareness, the modernist movement rejected the past and expressed anxiety about the present and future. It is a culmination of what preceded it—revolutionary wars, industrialization, urbanization, technological changes, religious doubt, scientific discovery, blurred gender roles—and a response to contemporary events. For example, Sigmund Freud's studies on psychoanalysis and the unconscious mind in the late 1800s and early 1900s influenced how modernist writers conveyed human psychology. Similarly, Einstein's theories of relativity radically transformed conceptions of space and time, inspiring many modernist writers to depict a reality that was unique and relative to an individual.

Unlike the image of the heroic, solitary, overlooked writer of the past, the modernist writer was a prominent, radical, defiant presence who communicated with an audience but remained separate from it. Among the most prominent and influential modernists are D.H. Lawrence, James Joyce, and Virginia Woolf. Joseph Conrad, E.M. Forster, Ford Madox Ford, T.S. Eliot, and W.B. Yeats also reflected the principles of modernism. Driven by a desire to make sense of the world through art, these writers and others sought to create unity through fragmentation and capture consciousness itself. Whereas Victorian novelists portrayed material realism, Modernists emphasized subjectivity. They turned their attention decisively inward, downplaying the social world in favor of individual consciousness. Modernist literature embraces instability and discontinuity, often toying with the reader's perception of time or changing locations without warning. Recurring symbols compel readers to derive meaning from the speaker's or narrator's associations and observations.

Language, to many Modernists, failed to transparently express what people need it to express. Many writers and artists dedicated their efforts to finding new ways of explaining the world. Prosaists questioned language itself and constantly reassessed its use. Some poets relinquished metrical restrictions, instead preferring free verse. The American writer Ezra Pound helped found imagism, a movement that recognized and understood the history of poetry but invented new poetic styles. Filled with concrete, vivid images, modernist poets often sought to revolutionize the English language, stripping it down to its simplest, sparest form. Novelists, too, wanted to transform their genre. Developing methods to accurately depict consciousness, perception, and emotion lay at the core of novels from this time. A character no longer observed and passively described an event. Instead, a character participated in an event. The narrative style could convey a character's thoughts, feelings, and perspective. Some writers eventually experimented with stream of consciousness, a technique that provides a person's thoughts and reactions in a continuous flow. Joyce's famously utilizes stream of consciousness in *Ulysses*, while Virginia Woolf developed a similar technique called "tunneling," in which she recalls her characters' memories.

Modernists pieces entered the mass market thanks to journals and "little magazines," which published experimental works and shared literature that was not strictly commercial. Many magazines had women editors, making women an instrumental component to the evolution and spread of Modernism. Journals serialized longer modernist texts. Censorship could be problematic, but publishers more so contended with the cultural question of what was appropriate to share. Some publishers grew concerned that printing unreasonable material would encourage people to believe in fantasy.

Modernism reached its height during the 1920s, and it was also during this decade that literary study became a professional field. Critics began questioning what constitutes as "good" literature and considered a text's complexity, richness, and seriousness when assessing its status. Scholars realized that writers expressed moral and social values through the individual words and sentences of their works. The 1930s saw the tail end of modernism. Social concerns changed as unemployment rose and a global depression set it. After World War II, people became increasingly cognizant that wealthy, first-world nations were capable of extreme brutality. When the United States dropped the atomic bombs, people witnessed not only the end of the war, but also a decisive shift in thinking. Widespread destruction was a reality; one's cozy middle-class life, insulated from catastrophe, could vanish in mere seconds. Postmodernism and neo-modernism ensued as writers began crafting highly-experimental literature.

CONTEXTS		TEXTS
1902		Joseph Conrad, *Heart of Darkness*
1904	Abbey Theatre opens in Dublin	
1905	Albert Einstein's Theory of Special Relativity formulated	
1910		E.M. Forster, *Howards End*
1914–18	World War I	
1914	Irish Home Rule Act	James Joyce, *Dubliners*
1915	Albert Einstein's Theory of General Relativity formulated	D.H. Lawrence, *The Rainbow*
		Dorothy Richardson, *Pointed Roofs*
		Ford Maddox Ford, *The Good Soldier*
1916	Easter Uprising in Ireland	Joyce, *A Portrait of the Artist as a Young Man*
1918	All men over 21 and some women over 30 eligible to vote	Lytton Strachey, *Eminent Victorians*
1919	Treaty of Versailles	Richardson, *Interim*
1920	League of Nations formed	Lawrence, *Women in Love*
1922	British Broadcasting Corporation (BBC) founded	T.S. Eliot, *The Waste Land*
		Joyce, *Ulysses*
	Irish Free State founded	Virginia Woolf, *Jacob's Room*
1925		V. Woolf, *Mrs. Dalloway*
1927	Charles Lindbergh makes solo flight across the Atlantic Ocean	V. Woolf, *To the Lighthouse*

1928	All adult women eligible to vote	Lawrence, *Lady Chatterley's Lover*
	First television broadcast aired	
1929	The Great Depression begins in the U.S. and becomes global	Robert Graves, *Goodbye to All That*
1932		Aldous Huxley, *Brave New World*
1936	George V dies; Accession of Edward VIII	
1937	Edward VIII abdicates; Accession of George VI	J.R. R. Tolkien, *The Hobbit*
1939–45	World War II	
1939		Joyce, *Finnegans Wake*
1940	Winston Churchill becomes Prime Minister	
1941	Britain loses Eastern colonies to Japan	
1943	Benito Mussolini deposed in Italy	Eliot, *Four Quartets*
1945	Atomic bombs dropped on Hiroshima and Nagasaki	George Orwell, *Animal Farm*
	United Nations formed	

Thomas Hardy
1840–1928

R aised in Higher Bockhampton, Thomas Hardy largely spent his youth studying the landscape and culture that surrounded him. He attended various village schools until he was apprenticed to a local architect. After six years of service, he moved to London and became a draftsman for Arthur Blomfield, a respected and prominent architect who specialized in Gothic-style structures. Initially drawn to a religious vocation, Hardy contemplated a university education, but insufficient funds and wavering faith redirected him toward prose and poetry. He wrote his first novel, *The Poor Man and the Lady*, while still employed by Blomfield. Though publishers considered the piece, they ultimately rejected it. His next attempts, a sensational novel called *Desperate Remedies* and a romance novel titled *Under the Greenwood Tree*, were published in 1871 and 1872 respectively. His confidence thrived when his third published novel, *A Pair of Blue Eyes*, received favorable reviews. The book was heavily based on his courtship of Emma Gifford, whom he married against the wishes of both of their families in 1874. After the publication of *Far from the Madding Crowd* during the same year, Hardy quit architecture to write fiction full-time.

He described his fiction as a "series of seemings" involving both plot and symbolism. His novels blend together melodramatic, pastoral, and tragic elements; they further incorporate aspects of comedy. Hardy's humorous portrayals of rural, eccentric characters entertained his urban readers. He created a setting called "Wessex," a fictional amalgamation of the southwestern counties of England, and staged his novels there. *Tess of the d'Urbervilles*, one of his finest novels, reflects several of the subjects he addressed in his writing: sexual mores, the institution of marriage, and the British social class system. The story focuses on Tess, an impoverished country girl who is rejected by her husband after he learns she once had an illegitimate child. After a series of highly ironic events, she murders her original seducer and is subsequently sentenced to death by hanging. To Hardy's dismay, readers had moral objections to both *Tess* and *Jude the Obscure*. Many readers considered *Jude* risqué for its depiction of a non-traditional re-lationship. Hardy ceased writing novels entirely after its publication in 1895; financially well-off and eager to explore aesthetically, he transitioned to poetry, his preferred genre.

Hardy had published a single volume of poems (*Wessex Poems*) during his career as a novelist. He made his debut as a poet, however, with the publication of *Poems of the Past and Present* in 1901. Like subsequent collections of verse, poems from this volume were thematically grouped, either explicitly or implicitly. But because *Poems of the Past and Present* compiles pieces from various periods in Hardy's career as a writer, and many of the poems are undated, it is difficult to discern a clear evolution from poetic immaturity to maturity in Hardy's work. He experimented with various styles, composing lyrics, meditations, ballads, and dramatic monologues while additionally mixing together traditional genres. He also used complicated stanza forms and deliberately awkward phrasing, such as "Half-eased in that a Powerfuller than I" in "Hap." Hardy trusted in the irregularity of the spoken word, holding that the secret of poetry did not reside in "poetic veneer" or "the jewelled line," but in realism itself.

He used his verse as a vessel, exploring and expanding on his own intellectual uncertainties. Although he considered himself "churchy," he grappled with what has been called "the disappearance of God," particularly in his own life. Hardy questioned the existence of God, instead believing in a blind, unconscious force he termed the "Immanent Will." Because the Immanent Will governed the universe with purposeless movements, all human life was reduced to chance. Hardy grew frustrated with the senselessness that accompanies existence and fended off his sorrow with cutting irony. His attitude was dogged despite his cynicism; he insisted that the world could be bettered by human effort, a stance known as meliorism.

Although he somewhat shared the bleak late-Victorian attitude, Hardy was ultimately forward-looking. As his speaker notes in "The Darkling Thrush," "Some blessed Hope" awaited at the close of the nineteenth century, though the precise nature of that hope was unknown. Much of Hardy's poetry attests to the shift from Victorian conventions to the spontaneous, disjointed spirit that became emblematic of twentieth-century writing. His writing encompasses both a historical perspective and a sense of modernism. He was appointed to the Order of Merit in 1910 and had reached world-wide fame when he died in 1928. After public demands, his ashes were placed in the Poets' Corner of Westminster Abbey. His heart, which was removed before cremation, was buried in a local churchyard beside his deceased family members.

1840	Thomas Hardy born 2 June
1856–62	Apprenticeship to the architect John Hicks
1862–67	Works as draftsman for Arthur Blomsfield, a London architect
1873	*A Pair of Blue Eyes*
1874	Marries Emma Gifford; *Far from the Madding Crowd*
1885	Moves to Max Gate on the outskirts of Dorchester, Dorset, England, a house of his own design and construction
1886	*The Mayor of Casterbridge*
1888	*Wessex Tales*
1891	*Tess of the d'Urbervilles*
1895	*Jude the Obscure*
1898	*Wessex Poems*
1901	*Poems of the Past and Present*
1910	Appointed to the Order of Merit
1912	Emma suddenly dies 27 November
1914	Marries Florence Dugdale
1922	*Late Lyrics and Earlier with Many Other Verses*
1928	Hardy dies 11 January and his ashes are interred in Poets' Corner in Westminster Abbey; his heart is buried at the Higher Bockhampton parish alongside his wives and parents

HAP

If but some vengeful god would call to me
From up the sky, and laugh: 'Thou suffering thing,
Know that thy sorrow is my ecstasy,
That thy love's loss is my hate's profiting!'

Then would I bear, and clench myself, and die,   5
Steeled by the sense of ire unmerited;
Half-eased in that a Powerfuller than I
Had willed and meted me the tears I shed.

But not so. How arrives it joy lies slain,
And why unblooms the best hope ever sown?   10
—Crass Casualty obstructs the sun and rain,
And dicing Time for gladness casts a moan...
These purblind Doomsters had as readily strown
Blisses about my pilgrimage as pain.

1898

THE DARKLING THRUSH

Growing dark; characterized by darkness

I leant upon a coppice gate
  When Frost was spectre-gray,
And Winter's dregs made desolate
  The weakening eye of day.
The tangled bine-stems scored the sky   5
  Like strings from broken lyres,
And all mankind that haunted nigh
  Had sought their household fires.

The land's sharp features seemed to be
  The Century's corpse outleant,   10
His crypt the cloudy canopy,
  The wind his death-lament.
The ancient pulse of germ and birth
  Was shrunken hard and dry,
And every spirit upon earth   15
  Seemed fervourless as I.

At once a voice outburst among
  The bleak twigs overhead
In a full-hearted evensong
  Of joy illimited;   20
An aged thrush, frail, gaunt, and small,
  In blast-beruffled plume,
Had chosen thus to fling his soul
  Upon the growing gloom.

So little cause for carollings   25
  Of such ecstatic sound
Was written on terrestrial things
  Afar or nigh around,
That I could think there trembled through
  His happy good-night air   30
Some blessed Hope, whereof he knew
  And I was unaware.

1900

THE RUINED MAID

"O 'Melia, my dear, this does everything crown!
Who could have supposed I should meet you in Town?
And whence such fair garments, such prosperi-ty?"—
"O didn't you know I'd been ruined?" said she.

—"You left us in tatters, without shoes or socks,   5
Tired of digging potatoes, and spudding up docks;
And now you've gay bracelets and bright feathers three!"—
"Yes: that's how we dress when we're ruined," said she.

—"At home in the barton you said 'thee' and 'thou,'
And 'thik oon,' and 'theäs oon,' and 't'other'; but now   10
Your talking quite fits 'ee for high compa-ny!"—
"Some polish is gained with one's ruin," said she.

—"Your hands were like paws then, your face blue and bleak,
But now I'm bewitched by your delicate cheek,
And your little gloves fit as on any la-dy!"—   15
"We never do work when we're ruined," said she.

—"You used to call home-life a hag-ridden dream,
And you'd sigh, and you'd sock; but at present you seem
To know not of megrims or melancho-ly!"—
"True. There's an advantage in ruin," said she.   20

—"I wish I had feathers, a fine sweeping gown,
And a delicate face, and could strut about Town!"—
"My dear—a raw country girl, such as you be,
Isn't equal to that. You ain't ruined," said she.

1900

"AH, ARE YOU DIGGING ON MY GRAVE?"

"Ah, are you digging on my grave
        My beloved one?—planting rue?"
—"No: yesterday he went to wed
One of the brightest wealth has bred.
'It cannot hurt her now,' he said,   5
        'That I should not be true.'"

"Then who is digging on my grave?
        My nearest dearest kin?"
—"Ah, no; they sit and think, 'What use!
What good will planting flowers produce?   10
No tendance of her mound can loose
        Her spirit from Death's gin.'"

"But some one digs upon my grave?
        My enemy?—prodding sly?"
—"Nay: when she heard you had passed the Gate   15
That shuts on all flesh soon or late,
She thought you no more worth her hate,
        And cares not where you lie."

"Then, who is digging on my grave?
        Say—since I have not guessed!"   20
—"O it is I, my mistress dear,
Your little dog, who still lives near,
And much I hope my movements here
        Have not disturbed your rest?"

"Ah, yes! *You* dig upon my grave...   25
        Why flashed it not on me
That one true heart was left behind!
What feeling do we ever find
To equal among human kind
        A dog's fidelity!"   30

"Mistress, I dug upon your grave
   To bury a bone, in case
I should be hungry near this spot
When passing on my daily trot.
I am sorry, but I quite forgot   35
   It was your resting-place."

1914

THE CONVERGENCE OF THE TWAIN
(Lines on the loss of the "Titanic")

I.
In a solitude of the sea
   Deep from human vanity,
And the Pride of Life that planned her, stilly couches she.

II.
Steel chambers, late the pyres
   Of her salamandrine fires,   5
Cold currents thrid, and turn to rhythmic tidal lyres.

III.
Over the mirrors meant
   To glass the opulent
The sea-worm crawls—grotesque, slimed, dumb, indifferent.

IV.
Jewels in joy designed   10
   To ravish the sensuous mind
Lie lightless, all their sparkles bleared and black and blind.

V.

Dim moon-eyed fishes near
Gaze at the gilded gear
And query: "What does this vaingloriousness down here?"... 15

VI.

Well: while was fashioning
This creature of cleaving wing,
The Immanent Will that stirs and urges everything

VII.

Prepared a sinister mate
For her—so gaily great—   20
A Shape of Ice, for the time far and dissociate.

VIII.

And as the smart ship grew
In stature, grace, and hue,
In shadowy silent distance grew the Iceberg too.

IX.

Alien they seemed to be: 25
No mortal eye could see
The intimate welding of their later history,

X.

Or sign that they were bent
By paths coincident
On being anon twin halves of one august event,   30

XI.

Till the Spinner of the Years
Said "Now!" And each one hears,
And consummation comes, and jars two hemispheres.

1915

WILLIAM BUTLER YEATS
1865–1939

William Butler Yeats was born on the outskirts of Dublin. His family moved to London when he was two years old, but much of his youth was spent in Sligo, a seaport in western Ireland that was near his mother's birthplace. Yeats's father, J.B. Yeats, descended from a line of men who had graduated from Trinity College and become Protestant clergymen. J.B. himself believed only in the "religion of art" and had pursued a career as an artist despite his education as a lawyer. He taught Yeats until the boy could attend high school in Dublin where the family returned in 1880. Yeats briefly continued his studies at the Metropolitan School of Art before switching from visual art to poetry.

Yeats's family returned to London in the late 1880s, and the young writer quickly submerged himself in the city's social circles. His early aesthetic principles took shape as he encountered a range of eminent poets and artists. It was also in London that Yeats began his lifelong commitment to organizations focused on occultism, magic, religion, art, and politics. He was briefly a member of the famous Theosophical Society, a group that endorsed mysticism, and he later joined a secret society known as the Hermetic Order of the Golden Dawn that practiced ritual magic. He further helped found the Irish Literary Society of London and the National Literary Society in Dublin, both organizations which revived interest in native Irish writers and writing.

Yeats wanted to encourage the growth of a uniquely Irish literary conscience through his activities and writing alike. He was heavily influenced by Irish nationalism and revolutionist ideologies. His convictions were temporarily strengthened when he met Maud Gonne, a fiery nationalist and beautiful actress, in 1889. Hopelessly in love with her, he pledged himself to the Irish nationalist cause. Yeats interacted with numerous other leaders, including John O'Leary, a patriot who in 1885 returned to Ireland after a collective twenty years of imprisonment and exile in England for revolutionary actions. Yeats, however, increasingly understood that Irish culture had been hollowed out by political strife. He differed from many of his associates in that he believed in the intrinsic power and value of art. Additionally, although his poetry often contains political elements, he avoided writing for purely political ends.

His perspective was shared by Augusta, Lady Gregory, an aristocrat and playwright who found Irish lore fascinating and wholeheartedly promoted Irish literature. Yeats spent numerous summers at her country estate, Coole Park, which inspired his poem "The Wild Swans at Coole." In it, Yeats describes the ache of living at a time when "All's changed" and not even the somber beauty of nature can offer solace. With Lady Gregory's guidance, Yeats devoted himself to Irish drama. He founded a theater with her help (named the Abbey Theatre in 1904). Several of his plays, including *The Countess Cathleen*, *Cathleen ni Houlihan*, and *On Baile's Strand* were performed there. Yeats served as a prominent figure in the theater for nearly three decades, managing actors and actresses, conducting tours in America, and attending to other theater business.

In addition to penning plays, Yeats wrote lyrics, ballads, narrative poems, essays, prefaces, and notes. Although Yeats first communicated the "rhythm of my own music" in one of his earliest and most popular lyrics ("The Lake Isle of Innisfree"), his mid to late years produced many of his most powerful works. Between ages fifty and seventy-five, he adopted elements of Irish lore, mysticism, and mythology (such as the fairies in "The Stolen Child"), all of which galvanized his pieces. He also began reflecting on his experiences in Sligo, evoking the beauty of the land with ethereal descriptions of flora and fauna. But beginning at the turn of the twentieth century, Yeats abandoned the sentiments of the Romantic period, instead favoring a "cold and hard" style with simpler diction. As he remarked in "A Coat," his poetry did not need "embroideries" because "there's more enterprise / In walking naked." His departure from a less mannered style disappointed some readers who preferred more ornamental language. His verse assumed a new edge, but it never lost its inherent grace and musicality.

Yeats intermingled Irish traditions with English ideas, Indian meditations, and Japanese Noh theater. His sense of interconnectivity flourished both in terms of the connections between historical and contemporary societies and in the relationship between local issues and global concerns. For example, "Leda and the Swan," published in 1924, presents a parallel between Greek myth and the economic tensions that were occurring between Ireland and England. In "Easter, 1916," Yeats pays homage to fifteen Irish leaders who were executed after the Easter Rising of 1916, some of whom were close friends. Yeats reveals his assessment of the fight for Irish independence in this piece, and he continued to discuss the failed Easter Rising and the Irish civil war in *The Winding Stair*, a volume of poems published in 1929. Spiral staircases are fundamental symbols in Yeats's later poetry; they testify to the cyclical nature of history. Yeats explored this concept by devising a system of "gyres," interpenetrating cones that represent major personal and historical events. In his own lifetime, he witnessed "the widening gyre"—an event that signified the end of a two-thousand-year era dominated by Christianity—which he described in his prophetic poem "The Second Coming."

The interconnection between past, present, and future gripped Yeats, and he was adamant about discerning Ireland's role. From 1922 to 1928, he served as a senator of the newly-formed Irish Free State. His prominence as a political figure seconded his reputation as an accomplished writer; he received the Nobel Prize for Literature in 1923. Yeats interacted extensively with T.S. Eliot and Ezra Pound, who shared his initial allure to fascism. His interest in fascism was brief, and he eventually became repulsed by all political opinions. He did, however, remain committed to his country despite the political power struggles that arose. He renamed the ruined Norman tower on Lady Gregory's land (where he intermittently lived) Thoor (Castle) Ballylee, an Irish name, and restored it to its original state.

Yeats chose to assert his Irish nationality above all else, even though he had claim as a member of the powerful Anglo-Irish Protestant minority by birth. From early manhood onward, he endeavored "to show in a vision something of the face of Ireland" to his own people—to make a tradition built on customs and beliefs that existed separate from Ireland's religious history. He gradually embraced the themes and symbols knit into his heritage, crafting works that reverberate with passion. He died in southern France in 1939, shortly before the start of World War II. He was later buried in Drumcliff Cemetery, Ireland, near Sligo.

1865	William Butler Yeats born 13 June
1884–86	ttends Metropolitan School of Art, Dublin, Ireland
1890	"The Lake Isle of Innisfree"
1893	*The Celtic Twilight*
1899	*The Wind Among the Reeds*; Irish Literary Theater (later named Abbey Theater) established
1914	"A Coat"
1917	"The Wild Swans at Coole"; Marries Georgie (George) Hyde Lees
1920	"The Second Coming"
1921	"Easter, 1916"
1922–28	Serves as senator of Irish Free State
1923	Receives Nobel Prize for Literature
1924	"Leda and the Swan"
1939	Dies due to congestive heart failure on 28 January, and is buried in France
1948	Yeats is buried in Drumcliff Cemetery, Ireland

THE STOLEN CHILD

Where dips the rocky highland
Of Sleuth Wood in the lake,
There lies a leafy island
Where flapping herons wake
The drowsy water rats; 5
There we've hid our faery vats
Full of berries,
And of reddest stolen cherries.
Come away, O, human child!
To the woods and waters wild 10
With a faery, hand in hand,
For the world's more full of weeping than you can understand.

Where the wave of moonlight glosses
The dim grey sands with light,
Far off by furthest Rosses 15
We foot it all the night,
Weaving olden dances,
Mingling hands and mingling glances
Till the moon has taken flight;
To and fro we leap 20
And chase the frothy bubbles,
While the world is full of troubles
And is anxious in its sleep.
Come away, O, human child!
To the woods and waters wild 25
With a faery, hand in hand,
For the world's more full of weeping than you can understand.

Where the wandering water gushes
From the hills above Glen-Car,
In pools among the rushes, 30
That scarce could bathe a star,
We seek for slumbering trout,
And whispering in their ears

We give them evil dreams;
Leaning softly out   35
From ferns that drop their tears
Over the young streams.
Come away, O human child!
To the waters and the wild
With a faery, hand in hand,   40
For the world's more full of weeping than you can understand.

Away with us he's going,
The solemn-eyed:
He'll hear no more the lowing
Of the calves on the warm hillside;   45
Or the kettle on the hob
Sing peace into his breast,
Or see the brown mice bob
Round and round the oatmeal-chest.
For he comes, the human child,   50
To the waters and the wild
With a faery, hand in hand,
From a world more full of weeping than he can understand.

1889

THE LAKE ISLE OF INNISFREE

I will arise and go now, and go to Innisfree,
And a small cabin build there, of clay and wattles made;
Nine bean rows will I have there, a hive for the honey bee,
And live alone in the bee-loud glade.

And I shall have some peace there, for peace comes dropping slow, 5
Dropping from the veils of the morning to where the cricket sings;
There midnight's all a glimmer, and noon a purple glow,
And evening full of the linnet's wings.

I will arise and go now, for always night and day
I hear lake water lapping with low sounds by the shore;   10
While I stand on the roadway, or on the pavements gray,
I hear it in the deep heart's core.

1895

A COAT

I made my song a coat,
Covered with embroideries,
Out of old mythologies,
From heel to throat.
But the fools caught it,   5
Wore it in the world's eye,
As though they'd wrought it.
Song, let them take it,
For there's more enterprise
In walking naked.   10

1912

THE WILD SWANS AT COOLE

The trees are in their autumn beauty,
The woodland paths are dry,
Under the October twilight the water
Mirrors a still sky;
Upon the brimming water among the stones   5
Are nine and fifty swans.

The nineteenth Autumn has come upon me
Since I first made my count;
I saw, before I had well finished,
All suddenly mount   10
And scatter wheeling in great broken rings
Upon their clamorous wings.

I have looked upon those brilliant creatures,
And now my heart is sore.
All's changed since I, hearing at twilight,   15
The first time on this shore,
The bell-beat of their wings above my head,
Trod with a lighter tread.

Unwearied still, lover by lover,
They paddle in the cold,   20
Companionable streams or climb the air;
Their hearts have not grown old;
Passion or conquest, wander where they will,
Attend upon them still.

But now they drift on the still water   25
Mysterious, beautiful;
Among what rushes will they build,
By what lake's edge or pool
Delight men's eyes when I awake some day
To find they have flown away?   30

1919

[handwritten note, top margin: Violence /anarchy / "blood dimmed tide" specifically symbolizes WWI, Bolshevik Revolution, & widespread violence / threat of violence in Ireland at the time]

THE SECOND COMING

[handwritten left margin: Ref. to gyres theory / philosophy; falcon is order & aristocracy; loss of it's point of ref. = societal collapse / end of era.]

Turning and turning in the widening gyre
The falcon cannot hear the falconer;
Things fall apart; the centre cannot hold;

[handwritten right margin: Tennants of present society / Christianity can't control violence inherent in end of it's era]

Mere anarchy is loosed upon the world,
The blood-dimmed tide is loosed, and everywhere
The ceremony of innocence is drowned;

[handwritten left margin: End of era signaled by violence; double entendre of mere; innocence = trad. values]

The best lack all conviction, while the worst
Are full of passionate intensity.

[handwritten left margin: Paradox; echo & intensify preceding images & intent]

Surely some revelation is at hand;
Surely the Second Coming is at hand.
The Second Coming! Hardly are those words out

[handwritten left margin: Second coming meant to be heralded by violence, but Yeats sees this as beginning of new era instead]

When a vast image out of Spiritus Mundi
Troubles my sight: somewhere in sands of the desert

[handwritten right margin: 10 — Collection of symbols / images present across Ages]

A shape with lion body and the head of a man,
A gaze blank and pitiless as the sun,

[handwritten left margin: Sphynx is power / protection, strength, & nobility; connected to Horus, to whom the falcon was sacred; god of light &, symbol of rebirth]

Is moving its slow thighs, while all about it
Reel shadows of the indignant desert birds.

[handwritten right margin: Confusion over how exactly new era will be, no necissarily fear — Slow movement = slow emergence of new era]

The darkness drops again; but now I know
That twenty centuries of stony sleep

[handwritten left margin: Pitiless ≠ cruel, meant to establish sphynx & what it symbolizes as proud, stern, fearless contex of authority; keeps w/ bird & cyclical theme]

[handwritten right margin: — Ref. to gyre philosophy]

Were vexed to nightmare by a rocking cradle,
And what rough beast, its hour come round at last,
Slouches towards Bethlehem to be born?

[handwritten right margin: 20]

1919

[handwritten bottom margin: Fear + hope; paradox; fear related to emergence of new era; part of it's awe-inspiring & near-divine nature; rough beast's power & authority contrasts softer, nurturing vibe of Bethlehem]

EASTER, 1916

I have met them at close of day
Coming with vivid faces
From counter or desk among grey
Eighteenth-century houses.
I have passed with a nod of the head   5
Or polite meaningless words,
Or have lingered awhile and said
Polite meaningless words,
And thought before I had done
Of a mocking tale or a gibe   10
To please a companion
Around the fire at the club,
Being certain that they and I
But lived where motley is worn:
All changed, changed utterly: 15
A terrible beauty is born.

That woman's days were spent
In ignorant good will,
Her nights in argument
Until her voice grew shrill.   20
What voice more sweet than hers
When young and beautiful,
She rode to harriers?
This man had kept a school
And rode our winged horse;   25
This other his helper and friend
Was coming into his force;
He might have won fame in the end,
So sensitive his nature seemed,
So daring and sweet his thought.   30
This other man I had dreamed
A drunken, vainglorious lout.
He had done most bitter wrong
To some who are near my heart,

Yet I number him in the song;   35
He, too, has resigned his part
In the casual comedy;
He, too, has been changed in his turn,
Transformed utterly:
A terrible beauty is born.   40

Hearts with one purpose alone
Through summer and winter seem
Enchanted to a stone
To trouble the living stream.
The horse that comes from the road,   45
The rider, the birds that range
From cloud to tumbling cloud,
Minute by minute they change;
A shadow of cloud on the stream
Changes minute by minute;   50
A horse-hoof slides on the brim,
And a horse plashes within it
The long-legged moor-hens dive,
And hens to moor-cocks call.
Minute by minute they live: 55
The stone's in the midst of all.

Too long a sacrifice
Can make a stone of the heart.
O when may it suffice?
That is heaven's part, our part   60
To murmur name upon name,
As a mother names her child
When sleep at last has come
On limbs that had run wild.
What is it but nightfall?   65
No, no, not night but death;
Was it needless death after all?
For England may keep faith
For all that is done and said.
We know their dream; enough   70
To know they dreamed and are dead;
And what if excess of love
Bewildered them till they died?

I write it out in a verse—
MacDonagh and MacBride   75
And Connolly and Pearse
Now and in time to be,
Wherever green is worn,
Are changed, changed utterly:
A terrible beauty is born.   80

1921

LEDA AND THE SWAN

A sudden blow: the great wings beating still
Above the staggering girl, her thighs caressed
By the dark webs, her nape caught in his bill,
He holds her helpless breast upon his breast.

How can those terrified vague fingers push   5
The feathered glory from her loosening thighs?
And how can body, laid in that white rush,
But feel the strange heart beating where it lies?

A shudder in the loins engenders there
The broken wall, the burning roof and tower   10
And Agamemnon dead. ⁊ split line
                        Being so caught up,
So mastered by the brute blood of the air,
Did she put on his knowledge with his power
Before the indifferent beak could let her drop?

1924   Sonnet

JAMES JOYCE
1882–1941

Though James Joyce was born in Dublin and wrote extensively about Dublin, most of his life was spent outside of Ireland. In fact, his last visit to the country was in 1912, just two years before the publication of his famous work, *Dubliners*. The eldest of ten children, Joyce was favored by his father, a brilliant but irresponsible man whose alcoholism curtailed his prosperity. Throughout Joyce's adolescence, his family slipped deeper into unrecoverable debt; he lived in eight different houses, each with cruder conditions than the last, in a two-year timeframe. Joyce withdrew from boarding school in 1891 due to poverty and could only resume his formal education in 1893 because Father John Conmee, the prefect of studies at Belvedere College, recognized Joyce's academic aptitude and waived admission fees.

Joyce began studying for a degree at University College, Dublin, when he was sixteen years old. He showed an early inclination for history and literature, and in 1900, his critique of a play by Henrik Ibsen was published in the London magazine, *Fortnightly Review*. The Norwegian playwright himself read and praised the piece. After graduating, Joyce traveled to France with the intent of becoming a doctor but soon abandoned medicinal studies. Daily Parisian life proved arduous; at times too poor to clean his clothes or afford food, he survived by relying heavily on the generosity of family and friends. News of his mother's terminal illness drew him back to Dublin, and he stayed there for about a year before leaving the country with Nora Barnacle, an illiterate Irish woman whose compassion and ferocity enamored him.

Though Nora scorned intellectualism and found Joyce's work uninteresting, the two were mostly amicable companions. They moved restlessly between England and Switzerland before settling first in Pola, Austria-Hungary, then in Trieste, Italy, where their son and daughter were both born. Joyce predominantly worked as a teacher, but his family often grappled with poverty. Their circumstances were worsened by his heavy drinking, a habit that eventually led his brother Stanislaus to live with the family in order to chaperone Joyce's behavior. Eye diseases also troubled Joyce. He underwent twenty-five operations over the course of his life to alleviate pain and temporary blindness.

Adversity and anger compelled him to continue writing. His first publication, a collection of love poems titled *Chamber Music*, garnered the attention of T.S. Eliot and Ezra Pound in 1907. But a seven-year period of rejections ensued. Joyce's literary career did not gain momentum until the publication of *Dubliners*. Drafted during a six-month burst of creativity in 1904 and introduced to the public ten years later, *Dubliners* encompasses fifteen short stories. Each represents Joyce's attempt to recreate Dublin as it existed in his imagination, capturing and vivifying the city's essence through details and symbols. Constructed using Joyce's childhood memories, the stories embrace a range of themes including the relationship between innocence and experience, a yearning for beauty and adventure amid dullness and routine, and the intersection of life and death. Joyce believed that Dubliners were neither entirely alive nor dead but trapped in a state of suspension he termed "paralysis." Joyce had rejected this lifestyle by leaving Dublin. He accepted his decision in *A Portrait of the Artist as a Young Man*, an ironic and self-admiring work that underwent extensive revisions before its publication in 1916. Autobiographical in nature but fictitious in composition, *A Portrait of the Artist* charts the progression of Joyce's artistic development through the life story of the novel's protagonist, Stephen Dedalus.

Financial support, given chiefly from an American patron named Edith Rockefeller McCormick, eased some of Joyce's burdens. Further aid arrived from Harriet Shaw Weaver, the editor of the *Egoist* magazine and a formidable political activist who sponsored Joyce from 1917 until his death. Her efforts superseded financial assistance; she established the Egoist Press to publish some of Joyce's works herself. As his sole literary executor, Weaver tirelessly promoted his pieces to other publishers. Finding consistent, reliable publishers, however, was exasperating even with the plethora of acquaintances and connections Joyce had, and the process was rarely free of complications. Joyce constantly battled against editors who omitted entire sections of his work or refused to publish it at all. Publication of *Ulysses*, for example, immediately ceased in 1921 when the U.S. Post Office brought a charge of obscenity against the work. Though the novel had been serialized in the American magazine *The Little Review* since 1918, it was banned in both America and Britain until 1933.

Joyce wrote obstinately despite persistent publishing and censorship issues. His final project, an experimental novel he referred to only as "Work in Progress" until its publication, required more than fourteen years of writing. *Finnegans Wake*, as it was finally titled, appeared simultaneously in New York and London in 1939. Joyce claimed that it was his masterpiece, but some critics found it unintelligible. *Finnegans Wake* contains a complex storyline that juxtaposes reality with the world of dreams. Joyce's diction is particularly challenging; he combines words from multiple extant languages, creating and utilizing his own unique vernacular. His "thunder words," which consist of approximately one hundred letters each, offer a range of literary, historical, and artistic meanings. *Finnegans Wake* is still widely studied and scrutinized.

The Joyces fled from Paris shortly after the publication of Finnegans Wake. The city had been their home for nearly twenty years, but as the threat of war drew nearer, they were forced to relocate to Zürich. Joyce received international recognition at the time of his death in 1941. Using experimental techniques, he challenged many of the conventions of fiction and composed a body of work that was startling and witty. Though some of Joyce's works are branded as obscene or unreadable, Joyce is known as one of the greatest and most controversial writers of the twentieth century. He revealed the political and social issues Ireland faced, writing stories framed by contemporary forces such as the revivalist theatre and the formation of the Irish Free State. As an Irish emigre, he introduced Irish culture not only to continental Europe but to the U.S. as well.

1882	James Joyce born 2 February
1888–91	Attends Clongowes Wood College
1893	Enters Belvedere College
1898–1902	Attends University College, Dublin (then Royal University)
1903	Returns to Dublin during his mother's fatal illness; Mother dies
1905	Son Giorgio born
1907	*Chamber Music*; Daughter Lucia born
1912	Joyce's last trip to Ireland
1914	*Dubliners*
1916	*A Portrait of the Artist as a Young Man*
1917	Harriet Shaw Weaver begins lifelong financial support of Joyce
1918	*Exiles*; Edith Rockefeller McCormick provides financial support
1922	*Ulysses*
1931	Marries Nora Barnacle; Father dies
1936	*Collected Poems*
1939	*Finnegans Wake*
1941	Joyce dies from a perforated ulcer on 13 January and is buried in Fluntern Cemetery, Zürich, Switzerland

ARABY

NORTH RICHMOND STREET, being blind, was a quiet street except at the hour when the Christian Brothers' School set the boys free. An uninhabited house of two storys stood at the blind end, detached from its neighbours in a square ground. The other houses of the street, conscious of decent lives within them, gazed at one another with brown imperturbable faces.

The former tenant of our house, a priest, had died in the back drawing-room. Air, musty from having been long enclosed, hung in all the rooms, and the waste room behind the kitchen was littered with old useless papers. Among these I found a few paper-covered books, the pages of which were curled and damp: *The Abbot*, by Walter Scott, *The Devout Communicant* and *The Memoirs of Vidocq*. I liked the last best because its leaves were yellow. The wild garden behind the house contained a central apple-tree and a few straggling bushes under one of which I found the late tenant's rusty bicycle-pump. He had been a very charitable priest; in his will he had left all his money to institutions and the furniture of his house to his sister.

When the short days of winter came dusk fell before we had well eaten our dinners. When we met in the street the houses had grown sombre. The space of sky above us was the colour of ever-changing violet and towards it the lamps of the street lifted their feeble lanterns. The cold air stung us and we played till our bodies glowed. Our shouts echoed in the silent street. The career of our play brought us through the dark muddy lanes behind the houses where we ran the gauntlet of the rough tribes from the cottages, to the back doors of the dark dripping gardens where odours arose from the ashpits, to the dark odorous stables where a coachman smoothed and combed the horse or shook music from the buckled harness. When we returned to the street light from the kitchen windows had filled the areas. If my uncle was seen turning the corner we hid in the shadow until we had seen him safely housed. Or if Mangan's sister came out on the doorstep to call her brother in to his tea we watched her from our shadow peer up and down the street. We waited to see whether she would remain or go in and, if she remained, we left our shadow and walked up to Mangan's steps resignedly. She was waiting for us, her figure defined by the light from the half-opened door. Her brother always teased her before he obeyed and I stood by the railings looking at her. Her dress swung as she moved her body and the soft rope of her hair tossed from side to side.

Every morning I lay on the floor in the front parlour watching her door. The blind was pulled down to within an inch of the sash so that I could not be seen. When she came out on the doorstep my heart leaped. I ran to the hall, seized my books and followed her. I kept her brown figure always in my eye and, when we came near the point at which our ways diverged, I quickened my pace and passed her. This happened morning after morning. I had never spoken to her, except for a few casual words, and yet her name was like a summons to all my foolish blood.

Her image accompanied me even in places the most hostile to romance. On Saturday evenings when my aunt went marketing I had to go to carry some of the parcels. We walked through the flaring streets, jostled by drunken men and bargaining women, amid the curses of labourers, the shrill litanies of shopboys who stood on guard by the barrels of pigs' cheeks, the nasal chanting of street-singers, who sang a *come-all-you* about O'Donovan Rossa,[1] or a ballad about the troubles in our native land. These noises converged in a single sensation of life for me: I imagined that I bore my chalice safely through a throng of foes. Her name sprang to my lips at moments in strange prayers and praises which I myself did not understand. My eyes were often full of tears (I could not tell why) and at times a flood from my heart seemed to pour itself out into my bosom. I thought little of the future. I did not know whether I would ever speak to her or not or, if I spoke to her, how I could tell her of my confused adoration. But my body was like a harp and her words and gestures were like fingers running upon the wires.

One evening I went into the back drawing-room in which the priest had died. It was a dark rainy evening and there was no sound in the house. Through one of the broken panes I heard the rain impinge upon the earth, the fine incessant needles of water playing in the sodden beds. Some distant lamp or lighted window gleamed below me. I was thankful that I could see so little. All my senses seemed to desire to veil themselves and, feeling that I was about to slip from them, I pressed the palms of my hands together until they trembled, murmuring: "*O love! O love!*" many times.

At last she spoke to me. When she addressed the first words to me I was so confused that I did not know what to answer. She asked me was I going to *Araby*.[2] I forgot whether I answered yes or no. It would be a splendid bazaar, she said she would love to go.

"And why can't you?" I asked.

While she spoke she turned a silver bracelet round and round her wrist. She could not go, she said, because there would be a retreat that week in her convent.

---

1 Jeremiah O'Donovan Rossa (1831–1915) was a famous member of the Fenians, a 19th-century revolutionary Irish nationalist organization. Rossa wanted to resist British rule in Ireland and establish an Irish Republic.

2 The Araby bazaar opened in Dublin in May of 1894. The bazaar was staged to have an oriental, exotic atmosphere.

Her brother and two other boys were fighting for their caps and I was alone at the railings. She held one of the spikes, bowing her head towards me. The light from the lamp opposite our door caught the white curve of her neck, lit up her hair that rested there and, falling, lit up the hand upon the railing. It fell over one side of her dress and caught the white border of a petticoat, just visible as she stood at ease.

"It's well for you," she said.

"If I go," I said, "I will bring you something."

What innumerable follies laid waste my waking and sleeping thoughts after that evening! I wished to annihilate the tedious intervening days. I chafed against the work of school. At night in my bedroom and by day in the classroom her image came between me and the page I strove to read. The syllables of the word *Araby* were called to me through the silence in which my soul luxuriated and cast an Eastern enchantment over me. I asked for leave to go to the bazaar on Saturday night. My aunt was surprised and hoped it was not some Freemason affair. I answered few questions in class. I watched my master's face pass from amiability to sternness; he hoped I was not beginning to idle. I could not call my wandering thoughts together. I had hardly any patience with the serious work of life which, now that it stood between me and my desire, seemed to me child's play, ugly monotonous child's play.

On Saturday morning I reminded my uncle that I wished to go to the bazaar in the evening. He was fussing at the hallstand, looking for the hat-brush, and answered me curtly:

"Yes, boy, I know."

As he was in the hall I could not go into the front parlour and lie at the window. I left the house in bad humour and walked slowly towards the school. The air was pitilessly raw and already my heart misgave me.

When I came home to dinner my uncle had not yet been home. Still it was early. I sat staring at the clock for some time and, when its ticking began to irritate me, I left the room. I mounted the staircase and gained the upper part of the house. The high cold empty gloomy rooms liberated me and I went from room to room singing. From the front window I saw my companions playing below in the street. Their cries reached me weakened and indistinct and, leaning my forehead against the cool glass, I looked over at the dark house where she lived. I may have stood there for an hour, seeing nothing but the brown-clad figure cast by my imagination, touched discreetly by the lamplight at the curved neck, at the hand upon the railings and at the border below the dress.

When I came downstairs again I found Mrs Mercer sitting at the fire. She was an old garrulous woman, a pawnbroker's widow, who collected used stamps for some pious purpose. I had to endure the gossip of the tea-table. The meal was prolonged beyond an hour and still my uncle did not come. Mrs Mercer stood up to go: she was sorry she couldn't wait any longer, but it was after eight o'clock and she did not like to be out late, as the night air was bad for her. When she had gone I began to walk up and down the room, clenching my fists. My aunt said:

"I'm afraid you may put off your bazaar for this night of Our Lord."

At nine o'clock I heard my uncle's latchkey in the halldoor. I heard him talking to himself and heard the hallstand rocking when it had received the weight of his overcoat. I could interpret these signs. When he was midway through his dinner I asked him to give me the money to go to the bazaar. He had forgotten.

"The people are in bed and after their first sleep now," he said.

I did not smile. My aunt said to him energetically:

"Can't you give him the money and let him go? You've kept him late enough as it is."

My uncle said he was very sorry he had forgotten. He said he believed in the old saying: "All work and no play makes Jack a dull boy." He asked me where I was going and, when I had told him a second time he asked me did I know *The Arab's Farewell to his Steed*. When I left the kitchen he was about to recite the opening lines of the piece to my aunt.

I held a florin tightly in my hand as I strode down Buckingham Street towards the station. The sight of the streets thronged with buyers and glaring with gas recalled to me the purpose of my journey. I took my seat in a third-class carriage of a deserted train. After an intolerable delay the train moved out of the station slowly. It crept onward among ruinous houses and over the twinkling river. At Westland Row Station a crowd of people pressed to the carriage doors; but the porters moved them back, saying that it was a special train for the bazaar. I remained alone in the bare carriage. In a few minutes the train drew up beside an improvised wooden platform. I passed out on to the road and saw by the lighted dial of a clock that it was ten minutes to ten. In front of me was a large building which displayed the magical name.

I could not find any sixpenny entrance and, fearing that the bazaar would be closed, I passed in quickly through a turnstile, handing a shilling to a weary-looking man. I found myself in a big hall girdled at half its height by a gallery. Nearly all the stalls were closed and the greater part of the hall was in darkness. I recognised a silence like that which pervades a church after a service. I walked into the centre of the bazaar timidly. A few people were gathered about the stalls which were still open. Before a curtain, over which the words *Café Chantant* were written in coloured lamps, two men were counting money on a salver. I listened to the fall of the coins.

Remembering with difficulty why I had come I went over to one of the stalls and examined porcelain vases and flowered tea-sets. At the door of the stall a young lady was talking and laughing with two young gentlemen. I remarked their English accents and listened vaguely to their conversation.

"O, I never said such a thing!"

"O, but you did!"

"O, but I didn't!"

"Didn't she say that?"

"Yes. I heard her."

"O, there's a...fib!"

Observing me the young lady came over and asked me did I wish to buy anything. The tone of her voice was not encouraging; she seemed to have spoken to me out of a sense of duty. I looked humbly at the great jars that stood like eastern guards at either side of the dark entrance to the stall and murmured:

"No, thank you."

The young lady changed the position of one of the vases and went back to the two young men. They began to talk of the same subject. Once or twice the young lady glanced at me over her shoulder.

I lingered before her stall, though I knew my stay was useless, to make my interest in her wares seem the more real. Then I turned away slowly and walked down the middle of the bazaar. I allowed the two pennies to fall against the sixpence in my pocket. I heard a voice call from one end of the gallery that the light was out. The upper part of the hall was now completely dark.

Gazing up into the darkness I saw myself as a creature driven and derided by vanity; and my eyes burned with anguish and anger.

1914

THE DEAD

LILY, THE CARETAKER'S DAUGHTER, was literally run off her feet. Hardly had she brought one gentleman into the little pantry behind the office on the ground floor and helped him off with his overcoat than the wheezy hall-door bell clanged again and she had to scamper along the bare hallway to let in another guest. It was well for her she had not to attend to the ladies also. But Miss Kate and Miss Julia had thought of that and had converted the bathroom upstairs into a ladies' dressing-room. Miss Kate and Miss Julia were there, gossiping and laughing and fussing, walking after each other to the head of the stairs, peering down over the banisters and calling down to Lily to ask her who had come.

It was always a great affair, the Misses Morkan's annual dance. Everybody who knew them came to it, members of the family, old friends of the family, the members of Julia's choir, any of Kate's pupils that were grown up enough and even some of Mary Jane's pupils too. Never once had it fallen flat. For years and years it had gone off in splendid style as long as anyone could remember; ever since Kate and Julia, after the death of their brother Pat, had left the house in Stoney Batter and taken Mary Jane, their only niece, to live with them in the dark gaunt house on Usher's Island, the upper part of which they had rented from Mr. Fulham, the corn-factor on the ground floor. That was a good thirty years ago if it was a day. Mary Jane, who was then a little girl in short clothes, was now the main prop of the household for she had the organ in Haddington Road. She had been through the Academy and gave a pupils' concert every year in the upper room of the Antient Concert Rooms. Many of her pupils belonged to better-class families on the Kingstown and Dalkey line. Old as they were, her aunts also did their share. Julia, though she was quite grey, was still the leading soprano in Adam and Eve's, and Kate, being too feeble to go about much, gave music lessons to beginners on the old square piano in the back room. Lily, the caretaker's daughter, did housemaid's work for them. Though their life was modest they believed in eating well; the best of everything: diamond-bone sirloins, three-shilling tea and the best bottled stout. But Lily seldom made a mistake in the orders so that she got on well with her three mistresses. They were fussy, that was all. But the only thing they would not stand was back answers.

Of course they had good reason to be fussy on such a night. And then it was long after ten o'clock and yet there was no sign of Gabriel and his wife. Besides they were dreadfully afraid that Freddy Malins might turn up screwed. They would not wish for worlds that any of Mary Jane's pupils should see him under the influence; and when he was like that it was sometimes very hard to manage him. Freddy Malins always came late but they wondered what could be keeping Gabriel: and that was what brought them every two minutes to the banisters to ask Lily had Gabriel or Freddy come.

"O, Mr. Conroy," said Lily to Gabriel when she opened the door for him, "Miss Kate and Miss Julia thought you were never coming. Good-night, Mrs Conroy."

"I'll engage they did," said Gabriel, "but they forget that my wife here takes three mortal hours to dress herself." — *First words are critical & misogynistic*

He stood on the mat, scraping the snow from his goloshes, while Lily led his wife to the foot of the stairs and called out:

"Miss Kate, here's Mrs Conroy."

Kate and Julia came toddling down the dark stairs at once. Both of them kissed Gabriel's wife, said she must be perished alive and asked was Gabriel with her.

"Here I am as right as the mail, Aunt Kate! Go on up. I'll follow," called out Gabriel from the dark.

He continued scraping his feet vigorously while the three women went upstairs, laughing, to the ladies' dressing-room. A light fringe of snow lay like a cape on the shoulders of his overcoat and like toecaps on the toes of his goloshes; and, as the buttons of his overcoat slipped with a squeaking noise through the snow-stiffened frieze, a cold fragrant air from out-of-doors escaped from crevices and folds.

"Is it snowing again, Mr. Conroy?" asked Lily.

She had preceded him into the pantry to help him off with his overcoat. Gabriel smiled at the three syllables she had given his surname and glanced at her. She was a slim, growing girl, pale in complexion and with hay-coloured hair. The gas in the pantry made her look still paler. Gabriel had known her when she was a child and used to sit on the lowest step nursing a rag doll.

"Yes, Lily," he answered, "and I think we're in for a night of it."

He looked up at the pantry ceiling, which was shaking with the stamping and shuffling of feet on the floor above, listened for a moment to the piano and then glanced at the girl, who was folding his overcoat carefully at the end of a shelf.

"Tell me, Lily," he said in a friendly tone, "do you still go to school?"

"O no, sir," she answered. "I'm done schooling this year and more."

"O, then," said Gabriel gaily, "I suppose we'll be going to your wedding one of these fine days with your young man, eh?"

The girl glanced back at him over her shoulder and said with great bitterness:

"The men that is now is only all palaver and what they can get out of you."

Gabriel coloured as if he felt he had made a mistake and, without looking at her, kicked off his goloshes and flicked actively with his muffler at his patent-leather shoes.

He was a stout tallish young man. The high colour of his cheeks pushed upwards even to his forehead where it scattered itself in a few formless patches of pale red; and on his hairless face there scintillated restlessly the polished lenses and the bright gilt rims of the glasses which screened his delicate and restless eyes. His glossy black hair was parted in the middle and brushed in a long curve behind his ears where it curled slightly beneath the groove left by his hat.

When he had flicked lustre into his shoes he stood up and pulled his waistcoat down more tightly on his plump body. Then he took a coin rapidly from his pocket.

"O Lily," he said, thrusting it into her hands, "it's Christmas-time, isn't it? Just...here's a little..."

He walked rapidly towards the door.

"O no, sir!" cried the girl, following him. "Really, sir, I wouldn't take it."

"Christmas-time! Christmas-time!" said Gabriel, almost trotting to the stairs and waving his hand to her in deprecation.

The girl, seeing that he had gained the stairs, called out after him:

"Well, thank you, sir."

He waited outside the drawing-room door until the waltz should finish, listening to the skirts that swept against it and to the shuffling of feet. He was still discomposed by the girl's bitter and sudden retort. It had cast a gloom over him which he tried to dispel by arranging his cuffs and the bows of his tie. Then he took from his waistcoat pocket a little paper and glanced at the headings he had made for his speech. He was undecided about the lines from Robert Browning for he feared they would be above the heads of his hearers. Some quotation that they would recognise from Shakespeare or from the Melodies would be better. The indelicate clacking of the men's heels and the shuffling of their soles reminded him that their grade of culture differed from his. He would only make himself ridiculous by quoting poetry to them which they could not understand. They would think that he was airing his superior education. He would fail with them just as he had failed with the girl in the pantry. He had taken up a wrong tone. His whole speech was a mistake from first to last, an utter failure.

Just then his aunts and his wife came out of the ladies' dressing-room. His aunts were two small plainly dressed old women. Aunt Julia was an inch or so the taller. Her hair, drawn low over the tops of her ears, was grey; and grey also, with darker shadows, was her large flaccid face. Though she was stout in build and stood erect her slow eyes and parted lips gave her the appearance of a woman who did not know where she was or where she was going. Aunt Kate was more vivacious. Her face, healthier than her sister's, was all puckers and creases, like a shrivelled red apple, and her hair, braided in the same old-fashioned way, had not lost its ripe nut colour.

They both kissed Gabriel frankly. He was their favourite nephew, the son of their dead elder sister, Ellen, who had married T. J. Conroy of the Port and Docks.

"Gretta tells me you're not going to take a cab back to Monkstown to-night, Gabriel," said Aunt Kate.

"No," said Gabriel, turning to his wife, "we had quite enough of that last year, hadn't we? Don't you remember, Aunt Kate, what a cold Gretta got out of it? Cab windows rattling all the way, and the east wind blowing in after we passed Merrion. Very jolly it was. Gretta caught a dreadful cold."

Aunt Kate frowned severely and nodded her head at every word.

"Quite right, Gabriel, quite right," she said. "You can't be too careful."

"But as for Gretta there," said Gabriel, "she'd walk home in the snow if she were let."

Mrs Conroy laughed.

"Don't mind him, Aunt Kate," she said. "He's really an awful bother, what with green shades for Tom's eyes at night and making him do the dumb-bells, and forcing Eva to eat the stirabout. The poor child! And she simply hates the sight of it!...O, but you'll never guess what he makes me wear now!"

She broke out into a peal of laughter and glanced at her husband, whose admiring and happy eyes had been wandering from her dress to her face and hair. The two aunts laughed heartily too, for Gabriel's solicitude was a standing joke with them.

"Goloshes!" said Mrs Conroy. "That's the latest. Whenever it's wet underfoot I must put on my goloshes. To-night even he wanted me to put them on, but I wouldn't. The next thing he'll buy me will be a diving suit."

Gabriel laughed nervously and patted his tie reassuringly while Aunt Kate nearly doubled herself, so heartily did she enjoy the joke. The smile soon faded from Aunt Julia's face and her mirthless eyes were directed towards her nephew's face. After a pause she asked:

"And what are goloshes, Gabriel?"

"Goloshes, Julia!" exclaimed her sister. "Goodness me, don't you know what goloshes are? You wear them over your...over your boots, Gretta, isn't it?"

"Yes," said Mrs Conroy. "Guttapercha[1] things. We both have a pair now. Gabriel says everyone wears them on the continent."

"O, on the continent," murmured Aunt Julia, nodding her head slowly.

Gabriel knitted his brows and said, as if he were slightly angered:

"It's nothing very wonderful but Gretta thinks it very funny because she says the word reminds her of Christy Minstrels."

"But tell me, Gabriel," said Aunt Kate, with brisk tact. "Of course, you've seen about the room. Gretta was saying..."

"O, the room is all right," replied Gabriel. "I've taken one in the Gresham."

---

1 A tough, rubberlike substance made from various Malaysian trees.

"To be sure," said Aunt Kate, "by far the best thing to do. And the children, Gretta, you're not anxious about them?"

"O, for one night," said Mrs Conroy. "Besides, Bessie will look after them."

"To be sure," said Aunt Kate again. "What a comfort it is to have a girl like that, one you can depend on! There's that Lily, I'm sure I don't know what has come over her lately. She's not the girl she was at all."

Gabriel was about to ask his aunt some questions on this point but she broke off suddenly to gaze after her sister who had wandered down the stairs and was craning her neck over the banisters.

"Now, I ask you," she said almost testily, "where is Julia going. Julia! Julia! Where are you going?"

Julia, who had gone half way down one flight, came back and announced blandly:

"Here's Freddy."

At the same moment a clapping of hands and a final flourish of the pianist told that the waltz had ended. The drawing-room door was opened from within and some couples came out. Aunt Kate drew Gabriel aside hurriedly and whispered into his ear:

"Slip down, Gabriel, like a good fellow and see if he's all right, and don't let him up if he's screwed. I'm sure he's screwed. I'm sure he is."

Gabriel went to the stairs and listened over the banisters. He could hear two persons talking in the pantry. Then he recognised Freddy Malins' laugh. He went down the stairs noisily.

"It's such a relief," said Aunt Kate to Mrs Conroy, "that Gabriel is here. I always feel easier in my mind when he's here...Julia, there's Miss Daly and Miss Power will take some refreshment. Thanks for your beautiful waltz, Miss Daly. It made lovely time."

A tall wizen-faced man, with a stiff grizzled moustache and swarthy skin, who was passing out with his partner said:

"And may we have some refreshment, too, Miss Morkan?"

"Julia," said Aunt Kate summarily, "and here's Mr. Browne and Miss Furlong. Take them in, Julia, with Miss Daly and Miss Power."

"I'm the man for the ladies," said Mr. Browne, pursing his lips until his moustache bristled and smiling in all his wrinkles. "You know, Miss Morkan, the reason they are so fond of me is—"

He did not finish his sentence, but, seeing that Aunt Kate was out of earshot, at once led the three young ladies into the back room. The middle of the room was occupied by two square tables placed end to end, and on these Aunt Julia and the caretaker were straightening and smoothing a large cloth. On the sideboard were arrayed dishes and plates, and glasses and bundles of knives and forks and spoons. The top of the closed square piano served also as a sideboard for viands and sweets. At a smaller sideboard in one corner two young men were standing, drinking hop-bitters.

Mr. Browne led his charges thither and invited them all, in jest, to some ladies' punch, hot, strong and sweet. As they said they never took anything strong he opened three bottles of lemonade for them. Then he asked one of the young men to move aside, and, taking hold of the decanter, filled out for himself a goodly measure of whisky. The young men eyed him respectfully while he took a trial sip.

"God help me," he said, smiling, "it's the doctor's orders."

His wizened face broke into a broader smile, and the three young ladies laughed in musical echo to his pleasantry, swaying their bodies to and fro, with nervous jerks of their shoulders. The boldest said:

"O, now, Mr. Browne, I'm sure the doctor never ordered anything of the kind."

Mr. Browne took another sip of his whisky and said, with sidling mimicry:

"Well, you see, I'm like the famous Mrs. Cassidy, who is reported to have said: 'Now, Mary Grimes, if I don't take it, make me take it, for I feel I want it.'"

His hot face had leaned forward a little too confidentially and he had assumed a very low Dublin accent so that the young ladies, with one instinct, received his speech in silence. Miss Furlong, who was one of Mary Jane's pupils, asked Miss Daly what was the name of the pretty waltz she had played; and Mr. Browne, seeing that he was ignored, turned promptly to the two young men who were more appreciative.

A red-faced young woman, dressed in pansy, came into the room, excitedly clapping her hands and crying:

"Quadrilles! Quadrilles![1]"

Close on her heels came Aunt Kate, crying:

"Two gentlemen and three ladies, Mary Jane!"

"O, here's Mr. Bergin and Mr. Kerrigan," said Mary Jane. "Mr. Kerrigan, will you take Miss Power? Miss Furlong, may I get you a partner, Mr. Bergin. O, that'll just do now."

"Three ladies, Mary Jane," said Aunt Kate.

The two young gentlemen asked the ladies if they might have the pleasure, and Mary Jane turned to Miss Daly.

"O, Miss Daly, you're really awfully good, after playing for the last two dances, but really we're so short of ladies tonight."

"I don't mind in the least, Miss Morkan."

"But I've a nice partner for you, Mr. Bartell D'Arcy, the tenor. I'll get him to sing later on. All Dublin is raving about him."

"Lovely voice, lovely voice!" said Aunt Kate.

---

1 Square dance.

As the piano had twice begun the prelude to the first figure Mary Jane led her recruits quickly from the room. They had hardly gone when Aunt Julia wandered slowly into the room, looking behind her at something.

"What is the matter, Julia?" asked Aunt Kate anxiously. "Who is it?"

Julia, who was carrying in a column of table-napkins, turned to her sister and said, simply, as if the question had surprised her:

"It's only Freddy, Kate, and Gabriel with him."

In fact right behind her Gabriel could be seen piloting Freddy Malins across the landing. The latter, a young man of about forty, was of Gabriel's size and build, with very round shoulders. His face was fleshy and pallid, touched with colour only at the thick hanging lobes of his ears and at the wide wings of his nose. He had coarse features, a blunt nose, a convex and receding brow, tumid and protruded lips. His heavy-lidded eyes and the disorder of his scanty hair made him look sleepy. He was laughing heartily in a high key at a story which he had been telling Gabriel on the stairs and at the same time rubbing the knuckles of his left fist backwards and forwards into his left eye.

"Good-evening, Freddy," said Aunt Julia.

Freddy Malins bade the Misses Morkan good-evening in what seemed an offhand fashion by reason of the habitual catch in his voice and then, seeing that Mr. Browne was grinning at him from the sideboard, crossed the room on rather shaky legs and began to repeat in an undertone the story he had just told to Gabriel.

"He's not so bad, is he?" said Aunt Kate to Gabriel.

Gabriel's brows were dark but he raised them quickly and answered:

"O no, hardly noticeable."

"Now, isn't he a terrible fellow!" she said. "And his poor mother made him take the pledge on New Year's Eve. But come on, Gabriel, into the drawing-room."

Before leaving the room with Gabriel she signalled to Mr. Browne by frowning and shaking her forefinger in warning to and fro. Mr. Browne nodded in answer and, when she had gone, said to Freddy Malins:

"Now, then, Teddy, I'm going to fill you out a good glass of lemonade just to buck you up."

Freddy Malins, who was nearing the climax of his story, waved the offer aside impatiently but Mr. Browne, having first called Freddy Malins' attention to a disarray in his dress, filled out and handed him a full glass of lemonade. Freddy Malins' left hand accepted the glass mechanically, his right hand being engaged in the mechanical readjustment of his dress. Mr. Browne, whose face was once more wrinkling with mirth, poured out for himself a glass of whisky while Freddy Malins exploded, before he had well reached the climax of his story, in a kink of high-pitched bronchitic laughter and, setting down his untasted and overflowing glass, began to rub the knuckles of his left fist backwards and forwards into his left eye, repeating words of his last phrase as well as his fit of laughter would allow him.

Gabriel could not listen while Mary Jane was playing her Academy piece, full of runs and difficult passages, to the hushed drawing-room. He liked music but the piece she was playing had no melody for him and he doubted whether it had any melody for the other listeners, though they had begged Mary Jane to play something. Four young men, who had come from the refreshment-room to stand in the doorway at the sound of the piano, had gone away quietly in couples after a few minutes. The only persons who seemed to follow the music were Mary Jane herself, her hands racing along the keyboard or lifted from it at the pauses like those of a priestess in momentary imprecation, and Aunt Kate standing at her elbow to turn the page.

Gabriel's eyes, irritated by the floor, which glittered with beeswax under the heavy chandelier, wandered to the wall above the piano. A picture of the balcony scene in *Romeo and Juliet* hung there and beside it was a picture of the two murdered princes in the Tower[1] which Aunt Julia had worked in red, blue and brown wools when she was a girl. Probably in the school they had gone to as girls that kind of work had been taught for one year. His mother had worked for him as a birthday present a waistcoat of purple tabinet, with little foxes' heads upon it, lined with brown satin and having round mulberry buttons. It was strange that his mother had had no musical talent though Aunt Kate used to call her the brains carrier of the Morkan family. Both she and Julia had always seemed a little proud of their serious and matronly sister. Her photograph stood before the pierglass. She held an open book on her knees and was pointing out something in it to Constantine who, dressed in a man-o'-war suit, lay at her feet. It was she who had chosen the names for her sons for she was very sensible of the dignity of family life. Thanks to her, Constantine was now senior curate in Balbriggan and, thanks to her, Gabriel himself had taken his degree in the Royal University. A shadow passed over his face as he remembered her sullen opposition to his marriage. Some slighting phrases she had used still rankled in his memory; she had once spoken of Gretta as being country cute and that was not true of Gretta at all. It was Gretta who had nursed her during all her last long illness in their house at Monkstown.

He knew that Mary Jane must be near the end of her piece for she was playing again the opening melody with runs of scales after every bar and while he waited for the end the resentment died down in his heart. The piece ended with a trill

---

1 The two sons of King Edward IV were murdered in the Tower of London, likely by orders from their uncle, Richard III.

of octaves in the treble and a final deep octave in the bass. Great applause greeted Mary Jane as, blushing and rolling up her music nervously, she escaped from the room. The most vigorous clapping came from the four young men in the doorway who had gone away to the refreshment-room at the beginning of the piece but had come back when the piano had stopped.

Lancers were arranged. Gabriel found himself partnered with Miss Ivors. She was a frank-mannered talkative young lady, with a freckled face and prominent brown eyes. She did not wear a low-cut bodice and the large brooch which was fixed in the front of her collar bore on it an Irish device and motto.

When they had taken their places she said abruptly:

"I have a crow to pluck with you."

"With me?" said Gabriel.

She nodded her head gravely.

"What is it?" asked Gabriel, smiling at her solemn manner.

"Who is G. C.?" answered Miss Ivors, turning her eyes upon him.

Gabriel coloured and was about to knit his brows, as if he did not understand, when she said bluntly:

"O, innocent Amy! I have found out that you write for *The Daily Express.*[1] Now, aren't you ashamed of yourself?"

"Why should I be ashamed of myself?" asked Gabriel, blinking his eyes and trying to smile.

"Well, I'm ashamed of you," said Miss Ivors frankly. "To say you'd write for a paper like that. I didn't think you were a West Briton."[2]

A look of perplexity appeared on Gabriel's face. It was true that he wrote a literary column every Wednesday in *The Daily Express*, for which he was paid fifteen shillings. But that did not make him a West Briton surely. The books he received for review were almost more welcome than the paltry cheque. He loved to feel the covers and turn over the pages of newly printed books. Nearly every day when his teaching in the college was ended he used to wander down the quays to the second-hand booksellers, to Hickey's on Bachelor's Walk, to Webb's or Massey's on Aston's Quay, or to O'Clohissey's in the by-street. He did not know how to meet her charge. He wanted to say that literature was above politics. But they were friends of many years' standing and their careers had been parallel, first at the university and then as teachers: he could not risk a grandiose phrase with her. He continued blinking his eyes and trying to smile and murmured lamely that he saw nothing political in writing reviews of books.

When their turn to cross had come he was still perplexed and inattentive. Miss Ivors promptly took his hand in a warm grasp and said in a soft friendly tone:

---

1 *The Dublin Daily Express* discouraged Irish nationalism.

2 A derogatory term for a native of Ireland who supports or sympathizes with Britain.

"Of course, I was only joking. Come, we cross now."

When they were together again she spoke of the University question[3] and Gabriel felt more at ease. A friend of hers had shown her his review of Browning's poems. That was how she had found out the secret: but she liked the review immensely. Then she said suddenly:

"O, Mr. Conroy, will you come for an excursion to the Aran Isles this summer? We're going to stay there a whole month. It will be splendid out in the Atlantic. You ought to come. Mr. Clancy is coming, and Mr. Kilkelly and Kathleen Kearney. It would be splendid for Gretta too if she'd come. She's from Connacht, isn't she?"

"Her people are," said Gabriel shortly.

"But you will come, won't you?" said Miss Ivors, laying her warm hand eagerly on his arm.

"The fact is," said Gabriel, "I have just arranged to go—"

"Go where?" asked Miss Ivors.

"Well, you know, every year I go for a cycling tour with some fellows and so—"

"But where?" asked Miss Ivors.

"Well, we usually go to France or Belgium or perhaps Germany," said Gabriel awkwardly.

"And why do you go to France and Belgium," said Miss Ivors, "instead of visiting your own land?"

"Well," said Gabriel, "it's partly to keep in touch with the languages and partly for a change."

"And haven't you your own language to keep in touch with—Irish?" asked Miss Ivors.

"Well," said Gabriel, "if it comes to that, you know, Irish is not my language."

Their neighbours had turned to listen to the cross-examination. Gabriel glanced right and left nervously and tried to keep his good humour under the ordeal which was making a blush invade his forehead.

"And haven't you your own land to visit," continued Miss Ivors, "that you know nothing of, your own people, and your own country?"

"O, to tell you the truth," retorted Gabriel suddenly, "I'm sick of my own country, sick of it!"

"Why?" asked Miss Ivors.

Gabriel did not answer for his retort had heated him.

"Why?" repeated Miss Ivors.

They had to go visiting together and, as he had not answered her, Miss Ivors said warmly:

---

3 The University question of the nineteenth century discussed whether the British government should endow the formation of a Catholic university in Ireland. Ireland's two extant institutions admitted Irish Protestants only; as a result, Irish Catholics, who could not attend university unless they compromised their beliefs, lacked equal social, political, economic, and professional opportunities.

"Of course, you've no answer."

Gabriel tried to cover his agitation by taking part in the dance with great energy. He avoided her eyes for he had seen a sour expression on her face. But when they met in the long chain he was surprised to feel his hand firmly pressed. She looked at him from under her brows for a moment quizzically until he smiled. Then, just as the chain was about to start again, she stood on tiptoe and whispered into his ear:

"West Briton!"

When the lancers were over Gabriel went away to a remote corner of the room where Freddy Malins' mother was sitting. She was a stout feeble old woman with white hair. Her voice had a catch in it like her son's and she stuttered slightly. She had been told that Freddy had come and that he was nearly all right. Gabriel asked her whether she had had a good crossing. She lived with her married daughter in Glasgow and came to Dublin on a visit once a year. She answered placidly that she had had a beautiful crossing and that the captain had been most attentive to her. She spoke also of the beautiful house her daughter kept in Glasgow, and of all the friends they had there. While her tongue rambled on Gabriel tried to banish from his mind all memory of the unpleasant incident with Miss Ivors. Of course the girl or woman, or whatever she was, was an enthusiast but there was a time for all things. Perhaps he ought not to have answered her like that. But she had no right to call him a West Briton before people, even in joke. She had tried to make him ridiculous before people, heckling him and staring at him with her rabbit's eyes.

He saw his wife making her way towards him through the waltzing couples. When she reached him she said into his ear:

"Gabriel, Aunt Kate wants to know won't you carve the goose as usual. Miss Daly will carve the ham and I'll do the pudding."

"All right," said Gabriel.

"She's sending in the younger ones first as soon as this waltz is over so that we'll have the table to ourselves."

"Were you dancing?" asked Gabriel.

"Of course I was. Didn't you see me? What row had you with Molly Ivors?"

"No row. Why? Did she say so?"

"Something like that. I'm trying to get that Mr. D'Arcy to sing. He's full of conceit, I think."

"There was no row," said Gabriel moodily, "only she wanted me to go for a trip to the west of Ireland and I said I wouldn't."

His wife clasped her hands excitedly and gave a little jump.

"O, do go, Gabriel," she cried. "I'd love to see Galway again."

"You can go if you like," said Gabriel coldly.

She looked at him for a moment, then turned to Mrs. Malins and said:

"There's a nice husband for you, Mrs. Malins."

While she was threading her way back across the room Mrs. Malins, without adverting to the interruption, went on to tell Gabriel what beautiful places there were in Scotland and beautiful scenery. Her son-in-law brought them every year to the lakes and they used to go fishing. Her son-in-law was a splendid fisher. One day he caught a beautiful big fish and the man in the hotel cooked it for their dinner.

Gabriel hardly heard what she said. Now that supper was coming near he began to think again about his speech and about the quotation. When he saw Freddy Malins coming across the room to visit his mother Gabriel left the chair free for him and retired into the embrasure of the window. The room had already cleared and from the back room came the clatter of plates and knives. Those who still remained in the drawing-room seemed tired of dancing and were conversing quietly in little groups. Gabriel's warm trembling fingers tapped the cold pane of the window. How cool it must be outside! How pleasant it would be to walk out alone, first along by the river and then through the park! The snow would be lying on the branches of the trees and forming a bright cap on the top of the Wellington Monument. How much more pleasant it would be there than at the supper-table!

He ran over the headings of his speech: Irish hospitality, sad memories, the Three Graces,[1] Paris,[2] the quotation from Browning. He repeated to himself a phrase he had written in his review: "One feels that one is listening to a thought-tormented music." Miss Ivors had praised the review. Was she sincere? Had she really any life of her own behind all her propagandism? There had never been any ill-feeling between them until that night. It unnerved him to think that she would be at the supper-table, looking up at him while he spoke with her critical quizzing eyes. Perhaps she would not be sorry to see him fail in his speech. An idea came into his mind and gave him courage. He would say, alluding to Aunt Kate and Aunt Julia: "Ladies and Gentlemen, the generation which is now on the wane among us may have had its faults but for my part I think it had certain qualities of hospitality, of humour, of humanity, which the new and very serious and hypereducated generation that is growing up around us seems to me to lack." Very good: that was one for Miss Ivors. What did he care that his aunts were only two ignorant old women?

A murmur in the room attracted his attention. Mr. Browne was advancing from the door, gallantly escorting Aunt Julia, who leaned upon his arm, smiling and hanging her head. An irregular musketry of applause escorted her also as far as the piano and then, as Mary Jane seated herself on the stool, and Aunt

---

1 The three sister goddesses represent charm, beauty, and grace.

2 According to Greek legend, Zeus asked Paris, a prince raised as a shepherd, to judge which of three goddesses was the most beautiful. Paris chose Aphrodite, who in turn helped him win the Spartan king's wife, Helen. Paris refused to return Helen and started the Trojan War.

Julia, no longer smiling, half turned so as to pitch her voice fairly into the room, gradually ceased. Gabriel recognised the prelude. It was that of an old song of Aunt Julia's—*Arrayed for the Bridal*. Her voice, strong and clear in tone, attacked with great spirit the runs which embellish the air and though she sang very rapidly she did not miss even the smallest of the grace notes. To follow the voice, without looking at the singer's face, was to feel and share the excitement of swift and secure flight. Gabriel applauded loudly with all the others at the close of the song and loud applause was borne in from the invisible supper-table. It sounded so genuine that a little colour struggled into Aunt Julia's face as she bent to replace in the music-stand the old leather-bound song-book that had her initials on the cover. Freddy Malins, who had listened with his head perched sideways to hear her better, was still applauding when everyone else had ceased and talking animatedly to his mother who nodded her head gravely and slowly in acquiescence. At last, when he could clap no more, he stood up suddenly and hurried across the room to Aunt Julia whose hand he seized and held in both his hands, shaking it when words failed him or the catch in his voice proved too much for him.

"I was just telling my mother," he said, "I never heard you sing so well, never. No, I never heard your voice so good as it is to-night. Now! Would you believe that now? That's the truth. Upon my word and honour that's the truth. I never heard your voice sound so fresh and so...so clear and fresh, never."

Aunt Julia smiled broadly and murmured something about compliments as she released her hand from his grasp. Mr. Browne extended his open hand towards her and said to those who were near him in the manner of a showman introducing a prodigy to an audience:

"Miss Julia Morkan, my latest discovery!"

He was laughing very heartily at this himself when Freddy Malins turned to him and said:

"Well, Browne, if you're serious you might make a worse discovery. All I can say is I never heard her sing half so well as long as I am coming here. And that's the honest truth."

"Neither did I," said Mr. Browne. "I think her voice has greatly improved."

Aunt Julia shrugged her shoulders and said with meek pride:

"Thirty years ago I hadn't a bad voice as voices go."

"I often told Julia," said Aunt Kate emphatically, "that she was simply thrown away in that choir. But she never would be said by me."

She turned as if to appeal to the good sense of the others against a refractory child while Aunt Julia gazed in front of her, a vague smile of reminiscence playing on her face.

"No," continued Aunt Kate, "she wouldn't be said or led by anyone, slaving there in that choir night and day, night and day. Six o'clock on Christmas morning! And all for what?"

"Well, isn't it for the honour of God, Aunt Kate?" asked Mary Jane, twisting round on the piano-stool and smiling.

Aunt Kate turned fiercely on her niece and said:

"I know all about the honour of God, Mary Jane, but I think it's not at all honourable for the pope to turn out the women out of the choirs[1] that have slaved there all their lives and put little whipper-snappers of boys over their heads. I suppose it is for the good of the Church if the pope does it. But it's not just, Mary Jane, and it's not right."

She had worked herself into a passion and would have continued in defence of her sister for it was a sore subject with her but Mary Jane, seeing that all the dancers had come back, intervened pacifically:

"Now, Aunt Kate, you're giving scandal to Mr. Browne who is of the other persuasion."

Aunt Kate turned to Mr. Browne, who was grinning at this allusion to his religion, and said hastily:

"O, I don't question the pope's being right. I'm only a stupid old woman and I wouldn't presume to do such a thing. But there's such a thing as common everyday politeness and gratitude. And if I were in Julia's place I'd tell that Father Healey straight up to his face..."

"And besides, Aunt Kate," said Mary Jane, "we really are all hungry and when we are hungry we are all very quarrelsome."

"And when we are thirsty we are also quarrelsome," added Mr. Browne.

"So that we had better go to supper," said Mary Jane, "and finish the discussion afterwards."

On the landing outside the drawing-room Gabriel found his wife and Mary Jane trying to persuade Miss Ivors to stay for supper. But Miss Ivors, who had put on her hat and was buttoning her cloak, would not stay. She did not feel in the least hungry and she had already overstayed her time.

"But only for ten minutes, Molly," said Mrs. Conroy. "That won't delay you."

"To take a pick itself," said Mary Jane, "after all your dancing."

"I really couldn't," said Miss Ivors.

"I am afraid you didn't enjoy yourself at all," said Mary Jane hopelessly.

"Ever so much, I assure you," said Miss Ivors, "but you really must let me run off now."

"But how can you get home?" asked Mrs. Conroy.

"O, it's only two steps up the quay."

Gabriel hesitated a moment and said:

---

1 In the early twentieth century, Pope Pius X (1835-1914) forbid women and girls from singing in church choirs.

"If you will allow me, Miss Ivors, I'll see you home if you are really obliged to go."

But Miss Ivors broke away from them.

"I won't hear of it," she cried. "For goodness sake go in to your suppers and don't mind me. I'm quite well able to take care of myself."

"Well, you're the comical girl, Molly," said Mrs. Conroy frankly.

"*Beannacht libh*," cried Miss Ivors, with a laugh, as she ran down the staircase.

Mary Jane gazed after her, a moody puzzled expression on her face, while Mrs Conroy leaned over the banisters to listen for the hall-door. Gabriel asked himself was he the cause of her abrupt departure. But she did not seem to be in ill humour: she had gone away laughing. He stared blankly down the staircase.

At the moment Aunt Kate came toddling out of the supper-room, almost wringing her hands in despair.

"Where is Gabriel?" she cried. "Where on earth is Gabriel? There's everyone waiting in there, stage to let, and nobody to carve the goose!"

"Here I am, Aunt Kate!" cried Gabriel, with sudden animation, "ready to carve a flock of geese, if necessary."

A fat brown goose lay at one end of the table and at the other end, on a bed of creased paper strewn with sprigs of parsley, lay a great ham, stripped of its outer skin and peppered over with crust crumbs, a neat paper frill round its shin and beside this was a round of spiced beef. Between these rival ends ran parallel lines of side-dishes: two little minsters of jelly, red and yellow; a shallow dish full of blocks of blancmange and red jam, a large green leaf-shaped dish with a stalk-shaped handle, on which lay bunches of purple raisins and peeled almonds, a companion dish on which lay a solid rectangle of Smyrna figs, a dish of custard topped with grated nutmeg, a small bowl full of chocolates and sweets wrapped in gold and silver papers and a glass vase in which stood some tall celery stalks. In the centre of the table there stood, as sentries to a fruit-stand which upheld a pyramid of oranges and American apples, two squat old-fashioned decanters of cut glass, one containing port and the other dark sherry. On the closed square piano a pudding in a huge yellow dish lay in waiting and behind it were three squads of bottles of stout and ale and minerals, drawn up according to the colours of their uniforms, the first two black, with brown and red labels, the third and smallest squad white, with transverse green sashes.

Gabriel took his seat boldly at the head of the table and, having looked to the edge of the carver, plunged his fork firmly into the goose. He felt quite at ease now for he was an expert carver and liked nothing better than to find himself at the head of a well-laden table.

"Miss Furlong, what shall I send you?" he asked. "A wing or a slice of the breast?"

"Just a small slice of the breast."

"Miss Higgins, what for you?"

"O, anything at all, Mr. Conroy."

While Gabriel and Miss Daly exchanged plates of goose and plates of ham and spiced beef Lily went from guest to guest with a dish of hot floury potatoes wrapped in a white napkin. This was Mary Jane's idea and she had also suggested apple sauce for the goose but Aunt Kate had said that plain roast goose without any apple sauce had always been good enough for her and she hoped she might never eat worse. Mary Jane waited on her pupils and saw that they got the best slices and Aunt Kate and Aunt Julia opened and carried across from the piano bottles of stout and ale for the gentlemen and bottles of minerals for the ladies. There was a great deal of confusion and laughter and noise, the noise of orders and counter-orders, of knives and forks, of corks and glass-stoppers. Gabriel began to carve second helpings as soon as he had finished the first round without serving himself. Everyone protested loudly so that he compromised by taking a long draught of stout for he had found the carving hot work. Mary Jane settled down quietly to her supper but Aunt Kate and Aunt Julia were still toddling round the table, walking on each other's heels, getting in each other's way and giving each other unheeded orders. Mr. Browne begged of them to sit down and eat their suppers and so did Gabriel but they said they were time enough so that, at last, Freddy Malins stood up and, capturing Aunt Kate, plumped her down on her chair amid general laughter.

When everyone had been well served Gabriel said, smiling:

"Now, if anyone wants a little more of what vulgar people call stuffing let him or her speak."

A chorus of voices invited him to begin his own supper and Lily came forward with three potatoes which she had reserved for him.

"Very well," said Gabriel amiably, as he took another preparatory draught, "kindly forget my existence, ladies and gentlemen, for a few minutes."

He set to his supper and took no part in the conversation with which the table covered Lily's removal of the plates. The subject of talk was the opera company which was then at the Theatre Royal. Mr. Bartell D'Arcy, the tenor, a dark-complexioned young man with a smart moustache, praised very highly the leading contralto of the company but Miss Furlong thought she had a rather vulgar style of production. Freddy Malins said there was a negro chieftain singing in the second part of the Gaiety[1] pantomime who had one of the finest tenor voices he had ever heard.

"Have you heard him?" he asked Mr. Bartell D'Arcy across the table.

"No," answered Mr. Bartell D'Arcy carelessly.

---

1 A Theatre in Dublin.

"Because," Freddy Malins explained, "now I'd be curious to hear your opinion of him. I think he has a grand voice."

"It takes Teddy to find out the really good things," said Mr. Browne familiarly to the table.

"And why couldn't he have a voice too?" asked Freddy Malins sharply. "Is it because he's only a black?"

Nobody answered this question and Mary Jane led the table back to the legitimate opera. One of her pupils had given her a pass for *Mignon*. Of course it was very fine, she said, but it made her think of poor Georgina Burns. Mr. Browne could go back farther still, to the old Italian companies that used to come to Dublin—Tietjens, Ilma de Murzka, Campanini, the great Trebelli Giuglini, Ravelli, Aramburo. Those were the days, he said, when there was something like singing to be heard in Dublin. He told too of how the top gallery of the old Royal used to be packed night after night, of how one night an Italian tenor had sung five encores to *Let me like a Soldier fall*, introducing a high C every time, and of how the gallery boys would sometimes in their enthusiasm unyoke the horses from the carriage of some great *prima donna* and pull her themselves through the streets to her hotel. Why did they never play the grand old operas now, he asked, "*Dinorah, Lucrezia Borgia*? Because they could not get the voices to sing them: that was why."

"Oh, well," said Mr. Bartell D'Arcy, "I presume there are as good singers to-day as there were then."

"Where are they?" asked Mr. Browne defiantly.

"In London, Paris, Milan," said Mr. Bartell D'Arcy warmly. "I suppose Caruso, for example, is quite as good, if not better than any of the men you have mentioned."

"Maybe so," said Mr. Browne. "But I may tell you I doubt it strongly."

"O, I'd give anything to hear Caruso sing," said Mary Jane.

"For me," said Aunt Kate, who had been picking a bone, "there was only one tenor. To please me, I mean. But I suppose none of you ever heard of him."

"Who was he, Miss Morkan?" asked Mr. Bartell D'Arcy politely.

"His name," said Aunt Kate, "was Parkinson. I heard him when he was in his prime and I think he had then the purest tenor voice that was ever put into a man's throat."

"Strange," said Mr. Bartell D'Arcy. "I never even heard of him."

"Yes, yes, Miss Morkan is right," said Mr. Browne. "I remember hearing of old Parkinson but he's too far back for me."

"A beautiful pure sweet mellow English tenor," said Aunt Kate with enthusiasm.

Gabriel having finished, the huge pudding was transferred to the table. The clatter of forks and spoons began again. Gabriel's wife served out spoonfuls of the pudding and passed the plates down the table. Midway down they were held up by

Mary Jane, who replenished them with raspberry or orange jelly or with blancmange and jam. The pudding was of Aunt Julia's making and she received praises for it from all quarters. She herself said that it was not quite brown enough.

"Well, I hope, Miss Morkan," said Mr. Browne, "that I'm brown enough for you because, you know, I'm all brown."

All the gentlemen, except Gabriel, ate some of the pudding out of compliment to Aunt Julia. As Gabriel never ate sweets the celery had been left for him. Freddy Malins also took a stalk of celery and ate it with his pudding. He had been told that celery was a capital thing for the blood and he was just then under doctor's care. Mrs. Malins, who had been silent all through the supper, said that her son was going down to Mount Melleray in a week or so. The table then spoke of Mount Melleray, how bracing the air was down there, how hospitable the monks were and how they never asked for a penny-piece from their guests.

"And do you mean to say," asked Mr. Browne incredulously, "that a chap can go down there and put up there as if it were a hotel and live on the fat of the land and then come away without paying anything?"

"O, most people give some donation to the monastery when they leave," said Mary Jane.

"I wish we had an institution like that in our Church," said Mr. Browne candidly.

He was astonished to hear that the monks never spoke, got up at two in the morning and slept in their coffins. He asked what they did it for.

"That's the rule of the order," said Aunt Kate firmly.

"Yes, but why?" asked Mr. Browne.

Aunt Kate repeated that it was the rule, that was all. Mr. Browne still seemed not to understand. Freddy Malins explained to him, as best he could, that the monks were trying to make up for the sins committed by all the sinners in the outside world. The explanation was not very clear for Mr. Browne grinned and said:

"I like that idea very much but wouldn't a comfortable spring bed do them as well as a coffin?"

"The coffin," said Mary Jane, "is to remind them of their last end."

As the subject had grown lugubrious it was buried in a silence of the table during which Mrs Malins could be heard saying to her neighbour in an indistinct undertone:

"They are very good men, the monks, very pious men."

The raisins and almonds and figs and apples and oranges and chocolates and sweets were now passed about the table and Aunt Julia invited all the guests to have either port or sherry. At first Mr. Bartell D'Arcy refused to take either but one of his neighbours nudged him and whispered something to him upon which he allowed his glass to be filled. Gradually as the last glasses were being filled the conversation ceased. A pause followed, broken only by the noise of the wine and by unsettlings of chairs. The Misses Morkan, all three, looked down at the tablecloth. Someone coughed once or twice and then a few gentlemen patted the table gently as a signal for silence. The silence came and Gabriel pushed back his chair and stood up.

The patting at once grew louder in encouragement and then ceased altogether. Gabriel leaned his ten trembling fingers on the tablecloth and smiled nervously at the company. Meeting a row of upturned faces he raised his eyes to the chandelier. The piano was playing a waltz tune and he could hear the skirts sweeping against the drawing-room door. People, perhaps, were standing in the snow on the quay outside, gazing up at the lighted windows and listening to the waltz music. The air was pure there. In the distance lay the park where the trees were weighted with snow. The Wellington Monument wore a gleaming cap of snow that flashed westward over the white field of Fifteen Acres.

He began:

"Ladies and Gentlemen,

"It has fallen to my lot this evening, as in years past, to perform a very pleasing task but a task for which I am afraid my poor powers as a speaker are all too inadequate."

"No, no!" said Mr. Browne.   ⌐ Fishing for complements

"But, however that may be, I can only ask you to-night to take the will for the deed and to lend me your attention for a few moments while I endeavour to express to you in words what my feelings are on this occasion.

"Ladies and Gentlemen, it is not the first time that we have gathered together under this hospitable roof, around this hospitable board. It is not the first time that we have been the recipients—or perhaps, I had better say, the victims—of the hospitality of certain good ladies."

He made a circle in the air with his arm and paused. Everyone laughed or smiled at Aunt Kate and Aunt Julia and Mary Jane who all turned crimson with pleasure. Gabriel went on more boldly:

"I feel more strongly with every recurring year that our country has no tradition which does it so much honour and which it should guard so jealously as that of its hospitality. It is a tradition that is unique as far as my experience goes (and I have visited not a few places abroad) among the modern nations. Some would say, perhaps, that with us it is rather a failing than anything to be boasted of. But granted even that, it is, to my mind, a princely failing, and one that I trust will long be cultivated among us. Of one thing, at least, I am sure. As long as this one roof shelters the good ladies aforesaid—and I wish from my heart it may do so for many and many a long year to come—the tradition of genuine warm-hearted courteous Irish hospitality, which our forefathers have handed down to us and which we in turn must hand down to our descendants, is still alive among us."

A hearty murmur of assent ran round the table. It shot through Gabriel's mind that Miss Ivors was not there and that she had gone away discourteously: and he said with confidence in himself:

"Ladies and Gentlemen,

"A new generation is growing up in our midst, a generation actuated by new ideas and new principles. It is serious and enthusiastic for these new ideas and its enthusiasm, even when it is misdirected, is, I believe, in the main sincere. But we are living in a sceptical and, if I may use the phrase, a thought-tormented age: and sometimes I fear that this new generation, educated or hypereducated as it is, will lack those qualities of humanity, of hospitality, of kindly humour which belonged to an older day. Listening to-night to the names of all those great singers of the past it seemed to me, I must confess, that we were living in a less spacious age. Those days might, without exaggeration, be called spacious days: and if they are gone beyond recall let us hope, at least, that in gatherings such as this we shall still speak of them with pride and affection, still cherish in our hearts the memory of those dead and gone great ones whose fame the world will not willingly let die."

"Hear, hear!" said Mr. Browne loudly.

"But yet," continued Gabriel, his voice falling into a softer inflection, "there are always in gatherings such as this sadder thoughts that will recur to our minds: thoughts of the past, of youth, of changes, of absent faces that we miss here to-night. Our path through life is strewn with many such sad memories: and were we to brood upon them always we could not find the heart to go on bravely with our work among the living. We have all of us living duties and living affections which claim, and rightly claim, our strenuous endeavours.

"Therefore, I will not linger on the past. I will not let any gloomy moralising intrude upon us here to-night. Here we are gathered together for a brief moment from the bustle and rush of our everyday routine. We are met here as friends, in the spirit of good-fellowship, as colleagues, also to a certain extent, in the true spirit of *camaraderie*, and as the guests of—what shall I call them?—the Three Graces of the Dublin musical world."

The table burst into applause and laughter at this allusion. Aunt Julia vainly asked each of her neighbours in turn to tell her what Gabriel had said.

"He says we are the Three Graces, Aunt Julia," said Mary Jane.

Aunt Julia did not understand but she looked up, smiling, at Gabriel, who continued in the same vein:

"Ladies and Gentlemen,

"I will not attempt to play to-night the part that Paris played on another occasion. I will not attempt to choose between them. The task would be an invidious one and one beyond my poor powers. For when I view them in turn, whether it be our chief hostess herself, whose good heart, whose too good heart, has become a byword with all who know her, or her sister, who seems to be gifted with perennial youth and whose singing must have been a surprise and a revelation to us all to-night, or, last but not least, when I consider our youngest hostess, talented, cheerful, hard-working and the best of nieces, I confess, Ladies and Gentlemen, that I do not know to which of them I should award the prize."

Gabriel glanced down at his aunts and, seeing the large smile on Aunt Julia's face and the tears which had risen to Aunt Kate's eyes, hastened to his close. He raised his glass of port gallantly, while every member of the company fingered a glass expectantly, and said loudly:

"Let us toast them all three together. Let us drink to their health, wealth, long life, happiness and prosperity and may they long continue to hold the proud and self-won position which they hold in their profession and the position of honour and affection which they hold in our hearts."

All the guests stood up, glass in hand, and, turning towards the three seated ladies, sang in unison, with Mr. Browne as leader:

> "For they are jolly gay fellows,
> For they are jolly gay fellows,
> For they are jolly gay fellows,
> Which nobody can deny."

Aunt Kate was making frank use of her handkerchief and even Aunt Julia seemed moved. Freddy Malins beat time with his pudding-fork and the singers turned towards one another, as if in melodious conference, while they sang with emphasis:

> "Unless he tells a lie,
> Unless he tells a lie."

Then, turning once more towards their hostesses, they sang:

> "For they are jolly gay fellows,
> For they are jolly gay fellows,
> For they are jolly gay fellows,
> Which nobody can deny."

The acclamation which followed was taken up beyond the door of the supper-room by many of the other guests and renewed time after time, Freddy Malins acting as officer with his fork on high.

The piercing morning air came into the hall where they were standing so that Aunt Kate said:

"Close the door, somebody. Mrs. Malins will get her death of cold."

"Browne is out there, Aunt Kate," said Mary Jane.

"Browne is everywhere," said Aunt Kate, lowering her voice.

Mary Jane laughed at her tone.

"Really," she said archly, "he is very attentive."

"He has been laid on here like the gas," said Aunt Kate in the same tone, "all during the Christmas."

She laughed herself this time good-humouredly and then added quickly:

"But tell him to come in, Mary Jane, and close the door. I hope to goodness he didn't hear me."

At that moment the hall-door was opened and Mr. Browne came in from the doorstep, laughing as if his heart would break. He was dressed in a long green overcoat with mock astrakhan cuffs and collar and wore on his head an oval fur cap. He pointed down the snow-covered quay from where the sound of shrill prolonged whistling was borne in.

"Teddy will have all the cabs in Dublin out," he said.

Gabriel advanced from the little pantry behind the office, struggling into his overcoat and, looking round the hall, said:

"Gretta not down yet?"

"She's getting on her things, Gabriel," said Aunt Kate.

"Who's playing up there?" asked Gabriel.

"Nobody. They're all gone."

"O no, Aunt Kate," said Mary Jane. "Bartell D'Arcy and Miss O'Callaghan aren't gone yet."

"Someone is fooling at the piano, anyhow," said Gabriel.

Mary Jane glanced at Gabriel and Mr. Browne and said with a shiver:

"It makes me feel cold to look at you two gentlemen muffled up like that. I wouldn't like to face your journey home at this hour."

"I'd like nothing better this minute," said Mr. Browne stoutly, "than a rattling fine walk in the country or a fast drive with a good spanking goer between the shafts."

"We used to have a very good horse and trap[1] at home," said Aunt Julia sadly.

"The never-to-be-forgotten Johnny," said Mary Jane, laughing.

Aunt Kate and Gabriel laughed too.

"Why, what was wonderful about Johnny?" asked Mr. Browne.

"The late lamented Patrick Morkan, our grandfather, that is," explained Gabriel, "commonly known in his later years as the old gentleman, was a glue-boiler."

"O, now, Gabriel," said Aunt Kate, laughing, "he had a starch mill."

"Well, glue or starch," said Gabriel, "the old gentleman had a horse by the name of Johnny. And Johnny used to work in the old gentleman's mill, walking round and round in order to drive the mill. That was all very well; but now comes the tragic part about Johnny. One fine day the old gentleman thought he'd like to drive out with the quality to a military review in the park."

"The Lord have mercy on his soul," said Aunt Kate compassionately.

"Amen," said Gabriel. "So the old gentleman, as I said, harnessed Johnny and put on his very best tall hat and his very best stock collar and drove out in grand style from his ancestral mansion somewhere near Back Lane, I think."

---

1 A two-wheeled carriage.

Everyone laughed, even Mrs. Malins, at Gabriel's manner and Aunt Kate said:

"O now, Gabriel, he didn't live in Back Lane, really. Only the mill was there."

"Out from the mansion of his forefathers," continued Gabriel, "he drove with Johnny. And everything went on beautifully until Johnny came in sight of King Billy's statue: and whether he fell in love with the horse King Billy sits on or whether he thought he was back again in the mill, anyhow he began to walk round the statue."

Gabriel paced in a circle round the hall in his goloshes amid the laughter of the others.

"Round and round he went," said Gabriel, "and the old gentleman, who was a very pompous old gentleman, was highly indignant. 'Go on, sir! What do you mean, sir? Johnny! Johnny! Most extraordinary conduct! Can't understand the horse!'"

The peals of laughter which followed Gabriel's imitation of the incident was interrupted by a resounding knock at the hall-door. Mary Jane ran to open it and let in Freddy Malins. Freddy Malins, with his hat well back on his head and his shoulders humped with cold, was puffing and steaming after his exertions.

"I could only get one cab," he said.

"O, we'll find another along the quay," said Gabriel.

"Yes," said Aunt Kate. "Better not keep Mrs. Malins standing in the draught."

Mrs. Malins was helped down the front steps by her son and Mr. Browne and, after many manœuvres, hoisted into the cab. Freddy Malins clambered in after her and spent a long time settling her on the seat, Mr. Browne helping him with advice. At last she was settled comfortably and Freddy Malins invited Mr. Browne into the cab. There was a good deal of confused talk, and then Mr. Browne got into the cab. The cabman settled his rug over his knees, and bent down for the address. The confusion grew greater and the cabman was directed differently by Freddy Malins and Mr. Browne, each of whom had his head out through a window of the cab. The difficulty was to know where to drop Mr. Browne along the route and Aunt Kate, Aunt Julia and Mary Jane helped the discussion from the doorstep with cross-directions and contradictions and abundance of laughter. As for Freddy Malins he was speechless with laughter. He popped his head in and out of the window every moment, to the great danger of his hat, and told his mother how the discussion was progressing, till at last Mr. Browne shouted to the bewildered cabman above the din of everybody's laughter:

"Do you know Trinity College?"

"Yes, sir," said the cabman.

"Well, drive bang up against Trinity College gates," said Mr. Browne, "and then we'll tell you where to go. You understand now?"

"Yes, sir," said the cabman.

"Make like a bird for Trinity College."

"Right, sir," said the cabman.

The horse was whipped up and the cab rattled off along the quay amid a chorus of laughter and adieus.

Gabriel had not gone to the door with the others. He was in a dark part of the hall gazing up the staircase. A woman was standing near the top of the first flight, in the shadow also. He could not see her face but he could see the terracotta and salmon-pink panels of her skirt which the shadow made appear black and white. It was his wife. She was leaning on the banisters, listening to something. Gabriel was surprised at her stillness and strained his ear to listen also. But he could hear little save the noise of laughter and dispute on the front steps, a few chords struck on the piano and a few notes of a man's voice singing.

He stood still in the gloom of the hall, trying to catch the air that the voice was singing and gazing up at his wife. There was grace and mystery in her attitude as if she were a symbol of something. He asked himself what is a woman standing on the stairs in the shadow, listening to distant music, a symbol of. If he were a painter he would paint her in that attitude. Her blue felt hat would show off the bronze of her hair against the darkness and the dark panels of her skirt would show off the light ones. *Distant Music* he would call the picture if he were a painter.

The hall-door was closed; and Aunt Kate, Aunt Julia and Mary Jane came down the hall, still laughing.

"Well, isn't Freddy terrible?" said Mary Jane. "He's really terrible."

Gabriel said nothing but pointed up the stairs towards where his wife was standing. Now that the hall-door was closed the voice and the piano could be heard more clearly. Gabriel held up his hand for them to be silent. The song seemed to be in the old Irish tonality and the singer seemed uncertain both of his words and of his voice. The voice, made plaintive by distance and by the singer's hoarseness, faintly illuminated the cadence of the air with words expressing grief:

> "O, the rain falls on my heavy locks
> And the dew wets my skin,
> My babe lies cold..."

"O," exclaimed Mary Jane. "It's Bartell D'Arcy singing and he wouldn't sing all the night. O, I'll get him to sing a song before he goes."

"O do, Mary Jane," said Aunt Kate.

Mary Jane brushed past the others and ran to the staircase but before she reached it the singing stopped and the piano was closed abruptly.

"O, what a pity!" she cried. "Is he coming down, Gretta?"

Gabriel heard his wife answer yes and saw her come down towards them. A few steps behind her were Mr. Bartell D'Arcy and Miss O'Callaghan.

"O, Mr. D'Arcy," cried Mary Jane, "it's downright mean of you to break off like that when we were all in raptures listening to you."

"I have been at him all the evening," said Miss O'Callaghan, "and Mrs. Conroy too and he told us he had a dreadful cold and couldn't sing."

"O, Mr. D'Arcy," said Aunt Kate, "now that was a great fib to tell."

"Can't you see that I'm as hoarse as a crow?" said Mr. D'Arcy roughly.

He went into the pantry hastily and put on his overcoat. The others, taken aback by his rude speech, could find nothing to say. Aunt Kate wrinkled her brows and made signs to the others to drop the subject. Mr. D'Arcy stood swathing his neck carefully and frowning.

"It's the weather," said Aunt Julia, after a pause.

"Yes, everybody has colds," said Aunt Kate readily, "everybody."

"They say," said Mary Jane, "we haven't had snow like it for thirty years; and I read this morning in the newspapers that the snow is general all over Ireland."

"I love the look of snow," said Aunt Julia sadly.

"So do I," said Miss O'Callaghan. "I think Christmas is never really Christmas unless we have the snow on the ground."

"But poor Mr. D'Arcy doesn't like the snow," said Aunt Kate, smiling.

Mr. D'Arcy came from the pantry, fully swathed and buttoned, and in a repentant tone told them the history of his cold. Everyone gave him advice and said it was a great pity and urged him to be very careful of his throat in the night air. Gabriel watched his wife who did not join in the conversation. She was standing right under the dusty fanlight and the flame of the gas lit up the rich bronze of her hair which he had seen her drying at the fire a few days before. She was in the same attitude and seemed unaware of the talk about her. At last she turned towards them and Gabriel saw that there was colour on her cheeks and that her eyes were shining. A sudden tide of joy went leaping out of his heart.

"Mr. D'Arcy," she said, "what is the name of that song you were singing?"

"It's called *The Lass of Aughrim*," said Mr. D'Arcy, "but I couldn't remember it properly. Why? Do you know it?"

"*The Lass of Aughrim*," she repeated. "I couldn't think of the name."

"It's a very nice air," said Mary Jane. "I'm sorry you were not in voice tonight."

"Now, Mary Jane," said Aunt Kate, "don't annoy Mr. D'Arcy. I won't have him annoyed."

Seeing that all were ready to start she shepherded them to the door where good-night was said:

"Well, good-night, Aunt Kate, and thanks for the pleasant evening."

"Good-night, Gabriel. Good-night, Gretta!"

"Good-night, Aunt Kate, and thanks ever so much. Good-night, Aunt Julia."

"O, good-night, Gretta, I didn't see you."

"Good-night, Mr. D'Arcy. Good-night, Miss O'Callaghan."

"Good-night, Miss Morkan."

"Good-night, again."

"Good-night, all. Safe home."

"Good-night. Good-night."

The morning was still dark. A dull yellow light brooded over the houses and the river; and the sky seemed to be descending. It was slushy underfoot; and only streaks and patches of snow lay on the roofs, on the parapets of the quay and on the area railings. The lamps were still burning redly in the murky air and, across the river, the palace of the Four Courts stood out menacingly against the heavy sky.

She was walking on before him with Mr. Bartell D'Arcy, her shoes in a brown parcel tucked under one arm and her hands holding her skirt up from the slush. She had no longer any grace of attitude but Gabriel's eyes were still bright with happiness. The blood went bounding along his veins; and the thoughts went rioting through his brain, proud, joyful, tender, valorous.

She was walking on before him so lightly and so erect that he longed to run after her noiselessly, catch her by the shoulders and say something foolish and affectionate into her ear. She seemed to him so frail that he longed to defend her against something and then to be alone with her. Moments of their secret life together burst like stars upon his memory. A heliotrope[1] envelope was lying beside his breakfast-cup and he was caressing it with his hand. Birds were twittering in the ivy and the sunny web of the curtain was shimmering along the floor: he could not eat for happiness. They were standing on the crowded platform and he was placing a ticket inside the warm palm of her glove. He was standing with her in the cold, looking in through a grated window at a man making bottles in a roaring furnace. It was very cold. Her face, fragrant in the cold air, was quite close to his; and suddenly he called out to the man at the furnace:

"Is the fire hot, sir?"

But the man could not hear with the noise of the furnace. It was just as well. He might have answered rudely.

A wave of yet more tender joy escaped from his heart and went coursing in warm flood along his arteries. Like the tender fire of stars moments of their life together, that no one knew of or would ever know of, broke upon and illumined his memory. He longed to recall to her those moments, to make her forget the years of their dull existence together and remember only their moments of ecstasy. For the years, he felt, had not quenched his soul or hers. Their children, his writing, her household cares had not quenched all their souls' tender fire. In one letter that he had written to her then he had said: "Why is it that words like these seem to me so dull and cold? Is it because there is no word tender enough to be your name?"

Like distant music these words that he had written years before were borne towards him from the past. He longed to be alone with her. When the others had gone away, when he and she were in their room in the hotel, then they would be alone together. He would call her softly:

---

1 A reddish-purple color.

"Gretta!"

Perhaps she would not hear at once: she would be undressing. Then something in his voice would strike her. She would turn and look at him....

At the corner of Winetavern Street they met a cab. He was glad of its rattling noise as it saved him from conversation. She was looking out of the window and seemed tired. The others spoke only a few words, pointing out some building or street. The horse galloped along wearily under the murky morning sky, dragging his old rattling box after his heels, and Gabriel was again in a cab with her, galloping to catch the boat, galloping to their honeymoon.

As the cab drove across O'Connell Bridge Miss O'Callaghan said:

"They say you never cross O'Connell Bridge without seeing a white horse."

"I see a white man this time," said Gabriel.

"Where?" asked Mr. Bartell D'Arcy.

Gabriel pointed to the statue, on which lay patches of snow. Then he nodded familiarly to it and waved his hand.

"Good-night, Dan," he said gaily.

When the cab drew up before the hotel Gabriel jumped out and, in spite of Mr. Bartell D'Arcy's protest, paid the driver. He gave the man a shilling over his fare. The man saluted and said:

"A prosperous New Year to you, sir."

"The same to you," said Gabriel cordially.

She leaned for a moment on his arm in getting out of the cab and while standing at the curbstone, bidding the others good-night. She leaned lightly on his arm, as lightly as when she had danced with him a few hours before. He had felt proud and happy then, happy that she was his, proud of her grace and wifely carriage. But now, after the kindling again of so many memories, the first touch of her body, musical and strange and perfumed, sent through him a keen pang of lust. Under cover of her silence he pressed her arm closely to his side; and, as they stood at the hotel door, he felt that they had escaped from their lives and duties, escaped from home and friends and run away together with wild and radiant hearts to a new adventure.

An old man was dozing in a great hooded chair in the hall. He lit a candle in the office and went before them to the stairs. They followed him in silence, their feet falling in soft thuds on the thickly carpeted stairs. She mounted the stairs behind the porter, her head bowed in the ascent, her frail shoulders curved as with a burden, her skirt girt tightly about her. He could have flung his arms about her hips and held her still for his arms were trembling with desire to seize her and only the stress of his nails against the palms of his hands held the wild impulse of his body in check. The porter halted on the stairs to settle his guttering candle. They halted too on the steps below him. In the silence Gabriel could hear the falling of the molten wax into the tray and the thumping of his own heart against his ribs.

The porter led them along a corridor and opened a door. Then he set his unstable candle down on a toilet-table and asked at what hour they were to be called in the morning.

"Eight," said Gabriel.

The porter pointed to the tap of the electric-light and began a muttered apology but Gabriel cut him short.

"We don't want any light. We have light enough from the street. And I say," he added, pointing to the candle, "you might remove that handsome article, like a good man."

The porter took up his candle again, but slowly for he was surprised by such a novel idea. Then he mumbled good-night and went out. Gabriel shot the lock too.

A ghostly light from the street lamp lay in a long shaft from one window to the door. Gabriel threw his overcoat and hat on a couch and crossed the room towards the window. He looked down into the street in order that his emotion might calm a little. Then he turned and leaned against a chest of drawers with his back to the light. She had taken off her hat and cloak and was standing before a large swinging mirror, unhooking her waist. Gabriel paused for a few moments, watching her, and then said:

"Gretta!"

She turned away from the mirror slowly and walked along the shaft of light towards him. Her face looked so serious and weary that the words would not pass Gabriel's lips. No, it was not the moment yet.

"You looked tired," he said.

"I am a little," she answered.

"You don't feel ill or weak?"

"No, tired: that's all."

She went on to the window and stood there, looking out. Gabriel waited again and then, fearing that diffidence was about to conquer him, he said abruptly:

"By the way, Gretta!"

"What is it?"

"You know that poor fellow Malins?" he said quickly.

"Yes. What about him?"

"Well, poor fellow, he's a decent sort of chap after all," continued Gabriel in a false voice. "He gave me back that sovereign I lent him and I didn't expect it really. It's a pity he wouldn't keep away from that Browne because he's not a bad fellow really."

He was trembling now with annoyance. Why did she seem so abstracted? He did not know how he could begin. Was she annoyed, too, about something? If she would only turn to him or come to him of her own accord! To take her as she was would be brutal. No, he must see some ardour in her eyes first. He longed to be master of her strange mood.

"When did you lend him the pound?" she asked, after a pause.

Gabriel strove to restrain himself from breaking out into brutal language about the sottish Malins and his pound. He longed to cry to her from his soul, to crush her body against his, to overmaster her. But he said:

"O, at Christmas, when he opened that little Christmas-card shop in Henry Street."

He was in such a fever of rage and desire that he did not hear her come from the window. She stood before him for an instant, looking at him strangely. Then, suddenly raising herself on tiptoe and resting her hands lightly on his shoulders, she kissed him.

"You are a very generous person, Gabriel," she said.

Gabriel, trembling with delight at her sudden kiss and at the quaintness of her phrase, put his hands on her hair and began smoothing it back, scarcely touching it with his fingers. The washing had made it fine and brilliant. His heart was brimming over with happiness. Just when he was wishing for it she had come to him of her own accord. Perhaps her thoughts had been running with his. Perhaps she had felt the impetuous desire that was in him and then the yielding mood had come upon her. Now that she had fallen to him so easily he wondered why he had been so diffident.

He stood, holding her head between his hands. Then, slipping one arm swiftly about her body and drawing her towards him, he said softly:

"Gretta dear, what are you thinking about?"

She did not answer nor yield wholly to his arm. He said again, softly:

"Tell me what it is, Gretta. I think I know what is the matter. Do I know?"

She did not answer at once. Then she said in an outburst of tears:

"O, I am thinking about that song, *The Lass of Aughrim*."

She broke loose from him and ran to the bed and, throwing her arms across the bed-rail, hid her face. Gabriel stood stock-still for a moment in astonishment and then followed her. As he passed in the way of the cheval-glass he caught sight of himself in full length, his broad, well-filled shirt-front, the face whose expression always puzzled him when he saw it in a mirror and his glimmering gilt-rimmed eyeglasses. He halted a few paces from her and said:

"What about the song? Why does that make you cry?"

She raised her head from her arms and dried her eyes with the back of her hand like a child. A kinder note than he had intended went into his voice.

"Why, Gretta?" he asked.

"I am thinking about a person long ago who used to sing that song."

"And who was the person long ago?" asked Gabriel, smiling.

"It was a person I used to know in Galway when I was living with my grandmother," she said.

The smile passed away from Gabriel's face. A dull anger began to gather again at the back of his mind and the dull fires of his lust began to glow angrily in his veins.

"Someone you were in love with?" he asked ironically.

"It was a young boy I used to know," she answered, "named Michael Furey. He used to sing that song, *The Lass of Aughrim*. He was very delicate."

Gabriel was silent. He did not wish her to think that he was interested in this delicate boy.

"I can see him so plainly," she said after a moment. "Such eyes as he had: big, dark eyes! And such an expression in them—an expression!"

"O then, you were in love with him?" said Gabriel.

"I used to go out walking with him," she said, "when I was in Galway."

A thought flew across Gabriel's mind.

"Perhaps that was why you wanted to go to Galway with that Ivors girl?" he said coldly.

She looked at him and asked in surprise:

"What for?"

Her eyes made Gabriel feel awkward. He shrugged his shoulders and said:

"How do I know? To see him perhaps."

She looked away from him along the shaft of light towards the window in silence.

"He is dead," she said at length. "He died when he was only seventeen. Isn't it a terrible thing to die so young as that?"

"What was he?" asked Gabriel, still ironically.

"He was in the gasworks," she said.

Gabriel felt humiliated by the failure of his irony and by the evocation of this figure from the dead, a boy in the gasworks. While he had been full of memories of their secret life together, full of tenderness and joy and desire, she had been comparing him in her mind with another. A shameful consciousness of his own person assailed him. He saw himself as a ludicrous figure, acting as a pennyboy[1] for his aunts, a nervous well-meaning sentimentalist, orating to vulgarians and idealising his own clownish lusts, the pitiable fatuous fellow he had caught a glimpse of in the mirror. Instinctively he turned his back more to the light lest she might see the shame that burned upon his forehead.

He tried to keep up his tone of cold interrogation but his voice when he spoke was humble and indifferent.

"I suppose you were in love with this Michael Furey, Gretta," he said.

"I was great with him at that time," she said.

Her voice was veiled and sad. Gabriel, feeling now how vain it would be to try to lead her whither he had purposed, caressed one of her hands and said, also sadly:

"And what did he die of so young, Gretta? Consumption, was it?"

1 A person tasked with menial duties.

"I think he died for me," she answered.

A vague terror seized Gabriel at this answer as if, at that hour when he had hoped to triumph, some impalpable and vindictive being was coming against him, gathering forces against him in its vague world. But he shook himself free of it with an effort of reason and continued to caress her hand. He did not question her again for he felt that she would tell him of herself. Her hand was warm and moist: it did not respond to his touch but he continued to caress it just as he had caressed her first letter to him that spring morning.

"It was in the winter," she said, "about the beginning of the winter when I was going to leave my grandmother's and come up here to the convent. And he was ill at the time in his lodgings in Galway and wouldn't be let out and his people in Oughterard were written to. He was in decline, they said, or something like that. I never knew rightly."

She paused for a moment and sighed.

"Poor fellow," she said. "He was very fond of me and he was such a gentle boy. We used to go out together, walking, you know, Gabriel, like the way they do in the country. He was going to study singing only for his health. He had a very good voice, poor Michael Furey."

"Well; and then?" asked Gabriel.

"And then when it came to the time for me to leave Galway and come up to the convent he was much worse and I wouldn't be let see him so I wrote him a letter saying I was going up to Dublin and would be back in the summer and hoping he would be better then."

She paused for a moment to get her voice under control and then went on:

"Then the night before I left I was in my grandmother's house in Nuns' Island, packing up, and I heard gravel thrown up against the window. The window was so wet I couldn't see so I ran downstairs as I was and slipped out the back into the garden and there was the poor fellow at the end of the garden, shivering."

"And did you not tell him to go back?" asked Gabriel.

"I implored of him to go home at once and told him he would get his death in the rain. But he said he did not want to live. I can see his eyes as well as well! He was standing at the end of the wall where there was a tree."

"And did he go home?" asked Gabriel.

"Yes, he went home. And when I was only a week in the convent he died and he was buried in Oughterard where his people came from. O, the day I heard that, that he was dead!"

She stopped, choking with sobs, and, overcome by emotion, flung herself face downward on the bed, sobbing in the quilt. Gabriel held her hand for a moment longer, irresolutely, and then, shy of intruding on her grief, let it fall gently and walked quietly to the window.

She was fast asleep.

Gabriel, leaning on his elbow, looked for a few moments unresentfully on her tangled hair and half-open mouth, listening to her deep-drawn breath. So she had had that romance in her life: a man had died for her sake. It hardly pained him now to think how poor a part he, her husband, had played in her life. He watched her while she slept as though he and she had never lived together as man and wife. His curious eyes rested long upon her face and on her hair: and, as he thought of what she must have been then, in that time of her first girlish beauty, a strange friendly pity for her entered his soul. He did not like to say even to himself that her face was no longer beautiful but he knew that it was no longer the face for which Michael Furey had braved death.

Perhaps she had not told him all the story. His eyes moved to the chair over which she had thrown some of her clothes. A petticoat string dangled to the floor. One boot stood upright, its limp upper fallen down: the fellow of it lay upon its side. He wondered at his riot of emotions of an hour before. From what had it proceeded? From his aunt's supper, from his own foolish speech, from the wine and dancing, the merry-making when saying good-night in the hall, the pleasure of the walk along the river in the snow. Poor Aunt Julia! She, too, would soon be a shade with the shade of Patrick Morkan and his horse. He had caught that haggard look upon her face for a moment when she was singing *Arrayed for the Bridal*. Soon, perhaps, he would be sitting in that same drawing-room, dressed in black, his silk hat on his knees. The blinds would be drawn down and Aunt Kate would be sitting beside him, crying and blowing her nose and telling him how Julia had died. He would cast about in his mind for some words that might console her, and would find only lame and useless ones. Yes, yes: that would happen very soon.

The air of the room chilled his shoulders. He stretched himself cautiously along under the sheets and lay down beside his wife. One by one they were all becoming shades. Better pass boldly into that other world, in the full glory of some passion, than fade and wither dismally with age. He thought of how she who lay beside him had locked in her heart for so many years that image of her lover's eyes when he had told her that he did not wish to live.

Generous tears filled Gabriel's eyes. He had never felt like that himself towards any woman but he knew that such a feeling must be love. The tears gathered more thickly in his eyes and in the partial darkness he imagined he saw the form of a young man standing under a dripping tree. Other forms were near. His soul had approached that region where dwell the vast hosts of the dead. He was conscious of, but could not apprehend, their wayward and flickering existence. His own identity was fading out into a grey impalpable world: the solid world itself which these dead had one time reared and lived in was dissolving and dwindling.

A few light taps upon the pane made him turn to the window. It had begun to snow again. He watched sleepily the flakes, silver and dark, falling obliquely against the lamplight. The time had come for him to set out on his journey westward. Yes, the newspapers were right: snow was general all over Ireland. It was falling on every part of the dark central plain, on the treeless hills, falling softly upon the Bog of Allen and, farther westward, softly falling into the dark mutinous Shannon waves. It was falling, too, upon every part of the lonely churchyard on the hill where Michael Furey lay buried. It lay thickly drifted on the crooked crosses and headstones, on the spears of the little gate, on the barren thorns. His soul swooned slowly as he heard the snow falling faintly through the universe and faintly falling, like the descent of their last end, upon all the living and the dead.

1914

VIRGINIA WOOLF
1882–1941

VIRGINIA WOOLF (née Stephen) was born into a large family with ample social and artistic connections. Both of her parents were widowers; her mother, Julia Duckworth, had three children of her own when she married Leslie (later Sir Leslie) Stephen, an essayist, historian, and mountaineer who had a daughter with his first wife. The couple had four more children together, all of whom were intellectual and talented. Despite recurrent bouts of sibling rivalry, Woolf, her sister, and her two brothers shared close familial bonds that helped them cope with the misfortunes that wracked their early years.

As a girl, Woolf's world was predictable and ordered. She spent summers in a country house by the Cornwall coast and all other seasons confined to the dusky rooms of a London townhouse. Her sense of security, however, was ruptured when her older half-brother sexually abused her. She was later left vulnerable and grieving after her mother's unexpected death in 1895, followed by the loss of her affectionate half-sister two years later. When her father died in 1904, she suffered a severe breakdown and attempted suicide. The family relocated to Bloomsbury, a bohemian section of London that offered a less repressive atmosphere. Spacious and bright, the new house became symbolic of modernity and personal freedom.

There the Stephens formed the Old Bloomsbury Group, a circle composed of liberally-minded individuals who breached drawing room etiquette, ridiculed social, religious, and moral components of Victorian society, and openly discussed sexuality. Woolf's interactions and relationships shaped her assessment of gender and provided critical material for writing. Her novel, *Orlando: A Biography*, for instance, centers on a protagonist who alternates between masculine and feminine identities through the ages. It was partially inspired by Virginia's own extra-marital affair with Vita (Victoria) Sackville-West, a bisexual aristocrat and poet. Bloomsbury meetings continued at a new address after Virginia's younger brother, who had instigated the group's formation, died of typhoid in 1906. The group members permanently impacted her life and writing; they were linked to one another as friends and lovers. For example, Woolf's sister Vanessa and her brother Adrian had affairs with the painter Duncan Grant, and both Vanessa and Woolf eventually married fellow members.

In 1912, Virginia married Leonard Woolf, an author who emotionally and intellectually supported her through her best and worst moments. By her mid-twenties, she solidified her theory as a writer. Eager to strike the nerves of her readers and reach the depths of her topics, she endeavored to "re-form" the Victorian novel. Rather than relying on external plot-intensive events, she concentrated heavily on the inner, unseen mechanisms of her characters. As she remarked in her lengthy 1924 pamphlet *Mr. Bennet and Mrs. Brown*,

> I believe that all novels, that is to say, deal with character, and that
> it is to express character—not to preach doctrines, sing songs, or
> celebrate the glories of the British Empire, that the form of the
> novel, so clumsy, verbose, and undramatic, so rich, elastic, and
> alive, has been evolved.

Her pieces, often bereft of dramatic outward activity, encompass unmistakable psychological complexity. The desire to decipher and replicate human consciousness flows through her work.

"The Mark on the Wall," the first piece published using the Hogarth Press, a printing press the Woolfs purchased in 1917, illuminates Woolf's ambitions. In a stream-of-consciousness monologue, the narrator contemplates religion, nature, and other themes while simply sitting and staring at an undistinguished mark. In "The Mark" and other works alike, Woolf established a host of characters whose thoughts and observations allow them to extract meaningful revelations from ordinary domestic activities.

Domesticity also factored into another focus of Woolf's work: gender. The "woman question," which debated the nature and roles of women, remained at the forefront of her mind, as did demands for education, political rights, and professional opportunities brought about by the "New Woman." She wrote for *The Guardian*, a women's paper, and supported the women's suffrage movement. Though she established herself as a spokeswoman on some gender issues, her stances were at times ambivalent, warranting criticism from her more fervent feminist and political friends. She nevertheless asserted that old-fashioned trends and power biases severely hindered female potential. She expounded the need for women to have the time, money, and space necessary to write in *A Room of One's Own*, an essay that sprouted from two separate addresses delivered to female undergraduates. It soon morphed into an attempt to establish a new tradition for women that did not renounce the history of traditional womanhood.

Woolf bolstered the feminist cause in *Three Guineas*, a novel that critiques male power. Published on the eve of World War II, Woolf controversially described war as a male pastime. As the threat of the Nazi invasion of England drew nearer, Woolf fell into dread and despair; in the event of invasion, Leonard, who was

Jewish, would be arrested by the Gestapo, and she would also be detained. Writing for Woolf had always served as a remedy to her troubles, yet she grew to believe that her writing was powerless against war and feared that she could never reach a wide enough audience to advance her cause. She committed suicide in a river near her home in 1941.

Woolf left an overwhelming quantity of writing, both finished and unfinished, behind. *Between the Acts,* her final novel, was published posthumously and eventually joined by a plethora of letters, essays, and journal entries. She fully submerged herself in her work, frequently suffering extreme depressive episodes after completing novels. Splicing together narratives from fragments, manipulating sensory details, and evoking tangible emotion, Woolf consistently drove at the structures of personality, identity, and personal relationships.

1882	Adeline Virginia Stephen born 25 January
1912	Marries Leonard Woolf
1915	*The Voyage Out*
1917	"A Mark on the Wall"
1922	*Jacob's Room*
1925	*Mrs. Dalloway*
1927	*To the Lighthouse*
1928	*Orlando: A Biography*
1929	*A Room of One's Own*
1931	*The Waves*
1937	*The Years*
1938	*Three Guineas*
1941	Woolf commits suicide on 28 March and is buried at Monk's House, the Woolfs' country residence; *Between the Acts*

MODERN NOVELS

I N MAKING ANY SURVEY, even the freest and loosest, of modern fiction, it is difficult not to take it for granted that the modern practice of the art is somehow an improvement upon the old. With their simple tools and primitive materials, it might be said, Fielding did well and Jane Austen even better, but compare their opportunities with ours! Their masterpieces certainly have a strange air of simplicity. And yet the analogy between literature and the process, to choose an example, of making bicycles scarcely holds good beyond the first glance. It is doubtful whether in the course of the centuries, though we have learnt much about making machines, we have learnt anything about making literature. We do not come to write better; all that we can be said to do is to keep moving, now a little in this direction, now in that, but with a circular tendency should the whole course of the track be viewed from a sufficiently lofty pinnacle. It need scarcely be said that we make no claim to stand even momentarily upon that vantage ground; we seem to see ourselves on the flat, in the crowd, half blind with dust, and looking back with a sort of envy to those happy warriors whose battle is won and whose achievements wear so serene an air of accomplishment that in our envy we can scarcely refrain from whispering that the prize was not so rare, nor the battle so fierce, as our own. Let the historian of literature decide. It is for him, too, to ascertain whether we are now at the beginning, or middle, or end, of a great period of prose fiction; all that we ourselves can know is that, whatever stage we have reached, we are still in the thick of the battle. This very sense of heights reached by others and unassailable by us, this envious belief that Fielding, Thackeray, or Jane Austen were set an easier problem, however triumphantly they may have solved it, is a proof, not that we have improved upon them, still less that we have given up the game and left them the victors, but only that we still strive and press on.

Our quarrel, then, is not with the classics, and if we speak of quarrelling with Mr. Wells, Mr. Bennett, and Mr. Galsworthy it is partly that by the mere fact of their existence in the flesh their work has a living, breathing, every-day imperfection which bids us take what liberties with it we choose. But it is also true that, while we thank them for a thousand gifts, we reserve our unconditional gratitude for Mr. Hardy, for Mr. Conrad, and in a much lesser degree for the Mr. Hudson, of *The Purple Land, Green Mansions*, and *Far Away and Long Ago*. The former, differently and in different measures, have excited so many hopes and disappointed them so persistently that our gratitude largely takes the form of thanking them for having shown us what it is that we certainly could not do, but as certainly, perhaps, do not wish to do. No single phrase will sum up the charge or grievance which we have to bring against a mass of work so large in its volume and embodying so many qualities, both admirable and the reverse. If we tried to formulate our meaning in one word we should say that these three writers are materialists, and for that reason have disappointed us and left us with the feeling that the sooner English fiction turns its back upon them, as politely as may be, and marches, if only into the desert, the better for its soul. Of course, no single word reaches the centre of three separate targets. In the case of Mr. Wells it falls notably wide of the mark. And yet even in his case it indicates to our thinking the fatal alloy in his genius, the great clod of clay that has got itself mixed up with the purity of his inspiration. But Mr. Bennett is perhaps the worst culprit of the three, inasmuch as he is by far the best workman. He can make a book so well constructed and solid in its craftsmanship that it is difficult for the most exacting of critics to see through what chink or crevice decay can creep in. There is not so much as a draught between the frames of the windows, or a crack in the boards. And yet—if life should refuse to live there? That is a risk which the creator of *The Old Wives' Tale*, George Cannon, Edwin Clayhanger, and hosts of other figures, may well claim to have surmounted. His characters live abundantly, even unexpectedly, but it remains to ask how do they live, and what do they live for? More and more they seem to us, deserting even the well-built villa in the Five Towns,[1] to spend their time in some softly padded first-class railway carriage, fitted with bells and buttons innumerable; and the destiny to which they travel so luxuriously becomes more and more unquestionably an eternity of bliss spent in the very best hotel in Brighton. It can scarcely be said of Mr. Wells that he is a materialist in the sense that he takes too much delight in the solidity of his fabric. His mind is too generous in its sympathies to allow him to spend much time in making things shipshape and substantial. He is a materialist from sheer goodness of heart, taking upon his shoulders the work that ought to have been discharged by Government officials, and in the plethora of his ideas and facts scarcely having leisure to realize, or forgetting to think important, the crudity and coarseness of his human beings. Yet what more damaging criticism can there be both of his earth and of his Heaven than that they are to be inhabited here and hereafter by his Joans and his Peters? Does not the inferiority of their natures tarnish whatever institutions and ideals may be provided for them by the generosity of their Creator? Nor, profoundly though we respect the integrity and humanity of Mr. Galsworthy, shall we find what we seek in his pages.

---

1 Arnold Bennett's Five Towns novels and short stories are set in the Five Towns, fictional locations closely based on his birthplace.

We have to admit that we are exacting, and, further, that we find it difficult
to justify our discontent by explaining what it is that we exact. We frame our
question differently at different times. But it reappears most persistently as we
drop the finished novel on the crest of a sigh—Is it worth while? What is the point
of it all? Can it be that owing to one of those little deviations which the human
spirit seems to make from time to time Mr. Bennett has come down with his
magnificent apparatus for catching life just an inch or two on the wrong side? Life
escapes; and perhaps without life nothing else is worth while. It is a confession of
vagueness to have to make use of such a figure as this, but we scarcely better the
matter by speaking as critics are prone to do of reality. Admitting the vagueness,
let us hazard the opinion that for us at this moment the form of fiction most in
vogue more often misses than secures the thing we seek. Whether we call it life or
spirit, truth or reality, this, the essential thing, has moved off, or on, and refuses to
be contained any longer in such ill-fitting vestments as we provide. Nevertheless we
go on perseveringly, conscientiously, constructing our thirty-two chapters after
a design which more and more ceases to resemble the vision in our minds. So
much of the enormous labour of proving the solidity, the likeness to life, of the
story is not merely labour thrown away but labour misplaced to the extent of
obscuring and blotting out the light of the conception. The mediocrity of most
novels seems to arise from a conviction on the part of the writer that unless his
plot provides scenes of tragedy, comedy, and excitement, an air of probability so
impeccable that if all his figures were to come to life they would find themselves
dressed down to the last button in the fashion of the hour, he has failed in his
duty to the public. If this, roughly as we have stated it, represents his vision,
his mediocrity may be said to be natural rather than imposed; but as often as
not we may suspect some moment of hesitation in which the question suggests
itself whether life is like this after all? Is it not possible that the accent falls a
little differently, that the moment of importance came before or after, that, if
one were free and could set down what one chose, there would be no plot, little
probability, and a vague general confusion in which the clear-cut features of
the tragic, the comic, the passionate, and the lyrical were dissolved beyond the
possibility of separate recognition? The mind, exposed to the ordinary course of
life, receives upon its surface a myriad impressions—trivial, fantastic, evanescent,
or engraved with the sharpness of steel. From all sides they come, an incessant
shower of innumerable atoms, composing in their sum what we might venture to
call life itself; and to figure further as the semi-transparent envelope, or luminous
halo, surrounding us from the beginning of consciousness to the end. Is it not
perhaps the chief task of the novelist to convey this incessantly varying spirit with
whatever stress of sudden deviation it may display, and as little admixture of the
alien and external as possible? We are not pleading merely for courage and sincerity;

but suggesting that the proper stuff for fiction is a little other than custom would have us believe it.

In some such fashion as this that we seek to define the element which distinguishes the work of several young writers, among whom Mr. James Joyce is the most notable, from that of their predecessors. It attempts to come closer to life, and to preserve more sincerely and exactly what interests and moves them by discarding most of the conventions which are commonly observed by the novelists. Let us record the atoms as they fall upon the mind in the order in which they fall, let us trace the pattern, however disconnected and incoherent in appearance, which each sight or incident scores upon the consciousness. Let us not take it for granted that life exists more in what is commonly thought small. Any one who has read *The Portrait of the Artist as a Young Man* or what promises to be a far more interesting work, *Ulysses*, now appearing in the *Little Review*, will have hazarded some theory of this nature as to Mr. Joyce's intention. On our part it is hazarded rather than affirmed; but whatever the exact intention there can be no question but that it is of the utmost sincerity and that the result, difficult or unpleasant as we may judge it, is undeniably important. In contrast to those whom we have called materialists Mr. Joyce is spiritual; concerned at all costs to reveal the flickerings of that innermost flame which flashes its myriad messages through the brain, he disregards with complete courage whatever seems to him adventitious, though it be probability or coherence or any other of the handrails to which we cling for support when we set our imaginations free. Faced, as in the Cemetery scene, by so much that, in its restless scintillations, in its irrelevance, its flashes of deep significance succeeded by incoherent inanities, seems to be life itself, we have to fumble rather awkwardly if we want to say what else we wish; and for what reason a work of such originality yet fails to compare, for we must take high examples, with *Youth* or *Jude the Obscure*. If fails, one might say simply, because of the comparative poverty of the writer's mind. But it is possible to press a little further and wonder whether we may not refer our sense of being in a bright and yet somehow strictly confined apartment rather than at large beneath the sky to some limitation imposed by the method as well as by the mind. Is it due to the method that we feel neither jovial nor magnanimous, but centred in a self which in spite of its tremor of susceptibility never reaches out or embraces or comprehends what is outside itself and beyond? Does the emphasis laid perhaps didactically upon indecency contribute to this effect of angular and isolated? Or is it merely that in any effort of such courage the faults as well as the virtues are left naked to the view? In any case we need not attribute too much importance to the method. Any method is right, every method is right, that expresses what we wish to express. This one has the merit of giving closer shape to what we were prepared to call life itself; did not the reading of *Ulysses* suggest how much of life is excluded and ignored, and did it not come with a shock to open *Tristram Shandy* or even

Pendennis, and be by them convinced that there are not only other aspects of life, and larger ones into the bargain?

However this may be, the problem before the novelist at present, as we suppose it to have been in the past, is to contrive a means of being free to set down what he chooses. He has to have the courage to say that what interests him is no longer this, but that; out of "that" alone must he construct his work. The tendency of the moderns and part of their perplexity is no doubt that they find their interest more and more in the dark region of psychology. At once therefore the accent falls a little differently; it becomes apparent that the emphasis is upon something hitherto ignored or unstressed in that relation, a feeling, a point of view suggesting a different and obscure outline of form, incomprehensible to our predecessors. No one but a modern, perhaps no one but a Russian, would have felt the interest of the situation which Tchekov has made into the short story which he calls "Gusev." Some Russian soldiers are lying ill in the hospital of a ship which is taking them back to Russia. We are given scraps of their talk; a few of their thoughts; then one of the soldiers dies, and is taken away; the talk goes on among the others for a time; until Gusev himself dies and, looking "like a carrot or a radish," is thrown overboard. The emphasis is laid upon such unexpected places that at first it seems as if there were no emphasis at all; and then, as the eyes accustom themselves to twilight and discern the shapes of things in a room, we see how complete the story is, how profound, and how truly in obedience to his vision Tchekov has chosen this, that, and the other, and placed them together to compose something new. But it is impossible to say that this is humorous or that tragic, or even that it is proper to call the whole a short story, since the writer seems careless of brevity and intensity, and leaves us with the suggestion that the strange chords he has struck sound on and on. There is, perhaps, no need that a short story should be brief and intense, as there is perhaps no answer to the questions which it raises.

The most inconclusive remarks upon modern English fiction can hardly avoid some mention of the Russian influence, and if the Russians are mentioned one runs the risk of feeling that to write of any fiction save theirs is waste of time. If we want understanding of the soul and heart where else shall we find it of comparable profundity? If we are sick of our own materialism the least considerable of their novelists has by right of birth a natural reverence for the human spirit. "Learn to make yourself akin to people.... But let this sympathy be not with the mind—for it is easy with the mind—but with the heart, with love towards them." In every great Russian writer we seem to discern the features of a saint, if sympathy for the sufferings of others, love towards them, endeavour to reach some goal worthy of the most exacting demands of the spirit constitute saintliness. It is the saint in them which confounds us with a feeling of our own irreligious triviality, and turns so many of our famous novels to tinsel and trickery. The conclusions of the

Russian mind, thus comprehensive and compassionate, are inevitably perhaps of the utmost sadness. It might indeed be more true to speak of the inconclusiveness of the Russian mind. It is the sense that there is no answer, that if honestly examined life presents question after question which must be left to sound on and on after the story is over in hopeless interrogation that fills us with a deep, and finally it may be with a resentful, despair. They are right perhaps; unquestionably they see further than we do and without our gross impediments of vision. But perhaps we see something that escapes them, or why should this voice of protest mix itself with our gloom? The voice of protest is the voice of another and an ancient civilization which seems to have bred in us the instinct to enjoy and fight rather than to suffer and understand. English fiction from Sterne to Meredith bears witness to our natural delight in humour and comedy, in the beauty of earth, in the activities of the intellect, and in the splendour of the body. But any deductions that we may draw from the comparison of one fiction with another are futile, save as they flood us with a view of the infinite possibilities, assure us that there is no bound to the horizon, and nothing forbidden but falsity and pretence. "The proper stuff of fiction" does not exist; everything is the proper stuff of fiction; whatever one honestly thinks, whatever one honestly feels. No perception comes amiss; every good quality whether of the mind or spirit is drawn upon and used and turned by the magic of art to something little or large, but endlessly different, everlastingly new. All that fiction asks of us is that we should break her and bully her, honour and love her, till she yields to our bidding, for so her youth is perpetually renewed and her sovereignty assured.

1919

AN UNWRITTEN NOVEL

S UCH AN EXPRESSION of unhappiness was enough by itself to make one's eyes
slide above the paper's edge to the poor woman's face—insignificant without
that look, almost a symbol of human destiny with it. Life's what you see in
people's eyes; life's what they learn, and, having learnt it, never, though they seek
to hide it, cease to be aware of—what? That life's like that, it seems. Five faces
opposite—five mature faces—and the knowledge in each face. Strange, though,
how people want to conceal it! Marks of reticence are on all those faces: lips shut,
eyes shaded, each one of the five doing something to hide or stultify his knowledge.
One smokes; another reads; a third checks entries in a pocket book; a fourth stares
at the map of the line framed opposite; and the fifth—the terrible thing about the
fifth is that she does nothing at all. She looks at life. Ah, but my poor, unfortunate
woman, do play the game—do, for all our sakes, conceal it!

As if she heard me, she looked up, shifted slightly in her seat and sighed. She
seemed to apologise and at the same time to say to me, "If only you knew!" Then
she looked at life again. "But I do know," I answered silently, glancing at the *Times*
for manners' sake. "I know the whole business. 'Peace between Germany and the
Allied Powers was yesterday officially ushered in at Paris—Signor Nitti, the Italian
Prime Minister—a passenger train at Doncaster was in collision with a goods
train...' We all know—the *Times* knows—but we pretend we don't." My eyes had
once more crept over the paper's rim. She shuddered, twitched her arm queerly to
the middle of her back and shook her head. Again I dipped into my great reser-
voir of life. "Take what you like," I continued, "births, deaths, marriages, Court
Circular, the habits of birds, Leonardo da Vinci, the Sandhills murder, high wages
and the cost of living—oh, take what you like," I repeated, "it's all in the *Times*!"
Again with infinite weariness she moved her head from side to side until, like a top
exhausted with spinning, it settled on her neck.

The *Times* was no protection against such sorrow as hers. But other human
beings forbade intercourse. The best thing to do against life was to fold the paper
so that it made a perfect square, crisp, thick, impervious even to life. This done, I
glanced up quickly, armed with a shield of my own. She pierced through my shield;
she gazed into my eyes as if searching any sediment of courage at the depths of them
and damping it to clay. Her twitch alone denied all hope, discounted all illusion.

So we rattled through Surrey and across the border into Sussex. But with my eyes upon life I did not see that the other travellers had left, one by one, till, save for the man who read, we were alone together. Here was Three Bridges station. We drew slowly down the platform and stopped. Was he going to leave us? I prayed both ways—I prayed last that he might stay. At that instant he roused himself, crumpled his paper contemptuously, like a thing done with, burst open the door, and left us alone.

The unhappy woman, leaning a little forward, palely and colourlessly addressed me—talked of stations and holidays, of brothers at Eastbourne, and the time of year, which was, I forget now, early or late. But at last looking from the window and seeing, I knew, only life, she breathed, "Staying away—that's the drawback of it—" Ah, now we approached the catastrophe, "My sister-in-law"—the bitterness of her tone was like lemon on cold steel, and speaking, not to me, but to herself, she muttered, "nonsense, she would say—that's what they all say," and while she spoke she fidgeted as though the skin on her back were as a plucked fowl's in a poulterer's shop-window.

"Oh, that cow!" she broke off nervously, as though the great wooden cow in the meadow had shocked her and saved her from some indiscretion. Then she shuddered, and then she made the awkward angular movement that I had seen before, as if, after the spasm, some spot between the shoulders burnt or itched. Then again she looked the most unhappy woman in the world, and I once more reproached her, though not with the same conviction, for if there were a reason, and if I knew the reason, the stigma was removed from life.

"Sisters-in-law," I said—

Her lips pursed as if to spit venom at the word; pursed they remained. All she did was to take her glove and rub hard at a spot on the window-pane. She rubbed as if she would rub something out for ever—some stain, some indelible contamination. Indeed, the spot remained for all her rubbing, and back she sank with the shudder and the clutch of the arm I had come to expect. Something impelled me to take my glove and rub my window. There, too, was a little speck on the glass. For all my rubbing it remained. And then the spasm went through me; I crooked my arm and plucked at the middle of my back. My skin, too, felt like the damp chicken's skin in the poulterer's shop-window; one spot between the shoulders itched and irritated, felt clammy, felt raw. Could I reach it? Surreptitiously I tried. She saw me. A smile of infinite irony, infinite sorrow, flitted and faded from her face. But she had communicated, shared her secret, passed her poison; she would speak no more. Leaning back in my corner, shielding my eyes from her eyes, seeing only the slopes and hollows, greys and purples, of the winter's landscape, I read her message, deciphered her secret, reading it beneath her gaze.

Hilda's the sister-in-law. Hilda? Hilda? Hilda Marsh—Hilda the blooming, the full bosomed, the matronly. Hilda stands at the door as the cab draws up, holding a coin. "Poor Minnie, more of a grasshopper than ever—old cloak she had last year. Well, well, with two children these days one can't do more. No, Minnie, I've got it; here you are, cabby—none of your ways with me. Come in, Minnie. Oh, I could carry *you*, let alone your basket!" So they go into the dining-room. "Aunt Minnie, children."

Slowly the knives and forks sink from the upright. Down they get (Bob and Barbara), hold out hands stiffly; back again to their chairs, staring between the resumed mouthfuls. [But this we'll skip; ornaments, curtains, trefoil china plate, yellow oblongs of cheese, white squares of biscuit—skip—oh, but wait! Halfway through luncheon one of those shivers; Bob stares at her, spoon in mouth. "Get on with your pudding, Bob;" but Hilda disapproves. "Why *should* she twitch?" Skip, skip, till we reach the landing on the upper floor; stairs brass-bound; linoleum worn; oh, yes! little bedroom looking out over the roofs of Eastbourne—zigzagging roofs like the spines of caterpillars, this way, that way, striped red and yellow, with blue-black slating]. Now, Minnie, the door's shut; Hilda heavily descends to the basement; you unstrap the straps of your basket, lay on the bed a meagre night-gown, stand side by side furred felt slippers. The looking-glass—no, you avoid the looking-glass. Some methodical disposition of hat-pins. Perhaps the shell box has something in it? You shake it; it's the pearl stud there was last year—that's all. And then the sniff, the sigh, the sitting by the window. Three o'clock on a December afternoon; the rain drizzling; one light low in the skylight of a drapery emporium; another high in a servant's bedroom—this one goes out. That gives her nothing to look at. A moment's blankness—then, what are you thinking? (Let me peep across at her opposite; she's asleep or pretending it; so what would she think about sitting at the window at three o'clock in the afternoon? Health, money, hills, her God?) Yes, sitting on the very edge of the chair looking over the roofs of Eastbourne, Minnie Marsh prays to God. That's all very well; and she may rub the pane too, as though to see God better; but what God does she see? Who's the God of Minnie Marsh, the God of the back streets of Eastbourne, the God of three o'clock in the afternoon? I, too, see roofs, I see sky; but, oh, dear—this seeing of Gods! More like President Kruger than Prince Albert—that's the best I can do for him; and I see him on a chair, in a black frock-coat, not so very high up either; I can manage a cloud or two for him to sit on; and then his hand trailing in the cloud holds a rod, a truncheon is it?—black, thick, thorned—a brutal old bully—Minnie's God! Did he send the itch and the patch and the twitch? Is that why she prays? What she rubs on the window is the stain of sin. Oh, she committed some crime!

I have my choice of crimes. The woods flit and fly—in summer there are blue-bells; in the opening there, when Spring comes, primroses. A parting, was it, twenty years ago? Vows broken? Not Minnie's!... She was faithful. How she nursed her mother! All her savings on the tombstone—wreaths under glass—daffodils in jars.

But I'm off the track. A crime…. They would say she kept her sorrow, suppressed her secret—her sex, they'd say—the scientific people. But what flummery to saddle *her* with sex! No—more like this. Passing down the streets of Croydon twenty years ago, the violet loops of ribbon in the draper's window spangled in the electric light catch her eye. She lingers—past six. Still by running she can reach home. She pushes through the glass swing door. It's sale-time. Shallow trays brim with ribbons. She pauses, pulls this, fingers that with the raised roses on it—no need to choose, no need to buy, and each tray with its surprises. "We don't shut till seven," and then it *is* seven. She runs, she rushes, home she reaches, but too late. Neighbours—the doctor—baby brother—the kettle—scalded—hospital—dead—or only the shock of it, the blame? Ah, but the detail matters nothing! It's what she carries with her; the spot, the crime, the thing to expiate, always there between her shoulders. "Yes," she seems to nod to me, "it's the thing I did."

Whether you did, or what you did, I don't mind; it's not the thing I want. The draper's window looped with violet—that'll do; a little cheap perhaps, a little commonplace—since one has a choice of crimes, but then so many (let me peep across again—still sleeping, or pretending sleep! white, worn, the mouth closed—a touch of obstinacy, more than one would think—no hint of sex)—so many crimes aren't *your* crime; your crime was cheap; only the retribution solemn; for now the church door opens, the hard wooden pew receives her; on the brown tiles she kneels; every day, winter, summer, dusk, dawn (here she's at it) prays. All her sins fall, fall, for ever fall. The spot receives them. It's raised, it's red, it's burning. Next she twitches. Small boys point. "Bob at lunch to-day"—But elderly women are the worst.

Indeed now you can't sit praying any longer. Kruger's sunk beneath the clouds—washed over as with a painter's brush of liquid grey, to which he adds a tinge of black—even the tip of the truncheon gone now. That's what always happens! Just as you've seen him, felt him, someone interrupts. It's Hilda now.

How you hate her! She'll even lock the bathroom door overnight, too, though it's only cold water you want, and sometimes when the night's been bad it seems as if washing helped. And John at breakfast—the children—meals are worst, and sometimes there are friends—ferns don't altogether hide 'em—they guess, too; so out you go along the front, where the waves are grey, and the papers blow, and the glass shelters green and draughty, and the chairs cost tuppence—too much—for there must be preachers along the sands. Ah, that's a nigger—that's a funny man—that's a man with parakeets—poor little creatures! Is there no one here who thinks of God?—just up there, over the pier, with his rod—but no—there's nothing but grey in the sky or if it's blue the white clouds hide him, and the music—it's military music—and what they are fishing for? Do they catch them? How the children stare! Well, then home a back way—"Home a back way!" The

words have meaning; might have been spoken by the old man with whiskers—
no, no, he didn't really speak; but everything has meaning—placards leaning
against doorways—names above shop-windows—red fruit in baskets—women's
heads in the hairdresser's—all say "Minnie Marsh!" But here's a jerk. "Eggs are
cheaper!" That's what always happens! I was heading her over the waterfall, straight
for madness, when, like a flock of dream sheep, she turns t'other way and runs
between my fingers. Eggs are cheaper. Tethered to the shores of the world, none
of the crimes, sorrows, rhapsodies, or insanities for poor Minnie Marsh; never
late for luncheon; never caught in a storm without a mackintosh; never utterly
unconscious of the cheapness of eggs. So she reaches home—scrapes her boots.

Have I read you right? But the human face—the human face at the top of the
fullest sheet of print holds more, withholds more. Now, eyes open, she looks out;
and in the human eye—how d'you define it?—there's a break—a division—so
that when you've grasped the stem the butterfly's off—the moth that hangs in
the evening over the yellow flower—move, raise your hand, off, high, away. I
won't raise my hand. Hang still, then, quiver, life, soul, spirit, whatever you are of
Minnie Marsh—I, too, on my flower—the hawk over the down—alone, or what
were the worth of life? To rise; hang still in the evening, in the midday; hang still
over the down. The flicker of a hand—off, up! then poised again. Alone, unseen;
seeing all so still down there, all so lovely. None seeing, none caring. The eyes of
others our prisons; their thoughts our cages. Air above, air below. And the moon
and immortality.... Oh, but I drop to the turf! Are you down too, you in the
corner, what's your name—woman—Minnie Marsh; some such name as that?
There she is, tight to her blossom; opening her hand-bag, from which she takes a
hollow shell—an egg—who was saying that eggs were cheaper? You or I? Oh, it
was you who said it on the way home, you remember, when the old gentleman,
suddenly opening his umbrella—or sneezing was it? Anyhow, Kruger went, and
you came "home a back way," and scraped your boots. Yes. And now you lay
across your knees a pocket-handkerchief into which drop little angular fragments
of eggshell—fragments of a map—a puzzle. I wish I could piece them together!
If you would only sit still. She's moved her knees—the map's in bits again. Down
the slopes of the Andes the white blocks of marble go bounding and hurtling,
crushing to death a whole troop of Spanish muleteers, with their convoy—Drake's
booty, gold and silver. But to return—

To what, to where? She opened the door, and, putting her umbrella in the
stand—that goes without saying; so, too, the whiff of beef from the basement; dot,
dot, dot. But what I cannot thus eliminate, what I must, head down, eyes shut,
with the courage of a battalion and the blindness of a bull, charge and disperse
are, indubitably, the figures behind the ferns, commercial travellers. There I've
hidden them all this time in the hope that somehow they'd disappear, or better

still emerge, as indeed they must, if the story's to go on gathering richness and rotundity, destiny and tragedy, as stories should, rolling along with it two, if not three, commercial travellers and a whole grove of aspidistra. "The fronds of the aspidistra only partly concealed the commercial traveller—" Rhododendrons would conceal him utterly, and into the bargain give me my fling of red and white, for which I starve and strive; but rhododendrons in Eastbourne—in December— on the Marshes' table—no, no, I dare not; it's all a matter of crusts and cruets, frills and ferns. Perhaps there'll be a moment later by the sea. Moreover, I feel, pleasantly pricking through the green fretwork and over the glacis of cut glass, a desire to peer and peep at the man opposite—one's as much as I can manage. James Moggridge is it, whom the Marshes call Jimmy? [Minnie, you must promise not to twitch till I've got this straight]. James Moggridge travels in—shall we say buttons?—but the time's not come for bringing *them* in—the big and the little on the long cards, some peacock-eyed, others dull gold; cairngorms some, and others coral sprays—but I say the time's not come. He travels, and on Thursdays, his Eastbourne day, takes his meals with the Marshes. His red face, his little steady eyes—by no means altogether commonplace—his enormous appetite (that's safe; he won't look at Minnie till the bread's swamped the gravy dry), napkin tucked diamond-wise—but this is primitive, and, whatever it may do the reader, don't take me in. Let's dodge to the Moggridge household, set that in motion. Well, the family boots are mended on Sundays by James himself. He reads *Truth*. But his passion? Roses—and his wife a retired hospital nurse—interesting—for God's sake let me have one woman with a name I like! But no; she's of the unborn children of the mind, illicit, none the less loved, like my rhododendrons. How many die in every novel that's written—the best, the dearest, while Moggridge lives. It's life's fault. Here's Minnie eating her egg at the moment opposite and at t'other end of the line—are we past Lewes?—there must be Jimmy—or what's her twitch for?

There must be Moggridge—life's fault. Life imposes her laws; life blocks the way; life's behind the fern; life's the tyrant; oh, but not the bully! No, for I assure you I come willingly; I come wooed by Heaven knows what compulsion across ferns and cruets, table splashed and bottles smeared. I come irresistibly to lodge myself somewhere on the firm flesh, in the robust spine, wherever I can penetrate or find foothold on the person, in the soul, of Moggridge the man. The enormous stability of the fabric; the spine tough as whalebone, straight as oak-tree; the ribs radiating branches; the flesh taut tarpaulin; the red hollows; the suck and regurgitation of the heart; while from above meat falls in brown cubes and beer gushes to be churned to blood again—and so we reach the eyes. Behind the aspidistra they see something: black, white, dismal; now the plate again; behind the aspidistra they see elderly woman; "Marsh's sister, Hilda's more my sort;" the tablecloth now. "Marsh would know what's wrong with Morrises..." talk that over; cheese has come; the plate again; turn it round—the enormous fingers; now the woman opposite. "Marsh's sister—not a bit like Marsh; wretched, elderly female.... You should feed your hens.... God's truth, what's set her twitching? Not what *I* said? Dear, dear, dear! these elderly women. Dear, dear!"

[Yes, Minnie; I know you've twitched, but one moment—James Moggridge.]

"Dear, dear, dear!" How beautiful the sound is! like the knock of a mallet on seasoned timber, like the throb of the heart of an ancient whaler when the seas press thick and the green is clouded. "Dear, dear!" what a passing bell for the souls of the fretful to soothe them and solace them, lap them in linen, saying, "So long. Good luck to you!" and then, "What's your pleasure?" for though Moggridge would pluck his rose for her, that's done, that's over. Now what's the next thing? "Madam, you'll miss your train," for they don't linger.

That's the man's way; that's the sound that reverberates; that's St. Paul's and the motor-omnibuses. But we're brushing the crumbs off. Oh, Moggridge, you won't stay? You must be off? Are you driving through Eastbourne this afternoon in one of those little carriages? Are you the man who's walled up in green card-board boxes, and sometimes has the blinds down, and sometimes sits so solemn staring like a sphinx, and always there's a look of the sepulchral, something of the undertaker, the coffin, and the dusk about horse and driver? Do tell me—but the doors slammed. We shall never meet again. Moggridge, farewell!

Yes, yes, I'm coming. Right up to the top of the house. One moment I'll linger. How the mud goes round in the mind—what a swirl these monsters leave, the waters rocking, the weeds waving and green here, black there, striking to the sand, till by degrees the atoms reassemble, the deposit sifts itself, and again through the eyes one sees clear and still, and there comes to the lips some prayer for the departed, some obsequy for the souls of those one nods to, the people one never meets again.

James Moggridge is dead now, gone for ever. Well, Minnie— "I can face it no longer." If she said that—(Let me look at her. She is brushing the eggshell into deep declivities). She said it certainly, leaning against the wall of the bedroom, and plucking at the little balls which edge the claret-coloured curtain. But when the self speaks to the self, who is speaking?—the entombed soul, the spirit driven in, in, in to the central catacomb; the self that took the veil and left the world—a coward perhaps, yet somehow beautiful, as it flits with its lantern restlessly up and down the dark corridors. "I can bear it no longer," her spirit says. "That man at lunch—Hilda—the children." Oh, heavens, her sob! It's the spirit wailing its destiny, the spirit driven hither, thither, lodging on the diminishing carpets—meagre footholds—shrunken shreds of all the vanishing universe—love, life, faith, husband, children, I know not what splendours and pageantries glimpsed in girlhood. "Not for me—not for me."

But then—the muffins, the bald elderly dog? Bead mats I should fancy and the consolation of underlinen. If Minnie Marsh were run over and taken to hospital, nurses and doctors themselves would exclaim.... There's the vista and the vision— there's the distance—the blue blot at the end of the avenue, while, after all, the tea is rich, the muffin hot, and the dog—"Benny, to your basket, sir, and see what mother's brought you!" So, taking the glove with the worn thumb, defying once more the encroaching demon of what's called going in holes, you renew the fortifications, threading the grey wool, running it in and out.

Running it in and out, across and over, spinning a web through which God himself—hush, don't think of God! How firm the stitches are! You must be proud of your darning. Let nothing disturb her. Let the light fall gently, and the clouds show an inner vest of the first green leaf. Let the sparrow perch on the twig and shake the raindrop hanging to the twig's elbow.... Why look up? Was it a sound, a thought? Oh, heavens! Back again to the thing you did, the plate glass with the violet loops? But Hilda will come. Ignominies, humiliations, oh! Close the breach.

Having mended her glove, Minnie Marsh lays it in the drawer. She shuts the drawer with decision. I catch sight of her face in the glass. Lips are pursed. Chin held high. Next she laces her shoes. Then she touches her throat. What's your brooch? Mistletoe or merry-thought? And what is happening? Unless I'm much mistaken, the pulse's quickened, the moment's coming, the threads are racing, Niagara's ahead. Here's the crisis! Heaven be with you! Down she goes. Courage, courage! Face it, be it! For God's sake don't wait on the mat now! There's the door! I'm on your side. Speak! Confront her, confound her soul!

"Oh, I beg your pardon! Yes, this is Eastbourne. I'll reach it down for you. Let me try the handle." [But, Minnie, though we keep up pretences, I've read you right—I'm with you now].

"That's all your luggage?"

"Much obliged, I'm sure."

(But why do you look about you? Hilda won't come to the station, nor John; and Moggridge is driving at the far side of Eastbourne).

"I'll wait by my bag, ma'am, that's safest. He said he'd meet me.... Oh, there he is! That's my son."

So they walk off together.

Well, but I'm confounded.... Surely, Minnie, you know better! A strange young man.... Stop! I'll tell him—Minnie!—Miss Marsh!—I don't know though. There's something queer in her cloak as it blows. Oh, but it's untrue, it's indecent.... Look how he bends as they reach the gateway. She finds her ticket. What's the joke? Off they go, down the road, side by side.... Well, my world's done for! What do I stand on? What do I know? That's not Minnie. There never was Moggridge. Who am I? Life's bare as bone.

And yet the last look of them—he stepping from the kerb and she following him round the edge of the big building brims me with wonder—floods me anew. Mysterious figures! Mother and son. Who are you? Why do you walk down the street? Where to-night will you sleep, and then, to-morrow? Oh, how it whirls and surges—floats me afresh! I start after them. People drive this way and that. The white light splutters and pours. Plate-glass windows. Carnations; chrysanthemums. Ivy in dark gardens. Milk carts at the door. Wherever I go, mysterious figures, I see you, turning the corner, mothers and sons; you, you, you. I hasten, I follow. This, I fancy, must be the sea. Grey is the landscape; dim as ashes; the water murmurs and moves. If I fall on my knees, if I go through the ritual, the ancient antics, it's you, unknown figures, you I adore; if I open my arms, it's you I embrace, you I draw to me—adorable world!

1921

THE MARK ON THE WALL

PERHAPS IT WAS THE MIDDLE OF JANUARY in the present year that I first looked up and saw the mark on the wall. In order to fix a date it is necessary to remember what one saw. So now I think of the fire; the steady film of yellow light upon the page of my book; the three chrysanthemums in the round glass bowl on the mantelpiece. Yes, it must have been the winter time, and we had just finished our tea, for I remember that I was smoking a cigarette when I looked up and saw the mark on the wall for the first time. I looked up through the smoke of my cigarette and my eye lodged for a moment upon the burning coals, and that old fancy of the crimson flag flapping from the castle tower came into my mind, and I thought of the cavalcade of red knights riding up the side of the black rock. Rather to my relief the sight of the mark interrupted the fancy, for it is an old fancy, an automatic fancy, made as a child perhaps. The mark was a small round mark, black upon the white wall, about six or seven inches above the mantelpiece.

How readily our thoughts swarm upon a new object, lifting it a little way, as ants carry a blade of straw so feverishly, and then leave it…. If that mark was made by a nail, it can't have been for a picture, it must have been for a miniature—the miniature of a lady with white powdered curls, powder-dusted cheeks, and lips like red carnations. A fraud of course, for the people who had this house before us would have chosen pictures in that way—an old picture for an old room. That is the sort of people they were—very interesting people, and I think of them so often, in such queer places, because one will never see them again, never know what happened next. They wanted to leave this house because they wanted to change their style of furniture, so he said, and he was in process of saying that in his opinion art should have ideas behind it when we were torn asunder, as one is torn from the old lady about to pour out tea and the young man about to hit the tennis ball in the back garden of the suburban villa as one rushes past in the train.

But as for that mark, I'm not sure about it; I don't believe it was made by a nail after all; it's too big, too round, for that. I might get up, but if I got up and looked at it, ten to one I shouldn't be able to say for certain; because once a thing's done, no one ever knows how it happened. Oh! dear me, the mystery of life; The inaccuracy of thought! The ignorance of humanity! To show how very little control of our possessions we have—what an accidental affair this living is after all our civilization—let me just count over a few of the things lost in one lifetime, beginning, for that seems always the most mysterious of losses—what cat would gnaw, what rat would nibble—three pale blue canisters of book-binding tools? Then there were the bird cages, the iron hoops, the steel skates, the Queen Anne coal-scuttle, the bagatelle board, the hand organ—all gone, and jewels, too. Opals and emeralds, they lie about the roots of turnips. What a scraping paring affair it is to be sure! The wonder is that I've any clothes on my back, that I sit surrounded by solid furniture at this moment. Why, if one wants to compare life to anything, one must liken it to being blown through the Tube at fifty miles an hour—landing at the other end without a single hairpin in one's hair! Shot out at the feet of God entirely naked! Tumbling head over heels in the asphodel meadows like brown paper parcels pitched down a shoot in the post office! With one's hair flying back like the tail of a race-horse. Yes, that seems to express the rapidity of life, the perpetual waste and repair; all so casual, all so haphazard....

But after life. The slow pulling down of thick green stalks so that the cup of the flower, as it turns over, deluges one with purple and red light. Why, after all, should one not be born there as one is born here, helpless, speechless, unable to focus one's eyesight, groping at the roots of the grass, at the toes of the Giants? As for saying which are trees, and which are men and women, or whether there are such things, that one won't be in a condition to do for fifty years or so. There will be nothing but spaces of light and dark, intersected by thick stalks, and rather higher up perhaps, rose-shaped blots of an indistinct colour—dim pinks and blues—which will, as time goes on, become more definite, become—I don't know what....

And yet that mark on the wall is not a hole at all. It may even be caused by some round black substance, such as a small rose leaf, left over from the summer, and I, not being a very vigilant housekeeper—look at the dust on the mantelpiece, for example, the dust which, so they say, buried Troy three times over, only fragments of pots utterly refusing annihilation, as one can believe.

The tree outside the window taps very gently on the pane.... I want to think quietly, calmly, spaciously, never to be interrupted, never to have to rise from my chair, to slip easily from one thing to another, without any sense of hostility, or obstacle. I want to sink deeper and deeper, away from the surface, with its hard separate facts. To steady myself, let me catch hold of the first idea that passes.... Shakespeare.... Well, he will do as well as another. A man who sat himself solidly in an arm-chair, and looked into the fire, so— A shower of ideas fell perpetually from some very high Heaven down through his mind. He leant his forehead on his hand, and people, looking in through the open door,—for this scene is supposed to take place on a summer's evening—But how dull this is, this historical fiction! It doesn't interest me at all. I wish I could hit upon a pleasant track of thought, a track indirectly reflecting credit upon myself, for those are the pleasantest thoughts, and very frequent even in the minds of modest mouse-coloured people, who believe genuinely that they dislike to hear their own praises. They are not thoughts directly praising oneself; that is the beauty of them; they are thoughts like this:

"And then I came into the room. They were discussing botany. I said how I'd seen a flower growing on a dust heap on the site of an old house in Kingsway. The seed, I said, must have been sown in the reign of Charles the First. What flowers grew in the reign of Charles the First?" I asked—(but I don't remember the answer). Tall flowers with purple tassels to them perhaps. And so it goes on. All the time I'm dressing up the figure of myself in my own mind, lovingly, stealthily, not openly adoring it, for if I did that, I should catch myself out, and stretch my hand at once for a book in self-protection. Indeed, it is curious how instinctively one protects the image of oneself from idolatry or any other handling that could make it ridiculous, or too unlike the original to be believed in any longer. Or is it not so very curious after all? It is a matter of great importance. Suppose the looking glass smashes, the image disappears, and the romantic figure with the green of forest depths all about it is there no longer, but only that shell of a person which is seen by other people—what an airless, shallow, bald, prominent world it becomes! A world not to be lived in. As we face each other in omnibuses and underground railways we are looking into the mirror; that accounts for the vagueness, the gleam of glassiness, in our eyes. And the novelists in future will realize more and more the importance of these reflections, for of course there is not one reflection but an almost infinite number; those are the depths they will explore, those the phantoms they will pursue, leaving the description of reality more and more out of their stories, taking a knowledge of it for granted, as the Greeks did and Shakespeare perhaps—but these generalizations are very worthless. The military sound of the word is enough. It recalls leading articles, cabinet ministers—a whole class of things indeed which as a child one thought the thing itself, the standard thing, the real thing, from which one could not depart save at the risk of nameless damnation. Generalizations bring back somehow Sunday in London, Sunday afternoon walks, Sunday luncheons, and also ways of speaking of the dead, clothes, and habits—like the habit of sitting all together in one room until a certain hour, although nobody liked it. There was a rule for everything. The rule for tablecloths at that particular period was that they should be made of tapestry with little yellow compartments marked upon them, such as you may see in photographs of the carpets in the corridors of the royal palaces. Tablecloths of a different kind were not real tablecloths. How shocking, and yet how wonderful it was to discover that these real things, Sunday luncheons, Sunday walks, country houses, and tablecloths were not entirely real, were indeed half phantoms, and the damnation which visited the disbeliever in them was only a sense of illegitimate freedom. What now takes the place of those things I wonder, those real standard things? Men perhaps, should you be a woman; the masculine point of view which governs our lives, which sets the standard, which establishes

Whitaker's Table of Precedency, which has become, I suppose, since the war half a phantom to many men and women, which soon, one may hope, will be laughed into the dustbin where the phantoms go, the mahogany sideboards and the Landseer prints, Gods and Devils, Hell and so forth, leaving us all with an intoxicating sense of illegitimate freedom—if freedom exists....

In certain lights that mark on the wall seems actually to project from the wall. Nor is it entirely circular. I cannot be sure, but it seems to cast a perceptible shadow, suggesting that if I ran my finger down that strip of the wall it would, at a certain point, mount and descend a small tumulus, a smooth tumulus like those barrows on the South Downs which are, they say, either tombs or camps. Of the two I should prefer them to be tombs, desiring melancholy like most English people, and finding it natural at the end of a walk to think of the bones stretched beneath the turf....There must be some book about it. Some antiquary must have dug up those bones and given them a name....What sort of a man is an antiquary, I wonder? Retired Colonels for the most part, I daresay, leading parties of aged labourers to the top here, examining clods of earth and stone, and getting into correspondence with the neighbouring clergy, which, being opened at breakfast time, gives them a feeling of importance, and the comparison of arrow-heads necessitates cross-country journeys to the county towns, an agreeable necessity both to them and to their elderly wives, who wish to make plum jam or to clean out the study, and have every reason for keeping that great question of the camp or the tomb in perpetual suspension, while the Colonel himself feels agreeably philosophic in accumulating evidence on both sides of the question. It is true that he does finally incline to believe in the camp; and, being opposed, indites a pamphlet which he is about to read at the quarterly meeting of the local society when a stroke lays him low, and his last conscious thoughts are not of wife or child, but of the camp and that arrowhead there, which is now in the case at the local museum, together with the foot of a Chinese murderess, a handful of Elizabethan nails, a great many Tudor clay pipes, a piece of Roman pottery, and the wine-glass that Nelson drank out of—proving I really don't know what.

No, no, nothing is proved, nothing is known. And if I were to get up at this very moment and ascertain that the mark on the wall is really—what shall we say?—the head of a gigantic old nail, driven in two hundred years ago, which has now, owing to the patient attrition of many generations of housemaids, revealed its head above the coat of paint, and is taking its first view of modern life in the sight of a white-walled fire-lit room, what should I gain?—Knowledge? Matter for further speculation? I can think sitting still as well as standing up. And what is knowledge? What are our learned men save the descendants of witches and hermits who crouched in caves and in woods brewing herbs, interrogating shrew-mice and writing down the language of the stars? And the less we honour them as our su-

perstitions dwindle and our respect for beauty and health of mind increases.....
Yes, one could imagine a very pleasant world. A quiet, spacious world, with the
flowers so red and blue in the open fields. A world without professors or specialists
or house-keepers with the profiles of policemen, a world which one could slice
with one's thought as a fish slices the water with his fin, grazing the stems of the
water-lilies, hanging suspended over nests of white sea eggs....How peaceful it
is down here, rooted in the centre of the world and gazing up through the grey
waters, with their sudden gleams of light, and their reflections—if it were not for
Whitaker's Almanack—if it were not for the Table of Precedency!

I must jump up and see for myself what that mark on the wall really is—a
nail, a rose-leaf, a crack in the wood?

Here is nature once more at her old game of self-preservation. This train of
thought, she perceives, is threatening mere waste of energy, even some collision
with reality, for who will ever be able to lift a finger against Whitaker's Table
of Precedency? The Archbishop of Canterbury is followed by the Lord High
Chancellor; the Lord High Chancellor is followed by the Archbishop of York.
Everybody follows somebody, such is the philosophy of Whitaker; and the great
thing is to know who follows whom. Whitaker knows, and let that, so Nature
counsels, comfort you, instead of enraging you; and if you can't be comforted, if
you must shatter this hour of peace, think of the mark on the wall.

I understand Nature's game—her prompting to take action as a way of ending
any thought that threatens to excite or to pain. Hence, I suppose, comes our slight
contempt for men of action—men, we assume, who don't think. Still, there's no
harm in putting a full stop to one's disagreeable thoughts by looking at a mark on
the wall.

Indeed, now that I have fixed my eyes upon it, I feel that I have grasped a
plank in the sea; I feel a satisfying sense of reality which at once turns the two
Archbishops and the Lord High Chancellor to the shadows of shades. Here is
something definite, something real. Thus, waking from a midnight dream of horror,
one hastily turns on the light and lies quiescent, worshipping the chest of drawers,
worshipping solidity, worshipping reality, worshipping the impersonal world which
is a proof of some existence other than ours. That is what one wants to be sure of....
Wood is a pleasant thing to think about. It comes from a tree; and trees grow, and
we don't know how they grow. For years and years they grow, without paying any
attention to us, in meadows, in forests, and by the side of rivers—all things one
likes to think about. The cows swish their tails beneath them on hot afternoons;
they paint rivers so green that when a moorhen dives one expects to see its feathers
all green when it comes up again. I like to think of the fish balanced against the
stream like flags blown out; and of water-beetles slowly raising domes of mud upon
the bed of the river. I like to think of the tree itself: first the close dry sensation of

being wood; then the grinding of the storm; then the slow, delicious ooze of sap. I like to think of it, too, on winter's nights standing in the empty field with all leaves close-furled, nothing tender exposed to the iron bullets of the moon, a naked mast upon an earth that goes tumbling, tumbling, all night long. The song of birds must sound very loud and strange in June; and how cold the feet of insects must feel upon it, as they make laborious progresses up the creases of the bark, or sun themselves upon the thin green awning of the leaves, and look straight in front of them with diamond-cut red eyes.... One by one the fibres snap beneath the immense cold pressure of the earth, then the last storm comes and, falling, the highest branches drive deep into the ground again. Even so, life isn't done with; there are a million patient, watchful lives still for a tree, all over the world, in bedrooms, in ships, on the pavement, lining rooms, where men and women sit after tea, smoking cigarettes. It is full of peaceful thoughts, happy thoughts, this tree. I should like to take each one separately—but something is getting in the way....Where was I? What has it all been about? A tree? A river? The Downs? Whitaker's Almanack? The fields of asphodel? I can't remember a thing. Every-thing's moving, falling, slipping, vanishing.... There is a vast upheaval of matter. Someone is standing over me and saying—

"I'm going out to buy a newspaper."

"Yes?"

"Though it's no good buying newspapers.... Nothing ever happens. Curse this war; God damn this war!... All the same, I don't see why we should have a snail on our wall."

Ah, the mark on the wall! It was a snail.

1921

T.S. Eliot
1888–1965

Thomas Stearns Eliot was born in St. Louis, Missouri, and became a naturalized British citizen when he was nearly forty years old. His parents were distinguished New England transplants, and Eliot's childhood ventures brought him from his Midwestern home state to harbor-side towns in northern Massachusetts. While at Harvard University from 1906 to 1909, he studied under George Santayana, a philosopher and poet who curated Eliot's ambitions. Irving Babbitt, another Harvard figure, helped lay the groundwork for Eliot's opposition to Romanticism and sentimentality. Eliot also spent a year studying abroad in France and Germany. After learning philosophy, Indic philology, and Sanskrit, Eliot had intentions of returning to Harvard to receive his PhD, but the outbreak of World War I prevented him from completing the degree. Instead, he stayed in England and continued to study Greek philosophy at the University of Oxford.

After holding various teaching jobs, Eliot obtained a post in the Colonial and Foreign Department of Lloyds Bank in London. There he learned the destruction the Great War exacted on central Europe. His occupation kept him busy, but he dedicated his evenings to writing. Though his literary ambitions were not usually politically-oriented, the chaos of post-war Europe haunts much of his work. *The Waste Land*, the long poem he struggled to draft while working at the bank, is still recognized as one of the most robust, poignant pieces of Modernist literature about World War I. Eliot, like many of his contemporaries, felt gravely disillusioned and repulsed by the conflict.

Disillusionment and conflict also governed Eliot's personal life. Nearing a nervous breakdown, he took three months' leave from the bank and left for Switzerland at the end of 1921. In addition to work stresses, Eliot contended with a disagreeable home life; he married Vivien Haigh-Wood in 1915 within weeks of meeting her, and though they initially enjoyed a congenial companionship, their marriage became physically and mentally painful for both parties. Vivien faced serious and demanding health problems, and Eliot, who was utterly squeamish, once confessed to his friends Virginia and Leonard Woolf that he could not imagine shaving in Vivien's presence. In a reaction to their obvious incompatibility, Vivien had an affair. Their union, Eliot quickly realized, had been a terrible mistake. Still, he refused to separate from his wife until 1932. After their divorce, Vivien's behavior grew so peculiar and unstable that she was committed to a private mental hospital where she died in 1947. Ten years later, Eliot married his secretary Valerie Fletcher, a woman nearly forty years younger than him, who brought him immense happiness.

The years following Eliot's separation from Vivien marked intense periods of literary activity. Since the publication of "The Love Song of J. Alfred Prufrock" (which first appeared in 1915 but was individually republished two years later with greater success) and *The Waste Land*, Eliot had earned a reputation as one of the greatest poets of the century. His life thereafter largely consisted of lectures and awards. He took up the Charles Eliot Norton professorship at Harvard and delivered numerous lectures at prestigious American colleges. He also lectured before a crowd of fourteen thousand people in Minneapolis, Minnesota. Eliot addressed listeners abroad as well, partaking in a six-week lecture tour in Germany and speaking in England on numerous occasions. Throughout his lecturing career, his speeches spanned a range of topics including Elizabethan literature and the metaphysical poetry of the seventeenth century. Since most of Eliot's lectures were written hastily, however, reading them is an arduous experience. Contemporary critics gave them mixed reviews, and it is generally agreed that Eliot's essays are far more focused than his addresses. By the end of his career as a poet, playwright, and critic, Eliot had been featured on the cover of *Time* magazine, awarded the Order of Merit, and received a Nobel Prize.

Eliot's career was not without its blunders. Though he was immensely popular, his character came under scrutiny. Despite Eliot's attempts to disprove or evade the accusations against him, repeated charges of fascist sympathies, misogyny, and anti-Semitism peppered his reputation then and still receive critical debate. His potential fascism was largely disproved during his own lifetime; many scholars agree that the allegations were a consequence of Eliot's friendships with far right-wing sympathizers. His misogynistic tendencies and anti-Semitism are more challenging to negate, for evidence of both can be identified throughout his works. Some of Eliot's detractors also insist that his success was built on a deliberate calculation of the literary market and by imitating other writers' ideas. James Joyce, for instance, constantly accused Eliot of stealing concepts and techniques from *Ulysses* and using them in *The Waste Land*. While Eliot is well-known for his self-advancing disposition, he is dually recognized as a man of intense secrecy and reservation. Eliot meekly describes himself in his 1961 essay "To Criticise the Critic" as "the mild-mannered man safely entrenched behind his typewriter."

Eliot may have lived a quiet outer life, but what he feared was not living fully, either spiritually or physically, and this fear echoes throughout his works. "The Hollow Men," for example, focuses on beings who are trapped between heaven and hell because they lived empty, meaningless lives. Eliot rejected the Romantic idea that the contemplative life was better than the active one and explored a multiplicity of lives, including those that previously occurred and inner, hidden lives. Eliot also gained inspiration from the Waste Land, his metaphor for the cultural and moral decay of the Western world that resulted from World War I. Though Eliot depicts the Waste Land as a physical place of utter barrenness and desolation, it more so symbolizes a psychological or spiritual space of unfulfillment.

Eliot's poetry struck readers as wildly experimental and challenging to read when it was first published. Many of his works lack smooth transitions or clear speakers, and he incorporates allusions to other pieces of literature which are not always English in origin. The American poet Ezra Pound, who Eliot had met and befriended in 1914, curtailed some of Eliot's poetic shortcomings. Pound's friendship proved invaluable throughout Eliot's career; it was at Pound's insistence that Eliot first published his poetry, and it was Pound, too, who fostered publishing connections for Eliot in Britain as well as the United States. Eliot's esteem as a poet and critic in both nations was colossal from the 1920s onward, and at the time of his death in 1965, many readers conceded that he was the most significant literary figure in the world.

1888	Thomas Stearns (T.S.) Eliot born 26 September in St. Louis, Missouri, U.S.A.
1898	Enters Smith Academy, St. Louis
1905	Enters Milton Academy
1906–10	Attends Harvard University and earns his BA and MA in English Literature
1911–14	Studies for his PhD at Harvard University
1914	Begins thesis work at Merton College, University of Oxford; meets Ezra Pound
1915	Marries Vivien Haigh-Wood
1917	*Prufrock and Other Observations*
1922	*The Waste Land*
1927	Eliot is received into the Church of England; Eliot takes British citizenship
1932	Separates from Vivien
1944	*Four Quartets*
1948	Awarded Nobel Prize and Order of Merit
1957	Marries Valerie Fletcher
1965	Eliot dies 4 January after a long illness, and his ashes are buried in East Coker

THE LOVE SONG OF J. ALFRED PRUFROCK

S'io credesse che mia risposta fosse
A persona che mai tornasse al mondo,
Questa fiamma staria senza piu scosse.
Ma perciocche giammai di questo fondo
Non torno vivo alcun, s'i'odo il vero,
Senza tema d'infamia ti rispondo.[1]

Let us go then, you and I,
When the evening is spread out against the sky
Like a patient etherized upon a table;
Let us go, through certain half-deserted streets,
The muttering retreats   5
Of restless nights in one-night cheap hotels
And sawdust restaurants with oyster-shells:
Streets that follow like a tedious argument
Of insidious intent
To lead you to an overwhelming question....   10
Oh, do not ask, "What is it?"
Let us go and make our visit.

In the room the women come and go
Talking of Michelangelo.[2]

The yellow fog that rubs its back upon the window-panes,   15
The yellow smoke that rubs its muzzle on the window-panes,
Licked its tongue into the corners of the evening,
Lingered upon the pools that stand in drains,
Let fall upon its back the soot that falls from chimneys,
Slipped by the terrace, made a sudden leap,   20
And seeing that it was a soft October night,
Curled once about the house, and fell asleep.

---

1 Did I believe my answer now were made to one again to tread the upper world, then should this
flame flicker and wave no more; but since there never from this utter depth return'd one living thing,
if such the truth, then will I answer thee and fear no shame [Dante, *Inferno* XXVII 61-66].

2 Michelangelo (1475-1564) was an Italian Renaissance sculptor, painter, and poet.

And indeed there will be time
For the yellow smoke that slides along the street,
Rubbing its back upon the window-panes;   25
There will be time, there will be time
To prepare a face to meet the faces that you meet;
There will be time to murder and create,
And time for all the works and days of hands
That lift and drop a question on your plate;   30
Time for you and time for me,
And time yet for a hundred indecisions,
And for a hundred visions and revisions,
Before the taking of a toast and tea.

In the room the women come and go   35
Talking of Michelangelo.

And indeed there will be time
To wonder, "Do I dare?" and, "Do I dare?"
Time to turn back and descend the stair,
With a bald spot in the middle of my hair—   40
(They will say: "How his hair is growing thin!")
My morning coat, my collar mounting firmly to the chin,
My necktie rich and modest, but asserted by a simple pin—
(They will say: "But how his arms and legs are thin!")
Do I dare   45
Disturb the universe?
In a minute there is time
For decisions and revisions which a minute will reverse.

For I have known them all already, known them all:
Have known the evenings, mornings, afternoons,   50
I have measured out my life with coffee spoons;
I know the voices dying with a dying fall
Beneath the music from a farther room.
       So how should I presume?

And I have known the eyes already, known them all—   55
The eyes that fix you in a formulated phrase,

And when I am formulated, sprawling on a pin,
When I am pinned and wriggling on the wall,
Then how should I begin
To spit out all the butt-ends of my days and ways?   60
    And how should I presume?

And I have known the arms already, known them all—
Arms that are braceleted and white and bare
(But in the lamplight, downed with light brown hair!)
Is it perfume from a dress   65
That makes me so digress?
Arms that lie along a table, or wrap about a shawl.
    And should I then presume?
    And how should I begin?

      *   *   *   *

Shall I say, I have gone at dusk through narrow streets   70
And watched the smoke that rises from the pipes
Of lonely men in shirt-sleeves, leaning out of windows?...

I should have been a pair of ragged claws
Scuttling across the floors of silent seas.

      *   *   *   *

And the afternoon, the evening, sleeps so peacefully!   75
Smoothed by long fingers,
Asleep...tired...or it malingers,
Stretched on the floor, here beside you and me.
Should I, after tea and cakes and ices,
Have the strength to force the moment to its crisis?   80
But though I have wept and fasted, wept and prayed,
Though I have seen my head (grown slightly bald) brought in
    upon a platter,[1]
I am no prophet—and here's no great matter;
I have seen the moment of my greatness flicker,
And I have seen the eternal Footman hold my coat,
    and snicker,   85
And in short, I was afraid.

---

1 An allusion to the Jewish prophet John the Baptist, whose head was brought before the queen of Galilee on a silver platter.

And would it have been worth it, after all,
After the cups, the marmalade, the tea,
Among the porcelain, among some talk of you and me,
Would it have been worth while,   90
To have bitten off the matter with a smile,
To have squeezed the universe into a ball
To roll it toward some overwhelming question,
To say: "I am Lazarus, come from the dead,[1]
 Come back to tell you all, I shall tell you all"—   95
 If one, settling a pillow by her head,
    Should say: "That is not what I meant at all;
    That is not it, at all."

And would it have been worth it, after all,
Would it have been worth while,   100
After the sunsets and the dooryards and the sprinkled streets,
After the novels, after the teacups, after the skirts that trail along
        the floor—
And this, and so much more?—
It is impossible to say just what I mean!
But as if a magic lantern threw the nerves in patterns on
        a screen: 105
Would it have been worth while
If one, settling a pillow or throwing off a shawl,
And turning toward the window, should say:
    "That is not it at all,
    That is not what I meant, at all."   110

                        *   *   *   *

No! I am not Prince Hamlet, nor was meant to be;[2]
Am an attendant lord, one that will do
To swell a progress, start a scene or two,
Advise the prince; no doubt, an easy tool,
Deferential, glad to be of use,   115
Politic, cautious, and meticulous;

---

1 Four days after Lazarus' entombment, Jesus raised him from the dead.

2 Eliot alludes to Hamlet's famous "To be, or not to be" soliloquy in Shakespeare's *Hamlet*. Miserable and unsure, Hamlet contemplates if life is worth living.

Full of high sentence, but a bit obtuse;
At times, indeed, almost ridiculous—
Almost, at times, the Fool.[3] →> Yorrick (Hamlet's dead fool)

I grow old... I grow old...   120
I shall wear the bottoms of my trousers rolled.

Shall I part my hair behind? Do I dare to eat a peach?
I shall wear white flannel trousers, and walk upon the beach.
I have heard the mermaids singing, each to each.

I do not think that they will sing to me.   125

I have seen them riding seaward on the waves
Combing the white hair of the waves blown back   } Ophelia-esque
When the wind blows the water white and black.
We have lingered in the chambers of the sea
By sea-girls wreathed with seaweed red and brown   130
Till human voices wake us, and we drown.

1915

---

3 Shakespearean fools are generally divided into natural fools, who lack common sense, and wise
fools, who entertain and outwit others.

Suggested Reading

Brown, Judith, editor. *The Oxford History of the British Empire: Volume IV: The Twentieth Century*, Oxford University Press USA - OSO, 1999.

McCord, Norman, et al. *British History 1815-1914*, Oxford University Press USA - OSO, 2007.

Mee, Jon, et al. *British Culture, 1776-1832: British Culture, 1776-1832*, edited by Iain McCalman, Oxford University Press USA - OSO, 2001.

Printed in the USA
CPSIA information can be obtained
at www.ICGtesting.com
LVHW010552191223
766839LV00004B/37

9 781943 115358